Small Business Management in the 21st Century Version 1.0

By

David T. Cadden and Sandra L. Lueder

S-184788-BW-2

9 781453 345542

Small Business Management in the 21st Century Version 1.0

David T. Cadden and Sandra L. Lueder

Published by:

Flat World Knowledge, Inc.
1111 19th St NW, Suite 1180
Washington, DC 20036

Brief Contents

About the Authors

Acknowledgments

Dedications

Preface

Chapter 1   Foundations for Small Business

Chapter 2   Your Business Idea: The Quest for Value

Chapter 3   Family Businesses

Chapter 4   E-Business and E-Commerce

Chapter 5   The Business Plan

Chapter 6   Marketing Basics

Chapter 7   Marketing Strategy

Chapter 8   The Marketing Plan

Chapter 9   Accounting and Cash Flow

Chapter 10   Financial Management

Chapter 11   Supply Chain Management: You Better Get It Right

Chapter 12   People and Organization

Chapter 13   The Search for Efficiency and Effectiveness

Chapter 14   Icebergs and Escapes

Chapter 15   Going Global: Yes or No?

Chapter 16   Appendix: A Sample Business Plan

Index

Contents

About the Authors   1

Acknowledgments   2

Dedications   3

Preface   4

Chapter 1   Foundations for Small Business   5

              Small Business in the US Economy   6
              Success and Failure in Small Businesses   11
              Evolution   16
              Ethics   19
              The Three Threads   24
              Endnotes   31

Chapter 2   Your Business Idea: The Quest for Value   35

              Defining the Customer's Concept of Value   36
              Knowing Your Customers   46
              Sources of Business Ideas   55
              The Three Threads   61
              Endnotes   66

Chapter 3   Family Businesses   67

              Family Business: An Overview   68
              Family Business Issues   73
              Conflict   82
              The Three Threads   85
              Endnotes   88

Chapter 4   E-Business and E-Commerce   91

              E-Business and E-Commerce: The Difference   92
              E-Commerce Operations   99
              E-Commerce Technology   108
              The Three Threads   112
              Endnotes   115

Chapter 5   The Business Plan   119

              Developing Your Strategy   120
              The Necessity for a Business Plan   129
              Building a Plan   133

		The Three Threads	149
		Endnotes	152
Chapter 6	**Marketing Basics**		**153**
		What Marketing Is All About	154
		The Customer	163
		Marketing Research	173
		The Three Threads	178
		Endnotes	181
Chapter 7	**Marketing Strategy**		**183**
		The Importance of a Marketing Strategy	184
		The Marketing Strategy Process	185
		Segmentation and the Target Market	187
		Differentiation and Positioning	189
		Marketing Strategy and Product	194
		Marketing Strategy and Price	208
		Marketing Strategy and Place	211
		Marketing Strategy and Promotion	218
		The Three Threads	227
		Endnotes	230
Chapter 8	**The Marketing Plan**		**235**
		The Need for a Marketing Plan	236
		The Marketing Plan	239
		The Three Threads	262
		Endnotes	264
Chapter 9	**Accounting and Cash Flow**		**267**
		Understanding the Need for Accounting Systems	268
		Financial Accounting Statements	273
		Financial Ratio Analysis	290
		The Three Threads	295
		Endnotes	300
Chapter 10	**Financial Management**		**301**
		The Importance of Financial Management in Small Business	302
		Financial Control	311
		Financial Decision Making	313
		The Three Threads	322
		Endnotes	326
Chapter 11	**Supply Chain Management: You Better Get It Right**		**327**
		The Supply Chain and a Firm's Role in It	328
		A Firm's Role in the Supply Chain	338

The Benefits and the Risks of Participating in a Supply Chain 344

The Three Threads 346

Endnotes 352

Chapter 12   People and Organization   353

Principles of Management and Organization 354

Organizational Design 361

Legal Forms of Organization for the Small Business 370

People 375

The Three Threads 386

Endnotes 389

Chapter 13   The Search for Efficiency and Effectiveness   393

Personal Efficiency and Effectiveness 394

Creativity 400

Organizational Efficiency 405

Going Lean 416

Personnel Efficiency 422

The Three Threads 427

Endnotes 431

Chapter 14   Icebergs and Escapes   433

Icebergs 434

Disaster Assistance 440

Escapes: Getting Out of the Business 442

Exit Strategies 445

Endnotes 454

Chapter 15   Going Global: Yes or No?   457

US Small Business in the Global Environment 457

What You Should Know Before Going Global 462

Key Management Decisions and Considerations 475

The Three Threads 481

Endnotes 484

Chapter 16   Appendix: A Sample Business Plan   487

Executive Summary 487

Index   505

About the Authors

DAVID T. CADDEN

Dr. David Cadden was born in New York and received his undergraduate degree in engineering from the Brooklyn Polytechnic Institute. He received an MS in management from the same institution. He attended Baruch College, which is part of the City University of New York, where he received his MBA and earned his PhD in management planning systems.

Dr. Cadden is the author of many journal articles, book chapters, and proceedings publications. For several years he ran a program at Quinnipiac University where students traveled to Nicaragua to assist local small businesses in improving their operations. He teaches in the areas of operations and strategy and places special emphasis in these courses on the unique demands of small businesses. Dr. Cadden has consulted with several firms, including McDonald-Douglas Aircraft and the Blue Cross and Blue Shield Association. Prior to coming to Quinnipiac, Dr. Cadden worked for Hazeltine Corporation, Baruch College, and Fairfield University.

SANDRA L. LUEDER

Dr. Sandra Lueder is an associate professor emeritus at Southern Connecticut State University. She has a PhD in marketing from the City University of New York (Baruch College), an MBA in management and marketing from the University of Connecticut, and a BA from the University of Wisconsin in Madison. She also taught at Sacred Heart University in Fairfield, Connecticut. Her noneducation employment includes working in government, small business, and United Engineers and Constructors, a large corporation that is a division of Raytheon. Dr. Lueder has been passionate about small business for more than twenty-five years. As the proud daughter of a twice-entrepreneur, she has lived the life and has seen the ups and downs of small business ownership. She has taught small business management courses and has integrated the small business perspective into most of the marketing and leadership courses that she teaches. Dr. Lueder has been published in the *New England Journal of Entrepreneurship* and *The E-Business Review*. She has also made many presentations at academic conferences.

Acknowledgments

We would like to thank the following reviewers. Their insightful feedback and suggestions for improving the material helped us make this a better text:

- Diane Denslow, University of North Florida
- Vada Grantham, Des Moines Area Community College
- Kirk C. Heriot, Columbus State University
- Richard Kimbrough, University of Nebraska-Lincoln
- Dr. Luis I. Molina, Miami-Dade College
- Dr. Donatus A. Okhomina, Fayetteville State University
- Dr. Marvin Anthony Parker, Fort Valley State University
- Brenda A. B. Smith, Southwest Tennessee Community College

Our acknowledgments cannot be complete without words of appreciation for the wonderful people at Flat World Knowledge. Michael Boezi saw our vision and was willing to take a chance on us. He supported us throughout the project in spite of many creative blocks. Jeff Shelstad and Eric Frank—how wonderful that their genius created Flat World Knowledge in the first place. It is the place where we realized our dream. Claire Hunter was our indispensable reviewer for the last few chapters, helping us refine our thinking. Becky Knauer, our project manager, was awesome! She kept us on track and showed compassion and understanding during the multiple hardships we experienced during this journey. We probably would not have made it had it not been for her. She kept us sane.

Dedications

DAVID T. CADDEN

To my grandmother, Helen Lane, whose love taught me what it means to be a real human being.

To my mother, Dorothy. I wouldn't be who I am or where I am without her constant support and love.

To my wife, Sandy, whose passion was the driving force behind this book and whose love and support made sure it would be completed.

To my daughter, Helena, who taught me more about learning than all my years in the classroom.

SANDRA L. LUEDER

To my Dad, a twice-entrepreneur, who instilled in me the love of small business and the importance of integrity in everything I do.

To my Mom, always the soldier in support of my Dad's entrepreneurial ventures. It wasn't easy. She was amazing!

To my husband, David, whose shared passion for small business helped to make this book a reality. This book is our dream.

To Helena, our beautiful daughter, who is very entrepreneurial in her own right. May she realize her dreams.

Preface

Imagine a text that your students might actually read. Imagine a book that is the core of your course without the bloat. Imagine a book that uses customer value, digital technology, and cash flow as key themes rather than afterthought add-ins. Imagine a text that contains extensive ancillary materials—PowerPoints, websites, videos, podcasts, and guides to software—all geared to enhancing the educational experience. Sound good? *Small Business Management in the 21st Century* is your text.

This text offers a unique perspective and set of capabilities for instructors. It is a text that believes "less can be more" and that small business management should not be treated as an abstract theoretical concept but as a practical human activity. It emphasizes clear illustrations and real-world examples.

The text has a format and structure that will be familiar to those who use other books on small business management, yet it brings a fresh perspective by incorporating three distinctive and unique themes that are embedded throughout the entire text. These themes ensure that students see the material in an integrated context rather than a stream of separate and distinct topics.

First, we incorporate the use of **technology and e-business** as a way to gain competitive advantage over larger rivals. Technology is omnipresent in today's business world. Small business must use it to its advantage. We provide practical discussions and examples of how a small business can use these technologies without having extensive expertise or expenditures.

Second, we explicitly acknowledge the constant need to examine how decisions affect **cash flow** by incorporating cash flow impact content in several chapters. As the life blood of all organizations, cash flow implications must be a factor in all business decision making.

Third, we recognize the need to clearly identify sources of **customer value** and bring that understanding to every decision. Decisions that do not add to customer value should be seriously reconsidered.

Another unique element of this text is the use of **Disaster Watch** scenarios. Few texts cover, in any detail, some of the major hazards that small business managers face. Disaster Watch scenarios, included in most chapters, cover topics that include financing, bankers, creditors, employees, economic downturns, and marketing challenges.

CHAPTER 1
Foundations for Small Business

The Twenty-First-Century Small-Business Owner

Source: Used with permission from Frank C. Trotta III.

Frank Trotta III is a recent college graduate, class of 2009, and an excellent example of the twenty-first-century small business owner. At 23, he is already running his own business and planning to open a second. This may be second nature because Frank III is a third-generation small business owner. His grandfather, Frank Trotta Sr., opened a supermarket in 1945. His son, Frank C. Trotta Jr., began his career by working in the supermarket. Soon he had his own hardware department within the store and was beginning to understand what it takes to be a successful grocer. He observed his dad interacting with his customers and providing value through customer service.

Frank Jr. now owns and operates one of Long Island's most successful travel companies: the Prime Time Travel Club. The experience Frank Jr. garnered from his father in customer service became the tenet of his business philosophy: give customers value through personal attention and service. At an early age, Frank III worked in his dad's office when he was not busy with school activities. He had a strong entrepreneurial leaning and became very interested in the travel industry. In high school, Frank III worked for his dad and learned different facets of the travel business. While attending a Connecticut university, Frank III reached out to other students on campus and started his own side business: booking spring break trips. The same people are now repeat customers who call him to book their vacations, honeymoons, and family trips.

In his junior year, Frank III created a travel site of his own: Cruisetoanywhere.com. He is involved with every aspect of the site: he takes all calls from the customer service number, produces all the marketing campaigns, and works on contracts with both major and smaller cruise lines. Although the site is still young, it has been very successful. Frank III is learning how larger competitors do business and from their successes and mistakes. Customer service and attention are his first priority. Frank III believes his competitive business edge comes from what he learned from his father's company and business skills such as planning and managing cash flow from his professors. In addition to his cruise website, Frank III plans to launch another site, Tourstoanywhere.com. He exemplifies the skill set that will characterize the twenty-first-century small business owner: a clear focus on creating value for his customers, a willingness to exploit the benefits of digital technology and e-commerce, and the ability to apply basic business skills to the effective operation of the firm.

1. SMALL BUSINESS IN THE US ECONOMY

It's an exciting time to be in small business. This is certainly not anything new, but you might not know it. Scan any issue of the popular business press, and in all probability, you will find a cover story on one of America's or the world's major corporations or a spotlight on their CEOs. Newspapers, talk radio, and television seem to have an unlimited supply of pundits and politicians eager to pontificate on firms that have been labeled as "too big to fail." Listen to any broadcast of a weekday's evening news program, and there will be a segment that highlights the ups and downs of the Dow Jones Industrial Average and the Standard and Poor's (S&P) 500. These market measures provide an insight into what is going on in Wall Street. However, they are clearly biased to not only large firms but also huge firms. This creates the false notion that "real" business is only about big business. It fails to recognize that small businesses are the overwhelming majority of all businesses in America; not only are the majority of jobs in small businesses, but small businesses have also been the major driving force in new job creation and innovation. Small business is *the* dynamo of innovation in our economy. In 2006, Thomas M. Sullivan, the chief counsel for advocacy of the Small Business Administration (SBA), said, "Small business is a major part of our economy,…small businesses innovate and create new jobs at a faster rate than their larger competitors. They are nimble, creative, and a vital part of every community across the country."[1]

This text is devoted to small business, not entrepreneurship. There has always been a challenge to distinguish—correctly—between the small business owner and the entrepreneur. Some argue that there is no difference between the two terms. The word *entrepreneur* is derived from a French word for "to undertake," which might indicate that entrepreneurs should be identified as those who start businesses.[2] However, this interpretation is too broad and is pointless as a means of distinguishing between the two. Some have tried to find differences based on background, education, or age.[3] Often one finds the argument that entrepreneurs have a different orientation toward risk than small business owners. The standard line is that entrepreneurs are willing to take great risks in starting an enterprise and/or willing to start again after a business failure.[4] Others try to make the distinction based on the issue of innovation or the degree of innovation. Given this focus, entrepreneurs need not even work for small business because they can come up with innovative products, services, production, or marketing processes in large organizations.[5] Perhaps the most common interpretation of the entrepreneur is an individual involved in a high-tech start-up who becomes a billionaire. That is not the focus of this text. It centers on the true driving force of America's economy—the small business.

This chapter gives a brief history of small business in the United States, the critical importance of small business to the American economy, the challenges facing small business owners as they struggle to survive and prosper, the requisite skills to be an effective small business owner, the critical importance of ethical behavior, and how these businesses may evolve over time. In addition, three critical success factors for the twenty-first-century small business are threaded through the text: (1) *identifying and providing customer value*, (2) *being able to exploit digital technologies with an emphasis on e-business and e-commerce*, and (3) *properly managing your cash flow*. These three threads are essential to the successful decision making of any contemporary small business and should be considered of paramount importance. They are everyday considerations.

1.1 A Brief History of Small Business

Throughout American history, from colonial times until today, most businesses were small businesses, and they have played a vital role in America's economic success and are a forge to our national identity. It would not be an exaggeration to say that the small businessperson has always held an important—even exalted—position in American life. Americans in the early republic were as suspicious of large economic enterprises as threats to their liberty as they were of large government. The historian James L. Houston discussed American suspicion of large economic enterprises: "Americans believed that if property was concentrated in the hands of a few in the republic, those few would use their wealth to control other citizens, seize political power, and warp the republic into an oligarchy."[6] In fact, much of the impetus behind the Boston Tea Party was the fear on the part of local merchants and tradesmen that the East India Company, at that time the world's largest corporation, was dumping low-priced tea in the colonies, which would have driven local business to ruin.[7] Jefferson's promotion of the yeoman farmer, which included small merchants, as the bulwark of democracy stemmed from his fear of large moneyed interests: "The end of democracy and the defeat of the American Revolution will occur when government falls into the hands of lending institutions and moneyed incorporations."[8] So great was the fear of the large aggregation of wealth that the colonies and the early republic placed severe restrictions on the creation of corporate forms. In the first decades of the nineteenth century, state governments restricted the corporate form by limiting its duration, geographic scope, size, and even profits.[9] This was done because of the concern that corporations had the potential of becoming monopolies that would drive entrepreneurs out of business.

Eventually, however, some businesses grew in size and power. Their growth and size necessitated the development of a professional management class that was distinct from entrepreneurs who started and ran their own businesses. However, not until the post–Civil War period did America see the true explosion in big businesses. This was brought about by several factors: the development of the mass market (facilitated by the railroads); increased capital requirement for mass production; and the 1886 Supreme Court case of *Santa Clara County v. Southern Pacific Railroad*, which granted corporations "personhood" by giving them protection under the Fourteenth Amendment.

The growth of corporations evoked several responses that were designed to protect small businesses from their larger competitors. The Interstate Commerce Act (1887) was a federal law designed to regulate the rates charged by railroads to protect small farmers and businesses. Other federal laws—the Sherman Act (1890) and the Clayton Act (1914)—were passed with the initial intent of restricting the unfair trading practices of trusts. In the early years, however, the Sherman Act was used more frequently against small business alliances and unions than against large businesses. Congress continued to support small businesses through the passage of legislation. The Robinson-Patman Act of 1936 and the Miller-Tydings Act of 1937 were designed to protect small retailers from large chain retailers.[10]

The Depression and the post–World War II environments posed special challenges to small business operations. The Hoover and Roosevelt administrations created organizations (the Reconstruction Finance Corporation in 1932 and the Small War Plants Corporation in 1942) to assist small firms. The functions of several government agencies were subsumed into the **Small Business Administration** in 1953. The designated purpose of the SBA was to "aid, counsel, assist and protect, insofar as is possible, the interests of small business concerns."[11] The SBA functions to ensure that small businesses have a fair chance at securing government contracts. It also has the responsibility of defining what constitutes a small business.

If anything is to be learned from the passage of all this legislation, it is that, as Conte (2006) eloquently put it, "Americans continued to revere small businesspeople for their self-reliance and independence."[12]

1.2 Definition of Small Business

The SBA definition of a small business has evolved over time and is dependent on the particular industry. In the 1950s, the SBA defined a **small business** firm as "independently owned and operated...and not dominant in its field of operation."[13] This is still part of their definition. At that time, the SBA classified a small firm as being limited to 250 employees for industrial organizations. Currently, this definition depends on the North American Industry Classification System (NAICS) for a business. The SBA recognizes that there are significant differences, across industries, with respect to competitiveness, entry and exit costs, distribution by size, growth rates, and technological change. Although the SBA defines 500 employees as the limit for the majority of industrial firms and receipts of $7 million for the majority of service, retail, and construction firms, there are different values for some industries. Table 1.1 presents a selection of different industries and their size limits.

Small Business Administration

The government agency that is charged with aiding, counseling, assisting, and protecting the interests of small business.

small business

A firm that is independently owned and operated and not dominant in its field of operation. There are variations across industries with respect to competitiveness, entry and exit costs, distribution by size, growth rates, and technological change.

TABLE 1.1   Examples of Size Limits for Small Businesses by the SBA

NAICS Code	NAICS US Industry Title	Size Standards (Millions of $)	Size Standards (Number of Employees)
111333	Strawberry farming	0.75	
113310	Timber tract operations	7.00	
114112	Shellfish fishing	4.00	
212210	Iron ore mining		500
236115	New single family housing construction	33.50	
311230	Breakfast cereal manufacturer		1,000
315991	Hat, cap, and millenary manufacturing		500
443111	Household appliance store	9.00	
454311	Heating oil dealers		50
483111	Deep sea freight transportation		500
484110	General freight trucking, local	25.50	
511130	Book publishers		500
512230	Music publishers		500
541214	Payroll services	8.50	
541362	Geophysical surveying and mapping services	4.50	
541712	Research and development in physical, engineering, and life sciences		500
	Except aircraft		1,500
722110	Full-service restaurants	7.00	
722310	Food service contractors	20.50	
811111	General automotive repair	7.00	
812320	Dry cleaning and laundry services	4.50	
813910	Business associations	7.00	

Source: "Table of Small Business Size Standards Matched to North American Industry Classification System Codes," US Small Business

Administration, August 22, 2008, accessed June 1, 2012, http://www.sba.gov/content/small-business-size-standards.

The SBA definition of what constitutes a small business has practical significance. Small businesses have access to an extensive support network provided by the SBA. It runs the SCORE program, which has more than 12,000 volunteers who assist small firms with counseling and training. The SBA also operates Small Business Development Centers, Export Assistance Centers, and Women's Business Centers. These centers provide comprehensive assistance to small firms. There can be significant economic support for small firms from the SBA. It offers a variety of guaranteed loan programs to start-ups and small firms. It assists small firms in acquiring access to nearly half a trillion dollars in federal contracts. In fact, legislation attempts to target 23 percent of this value for small firms. The SBA can also assist with financial aid following a disaster.

1.3   Small Business in the American Economy

In 1958, small business contributed 57 percent of the nation's gross domestic product (GDP). This value dropped to 50 percent by 1980. What is remarkable is that this 50 percent figure has essentially held steady for the last thirty years.[14] It is interesting to note that the contribution of small businesses to the GDP can vary considerably based on particular industries. Table 1.2 presents data for selected industries for the period 1998–2004. It can be seen that in some industries—construction and real estate—80 percent or more of that industry's contribution to the GDP comes from small businesses, while in the information industry that number is 20 percent or less.

Few people realize that the overwhelming majority of businesses in the United States are small businesses with fewer than five hundred employees. The SBA puts the number of small businesses at 99.7 percent of the total number of businesses in the United States. However, most of the businesses are nonemployee businesses (i.e., no paid employees) and are home based.

TABLE 1.2 Small Businesses' Component of Industry Contribution to GDP

Year	Construction (%)	Real Estate and Leasing (%)	Wholesale Trade (%)	Transportation and Warehousing (%)	Information (%)
1998	88.0	80.4	59.1	39.1	26.4
1999	87.2	80.0	57.5	39.4	25.4
2000	85.4	79.8	56.8	39.0	22.7
2001	85.1	80.3	55.3	41.1	19.7
2002	84.6	79.4	56.3	41.0	20.3
2003	85.4	79.5	54.6	39.1	20.3
2004	85.6	79.6	55.4	38.6	18.0

Source: Katherine Kobe, "Small Business Share of GDP (Contract No. SBAHQ-05-M-0413)," SBA Office of Advocacy, April 2007, accessed October 7, 2011, http://archive.sba.gov/advo/research/rs299tot.pdf.

One area where the public has a better understanding of the strength of small business is in the area of innovation. Evidence dating back to the 1970s indicates that small businesses disproportionately produce innovations.[15] It has been estimated that 40 percent of America's scientific and engineering talent is employed by small businesses. The same study found that small businesses that pursue patents produce thirteen to fourteen times as many patents per employee as their larger counterparts. Further, it has been found that these patents are twice as likely to be in the top 1 percent of highest impact patents.[16]

It is possible that small size might pose an advantage with respect to being more innovative. The reasons for this have been attributed to several factors:

- **Passion.** Small-business owners are interested in making businesses successful and are more open to new concepts and ideas to achieve that end.
- **Customer connection.** Being small, these firms better know their customers' needs and therefore are better positioned to meet them.
- **Agility.** Being small, these firms can adapt more readily to changing environment.
- **Willingness to experiment.** Small-business owners are willing to risk failure on some experiments.
- **Resource limitation.** Having fewer resources, small businesses become adept at doing more with less.
- **Information sharing.** Smaller size may mean that there is a tighter social network for sharing ideas.[17]

Regardless of the reasons, small businesses, particularly in high-tech industries, play a critical role in preserving American global competitiveness.

1.4 Small Business and National Employment

The majority—approximately 50.2 percent in 2006—of private sector employees work for small businesses. A breakdown of the percentage of private sector employees by firm size for the period 1988 to 2006 is provided in Table 1.3. For 2006, slightly more than 18 percent of the entire private sector workforce was employed by firms with fewer than twenty employees. It is interesting to note that there can be significant difference in the percentage of employment by small business across states. Although the national average was 50.2 percent in 2006, the state with the lowest percentage working for small businesses was Florida with 44.0 percent, while the state with the highest percentage was Montana with a remarkable 69.8 percent.[18]

TABLE 1.3 Percentage of Private Sector Employees by Firm Size

Year	0–4 Employees	5–9 Employees	10–19 Employees	20–99 Employees	100–499 Employees	500+ Employees
1988	5.70%	6.90%%	8.26%	19.16%	14.53%	45.45%
1991	5.58%	6.69%	8.00%	18.58%	14.24%	46.91%
1994	5.50%	6.55%	7.80%	18.29%	14.60%	47.26%
1997	5.20%	4.95%	6.36%	16.23%	13.73%	53.54%
2000	4.90%	5.88%	7.26%	17.78%	14.26%	49.92%
2003	5.09%	5.94%	7.35%	17.80%	14.49%	49.34%
2006	4.97%	5.82%	7.24%	17.58%	14.62%	49.78%

Source: US Census Bureau, "Statistics of U.S. Business," accessed October 7, 2011, http://www.census.gov/econ/susb.

Small business is the great generator of jobs. Recent data indicate that small businesses produced 64 percent of the net new jobs from 1993 to the third quarter of 2008.[19] This is not a recent phenomenon. Thirty years of research studies have consistently indicated that the driving force in fostering new job creation is the birth of new companies and the net additions coming from small businesses. In the 1990s, firms with fewer than twenty employees produced far more net jobs proportionally to their size, and two to three times as many jobs were created through new business formation than through job expansion in small businesses.[20] The US Census Bureau's Business Dynamics Statistics data confirm that the greatest number of new jobs comes from the creation of new businesses. One can get a sense of the extent of net job change by business size in Table 1.4.

An additional point needs to be made about job creation and loss by small businesses in the context of overall economic conditions. Government data show that of the "net 1.5 million jobs lost in 2008, 64 percent were from small firms."[21] However, the same study had some interesting results from the past two recessions. In the 2001 recession, small businesses with fewer than 20 employees experienced 7 percent of the total reduction in jobs, firms with between 20 and 500 employees were responsible for 43 percent of the job losses, and the rest of the job losses came from large firms. As the economy recovered in the following year, firms with fewer than 20 employees created jobs, while the other two groups continued to shed jobs. Following the 1991 recession, it was firms with 20 to 500 employees that were responsible for more than 56 percent of the jobs that were added.

TABLE 1.4 Job Creation by Firm Size

Years	1–4	5–9	10–19	20–99	100–499	500+
2002–2003	1,106,977	307,690	158,795	304,162	112,702	(994,667)
2003–2004	1,087,128	336,236	201,247	199,298	66,209	(214,233)
2004–2005	897,296	141,057	(11,959)	(131,095)	83,803	262,326
2005–2006	1,001,960	295,521	292,065	590,139	345,925	1,072,710

Source: "Small Business Profile," SBA Office of Advocacy, 2009, http://archive.sba.gov/advo/research/data.html.

One last area concerning the small business contribution to American employment is its role with respect to minority ownership and employment. During the last decade, there has been a remarkable increase in the number of self-employed individuals. From 2000 to 2007, the number of women who were self-employed increased by 9.7 percent. The number of African Americans who were self-employed increased by 36.6 percent for the same time range. However, the most remarkable number was an increase of nearly 110 percent for Hispanics. It is clear that small business has become an increasingly attractive option for minority groups.[22] Women and Hispanics are also employed by small businesses at a higher rate than the national average.

KEY TAKEAWAYS

- Small businesses have always played a key role in the US economy.
- Small businesses are responsible for more than half the employment in the United States.
- Small businesses have a prominent role in innovation and minority employment.

EXERCISES

1. Throughout this text, you will be given several assignments. It would be useful if these assignments had some degree of consistency. Select a type of business that interests you and plan on using it throughout some of the chapter assignments. After selecting your business, go to www.sba.gov/content/ table-small-business-size-standards and determine the size of the business.

2. In the United States, 50 percent of those employed are working for small businesses. There are considerable differences across states. Go to www.census.gov/econ/susb/ and compute the percentage for your state. What factors might account for the differences across states?

2. SUCCESS AND FAILURE IN SMALL BUSINESSES

LEARNING OBJECTIVES

1. Be able to explain what is meant by business success.
2. Be able to describe the different components of business failure.
3. Understand that statistics on business failure can be confusing and contradictory.
4. Understand that small business failure can be traced to managerial inadequacy, financial issues, and the external environment.
5. Understand that small business owners need to be able to formally plan and understand the accounting and finance needs of their firms.

There are no easy answers to questions about success and failure in a small business. The different points of view are all over the map.

2.1 What Is a Successful Small Business?

Ask the average person what the purpose of a business is or how he or she would define a successful business, and the most likely response would be "one that makes a profit." A more sophisticated reply might extend that to "one that makes an acceptable profit now and in the future." Ask anyone in the finance department of a publicly held firm, and his or her answer would be "one that maximizes shareholder wealth." The management guru Peter Drucker said that for businesses to succeed, they needed to create customers, while W. E. Deming, the quality guru, advocated that business success required "delighting" customers. No one can argue, specifically, with any of these definitions of **small business success**, but they miss an important element of the definition of success for the small business owner: *to be free and independent.*

Many people have studied whether there is any significant difference between the small business owner and the entrepreneur. Some entrepreneurs place more emphasis on growth in their definition of success.[23] However, it is clear that entrepreneurs and small business owners define much of their personal and their firm's success in the context of providing them with independence. For many small business owners, being in charge of their own life is the prime motivator: a "fervently guarded sense of independence," and money is seen as a beneficial by-product.[24],[25],[26] Oftentimes, financial performance is seen as an important measure of success. However, small businesses are reluctant to report their financial information, so this will always be an imperfect and incomplete measure of success.[27]

Three types of small business operators can be identified based on what they see as constituting success:

1. An artisan whose intrinsic satisfaction comes from performing the business activity

2. The entrepreneur who seeks growth

3. The owner who seeks independence[28]

small business success

The need for independence by small business owners.

Video Clip 1.1

Popchips
The story of Popchips, a small business success.

View the video online at: http://www.youtube.com/v/27Ckl8qb7cQ
Source: CNN's Small Business Success.

2.2   Failure Rates for Small Business

When discussing failure rates in small business, there is only one appropriate word: *confusion*. There are wildly different values, from 90 percent to 1 percent, with a wide range of values in between.[29] Obviously, there is a problem with these results, or some factor is missing. One factor that would explain this discrepancy is the different definitions of the term *failure*. A second factor is that of timeline. When will a firm fail after it starts operation?

The term *failure* can have several meanings.[30] **Small-business failure** is often measured by the cessation of a firm's operation, but this can be brought about by several things:

small business failure

A broad term covering several types of failure: (1) discontinuance, (2) failure of opportunity cost, (3) avoidance of loss to creditors, (4) losses to creditors, and (5) bankruptcy.

- An owner can die or simply choose to discontinue operations.
- The owner may recognize that the business is not generating sufficient return to warrant the effort that is being put into it. This is sometimes referred to as the failure of opportunity cost.
- A firm that is losing money may be terminated to avoid losses to its creditors.
- There can be losses to creditors that bring about cessations of the firm's operations.
- The firm can experience bankruptcy. Bankruptcy is probably what most people think of when they hear the term *business failure*. However, the evidence indicates that bankruptcies constitute only a minor reason for failure.

Failure can therefore be thought of in terms of a cascading series of outcomes (see Figure 1.1). There are even times when small business owners involved in a closure consider the firm successful at its closing.[31] Then there is the complication of considering the industry of the small business when examining failure and bankruptcy. The rates of failure can vary considerably across different industries; in the fourth quarter of 2009, the failure rates for service firms were half that of transportation firms.[32]

FIGURE 1.1 Types of Business Failures

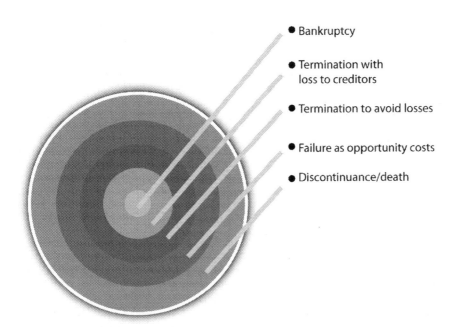

- Bankruptcy
- Termination with loss to creditors
- Termination to avoid losses
- Failure as opportunity costs
- Discontinuance/death

The second issue associated with small business failure is a consideration of the time horizon. Again, there are wildly different viewpoints. The Dan River Small Business Development Center presented data that indicated that 95 percent of small businesses fail within five years.[33] Dun and Bradstreet reported that companies with fewer than twenty employees have only a 37 percent chance of surviving four years, but only 10 percent will go bankrupt.[34] The US Bureau of Labor Statistics indicated that 66 percent of new establishments survive for two years, and that number drops to 44 percent two years later.[35] It appears that the longer you survive, the higher the probability of your continued existence. This makes sense, but it is no guarantee. Any business can fail after many years of success.

2.3 Why Do Small Businesses Fail?

There is no more puzzling or better studied issue in the field of small business than what causes them to fail. Given the critical role of small businesses in the US economy, the economic consequences of failure can be significant. Yet there is no definitive answer to the question.

Three broad categories of causes of failure have been identified: managerial inadequacy, financial inadequacy, and external factors. The first cause, **managerial inadequacy**, is the most frequently mentioned reason for firm failure.[36] Unfortunately, it is an all-inclusive explanation, much like explaining that all plane crashes are due to pilot failure. Over thirty years ago, it was observed that "while everyone agrees that bad management is the prime cause of failure, no one agrees what 'bad management' means nor how it can be recognized except that the company has collapsed—then everyone agrees that how badly managed it was."[37] This observation remains true today.

The second most common explanation cites **financial inadequacy**, or a lack of financial strength in a firm. A third set of explanations center on environmental or **external factors**, such as a significant decline in the economy.

Because it is important that small firms succeed, not fail, each factor will be discussed in detail. However, these factors are not independent elements distinct from each other. A declining economy will depress a firm's sales, which negatively affects a firm's cash flow. An owner who lacks the knowledge and experience to manage this cash flow problem will see his or her firm fail.

Managerial inadequacy is generally perceived as the major cause of small business failure. Unfortunately, this term encompasses a very broad set of issues. It has been estimated that two thirds of small business failures are due to the incompetence of the owner-manager.[38] The identified problems cover behavioral issues, a lack of business skills, a lack of specific technical skills, and marketing myopia. Specifying every limitation of these owners would be prohibitive. However, some limitations are mentioned with remarkable consistency. Having poor communication skills, with employees and/or customers, appears to be a marker for failure.[39] The inability to listen to criticism or divergent views is a marker for failure, as is the inability to be flexible in one's thinking.[40]

managerial inadequacy

The failure of a firm is based on the limitations of its owner, such as a lack of business skills or a lack of behavior skills.

financial inadequacy

The failure of a firm is based on financial issues, such as having inadequate financing at the beginning, inadequate financial controls, poor cash-flow management, and the inability to raise additional capital.

external factors

The failure of the firm is based on external factors, such as a downturn in the economy, rising interest rates, or changes in customer demand.

Ask many small business owners where their strategic plans exist, and they may point to their foreheads. The failure to conduct formal planning may be the most frequently mentioned item with respect to small business failure. Given the relative lack of resources, it is not surprising that small firms tend to opt for intuitive approaches to planning.[41],[42] Formal approaches to planning are seen as a waste of time,[43] or they are seen as too theoretical.[44] The end result is that many small business owners fail to conduct formal strategic planning in a meaningful way.[45],[46] In fact, many fail to conduct any planning;[47],[48] others may fail to conduct operational planning, such as marketing strategies.[49] The evidence appears to clearly indicate that a small firm that wishes to be successful needs to not only develop an initial strategic plan but also conduct an ongoing process of strategic renewal through planning.

Many managers do not have the ability to correctly select staff or manage them.[50] Other managerial failings appear to be in limitations in the functional area of marketing. Failing firms tend to ignore the changing demands of their customers, something that can have devastating effects.[51] The failure to understand what customers value and being able to adapt to changing customer needs often leads to business failure.[52]

The second major cause of small business failure is finance. Financial problems fall into three categories: start-up, cash flow, and financial management. When a firm begins operation (start-up), it will require capital. Unfortunately, many small business owners initially underestimate the amount of capital that should be available for operations.[53] This may explain why most small firms that fail do so within the first few years of their creation. The failure to start with sufficient capital can be attributed to the inability of the owner to acquire the needed capital. It can also be due to the owner's failure to sufficiently plan for his or her capital needs. Here we see the possible interactions among the major causes of firm failure. Cash-flow management has been identified as a prime cause for failure.[54],[55] Good cash-flow management is essential for the survival of any firm, but small firms in particular must pay close attention to this process. Small businesses must develop and maintain effective financial controls, such as credit controls.[56] For very small businesses, this translates into having an owner who has at least a fundamental familiarity with accounting and finance.[57] In addition, the small firm will need either an in-house or an outsourced accountant.[58] Unfortunately, many owners fail to fully use their accountants' advice to manage their businesses.[59]

The last major factor identified with the failure of small businesses is the external environment. There is a potentially infinite list of causes, but the economic environment tends to be most prominent. Here again, however, *confusing* appears to describe the list. Some argue that economic conditions contribute to between 30 percent and 50 percent of small business failures, in direct contradiction to the belief that managerial incompetence is the major cause.[60] Two economic measures appear to affect failure rates: interest rates, which appear to be tied to bankruptcies, and the unemployment rate, which appears to be tied to discontinuance.[61] The potential impact of these external economic variables might be that small business owners need to be either planners to cover potential contingencies or lucky.

Even given the confusing and sometimes conflicting results with respect to failure in small businesses, some common themes can be identified. The reasons for failure fall into three broad categories: managerial inadequacy, finance, and environmental. They, in turn, have some consistently mentioned factors (see Table 1.5). These factors should be viewed as warning signs—danger areas that need to be avoided if you wish to survive. Although small business owners cannot directly affect environmental conditions, they can recognize the potential problems that they might bring. This text will provide guidance on how the small business owner can minimize these threats through proactive leadership.

TABLE 1.5 Reasons for Small Business Failure

Managerial Inadequacy	Financial Inadequacy	External Factors
<ul><li>Failure in planning (initial start-up plan and subsequent plans)</li><li>Inexperience with managing business operation</li><li>Ineffective staffing</li><li>Poor communication skills</li><li>Failure to seek or respond to criticism</li><li>Failure to learn from past failures</li><li>Ignoring customers' needs</li><li>Ignoring competition</li><li>Failure to diversify customer base</li><li>Failure to innovate</li><li>Ineffective marketing strategies</li></ul>	<ul><li>Cash-flow problems</li><li>Insufficient initial capitalization</li><li>Inadequate financial records</li><li>Not using accountants' insights</li><li>Inadequate capital acquisition strategies</li><li>Failure to deal with financial issues brought about by growth</li></ul>	<ul><li>Downturn in economy</li><li>Rising unemployment</li><li>Rising interest rates</li><li>Product or service no longer desired by customers</li><li>Unmatchable foreign competition</li><li>Fraud</li><li>Disaster</li></ul>

Ultimately, business failure will be a company-specific combination of factors. Monitor101, a company that developed an Internet information monitoring product for institutional investors in 2005, failed badly. One of the cofounders identified the following seven mistakes that were made, most of which can be linked to managerial inadequacy:[62]

1. The lack of a single "the buck stops here" leader until too late in the game
2. No separation between the technology organization and the product organization
3. Too much public relations, too early
4. Too much money
5. Not close enough to the customer
6. Slowness to adapt to market reality
7. Disagreement on strategy within the company and with the board

"Entrepreneurs Turn Business Failure into Success"

Bloomberg Businessweek's 2008 cover story highlights owners who turn business failure into success.

http://www.businessweek.com/magazine/content/08_70/s0810040731198.htm

KEY TAKEAWAYS

- There is no universal definition for small business success. However, many small business owners see success as their own independence.
- The failure rates for small businesses are wide ranging. There is no consensus.
- Three broad categories of factors are thought to contribute to small business failure: managerial inadequacy, financial inadequacy, and external forces, most notably the economic environment.

1. Starting a business can be a daunting task. It can be made even more daunting if the type of business you choose is particularly risky. Go to www.forbes.com/2007/01/18/ fairisaac-nordstrom-verizon-ent-fin-cx_mf_0118risky_slide.html?thisSpeed=undefined, where the ten riskiest businesses are identified. Select any two of these businesses and address why you think they are risky.

2. Amy Knaup is the author of a 2005 study "Survival and Longevity in the Business Employment Dynamics Data" (see www.bls.gov/opub/mlr/2005/05/ressum.pdf). The article points to different survival rates for ten different industries. Discuss why there are significant differences in the survival rates among these industries.

3. EVOLUTION

LEARNING OBJECTIVES

1. Define the five stages of small business growth.
2. Identify the stages of the organizational life cycle.
3. Characterize the industry life cycle and its impact on small business.

Small businesses come in all shapes and sizes. One thing that they all share, however, is experience with common problems that arise at similar stages in their growth and organizational evolution. Predictable patterns can be seen. These patterns "tend to be sequential, occur as a hierarchical progression that is not easily reversed, and involve a broad range of organizational activities and structures."[63] The industry life cycle adds further complications. The success of any small business will depend on its ability to adapt to evolutionary changes, each of which will be characterized by different requirements, opportunities, challenges, risks, and internal and external threats. The decisions that need to be made and the priorities that are established will differ through this evolution.

3.1 Stages of Growth

small business growth stages

The five stages that small businesses may go through: existence, survival, success, take-off, and resource maturity.

Understanding the **small business growth stages** can be invaluable as a framework for anticipating resource needs and problems, assessing risk, and formulating business strategies (e.g., evaluating and responding to the impact of a new tax). However, the growth stages will not be applicable to all small businesses because not all small businesses will be looking to grow. Business success is commonly associated with growth and financial performance, but these are not necessarily synonymous—especially for small businesses. People become business owners for different reasons, so judgments about the success of their businesses may be related to any of those reasons.[64] A classic study by Churchill and Lewis identified five stages of small business growth: existence, survival, success, take-off, and resource maturity.[65] Each stage has its own challenges.

- **Stage I: Existence.**[66] This is the beginning. The business is up and running. The primary problems will be obtaining customers and establishing a customer base, producing products or services, and tracking and conserving cash flow.[67] The organization is simple, with the owner doing everything, including directly supervising a small number of subordinates. Systems and formal planning do not exist. The company strategy? *Staying alive*. The companies that stay in business move to Stage II.

- **Stage II: Survival.**[68] The business is now a viable operation. There are enough customers, and they are being satisfied well enough for them to stay with the business. The company's focal point shifts to the relationship between revenues and expenses. Owners will be concerned with (1) whether they can generate enough cash in the short run to break even and cover the repair/replacement of basic assets and (2) whether they can get enough cash flow to stay in business and finance growth to earn an economic return on assets and labor. The organizational structure remains simple. Little systems development is evident, cash forecasting is the focus of formal planning, and the owner still runs everything.

- **Stage III: Success.**[69] The business is now economically healthy, and the owners are considering whether to leverage the company for growth or consider the company as a means of support for them as they disengage from the company.[70] There are two tracks within the success stage. The first track is the **success-growth substage**, where the small business owner pulls all the company resources together and risks them all in financing growth. Systems are installed with forthcoming needs in mind. Operational planning focuses on budgets. Strategic planning is extensive, and the owner is deeply involved. The management style is functional, but the owner is active in all phases of the company's business. The second track is the **success-disengagement substage**, where managers take over the owner's operational duties, and the strategy focuses on maintaining the status quo. Cash is plentiful, so the company should be able to maintain itself indefinitely, barring external environmental changes. The owners benefit indefinitely from the positive cash flow or prepare for a sale or a merger. The first professional managers are hired, and basic financial, marketing, and production systems are in place.

- **Stage IV: Take-off.**[71] This is a critical time in a company's life. The business is becoming increasingly complex. The owners must decide how to grow rapidly and how to finance that growth. There are two key questions: (1) Can the owner delegate responsibility to others to improve managerial effectiveness? (2) Will there be enough cash to satisfy the demands of growth? The organization is decentralized and may have some divisions in place. Both operational planning and strategic planning are being conducted and involve specific managers. If the owner rises to the challenges of growth, it can become a very successful big business. If not, it can usually be sold at a profit.

- **Stage V: Resource Maturity.**[72] The company has arrived. It has the staff and financial resources to engage in detailed operational and strategic planning. The management structure is decentralized, with experienced senior staff, and all necessary systems are in place. The owner and the business have separated both financially and operationally. The concerns at this stage are to (1) consolidate and control the financial gains that have been brought on by the rapid growth and (2) retain the advantage of a small size (e.g., response flexibility and the entrepreneurial spirit). If the entrepreneurial spirit can be maintained, there is a strong probability of continued growth and success. If not, the company may find itself in a state of **ossification**. This occurs when there is a lack of innovation and risk aversion that, in turn, will contribute to stalled or halted growth. These are common traits in large corporations.

3.2 Organizational Life Cycle

Superimposed on the stages of small business growth is the **organizational life cycle (OLC)**, a concept that specifically acknowledges that organizations go through different life cycles, just like people do.[73] "They are born (established or formed), they grow and develop, they reach maturity, they begin to decline and age, and finally, in many cases, they die."[74] The changes that occur in organizations have a predictable pattern,[75] and this predictability will be very helpful in formulating the objectives and strategies of a small business, altering managerial processes, identifying the sources of risk, and managing organizational change.[76],[77] Because not all small businesses are looking to grow, however, it is likely that many small companies will retain simple organizational structures.

For those small businesses that are looking to grow, the move from one OLC stage to another occurs because the fit between the organization and its environment is so inadequate that either the organization's efficiency and/or effectiveness is seriously impaired or the organization's very survival is

existence

A business is up and running, and the strategy is to stay alive.

survival

A business is viable, and the focus shifts to revenues and expenses.

success

A business is economically healthy. The owners are considering leveraging the company for growth or using the company as a means of support while disengaging.

success-growth substage

An owner risks all resources in financing growth.

success-disengagement substage

An owner's operational duties are assumed by managers. The focus is on maintaining the status quo.

take-off

A business becomes increasingly complex. The owner must decide how to grow rapidly and finance growth.

resource maturity

A business has demonstrated success. There is a strong chance of continued growth and success if entrepreneurial spirit can be maintained.

ossification

If innovation is lacking, risk aversion is prevalent, and the entrepreneurial spirit is gone, a business may exhibit stalled or halted growth.

organizational life cycle (OLC)

The four stages that organizations go through in their development: birth, youth, midlife, and maturity.

threatened. Pressure will come from changes in the nature and number of requirements, opportunities, and threats.[78]

Four OLC stages can be observed: birth, youth, midlife, and maturity.[79] In the **birth** stage, a small business will have a very simple organizational structure, one in which the owner does everything. There are few, if any, subordinates. As the business moves through **youth** and **midlife**, more sophisticated structures will be adopted, and authority will be decentralized to middle- and lower-level managers. At maturity, firms will demonstrate significantly more concern for internal efficiency, install more control mechanisms and processes, and become very bureaucratic. There are other features as well that characterize the movement of an organization from birth to maturity, which are summarized in Table 1.6.

TABLE 1.6 Organizational Life Cycle Features

Feature	Birth Cycle	Youth Cycle	Midlife Cycle	Maturity Cycle
Size	Small	Medium	Large	Very large
Bureaucratic	Nonbureaucratic	Prebureaucratic	Bureaucratic	Very bureaucratic
Division of labor	Overlapping tasks	Some departments	Many departments	Extensive, with small jobs and many descriptions
Centralization	One-person rule	Two leaders rule	Two department heads	Top-management heavy
Formalization	No written rules	Few rules	Policy and procedure manuals	Extensive
Administrative intensity	Secretary, no professional staff	Increasing clerical and maintenance	Increasing professional and staff support	Large-multiple departments
Internal systems	Nonexistent	Crude budget and information	Control systems in place: budget, performance, reports, etc.	Extensive planning, financial, and personnel added
Lateral teams, task forces for coordination	None	Top leaders only	Some use of integrators and task	Frequent at lower levels to break down bureaucracy

Source: Richard L. Daft, Organizational Theory and Design (St. Paul, MN: West Publishing, 1992), as cited in Carter McNamara, "Basic Overview of Organizational Life Cycles," accessed October 7, 2011, http://managementhelp.org/organizations/life-cycles.htm.

A small business will always be somewhere on the OLC continuum. Business success will often be based on recognizing where the business is situated along that continuum and adopting strategies best suited to that place in the cycle.

3.3 Industry Life Cycle

The industry life cycle (ILC) is another dimension of small business evolution, which needs to be understood and assessed in concert with the stages of small business growth and the OLC. All small businesses compete in an industry, and that industry will experience a life cycle just as products and organizations do. Although there may be overlap in the names of the ILC stages, the meaning and implications of each stage are different.

The **industry life cycle** refers to the continuum along which an industry is born, grows, matures, and eventually experiences decline and then dies. Although the pattern is predictable, the duration of each stage in the cycle is not. The stages are the same for all industries, but every industry will experience the stages differently. The stages will last longer for some and pass quickly for others; even within the same industry various small businesses may find themselves at different life cycle stages.[80] However, no matter where a small business finds itself along the ILC continuum, the strategic planning of that business will be influenced in important ways.

According to one study, the ILC, charted on the basis of the growth of an industry's sales over time, can be observed as having four stages: introduction, growth, maturity, and decline.[81] The **introduction** stage[82] finds the industry in its infancy. Although it is possible for a small business to be alone in the industry as a result of having developed and introduced something new to the marketplace, this is not the usual situation. The business strategy will focus on stressing the uniqueness of the product or the service to a small group of customers, commonly referred to as innovators or early adopters. A significant amount of capital is required. Profits are usually negative for both the firm and the industry.

The **growth** stage[83] is the second ILC stage. This stage also requires a significant amount of capital, but increasing product standardization may lead to economies of scale that will, in turn, increase profitability. The strategic focus is product differentiation, with an increased focus on responding to customer needs and interests. Intense competition will result as more new competitors join the industry, but many firms will be profitable. The duration of the growth stage will be industry dependent.

The **maturity** stage[84] will see some competition from late entrants that will try to take market share away from existing companies. This means that the marketing effort must continue to focus on product or service differentiation. There will be fewer firms in mature industries, so those that survive will be larger and more dominant. Many small businesses may move into the ranks of midsize or big businesses.

The **decline** stage[85] occurs in most industries. It is typically triggered by a product or service innovation that renders the industry obsolete. Sales will suffer, and the business goes into decline. Some companies will leave the industry, but others will remain to compete in the smaller market. The smaller businesses may be more agile for competing in a declining industry, but they will need to carefully formulate their business strategies to remain viable.

growth

An industry in which significant capital is required, economies of scale kick in, and many firms are profitable.

maturity

A business is very large, very bureaucratic, and top-management heavy. An industry in which there is competition from late entrants and where the marketing focus is on differentiation.

decline

An industry that is triggered by product or service innovation. The industry becomes obsolete, sales suffer, and many companies leave.

KEY TAKEAWAYS

- Small-business management should consider the growth stages, the OLC, and the ILC in its planning.
- There are five stages of small business growth: existence, survival, success, take-off, and resource maturity. The success stage includes two substages, growth and disengagement. Ossification may result if a mature small business loses its entrepreneurial spirit and becomes more risk averse.
- Some small businesses may not be looking to grow, so they may remain in the survival stage.
- The OLC refers to the four stages of development that organizations go through: birth, youth, midlife, and maturity.
- Some small businesses may stick with the very simple organizational structures because they are not interested in growing to the point where more complicated structures are required.
- The ILC is the time continuum along which an industry is born, grows, matures, declines, and dies.
- There are four stages in the ILC: introduction, growth, maturity, and decline.

EXERCISE

1. Interview the owners of three small businesses in your community, each a different type and size. Where would you put each business with respect to the five stages of small business growth? Justify your answer.

4. ETHICS

LEARNING OBJECTIVES

1. Define ethics.
2. Explain business ethics.
3. Describe small business ethics.
4. Understand why a small business should have an ethics policy.

Ethics are about doing the right thing. They are about well-based standards of right and wrong that prescribe what humans ought to do—usually in terms of rights, obligations, benefits to society, fairness, or specific virtues.[86] They serve as guidelines for making decisions about how to behave in specific

ethics

Standards of right and wrong.

situations; they also guide us in evaluating the actions of others.[87] Hopefully, they will provide us with a good understanding of how to react to situations long before those situations occur.

4.1   What Ethics Are Not

It is important to understand what ethics are *not*.[88]

values

Enduring beliefs that a given behavior or outcome is desirable or good.

- **Ethics are not the same as our feelings.** Our feelings are not always accurate indicators about a particular action being unethical (e.g., taking a long lunch or spending too much personal time on the Internet while at work). We all develop defense mechanisms to protect ourselves, so we may not feel badly about a particular unethical act. Some people may actually feel good about behaving unethically.
- **Ethics are not the same as religion.** Most religions champion high ethical standards, but not everyone is religious. Ethics apply to everyone.
- **Ethics are not necessarily synonymous with the law.** There will be instances in which ethical behavior and the law are the same (e.g., in the cases of murder, discrimination, whistleblower protection, and fraud). Such instances are illustrative of a good legal system. There will, however, be times when the law takes a different path than ethics—the result being ethical corruption that serves only the interests of small groups.
- **Ethics are not about following cultural norms.** Following cultural norms works only for ethical cultures. Although most cultures probably like to see themselves as ethical, all societies have been and will be plagued with norms that are unethical (e.g., slavery in the United States prior to the Civil War and sweatshops in developing countries).
- **Ethics are not synonymous with science.** Science cannot tell us what to do. The sciences can provide us with insights into human behavior, but ethics provides the reasons and the guidance for what we should do.
- **Ethics are not the same as values.** Although values are essential to ethics, the two are not synonymous. **Values** are enduring beliefs that a given behavior or outcome is desirable or good.[89] They create internal judgments that will determine how a person actually behaves. Ethics determine which values should be pursued and which should not.[90]

4.2   Why Ethics Are Important

Ethics are important because they provide structure and stabilization for society. They help us to understand what is good and bad, and this helps us to choose between right and wrong actions. Without ethics, our actions would be "random and aimless, with no way to work toward a goal because there would be no way to pick between a limitless number of goals."[91] Ethics do not provide easy answers to hard questions, but they do provide a framework within which to seek the answers.

4.3   Business Ethics

business ethics

Applying the virtue and discipline of ethics to business behavior.

Business ethics is applying the virtues and discipline of ethics to business behavior. They set the standard for how your business is conducted and define the value system of how you operate in the marketplace and within your business.[92] They are relevant to any and all aspects of business conduct: workplace issues, product and brand, corporate wrongdoing, professional ethics, and global business ethics. They apply equally to the individual who works for the company and to the company itself because all ethical and unethical business behavior eventually finds its way to the bottom line. It is almost a certainty that someone will encounter an ethical dilemma at some point in his or her professional life.

Video Link 1.1

Business Ethics in the Twenty-First Century

A PBS documentary about business ethics and social responsibility.

http://watch.wliw.org/video/1316867588

Do Business Ethics Pay?

Asking whether business ethics pay may be the wrong question to ask. Behaving ethically should happen because it is the right thing to do. However, companies large and small are in the business of making money, so the question is not an unreasonable one. Good ethics carry many benefits, not the least of which is financial good health. Companies that "outbehave" the competition ethically will also tend to outperform them financially.[93] According to an Institute of Business Ethics report, companies with a code of conduct generated significantly more economic value added and market value added than those companies without a code, experienced less price to earnings volatility, and showed a 50 percent increase in average return on capital employed.[94]

Business ethics also pay in other ways that will improve the workplace climate and, ultimately, positively impact the bottom line. They can "reduce incidents of corruption, fraud, and other malpractices; enhance the trust of customers, suppliers and contractors; enhance the credibility of buyers and salespersons; and enhance the loyalty and goodwill of employees, shareholders and customers."[95]

The Costs of Unethical Business Conduct

By contrast, the costs of unethical business behavior can be staggering. Some of the costs include the loss of physical assets, increased security, the loss of customers, the loss of employees, the loss of reputation, legal costs, the loss of investor confidence, regulatory intrusion, and the costs of bankruptcy. According to a report by the Josephson Institute,[96] unethical business behavior has an adverse impact on sales, stock prices, productivity, the performance of the highly skilled employees, efficiency, communication, and employee retention and recruiting plus the risks from scandal and employee fraud.

The costs of employee theft are particularly daunting. An estimated 75 percent of employees steal from the workplace, and most do so repeatedly. One third of all US corporate bankruptcies are caused directly by employee theft; US companies lose nearly $400 billion per year in lost productivity due to "time theft" or loafing; and an estimated 20 percent of every dollar earned by a US company is lost to employee theft.[97] Office supplies, money, and merchandise are the most frequently stolen items.[98] Employee theft may be even more of a concern to small businesses because many small businesses operate so close to the margin. It has been estimated that theft by small business employees totals nearly $40 billion each year.[99]

 Video Clip 1.2

Business Ethics with Sound
Do not steal time at work.

View the video online at: http://www.youtube.com/v/02kziRS5tZl

4.4 Small Business Ethics

In business, it is common for there to be conflicts between business success and ethical behavior. When faced with an ethical dilemma, the decision may be unduly influenced by profits and legality. This challenge is particularly acute for small business owners because they are so much closer to the employees and the customers. The results of ethical decisions will be felt more immediately by the entire company.[100]

Small-business owners will find themselves confronted more often with ethical choices because of the decision-making autonomy that they have; there is no need to answer to a large number of employees, corporate management, or a corporate board. The ethical choices that are made will likely impact a far greater number of people than will the ethical decisions of individual employees. Many business decisions will pose ethical challenges—examples being whether to use inferior materials to produce products because of competition with larger businesses, employee and workplace problems, product quality and pricing, legal problems, and government regulatory concerns.[101] The pressure to make an unethical choice on behalf of the small business can be very powerful, especially when the health and vitality of the business may be at stake.[102] Fortunately, the chances of an unethical decision being made in a small business are lower because the individual or individuals who are harmed will always be more visible. It is more difficult for the small business owner to be unethical. Ultimately, small business owners will behave in accordance with "their own moral compass, sense of fair play and inclination to deal in good faith."[103]

According to one study,[104] small businesses see norms and pressures from the community and peers as having more influence on their ethics than moral or religious principles, the anticipation of rewards, upholding the law, or the fear of punishment. This leads to the conclusion that small business is influenced significantly by the communities in which their businesses are located. Socially responsive behavior is visible and it is "rewarded or sanctioned by local residents through changes in employee morale, performance, and turnover; customer loyalty; and positive interactions with business service professionals, suppliers, local government officials, and business colleagues. These local sanctioning mechanisms [in turn affected] the success of the business."[105]

Because of this community influence, customer relationships are and must be based on trust and the relatively immediate visibility of ethical behavior. It is perhaps not surprising that people in small business are ranked number one on ethical standards ahead of physicians, people in big business, and government officials.[106]

4.5 Developing an Ethics Policy

ethics policy (code of conduct or code of ethics)

The rules and expectations about workplace behavior.

The small business owner is in a unique position to set the ethical tone for the business. Employees will follow the lead of the owner when executing their duties and tending to their responsibilities, so it is critical that the owner establish an ethical work environment.[107] Establishing an **ethics policy (code of conduct or code of ethics)** is an important step in creating that environment. Employees who work in companies with active ethics programs; who observe leaders modeling ethical behavior; and who see honesty, respect, and trust applied frequently in the workplace have reported more positive experiences that include the following:[108]

- Less pressure on employees to compromise ethics standards
- Less observed misconduct at work
- Greater willingness to report misconduct
- Greater satisfaction with their organization's response to misconduct they report
- Greater overall satisfaction with their organizations
- Greater likelihood of "feeling valued" by their organizations

These positive work experiences would be even more notable in small businesses because of the smaller number of employees.

Employee perceptions of their organization's ethical leadership may well be the most important driver of employee trust and loyalty.[109] Having an ethical culture should, therefore, be a top priority for every small business.

Many small business owners may feel that a code of ethics is unnecessary. However, the benefit of having such a code is higher employee morale and commitment, more loyal customers, and a more supportive community. Even the nonemployee small business benefits. A code of ethics puts your business in a more positive, proactive light, and it spells out to customers and employees what behavior is and is not appropriate.[110]

There is no recipe for developing an ethics policy. Its development may involve no one other than the small business owner, but it should involve several people. The contents should be specific to the values, goals, and culture of each company, and it should be "a central guide and reference for users in support of day-to-day decision making. It is meant to clarify an organization's mission, values, and principles, linking them with the standards of professional conduct."[111] Small-business owners must decide what will make the most sense for their companies. Jeff Wuorio offered the following eight guidelines:[112]

1. **Focus on business practices and specific issues.** The content of one company's code of ethics will differ from that of another.
2. **Tailor it to fit your business.** One size does not fit all. Make sure your code of ethics reflects the values and mission of your company.

3. **Include employees in developing a code of ethics.** A mandate from the small business owner will not be effective. Get input from your employees whenever possible. They will be more accepting of the ethics policy.

4. **Train your people to be ethical.** The extent and nature of employee education and training will depend on the size of the small business. Even the smallest business, however, will benefit from some ethics training.

5. **Post your code of ethics internally and set up a reporting system.** Employees need a way to let someone know about ethics violations. Both an open-door policy and an anonymous reporting system will be helpful.

6. **Consider appointing a compliance person.** This would probably not be appropriate for the very small businesses. However, it would be worth considering if the business has fifty or more employees. Having someone to whom employees can report suspected ethical problems would make things much simpler.

7. **Follow up on any ethics violations you uncover.** Make sure that everyone understands the ramifications of ethics policy violations. Include an appeals process. If a small business owner fails to act on ethics violations, employees will not take the policy seriously.

8. **Live it from the top down.** The small business owner must walk the talk. No one should appear to be above the code of ethics. Good role modeling is critical.

The actual development of a code of ethics can be done by starting from scratch, hiring a consultant, or customizing a code from another organization. Before making a choice, it would be worth doing some research. A good place to start would be www.conductcode.com, a website that looks at codes of conduct from a practitioner approach. A search of the Internet will provide examples of codes of ethics, but there is a bias toward larger companies, so small business owners will have to pick and choose what will be best suited to their respective companies.

Ethical Behavior Survey

The Ethics Resource Center conducted a survey of employees at large and small businesses and found the following:

- Fifty-six percent of the employees had witnessed misconduct by other employees that violated the firm's ethics standards or policies or the law.
- Fifty-four percent of the employees who had witnessed misconduct believed that reporting the misconduct would not lead to corrective action.
- Forty-two percent of the employees who had witnessed misconduct reported it. The percentage rose to 61 percent for employees whose employers have a well-implemented ethics and compliance program.
- Thirty-six percent of the employees who had witnessed misconduct but did not report it cited fear of retaliation as their reason for not reporting it.[113]

KEY TAKEAWAYS

- Ethics are about doing the right thing. They are about standards that help us decide between right and wrong. They are not the same as our feelings, religion, the law, cultural norms, science, or values.
- Ethics are important because they provide structure and stabilization for society.
- Business ethics are about applying the virtues and discipline of ethics to business behavior. They set the standard for how your business is conducted and define the value system of how you operate in the marketplace and within your business.
- Companies that "outbehave" the competition ethically tend to outperform them financially.
- Ethical behavior in business improves the workplace climate and will ultimately improve the bottom line. The cost of unethical behavior can be staggering.
- Small-business owners have the opportunity to set the ethical tone for their companies. Modeling ethical behavior is key. The community and peers heavily influence small business ethics.
- Establishing an ethics policy is critical for creating an ethical work environment. The contents of the policy should be specific to the values, goals, and culture of each company. One size does not fit all.

1. MaryAnn's marketing team just presented a "Less Sugar" ad campaign to the cereal brand manager for three of her brands. The packages shouted "75% LESS SUGAR" in large and colorful type so that it would catch the parent's eye and increase sales. With all the recent attention about childhood obesity, the company thought that parents would purchase the cereal to help their children attain and keep a healthy weight. A side-by-side comparison of the less-sugar and the high-sugar versions of the cereals, however, revealed that the carbohydrate content of the cereals was essentially the same. At best, the less-sugar version had only ten fewer calories per bowl. It offered no weight-loss advantage. The brand manager correctly concluded that the marketing campaign was unethical.[114] Was the campaign illegal? What should the cereal brand manager do?

2. An office supplies business with fifty employees has been doing well, but lately there have been suspicions by some of the employees. No names are known, but it is known that merchandise has been disappearing without explanation, and expensive gifts have been accepted from some vendors. The owner thinks it is time to create and implement a code of ethics. She has asked you for advice. You told her that it would be important to involve the employees in the development of the code, but you committed to do two things for her in preparation for that involvement: (1) search the Internet for a code of ethics that could be tailored to her needs and (2) prepare a preliminary list of topics that should be included in the code. She thanked you and asked that you submit your ideas within the week. She reminded you that her business is small, so a code of ethics for a large corporation would not be suitable.

5. THE THREE THREADS

1. Define customer value and explain why it is important to small business competitiveness.
2. Define digital technology and explain its role in small business competitiveness.
3. Define e-business and explain why e-business is important to small businesses.
4. Define e-commerce and explain why e-commerce should be integrated into small businesses.

There are three threads that flow throughout this text: customer value, cash flow, and digital resources and e-environments. These threads can be likened to the human body. Cash flow is the circulatory system, without which there can be no life. Digital technology and e-business are the internal organs that carry out daily processes. E-commerce is the sensory system that enables business to observe and interact with the external environment. Customer value is overall health. These threads must figure prominently in all small business decision making. Although they are necessary but not sufficient conditions for small business survival, the chances for survival will be reduced significantly if they are not used.

5.1 Customer Value

In 1916, Nathan Hanwerker was an employee at one of the largest restaurants on Coney Island—but he had a vision. Using his wife's recipe, he and his wife opened a hot dog stand. He believed that the combination of a better tasting hot dog and the nickel price, half that of his competitors, was his recipe for success. He was wrong. Unfortunately for Nathan, Upton Sinclair's book *The Jungle* a decade before had made the public suspicious of low-cost meat products. Nathan discovered that his initial business model was not working. Customers valued taste and cost, but they also valued the quality of a safe product. To convince customers that his hot dogs were safe, he secured several doctors' smocks and had people wear them. The sight of "doctors" consuming Nathan's hot dogs gave customers the extra value that they needed. It was all about the perception of quality. If doctors were eating the hot dogs, they must be OK. Today there are over 20,000 outlets serving Nathan's hot dogs.[115]

In principle, **customer value** is a very simple concept. It is the difference between the benefits that a customer receives from a product or a service and the costs associated with obtaining that product or service. **Total customer benefit** refers to the perceived monetary value of the bundle of economic, functional, and psychological benefits customers expect from a product or a service because of the products, services, personnel, and images involved. **Total customer cost**, the perceived bundle of costs that customers expect to occur when they evaluate, obtain, use, and dispose of the product or use the service, include monetary, time, energy, and psychological costs.[116] In short, it is all about what customers get and what they have to give up.

In reality, the creation of customer value will always be a challenge—particularly because it almost always needs to be defined on the customer's terms.[117] Nonetheless, "the number one goal of business should be to 'maximize customer value and strive to increase value continuously.' If a firm maximizes customer value, relative to competitors, success will follow. If a firm's products are viewed as conveying little customer value, the firm will eventually atrophy and fail."[118] This will certainly be true for the small business that is much closer to its customers than the large business.

The small business owner needs to be thinking about customer value every day: what is offered now, how it can be made better, and what the competition is doing that is offering more value. It is not easy, but it is essential. All business decisions will add to or detract from the value that can be offered to the customer. If your product or service is perceived to offer more value than that of the competition, you will get the sale. Otherwise, you will not get the sale.

5.2 Cash Flow

Revenue is vanity…margin is sanity…cash is king.
 - Unknown.

Most people would define success with respect to profits or sales. This misses a critical point. The survival of a firm hinges not so much on sales or profits, although these are vitally important, as it does on the firm's ability to meet its financial obligations. A firm must learn to properly manage its **cash flow**, defined as the money coming into and flowing from a business because cash is more than king. *It is a firm's lifeblood.* As the North Dakota Small Business Development Center put it, "Failure to properly plan cash flow is one of the leading causes for small business failure."[119]

An understanding of cash flow requires some understanding of accounting systems. There are two types: cash based and accrual. In a **cash-based accounting** system, sales are recorded when you receive the money. This type of system is really meant for small firms with sales totaling less than $1 million. **Accrual accounting** systems, by contrast, are systems that focus on measuring profits. They assume that when you make a sale, you are paid at that point. However, almost all firms make sales on credit, and they also make purchases on credit. Add in that sales are seldom constant, and you begin to see how easily and often cash inflows and outflows can fall out of sync. This can reduce a firm's **liquidity**, which is its ability to pay its bills. Envision the following scenario: A firm generates tremendous sales by using easy credit terms: 10 percent down and one year to pay the remaining 90 percent. However, the firm purchases its materials under tight credit terms. In an accrual accounting system, this might appear to produce significant profits. However, the firm may be unable to pay its bills and salaries. In this type of situation, the firm, particularly the small firm, can easily fail.

There are other reasons why cash flow is critically important. Firms need to have the money to buy new materials or expand. In addition, firms should have cash available to meet unexpected contingencies or investment opportunities.

Cash-flow management requires a future-focused orientation. You have to anticipate your future cash inflows and outflows and what actions you may need to take to preserve your liquidity. Today, even the nonemployee firm can begin this process with simple spreadsheet software. Slightly larger firms could opt for the user-dedicated software. In either case, cash-flow analysis requires the owner to focus on the future and to develop effective planning skills.

Cash-flow management also involves activities such as expense control, receivables management, inventory control, and developing a close relationship with commercial lenders. The small business owner needs to think about these things every day. Their requirements may tax many small business operators, but they are essential skills.

customer value

The difference between the benefits a customer receives from a product or a service and the costs associated with obtaining the product or the service.

Total customer benefit

The perceived monetary value of economic, functional, and psychological benefits customers expect from a product or a service because of the products, services, personnel, and images involved.

Total customer cost

The perceived bundle of costs customers expect to incur when they evaluate, obtain, use, and dispose of the product or the service.

cash flow

The money coming into and exiting a business.

cash-based accounting

Sales are recorded when the money is received.

accrual accounting

The focus is on measuring profits.

liquidity

The ability of a small business to pay its bills.

cash-flow management

Expense control, receivables management, inventory control, and developing a close relationship with commercial lenders.

expense control

Seeking out efficiencies and cost-reduction strategies.

receivables management

Trying to receive customer payments as quickly as possible.

inventory control

Understanding the ABC classification system and determining order quantities and reorder points.

ABC classification system

A method of inventory management by which items are ranked according to their volume and value.

lean inventory management

Minimizing inventory by eliminating sources of waste.

equity loans

Pledging physical assets for cash.

digital technology

The broad spectrum of computer hardware, software, information retrieval and manipulation systems, and communication systems.

e-environment

A catchall term that includes e-business and e-commerce.

enterprise resource planning (ERP)

A system that integrates multiple business functions from purchasing to sales, billings, accounting records, and payroll.

- **Expense control** requires owners or operators to think in terms of constantly seeking out efficiencies and cost-reduction strategies.
- **Receivables management** forces owners to think about how to walk the delicate balance of offering customers the benefits of credit while trying to receive the payments as quickly as possible. They can use technology and e-business to expedite the cash inflow.
- Effective **inventory control** translates into an understanding of the **ABC classification system** (sorting inventory by volume and value), and determining order quantities and reorder points. Inevitably, any serious consideration of inventory management leads one to the study of "lean" philosophies. **Lean inventory management** refers to approaches that focus on minimizing inventory by eliminating all sources of waste. Lean inventory management inevitably leads its practitioners to adopt a new process-driven view of the firm and its operations.
- Lastly, attention to cash-flow management recognizes that there may well be periods when cash outflows will exceed cash inflows. You may have to use commercial loans, **equity loans** (pledging physical assets for cash), and/or lines of credit. These may not be offered by a lender at the drop of a hat. Small-business owners need to anticipate these cash shortfalls and should already have an established working relationship with a commercial lender.

A small business needs to be profitable over the long term if it is going to survive. However, this becomes problematic if the business is not generating enough cash to pay its way on a daily basis.[120] Cash flow can be a sign of the health—or pending death—of a small business. The need to ensure that cash is properly managed must therefore be a top priority for the business.[121] This is why cash-flow implications must be considered when making all business decisions. Everything will be a cash flow factor one way or the other. Fred Adler, a venture capitalist, could not have said it better when he said, "Happiness is a positive cash flow."[122]

5.3   Digital Technology and the E-Environment

Digital technology and the e-environment continue to change the way small and large businesses operate. **Digital technology** refers to a broad spectrum of computer hardware, software, and information retrieval and manipulation systems. The **e-environment** is a catchall term that includes e-business and e-commerce. The Internet in particular has had a powerful impact on the demands of customers, suppliers, and vendors, each of whom is ready—perhaps even expects—to do business 24/7.

Why Digital Technology?

With the advent of the personal computer and the Internet, small firms may be able to compete on a more equal footing with larger firms through their intelligent use of digital technologies. It would be impossible to list all the types of software that can enhance small business operations, so the focus will be on the major types of aids.

Today, even the smallest of firms can acquire a complete accounting system at a reasonable price. These packages can be tailored for specific industries and are designed to grow with the company. They not only generate standard accounting and financial reports but also assist with management decision making. Information about accounting software for small businesses is easily available on the Internet.

Small-business operations have also benefited greatly from affordable software that can handle forecasting, inventory control and purchasing, customer relations, and shipping and receiving. In fact, the software has advanced to the point where a small firm can cost-effectively possess its own **enterprise resource planning (ERP)** system. Only a few years ago, ERP systems were out of reach for all but the largest firms. ERP systems integrate multiple business functions, from purchasing to sales, billings, accounting records, and payroll (see Figure 1.2). These advances now give small firms the capability and opportunity to participate in global supply chains, thus broadening their customer base.

FIGURE 1.2 Broad Schematic of an ERP System

Touch screen computers, smartphones, or iPads can bring a new level of sophistication to data entry and manipulation and communications. Smartphones can boost productivity, especially when out of the office.[123] It is predicted that the iPad will change how we build business relationships, particularly with respect to connecting with prospects in a more meaningful way.[124] Inventory control may soon be revolutionized by a technology known as **radio-frequency identity devices (RFIDs)**. These small devices enable the tracking of inventory items. These same devices may change retailing by curtailing time at checkout and eliminating pilferage.[125]

radio-frequency identity device (RFID)

A small device that enables the tracking of inventory items.

Using Smartphones in Your Business

Lloyd's Construction is a 100-person demolition and carting firm in Eagan, Minnesota. This small, family-owned business is not your typical candidate for a firm that exploits cutting-edge technology. At the suggestion of the president's 17-year-old daughter, the firm switched to a smartphone system that allows for integrated data entry and communication. This system allowed the firm to reduce its routing and fuel costs by as much as 30 percent. The firm was also able to further reduce accounting and dispatch costs. On an investment of $50,000, the firm estimated that it saved $1 million in 2007.[126]

Video Clip 1.3

RFID Technology
How RFIDs work.

View the video online at: http://www.youtube.com/v/4Zj7txoDxbE

Video Clip 1.4

The Future Market
How grocery shopping may change with RFID.

View the video online at: http://www.youtube.com/v/eob532iEpqk

All these technologies, and others, are within the reach of the small business, but careful analysis must determine which technologies are best suited for a company. Given the speed of digital technology development, this analysis is something that should be conducted on a frequent basis. It is in the best interest of every small business to introduce digital technologies into the business as quickly as is practical and affordable. There should always be an interest in doing things better and faster. Through technology, a small business owner will be able to do so much more: grow the business (if desired), work smarter, attract more customers, enhance customer service, and stay ahead of the competition.[127]

The smaller the business, the more efficient it needs to be. Digital technology can help. Digital technologies, with their relatively low cost, ease of implementation, and power, can offer small businesses the rare opportunity to compete with larger rivals. If smaller firms are able to fully use the capabilities of these technologies along with exploiting their faster decision-making cycle, they can be the ones that secure competitive advantage.

Why E-business?

e-business

The use of the Internet and online technologies to create operational efficiencies.

E-business is a term that is often used interchangeably with e-commerce, but this is not accurate. **E-business** uses the Internet and online technologies to create operational efficiencies, thereby increasing value to the customer.[128] Its focus is internal—for example, online inventory control systems; accounting systems; procurement processes; supplier performance evaluation processes; tools to increase supply chain efficiency; processing requests for machine repairs; and the integration of planning, sourcing, and manufacturing. Critical business systems are connected to critical constituencies—customers, vendors, and suppliers—via the Internet, extranets, and intranets.[129] No revenue is generated, but "e-business applications turn into e-commerce precisely when an exchange of value occurs."[130]

E-business processes should be introduced wherever there is a process that is currently working OK but is costing unnecessary time and money to implement via paper. This would certainly apply to the small business that finds itself drowning in paperwork. Small businesses should always consider that e-business processes could improve their operational and cost efficiencies overall, so thinking about e-business implications should be part of many decisions. E-business can work for any small business "because it involves the whole business cycle for production, procurement, distribution, sales, payment, fulfillment, restocking and marketing. It's about relationships with customers, employees, suppliers and distributors. It involves support services like banks, lawyers, accountants and government agencies."[131] The way you do business and your future profitability will be affected by e-business. Converting your current business into e-business may require some redesign and reshaping, depending on the size of your company. However, e-business integration should be seen as an essential element in the efforts of a small business to increase its agility in responding to customer, market, and other strategic requirements.[132]

Why E-commerce?

E-commerce, the marketing, selling, and buying of goods and services online, is a subset of e-business. It generates revenue, whereas other areas of e-business do not. E-commerce has experienced extraordinary and rapid growth and will continue to grab more market share.[133]

In a survey of 400 small businesses, each with fewer than 100 employees, it was reported that the Internet had significantly improved growth and profitability while helping to reduce costs. Some businesses even indicated that they rely on the Internet to survive. Interestingly, the survey participants themselves took advantage of e-commerce to purchase computers and office technology online (54 percent), capital equipment and supplies (48 percent), and office furnishings (21 percent); one third bought inventory for online resale, and 59 percent purchased other business-related goods online.[134] E-commerce offers many benefits to small businesses, including the following:[135]

> **e-commerce**
>
> The subset of e-business that involves the marketing, selling, and buying of goods and services online.

- **Lower business costs.** It may not be necessary to maintain as much physical space and staff.
- **Greater accessibility.** Customers can shop when they want to.
- **The ability to provide customized service.** Like Amazon.com, companies can address their customers on a personal level by recognizing and greeting repeat shoppers.
- **Increased customer loyalty.** Companies can give information to customers while offering something of value (e.g., a coupon for use on the next purchase or helpful hints about using a product).

These benefits make it possible for a small business to compete with, perhaps even overtake, larger companies that do not have the agility and innovation of a smaller company.

The realities of Internet usage make a strong case for small businesses to integrate e-commerce into their operations, including the following:

- Seventy-four percent of American adults use the Internet.
- Eighty-one percent use the Internet for information online about a service or product they are thinking of buying.
- Seventy-one percent buy products online.[136]
- Sixty-six percent of adults have home broadband.[137]
- American small businesses have embraced broadband.[138]
- Fifty-five percent of American adults connect to the Internet wirelessly.[139]
- All income groups have high Internet usage, from 65 percent (less than $30,000 per year) to 98 percent ($75,000 per year or more).[140]
- Forty-six percent of small business owners plan to grow their businesses by creating or improving their company's online presence.[141]
- Almost half (49 percent) of online adults have used online classified ads.[142]

We live in a society of 24/7 immediacy, where the equivalent of foot traffic is increasingly becoming eyeballs on a website.[143] People and businesses turn to the Internet to solve problems and address the needs that they have. Embracing this change and moving existing small business practices to include e-commerce would not seem to be an option. Rather, it is increasingly becoming a requirement for survival. Even so, small business must think carefully about how to enter the e-commerce world or, if already there, how to best take advantage of the opportunities. Both situations will require careful and deliberate decision making that takes e-commerce implications into consideration regularly.

KEY TAKEAWAYS

- The creation of customer value must be a top priority for small business. The small business owner should be thinking about it every day.
- Cash flow is a firm's lifeblood. Without a positive cash flow, a small business cannot survive. All business decisions will have an impact on cash flow—which is why small business owners must think about it every day.
- A cash-based accounting system is for small firms with sales totaling less than $1 million. Accrual accounting systems measure profits instead of cash.
- Digital technologies are very important to small businesses. They can improve efficiencies, help create greater customer value, and make the business more competitive. Digital technology integration should be something that small business owners think about regularly.
- It is not correct to use the terms *e-business* and *e-commerce* interchangeably. E-commerce is a subset of e-business.
- E-business can work for any small business.
- E-commerce generates revenue. E-business does not.
- Moving existing small business practices to e-commerce is increasingly becoming a requirement for survival.

EXERCISES

1. "A customer calls L.L. Bean about a favorite jacket he purchased more than 10 years ago and has recently lost. In a matter of minutes, the sales agent identifies the old jacket, locates a replacement model in the current catalog, suggests a matching size and color, and orders the jacket. The replacement jacket arrives three days later."[144] How has L.L. Bean added to the customer's perception of value?

2. When thinking about customer value, you should plan to address three questions: (a) What do my customers truly value? (b) What do I provide? and (c) How does what I provide differ from my competitors? Select a small business and interview the owner to see how he or she answered these questions. Pay particular attention to the first question.

3. Intuit QuickBooks, Peachtree, and AccountEdge are three popular accounting packages. Gather information from their websites and conduct a comparative analysis as though you were a new small business looking to buy one of them.

ENDNOTES

1. "Small Business by the Numbers," *National Small Business Administration*, accessed October 7, 2011, www.nsba.biz/docs/bythenumbers.pdf.

2. "A Definition of Entrepreneurship," *QuickMBA.com*, accessed October 7, 2011, www.quickmba.com/entre/definition.

3. Nick Leiber, "The Anatomy of an Entrepreneur," *Bloomberg BusinessWeek*, July 8, 2009, accessed October 7, 2011, www.BusinessWeek.com/smallbiz/running_small_business/archives/2009/07/anatomy_of_an_e.html.

4. "Entrepreneur vs. Small Business Owner: What's the Difference?," *Mills Communication Group*, July 22, 2009, accessed October 7, 2011, www.millscommgroup.com/blog/2009/06/entrepreneur-vs-small-business-owner-whats-the-difference.

5. Dale Beermann, "Entrepreneur or Small Business Owner? Does It Matter?," *Brazen Careerist*, January 30, 2009, accessed October 7, 2011, www.brazencareerist.com/2009/01/29/entrepreneur-or-small-business-owner-does-it-matter.

6. Jack Beatty, *The Age of Betrayal: The Triumph of Money in America 1865–1900* (New York: Alfred A. Knopf, 2007), 11.

7. Ted Nace, *The Gangs of America: The Rise of Corporate Power and the Disabling of Democracy* (San Francisco: Berrett-Koehler Publishers, 2003), 44.

8. Bob Higgins, "Like Lincoln, Jefferson, Madison—Americans Fear Corporate Control of Public Policy," *TPMCafe*, February 17, 2011, accessed October 23, 2011, tpmcafe.talkingpointsmemo.com/talk/blogs/h/l/rlh974/2010/02/like-lincoln-jefferson-madison.php.

9. Ted Nace, *The Gangs of America: The Rise of Corporate Power and the Disabling of Democracy* (San Francisco, Berrett-Koehler Publishers, 2003), 44.

10. Mansel Blackford, *The History of Small Business in America*, 2nd ed. (Chapel Hill, NC: University of North Carolina Press, 2003), 4.

11. "What We Do," *Small Business Administration*, accessed October 7, 2011, www.sba.gov/about-sba-services/what-we-do.

12. Christopher Conte, "Small Business in U.S. History," *America.gov*, January 3, 2006, accessed October 7, 2011, www.america.gov/st/business-english/2008/July/20080814215602XJyrreP0.6187664.html.

13. Mansel Blackford, *The History of Small Business in America*, 2nd ed. (Chapel Hill, NC: University of North Carolina Press, 2003), 4.

14. Katherine Kobe, "The Small Business Share of GDP, 1998–2004," *Small Business Research Summary*, April 2007, accessed October 7, 2011, http://archive.sba.gov/advo/research/rs299tot.pdf.

15. Zoltan J. Acs and David B. Audretsch. "Innovation in Large and Small Firms: An Empirical Analysis," *American Economic Review* 78, no. 4 (1988): 678–90.

16. "Small Business by the Numbers," *National Small Business Administration*, accessed October 7, 2011, www.nsba.biz/docs/bythenumbers.pdf.

17. Jeff Cornwall, "Innovation in Small Business," *The Entrepreneurial Mind*, March 16, 2009, accessed June 1, 2012, http://www.drjeffcornwall.com/2009/03/16/innovation_in_small_business/.

18. "Small Business by the Numbers," *National Small Business Administration*, accessed October 7, 2011, www.nsba.biz/docs/bythenumbers.pdf.

19. "Statistics of U.S. Businesses," *US Census Bureau*, April 13, 2010, accessed October 7, 2011, www.census.gov/econ/susb.

20. William J Dennis Jr., Bruce D. Phillips, and Edward Starr, "Small Business Job Creation: The Findings and Their Critics", *Business Economics* 29, no. 3 (1994): 23–30.

21. Brian Headd, "An Analysis of Small Business and Jobs," *Small Business Administration*, March 2010, accessed October 7, 2011, www.sba.gov/advo/research/rs359tot.pdf (p. 10).

22. "Statistics of U.S. Businesses," *US Census Bureau*, April 13, 2010, accessed October 7, 2011, www.census.gov/econ/susb.

23. William Dunkelberg and A. C. Cooper. "Entrepreneurial Typologies: An Empirical Study," *Frontiers of Entrepreneurial Research*, ed. K. H. Vesper (Wellesley, MA: Babson College, Centre for Entrepreneurial Studies, 1982), 1–15.

24. "Report on the Commission or Enquiry on Small Firms," *Bolton Report*, vol. 339 (London: HMSO, February 1973), 156–73.

25. Paul Burns and Christopher Dewhurst, *Small Business and Entrepreneurship*, 2nd ed. (Basingstoke, UK: Macmillan, 1996), 17.

26. Graham Beaver, *Business, Entrepreneurship and Enterprise Development* (Englewood Cliffs, NJ: Prentice Hall, 2002), 33.

27. Terry L. Besser, "Community Involvement and the Perception of Success Among Small Business Operators in Small Towns," *Journal of Small Business Management* 37, no 4 (1999): 16.

28. M. K. J. Stanworth and J. Curran, "Growth and the Small Firm: An Alternative View," *Journal of Management Studies* 13, no. 2 (1976): 95–111.

29. Roger Dickinson, "Business Failure Rate," *American Journal of Small Business* 6, no. 2 (1981): 17–25.

30. A. B. Cochran, "Small Business Failure Rates: A Review of the Literature," *Journal of Small Business Management* 19, no. 4, (1981): 50–59.

31. Don Bradley and Chris Cowdery, "Small Business: Causes of Bankruptcy," July 26, 2004, accessed October 7, 2011, www.sbaer.uca.edu/research/asbe/2004_fall/16.pdf.

32. "Equifax Study Shows the Ups and Downs of Commercial Credit Trends," *Equifax*, 2010, accessed October 7, 2011, www.equifax.com/PR/pdfs/CommercialFactSheetFN3810.pdf.

33. Don Bradley and Chris Cowdery, "Small Business: Causes of Bankruptcy," July 26, 2004, accessed October 7, 2011, www.sbaer.uca.edu/research/asbe/2004_fall/16.pdf.

34. Don Bradley and Chris Cowdery, "Small Business: Causes of Bankruptcy," July 26, 2004, accessed October 7, 2011, www.sbaer.uca.edu/research/asbe/2004_fall/16.pdf.

35. Anita Campbell, "Business Failure Rates Is Highest in First Two Years," *Small Business Trends*, July 7, 2005, accessed October 7, 2011, smallbiztrends.com/2005/07/business-failure-rates-highest-in.html.

36. T. C. Carbone, "The Challenges of Small Business Management," *Management World* 9, no. 10 (1980): 36.

37. John Argenti, *Corporate Collapse: The Causes and Symptoms* (New York: McGraw-Hill, 1976), 45.

38. Graham Beaver, "Small Business: Success and Failure," *Strategic Change* 12, no. 3 (2003): 115–22.

39. Sharon Nelton, "Ten Key Threats to Success," *Nation's Business* 80, no. 6 (1992): 18–24.

40. Robert N. Steck, "Why New Businesses Fail," *Dun and Bradstreet Reports* 33, no. 6 (1985): 34–38.

41. G. E. Tibbits, "Small Business Management: A Normative Approach," in *Small Business Perspectives*, ed. Peter Gorb, Phillip Dowell, and Peter Wilson (London: Armstrong Publishing, 1981), 105.

42. Jim Brown, *Business Growth Action Kit* (London: Kogan Page, 1995), 26.

43. Christopher Orpen, "Strategic Planning, Scanning Activities and the Financial Performance of Small Firms," *Journal of Strategic Change* 3, no. 1 (1994): 45–55.

44. Sandra Hogarth-Scott, Kathryn Watson, and Nicholas Wilson, "Do Small Business Have to Practice Marketing to Survive and Grow?," *Marketing Intelligence and Planning* 14, no 1 (1995): 6–18.

45. Isaiah A. Litvak and Christopher J. Maule, "Entrepreneurial Success or Failure—Ten Years Later," *Business Quarterly* 45, no. 4 (1980): 65.

46. Hans J. Pleitner, "Strategic Behavior in Small and Medium-Sized Firms: Preliminary Considerations," *Journal of Small Business Management* 27, no. 4 (1989): 70–75.

47. Richard Monk, "Why Small Businesses Fail," *CMA Management* 74, no. 6 (2000): 12.

48. Anonymous, "Top-10 Deadly Mistakes for Small Business," *Green Industry Pro* 19, no. 7 (2007): 58.

49. Rubik Atamian and Neal R. VanZante, "Continuing Education: A Vital Ingredient of the 'Success Plan' for Business," *Journal of Business and Economic Research* 8, no. 3 (2010): 37–42.

50. T. Carbone, "Four Common Management Failures—And How to Avoid Them," *Management World* 10, no. 8 (1981): 38–39.

51. Anonymous, "Top-10 Deadly Mistakes for Small Business," *Green Industry Pro* 19, no. 7 (2007): 58.

52. Rubik Atamian and Neal R. VanZante, "Continuing Education: A Vital Ingredient of the 'Success Plan' for Business," *Journal of Business and Economic Research* 8, no. 3 (2010): 37–42.

53. Howard Upton, "Management Mistakes in a New Business," *National Petroleum News* 84, no. 10 (1992): 50.

54. Rubik Atamian and Neal R. VanZante, "Continuing Education: A Vital Ingredient of the 'Success Plan' for Business," *Journal of Business and Economic Research* 8, no. 3 (2010): 37–42.

55. Arthur R. DeThomas and William B. Fredenberger, "Accounting Needs of Very Small Business," *The CPA Journal* 55, no. 10 (1985): 14–20.

56. Roger Brown, "Keeping Control of Your Credit," *Motor Transportation*, April 2009, 8.

57. Arthur R. DeThomas and William B. Fredenberger, "Accounting Needs of Very Small Business," *The CPA Journal* 55, no. 10 (1985): 14–20.

58. Hugh M. O'Neill and Jacob Duker, "Survival and Failure in Small Business," *Journal of Small Business Management* 24, no. 1 (1986): 30–37.

59. Arthur R. DeThomas and William B. Fredenberger, "Accounting Needs of Very Small Business," *The CPA Journal* 55, no. 10 (1985): 14–20.

60. Jim Everett and John Watson, "Small Business Failures and External Risk Factors," *Small Business Economics* 11, no. 4 (1998): 371–90.

61. Jim Everett and John Watson, "Small Business Failures and External Risk Factors," *Small Business Economics* 11, no. 4 (1998): 371–90.

62. Roger Ehrenberg, "Monitor 110: A Post Mortem—Turning Failure into Learning," *Making It!*, August 27, 2009, accessed June 1, 2012, http://www.makingittv.com/Small-Business-Entrepreneur-Story-Failure.htm.

63. "Organizational Life Cycle," *Inc.*, 2010, accessed October 7, 2011, www.inc.com/encyclopedia/organizational-life-cycle.html.

64. B. Kotey and G. G. Meredith, "Relationships among Owner/Manager Personal Values, Business Strategies, and Enterprise Performance," *Journal of Small Business Management* 35, no. 2 (1997): 37–65.

65. Neil C. Churchill and Virginia L. Lewis, "The Five Stages of Small Business Growth," *Harvard Business Review* 61, no. 3 (1983): 30–44, 48–50.

66. Neil C. Churchill and Virginia L. Lewis, "The Five Stages of Small Business Growth," *Harvard Business Review* 61, no. 3 (1983): 30–44, 48–50.

67. Darrell Zahorsky, "Find Your Business Life Cycle," accessed October 7, 2011, sbinformation.about.com/cs/marketing/a/a040603.htm.

68. Neil C. Churchill and Virginia L. Lewis, "The Five Stages of Small Business Growth," *Harvard Business Review* 61, no. 3 (1983): 30–44, 48–50.

69. Neil C. Churchill and Virginia L. Lewis, "The Five Stages of Small Business Growth," *Harvard Business Review* 61, no. 3 (1983): 30–44, 48–50.

70. Shivonne Byrne, "Empowering Small Business," *Innuity*, June 25, 2007, accessed October 7, 2011, innuity.typepad.com/innuity_empowers_small_bu/2007/06/five-stages-of.html.

71. Neil C. Churchill and Virginia L. Lewis, "The Five Stages of Small Business Growth," *Harvard Business Review* 61, no. 3 (1983): 30–44, 48–50.

72. Neil C. Churchill and Virginia L. Lewis, "The Five Stages of Small Business Growth," *Harvard Business Review* 61, no. 3 (1983): 30–44, 48–50.

73. Carter McNamara, "Basic Overview of Organizational Life Cycles," accessed October 7, 2011, http://managementhelp.org/organizations/life-cycles.htm.

74. "Organizational Life Cycle," *Inc.*, 2010, accessed October 7, 2011, www.inc.com/encyclopedia/organizational-life-cycle.html.

75. Robert E. Quinn and Kim Cameron, "Organizational Life Cycles and Shifting Criteria of Effectiveness: Some Preliminary Evidence," *Management Science* 29, no. 1 (1983): 33–51.

76. "Organizational Life Cycle," *Inc.*, 2010, accessed October 7, 2011, www.inc.com/encyclopedia/organizational-life-cycle.html.

77. Yash P. Gupta and David C. W. Chin, "Organizational Life Cycle: A Review and Proposed Directions for Research," *The Mid-Atlantic Journal of Business* 30, no. 3 (December 1994): 269–94.

78. "Organizational Life Cycle," *Inc.*, 2010, accessed October 7, 2011, www.inc.com/encyclopedia/organizational-life-cycle.html.

79. Carter McNamara, "Basic Overview of Organizational Life Cycles," accessed October 7, 2011, http://managementhelp.org/organizations/life-cycles.htm.

80. "Industry Life Cycle," *Inc.*, 2010, accessed June 1, 2012, www.inc.com/encyclopedia/industry-life-cycle.html.

81. "Industry Life Cycle," *Inc.*, 2010, accessed June 1, 2012, www.inc.com/encyclopedia/industry-life-cycle.html.

82. "Organizational Life Cycle," *Inc.*, 2010, accessed October 7, 2011, www.inc.com/encyclopedia/organizational-life-cycle.html.

83. "Organizational Life Cycle," *Inc.*, 2010, accessed October 7, 2011, www.inc.com/encyclopedia/organizational-life-cycle.html.

84. "Organizational Life Cycle," *Inc.*, 2010, accessed October 7, 2011, www.inc.com/encyclopedia/organizational-life-cycle.html.

85. "Organizational Life Cycle," *Inc.*, 2010, accessed October 7, 2011, www.inc.com/encyclopedia/organizational-life-cycle.html.

86. Manuel Velasquez et al., "What Is Ethics?," *Santa Clara University: Markula Center for Applied Ethics*, 2010, accessed October 7, 2011, www.scu.edu/ethics/practicing/decision/whatisethics.html.

87. Daniel J. Brown and Jonathan B. King, "Small Business Ethics: Influences and Perceptions," *Journal of Small Business Management* 11, no. 8 (1982): 11–18.

88. "A Framework for Thinking Ethically," *Santa Clara University: Markula Center for Applied Ethics*, 2009, accessed October 7, 2011, www.scu.edu/ethics/practicing/decision/framework.html.

89. Milton Rokeach, *The Nature of Human Values* (New York: Free Press, 1973), 5, as cited in Wayne D. Hoyer and Deborah J. MacInnis, *Consumer Behavior* (Boston: Houghton Mifflin, 2001), 416.

90. Jeff Landauer and Joseph Rowlands, "Values," *Importance of Philosophy*, 2001, accessed October 7, 2011, www.importanceofphilosophy.com/Ethics_Values.html.

91. Jeff Landauer and Joseph Rowlands, "Values," *Importance of Philosophy*, 2001, accessed October 7, 2011, www.importanceofphilosophy.com/Ethics_Values.html.

92. "Business Ethics," *Small Business Notes*, accessed October 7, 2011, www.smallbusinessnotes.com/operating/leadership/ethics.html.

93. Richard McGill Murphy, "Why Doing Good Is Good for Business," *CNNMoney.com*, February 2, 2010, accessed October 7, 2011, money.cnn.com/2010/02/01/news/companies/dov_seidman_lrn.fortune.

94. Simon Webley and Elise More, "Does Business Ethics Pay?," *Institute of Business Ethics*, 2003, accessed October 7, 2011, www.ibe.org.uk/userfiles/doesbusethicspaysumm.pdf.

95. Simon Webley and Elise More, "Does Business Ethics Pay?," *Institute of Business Ethics*, 2003, accessed October 7, 2011, www.ibe.org.uk/userfiles/doesbusethicspaysumm.pdf.

96. "The Hidden Costs of Unethical Behavior," *Josephson Institute*, 2004, accessed October 7, 2011, josephsoninstitute.org/pdf/Report_HiddenCostsUnethicalBehavior.pdf.

97. Terrence Shulman, "Employee Theft Statistics," *Employee Theft Solutions*, 2007, accessed October 7, 2011, www.employeetheftsolutions.com.

98. Leslie Taylor, "Four in 10 Managers Have Fired Employees for Theft," *Inc.*, September 1, 2006, accessed October 7, 2011, www.inc.com/news/articles/200609/theft.html?partner=rss.

99. Mary Paulsell, "The Problem of Employee Theft," *MissouriBusiness.net*, October 10, 2007, accessed October 7, 2011, www.missouribusiness.net/sbtdc/docs/problem_employee_theft.asp.

100. Karen E. Klein, "Making the Case for Business Ethics," *Bloomberg BusinessWeek*, April 26, 2010, accessed October 7, 2011, www.BusinessWeek.com/smallbiz/content/dec2008/sb20081230_999118.htm.

101. Jeffrey S. Hornsby et al., "The Ethical Perceptions of Small Business Owners: A Factor Analytic Study," *Journal of Small Business Management* 32 (1994): 9–16, adapted.

102. "Business Ethics," *Answers.com*, 2001, accessed October 7, 2011, www.answers.com/topic/business-ethics.

103. Jim Blasingame, "Small Business Ethics," *Small Business Advocate*, August 13, 2001, accessed October 7, 2011, www.smallbusinessadvocate.com/motivational-minutes/small-business-ethics-22.

104. Daniel J. Brown and Jonathan B. King, "Small Business Ethics: Influences and Perceptions," *Journal of Small Business Management* 11, no. 8 (1982): 11–18.

105. Terry L. Besser, "Community Involvement and the Perception of Success among Small Business Operators in Small Towns," *Journal of Small Business Management* 37, no. 4 (1999): 16–29.

106. Daniel J. Brown and Jonathan B. King, "Small Business Ethics: Influences and Perceptions," *Journal of Small Business Management* 11, no. 8 (1982): 11–18.

107. "Business Ethics," *Answers.com*, 2001, accessed October 7, 2011, www.answers.com/topic/business-ethics.

108. Natalie Rhoden, "Ethics in the Workplace," *Articlesbase*, November 5, 2008, accessed October 7, 2011, www.articlesbase.com/human-resources-articles/ethics-in-the-workplace-629384.html.

109. Jennifer Schramm, "Perceptions on Ethics," *HR Magazine*, November 2004, 176.

110. Jeff Wuorio, "Put It in Writing: Your Business Has Ethics," *Microsoft Small Business*, 2011, accessed October 7, 2011, www.microsoft.com/business/en-us/resources/management/leadership-training/put-it-in-writing-your-business-has-ethics.aspx?fbid=WTbndqFrlli.

111. "Why Have a Code of Conduct," *Ethics Resource Center*, May 29, 2009, accessed October 7, 2011, www.ethics.org/resource/why-have-code-conduct.

112. Jeff Wuorio, "Put It in Writing: Your Business Has Ethics," *Microsoft Small Business*, 2011, accessed October 7, 2011, www.microsoft.com/business/en-us/resources/management/leadership-training/put-it-in-writing-your-business-has-ethics.aspx?fbid=WTbndqFrlli.

113. Reported in Jeff Madura, *Introduction to Business* (St. Paul, MN: Paradigm Publishing, 2010), 52.

114. J. Brooke Hamilton III, "Case Example 1: 'Less Sugar' Marketing," *Operationalizing Ethics in Business Settings*, 2009, accessed June 1, 2012, ethicsops.com/LessSugarMarketingCase.php.

115. John A. Jakle and Keith A. Sculle, *Fast Food* (Baltimore: Johns Hopkins University Press, 1999), 163–64.

116. Philip Kotler and Kevin Lane, *Marketing Management* (Upper Saddle River, NJ: Pearson Prentice-Hall, 2009), 121.

117. H. Whitelock, "How to Create Customer Value," *eZine Articles*, March 16, 2007, accessed October 7, 2011, ezinearticles.com/?How-to-Create-Customer-Value&id=491697.

118. Earl Nauman, *Creating Customer Value: The Path to Sustainable Competitive Advantage* (New York: Free Press, 1995), 16.

119. "Why Is Cash Flow So Important?," *North Dakota Small Business Development Center*, 2005, accessed October 7, 2011, www.ndsbdc.org/faq/default.asp?ID=323.

120. Barry Minnery, "Don't Question the Importance of Cash Flow: Making a Profit Is the Goal but Day-to-Day Costs Must Be Met in Order to Keep a Business Afloat," *The Independent.com*, May 28, 2010, accessed October 7, 2011, http://www.articlesezinedaily.com/dont-question-the-importance-of-cash-flow/.

121. Barry Minnery, "Don't Question the Importance of Cash Flow: Making a Profit Is the Goal but Day-to-Day Costs Must Be Met in Order to Keep a Business Afloat," *The Independent.com*, May 28, 2010, accessed October 7, 2011, http://www.articlesezinedaily.com/dont-question-the-importance-of-cash-flow/.

122. Fred Adler, *QuotationsBook.com*, accessed October 7, 2011, quotationsbook.com/quote/18235.

123. Christopher Elliott, "5 Ways Smartphones & Servers Boost Productivity," *Microsoft Small Business Center*, 2010, accessed October 7, 2011, www.microsoft.com/business/en-us/resources/technology/communications/smartphones-and-business-productivity.aspx?fbid=WTbndqFrlli.

124. Brent Leary, "The iPad: Changing How We Build Business Relationships," *Inc.*, accessed October 7, 2011, www.inc.com/hardware/articles/201005/leary.html.

125. Kevin Bonsor, Candace Keener, and Wesley Fenlon, "How RFID Works," *HowStuffWorks.com*, accessed October 23, 2011, electronics.howstuffworks.com/gadgets/high-tech-gadgets/rfid.htm.

126. Jonathan Blum, "Running an Entire Business from Smartphones: Mobile Software Helps Track Equipment, Accounts—and Employee Lunch Breaks," *CNNMoney.com*, March 12, 2008, accessed October 7, 2011, money.cnn.com/2008/03/11/smbusiness/mobile_phone_software.fsb/index.htm.

127. "Technology: Your Roadmap to Small Business Success," *Intel*, 2009, accessed October 7, 2011, www.intel.com/content/www/us/en/world-ahead/world-ahead-small-business-success-article.html.

128. Kelly Wright, "E-Commerce vs. E-Business," *Supply Chain Resource Cooperative*, November 27, 2002, accessed October 7, 2011, scm.ncsu.edu/public/lessons/less021127.html.

129. Elias M. Awad, *Electronic Commerce: From Vision to Fulfillment* (Upper Saddle River, NJ: Pearson Education, 2004), 4.

130. Kenneth C. Laudon and Carol Guercio Traver, *E-commerce: Business, Technology, Society* (Upper Saddle River, NJ: Pearson Prentice Hall, 2007), 11.

131. "Making Money on the Internet," *BizBeginners.biz*, accessed October 23, 2011, bizbeginners.biz/e_business.html.

132. William M. Ulrich, "E-Business Integration: A Framework for Success," *Software Magazine*, August 2001, accessed October 7, 2011, findarticles.com/p/articles/mi_m0SMG/is_4_21/ai_73436110.

133. Heather Green, "US Ecommerce Growth to Pick up in 2010, But Hit Mature Stride," *Bloomberg BusinessWeek*, February 2, 2009, accessed June 1, 2012, http://www.businessweek.com/the_thread/the_thread_05272011/blogspotting/archives/2009/02/us_ecommerce_gr.html.

134. Robyn Greenspan, "Net Drives Profits to Small Biz," *ClickZ*, March 25, 2004, accessed October 7, 2011, www.clickz.com/clickz/stats/1719145/net-drives-profits-small-biz.

135. "E-commerce: Small Businesses Become Virtual Giants on the Internet," *SCORE*, accessed October 7, 2011, www.score.org/system/files/become_a_virtual_giant.pdf.

136. "Trend Data: What Internet Users Do Online," *Pew Internet & American Life Project*, May 1, 2011, accessed June 1, 2012, http://www.pewinternet.org/Trend-Data-%28Adults%29/Online-Activites-Total.aspx.

137. "Home Broadband Adoption Since 2000," *Pew Internet & American Life Project*, 2010, accessed June 1, 2012, http://www.pewinternet.org/Static-Pages/Trend-Data-(Adults)/Home-Broadband-Adoption.aspx.

138. Robyn Greenspan, "Small Biz Gets Up to Speed," *ClickZ.com*, January 26, 2004, accessed October 7, 2011, www.clickz.com/clickz/stats/1704631/small-biz-gets-up-to-speed.

139. Lee Rainie, "Internet, Broadband, and Cell Phone Statistics," *Pew Internet & American Life Project*, January 5, 2010, accessed October 7, 2011, pewinternet.org/~/media/Files/Reports/2010/PIP_December09_update.pdf.

140. "Demographics of Internet Users," *Pew Internet & American Life Project*, 2012, accessed June 21, 2012, http://www.pewinternet.org/Static-Pages/Trend-Data-%28Adults%29/Whos-Online.aspx.

141. "Small Biz Plans to Grow with Social," *eMarketer.com*, 2010, accessed October 7, 2011, www.emarketer.com/Article.aspx?R=1007706.

142. Sydney Jones, "Online Classifieds," *Pew Internet & American Life Project*, 2010, accessed June 1, 2012, http://www.pewinternet.org/Reports/2009/7--Online-Classifieds/1-Overview.aspx.

143. Sramana Mitra, "The Promise of E-Commerce," *Forbes.com*, April 9, 2010, accessed October 7, 2011, www.forbes.com/2010/04/08/retailing-entreprenuers-online-intelligent-technology-ecommerce.html.

144. Peter Kolesar, Garrett van Rysin, and Wayne Cutler, "Creating Customer Value through Industrialized Intimacy," *Strategy + Business*, July 1, 1998, accessed October 7, 2011, www.strategy-business.com/article/19127?gko=81aa7.

CHAPTER 2
Your Business Idea: The Quest for Value

Cheshire Package Store

Source: Used with permission from Robert Brown.

Robert Brown has been the owner and operator of the Cheshire Package Store for 25 years. It is one of several liquor stores in this town of 25,000 people. Some of his competitors are smaller or approximately the same size, and one is significantly larger. Robert is very clear in his understanding of what gives his store a competitive edge. He believes his establishment provides the setting that makes a customer feel at home. "My feeling has always been that small businesses must have a feeling of comfort. If your customers do not feel that they can ask you questions about the product or if they feel that they are imposing on you, then they are not likely to return."

Robert took every opportunity available to better understand his customers and provide them with value. One way his business does this is by developing a personal relationship with its customers. This may mean carefully looking at checks or credit cards, not for security reasons, but to identify customers by name. Robert points out that he always pays careful attention to what customers like and dislike; by doing so, they develop confidence in his suggestions. To foster this confidence, he and his family actively engage their customers in conversations. Customers, Robert, and the employees share stories, which is a key way to build better customer relationships. By listening to his customers, Robert can identify what they are looking for and assist him in knowing what new products he might offer.

In addition to this personalized level of service, the Cheshire Package Store also recognizes the importance of other factors. Robert talks about the importance of maintaining a well-lit store with spacious aisles, making it an inviting place in which to shop. He is careful about even minor details, such as assuring that there are open parking spaces near the entrance to his store. He recognizes that even walking short distances to or from the store might be a burden or deterrent for his customers. Robert's store possesses a cutting-edge inventory software package designed specifically for liquor stores. It enables him to track inventory levels, which can provide estimates for future inventory levels of different products; however, he sees this as a guide only. As he puts it, "Your knowledge of your customers will be the key determinant for your success."

Robert also strongly believes that the success of a small business depends on the owner being there. Stores have their own personality, in his view, and that personality is created by the owner. This personality imparted by the owner impacts all operational aspects of the business—"Your employees will pick up on what you expect, and they will know what your customers deserve."

1. DEFINING THE CUSTOMER'S CONCEPT OF VALUE

LEARNING OBJECTIVES

1. Define customer value.
2. Understand the five sources of perceived customer benefits.
3. Understand the three sources of perceived costs.

Look beneath the surface; let not the several qualities of neither the thing, nor its worth escape thee.
- *Marcus Aurelius Antoninus*

customer value

The difference between the benefits a customer receives from a product or a service and the costs associated with obtaining the product or the service.

In the previous chapter, Peter Drucker and W. Edward Deming placed the customer at the center of their definitions of the purpose of a business. They used the customer as being at the core of that purpose rather than focusing on financial measures such as profit, return on investment (ROI), or shareholders' wealth. Drucker's logic was that if a business did not create a sufficient number of customers, there never would be a profit with the business. Deming argued that delighting customers would become the basis for them to consistently return, and loyalty would ensure that the business would have a higher probability of surviving in the long term. The clearest way of doing that is by focusing on providing your customers with a clear sense of value. This emphasis on value will produce economic benefits. Gale Consulting explains the notion of value this way, "If customers don't get good value from you, they will shop around to find a better deal."[1] A recent study put it this way, "These firms have been successful...by consistently creating superior **customer value**—and profiting handsomely from that customer value."[2]

Strong evidence indicates that this focus on making the customer central to defining the business translates into economic success. It has been estimated that the cost of gaining a new customer over retaining a current customer is a multiple of five. The costs of regaining a dissatisfied customer over the cost of retaining a customer are ten times as much.[3] So a key question for any business then becomes, "How does one then go about making the customer the center of one's business?"

1.1 What Is Value?

It is essential to recognize that value is not just price. Value is a much richer concept. Fundamentally, the notion of customer value is fairly basic and relatively simple to understand; however, implementing this concept can prove to be tremendously challenging. It is a challenge because customer value is highly dynamic and can change for a variety of reasons, including the following: the business may change elements that are important to the customer value calculation, customers' preferences and perceptions may change over time, and competitors may change what they offer to customers. One author states that the challenge is to "understand the ever changing customer needs and innovate to gratify those needs."[4]

The simple version of the concept of customer value is that individuals evaluate the perceived benefits of some product or service and then compare that with their perceived cost of acquiring that product or service. If the benefits outweigh the cost, the product or the service is then seen as attractive (see Figure 2.1). This concept is often expressed as a straightforward equation that measures the difference between these two values:

customer value = perceived benefits − perceived cost.

FIGURE 2.1 Perceived Cost versus Perceived Benefits

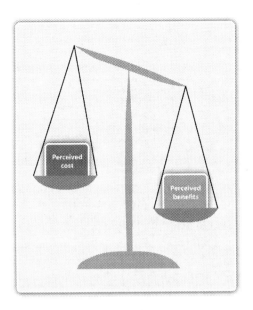

Some researchers express this idea of customer value not as a difference but as a ratio of these two factors.[5] Either way, it needs to be understood that customers do not evaluate these factors in isolation. They evaluate them with respect to their expectations and the competition.

Firms that provide greater customer value relative to their competitors should expect to see higher revenues and superior returns. Robert Buzzell and Bradley Gale, reporting on one finding in the Profit Impact through Marketing Strategy study, a massive research project involving 2,800 businesses, showed that firms with superior customer value outperform their competitors on ROI and market share gains.[6]

Given this importance, it is critical to understand what makes up the perceived benefits and the perceived costs in the eyes of the consumer. These critical issues have produced a considerable body of research. Some of the major themes in customer value are evolving, and there is no universal consensus or agreement on all aspects of defining these two components. First, there are approaches that provide richly detailed and academically flavored definitions; others provide simpler and more practical definitions. These latter definitions tend to be ones that are closer to the aforementioned equation approach, where customers evaluate the benefits they gain from the purchase versus what it costs them to purchase. However, one is still left with the issue of identifying the specific components of these benefits and costs. In looking at the benefits portion of the value equation, most researchers find that customer needs define the benefits component of value. But there still is no consensus as to what specific needs should be considered. Park, Jaworski, and McGinnis (1986) specified three broad types of needs of consumers that determine or impact value.[7] Seth, Newman, and Gross (1991)[8] provided five types of value, as did Woodall (2003), although he did not identify the same five values.[9] To add to the confusion, Heard (1993–94)[10] identified three factors, while Ulaga (2003)[11] specified eight categories of value; and Gentile, Spiller, and Noci (2007) mentioned six components of value.[12] Smith and Colgate (2007) attempted to place the discussion of customer value in a pragmatic context that might aid practitioners. They identified four types of values and five sources of value. Their purpose was to provide "a foundation for measuring or assessing value creation strategies."[13] In some of these works, the components or dimensions of value singularly consider the benefits side of the equation, while others incorporate cost dimensions as part of value.

From the standpoint of small businesses, what sense can be made of all this confusion? First, the components of the benefits portion of customer value need to be identified in a way that has significance for small businesses. Second, cost components also need to be identified. Seth, Newman, and Gross's five types of value provide a solid basis for considering perceived benefits (see Figure 2.2). Before specifying the five types of value, it is critical to emphasize that a business should not intend to compete on only one type of value. It must consider the mix of values that it will offer its customers. (In discussing these five values, it is important to provide the reader with examples. Most of our examples will relate to small business, but in some cases, good examples will have to be drawn from larger firms because they are better known.)

FIGURE 2.2 Five Types of Value

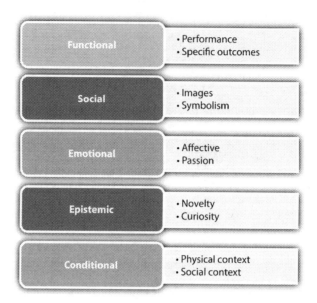

The five types of value are as follows:

functional value

A basis of value that relates to a product's or a service's ability to perform its utilitarian purpose.

social value

A basis of value that involves a sense of relationship with other groups by using images or symbols.

emotional value

A basis of value that is derived from the ability to evoke an emotional or an affective response.

epistemic value

A basis of value that is generated by a sense of novelty or simple fun.

conditional value

A basis of value that is derived from a particular context or a sociocultural setting.

1. **Functional value** relates to the product's or the service's ability to perform its utilitarian purpose. Woodruff (1997) identified that functional value can have several dimensions.[14] One dimension would be performance related. This relates to characteristics that would have some degree of measurability, such as appropriate performance, speed of service, quality, or reliability. A car may be judged on its miles per gallon or the time to go from zero to sixty miles per hour. These concepts can also be seen when evaluating a garage that is performing auto repairs. Customers have an expectation that the repairs will be done correctly, that the car will not have to be brought back for additional work on the same problem, and that the repairs will be done in a reasonable amount of time. Another dimension of functional value might consider the extent to which the product or the service has the correct features or characteristics. In considering the purchase of a laptop computer, customers may compare different models on the basis of weight, battery lifetime, or speed. The notion of features or characteristics can be, at times, quite broad. Features might include aesthetics or an innovation component. Some restaurants will be judged on their ambiance; others may be judged on the creativity of their cuisine. Another dimension of functional value may be related to the final outcomes produced by a business. A hospital might be evaluated by its number of successes in carrying out a particular surgical procedure.

2. **Social value** involves a sense of relationship with other groups by using images or symbols. This may appear to be a rather abstract concept, but it is used by many businesses in many ways. Boutique clothing stores often try to convey a chic or trendy environment so that customers feel that they are on the cutting edge of fashion. Rolex watches try to convey the sense that their owners are members of an economic elite. Restaurants may alter their menus and decorations to reflect a particular ethnic cuisine. Some businesses may wish to be identified with particular causes. Local businesses may support local Little League teams. They may promote fundraising for a particular charity that they support. A business, such as Ben & Jerry's Ice Cream, may emphasize a commitment to the environment or sustainability.

3. **Emotional value** is derived from the ability to evoke an emotional or an affective response. This can cover a wide range of emotional responses. Insurance companies and security alarm businesses are able to tap into both fear and the need for security to provide value. Some theme parks emphasize the excitement that customers will experience with a range of rides. A restaurant may seek to create a romantic environment for diners. This might entail the presence of music or candlelight. Some businesses try to remind customers of a particular emotional state. Food companies and restaurants may wish to stimulate childhood memories or the comfort associated with a home-cooked meal. Häagen-Dazs is currently producing a line of all-natural ice cream with a limited number of natural flavors. It is designed to appeal to consumers' sense of nostalgia.[15]

4. **Epistemic value** is generated by a sense of novelty or simple fun, which can be derived by inducing curiosity or a desire to learn more about a product or a service. Stew Leonard's began in the 1920s as a small dairy in Norwalk, Connecticut. Today, it is a $300 million per year enterprise of consisting of four grocery stores. It has been discussed in major management textbooks. These

accomplishments are due to the desire to turn grocery shopping into a "fun" experience. Stew Leonard's uses a petting zoo, animatronic figures, and costumed characters to create a unique shopping environment. They use a different form of layout from other grocery stores. Customers are required to follow a fixed path that takes them through the entire store. Thus customers are exposed to all items in the store. In 1992, they were awarded a Guinness Book world record for generating more sales per square foot than any food store in the United States.[16] Another example of a business that employs epistemic value is Rosetta Stone, a company that sells language-learning software. Rosetta Stone emphasizes the ease of learning and the importance of acquiring fluency in another language through its innovative approach.

5. **Conditional value** is derived from a particular context or a sociocultural setting. Many businesses learn to draw on shared traditions, such as holidays. For the vast majority of Americans, Thanksgiving means eating turkey with the family. Supermarkets and grocery stores recognize this and increase their inventory of turkeys and other foods associated with this period of the year. Holidays become a basis for many retail businesses to tap into conditional value.

Another way businesses may think about conditional value is to introduce a focus on emphasizing or creating a sociocultural context. Business may want to introduce a "tribal" element into their customer base, by using efforts that cause customers to view themselves as a member of a special group. Apple Computer does this quite well. Many owners of Apple computers view themselves as a special breed set apart from other computer users. This sense of special identity helps Apple in the sale of its other electronic consumer products. They reinforce this notion in the design and setup of Apple stores. Harley-Davidson does not just sell motorcycles; it sells a lifestyle. Harley-Davidson also has a lucrative side business selling accessories and apparel. The company supports owner groups around the world. All of this reinforces, among its customers, a sense of shared identity.

It should be readily seen that these five sources of value benefits are not rigorously distinct from each other. A notion of aesthetics might be applied, in different ways, across several of these value benefits. It also should be obvious that no business should plan to compete on the basis of only one source of value benefits. Likewise, it may be impossible for many businesses, particularly start-ups, to attempt to use all five dimensions. Each business, after identifying its customer base, must determine its own mix of these value benefits.

As previously pointed out, the notion of perceived customer value has two components—perceived value benefits and perceived value costs. When examining the cost component, customers need to recognize that it is more than just the cost of purchasing a product or a service. Perceived cost should also be seen having multiple dimensions (see Figure 2.3).

FIGURE 2.3 Components of Customer Value

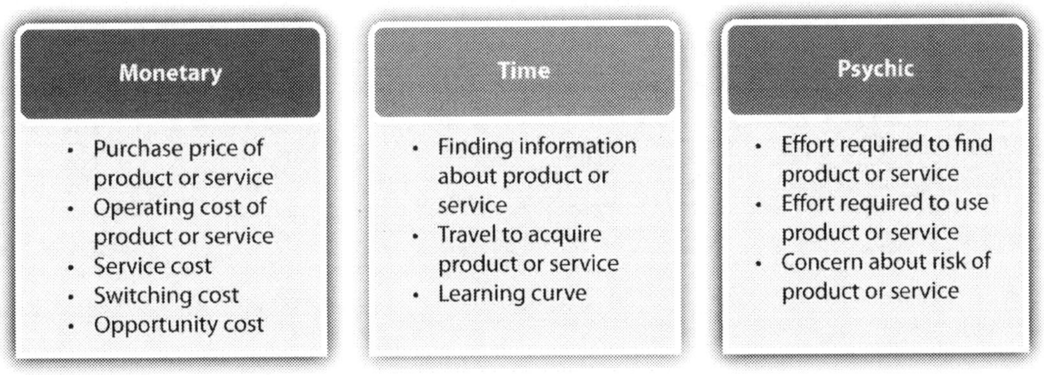

Monetary	Time	Psychic
• Purchase price of product or service • Operating cost of product or service • Service cost • Switching cost • Opportunity cost	• Finding information about product or service • Travel to acquire product or service • Learning curve	• Effort required to find product or service • Effort required to use product or service • Concern about risk of product or service

Perceived costs can be seen as being monetary, time, and psychic. The **monetary component** of perceived costs should, in turn, be broken down into its constituent elements. Obviously, the first component is the purchase price of the product or the service. Many would mistakenly think that this is the only element to be considered as part of the cost component. They fail to consider several other cost components that are quite often of equal—if not greater—importance to customers. Many customers will consider the operating cost of a product or a service. A television cable company may promote an introductory offer with a very low price for the cable box and its installation. Most customers will consider the monthly fees for cable service rather than just looking at the installation cost. They often use service costs when evaluating the value proposition. Customers have discovered that there are high costs associated with servicing a product. If there are service costs, particularly if they are hidden costs, then customers will find significantly less value from that product or service. Two other costs also need

monetary component of cost

A component that consists of the purchase, operating, service, switching, and opportunity costs associated with any product or service.

to be considered. Switching cost is associated with moving from one provider to another. In some parts of the country, the cost of heating one's home with propane gas might be significantly less than using home heating oil on an annualized basis. However, this switch from heating oil to propane would require the homeowner to install a new type of furnace. That cost might deter the homeowner from moving to the cheaper form of energy. Opportunity cost involves selecting among alternative purchases. A customer may be looking at an expensive piece of jewelry that he wishes to buy for his wife. If he buys the jewelry, he may have to forgo the purchase of a new television. The jewelry would then be the opportunity cost for the television; likewise, the television would be the opportunity cost for the piece of jewelry. When considering the cost component of the value equation, businesspeople should view each cost as part of an integrated package to be set forth before customers. More and more car dealerships are trying to win customers by not only lowering the sticker price but also offering low-cost or free maintenance during a significant portion of the lifetime of the vehicle.

time component

The time required to evaluate, acquire, and purchase a product or a service.

These monetary components are what we most often think of when we discuss the term *cost*, and, of course, they will influence the decision of customers; however, the **time component** is also vital to the decision-making process. Customers may have to expend time acquiring information about the nature of the product or the service or make comparisons between competing products and services. Time must be expended to acquire the product or the service. This notion of time would be associated with learning where the product or the service could be purchased. It would include time spent traveling to the location where the item would be purchased or the time it takes to have the item delivered to the customer. One also must consider the time that might be required to learn how to use the product or the service. Any product or service with a steep learning curve might deter customers from purchasing it. Firms can provide additional value by reducing the time component. They could simplify access to the product or the service. They may offer a wide number of locations. Easy-to-understand instructions or simplicity in operations may reduce the amount of time that is required to learn how to properly use the product or the service.

psychic component

The element of cost that is associated with factors that might induce stress in a customer.

The **psychic component** of cost can be associated with those factors that might induce stress on the customer. There can be stress associated with finding or evaluating products and services. In addition, products or services that are difficult to use or require a long time to learn how to use properly can cause stress on customers. Campbell's soup introduced a meal product called Souper Combos, which consisted of a sandwich and a cup of soup. At face value, one would think that this would be a successful product. Unfortunately, there were problems with the demands that this product placed on the customer in terms of preparing the meal. The frozen soup took twice as long to microwave as anticipated, and the consumer had to repeatedly insert and remove both the soup and the sandwich from the microwave.[17]

In summary, business owners need to constantly consider how they can enhance the benefits component while reducing the cost components of the value equation. Table 2.1 summarizes the subcomponents of perceived value, the types of firms that emphasize those components, and the activities that might be necessary to either enhance benefits or reduce costs.

TABLE 2.1 Components of Perceived Benefit and Perceived Cost

Component	Aspects	Activities to Deliver
Components of Perceived Benefit		
Functional	<ul><li>Measurable quality</li><li>Performance</li><li>Reliability</li><li>Support network</li></ul>	<ul><li>Quality assurance in product and services</li><li>Superior product and process design</li><li>Selection of correct attributes</li><li>Ability to improve product and operations</li><li>Management of value chain</li></ul>
Social	<ul><li>Builds identification with social, ethnic, or class group</li><li>Emphasize lifestyle</li><li>Development of interaction among people</li><li>Build bonds within groups</li></ul>	<ul><li>Market research correctly identifies customer base(s)</li><li>Ability to build social community among customers</li></ul>
Emotional	<ul><li>Assist in making one feel good about themselves</li><li>Attachment to product or service</li><li>Produces a change in how others see the user</li><li>Trustworthiness</li><li>Profound customer experience</li><li>Aesthetics</li></ul>	<ul><li>Market research understands psychological dimensions of customer base(s)</li><li>Marketing content emphasizes desired psychological dimensions</li><li>Reliability between marketing message and delivery</li></ul>
Epistemic	<ul><li>Novelty</li><li>Fun</li><li>Evoke interest in product or service</li><li>Interest in learning</li><li>Produces a willing suspension of disbelief</li></ul>	<ul><li>Creative personnel</li><li>Creative product or process development</li><li>Commitment to innovation</li><li>Willingness to experiment</li></ul>
Conditional	<ul><li>Produces meaning in a specific context</li><li>Tied to particular events</li><li>Tied to holidays</li><li>Demonstrates social responsibility</li></ul>	<ul><li>Flexibility (can alter physical facilities or marketing message depending on context)</li><li>Management commitment to responsible action</li></ul>
Components of Perceived Cost		
Monetary	<ul><li>Reduce purchase price</li><li>Reduce operating costs</li><li>Reduce maintenance costs</li><li>Reduce opportunity costs</li></ul>	<ul><li>Superior design</li><li>Operational efficiency</li><li>Cost containment</li><li>Quality control and assurance</li><li>Easy acquisition</li></ul>
Time	<ul><li>Reduce time to search for product or service</li><li>Reduce time to purchase</li><li>Reduced learning curve</li></ul>	<ul><li>Broad distribution channels</li><li>Web-based purchasing option</li><li>Web-based information</li><li>Superior design</li></ul>
Psychic	<ul><li>Simplified use</li><li>"Comfortable" feeling with regard to product or service use</li></ul>	<ul><li>Superior design</li><li>Ability to write clear instructions</li></ul>

Video Clip 2.1

Customer Value
What creates a customer experience of value?

View the video online at: http://www.youtube.com/v/jSHuU_HdKFU

 ### Video Clip 2.2

Creating Customer Value
Creating value is the essence of a start-up. This video reviews the product and value created by a watch with no hands.

View the video online at: http://www.youtube.com/v/cwXKOfsaFjM

 ### Video Clip 2.3

Simple Rules: Three Logics of Value Creation
Three core logics of the value proposition.

View the video online at: http://www.youtube.com/v/K8suroYpAHc

Video Clip 2.4

Articulating Your Value Proposition
A video on how to better articulate your value proposition. This is informative but very long (about one hour).

View the video online at: http://www.youtube.com/v/PyG5k0QtKOQ

1.2 Different Customers—Different Definitions

It is a cliché to say that people are different; nonetheless, it is true to a certain extent. If all people were totally distinct individuals, the notion of customer value might be an interesting intellectual exercise, but it would be absolutely useless from the standpoint of business because it would be impossible to identify a very unique definition of value for every individual. Fortunately, although people are individuals, they often operate as members of groups that share similar traits, insights, and interests. This notion of customers being members of some type of group becomes the basis of the concept known as **market segmentation**. This involves dividing the market into several portions that are different from each other.[18] It simply involves recognizing that the market at large is not homogeneous. There can be several dimensions along which a market may be segmented: geography, demographics, psychographics, or purchasing behavior. Geographic segmentation can be done by global or national region, population size or density, or even climate. Demographic segmentation divides a market on factors such as gender, age, income, ethnicity, or occupation. Psychographic segmentation is carried out on dimensions that reflect differences in personality, opinions, values, or lifestyle. Purchasing behavior can be another basis for segmentation. Differences among customers are determined based on a customer's usage of the product or the service, the frequency of purchases, the average value of purchases, and the status as a customer—major purchaser, first-time user, or infrequent customer. In the business-to-business (B2B) environment, one might want to segment customers on the basis of the type of company.

Market segmentation recognizes that not all people of the same segment are identical; it facilitates a better understanding of the needs and wants of particular customer groups. This comprehension should enable a business to provide greater customer value. There are several reasons why a small business should be concerned with market segmentation. The main reason centers on providing better customer value. This may be the main source of competitive advantage for a small business over its larger rivals. Segmentation may also indicate that a small business should focus on particular subsets of customers. Not all customers are equally attractive. Some customers may be the source of most of the profits of a business, while others may represent a net loss to a business. The requirements for providing value to a first-time buyer may differ significantly from the value notions for long time, valued customer. A failure to recognize differences among customers may lead to significant waste of resources and might even be a threat to the very existence of a firm.

market segmentation

Dividing the market into several portions that are different from each other. It involves recognizing that the market at large is not homogeneous.

Video Clip 2.5

Tom Peters: The Biggest Underserved Markets

Tom Peters, a self-described "professional loudmouth" who has been compared to Ralph Waldo Emerson, Walt Whitman, Henry David Thoreau, and H. L. (Henry Louis) Mencken, declares war on the worthless rules and absurd organizational barriers that stand in the way of creativity and success. In a totally outrageous, in-your-face presentation, Peters reveals the following: a reimagining of American business; two big markets—underserved and worth trillions; the top qualities of leadership excellence; and why passion, talent, and action must rule business today.

View the video online at: http://www.youtube.com/v/UyVMS5q7zkg

KEY TAKEAWAYS

- Essential to the success of any business is the need to correctly identify customer value.
- Customer value can be seen as the difference between a customer's perceived benefits and the perceived costs.
- Perceived benefits can be derived from five value sources: functional, social, emotional, epistemic, and conditional.
- Perceived costs can be seen as having three elements: monetary, time, and psychic.
- To better provide value to customers, it may be necessary to segment the market.
- Market segmentation can be done on the basis of demographics, psychographics, or purchasing behavior.

EXERCISES

Frank's All-American BarBeQue

Robert Rainsford is a twenty-eight-year-old facing a major turning point in his life. He has found himself unemployed for the first time since he was fifteen years old. Robert holds a BS degree in marketing from the University of Rhode Island. After graduation, a firm that specialized in developing web presences for other companies hired him. He worked for that firm for the last seven years in New York City. Robert rose rapidly through the company's ranks, eventually becoming one of the firm's vice presidents. Unfortunately, during the last recession, the firm suffered significant losses and engaged in extensive downsizing, so Robert lost his job. He spent months looking for a comparable position, yet even with an excellent résumé, nothing seemed to be on the horizon. Not wanting to exhaust his savings and finding it impossible to maintain a low-cost residence in New York City, he returned to his hometown in Fairfield, Connecticut, a suburban community not too far from the New York state border.

He found a small apartment near his parents. As a stopgap measure, he went back to work with his father, who is the owner of a restaurant—Frank's All-American BarBeQue. His father, Frank, started the restaurant in 1972. It is a midsize restaurant—with about eighty seats—that Frank has built up into a relatively successful and locally well-known enterprise. The restaurant has been at its present location since the early 1980s. It shares a parking lot with several other stores in the small mall where it is located. The restaurant places an emphasis on featuring the food and had a highly simplified décor, where tables are covered with butcher paper rather than linen tablecloths. Robert's father has won many awards at regional and national barbecue cook-offs, which is unusual for a business in New England. He has won for both his barbecue food and his sauces. The restaurant has been repeatedly written up in the local and New York papers for the quality of its food and the four special Frank's All-American BarBeQue sauces. The four sauces correspond to America's four styles of barbecue—Texan, Memphis, Kansas City, and Carolina. In the last few years, Frank had sold small lots of these sauces in the local supermarket.

As a teenager, Robert, along with his older sister Susan, worked in his father's restaurant. During summer vacations while attending college, he continued to work in the restaurant. Robert had never anticipated working full-time in the family business, even though he knew his father had hoped that he would do so. By the time he returned to his hometown, his father had accepted that neither Robert nor Susan would be interested in taking over the family business. In fact, Frank had started to think about selling the business and retiring. However, Robert concluded that his situation called for what he saw as desperate measures.

Initially, Robert thought his employment at his father's business was a temporary measure while he continued his job search. Interestingly, within the first few weeks he returned to the business, he felt that he could bring his expertise in marketing—particularly his web marketing focus—to his father's business. Robert became very enthusiastic about the possibility of fully participating in the family business. He thought about either expanding the size of the restaurant, adding a takeout option, or creating other locations outside his hometown. Robert looked at the possibility of securing a much larger site within his hometown to expand the restaurant's operations. He began to scout surrounding communities for possible locations. He also began to map out a program to effectively use the web to market Frank's All-American BarBeQue sauce and, in fact, to build it up to a whole new level of operational sophistication in marketing.

Robert recognized that the restaurant was as much of a child to his father as he and his sister were. He knew that if he were to approach his father with his ideas concerning expanding Frank's All-American BarBeQue, he would have to think very carefully about the options and proposals he would present to his father. Frank's All-American BarBeQue was one of many restaurants in Fairfield, but it is the only one that specializes in barbecue. Given the turnover in restaurants, it was amazing that Frank had been able to not only survive but also prosper. Robert recognized that his father was obviously doing something right. As a teenager, he would always hear his father saying the restaurant's success was based on "giving people great simple food at a reasonable price in a place where they feel comfortable." He wanted to make sure that the proposals he would present to his father would not destroy Frank's recipe for success.

1. Discuss how Robert should explicitly consider the customer value currently offered by Frank's All-American BarBeQue. In your discussion, comment on the five value benefits and the perceived costs.

2. Robert has several possible options for expanding his father's business—find a larger location in Fairfield, add a takeout option, open more restaurants in surrounding communities, incorporate web marketing concepts, and expand the sales of sauces. Review each in terms of value benefits.

3. What would be the costs associated with those options?

2. KNOWING YOUR CUSTOMERS

voice of the customer (VOC)

Any and all attempts to identify the *real* wants and needs of a customer.

The perceived value proposition offers a significant challenge to any business. It requires that a business have a fairly complete understanding of the customer's perception of benefits and costs. Although market segmentation may help a business better understand some segments of the market, the challenge is still getting to understand the customer. In many cases, customers themselves may have difficulty in clearly understanding what they perceive as the benefits and costs of any offer. How then is a business, particularly a small business, to identify this vital requirement? The simple answer is that a business must be open to every opportunity to listen to the **voice of the customer (VOC)**. This may involve actively talking to your customers on a one-to-one basis, as illustrated by Robert Brown, the small business owner highlighted at the beginning of this chapter. It may involve other methods of soliciting feedback from your customers, such as satisfaction surveys or using the company's website. Businesses may engage in market research projects to better understand their customers or evaluate proposed new products and services. Regardless of what mechanism is used, it should serve one purpose—to better understand the needs and wants of your customers.

 Video Clip 2.6

Robin Lawton—Voice of the Customer—What Do Customers Value?
International Management Technologies introduces Robin Lawton on the topic of "What Do Customers Value?"

View the video online at: http://www.youtube.com/v/wFNhw5xOnRg

Video Clip 2.7

Robin Lawton—Voice of the Customer—Basis for Satisfaction Keynote
The customer-centered organization begins the transformation process by understanding how to uncover and understand the VOC.

View the video online at: http://www.youtube.com/v/t9qynrMaBFU

2.1   Research

Chapter 6 of this text will focus on the topic of marketing for small business. Naturally, it will include significant materials on the subject of market research. In this section, the focus will be on how a business may gain better insight into what constitutes the benefits and the costs for particular customers. It will take a broad view and leave the details of market research for Chapter 6.

Good research in the area of customer value simply means that one must stop talking to the customer—talking through displays, advertising, and/or a website. It means that one is always open to listening carefully to the VOC. Active listening in the service of better identifying customer value means that one is always open to the question of how your business can better solve the problems of particular customers.

If businesses are to become better listeners, what should they be listening for? What types of questions should they be asking their customers? Businesses should address the following questions when they attempt to make customer value the focus of their existence:

- What needs of our customers are we currently meeting?
- What needs of our customers are we currently failing to meet?
- Do our customers understand their own needs and are they aware of them?
- How are we going to identify those unmet customer needs?
- How are we going to listen to the VOC?
- How are we going to let the customer talk to us?
- What is the current value proposition that is desired by customers?
- How is the value proposition different for different customers?
- How—exactly—is our value proposition different from our competitors?
- Do I know why customers have left our business for our competitors?

2.2   Who Your Customer Is—and Is Not

At the beginning of this chapter, it was argued that your central focus must be the customer. One critical way that this might be achieved is by providing a customer with superior value. However, creating this value must be done in a way that assures that the business makes money. One way of doing this is by identifying and selecting those customers who will be profitable. Some have put forth the concept of **customer lifetime value**, a measure of the revenue generated by a customer, the cost generated for that particular customer, and the projected retention rate of that customer over his or her lifetime.[19] ,[20]

customer lifetime value

A measure of the revenue generated by a customer, the cost generated for that particular customer, and the projected retention rate of that customer over his or her lifetime.

net present value

A value that discounts the value of future cash flows. It recognizes the time value of money.

This concept is popular enough that there are lifetime value calculator templates available on the web. The Harvard Business School created the calculator used in Exercise 2.1. It looks at the cost of acquiring a customer and then computes the **net present value** of the customer during his or her lifetime. Net present value discounts the value of future cash flows. It recognizes the time value of money. You can use one of two models: a simple model that examines a single product or a more complex model with additional variables. One of the great benefits in conducting customer lifetime value analysis is combining it with the notion of market segmentation. The use of market segmentation allows for recognizing that certain classes of customers may produce significantly different profits during their lifetimes. Not all customers are the same.

Let us look at a simple case of segmentation based on behavioral factors. Some customers make more frequent purchases; these loyal customers may generate a disproportionate contribution of a firm's overall profit. It has been estimated that only 15 percent of American customers have loyalty to a single retailer, yet these customers generate between 55 percent and 70 percent of retail sales.[21] Likewise, a lifetime-based economic analysis of different customer segments may show that certain groups of customers actually cost more than the revenues that they generate.

Having segmented your customers, you will probably find that some require more handholding during and after the sale. Some customer groups may need you to "tailor" your product or service to their needs.[22] As previously mentioned, market segmentation can be done along several dimensions. Today, some firms use data mining to determine the basis of segmentation, but that often requires extensive databases, software, and statisticians. One simple way to segment your customers is the customer value matrix that is well suited for small retail and service businesses. It uses just three variables: recency, frequency, and monetary value. Its data requirements are basic. It needs customer identification, the date of purchase, and the total amount of purchase. This enables one to easily calculate the average purchase amount of each customer. From this, you can create programs that reach out to particular segments.[23]

 Video Clip 2.8

Customer Lifetime Value

Jack Daly presents the "client for life" concept, featuring Continuity Programs BCL programs of customer loyalty outsourced service.

View the video online at: http://www.youtube.com/v/p2CRhF9az74

Video Clip 2.9

Lifetime Customer Value
Patrick McTigue explains how critical the lifetime value of a customer is to your business. He covers some tips to integrate superb customer service into your business model.

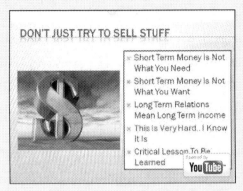

View the video online at: http://www.youtube.com/v/-1inNGaghNI

2.3   What Your Gut Tells You

The role of market research was already discussed in this chapter. For many small businesses, particularly very small businesses, formal market research may pose a problem. In many small businesses, there may be a conflict between decision making made on a professional basis and decision making made on an instinctual basis.[24] Some small business owners will always decide based on a gut instinct. We can point to many instances in which gut instinct concerning the possible success in product paid off, whereas a formal market research evaluation might consider the product to be a nonstarter.

In 1975, California salesman Gary Dahl came up with the idea of the ideal pet—a pet that would require minimal care and cost to maintain. He developed the idea of the pet rock. This unlikely concept became a fad and a great success for Dahl. Ken Hakuta, also known as Dr. Fad, developed a toy known as the Wallwalker in 1983. It sold over 240 million units.[25] These and other fad products, such as the Cabbage Patch dolls and Rubik's Cube, are so peculiar that one would be hard pressed to think of any marketing research that would have indicated that they would be viable, let alone major successes.

Sometimes it is an issue of having a product idea and knowing where the correct market for the product will be. Jill Litwin created *Peas a Pie Pizza*, which is a natural food pizza pie with vegetables baked in the crust. She knew that the best place to market her unique product would be in the San Francisco area with its appreciation of organic foods.[26]

This notion of going with one's gut instinct is not limited to fad products. Think of the birth of Apple Computer. The objective situation was dealing with a company whose two major executives were college dropouts. The business was operating out of the garage of the mother of one of these two executives. They were producing a product that up to that point had only a limited number of hobbyists as a market. None of this would add up to very attractive prospect for investment. You could easily envision a venture capitalist considering a possible investment asking for a market research study that would identify the target market(s) for its computers. None existed at the company's birth. Even today, there is a strong indication that Apple does not rely heavily on formal marketing research. As Steve Jobs put it,

It's not about pop culture, it's not about fooling people, and it's not about convincing people that they want something they don't. We figure out what we want. And I think we're pretty good at having the right discipline to think through whether a lot of other people are going to want it, too. That's what we get paid to do. So you can't go out and ask people, you know, what's the next big [thing.] There is a great quote by Henry Ford, right? He said, "If I had asked my customers what they wanted, they would've told me 'A faster horse.'"[27]

2.4 The Voice of the Customer—QFD

Quality function deployment (QFD) is an approach that is meant to take the VOC concept seriously and uses it to help design new products and services or improve existing ones. It is an approach that was initially developed in Japan for manufacturing applications. It seeks "to transform user demands into design quality, to deploy the functions forming quality, and to deploy methods for achieving the design quality into subsystems and component parts, and ultimately to specific elements."[28] To put it more clearly, QFD takes the desires of consumers and explores how well the individual activities of the business are meeting those desires. It also considers how company activities interact with each other and how well the company is meeting those customer desires with respect to the competition. It achieves all these ends through the means of a schematic; see Figure 2.4, which is known as the house of quality. The schematic provides the backbone for the entire QFD process. A comprehensive design process may use several houses of quality, moving from the first house, which concentrates on the initial specification of customer desires, all the way down to developing a house that focuses on the specification for parts or processes. Any house is composed of several components:

- **Customer requirements (the *whats*).** Here you identify the elements desired by customers; this section also contains the relative importance of these needs as identified by customers.

- **Engineering characteristics (the *hows*).** This is the means by which an organization seeks to meet customer needs.

- **Relationship matrix.** This illustrates the correlations among customer requirements and engineering characteristics. The degree of the correlation may be represented by different symbols.

- **"Roof" of the house.** This section illustrates the correlations among the engineering characteristics and reveals synergies that might exist among the engineering characteristics.

- **Competitive assessment matrix.** This is used to evaluate the position of a business with respect to its competition.

- **"Basement."** This section is used for assessing the engineering characteristics or setting target values. The "basement" enables participants to instantly see the relative benefits of the activities undertaken by a company in meeting consumer desires by multiplying the values in each cell by the weight of the "why" and then adding the values together.

FIGURE 2.4 House of Quality

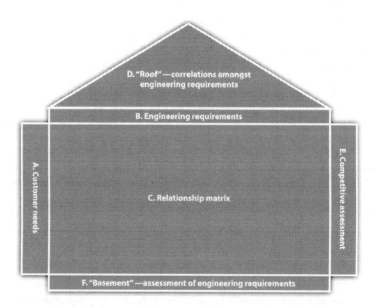

Although it might initially appear to be complex, QFD provides many benefits, including the following: (1) reduces time and effort during the design phase, (2) reduces alterations in design, (3) reduces the entire development time, (4) reduces the probability of inept design, (5) assists in team development, and (6) helps achieve common consensus.[29]

Unfortunately, QFD is most often associated with manufacturing. Few realize that it has found wide acceptance in many other areas—software development, services, education, amusement parks, restaurants, and food services. (For examples of these applications of QFD, go to http://www.mazur.net/publishe.htm.) Further, company size should not be seen as a limitation to its possible application. The QFD approach, in a simplified form, can be easily and successfully used by any business regardless of its size.[30] Its visual nature makes it extremely easy to comprehend, and it can convey to all members of the business the relative importance of the elements and what they do to help meet customers' expectations. Figure 2.5 illustrates this by providing a simplified house of quality chart for a restaurant.

FIGURE 2.5 Simplified House of Quality for a Restaurant

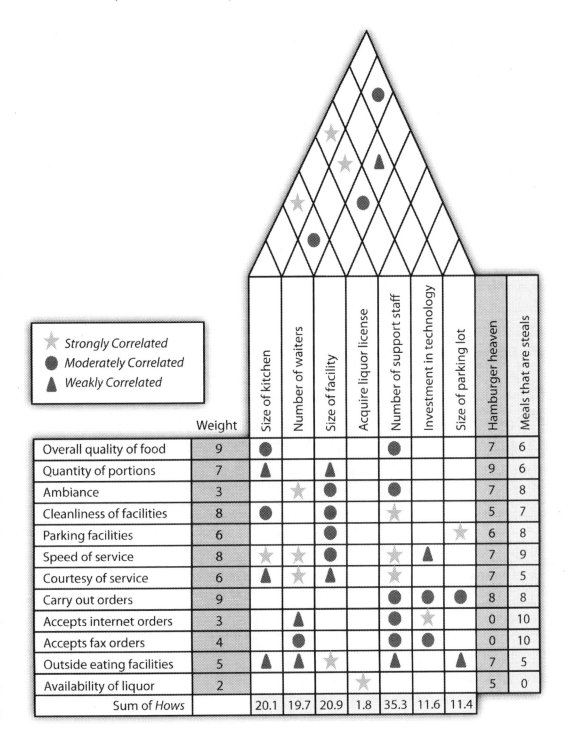

	Weight	Size of kitchen	Number of waiters	Size of facility	Acquire liquor license	Number of support staff	Investment in technology	Size of parking lot	Hamburger heaven	Meals that are steals
Overall quality of food	9	●				●			7	6
Quantity of portions	7	▲		▲					9	6
Ambiance	3		★	●		●			7	8
Cleanliness of facilities	8	●		●		★			5	7
Parking facilities	6			●				★	6	8
Speed of service	8	★	★	●		★	▲		7	9
Courtesy of service	6	▲	★	▲		★			7	5
Carry out orders	9					●	●	●	8	8
Accepts internet orders	3		▲			●	★		0	10
Accepts fax orders	4		●			●	●		0	10
Outside eating facilities	5	▲	▲	★		▲		▲	7	5
Availability of liquor	2				★				5	0
Sum of *Hows*		20.1	19.7	20.9	1.8	35.3	11.6	11.4		

Legend:
★ Strongly Correlated
● Moderately Correlated
▲ Weakly Correlated

Video Clip 2.10

Quality Function Deployment Tutorial
This gives a brief overview of QFD.

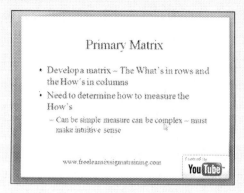

View the video online at: http://www.youtube.com/v/RCKIO2b1wCU

QFD Analysis and Excel

Some companies provide Excel-based software that can assist in conducting a QFD analysis. This shows a template in the QI Macros software to help structure your thinking, making sure nothing is left out. For more information and to download a 30-day trial of the QI Macros, including the QFD template, see www.qimacros.com/six-sigma-articles.html.

2.5 How to Become a Better Listener

Although some succeed by listening to their instincts—their inner voices—it is highly advisable to all businesses to be proactive in trying to listen to the VOC. Listening to the customer is the domain of market research. However, it should not be surprising that many small businesses have severe resource constraints that make it difficult for them to use complex and sophisticated marketing and market research approaches.[31] To some extent, this is changing with the introduction of powerful, yet relatively low cost, web-based tools and social media. These will be discussed in greater detail in Section 4 of this chapter. Another restriction that a small business may face in the area of marketing is that the owner's marketing skills and knowledge may not be very extensive. The owners of such firms may opt for several types of solutions. They may try to mimic the marketing techniques employed by larger organizations, drawing on what was just mentioned. They may opt for sophisticated but easy to use analytical tools, or they may just simply take marketing tools and techniques and apply them to the small business environment.[32]

The most basic and obvious way to listen to customers is by talking to them. All businesses should support programs in which employees talk to customers and then record what they have to say about the product or the service. It is important to centralize these observations.

Other ways of listening to customers are through comment cards and paper and online surveys. These approaches have their strengths and limitations (see "Video Clip 2.11"). Regardless of these limitations, they do provide an insight into your customers. Another way one can gather information about customers is through loyalty programs. Loyalty programs are used by 81 percent of US households.[33] Social media options—see Section 4—offer a tremendous opportunity to not only listen to your customer but also engage in an active dialog that can build a sustainable relationship with customers.

Video Clip 2.11

Listen to Your Customers and Express How Much You Care
This video details how easy and simple it is to show that you listen to your customers and care about them.

View the video online at: http://www.youtube.com/v/RyQiwLWZLpY

 ## Video Clip 2.12

Ask, Listen, and Retain Video #4: Listening and Analyzing What Your Customers Say?
This is the fourth in a series of videos on listening to customers. This video covers how to analyze any disengaged or disgruntled customers. Once a customer is identified, our process ensures that action is taken to reengage the customer by dealing with the concerns at hand. But most importantly, the process encourages the development of a relationship between the customer and branch level management.

View the video online at: http://www.youtube.com/v/_flGefvkT_0

Website

Cisco Website for Innovation

A web forum for small businesses to share information: communities.cisco.com/community/technology/collaboration/business/blog/tags/innovation.

KEY TAKEAWAYS

- Businesses must become proactive in attempting to identify the value proposition of their customers. They must know how to listen to the VOC.
- Businesses must make every effort to identify the unmet needs of their customers.
- Businesses should recognize that customer segmentation would enable them to better provide customer value to their various customers.
- Businesses should think in terms of computing the customer lifetime value within different customer segments.
- Intuition can play an important role in the development of new products and services.
- Tools and techniques such as QFD assist in the design of products and services so that a business may be better able to meet customer expectations.
- Innovation can play a key role in creating competitive advantage for small businesses.
- Innovation does not require a huge investment; it can be done by small firms by promoting creativity throughout the organization.
- Small businesses must be open to new social and consumer trends. Readily available technology can help them in identifying such trends.

EXERCISES

1. The Harvard Business School provides an online customer lifetime value calculator at hbsp.harvard.edu/ multimedia/flashtools/cltv/index.html. You provide some key values, and it computes the net present value of customer purchases. Go to the site and use the following data. What impact does changing the customer retention have on the value of the customer?

Average spent per purchase	$250.00
Average number of purchases per period	4
Direct marketing cost per period per year	$30
Average gross margin	20%
Average retention rate	**25%, 35%, 50%, 70%, 80%, and 90%**
Annual discount rate	10%

2. Imagine you are planning to open a boutique clothing store in the downtown section of a major city in the United States. You are interested in using a QFD chart to help you design the store. Identify the customer requirements (*whats*) in the engineering characteristics (*hows*). You need not to conduct a full-blown QFD analysis but at least show the degree of relationship between customer requirements and engineering characteristics.

3. You are the owner of a children's clothing store in a prosperous suburban community. What methods and techniques might you use to become more adept at listening to the VOC? Outline specific programs that go beyond just talking to your customer that might enable you to better understand their notion of value.

3.   SOURCES OF BUSINESS IDEAS

Small businesses have always been a driver of new products and services. Many products and inventions that we might commonly associate with large businesses were originally created by small businesses, including air-conditioners, Bakelite, the FM radio, the gyrocompass, the high resolution computed axial tomography scanner, the outboard engine, the pacemaker, the personal computer, frozen food, the safety razor, soft contact lenses, and the zipper.[34] This creativity and innovative capability probably stems from the fact that smaller businesses, which may lack extensive financial resources, bureaucratic restraints, or physical resources, may find a competitive edge by providing customers value by offering new products and services. It is therefore important to consider how small businesses can foster a commitment to creativity and innovation.

3.1   Creativity and Innovation

One way smaller firms may compete with their larger rivals is by being better at the process of innovation, which involves creating something that is new and different. It need not be limited to the creation of new products and services. **Innovation** can involve new ways in which a product or a service might be used. It can involve new ways of packaging a product or a service. Innovation can be associated with identifying new customers or new ways to reach customers. To put it simply, innovation centers on finding new ways to provide customer value.

Although some would argue that there is a difference between creativity and innovation (see "Video Clip 2.13"), one would be hard pressed to argue that creativity is not required to produce innovative means of constructing customer value. An entire chapter, even an entire book, could be devoted to fostering creativity in a small business. This text will take a different track; it will look at those factors that might inhibit or kill creativity. Alexander Hiam (1998) identified nine factors that can impede the creative mind-set in organizations:[35]

> **innovation**
>
> New ways in which a product or a service might be used, new ways of packaging a product or a service, or identifying new customers or new ways to reach customers.

1. **Failure to ask questions.** Small-business owners and their employees often fail to ask the required *why*-type questions.
2. **Failure to record ideas.** It does not help if individuals in an organization are creative and produce a large number of ideas but other members of the organization cannot evaluate these ideas. Therefore, it is important for you to record and share ideas.
3. **Failure to revisit ideas.** One of the benefits of recording ideas is that if they are not immediately implemented, they may become viable at some point in the future.
4. **Failure to express ideas.** Sometimes individuals are unwilling to express new ideas for fear of criticism. In some organizations, we are too willing to critique an idea before it is allowed to fully develop.
5. **Failure to think in new ways.** This is more than the cliché of "thinking outside the box." It involves new ways of approaching and looking at the problem of providing customer value.
6. **Failure to wish for more.** Satisfaction with the current state of affairs or with the means of solving particular problems translates into an inability to look at new ways of providing value to customers.
7. **Failure to try to be creative.** Many people mistakenly think that they are not at all creative. This means you will never try to produce new types of solutions to the ongoing problems.

8. **Failure to keep trying.** When attempting to provide new ways to create customer value, individuals are sometimes confronted with creative blocks. Then they simply give up. This is the surest way to destroy the creative thinking process.

9. **Failure to tolerate creative behavior.** Organizations often fail to nurture the creative process. They fail to give people time to think about problems; they fail to tolerate the "odd" suggestions from employees and limit creativity to a narrow domain.

One of the great mistakes associated with the concept of innovation is that innovation must be limited to highly creative individuals and organizations with large research and development (R&D) facilities.[36] The organization's size may have no bearing on its ability to produce new products and services. More than a decade ago, studies began to indicate that small manufacturing firms far exceeded their larger counterparts with respect to the number of innovations per employee.[37]

A more recent study, which covered the period from 2003 to 2007, showed that R&D performance by small US companies grew slightly faster than the comparable performance measures for larger US firms. During that period, small firms increased their R&D spending by more than 40 percent, compared to an approximate 33 percent increase for large companies. These smaller firms also increased their employment of scientists and engineers at a rate approximately 75 percent greater than larger companies. Further, the results of this study, which are presented in Figure 2.6, illustrate that particularly since 2004, smaller businesses have outpaced their larger rivals with respect to R&D intensity. The term R&D intensity refers to the current dollars spent on R&D divided by a company's reported sales revenue.[38]

FIGURE 2.6 R&D Intensity by Firm Size

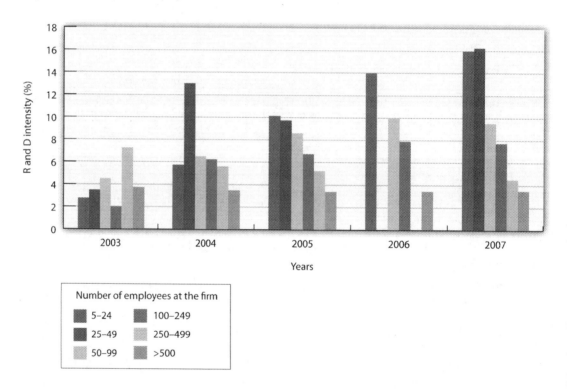

It cannot be over emphasized that innovation should not be limited to the creation of products or services. The following are just a few examples of innovation beyond the development of new products:

- In 1965, Thomas Angove, an Australian winemaker, developed the idea of packaging wine in boxes that had a polyethylene bladder. The package was not only more convenient to carry but also kept the wine fresher for a longer period of time.[39]

- Apple's iPod was certainly an innovative product, but its success was clearly tied to the creation of the iTunes website that provided content.

- Baker Tweet alerts customers via Twitter any time a fresh batch of baked goods emerge from a participating baker's oven.[40]

- Patrons at Wagaboo restaurants in Madrid can book specific tables online.[41]

- Restaurants often mark up bottles of wine by 200 percent to 300 percent. Several restaurants in New York, Sydney, and London have developed relationships with wine collectors. The collectors may have more wine than they can possibly drink, so they offer the wine for sale in the restaurant, with the restaurant selling it at a straightforward markup of 35 percent. This collaboration with customers is beneficial for the wine collector, the restaurant, and the customer.

 Video Clip 2.13

Vijay Govindarajan: Innovation Is Not Creativity
An interview with Vijay Govindarajan on the difference between creativity and innovation.

View the video online at: http://www.youtube.com/v/8EcCCm5Jz5E

 Video Clip 2.14

Where Good Ideas Come From
This cartoon was developed for Steven Johnson's book on innovation. He concluded that with today's tools and environment, radical innovation is extraordinarily accessible to those who know how to cultivate it. *Where Good Ideas Come From* is essential reading for anyone who wants to know how to come up with tomorrow's great ideas.

View the video online at: http://www.youtube.com/v/NugRZGDbPFU

Video Clip 2.15

Steven Johnson: Where Good Ideas Come From
This relatively long presentation (eighteen minutes) by Steven Johnson maps out the ideas presented in his book.

View the video online at: http://www.youtube.com/v/0af00UcTO-c

 Video Clip 2.16

Encouraging Innovation with Employees: Innovators Forum Guest Danika Davis
Danika Davis, Innovators Forum guest and CEO of the Northern California Human Resources Association, discusses the ways to reward innovation among employees and how to foster innovation in your small business. Discuss this and other topics at http://blogs.cisco.com/category/smallbusiness.

View the video online at: http://www.youtube.com/v/9m7zxmNG8YA

Video Clip 2.17

Creating an Innovation Mind-set
Vijay Govindarajan discusses that to create an innovation mind-set, managers must bring in fresh voices from outside the company, encourage collaboration, and consider how emerging market needs can spur ideas for innovative offerings.

View the video online at: http://www.youtube.com/v/sNzkmZdM4A4

 Video Clip 2.18

Tom Peters: Innovation Is Actually Easy!
Tom Peters declares war on the worthless rules and absurd organizational barriers that stand in the way of creativity and success.

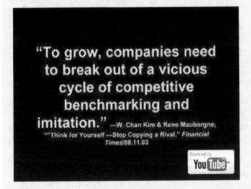

View the video online at: http://www.youtube.com/v/8AGTpu_i8sc

Video Clip 2.19

How to Spot Disruptive Innovation Opportunities
Disruptive innovation occurs when an innovator brings something to market that is simple, convenient, accessible, and affordable. Here are some tips to help you pinpoint disruptive opportunities within your organization.

View the video online at: http://www.youtube.com/v/KGzXWO_anLI

3.2 Social and Consumer Trends

Not all businesses have to concern themselves with social and consumer trends. Some businesses, and this would include many small businesses, operate in a relatively stable environment and provide a standard good or service. The local luncheonette is expected to provide standard fare on its menu. The men's haberdasher will be expected to provide mainline men's clothing. However, some businesses, particularly smaller businesses, could greatly benefit by recognizing an emerging social or consumer trend. Small businesses that focus on niche markets can gain sales if they can readily identify new social and consumer trends.

Trends differ from fads. Fads may delight customers, but by their very nature, they have a short shelf life. Trends, on the other hand, may be a portend of the future.[42] Smaller businesses may be in a position to better exploit trends. Their smaller size can give them greater flexibility; because they lack an extensive bureaucratic structure, they may be able to move with greater rapidity. The great challenge for small businesses is to be able to correctly identify these trends in a timely fashion. In the past, businesses had to rely on polling institutes for market research as a way of attempting to identify social trends. Harris Interactive produced a survey about the obesity epidemic in America. This study showed that the vast majority of Americans over the age of 25 are overweight. The percentage of those overweight has steadily increased since the early 1980s. The study also indicated that a majority of these people desired to lose weight. This information could be taken by the neighborhood gym, which could then create specialized weight-loss programs. Recognizing this trend could lead to a number of different products and services.[43]

In the past, the major challenge for smaller businesses to identify or track trends was the expense. These firms would have to use extensive market research or clipping services. Today, many of those capabilities can be provided online, either at no cost or a nominal cost.[44] Google Trends tracks how often a particular topic has been searched on Google for a particular time horizon. The system also allows you to track multiple topics, and it can be refined so that you can examine particular regions with these topics searched. The data are presented in graphical format that makes it easy to determine the existence of any particular trends. Google Checkout Trends monitors the sales of different products by brand. One could use this to determine if seasonality exists for any particular product type. Microsoft's AdCenter Labs offers two products that could be useful in tracking trends. One tool—Search Volume—tracks searches and also provides forecasts. Microsoft's second tool—Keyword Forecast—provides data on actual searches and breaks it down by key demographics. Facebook provides a tool called Lexicon. It tracks Facebook's communities' interests. (Check out the Unofficial Facebook Lexicon Blog for a description on how to fully use Lexicon.) The tool Twist tracks Twitter posts by subject areas. Trendpedia will identify articles online that refer to particular subject areas. These data can be presented as a trend line so that one can see the extent of public interest over time. The trend line is limited to the past three months. Trendrr tracks trends and is a great site for examining the existence of trends in many areas.

Online technology now provides even the smallest business with the opportunity to monitor and detect trends that can be translated into more successful business ventures.

Websites

- Google Trends: www.google.com/trends
- Microsoft AdCenter Labs: adlab.microsoft.com
- Microsoft AdCenter Labs Keyword Forecast: adlab.microsoft.com/Keyword-Forecast/default.aspx
- Unofficial Facebook Lexicon Blog: www.facebooklexicon.com
- Twitter Grader: http://tweet.grader.com
- Trendpedia: www.attentio.com
- BuzzMetrics: http://www.nmincite.com/wp-content/uploads/2010/06/MyBuzzMetrics.pdf
- NielsenBuzzMetrics: nielsen-online.com/products_buzz.jsp?section=pro_buzz
- Trendrr: www.trendrr.com
- Google Analytics: code.google.com/apis/checkout/developer/checkout_analytics_integration.html

KEY TAKEAWAYS

- Small businesses must be open to innovation with respect to products, services, marketing methods, and packaging.
- Creativity in any organization can be easily stifled by a variety of factors. These should be avoided at all cost.
- Small businesses should be sensitive to the emergence of new social and consumer trends.
- Online databases can provide even the smallest of businesses with valuable insights into the existence and emergence of social and consumer trends.

EXERCISES

1. Generate a new product or service idea. You should be able to describe it in two or three sentences. Work with your fellow students in groups of three to four and then ask them to review their ideas and select one for presentation in class. At the end of the presentation, everyone should write what he or she saw as occurring during the process of group decision making. Did it make the process more creative? Did it allow for the better evaluation of ideas? Do they see problems with this type of group innovation thinking?

2. In Exercise 1, students were asked to develop a new product or service. Repeat this exercise but now ask students to think up an innovation for an existing product in the area of either packaging or marketing. Again, ask them the following questions after the group decision-making process: (a) Did it make the process more creative? (b) Did it allow for the better evaluation of ideas? (c) Do they see problems with this type of group innovation thinking?

3. Consider that you are at the gym mentioned earlier in this section. This gym is considering adding a weight-loss program. Use some of the online tracking programs with respect to the term *weight loss program*. What useful information could be extracted from these searches?

4.   THE THREE THREADS

LEARNING OBJECTIVES

1. Understand that providing customer value can have a tremendous positive impact on a firm's cash flow.
2. Understand that determining customer value is critical to the survival of any business. Customer relationship marketing software, which previously was available only to the largest firms, is now priced so that even small firms can extract their benefit.

In Chapter 1, customer value, cash flow, and digital technology and the e-environment were compared to various parts of the human body and overall health. This analogy was made because these themes are viewed as essential to the survival of any small business in the twenty-first century. Individually, these threads may not ensure survival, but taken together, the probability of surviving and prospering increases tremendously. Their importance is so great for a twenty-first century enterprise that they are not only embedded in each chapter but also highlighted in each chapter. Throughout the text, each chapter's topic will be reviewed through the prism of these three threads.

4.1   Focusing on Providing Value to the Customer

The entire thrust of this chapter has been on the topic of customer value. The essence of the argument presented in this chapter has been that any business that fails to provide perceived customer value is a business that will probably fail.

Value's Impact on Cash Flow

It is not that difficult to envision how the successful creation of customer value can significantly enhance a firm's cash flow (see Figure 2.7). Firms that are successful in correctly identifying the sources of value should be able to provide superior customer value. This may produce a direct relationship with their customers. These relationships produce a back-and-forth flow of information that should enable the business to further enhance its ability to provide customer value. A successful relationship enhances the probability of customer loyalty, hopefully building a strong enough relationship to produce a customer for life.

Customer loyalty can have several positive outcomes. Loyalty will result in increased sales from particular customers. This does more than generate additional revenue; as the business comes to better understand its loyal customers, the cost of serving those customers will decrease. Increased sales, with declining costs, translate into a significant boost in cash flow. Customer loyalty also has the benefit of generating positive word-of-mouth support for a business. Word-of-mouth advertising can be one of the most powerful forms of advertising and can be seen as a form of free advertising. It has been estimated that word-of-mouth advertising is the primary factor in 20–50 percent of all purchasing decisions. A study by the US office of consumer affairs (formally known as the Federal Trade Commission) indicated that satisfied customers are likely to tell five other customers about their positive experiences.[45] It is particularly powerful in the case of first-time buyers or with expensive items and those items that require extensive research before purchase.[46] Positive word-of-mouth advertising coming from loyal customers can generate additional sales, which in turn enhances cash flow. The creation of superior customer value combined with an intelligent cost control system inevitably produces superior cash flow.

FIGURE 2.7   Superior Cash Flow as a Result of Superior Customer Value

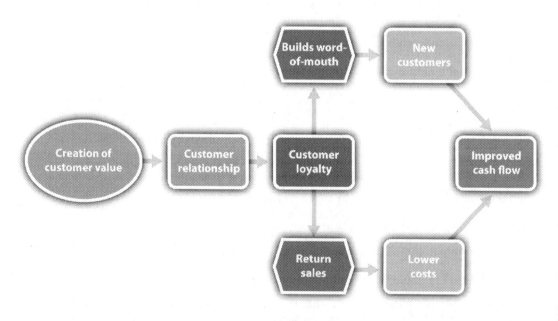

4.2   Digital Technology and E-Environment Implications

In the last decade, firms desiring to better understand the customer's notion of perceived value relied on customer relationship management (CRM) software. **Customer relationship management** refers to a service approach that hopes to build a long-term and sustainable relationship with customers that has value for both the customer and the company. It is a generic term covering different software and browser applications that collect information about customers and organize it in a way that may be used effectively by management. This term will be referred to repeatedly throughout this text. CRM can assist small businesses with respect to customer value in the following ways:[47]

- It can assist in identifying and targeting the best customers of a business.
- It can help a company develop individualized relationships with customers, thus improving customer satisfaction.
- It can improve customer service, particularly with the best customers.
- It can help management and employees better understand customers and therefore deliver better value to them.

> **customer relationship management**
>
> A service approach that hopes to build a long-term and sustainable relationship with customers that has value for both the customer and the company.

Although originally designed for large corporations with large budgets, CRM is now available to many firms in the small business environment. In addition to being expensive, original fees-first CRM packages were far too complex for small businesses.[48] Now there are many CRM packages that are specifically dedicated to the small business environment.

To maximize the benefits of the CRM package, several factors should be considered. Small businesses should have a clear idea as to their requirements for the CRM solution. Some questions that should be considered are as follows:[49]

- Is our focus on increasing the number of customers?
- Are we attempting to improve our relationships with our customers?
- Will the CRM package help us with e-mail marketing?
- How are we seeking to more effectively use the Internet to communicate with our customers?
- Will we be able to integrate social media?

In some ways, integrating the CRM package may be easier in the small business than in large business because you can overcome some bureaucratic hurdles. However, you must always recognize that the successful implementation of any software package is highly dependent on your employees.[50]

Perhaps the greatest incentive for small businesses to adopt CRM packages is the advent of cloud computing. **Cloud computing**, also known as SaaS (software as a service), refers to the situation in which vendor software does not reside on the computer system of a small business.[51] All aspects of the system, from maintenance to backups, are the responsibility of the vendor. This minimizes the need for computing capability by the small business. Cloud computing can significantly reduce the course of acquiring and maintaining such computer programs.

> **cloud computing**
>
> The situation in which vendor software does not reside on the computer system of a small business.

KEY TAKEAWAYS

- Focusing on customer value improves customer loyalty, which improves cash flow.
- Customer loyalty can translate into positive word-of-mouth advertising, which increases sales and cash flow.
- Customer value can be improved through the correct use of CRM software.
- CRM software was formerly so complex and expensive that it was suitable for large corporations only. Now it can be used by the smallest of businesses to improve customer value.

EXERCISE

1. Assume you are managing a small business that is experiencing a very rapid increase in sales. Unfortunately, this increase in sales has been accompanied by an increase in customer complaints that your company is letting "things slip between the cracks." You recognize that the old way of interacting with customers is no longer sufficient. You have a sales force of ten, and you would like to supply each with access to a basic CRM package. Go online and identify several CRM packages that might be appropriate for your business. Specify each package's capabilities and cost. How would you go about selecting one of these packages? Write a report outlining the information you collected and the logic of your selection.

Disaster Watch

The failure to accurately understand a customer's notion of perceived value is the surest recipe for complete disaster. This may be a large requirement because in many cases customers may be quite unsure about their own notion of value or have difficulty in explicitly articulating that notion. One would think that larger firms—those with much greater resources—would be in a better position to clearly identify their customers' notion of value. This does not seem to be the case, however, with all large firms. Even they may stumble in attempting to develop products and services that they believe will meet their customers' concept of value. In this feature, several noticeable product failures are identified. Almost every failure came from a large corporation. This is because we are much more familiar with the failures of large corporations that invest considerable time and effort into the introduction of new products and services. There is far less press given to the failures of small businesses that misread or misunderstand their customers' notion of perceived value.

When Your Notion of Value Is Not the Same as Your Customer's

Perhaps the most famous company failure to adequately gauge customers' notion of value revolved around the introduction of New Coke. In 1985, Coca-Cola was under great pressure, losing market share to its major rival, Pepsi. In an effort to recapture market share, particularly among the younger segment of the market, Coca-Cola initiated one of the largest market research projects of its time. It conducted extensive taste tests throughout the nation and investigated the possibility of introducing a new formula for Coke. The results from the taste tests were positively skewed toward a sweeter version. There was some debate whether this should be an additional option to the Coke line of products or whether it should replace the standard formula for Coke. Although there were some negative indications about this new formula from focus groups, Coke decided to begin a major introduction of New Coke, but it was universally considered a major disaster. Public reaction, particularly in the South, was very negative toward New Coke. A lot of this negative reaction stemmed from the fact that Coke had become an iconic product in the nation, particularly in southern regions. Hundreds of thousands of people called and wrote to Coca-Cola expressing their dissatisfaction with this decision.[52] Coca-Cola failed to recognize the emotional and social components of value for a significant number of its customers.

Many firms fail to realize that they have established, in the eyes of customers, a very strong sense of how a particular company provides value. These companies may wish to diversify their product or service line while at the same time attempting to exploit their brand name. However, customers may perceive the companies as being so closely identified with the original product that any attempt at diversification may be difficult, if not guaranteed to be a failure. Some examples of this are as follows: Smith & Wesson, noted for handguns, attempted to sell a line of mountain bikes in 2002; Coors beer attempted to sell bottled water; and Colgate toothpaste tried to produce a line of products known as Colgate Kitchen Entrées.[53]

Companies may produce products that run directly counter to their customers' notion of perceived value. McDonald's produces value for its customers by offering fast food and a family-friendly environment. Several years ago, in an effort to capture a different segment of the market, McDonald's introduced the Arch Deluxe hamburger, which was supposedly designed for more adult tastes. Even with a $100 million marketing campaign, McDonald's was unable to "sell" this product to its customers.

One health management organization invested more than one third of $1 million on a computerized member information service. The intention was that this would be more efficient, thus providing greater benefit value to customers. Their mistake was not recognizing that members preferred conversing with human beings. Customers did not want to use a computerized system.[54] Although customers of health-care organizations appreciate factors such as ease of access and reliability, they tend to view with greater importance and value the perceived expression of human compassion.

The dry cleaning business industry in the United States is extremely fragmented. The largest 50 firms control only 40 percent of the total industry's business. This translates into a simple fact: dry cleaning is still the domain of small business owners, with nearly 35,000 establishments throughout the United States. A decade ago, two firms wanted to change the structure of the industry. Both companies thought that they would be able to provide unique sources of value to customers. Mixell Technologies operates a franchise—Hanger's Cleaners—that focuses on environmentally responsible dry cleaning. Dry cleaning normally involves some fairly volatile chemicals. Hanger's Cleaners used a new process developed by Mixell Technology. The belief was that customers would respond to this much more environmentally friendly technology. Initially, the cost of this technology was two to three times the cost of normal dry cleaning equipment. One of the major investors in this firm was Ken Langone, a cofounder of Home Depot. In the same time frame, Tom Stemberg, the founder of Staples, was investing in a dry cleaning franchise called Zoots. Their focus on customer value was the ability to have employees pick up clothes for dry cleaning and drop off the clean clothes at the customer's home residence or work.[55] Neither business prospered. Mixell has moved on to other applications of its technologies. Zoots has significantly reduced its number of outlets. The reality was that dry cleaning establishments produce low margins and require long hours and close identification with customers. Unfortunately for both businesses, even though they had an experienced executive staff, they failed to correctly identify the true sources of customer value.[56]

ENDNOTES

1. "Why Customer Satisfaction Fails," *Gale Consulting*, accessed December 2, 2011, www.galeconsulting.com/index.php?option=com_content&view=article&id=18&itemid=23.

2. George Day and Christine Moorman, *Strategy from the Outside In* (New York: McGraw Hill, Kindle Edition, 2010), 104–10.

3. Forler Massnick, *The Customer Is CEO: How to Measure What Your Customers Want—and Make Sure They Get It* (New York: Amacom, 1997), 76.

4. Sudhakar Balachandran, "The Customer Centricity Culture: Drivers for Sustainable Profit," *Course Management* 21, no. 6 (2007): 12.

5. M. Christopher, "From Brand Value to Customer Value," *Journal of Marketing Practice: Applied Marketing Science* 2, no. 1 (1996): 55.

6. Robert D. Buzzell and Bradley T. Gale, *The PIMS Principles—Linking Strategy to Performance* (New York: Free Press, 1987), 106.

7. C. Whan Park, Bernard J. Jaworski, and Deborah J. MacInnis, "Strategic Brand Concept Image Management," *Journal of Marketing* 50 (1986): 135.

8. Jagdish N. Seth, Bruce I. Newman, and Barbara L. Gross, *Consumption Values and Market Choice: Theory and Applications* (Cincinnati, OH: Southwest Publishing, 1991), 77.

9. Tony Woodall, "Conceptualising 'Value for the Customer': An Attributional, Structural and Dispositional Analysis," *Academy of Marketing Science Review* 2003, no. 12 (2003), accessed October 7, 2011, www.amsreview.org/articles/woodall12-2003.pdf.

10. Ed Heard, "Walking the Talk of Customers Value," *National Productivity Review* 11 (1993–94): 21.

11. Wolfgang Ulaga, "Capturing Value Creation in Business Relationships: A Customer Perspective," *Industrial Marketing Management* 32, no. 8 (2003): 677.

12. Chiara Gentile, Nicola Spiller, and Giuliana Noci, "How to Sustain the Customer Experience: An Overview of Experience Components That Co-Create Value with the Customer," *European Management Journal* 25, no. 5 (2007): 395.

13. J. Brock Smith and Mark Colgate, "Customer Value Creation: A Practical Framework," *Journal of Marketing Theory and Practice* 15, no. 1 (2007): 7.

14. Robert B. Woodruff, "Customer Value: The Next Source of Competitive Advantage, *Journal of the Academy of Marketing Science* 25, no. 2 (1997): 139.

15. "Maturalism," *Trendwatching.com*, accessed June 1, 2012, http://trendwatching.com/trends/maturalism/.

16. "Company Story," *Stew Leonards*, accessed October 7, 2011, www.stewleonards.com/html/about.cfm.

17. Calvin L. Hodock, *Why Smart Companies Do Dumb Things* (Amherst, NY: Prometheus Books, 2007), 65.

18. "Market Segmentation," *NetMBA Business Knowledge Center*, accessed October 7, 2011, www.netmba.com/marketing/market/segmentation.

19. Jack Schmid, "How Much Are Your Customers Worth?," *Catalog Age* 18, no. 3 (2001): 63.

20. Jonathon Lee and Lawrence Feick, "Cooperating Word-of-Mouth Affection Estimating Customer Lifetime Value," *Journal of Database Marketing and Customer Strategy Management* 14 (2006): 29.

21. "Loyalty Promotions," *Little & King Integrated Marketing Group*, accessed December 5, 2011, www.littleandking.com/white_papers/loyalty_promotions.pdf.

22. "Determining Your Customer Perspective—Can You Satisfy These Customer Segments?," *Business901.com*, accessed October 8, 2011, business901.com/blog1/determining-your-customer-perspective-can-you-satisfy-these-customer-segments.

23. Claudio Marcus, "A Practical yet Meaningful Approach to Customer Segmentation," *Journal of Consumer Marketing* 15, no. 5 (1998): 494.

24. Malcolm Goodman, "The Pursuit of Value through Qualitative Market Research," *Qualitative Market Research: An International Journal* 2, no. 2 (1999): 111.

25. "What Are Wacky WallWalkers?," *DrFad.com*, accessed December 2, 2011, www.drfad.com/fad_facts/wallwalker.htm.

26. Susan Smith Hendrickson, "Mining Her Peas and Carrots Wins Investors," *Mississippi Business Journal* 32, no. 21 (2010): S4.

27. Alain Breillatt, "You Can't Innovate Like Apple," *Pragmatic Marketing* 6, no. 4, accessed October 8, 2011, www.pragmaticmarketing.com/publications/magazine/6/4/you_cant_innovate_like_apple.

28. Yoji Akao, *Quality Function Deployment: Integrating Customer Requirements into Product Design* (New York: Productivity Press, 1990), 17.

29. Gerson Tontini, "Deployment of Customer Needs in the QFD Using a Modified Kano Model," *Journal of the Academy of Business and Economics* 2, no. 1 (2003).

30. Glen Mazur, "QFD for Small Business: A Shortcut through the Maze of Matrices" (paper presented at the Sixth Symposium on Quality Function Deployment, Novi, MI, June 1994).

31. David Carson, Stanley Cromie, Pauric McGowan, Jimmy Hill, *Marketing and Entrepreneurship in Small and Midsize Enterprises* (Hemel Hempstead, UK: Prentice-Hall, 1995), 108.

32. Malcolm Goodman, "The Pursuit of Value through Qualitative Market Research," *Qualitative Market Research: An International Journal* 2, no. 2 (1999): 111.

33. Shallee Fitzgerald, "It's in the Cards," *Canadian Grocer* 118, no. 10 (2004/2005): 30.

34. Jerry Katz and Richard Green, *Entrepreneurial Small Business*, 2nd ed. (New York: McGraw-Hill, 2009), 17.

35. Alexander Hiam, *Creativity* (Amherst, MA: HRD Press, 1998), 6.

36. "Innovation Overload," *Trendwatching.com*, accessed December 2, 2011, trendwatching.com/trends/pdf/2006_08_innovation_overload.pdf.

37. A. Roy Thurik, "Introduction: Innovation in Small Business," *Small Business Economics* 8 (1996): 175.

38. L. Rausch, "Indicators of U.S. Small Business's Role in R&D," *National Science Foundation* (Info Brief NSF 10–304), March 2010.

39. Jancis Robinson, "The Oxford Companion to Wine," 2nd ed., *Wine Pros Archive*, accessed October 8, 2011, www.winepros.com.au/jsp/cda/reference/oxford_entry.jsp?entry_id=430.

40. "Innovation Jubilation," *Trendwatching.com*, accessed December 2, 2011, trendwatching.com/trends/innovationjubilation.

41. "Transparency Triumph," *Trendwatching.com*, accessed December 2, 2011, trendwatching.com/trends/transparencytriumph.

42. MakinBacon, "Why and How to Identify Real Trends," *HubPages*, accessed October 8, 2011, hubpages.com/hub/trendsanalysisforsuccess.

43. "Identifying and Understanding Trends in the Marketing Environment," *BrainMass*, accessed June 1, 2012, http://www.brainmass.com/library/viewposting.php?posting_id=51965.

44. Rocky Fu, "10 Excellent Online Tools to Identify Trends," *Rocky FU Social Media & Digital Strategies*, May 9, 2001, accessed October 8, 2011, www.rockyfu.com/blog/10-excellent-online-tools-to-identify-trends.

45. James L. Heskitt, W. Earl Sasser, and Leonard A. Schlesinger, *The Service Profit Chain* (New York: Free Press, 1997): 88.

46. Colette Weil, "Word-of-Mouth Marketing," *Home Care Magazine* 33, no. 1 (2010): 49.

47. "CRM (Customer Relationship Management," *About.com*, accessed October 8, 2011, sbinfocanada.about.com/cs/marketing/g/crm.htm.

48. Maria Verlengia, "CRM for the Small Business, Part 1: When Is It Time to Invest?," *CRMBuyer*, February 16, 2010, accessed October 8, 2011, www.crmbuyer.com/story/69349.html.

49. Maria Verlengia, "CRM for the Small Business, Part 2: Choosing the right CRM Tool," *CRMBuyer*, February 23, 2010, accessed October 8, 2011, www.crmbuyer.com/story/69402.html.

50. Maria Verlengia, "CRM for the Small Business, Part 4: Getting the New System Up and Running," *CRMBuyer*, March 9, 2010, accessed October 8, 2011, www.crmbuyer.com/story/69502.html%22.

51. "Great Customer Relations Management Tools," *St. Germane*, accessed June 1, 2012, http://www.stgermaine.ca/great-crm-customer-relationship-management-tools/.

52. Constance L. Hayes, *The Real Thing: Truth and Power at the Coca-Cola Company* (New York: Random House, 2004), 211.

53. "The Top 25 Biggest Product Flops of All Time," *Daily Finance*, accessed December 2, 2011, www.dailyfinance.com/photos/top-25-biggest-product-flops-of-all-time.

54. Scott MacStravic, "Questions of Value in Healthcare," *Marketing Health Services* 17, no. 4 (1997): 50.

55. "An Analysis of the Competitiveness Strategies of Zoots," *Cebu Ecommerce Writing Consultancy*, accessed June 1, 2012, http://cebuecommerce.info/an-analysis-of-the-competitive-strategies-of-zoots-the-cleaner-cleaner/.

56. *Companydatabase.org*, accessed June 1, 2012, http://companydatabase.org/c/recyclables-pick-up-service/products-services/zoots-corporation.html.

CHAPTER 3
Family Businesses

Westbrook Lobster

Source: Used with permission, Michael Larivere, manager, Westbrook Lobster, Wallingford, CT.

In 1957, Westbrook Lobster opened in Westbrook, Connecticut, as a specialized lobster and fish market. As time went on, the company expanded to offer a comprehensive range of fish, shrimp, and prepared foods. In 1989, Larry Larivere, who grew up near the docks of New Bedford, Massachusetts, bought the business and had a dream of expanding the business with a seafood restaurant.

Fast forward to 2004. Larry and his two sons, Michael (an environmental science major) and Matthew (a business major), opened up their second restaurant in Wallingford, Connecticut. It overlooks the Quinnipiac River in the historic Yale Brother's Mill built in the late 1670s. Originally a grain mill, later converted to a German and Britannia silver spoon factory, and finally converted into a restaurant, the building was rich with history.

Michael speaks easily about the value that Westbrook Lobster offers its customers: high quality food, great service…and visiting the tables while people are dining. He sees these visits as an important part of the relationships that he has built with his customers over the years. Westbrook customers eagerly await the monthly postcards that are sent out that feature dining specials, discounts, and coupons. He tries to get the postcards out early and actually receives phone calls if they are not received early. Many people have come to depend on them. Michael says that these postcards definitely give the restaurant its greatest return. The restaurant has a presence on Facebook, but that is geared to the bar crowd—a younger crowd.

Technology plays an important but mixed part in the restaurant's operations. Michael says that it is tough to run a restaurant these days without technology tools like POS (point of service) systems. These systems include touch screens for placing orders and paying for food items. Interestingly, however, most food vendors still do their business face to face (or telephone to telephone), choosing to stick with personal relationships. Only a few suppliers, such as liquor vendors, accept orders online.

The current Westbrook Lobster website was created by Michael and Matthew using services from intuit.com. They built the site themselves and are proud to note that restaurant gift cards can now be purchased directly from the site. This is a perfect example of Web 2.0 capabilities.

As far as running the business, currently fifty employees strong, Larry Larivere (Dad) is brought in on the big decisions. Otherwise, Michael and Mathew run the restaurants on their own. There are currently no other family members in the business.

Westbrook Lobster continues to provide the freshest seafood available at competitive prices. The daily selection includes everything from locally harvested shellfish to fresh fish from waters up and down the East Coast. They also offer several "healthy" options that are made without butter or bread crumbs. These menu items are very popular and are especially attractive for people with food allergies or people who just want to eat a bit lighter. All their efforts continue to pay off. Westbrook Lobster was voted "Best Seafood Restaurant Statewide" in *Connecticut Magazine* 2009 and "Best Seafood in New Haven County" in *Connecticut Magazine* 2009 and 2010.

Larry, Michael, and Matthew invite you to Westbrook Lobster when you are in the area. Once you are there, you are family.

Source: "The Lobster Tale," http://www.westbrooklobster.com/Wallingford/pages/wally_home.html (accessed on October 8, 2011) and interview with Michael Larivere, October 11, 2010.

1. FAMILY BUSINESS: AN OVERVIEW

LEARNING OBJECTIVES

1. Explain what a family business is.
2. Understand the role that family businesses play in the US economy.
3. Explain the advantages and disadvantages of family businesses.

"Family businesses are different."[1]
  - *BDO 2009 Report: "Focusing on Business Families"*

family business

A business that is actively owned and/or managed by more than one member of the same family.

There is no agreed-on definition of a family business. The percentage of ownership, the strategic control, the involvement of multiple generations, and the intention for the business to remain in the family are among the many criteria that experts use to distinguish family businesses from other types of businesses.[2] For the purposes of this chapter, however, a **family business** is defined as a business that is actively owned and/or managed by more than one member of the same family.[3] A family business can also be defined as the result of someone's dream:

> The story of every successful family business starts with someone who has the passion, confidence and courage to put his [or her] money where his [or her] mouth is…[These entrepreneurs] work incredibly hard, make things happen, are positive without being unrealistic and possess the resourcefulness to overcome all sorts of hurdles. They are also socially adept, capable of communicating effectively and good at inspiring others…[4]

Family business owners know that their roles are different from that of shareholders in companies owned by many public investors. In addition, "employees in family businesses know the difference that family control makes in their work lives, the company culture, and their career. Marketers appreciate the advantage that the image of a family business presents to customers. And families know that being in business together is a powerful part of their lives."[5]

1.1 Market and Employment Presence

Because of the private nature of most family businesses, it is difficult to obtain accurate information about them.[6] Complicating the situation is that most data sources do not distinguish between small family businesses, such as the local pizza parlor or deli, and large family businesses, such as Walmart, Mars, and Ford. "The reality is that family-based operations are represented across the full spectrum of American companies, from small businesses to large corporations."[7] Within this context, the following has been observed:[8]

- Family businesses account for a staggering 50 percent of the gross domestic product (GDP).
- Although it may seem that this GDP contribution comes from thousands of small operations, 35 percent of the *Fortune 500* companies are family companies.
- Family businesses account for 60 percent of US employment and 78 percent of the new jobs created.
- Family businesses represent one of the fastest growing sectors of the economy because their new job requirements outpace their current employment rates when compared to other types of businesses.

What this means is that family businesses continue to be a powerful economic force, no matter what their size and no matter how they are defined. "Family firms are the most common form of business structure; they employ many millions of people; and they generate a considerable amount of the world's wealth."[9]

The focus of this chapter is on the small family business.

Video Link 3.1

Mother and Daughter Partner in Family Business

A mother and daughter partner in a jewelry business.

video.answers.com/small-business-stories-mother-and-daughter-as-business-partner-132888892

1.2 Advantages and Disadvantages of the Family Business

There are benefits to a family business, but there are disadvantages that must be considered as well. Starting a family business is not for everyone.

Advantages

A family business offers the following advantages:

- One of the popular misconceptions about family businesses is that they are unable to adapt easily to increasing competitiveness and technological progress. The reality is that family businesses frequently have the advantage of entrepreneurial spirit, flexibility, and opportunism.[10]

- It is believed by some that family firms are "too soft" and rarely reach their potential. The reality is that family businesses actually outperform public companies. Oftentimes, the marketplace forces public companies to make short-term decisions, whereas a family business has the advantage of having more freedom to make its decisions. Family businesses can adapt to market fluctuations more easily because they can afford to be patient. They have common goals, shared values, and a commitment to brand building.[11]

- Family-owned businesses are often seen as ideal because family members form a "grounded and loyal foundation" for the company, and family members tend to exhibit more dedication to their common goals. "Having a certain level of intimacy among the owners of a business can help bring about familiarity with the company and having family members around provides a built-in support system that should ensure teamwork and solidarity."[12]

- The culture of a family business is very different from that of a company you will find on Wall Street. "Family businesses frequently take a very long-term point of view. They'll make investments that they don't expect to pay off for 5 or 15 or 25 years…Culture in a family business is more frequently based on very personal and emotional values. It's stronger because there are deeper roots and closer connections to the history of the company."[13]

- Family businesses are becoming more and more attractive to undergraduate business students who face a bleak job and salary outlook for new grads. These undergrads are choosing to return to their family businesses directly after graduation instead of trying to find a job in corporate America or on Wall Street.[14]

- There is a common misperception that family businesses are less professional and rigorous in their behavior because of the relational nature of the businesses.[15] However, like all other businesses, family businesses face global competition and rapidly changing markets. This creates more pressure on those who join to make sure that they produce. "This emphasis on professionalism has made family businesses both more daunting and more attractive—and has created new interest in them, from family members, outsiders, and business school students."[16]

- Many family-owned businesses tend to be stable and optimistic, even when economic times are uncertain. They seem to be better able to weather economic difficulties and stabilize the economy than their nonfamily counterparts.[17] However, this is a function of the industry and the size of the business.

- In general, family businesses feel that they are stronger because family members are involved in their activities. Family owners believe that their family members can be trusted, will work harder, and care more.[18] This can help create competitive advantage in the marketplace.

- Family businesses may be more open to flexible or part-time schedules or choosing your hours. This presents a very attractive work environment for people who need to tend to children, parents, or other family members in need.[19]

- Family businesses tend to operate more ethically. In fact, many family businesses believe that their ethical standards are more stringent than those of their competitors. In addition, family businesses are often deeply embedded in their communities, and this proximity is seen as an important factor that increases the likelihood of ethical decision making and moral behavior.[20]

As members of the local community, any ethical problems with a family business will be quickly visible.

- Family businesses also exhibit more social responsibility than their competitors. This has been attributed to their concern about image and local reputation [21] as well as their closeness to the community.
- Family businesses may incur lower costs because of the greater willingness of family members to make financial sacrifices for the sake of the business. Accepting lower pay than they would get elsewhere to help the business in the longer term or deferring wages in a cash-flow crisis are examples of family altruistic behavior. [22]
- Family businesses, in general, have greater independence of action because they have less (or no) pressure from the stock market and less (or no) takeover risk. [23]
- Family businesses tend to be more resilient in hard times because they are willing to plow profits back into the business. [24]
- Family businesses are less bureaucratic and less impersonal, which allows for greater flexibility and quicker decision making. [25]
- Family businesses offer the possibility of great financial success. [26] This can manifest itself in interesting ways. "As the family of a media conglomerate once mentioned, 'The name I have has certainly helped me to get access to top executives of companies, persons who under other circumstances would have kept their doors shut.'" [27]
- Family members have the chance to learn the business early. This extensive expertise can create an important competitive advantage. [28] "One executive recalled how as a child he would take long walks with his father, during which they would visit stores to look at competitor's products. Afterwards, his father would ask him which products he liked most, and this would lead to lengthy arguments about each product's quality. This man felt that the expertise he gained during those informal outings proved invaluable later in life." [29]

Video Link 3.2

Iron Horse Barbecue

A family-owned business that is helping other business fire up businesses of their own.

video.answers.com/small-business-stories-iron-horse-barbecue-124662002

Why Family Businesses Are So Special

"If family businesses are so common, how can they also be special? When Freud was asked what he considered to be the secret of a full life, he gave a three-word answer: 'Lieben und arbeiten [to love and to work].' For most people, the two most important things in their lives are their families and their work. It is easy to understand the compelling power of organizations that combine both. Being in a family firm affects all the participants. The role of chairman of the board is different when the company was founded by your father and when your mother and siblings sit around the table at board meetings, just as they sat around the dinner table. The job of a CEO is different when the vice president in the next office is also a younger sister. The role of partner is different when the other partner is a spouse or a child. The role of sales representative is different when you cover the same territory that your parent did twenty-five years earlier, and your grandparent twenty-five years before that. Even walking through the door on your first day of work on an assembly line or in a billing office is different if the name over the door is your own." [30]

Disadvantages

As attractive as family businesses are on many fronts, they have the following disadvantages:

succession

Passing the business to the next generation.

- Family businesses tend to be stable organizations. Although this is a good thing in many instances, stability can also make it difficult to change. A new, younger family member coming into the business will find tradition and structure. Changing that is not simple. The key to changing a family business lies in defining tradition in terms of the company's core values, not in specific ways of doing things. [31]
- Family closeness can lead to sibling rivalry or problems when both the parent and the child want control. By the third or fourth generation, with many cousins possibly sharing ownership, governance can become very complicated. [32]

- There may be times when the interests of a family member conflict with the interests of the business. One family member may want to expand the business, but other family members may not share this person's desire. The needs of the business are not in sync with the needs of the family.
- Family ties have a downside. Family members will frequently be expected to work harder, make more of a commitment, and get paid less than other employees in the business.[33]
- Family business owners may automatically promote someone from the family or give family members a job even if they do not have adequate skills for the job. A nonfamily employee may be better qualified.[34] This can cause dissension and resentment among other employees.
- Relationships between parents and children or among siblings have a tendency to deteriorate due to communication problems. "This dysfunctional behavior can result in judgments, criticism and lack of support."[35]
- The family business may be a breeding ground for jealousies, resentment, anger, and sabotage. Family problems may spill over into the workplace.[36]
- The business may be plagued with managerial incompetence, the lack of exposure to other businesses, and the inability to separate family and work.[37]
- Some family businesses may have difficulty attracting and keeping highly qualified managers. "Qualified managers may avoid family firms due to the exclusive **succession**, limited potential for professional growth, lack of perceived professionalism, and limitations on wealth transfer."[38] Succession refers to passing the business to the next generation.
- Family businesses have limited sources of external capital because they tend to avoid sharing equity with nonfamily members.[39] Having less access to capital markets may curtail growth.[40]
- Not all children of owner-managers may want to join the business. According to one study,[41] 80 percent of those who did not work in the family business did not intend to go into the business. This reluctance comes from several directions, such as the following:

  - My parents would not want me to join.
  - I could not work for my parents.
  - There are already too many family members in the business.
  - I am not interested in this particular business.
  - The business is too small for me.
  - The business would not allow me to use my talents.
  - The business would not allow me to use my training.
  - I can earn more elsewhere.
  - I am not interested in a business career.[42]

In Their Own Words

Why Some Children of Owner-Managers Do Not Want to Join the Business[43]

I see the pressure my dad is under—this does put me off slightly. I want to enjoy my job as well as enjoying life outside work.

A larger factor when working under a relative is the problem of self-worth. It is hard to feel like you are worth something when your father is an MD.

A business relationship with your father makes your family relationship harder.

I do not look to go into the family business straight away, as I feel this is giving a commitment to work there for the rest of my life.

I would join only because I am genuinely qualified, not because I am the owner's daughter.

The difference in my father's education and mine is a factor affecting why I have decided not to go into the business. I have more choice over what I want to do as a career, and my personal interests would not be met by my father's company. I am sure it would not have been his choice had he had the same educational choices as me.

As much as the route into the family business is seen by outsiders as an "easy route to wealth and inheritance," in my case it was also a liability. At 17, was I to be the fourth generation after 100 years that could not keep the company going?

- The "spoiled kid syndrome" often occurs in a family business. The business owner may feel guilty because his devotion to the business takes away from the attention he should be giving to his children. Out of a sense of guilt, he or she starts to bribe the children, "a kind of pay-off for not being available emotionally or otherwise."[44]

- Financial strain emanating from "family members milking the business and a disequilibrium between contribution and compensation"[45] can have a significant negative impact on the business.

- Nepotism that results in the "tolerance of inept family members as managers, inequitable reward systems, [and] greater difficulties in attracting professional management"[46] can easily lead to low morale among nonfamily members of the business, and it can ultimately result in business failure.

- Family businesses frequently have a confusing organization, with "messy structure and no clear division of tasks." Authority and responsibility lines are unclear; jobs may overlap; executives may hold a number of different jobs; and the decision-making hierarchy may be completely ignored, existing only to be bypassed.[47] This can create a dysfunctional working environment.

- Family businesses frequently have paternalistic or autocratic rule that is characterized by a resistance to change, secrecy, and the attraction of dependent personalities.[48]

KEY TAKEAWAYS

- Family businesses account for 50 percent of the GDP, 60 percent of US employment, and 78 percent of the new jobs that are created.
- A family business offers both advantages and disadvantages. It is important to understand both.

EXERCISE

1. In Chapter 2, Robert Rainsford was introduced in the *Frank's All-American BarBeQue* case. He has returned to the family business and is very enthusiastic about expanding the business. He has identified four options: (a) expanding the restaurant either at its current site or elsewhere in Fairfield; (b) opening several similar-sized restaurants in nearby towns; (c) using the Internet to expand sales; and (d) expanding the sales of Frank's sauces from a local store to a regional supermarket chain. Any one of these ideas would represent a change from his father's business model. Given that he had not expressed any interest in the management of the business, how should he go about approaching his father with these ideas? If the company expands, should Robert approach his sister and her husband about taking a more active role in the business? What should their roles be?

2. FAMILY BUSINESS ISSUES

> ## LEARNING OBJECTIVE
>
> 1. Explain why communication, employing family and nonfamily members, professional management, employment qualifications, salaries and compensation, succession, and ethics are important issues for all family businesses.

Looking at the vision and hard work of the founders, family businesses "take on their unique character as new members of the family enter the business. At best, the environment can be inspiring and motivating. At worst, it can result in routine business decisions becoming clouded by emotional issues."[49]

The owners and managers of family businesses face many unique challenges. These challenges stem from the overlap of family and business issues and include communication, employing family and nonfamily members, professional management, employment qualifications, salaries and compensation, and succession.

2.1 Communication

Communication is important in any business, but the complexities of communication in a family business are particularly problematic. Experts say that communication is one of the most difficult parts of running a family business.[50] The approach to communication needs to include commitment, the avoidance of secrecy, and an understanding of the risks of bad communication.

2.2 Commitment

In a family business, it is critical that there be a commitment to communicate effectively with family and nonfamily members of the business. "Business leaders should be open about their awareness of the potential for communication issues to evolve and their willingness to accept feedback and input from all employees about opportunities for improvement and areas of concern."[51]

One important issue is whether there should be a line drawn between family and business discussions. Some suggest that setting up strict guidelines from the start that draw a clear line between the different types of discussions is a good approach.[52] By contrast, the Praxity Family Business Survey[53] found that it is considered OK to talk about the business anywhere and at any time, whether at work or at home:

- Nineteen percent of the family businesses in the survey reported talking about business at home.
- Thirty-seven percent talk about it in the workplace.
- Forty-four percent talk about it when and wherever.

2.3 Secrecy

In family businesses, it is particularly important not to convey the impression that family members are more in the know than other employees. "…Even when this is not the case, the potential for the perception of exclusivity may exist. Steps should be taken to address any issues that may arise openly, honestly, and without preference for family members."[54]

2.4 Risks of Bad Communication

If good communication channels are not in place, the following can occur:

- "Family members assume they know what other family members feel or want."
- "Personal ties inhibit honest opinions being expressed."
- "The head of the family may automatically assume control of the business even if they don't have the best business skills."
- "One family member ends up dominating the business."

- "Family-member shareholders not active in the business fail to understand the objectives of those who are active and vice versa."
- "Personal resentments become business resentments and vice versa."[55]

These difficulties can be overcome if the family business makes a concerted effort to create and maintain an environment of open communication where people feel comfortable voicing opinions and concerns. It is important that family and nonfamily members have an equal opportunity to express their views.

2.5 Employing Family and Nonfamily Members

It is natural for a family business to employ family members, especially in management positions. Family members tend to be the first people hired when a small business gets started, and as the business grows, so do their roles.[56] There are both pros and cons to hiring family members. Both need to be considered carefully. Who to hire may well be the biggest management challenge that a family business owner faces.

Pros

On the positive side of things, several advantages can be identified for hiring family members:[57]

- Improved customer relations through family contact
- Intergenerational continuity
- Long-term stability
- Shared values
- Loyalty and commitment
- Inherent trust
- Willingness to sacrifice for the business
- Emotional attachment to the business; more willing to contribute to its success
- Share the same culture

"A family whose members work well together can also give the business a welcoming and friendly feel. It can encourage employees who aren't in the immediate family to work harder to gain acceptance by those employees who are."[58]

Cons

There are also quite a few disadvantages to hiring family members:[59]

- Families are not perfect, so a dispute among family members can spill from home into the workplace.
  - There is always the possibility of managerial incompetence.
  - It may not be possible to separate family and work.
  - Patterns of conflict will be rooted in early family experiences.
  - Communication may break down.
  - Sibling rivalry may create problems.
- Newly hired family members may feel that they do not have to earn their positions; their success will be seen as linked to their name instead of their abilities.
  - The company may be subject to charges of discriminatory hiring practices if job openings are not published.
  - Nonfamily members of the business may feel that family members get hiring preference.
  - Nonfamily members may feel that they will be automatically outvoted in decision making.
  - Hiring primarily family members for management positions may lead to hiring suboptimal people who cannot easily be dismissed. This could lead to greater conflict because of promotion criteria that are not based on merit.

Hiring Nonfamily Members

There will be times when the better decision may be to hire a nonfamily person for a particular job. Experience has shown that a family business is less likely to be successful if it employs only family members; bringing in the fresh thinking that comes with external expertise can be valuable at all levels of a business.[60] In addition, nonfamily members can offer stability to a family business by offering a fair and impartial perspective on business issues. The challenge is in attracting and retaining nonfamily employees because these employees "may find it difficult to deal with family conflicts on the job, limited opportunities for advancement, and the special treatment sometimes accorded family members. In addition, some family members may resent outsiders being brought into the firm and purposely make things unpleasant for nonfamily employees."[61] Because it is likely that a growing family business will need to hire people from the outside, it is important that the business come to terms with that necessity. Policies and procedures can help with the transition, but the most important thing is to prepare the family culture of the business to accept a nonfamily member. Not surprisingly, this is much easier said than done.

2.6   Professional Management

The decision to hire a **professional manager** is likely one of the most important and difficult hiring decisions that a family business owner will have to make. The typical definition of professional managers equates them with external, nonfamily, nonowner managers, thus declaring professional management and family management as mutually exclusive.[62] "A typical argument…is that professional non-family managers should be brought in to provide 'objectivity' and 'rationality' to the family firm."[63]

There are several problems with this way of thinking. First, it perpetuates the outdated notion that family members are not professional, that the smartest thing for a family business to do is to bring in professional management—as quickly as possible.[64]

Second, professional managers are not always prepared to deal with the special nature of family-owned businesses. "The influence of families on businesses they own and manage is often invisible to management theorists and business schools. The core topics of management education—organizational behavior, strategy, finance, marketing, production, and accounting—are taught without differentiating between family and nonfamily businesses."[65] This does an injustice to the unique workings of a family-owned business.

Third, a professional manager from the outside is not always prepared, perhaps not even most of the time, to deal with the special nature of family companies. The dominant view on professional management downplays the importance of the social and the cultural context. "This is a problem in family firms where family relations, norms, and values are crucial to the workings and development of the business."[66] It is argued that the meaning business families attach to their businesses is guided by family values and expectations—so much so that "anything or anyone that interrupts this fragility could send the business into chaos."[67]

The hiring of an outside manager, therefore, should include an assessment of both **formal competence** and **cultural competence**. Formal competence refers to formal education, training, and experience outside the family business. Although it is certainly helpful and appropriate, formal competence is not sufficient for managerial effectiveness. It needs to be supplemented with cultural competence, an understanding of the culture of a specific firm. Interestingly, most family businesses look only to formal competence when selecting a CEO.[68]

professional manager

An external, nonfamily, nonowner manager.

formal competence

Formal education, training, and experience outside the family business.

cultural competence

An understanding of the culture of a specific firm.

Culture and Nonfamily CEOs

It is extremely important to understand the culture of the family firm. It means that as a leader you have to be sensitive to the organization's reactions on the things you say and do. I have a long-term employee on my management team, and she is my guide in these issues. She can tell me how the organization will react and how things are likely to be received. We have to build on the past even though we have to do a lot of things in new and different ways. But because of the culture, this might be very sensitive. (The words of a nonfamily CEO in a family business.)

As a nonfamily CEO, you have to have in-depth respect for the invisible forces among the employees in the family firm. You cannot escape the fact that there will always be special bonds between the family firm and the owner. Always. (The words of a nonfamily CEO in a family business.)[69]

One concern of family businesses may be that the hiring of a nonfamily manager will result in the loss of their "familiness." However, one study found that, even with nonfamily managers bringing nonfamily management activities, styles, and characteristics, "the special and unique aspects and forces of the system of the family, its individual family members, and the business itself provide a synergistic force that offsets the outside influences of the [nonfamily managers]."[70] This same study acknowledged, however, that their research did not focus on understanding at what point, or percentage of nonfamily members, the feeling of "familiness" will begin to erode.[71]

2.7 Employment Qualifications

One of the more difficult challenges that a family business must face is determining employment qualifications for employees, both family and nonfamily. The lack of a clear employment policy and process can lead to major conflicts in the company. Unfortunately, it would appear that, despite their benefit, most family businesses have a family employment policy.[72] As a result, many family businesses may end up with more employees from the family than the company needs, and some of these people may not even be qualified or suitable for the jobs they have been given. "Some family businesses even find themselves acquiring businesses that have no relationship with their original business or keeping some unprofitable business lines just to make sure that everybody in the family gets a job within the company."[73] This kind of situation benefits no one.

A written family-business employment policy can solve a myriad of problems because it spells out the specific terms for family and nonfamily members with respect to recruiting, hiring, promoting, compensating, and terminating. One recommendation is that an ideal family employment policy should include the following:[74]

- "Explain the family employment policy's purpose and philosophy."
- "Describe how family members will apply and be considered for positions."
- "Cover the general conditions of employment, including compensation and supervision."
- "Outline the approach to be taken in developing and promoting family business members."
- Make clear that family members will be completing the same applications that other candidates will complete.
- Include an inspiring and upbeat reminder that the policy's purpose is to help the family business succeed and to support, develop, and motivate family members to lead successful and productive lives.
- Have all family business owners sign the policy, indicating they have read and agreed to it.

Others have recommended "that family members meet three qualifications before they are allowed to join the family business on a permanent basis: an appropriate educational background; three to five years' outside work experience; and an open, existing position in the firm that matches their background."[75]

There are no rules that dictate the content of a family business employment policy, so differences from one family business to another can be expected. However, it is very important "to set employment conditions that do not discriminate against or favor family members. This would help establish an atmosphere of fairness and motivation for all employees of the family business."[76]

The benefits of an employment policy notwithstanding, the idea may be met with resistance. There may be the feeling that hiring decisions for family members should be separate from the hiring decisions for nonfamily members because being a family member provides special qualifications that cannot be matched by someone outside the family. How to proceed will ultimately fall on the shoulders of the family business owner.

2.8   Salaries and Compensation

As difficult as hiring decisions may be for the family business, decisions about salaries and compensation are probably even worse. No matter how well intentioned and well designed the company's compensation plan may be, there will still be jealousies, hard feelings, severed sibling relationships, and even lawsuits, particularly among those family members who feel they have been treated unfairly.[77] This presents a daunting challenge: how to develop a compensation plan that will be fair to family members and good for the business:

> One of the greatest struggles of operating a family business is separating the family from the business. Oh yes, there are many great benefits to having family in the business and to being a family member in a family business, but the most difficult problems result when "family values" and issues take over, leaving business values and needs wanting. There is no greater source for family business problems—nor more fertile ground for their cure—than the family business compensation systems.[78]

Some of the Problems

Family businesses often make several common mistakes when developing their compensation plans.

- They consider fair compensation to be equal compensation for all family members, sometimes even for the owner. This creates a very sticky situation because all family members are not created equal. "It is sometimes difficult to assess and compare the talents of family members who are also employees. Nor do all family members contribute equally to the business. As a result of the stress that this causes, many family business owners ignore the problem and let compensation become a breeding ground for dissension in the family."[79]

- They do not compensate wives for the work they do. The reason often given? It saves on taxes. Not surprisingly, this approach leaves wives isolated from the business, invisible in the decision-making process, and unappreciated. This problem extends to the compensation of sons and daughters as well. A survey by Mass Mutual Insurance Company[80] reported a big discrepancy among the salaries of sons and daughters in family businesses across America. The average salary of the typical son in a family business was $115,000, while his sister earned only $19,000. This may be due to the tendency of sons being groomed for leadership, while daughters are groomed for the supportive roles that command lower salaries.

- The compensation for family members is higher than that for nonfamily members, but the differential is not tied to the actual job requirements or performance. This situation can lead to anger, reduced motivation, resentment, and eventual departure of the nonfamily member from the firm.

- The business overpays family members—for a variety of reasons:[81]
  - "Guilt, because mom & pop were so busy working when the kids were young."
  - "Fear of conflict, because someone's wife threatens not to come to the family picnic."
  - "Resistance to change, because 'That's the way we've always done it.'"
  - "Inability to confront family members who feel 'entitled' to inflated salaries."
  - "Determination to minimize estate taxes by transferring wealth through compensation."

- Emotional pressures are allowed to determine compensation policies. What this means is that compensation is not correctly determined by job requirements and performance in those jobs. When this happens, small problems develop centrifugal force:[82]
  - "Fighting between sibling/cousin partners increases."
  - "Hard-working family members and employees lose morale."
  - "Well-motivated competent employees leave the company."
  - "The company loses its competitive edge and growth potential."
  - "Family harmony decreases."
  - "The value of the company declines, or it is sold—for the wrong reasons."

Some of the Solutions

Developing a fair compensation plan for the family business is not easy. It requires good faith, trust, and good business sense. The dollar amounts offered to family members will be critical, but the more pressing issue is fairness.[83] Unfortunately, fairness is often construed as equality. This must be avoided.

There is no template for designing a compensation plan for family businesses, but there are several recommendations:[84]

- Develop accurate job descriptions for each employee that include responsibilities, level of authority, technical skills, level of experience and education required for the job, and goals for an annual performance review. In a performance-based company, the amount of stock owned by a family member will not be related to his or her compensation.
- Develop a clear philosophy of compensation so that everyone understands the standards that are used to pay people. The following is a sample of a written compensation plan philosophy that was developed by one family.

Family members employed in the business will be paid according to the standards in our region, as reported by our trade association, for a specific position, in companies of our size. In order to retain good employees we will pay all employed family members and other managers within the top quartile of our industry's standards. Additional compensation will be based on success in reaching specific company goals, with bonuses shared among all members of the management team. Individual incentives will be determined according to measurable goals for job performance determined each year, and reviewed by the appropriate manager.[85]

- Gather information about the salaries of similar positions in the industry of the family business in the applicable region of the country. Look at companies that are similar in the number of employees, revenue, and product. If possible, obtain salary and benefit information.
- Have the base salary for each position be consistent with the salaries and wages paid for comparable positions at similarly sized businesses. Paying at this market value will have an excellent effect on nonfamily members because they will feel that they are on an even playing field. There will be a positive effect on business morale.
- The family business owner might consider seeking outside help in determining compensation levels for individual family members. However, this assistance must be seen as truly objective, with no reason to favor one viewpoint over another.

Oh, Those Sleepless Nights!

A recent family business survey[86] reported that the following things keep family business owners awake at night.

Rank	The Nightmare	Percentage Citing as a Significant Concern (%)
1	Family members can never get away from work.	18
2	Business disagreements can put strain on family relationships.	17
3	Emotional aspects can get in the way of important business decisions.	16
4	Transition to the next generation is more difficult than a third-party sale.	10
5	There can often be conflicts regarding the fairness of reward for effort.	9
6	The business rewards are not necessarily based on merit.	8
7	Family members find it difficult to be individuals in their own right.	5
8	Difficulties arise in attracting professional management.	5
9	Children can be spoiled through inequitable rewards.	4
10	Outside shareholders do not contribute but take payouts from the business.	3
11	The family is always put before the business and therefore can be less efficient.	3
12	Past deeds are never forgotten and are brought up at inappropriate times.	2

Other urgent issues identified by a different family business survey included, in order of importance, the following:[87]

- Labor costs
- Health-care costs
- Finding qualified employees
- Foreign competition
- Labor union demands
- Domestic competition
- Oil prices
- Availability of credit from lenders
- Estate taxes

2.9 Succession

Another important issue that is particularly difficult for family businesses is **succession**. As mentioned earlier in this chapter, succession is about passing the business to the next generation. Decisions have to be made about who will take over the leadership and/or ownership of the company when the current generation dies or retires.[88] Interestingly, "only a third of all family businesses successfully make the transition to the second generation largely because succeeding generations either aren't interested in running the business or make drastic changes when they take the helm."[89] There are family businesses that manage the transition across generations quite easily because the succession process chooses only the children willing and able to join and work with the prevailing family, business values, and goals. Unfortunately, there are also instances in which children have had to leave school as soon as legally allowed, not equipped to manage either the business, their lives, or their family. These children spend many resentful years in the business until it fails.[90]

Passing the family business to the next generation is a difficult thing to do, but succession is a matter of some urgency because 40 percent of US businesses are facing the issue of succession at any given point in time.[91] This urgency notwithstanding, there are several forces that act against succession planning:[92]

1. Founder

- Fear of death

- Reluctance to let go of power and control
- Personal loss of identity
- Fear of losing work activity
- Feelings of jealousy and rivalry toward successor

2. Family

- Founder's spouse's reluctance to let go of role in firm
- Norms against discussing family's future beyond lifetime of parents
- Norms against favoring siblings
- Fear of parental death

3. Employees

- Reluctance to let go of personal relationship with founder
- Fears of differentiating among key managers
- Reluctance to establish formal controls
- Fear of change

4. Environmental

- Founder's colleagues and friends continue to work
- Dependence of clients on founder
- Cultural values that discourage succession planning

These are powerful forces working against succession planning, but they need to be overcome for the good of the founder, the family, and the business. It will be tricky to balance the needs of all three and fold them into a good succession plan.

2.10   The Succession Plan

Voyageur Transportation, a company in London, calls its successful succession planning program, "If you got hit by a beer truck, what would happen to your department?"[93] As a family business owner, you should pose this question in terms of yourself and your business. Hopefully, this will provide the impetus you need to develop a succession plan.

> *A good succession plan outlines how the succession will occur and what criteria will be used to judge when the successor is ready to take on the task. It eases the founder's concerns about transferring the firm to someone else and provides time in which to prepare for a major change in lifestyle. It encourages the heirs to work in the business, rather than embarking on alternative careers, because they can see what roles they will be able to play. And it endeavors to provide what is best for the business; in other words, it recognizes that managerial ability is more important than birthright, and that appointing an outside candidate may be wiser than entrusting the company to a relative who has no aptitude for the work.[94]*

A good succession plan will recognize and accept people's differences, not assume that the next generation wants the business; determine if heirs even have enough experience to run the business; consider fairness; and think and act like a business. The plan should also include a timetable of the transition stages, from the identification of a successor to the staged and then full transfer of responsibilities, and a contingency plan in case the unforeseen should happen, such as the departure or death of the intended successor or the intended successor declining the role.[95] It would also be helpful to get some good professional advice—from company advisors who have expertise in the industry as well as other family-run businesses.[96]

Although each succession plan will be different, the following components should be seen as necessary for a good succession plan:[97]

1. **Establish goals and objectives.** As the family business owner, you must establish your personal goals and vision for the business and your future role in its operation. You should include your retirement goals, family member goals, goals of other stakeholders (e.g., partners, shareholders, and employees), and goals relating to what should happen in the case of your illness, death, or disability.

2. **Family involvement in the decision-making process.** If the family and stakeholders who are involved in the decision-making process are kept informed of the decisions being made, many of the problems related to inheritance, management, and ownership issues will be alleviated. Communication, the process for handling family change and disputes, the family vision for the business, and the relationship between the family and the business should be addressed. The surest path to family discord is developing the succession plan on your own and then announcing it.[98]

3. **Identify successor(s).** This section of the plan will address the issue of who takes over ownership and management of the business. Identification of the potential successor(s), training of the successor(s), building support for the successor(s), and teaching the successor(s) to build vision for the business are included here. Working with your successor(s) for a year or two before you hand over the business will increase the chances for success.[99]

4. **Estate planning.** Estate planning is important if you are planning to retire or want to take precautionary measures regarding the future of the business in the event you are unable to continue operation of the family business due to illness, disability, or death. You should consult a lawyer, an accountant, a financial/estate planner, and a life insurance representative so that your benefits will be maximized. You will need to consider taxation, retirement income, provisions for other family members, and active/nonactive family members.

5. **Contingency planning.** Contingency planning is about unforeseen circumstances. It is about strategizing for the most likely "what if" scenarios (e.g., your death or disability). By thinking in terms of the unforeseen, you will be taking a proactive rather than reactive approach.

6. **Company structure and transfer methods.** This section of the succession plan involves the review and updating of the organizational and structural plan for the organization taking into account the strengths and weaknesses of the successor. The following needs to be identified: the roles and the responsibilities of the successor, the filling of key positions, structuring of the business to fit the successor, the potential roles for the retiring owner, any legal complications, and financial issues.

7. **Business valuation.** This section is relevant only if the business is being sold. Passing the business to a family member would not involve a business valuation.

8. **Exit strategy.** With any succession, ownership will be transferred, and you will remove yourself from the day-to-day operations of the business. Alternatives will be compared, and a framework for making your final choices will be developed. The transfer method and the timelines are decided. The exit plan should then be published and distributed to everyone who is involved in the succession process.

9. **Implementation and follow-up.** The succession plan should be reviewed regularly and revised as situations change. It should be a dynamic and a flexible document.

As difficult as the planning process can be, the goal should be a succession plan that will be in the best interests of all—or most—of the parties involved. Business interests should be put ahead of family interests, and merit should be emphasized over family position.[100]

The Family Business and Technology

In 2008, when R. Michael Johnson—Mikee to everyone who knows him—took over the pressure-treated lumber company his grandfather founded in 1952, he had a great idea: laptops for all managers and sales staff.

"'You would have thought the world was coming apart," says Johnson, CEO and president of Cox Industries in Orangeburg, South Carolina. One salesman—convinced that the computer would be used to track his movements outside the office—up and quit. A buyer who had been with the company for thirty-five years said he would like a fax machine but could not see why he needed a computer when he had managed just fine without one for so long.

And that was just the beginning. In an industry where some businesses still write delivery tickets by hand and tote them up on calculators, Johnson recently led the company through an ERP (enterprise resource planning) software conversion and distributed iPhones to the sales team so they can use the company's new customer relationship management (CRM) system.

"'Let's just say I have spent quite a few Sunday lunches after church explaining technology acronyms to Granddad and Grandmom," Johnson says.

The resistance to new technology quieted, however, after Johnson was able to point to market share growth of 35 percent at the $200 million business in the past year. "The numbers are starting to resonate," he says. "Five years ago, I couldn't even say what our market share was because we didn't have the technology to figure it."[101]

KEY TAKEAWAYS

- Important family issues include communication, employing family and nonfamily members, professional management, employment qualifications, salaries and compensation, and success. Each issue can create conflict.
- It is very important to understand the culture of the family business, especially by nonfamily CEOs.
- Succession planning is critical to the success of passing a business to family members.

EXERCISES

1. Select a family business in your area. Make arrangements to speak with three members of the family who work in the business. Develop a list of ten questions that cover a broad range of issues, such as the approach to compensation (but do not ask for specific salary or wage numbers), the process for hiring family and nonfamily members, and the plans for passing the business to the next generation. Ask each member of the business the same questions. Pull the answers together and compare them. Where did you find similarities? Where did you find differences? Did everyone know the answer to each question? Where were people reluctant to answer? Prepare a three- to five-page report on your findings.

2. The family business is looking to expand, and some members of the family, but not all, feel that it might be worth bringing in someone from the outside to fill one of the new management positions because the family talent has been pretty much exhausted. Design a process for hiring an external manager. What things should be considered? How might you get buy-in from all family members?

3. CONFLICT

LEARNING OBJECTIVES

1. Explain what conflict is.
2. Explain why positive or constructive conflict can be helpful to a family business.
3. Explain why negative or destructive conflict can damage a family business.
4. Identify sources of negative conflict in a family business.
5. Identify some ways in which negative conflict can be avoided.

positive or constructive conflict

Conflict that is beneficial to a family business.

negative or destructive conflict

Conflict that can hurt a family business.

All businesses have conflict. It can be a good thing or it can be a bad thing. **Positive or constructive conflict** can be beneficial to a family business when it increases opportunity recognition, produces high-quality decisions, encourages growth, strengthens groups and individuals, increases the learning necessary for entrepreneurial behavior, and increases the levels of commitment to the decisions being made.[102] An example of positive conflict is a disagreement between family members on the strategic direction of the family business, the result being a much-needed rethinking of the business plan and a new agreed-on vision for the company.[103]

By contrast, **negative or destructive conflict** can hurt a business by damaging the harmony and relationships of family members in the family business, discouraging learning, causing ongoing harm to groups and individuals in the business, frustrating adequate planning and rational decision making, and resulting in poor quality decisions.[104] "The absence of good conflict makes it that much harder to accurately evaluate business ideas and make important decisions...But conflict does not mean browbeating."[105] An example of a negative conflict would be arguments over the successor to the business. Ultimately, the failure to adequately control negative conflict may contribute to the high mortality rate of family-owned businesses.[106]

Because of the clash between business and emotional concerns in a family business, the potential for negative conflict can be greater than for other businesses.[107] The tension that exists among the personal lives and career pursuits of family members creates an **interrole conflict** (occurring when a family member has simultaneous roles with conflicting expectations) in which the role pressures from work and home are incompatible.[108] This conflict is difficult—if not impossible in some instances—to resolve. "Due to the interconnection and frequent contact among family members working in the business with those who are not but may still have an ownership stake, recurring conflict is highly probable in family firms."[109]

interrole conflict

A situation when a family member has simultaneous roles with conflicting expectations.

3.1 Sources of Conflict

The specific causes of conflict in a family business are many. Because the typical understanding of conflict in family businesses is that conflict refers to negative conflict that is unhealthy and disruptive, negative conflict is the focus of this section.

The PricewaterhouseCoopers Family Business Survey[110] identified a core group of issues that are likely to cause tension.

Issue Causing Tension	Causes Some Tension (%)	Causes a Lot of Tension (%)
Discussion about the future strategy of the business	25	9
Performance of family members actively involved in the business	19	8
Decisions about who can and cannot work in the business	19	7
Failure of family members actively involved in the business to consult the wider family on key issues	16	7
Decisions about the reinvestment of profits in the business versus the payment of dividends	15	7
The setting of remuneration levels for family members actively involved in the business	14	7
The role in-laws should or should not play in the business	14	7
Decisions about who can and cannot hold shares in the business	13	6
Discussions about the basis on which shares in the business should be valued	12	5
Rejection of chosen successor by other family members	10	5

Add to this the fact that "family firms are prone to psychodynamic effects like sibling rivalry, children's desire to differentiate themselves from their parents, marital discord, identity conflict, and succession and inheritance problems that nonfamily businesses do not suffer from,"[111] and it's easy to see how the family business is a fertile field for negative conflict.[112]

Several other sources of conflict can occur in a family-owned business. A sampling of those sources is discussed here. All have the potential to adversely impact family relationships, business operations, and business results.

- **Rivalry.** Harry Levinson from the Harvard Business School maintains that, "the fundamental psychological conflict in family businesses is rivalry, compounded by feelings of guilt, when more than one family member is involved."[113] This rivalry can occur between father and son, siblings, husband and wife, father and daughter, and in-laws with members of the family that own the business.

- **Differing vision.** Family members will often disagree with the founder and with each other about the vision and strategy for the business. These differences "can create fear, anger, and destructive attempts to control decisions that are divisive and counter-productive to making and implementing sound decisions."[114] Rivalries that spill into the workplace can get nasty, leading to destructive behaviors.

- **Jealousy.** There is always the potential for jealousy in the family business. It can arise from feelings of unfairness in such things as compensation, job responsibilities, promotions, "having the ear" of the business founder, and stock distributions. It can also arise with respect to the planned successor when there is a difference of opinion about who it should be. If it is not resolved, jealousy has the potential to divide the family and destroy the business.[115]

- **Succession.** Succession is always a big obstacle for a family business. In some cases, the founder may feel that his or her children are not capable of running the business. This will cause obvious tension between the parent and the child/children, such that the child or children may leave the business in frustration.[116] This, in turn, becomes problematic for succession. "Who gets what type of equity, benefit, title, or role can be major sources of explicit conflict or implicit but destructive behaviors."[117] It is also true that while the founder of the business wants to continue family ownership and leadership of the business, this may not be true of his or her immediate family or later-generation family members.[118] This can create substantive conflict during succession planning.

- **Playing by different rules.** This cause of negative conflict "often presents itself as a form of elitism or entitlement that exists simply by virtue of being in a family that owns a business. Examples show up in allowing one or more family members to exhibit deficient standards of conduct or performance that violate sound business practices or important requirements that all other employees are expected to follow. Such behaviors can be divisive and demoralizing to all employees and customers as well as harmful to the reputation of the business."[119]

- **Decision making.** If roles and responsibilities are not clearly defined, conflict will arise over who can make decisions and how decisions should be made. This will lead to confusion, uncertainty, and haphazard decisions that will put the company at risk.

- **Compensation and benefits.** "This is one of the most frequent sources of conflict, especially among members of the younger generation." A person's compensation is inextricably linked to his or her feelings of importance and self-worth. Compound that with the emotions associated with being a member of the family that owns the business, and you have the potential for explosive negative conflict. Clearly, this is not in the best interests of the business.[120]

3.2 Avoiding Conflict

Some measure of family squabbling is expected in a family business. Some of the arguments will be logical and necessary. However, "it's important that they remain professional and not personal, because squabbling among family members in a work environment can make the employees and customers feel extremely uncomfortable, and can give them grounds for legal claims against the business."[121] The negative effects of family squabbling are as follows:[122]

- **Unprofessional image.** Family squabbling conjures up images of children—immaturity and pettiness. This sends a signal to customers and other employees that they are not in a professional environment that focuses on the right things.

- **Uncomfortable environment.** It is embarrassing to witness squabbling. No one likes to be in an awkward atmosphere; squabbling can cost you customers and employees, and it may result in expensive and unpleasant lawsuits. This can affect your bottom line very quickly.

- **Discrimination.** Nepotism is one of the biggest dangers of working in a family business. Arguing with relatives will only reinforce to other employees that they are in a family business. This can quickly lead to feelings of disparate treatment which, in turn, can lead to discrimination charges.

- **Legal troubles.** In the worst cases of family squabbling, disagreements over business can lead to lawsuits. If one family member's role is minimized and his or her authority is restricted, this is violating the person's rights as a shareholder. This can lead to an oppressed minority shareholder suit against the family business. This would be expensive, it would be ugly, and it could lead to the demise of the company.

Avoiding conflict is no easy feat. However, there are several things that a family business should consider. First, there are consultants who engage in conflict resolution for a living. The possibilities should be checked out. If the budget can handle the costs of a consultant, it could be the best choice. A consultant, having no reason to take one side or the other, will bring the necessary objectivity to resolution of the conflict.

Second, emotional reactions should be differentiated from problem-solving reactions. Family members need to take a professional perspective rather than that of an irritated sibling, parent, son, or daughter.[123] It will probably be difficult to do this, but it is important that it be done.

Third, focus on the professional role instead of the family role. "Make sure it's clear what the expectations and attitudes of all your employees are…Because you're a small business, you might not have as strict a policy as a large corporation, but it would still be helpful to put it in writing, such as in an employee handbook, which carries legal responsibilities to both family and outside employees."[124]

Fourth, encourage honesty from the beginning. When first starting to work together, it is important that family members sit down together to talk about potential conflicts that might arise. Acknowledging that it will be more difficult to work together because of being family is a good beginning. Treating family members and the professional environment with respect and expecting honesty when someone steps over the line should make for a smoother process.[125]

Last, the founder should try to keep the conflict constructive. This means stimulating task-oriented disagreement and debate while trying to minimize interpersonal conflicts.[126] This will require a fair decision-making process. For people to believe that a process is fair, it means that they must[127]

- "Have ample opportunity to express their views and to discuss how and why they disagree with other [family] members";
- "Feel that the decision-making process has been transparent, i.e., deliberations have been relatively free of secretive, behind-the-scenes maneuvering";
- "Believe that the leader listened carefully to them and considered their views thoughtfully and seriously before making a decision";
- "Perceive that they had a genuine opportunity to influence the leader's final decision"; and
- "Have a clear understanding of the rationale for the final decision."

KEY TAKEAWAYS

- Conflict can be either positive or negative. Negative conflict can potentially harm the business.
- There are many sources of negative conflict in a family business. The fundamental psychological conflict in family businesses is rivalry.
- It is important to avoid negative conflict. In particular, family squabbling that is witnessed by others can cause damage to the firm. Employees and customers will feel uncomfortable, and there may ultimately be grounds for a lawsuit.

EXERCISE

1. The founder of XYZ company has decided to retire. He wants one of three children to take over leadership of the business—and he knows exactly who it should be. Other members of the family have their ideas as well. One segment of the family wants the oldest son, Michael, to take over, but the founder thinks Michael is a melon head. The second son, Christopher, is a well-meaning and hard-working part of the business, but he just does not have what it takes to be a leader. Nonetheless, he is favored by another group of family members. Samantha, the youngest child, is as sharp as a tack, with solid experience and accomplishments under her belt. On an objective basis, Samantha would be the best choice for the business. She is the founder's choice to take over the company and has other family supporters as well, although not as many as for Michael or Christopher. This is a situation tailor-made for conflict. How does the founder finesse the selection of Samantha and minimize the conflict that is bound to occur? Can he win?

4.   THE THREE THREADS

LEARNING OBJECTIVES

1. Explain how a family business adds to customer value.
2. Explain how being a family business can positively and negatively impact cash flow.
3. Explain how technology and the e-environment are impacting family businesses.

4.1   Customer Value Implications

When people think about family businesses, they usually think friendly, "quality, wholesome, and continuity." Customers feel that they have a connection to the business because they also have a family. It is something customers feel they can trust.[128] Customers are reminded that there is a family behind the business, not a faceless corporate entity.[129] These are important sources of customer value.

The high priority that family businesses place on community involvement and the "reputational capital attributed to the family name" also translate into a perception of greater value by the customer.[130] "Family business's identification with the family name motivates a greater emphasis on serving customers and consumers effectively, such as through providing quality products and customer services."[131] The emphasis of the family business on its family identity may, in fact, contribute to its competitive advantage. "It is conceivable that family businesses who promote their familiness build a reputation in the market place related to customers' positive perception of the family."[132] The long-term source of value for the customers of family businesses may rest with the belief that the businesses are customer-focused.

4.2 Cash-Flow Implications

A family business can help or hurt its cash flow depending on whether it compensates family members at market value. If a family member's compensation is based on "family values," such that the parents' compensation is excessive and the children's compensation is much less than their fair market value, this would give an inflated picture of the company's profitability.[133] However, it will help the company's cash flow because they will have more money to spend on the business. If, however, the children's compensation is excessive, often based on housing and family needs of the family members as opposed to their worth to the business, this would give an unrealistically low portrayal of the profitability of the business.[134] This will hurt the company's cash flow because the amount of money available to spend on the business will be reduced.

4.3 Digital Technology and E-Environment Implications

It is estimated that about 40 percent of US family-owned businesses survive into second generation businesses, but only about 13 percent are passed down successfully to a third generation. One of the main reasons for this is that technological change moves so swiftly that it bypasses the older generation. "Unless the next generation is poised to update, and can get buy-in from longtime employees wedded to 'the way we always did it,' a business can quickly become obsolete."[135] It is understood that family businesses will have different technology needs depending on their size, industry, and growth objectives. For many family businesses, however, the move to greater technology integration should be seen as a natural part of business evolution.

With respect to e-business and e-commerce, the commitment of a family business to digital technology will be a necessary precursor to the integration of e-business solutions. E-business is discussed in more detail in Chapter 4. The commitment to e-commerce should also be seen as a natural part of business evolution and a necessary response to the ubiquitous nature of the Internet. E-commerce for the small business is also discussed in greater detail in Chapter 4.

KEY TAKEAWAYS

- Family businesses offer increased customer value because they are associated with families instead of impersonal corporate entities.
- Not all family businesses may choose to integrate digital technology, e-business, and e-commerce into their planning and operations. The level of integration will occur on a continuum. Given the extent to which digital technology pervades business, however, it will be difficult to ignore it. The same is true for e-business and e-commerce.
- Overpaying or underpaying family members has an effect on cash flow.

EXERCISES

1. Select two family businesses in your area. Interview each business owner about how he or she currently uses technology in the business and what the plans are for future technology integration. Prepare a three- to five-page report on your findings.
2. Select three family businesses that you patronize. Think about what you see as the source(s) of customer value for each business. Interview the owner(s) of each business and ask them to describe the customer value that they offer. Compare your thoughts with what the owners said. Are they different? How? If they are different, what might account for the differences?

Disaster Watch

What Happens Now?

"From the day he opened his jewelry store in 1980, Michael Genovese, 57, expected his son Joseph, now 32, to come into and eventually take over the business. Joe started working there part time while still in junior high, engraving and polishing. 'Dad offered me a job, and I jumped at it,' he recalls. He did repairs, made jewelry, and worked in sales. 'He worked hard and did the dirtiest jobs' as he learned the business from the bottom up, says Mike."

"After graduating from college, Joe returned to the store, although Mike had urged him to first 'get some different experience working in another job.'"

"Back in the store, Joe was soon out-selling the other salespeople. Mike also began gradually training him in management duties—i.e., buying, working with vendors, personnel duties (like hiring and firing), financial matters, and managing sales staff—as he groomed him to lead the business. 'I never had a written [transition] plan, says Mike, 'but in my mind I planned this from the time he was a kid working here.'"

Then disaster struck. Mike had a serious heart attack. He was incapacitated by bypass surgery and months of recovery. Everything started going haywire. Joe's older brother, who never before had any interest, has now expressed an interest in the business. He has had several years of experience in another job and feels that it would be appropriate to come into the business at a high salary. In the meantime, the other salespeople are beginning to express dissatisfaction with their compensation and benefit plans, feeling that Joe has always received special treatment. There is a lot of dissension at the jewelry store. Joe is ready to tear his hair out. What should he do?[136]

ENDNOTES

1. "Focusing on Business Families," *BDO*, November 2009, accessed October 8, 2011, static.staging.bdo.defacto-cms.com/assets/documents/2010/04/Focusing_on_business_families.pdf.

2. Joseph H. Astrachan and Melissa Carey Shanker, "Family business's Contribution to the U.S. Economy: A Closer Look," *Family Business Review* 16, no. 3 (2003): 211–19.

3. "Family Businesses," *Entrepreneur*, 2010, accessed October 8, 2011, www.entrepreneur.com/encyclopedia/term/32060.html.

4. "Making a Difference: The PricewaterhouseCoopers Family Business Survey 2007/08," *PriceWaterhouseCoopers*, November 2007, accessed October 8, 2011, www.pwc.com/en_TH/th/publications/assets/pwc_fbs_survey.pdf.

5. Kelin E. Gersick et al., *Generation to Generation: Life Cycles of the Family Business* (Cambridge, MA: Owner Managed Business Institute, Harvard Business School Press, 1997), 1.

6. Joseph H. Astrachan and Shanker, "Family business's Contribution to the U.S. Economy: A Closer Look," *Family Business Review* 16, no. 3 (2003): 211–19.

7. "Family Business Statistics," *Gaebler.com: Resources for Entrepreneurs*, October 10, 2010, accessed October 8, 2011, www.gaebler.com/Family-Business-Statistics.htm.

8. "Family Business Statistics," *Gaebler.com: Resources for Entrepreneurs*, October 10, 2010, accessed October 8, 2011, www.gaebler.com/Family-Business-Statistics.htm; and Stacy Perman, "Taking the Pulse of Family Business," February 13, 2006, accessed October 8, 2011, www.BusinessWeek.com/smallbiz/content/feb2006/sb20060210_476491.htm.

9. "Making a Difference: The PricewaterhouseCoopers Family Business Survey 2007/08," *PriceWaterhouseCoopers*, November 2007, accessed October 8, 2011, www.pwc.com/en_TH/th/publications/assets/pwc_fbs_survey.pdf.

10. "Myths and Realities of Family Business," 2002, accessed October 8, 2011, www.insead.edu/discover_insead/publications/docs/iQ03.pdf.

11. "Myths and Realities of Family Business," 2002, accessed October 8, 2011, www.insead.edu/discover_insead/publications/docs/iQ03.pdf.

12. Alexis Writing, "Pros and Cons of Family Business," *Chron.com*, 2010, accessed October 8, 2011, smallbusiness.chron.com/pros-cons-family-business-409.html.

13. Margaret Steen, "The Decision Tree of Family Business," *Stanford Graduate School of Business*, August 2006, accessed June 21, 2012, www-prd-0.gsb.stanford.edu/news/bmag/sbsm0608/feature_familybiz.html.

14. Alison Damast, "Family Inc.: The New B-School Job Choice," *Bloomberg BusinessWeek*, April 12, 2010, accessed October 8, 2011, www.BusinessWeek.com/print/bschools/content/apr2010/bs20100412_706043.htm.

15. "American Family Business Survey," *Mass Mutual Financial Group*, 2007, accessed October 8, 2011, www.massmutual.com/mmfg/pdf/afbs.pdf.

16. Margaret Steen, "The Decision Tree of Family Business," *Stanford Graduate School of Business*, August 2006, accessed June 21, 2012, www-prd-0.gsb.stanford.edu/news/bmag/sbsm0608/feature_familybiz.html.

17. "American Family Business Survey," *Mass Mutual Financial Group*, 2007, accessed October 8, 2011, www.massmutual.com/mmfg/pdf/afbs.pdf.

18. "The Family Business Survey 2008/2009," *Praxity*, 2009, accessed October 8, 2011, http://praxityprod.awecomm.com/News/2009/Pages/UKFamilyBusinessSurvey.aspx.

19. Alexis Writing, "Pros and Cons of Family Business," *Chron.com*, 2010, accessed October 8, 2011, smallbusiness.chron.com/pros-cons-family-business-409.html.

20. "American Family Business Survey," *Mass Mutual Financial Group*, 2007, accessed October 8, 2011, www.massmutual.com/mmfg/pdf/afbs.pdf.

21. "American Family Business Survey," *Mass Mutual Financial Group*, 2007, accessed October 8, 2011, www.massmutual.com/mmfg/pdf/afbs.pdf.

22. "Advantages of Family Businesses," *Business Link*, accessed October 8, 2011, www.businesslink.gov.uk/bdotg/action/detail?itemId=1073792650&type=RESOURCES.

23. Manfred F. R. Kets de Vries, "The Dynamics of Family Controlled Firms: The Good and the Bad News," *Organizational Dynamics* 21, no. 3 (1993): 59–71.

24. Manfred F. R. Kets de Vries, "The Dynamics of Family Controlled Firms: The Good and the Bad News," *Organizational Dynamics* 21, no. 3 (1993): 59–71.

25. Manfred F. R. Kets de Vries, "The Dynamics of Family Controlled Firms: The Good and the Bad News," *Organizational Dynamics* 21, no. 3 (1993): 59–71.

26. Manfred F. R. Kets de Vries, "The Dynamics of Family Controlled Firms: The Good and the Bad News," *Organizational Dynamics* 21, no. 3 (1993): 59–71.

27. Manfred F. R. Kets de Vries, "The Dynamics of Family Controlled Firms: The Good and the Bad News," *Organizational Dynamics* 21, no. 3 (1993): 59–71.

28. Manfred F. R. Kets de Vries, "The Dynamics of Family Controlled Firms: The Good and the Bad News," *Organizational Dynamics* 21, no. 3 (1993): 59–71.

29. Manfred F. R. Kets de Vries, "The Dynamics of Family Controlled Firms: The Good and the Bad News," *Organizational Dynamics* 21, no. 3 (1993): 59–71.

30. Kelin E. Gersick et al., *Generation to Generation: Life Cycles of the Family Business* (Cambridge, MA: Owner Managed Business Institute, Harvard Business School Press, 1997), 2–3.

31. Margaret Steen, "The Decision Tree of Family Business," *Stanford Graduate School of Business*, August 2006, accessed June 21, 2012, www-prd-0.gsb.stanford.edu/news/bmag/sbsm0608/feature_familybiz.html.

32. Margaret Steen, "The Decision Tree of Family Business," *Stanford Graduate School of Business*, August 2006, accessed June 21, 2012, www-prd-0.gsb.stanford.edu/news/bmag/sbsm0608/feature_familybiz.html.

33. "The Family Business Survey 2008/2009," *Praxity*, 2009, accessed October 8, 2011, http://praxityprod.awecomm.com/News/2009/Pages/UKFamilyBusinessSurvey.aspx.

34. Alexis Writing, "Pros and Cons of Family Business," *Chron.com*, 2010, accessed October 8, 2011, smallbusiness.chron.com/pros-cons-family-business-409.html.

35. Alexis Writing, "Pros and Cons of Family Business," *Chron.com*, 2010, accessed October 8, 2011, smallbusiness.chron.com/pros-cons-family-business-409.html.

36. "Advantages and Disadvantages of a Family Business," September 6, 2009, accessed October 8, 2011, pinoynegosyo.blogspot.com/2009/09/advantages-and-disadvantages-of-family.html.

37. "Advantages and Disadvantages of a Family Business," September 6, 2009, accessed October 8, 2011, pinoynegosyo.blogspot.com/2009/09/advantages-and-disadvantages-of-family.html.

38. David G. Sirmon and Michael A. Hitt, "Managing Resources: Linking Unique Resources, Management, and Wealth Creation in Family Firms," *Entrepreneurship Theory and Practice*, Summer 2003, 339–58.

39. David G. Sirmon and Michael A. Hitt, "Managing Resources: Linking Unique Resources, Management, and Wealth Creation in Family Firms," *Entrepreneurship Theory and Practice*, Summer 2003, 339–58.

40. Manfred F. R. Kets de Vries, "The Dynamics of Family Controlled Firms: The Good and the Bad News," *Organizational Dynamics* 21, no. 3 (1993): 59–71.

41. Sue Birley, "Attitudes of Owner-Managers' Children towards Family and Business Issues," *Entrepreneurship Theory and Practice*, Spring 2002, 5–19.

42. Sue Birley, "Attitudes of Owner-Managers' Children towards Family and Business Issues," *Entrepreneurship Theory and Practice*, Spring 2002, 5–19.

43. Sue Birley, "Attitudes of Owner-Managers' Children towards Family and Business Issues," *Entrepreneurship Theory and Practice*, Spring 2002, 5–19.

44. Manfred F. R. Kets de Vries, "The Dynamics of Family Controlled Firms: The Good and the Bad News," *Organizational Dynamics* 21, no. 3 (1993): 59–71.

45. Manfred F. R. Kets de Vries, "The Dynamics of Family Controlled Firms: The Good and the Bad News," *Organizational Dynamics* 21, no. 3 (1993): 59–71.

46. Manfred F. R. Kets de Vries, "The Dynamics of Family Controlled Firms: The Good and the Bad News," *Organizational Dynamics* 21, no. 3 (1993): 59–71.

47. Manfred F. R. Kets de Vries, "The Dynamics of Family Controlled Firms: The Good and the Bad News," *Organizational Dynamics* 21, no. 3 (1993): 59–71.

48. Manfred F. R. Kets de Vries, "The Dynamics of Family Controlled Firms: The Good and the Bad News," *Organizational Dynamics* 21, no. 3 (1993): 59–71.

49. "Focusing on Business Families," *BDO*, November 2009, accessed October 8, 2011, static.staging.bdo.defacto-cms.com/assets/documents/2010/04/Focusing_on_business_families.pdf.

50. Christine Lagorio, "How to Run a Family Business," *Inc.*, March 5, 2010, accessed October 8, 2011, www.inc.com/guides/running-family-business.html.

51. Leigh Richards, "Family Owned Business and Communication," *Chron.com*, 2010, accessed June 1, 2012, http://smallbusiness.chron.com/family-owned-business-communication-3165.html.

52. Leigh Richards, "Family Owned Business and Communication," *Chron.com*, 2010, accessed October 8, 2011, smallbusiness.chron.com/family-owned-business-communication-3165.html.

53. "The Family Business Survey 2008/2009," *Praxity*, 2009, accessed October 8, 2011, http://praxityprod.awecomm.com/News/2009/Pages/UKFamilyBusinessSurvey.aspx.

54. Leigh Richards, "Family Owned Business and Communication," *Chron.com*, 2010, accessed October 8, 2011, smallbusiness.chron.com/family-owned-business-communication-3165.html.

55. "Communication and Family Businesses," *Business Link*, 2010, accessed October 8, 2011, www.businesslink.gov.uk/bdotg/action/detail?type=RESOURCES&itemId=1073792652.

56. Philip Keefe, "Hiring Family Members for the Family Business," March 30, 2010, accessed October 8, 2011, philip-keeffe.suite101.com/hiring-family-members-for-the-family-business-a220028.

57. Dean Fowler and Peg Masterson Edquist, "Evaluate the Pros and Cons of Employing Family Members," *Business Journal*, June 6, 2003, accessed October 8, 2011, www.bizjournals.com/milwaukee/stories/2003/06/09/smallb6.html; and Philip Keefe, "Hiring Family Members for the Family Business," March 30, 2010, accessed October 8, 2011, philip-keeffe.suite101.com/hiring-family-members-for-the-family-business-a220028.

58. Philip Keefe, "Hiring Family Members for the Family Business," March 30, 2010, accessed October 8, 2011, philip-keeffe.suite101.com/hiring-family-members-for-the-family-business-a220028.

59. Dean Fowler and Peg Masterson Edquist, "Evaluate the Pros and Cons of Employing Family Members," *Business Journal*, June 6, 2003, accessed October 8, 2011, www.bizjournals.com/milwaukee/stories/2003/06/09/smallb6.html; Philip Keefe, "Hiring Family Members for the Family Business," March 30, 2010, accessed October 8, 2011, philip-keeffe.suite101.com/hiring-family-members-for-the-family-business-a220028; Annika Hall and Mattias Nordqvist, "Professional Management in Family Businesses: Toward an Extended Understanding," *Family Business Review* 21, no. 1 (2008): 51–69; and Margaret Steen, "The Decision Tree of Family Business," *Stanford*

Graduate School of Business, August 2006, June 21, 2012, www-prd-0.gsb.stanford.edu/news/bmag/sbsm0608/feature_familybiz.html.

60. "Focusing on Business Families," *BDO*, November 2009, accessed October 8, 2011, static.staging.bdo.defacto-cms.com/assets/documents/2010/04/Focusing_on _business_families.pdf.

61. "Family Owned Businesses Law and Legal Definition," *USLegal.com*, 2010, accessed October 8, 2011, definitions.uslegal.com/f/family-owned-businesses.

62. Annika Hall and Mattias Nordqvist, "Professional Management in Family Businesses: Toward an Extended Understanding," *Family Business Review* 21, no. 1 (2008): 51–69.

63. Annika Hall and Mattias Nordqvist, "Professional Management in Family Businesses: Toward an Extended Understanding," *Family Business Review* 21, no. 1 (2008): 51–69.

64. Annika Hall and Mattias Nordqvist, "Professional Management in Family Businesses: Toward an Extended Understanding," *Family Business Review* 21, no. 1 (2008): 51–69.

65. Kelin E. Gersick et al., *Generation to Generation: Life Cycles of the Family Business* (Cambridge, MA: Owner Managed Business Institute, Harvard Business School Press, 1997), 4.

66. Annika Hall and Mattias Nordqvist, "Professional Management in Family Businesses: Toward an Extended Understanding," *Family Business Review* 21, no. 1 (2008): 51–69.

67. Annika Hall and Mattias Nordqvist, "Professional Management in Family Businesses: Toward an Extended Understanding," *Family Business Review* 21, no. 1 (2008): 51–69.

68. Annika Hall and Mattias Nordqvist, "Professional Management in Family Businesses: Toward an Extended Understanding," *Family Business Review* 21, no. 1 (2008): 51–69.

69. Annika Hall and Mattias Nordqvist, "Professional Management in Family Businesses: Toward an Extended Understanding," *Family Business Review* 21, no. 1 (2008): 51–69.

70. Matthew C. Sonfield and Robert N. Lussier, "Family-Member and Non-family-Member Managers in Family Businesses," *Journal of Small Business and Enterprise Development* 16, no. 2 (2009): 196–209.

71. Matthew C. Sonfield and Robert N. Lussier, "Family-Member and Non-family-Member Managers in Family Businesses," *Journal of Small Business and Enterprise Development* 16, no. 2 (2009): 196–209.

72. "GARBAGE IN—GARBAGE OUT: Family Employment Policies," *ReGENERATION Partners*, May 2002, accessed October 8, 2011, www.regeneration-partners.com/artman/ uploads/20-2002-may-news.pdf.

73. "Family Member Employment Policies (Case Study 1: SABIS)," *IFC Corporate Governance*, 2006, accessed October 8, 2011, www.smetoolkit.org/smetoolkit/en/ content/en/6742/Family-Member-Employment-Policies-Case-Study-1 -SABIS%C2%AE-.

74. "GARBAGE IN—GARBAGE OUT: Family Employment Policies," *ReGENERATION Partners*, May 2002, accessed October 8, 2011, www.regeneration-partners.com/artman/ uploads/20-2002-may-news.pdf.

75. Craig E. Aronoff and John L. Ward, *Family Business Succession: The Final Test of Greatness* (Marietta, GA: Business Owner Resources, 1992), as cited in "Nepotism," *Reference for Business.com*, 2010, accessed October 8, 2011, www.referenceforbusiness.com/ small/Mail-Op/Nepotism.html.

76. "Family Member Employment Policies (Case Study 1: SABIS)," *IFC Corporate Governance*, 2006, accessed October 8, 2011, www.smetoolkit.org/smetoolkit/en/ content/en/6742/Family-Member-Employment-Policies-Case-Study-1-SABIS%C2% AE-.

77. "Family Owned Businesses: Compensation in Family Businesses," *Gaebler.com Resources for Entrepreneurs*, 2010, accessed October 8, 2011, www.gaebler.com/ Compensation-in-Family-Businesses.htm.

78. Bernard J. D'Avella Jr. and Hannoch Weisman, "Why Compensation for Family Members Should Be at Market Value," *Fairleigh Dickinson University*, 2010, accessed October 8, 2011, view.fdu.edu/default.aspx?id=2344.

79. Kathy Marshack, "How to Arrive at Fair Compensation in a Family Business," *American Chronicle*, February 29, 2008, accessed October 8, 2011, www.americanchronicle.com/articles/view/53757.

80. Referenced in Kathy Marshack, "How to Arrive at Fair Compensation in a Family Business," *American Chronicle*, February 29, 2008, accessed October 8, 2011, www.americanchronicle.com/articles/view/53757.

81. Ellen Frankenberg, "Equal Isn't Always Fair: Making Tough Decisions about Transmitting Family Assets," Frankenberg Group, 2010, accessed October 8, 2011, www.frankenberggroup.com/equal-isnt-always-fair-making-tough-decisions-about -transmitting-family-assets.html.

82. Ellen Frankenberg, "Equal Isn't Always Fair: Making Tough Decisions about Transmitting Family Assets," Frankenberg Group, 2010, accessed October 8, 2011, www.frankenberggroup.com/equal-isnt-always-fair-making-tough-decisions-about -transmitting-family-assets.html.

83. Dean Fowler and Peg Masterson Edquist, "Evaluate the Pros and Cons of Employing Family Members," *Business Journal*, June 6, 2003, accessed October 8, 2011, www.bizjournals.com/milwaukee/stories/2003/06/09/smallb6.html.

84. Bernard J. D'Avella Jr. and Hannoch Weisman, "Why Compensation for Family Members Should Be at Market Value," *Fairleigh Dickinson University*, 2010, accessed October 8, 2011, view.fdu.edu/default.aspx?id=2344.

85. Ellen Frankenberg, "Equal Isn't Always Fair: Making Tough Decisions about Transmitting Family Assets," Frankenberg Group, 2010, accessed October 8, 2011, www.frankenberggroup.com/equal-isnt-always-fair-making-tough-decisions-about -transmitting-family-assets.html.

86. "The Family Business Survey 2008/2009," *Praxity*, 2009, accessed October 8, 2011, http://praxityprod.awecomm.com/News/2009/Pages/UKFamilyBusinessSurvey.aspx.

87. "American Family Business Survey," *Mass Mutual Financial Group*, 2007, accessed October 8, 2011, www.massmutual.com/mmfg/pdf/afbs.pdf.

88. "Family Owned Businesses Law and Legal Definition," *USLegal.com*, 2010, accessed October 8, 2011, definitions.uslegal.com/f/family-owned-businesses.

89. "Family Business Statistics," *Gaebler.com: Resources for Entrepreneurs*, October 10, 2010, accessed October 8, 2011, www.gaebler.com/Family-Business-Statistics.htm.

90. Sue Birley, "Attitudes of Owner-Managers' Children Towards Family and Business Issues," *Entrepreneurship Theory and Practice*, Spring 2002, 5–19.

91. Nancy Bowman-Upton, "Transferring Management in the Family-Owned Business," *Small Business Administration*, 1991, accessed October 8, 2011, www.sbaonline.sba.gov/idc/groups/public/documents/sba_homepage/serv_sbp _exit.pdf.

92. Ivan Lansberg, "The Succession Conspiracy," *Family Business Review* 1 (1981): 119–44, as cited in Nancy Bowman-Upton, "Transferring Management in the Family-Owned Business," *Small Business Administration*, 1991, accessed October 8, 2011, www.sbaonline.sba.gov/idc/groups/public/documents/sba_homepage/serv_sbp _exit.pdf.

93. "Sample Succession Planning Policy," accessed October 8, 2011, www.experienceworks.ca/pdf/successionpolicy.pdf.

94. "Making a Difference: The PricewaterhouseCoopers Family Business Survey 2007/08," *PriceWaterhouseCoopers*, November 2007, accessed October 8, 2011, www.pwc.com/ en_TH/th/publications/assets/pwc_fbs_survey.pdf.

95. "Family-Run Businesses: Succession Planning in Family Businesses," *Business Link*, accessed October 8, 2011, www.businesslink.gov.uk/bdotg/action/detail?type =RESOURCES&itemId=1074446767.

96. "Avoid Feuds When Handing Down the Family Business," 2010, *AllBusiness.com*, 2010, accessed October 8, 2011, www.allbusiness.com/buying-exiting-businesses/ exiting-a-business/2975479-1.html.

97. "Components of a Good Business Succession Plan," April 18, 2011, accessed October 8, 2011, www.entrepreneurshipsecret.com/components-of-a-good-business -succession-plan.

98. Susan Ward, "Six Business Succession Planning Tips," *About.com*, 2011, accessed October 8, 2011, sbinfocanada.about.com/cs/buysellabiz/a/succession1_2.htm.

99. Susan Ward, "Six Business Succession Planning Tips," *About.com*, 2011, accessed October 8, 2011, sbinfocanada.about.com/cs/buysellabiz/a/succession1_2.htm.

100. "Family Succession Plan First Then the Succession Plan for the Family's Business," *Family Business Experts*, 2011, accessed October 8, 2011, www.family-business-experts.com/family-succession-plan.html.

101. Karen E. Klein, "When the Third Generation Runs the Family Biz," *Bloomberg BusinessWeek*, April 9, 2010, accessed October 8, 2011, www.BusinessWeek.com/smallbiz/ content/apr2010/sb2010049_806426.htm.

102. George Ambler, "Constructive Conflict Is Essential for Creating Commitment to Decisions," May 15, 2007, accessed October 8, 2011; Kimberly A. Eddleston, Robert F. Otondo, and Franz Willi Kellermanns, "Conflict, Participative Decision-Making, and Generational Ownership Dispersion: A Multilevel Analysis," *Journal of Small Business Management* 46, no. 3 (2008): 456–84; and Suzi Quixley, "Understanding Constructive & Destructive Conflict," May 2008, accessed June 1, 2012, http://www.suziqconsulting.com.au/free_articles_files /CON%20-%20Constructive%20&%20Destructive%20-%20May08.pdf.

103. "Managing Conflict in Family Businesses," *Business Link*, 2010, accessed October 8, 2011, www.businesslink.gov.uk/bdotg/action/detail?type=RESOURCES&itemId= 1073792653.

104. Kimberly A. Eddleston, Robert F. Otondo, and Franz Willi Kellermanns, "Conflict, Participative Decision-Making, and Generational Ownership Dispersion: A Multilevel Analysis," *Journal of Small Business Management* 46, no. 3 (2008): 456–84; and Suzi Quixley, "Understanding Constructive & Destructive Conflict," May 2008, accessed June 1, 2012, http://www.suziqconsulting.com.au/free_articles_files /CON%20-%20Constructive%20&%20Destructive%20-%20May08.pdf.

105. Professor Michael Roberto from Harvard Business School, quoted in George Ambler, "Constructive Conflict Is Essential for Creating Commitment to Decisions," May 15, 2007, accessed October 8, 2011.

106. Nigel Finch, "Identifying and Addressing the Causes of Conflict in Family Business," Working Paper Series: University of Sydney, May 2005, accessed October 8, 2011, papers.ssrn.com/sol3/papers.cfm?abstract_id=717262.

107. "Managing Conflict in Family Businesses," *Business Link*, 2010, accessed October 8, 2011, www.businesslink.gov.uk/bdotg/action/detail?type=RESOURCES&itemId= 1073792653.

108. Nigel Finch, "Identifying and Addressing the Causes of Conflict in Family Business," Working Paper Series: University of Sydney, May 2005, accessed October 8, 2011, papers.ssrn.com/sol3/papers.cfm?abstract_id=717262.

109. Kimberly A. Eddleston, Robert F. Otondo, and Franz Willi Kellermanns, "Conflict, Participative Decision-Making, and Generational Ownership Dispersion: A Multilevel Analysis," *Journal of Small Business Management* 46, no. 3 (2008): 456–84.

110. "Making a Difference: The PricewaterhouseCoopers Family Business Survey 2007/08," *PriceWaterhouseCoopers*, November 2007, accessed October 8, 2011, www.pwc.com/ en_TH/th/publications/assets/pwc_fbs_survey.pdf.

111. Kimberly A. Eddleston, Robert F. Otondo, and Franz Willi Kellermanns, "Conflict, Participative Decision-Making, and Generational Ownership Dispersion: A Multilevel Analysis," *Journal of Small Business Management* 46, no. 3 (2008): 456–84.

112. Michael Harvey and Rodney E. Evans, "Family Business and Multiple Levels of Conflict," *Family Business Review* 7, no. 4 (1994): 331–48, as cited in Kimberly A. Eddleston, Robert F. Otondo, and Franz Willi Kellermanns, "Conflict, Participative Decision-

Making, and Generational Ownership Dispersion: A Multilevel Analysis," *Journal of Small Business Management* 46, no. 3 (2008): 456–84.

113. Harry Levinson, "Conflicts That Plague Family Businesses," *Harvard Business Review* 71 (1971): 90–98.

114. "Common Sources of Dysfunctional Conflict in Family Businesses," *RJW Consulting*, accessed October 8, 2011, www.rjweissconsulting.com/businessDevelopmentNewsDetail.asp?ID=2.

115. Nigel Finch, "Identifying and Addressing the Causes of Conflict in Family Business," Working Paper Series: University of Sydney, May 2005, accessed October 8, 2011, papers.ssrn.com/sol3/papers.cfm?abstract_id=717262.

116. Nigel Finch, "Identifying and Addressing the Causes of Conflict in Family Business," Working Paper Series: University of Sydney, May 2005, accessed October 8, 2011, papers.ssrn.com/sol3/papers.cfm?abstract_id=717262.

117. "Common Sources of Dysfunctional Conflict in Family Businesses," *RJW Consulting*, accessed October 8, 2011, www.rjweissconsulting.com/businessDevelopmentNewsDetail.asp?ID=2.

118. Peter S. Davis and Paula D. Harveston, "The Phenomenon of Substantive Conflict in the Family Firm: A Cross-Generational Study," *Journal of Small Business Management* 39, no. 1 (2001): 14–30.

119. "Common Sources of Dysfunctional Conflict in Family Businesses," *RJW Consulting*, accessed October 8, 2011, www.rjweissconsulting.com/businessDevelopmentNewsDetail.asp?ID=2.

120. Wayne Rivers, "Top 15 Sources of Conflict in Family Businesses," *Family Business Institute*, 2009, accessed October 8, 2011, www.familybusinessinstitute.com/index.php/volume-6-articles/top-15-sources-of-conflict-in-family-businesses.html.

121. "How Family Squabbling Affects Other Employees—and Customers," *National Federation of Independent Business*, 2010, accessed October 8, 2011, www.nfib.com/business-resources/business-resources-item?cmsid=52150.

122. "How Family Squabbling Affects Other Employees—and Customers," *National Federation of Independent Business*, 2010, accessed October 8, 2011, www.nfib.com/business-resources/business-resources-item?cmsid=52150.

123. "How Family Squabbling Affects Other Employees—and Customers," *National Federation of Independent Business*, 2010, accessed October 8, 2011, www.nfib.com/business-resources/business-resources-item?cmsid=52150.

124. "How Family Squabbling Affects Other Employees—and Customers," *National Federation of Independent Business*, 2010, accessed October 8, 2011, www.nfib.com/business-resources/business-resources-item?cmsid=52150.

125. "How Family Squabbling Affects Other Employees—and Customers," *National Federation of Independent Business*, 2010, accessed October 8, 2011, www.nfib.com/business-resources/business-resources-item?cmsid=52150.

126. George Ambler, "Constructive Conflict Is Essential for Creating Commitment to Decisions," May 15, 2007, accessed October 8, 2011.

127. George Ambler, "Constructive Conflict Is Essential for Creating Commitment to Decisions," May 15, 2007, accessed October 8, 2011.

128. "Promoting Family Brand Linked to Companies' Financial Success," *Austin Family Business Program*, September 15, 2008, accessed October 8, 2011, www.familybusinessonline.org/index.php?option=com_content&view+article&id=38:promoting-family-brand-linked-to-companies-financial-success-&catid=13:latest-news&Itemid=39.

129. Sahil Nagpal, "Family Businesses Perceived of Greater Value by Customers," *Top News*, August 15, 2008, accessed June 1, 2012, http://topnews.in/family-businesses-perceived-greater-value-customers-259364.

130. Sahil Nagpal, "Family Businesses Perceived of Greater Value by Customers," *Top News*, August 15, 2008, accessed October 8, 2011, topnews.in/family-businesses-perceived-greater-value-customers-259364.

131. Justin B. Craig, Clay Dibrell, and Peter S. Davis, "Leveraging Family-Based Identity to Enhance Firm Competitiveness and Performance in Family Businesses," *Journal of Small Business Management* 46, no. 3 (2008): 351–71.

132. Justin B. Craig, Clay Dibrell, and Peter S. Davis, "Leveraging Family-Based Identity to Enhance Firm Competitiveness and Performance in Family Businesses," *Journal of Small Business Management* 46, no. 3 (2008): 351–71.

133. Bernard J. D'Avella Jr. and Hannoch Weisman, "Why Compensation for Family Members Should Be at Market Value," *Fairleigh Dickinson University*, 2010, accessed October 8, 2011, view.fdu.edu/default.aspx?id=2344.

134. Bernard J. D'Avella Jr. and Hannoch Weisman, "Why Compensation for Family Members Should Be at Market Value," *Fairleigh Dickinson University*, 2010, accessed October 8, 2011, view.fdu.edu/default.aspx?id=2344.

135. Karen E. Klein, "When the Third Generation Runs the Family Biz," *Bloomberg BusinessWeek*, April 9, 2010, accessed October 8, 2011, www.BusinessWeek.com/smallbiz/content/apr2010/sb2010049_806426.htm.

136. William George Shuster, "Family Business in Crisis: Letting Go," *JCK Magazine*, March 2003, accessed October 8, 2011, www.jckonline.com/article/282706-Family_Business_in_Crisis_Letting_Go.php.

CHAPTER 4
E-Business and E-Commerce

Vermont Teddy Bear Company

Source: Used with permission from Vermont Teddy Bear.

In 1980, John Sortino got the idea for making teddy bears. He was playing with his young son, Graham, and noticed that none of Graham's 38 stuffed animals was made in the United States. This inspired John to make a teddy bear for Graham—named Bearcho. John then went on to make others, falling in love with the idea of making them by hand. Bearcho was soon followed by Buffy, Bearazar, and Fuzzy Wuzzy, all made in his wife's sewing room. By 1983, John was selling his bears from a gift cart at an open-air market in Burlington, Vermont. The sale of his first bear took 4 days, and it took 1 year to sell 200 bears.[1] Today, the Vermont Teddy Bear Company produces about 300,000 bears a year.

The Vermont Teddy Bear Company has tapped into America's long-standing love affair with teddy bears by creating a wide variety of customized teddy bears and shipping them to customers via the well-recognized Bear-Gram, "…a customized bear placed in a colorful box with an air hole and game printed on the inside, and enclosed with a personalized greeting and candy treat."[2] The company has experienced many changes, including John's departure in 1995 to pursue other interests and the addition of Pajamagram and Calyx Flowers as additional unique brands, but the Vermont Teddy Bear Company remains a household name and a Vermont icon.

Jay Bruns, vice president of branding, talks about the importance of knowing how to present the product so the company can grow further. Right now, a Vermont Teddy Bear is a unique gift item that promises quality for life, but the dynamics of gifting have changed. Same day or overnight delivery is not special anymore, so a Vermont Teddy Bear must offer something more than convenience. It needs to be a "go-to" gift of choice rather than an emergency or "last-minute" gift. This requires presenting the product as fresh and special.[3] E-commerce is an integral part of Vermont Teddy Bear's marketing strategy, with online sales accounting for more than one-half of its total sales. The company saw the growth in online buying and launched its website in October 1996 in an effort to reach the online consumer base. Elisabeth Robert, the CEO at the time, saw the potential synergy between radio and the Internet and used the power of the company's radio advertising "…to direct customers to the company's website where they could actually see the bears they were ordering."[4]

Victor Castro, director of e-commerce, describes the company's e-commerce strategy as direct marketing with a focus on easy ordering and the customer being able to interact with the brand. Convenience has become even more convenient, and the Vermont Teddy Bear Company makes things simple. As the consumer becomes more proficient online, it will be necessary to communicate properly what the Vermont Teddy Bear gift is all about (i.e., the experience of owning the bear). Castro says that the company has been very successful at that. However, the company's e-commerce strategy must evolve with changes in the online customer.[5]

To learn more about the Bear-Gram, go to www.vermontteddybear.com/Static/Bear-Grams.aspx. To take the online factory tour, go to www.vermontteddybear.com/Static/tour-welcomestation.aspx.

Video Clip 4.1

PBS Curiosity Quest—Vermont Teddy Bear
A tour of the Vermont Teddy Bear factory.

View the video online at: http://www.youtube.com/v/wqLz8BOaFio

1. E-BUSINESS AND E-COMMERCE: THE DIFFERENCE

LEARNING OBJECTIVES

1. Define e-business and e-commerce and explain the difference between them.
2. Understand that there are several different types of e-commerce and that a business can be engaged in more than one type at the same time.
3. Explain what a business model is and why the model that is selected is so important.

As stated in Chapter 1, e-business and e-commerce are terms that are often used interchangeably. But e-business and e-commerce are not the same. This section will elaborate on the differences between the two and some of the foundational knowledge that is critical to understanding and using e-commerce in particular.

1.1 E-Business

Chapter 1 talked about e-business in terms of using the Internet and online technologies to create operational efficiencies, thereby increasing customer value.[6] It is important that small businesses understand the nature of e-business and how it can facilitate operations as well as growth—if growth is desired. It has been said on other occasions, and it will continue to be said, that not all small businesses look for growth, choosing instead to happily remain small. For the small businesses that do want to grow, however, e-business can help them do it.

E-Business Components

E-business involves several major components:[7] business intelligence (BI), customer relationship management (CRM), supply chain management (SCM), enterprise resource planning (ERP), e-commerce, conducting electronic transactions within the firm, collaboration, and online activities among businesses.

FIGURE 4.1 Components of E-Business

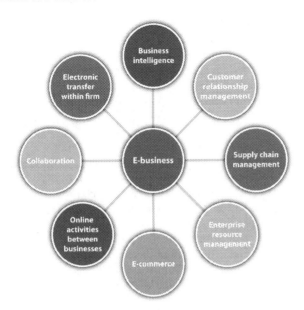

Business intelligence is about the activities that a small business may undertake to collect, store, access, and analyze information about its market or competition to help with decision making. When conducted online, BI is efficient and quick, helping companies to identify noteworthy trends and make better decisions faster. BI has been described as "the crystal ball of the 21st century."[8]

As defined in Chapter 2, **customer relationship management (CRM)** refers to "...a customer service approach that focuses on building long-term and sustainable customer relationships that add value for the customer and the company."[9] It is a company-wide strategy that brings together information from all data sources within an organization (and sometimes from external data sources) to give one holistic view of each customer in real time. The goal is to reduce costs and increase profitability while providing customer satisfaction.[10] CRM applications are available for even the smallest businesses.

Every small business has a supply chain, the network of vendors that provide the raw components that are needed to make a product or deliver a service. The management of this network is known as **supply chain management (SCM)**. SCM is about efficiently and effectively improving the way that a company finds those raw components and then delivers the product or the service to the customer.[11] SCM applications are now available for small businesses. More details about SCM are presented in Chapter 12.

Enterprise resource planning (ERP), as mentioned in Chapter 1, is about integrating all departments and functions across a company (sales, marketing, human resources, finance, accounting, production, engineering, etc.) into a single computer system that can serve the particular needs of each department. The objective is to provide information quickly and efficiently to those who need it. Small businesses have many vendor choices for ERP systems. There are more than thirty vendors in the field, and they are looking to small and midsize businesses as their primary growth market.[12] More details about ERP are provided in Chapter 12.

E-commerce, as defined in Chapter 1, is the marketing, selling, and buying of goods and services online. It generates revenue, which e-business does not. E-commerce is typically associated with e-marketing, discussed in Chapter 8, but most of this chapter is dedicated to the operational, nonmarketing dimensions of e-commerce.

Conducting electronic transactions within a firm can occur through an **intranet**, e-mail, and instant messaging. An intranet is a private network within a business that is used for information sharing, processing, and communication. The goal is to "streamline the workplace and allow easy information exchange within an organization."[13]

business intelligence

The activities that a small business may undertake to collect, store, access, and analyze information about its market or competition to help with decision making.

customer relationship management

A service approach that hopes to build a long-term and sustainable relationship with customers that has value for both the customer and the company.

supply chain management

Efficiently and effectively improving the way that a company finds raw components and then delivers the product or the service to the customer.

intranet

A private network within a business that is used for information sharing, processing, and communication.

wiki

A web page that can be
viewed and modified by
anybody with a web browser
and access to the Internet
unless it is password
protected.

extranet

The part of an intranet that is
made available to business
partners, vendors, or others
outside a company.

Collaboration can occur internally or externally, and it often involves business partners. The goal is to help teams or business partners communicate with each other more effectively and efficiently, manage projects and shared materials, save companies the costs of travel, and reduce travel-related productivity losses.[14] E-mail, instant messaging, newsgroups, bulletin boards, discussion boards, virtual team rooms, online meetings, and **wikis** are common means of collaboration. A wiki is a web page that can be viewed and modified by anybody with a web browser and access to the Internet unless it is password protected.[15] The most well-known wiki is *Wikipedia*.

Online activities between businesses focus on information sharing and communication via e-mail, online meetings, instant messaging, and **extranets**. An extranet is the part of an intranet that is made available to business partners, vendors, or others outside a company. It allows a business "to share documents, calendars, and project information with distributed employees, partners, and customers" and "it enables 24/7 private, secure access to collaborative tools with just an Internet connection."[16] They make communication easier, eliminate redundant processes, reduce paperwork, increase productivity, provide immediate updates and information, and provide quick response times to problems and questions.[17] The result is money and time saved for employees, the company, vendors, and your customers. Commercial transactions typically do not take place on extranets.

As integral as e-business may be to many small businesses, however, there will be small businesses that choose not to go the e-business route. Small businesses that are nonemployers and/or are very small operations that choose to stay that way—for example, local delis, gift shops, restaurants, dry cleaners, and ice cream shops can be and are successful without having to make a commitment to e-business. Therefore, a small business can choose to incorporate all, some, or none of the e-business components. Given the ways in which the Internet continues to transform small businesses, however, it would be virtually impossible for a small business to operate totally outside the realm of e-business.

1.2   E-Commerce

The moment that an exchange of value occurs, e-business becomes e-commerce.[18] E-commerce is the revenue generator for businesses that choose to use the Internet to sell their goods and services. Some small businesses rely on the Internet to grow and survive. As stated in Chapter 1, many small businesses also look to e-commerce for their own business needs, such as computers and office technology, capital equipment and supplies, office furnishings, inventory for online sale, or other business-related goods.[19] This is not surprising considering the pervasiveness of the Internet for business transactions of all shapes and sizes.

Types of E-Commerce

pure-play business

A business that has an online
presence only.

brick-and-click business

Businesses that combine a
physical presence with an
online presence.

Every Internet business is either **pure-play** or **brick-and-click**. A pure-play business, such as Amazon and Zappos, has an online presence only and uses the capabilities of the Internet to create a new business. Brick-and-click businesses, such as Barnes and Noble and Vermont Country Store, combine a physical presence with an online presence. These businesses use the Internet to supplement their existing businesses.[20]

There are several different types of e-commerce. A common classification system is with respect to the nature of transactions or the relationships among participants.[21] There are seven major types of e-commerce:

1. **Business-to-business (B2B)** e-commerce, where businesses focus on selling to other businesses or organizations, is the largest form of e-commerce.[22] Cisco, Staples, and Spiceworks (information technology [IT] and IT networks for the small- and medium-sized business) are all B2B companies.

2. **Business-to-consumer (B2C)** is the earliest form of e-commerce, but it is second in size to B2B. It refers to retail sales between businesses and individual consumers. Consumers gather information; purchase physical goods, such as books and clothing; purchase information goods, such as electronic material or digitized content, such as software; and, for information goods, receive products over an electronic network.[23]

3. **Consumer-to-consumer (C2C)** e-commerce is where consumers sell products and personal services to each other with the help of an **online market maker** to provide catalog, search engine, and transaction-clearing capabilities so that products can be easily displayed, discovered, and paid for. The most well-known C2C business is eBay, but there are many other online market makers as well. Craigslist is an extremely popular small e-commerce business for placing classified ads.

4. **Business-to-government (B2G)** e-commerce can generally be defined as transactions with the government. The Internet is used for procurement, filing taxes, licensing procedures, business registrations, and other government-related operations. This is an insignificant segment of e-commerce in terms of volume, but it is growing.

5. **Consumer-to-business (C2B)** e-commerce is between private individuals who use the Internet to sell products or services to organizations and individuals who seek sellers to bid on products or services.[24] Elance is an example of C2B where a consumer posts a project with a set budget deadline and within hours companies and/or individuals review the consumer's requirements and bid on the project. The consumer reviews the bids and selects the company or individual that will complete the project. Elance empowers consumers around the world by providing the meeting ground and platform for such transactions.[25] Priceline.com is a well-known example of C2B e-commerce.

6. **Mobile commerce (m-commerce)** refers to the purchase of goods and services through wireless technology, such as cell phones, and handheld devices, such as Blackberries and iPhones. Japan has the lead in m-commerce, but it is expected to grow rapidly in the United States over the next several years. eMarketer predicts mobile content revenues will grow to more than $3.53 billion in 2014, a compound annual growth rate of nearly 20 percent for the period 2009–2014, with the fastest growth coming from mobile music.[26]

7. **Peer-to-peer (P2P)** technology makes it possible for Internet users to share files and computer resources directly without having to go through a central web server. P2P began with Napster offering free music downloads via a file-sharing system.[27] Tamago launched the world's first P2P commerce system in 2005, which allowed people to sell every type of digital media directly from their computers to customers all over the world. People who publish videos, photos, music, e-books, and so forth can earn royalties, while buyers earn commissions for distributing media to others.[28]

---

business-to-business (B2B)

Sales among other businesses or organizations.

business-to-consumer (B2C)

Retail sales among businesses and individual consumers.

consumer-to-consumer (C2C)

Where consumers sell products and personal services to each other.

online market maker

An online company that provides catalog, search engine, and transaction-clearing capabilities so that products can be easily displayed, discovered, and paid for.

business-to-government (B2G)

Transactions with the government.

consumer-to-business (C2B)

Private individuals who use the Internet to sell products or services to organizations and individuals who seek sellers to bid on products or services.

mobile commerce (m-commerce)

The purchase of goods and services through wireless technology, such as cell phones and handheld devices..

peer-to-peer (P2P)

Internet users share files and computer resources directly without having to go through a central web server.

FIGURE 4.2　How P2P E-Commerce Works at Tamago.com

Source: "Peer to Peer Profit," http://www.tamago.us (accessed October 10, 2011).

Although these types of e-commerce have been discussed individually, there are many instances in which one company engages in multiple types. Office Depot and Staples are brick-and-click businesses that engage in B2B, B2C, and perhaps B2G e-commerce. Carbonite and Gourmet Gift Baskets are both pure-play small businesses that engage in B2C and B2B e-commerce.

1.3　E-Commerce Business Models

The decision to engage in e-commerce is an important one. The advantages are clear: lower business costs; 24/7 accessibility anywhere; the potential for stronger customer service; the ability to introduce a niche product; the ability to reach global markets on a more equalized basis with larger firms, making mass customization possible; and greater customer loyalty. But the risks are there as well. Internet problems, website problems, security and privacy breaches, intellectual property theft, legal liability, product and/or service failure, customer deceit, and customer dissatisfaction are but a few of the risks. Therefore, the choice of an e-commerce business model must be made carefully. Each model will have different implications in terms of business planning and strategy.

e-commerce business model

The method that a business uses to generate revenue online.

　　An **e-commerce business model** is the method that a business uses to generate revenue online. "The business model spells out how a company makes money by specifying where it is positioned in the value chain. Some models are quite simple. A company produces a good or service and sells it to customers. If all goes well, the revenues from sales exceed the cost of operation and the company realizes a profit. Other models can be more intricately woven."[29] Another way to look at a business model is that it "reflects management's hypothesis about what customers want, how they want it, and how the enterprise can organize to best meet those needs, get paid for doing so, and make a profit."[30] There are many models to choose from, and new models will continue to emerge as technology evolves and businesses look for new and creative ways to generate revenue. Some of the many e-commerce business models are as follows:[31]

- The **virtual merchant model** is used by online retailers that operate over the Internet only. FreshDirect is a small business that offers fresh food and brand-name groceries for home delivery in New York. Amazon is another example of a virtual merchant.

- The **brokerage model** brings buyers and sellers together and facilitates transactions. Supply Chain Connect is a small business that helps "companies optimize their purchasing and sales purchasing and sales processes through the use of e-commerce across a broad range of products including chemicals, plastics, wire and cable, and manufactured goods."[32]

- The **incentive marketing model** is a "customer loyalty program that provides incentives to customers such as redeemable points or coupons for making purchases from associated retailers."[33] Cool Savings, a small business that uses this model, wants to be its customers' free resource for valuable coupons, discounts, and special offers from their favorite brands and stores.

Because the business model will be at the center of the business plan, the model must be designed carefully. If a successful model is to be built, the model should effectively address the eight key elements listed in Table 4.1. Although value proposition and the revenue model may be the most important and easily identifiable aspects of a company's business model, the other six elements are equally important.[34]

virtual merchant model

Used by online retailers that operate only over the Internet.

brokerage model

Brings buyers and sellers together and facilitates transactions.

incentive marketing model

A customer loyalty program that provides incentives such as redeemable points or coupons.

TABLE 4.1 Key Elements of a Business Model

Components	Key Questions
Value proposition	Why should the customer buy from you?
Revenue model	How will you earn your money?
Market opportunity	What market space do you intend to serve, and what is its size?
Competitive environment	Who else occupies your intended market space?
Competitive advantage	What special advantages does your firm bring to the market space?
Market strategy	How do you plan to promote your products or services to attract your target audience?
Organizational development	What types of organizational structures within the firm are necessary to carry out the business plan?
Management team	What kinds of experiences and background are important for the company's leaders to have?

Source: Kenneth C. Laudon and Carol G. Traver, E-commerce: Business, Technology, Society (Upper Saddle River, NJ: Prentice Hall, 2007), 59.

1.4 E-Commerce Trends

For businesses already engaged in e-commerce and for those that are thinking about it, being aware of the latest e-commerce trends is important because they could have a long-term influence on the future of a company's market. This influence, in turn, could mean life or death for your e-commerce operations. Several general e-commerce trends can be identified, and they are relevant to all e-commerce operations.

- E-commerce will continue to grab more market share.[35]

- It is expected that, in some way, the web will influence 53 percent of all purchases made in 2014.[36]

- The lines between online and offline commerce will become less defined. If somebody buys from a mobile device in your store, is that a web sale or a store sale? Retailers need to think of some new ways that they can take the web's influence into account.[37]

- B2B e-commerce will continue to significantly outpace B2C e-commerce, representing more than 85 percent of all e-commerce.

- M-commerce is the fastest growing segment of visitors to e-commerce websites. If a business does not allow customers to both browse its catalog and conduct transactions on a mobile device, customers will seek out other brands that offer such experience.[38]

- Many businesses have increased their social marketing initiatives through a combination of Facebook pages, Twitter tweets, YouTube fan videos, and blogs. Any business that sells its products or services online without having a social strategy will suffer.[39]

The following e-commerce trends specifically apply to small businesses:

- The Internet will continue to create opportunities for small businesses. It is now possible to buy a wide range of specialized products and services that are not available elsewhere. The Internet has provided a lifeline for many small producers and has allowed entrepreneurs to enter retailing without having to invest heavily in physical outlets.[40] Small businesses can easily enter the e-commerce arena as pure-play businesses. Take Socrata, an online service that makes it easy to share data—anything from crime statistics to football schedules. This small start-up business discovered that federal agencies were the site's biggest users. "It became clear that a really good place for our technology was helping government organizations share data in the interest of transparency."[41]

- Broadband and wireless networks will be everywhere. Small businesses will need to factor in the effect of the broadband revolution on their businesses.[42] Consider the case of the small, ten-person shop in Seattle that engraves plaques and trophies. Today, 60 percent of its business is conducted online, with customers who live outside the Seattle area.[43]

- The Internet will continue to be a platform that provides small businesses with a wide range of new tools, services, and capabilities. Small businesses will find new ways to use the Internet, contributing to the blurred distinctions between the physical and the virtual worlds.[44]

- Small business relationships will become increasingly virtual as online social networks expand.[45] Many small businesses are promoting their presence on Facebook and Twitter. Westbrook Lobster and Arisco Farms are both small businesses in Connecticut that have an online social presence. Naked Pizza in New Orleans has a presence on Twitter that has proven to be a boon to its business.[46]

 Video Clip 4.2

Naked Pizza on Twitter
Naked Pizza can now be followed on Twitter.

View the video online at: http://www.youtube.com/v/wSfOsSSOT-M

1.5 Is E-Commerce for All Small Businesses?

Despite the popularity and pervasiveness of e-commerce, not all small businesses may be interested in pursuing e-commerce as a part of their businesses. Many small businesses survive without an online presence. However, business analysts have agreed for a long time "that for any company larger than a local mom and pop store, e-commerce is now a business requirement."[47]

KEY TAKEAWAYS

- E-business and e-commerce are not synonymous terms. E-commerce generates revenue. E-business does not.
- E-business and/or e-commerce may not be of interest to all small businesses. However, using technology well is proving to be one of the most prominent drivers of business success.
- E-business consists of several major components, one of which is e-commerce.
- Every Internet business is either pure-play (an Internet presence only) or brick-and-click (having both a physical and an online presence).
- The seven major types of e-commerce are B2B, B2C, C2C, B2G, C2B, m-commerce, and P2P.
- An e-commerce business model is the method that a business uses to generate revenue online. Some models are very simple; others are more complicated. New business models are being introduced all the time.
- E-commerce will continue to grab more market share, and the line between online and offline commerce will become less defined.

EXERCISES

1. In the Frank's All-American BarBeQue case in Chapter 2, the son, Robert Rainsford, wants to bring his expertise to improving the operations of the business. What other elements of digital technology, e-business, and e-commerce could be used to improve operations?

2. Joan Watson is the owner of Joan's Gourmet Baskets, a small brick-and-mortar business that specializes in gourmet gift and picnic baskets. Joan has been keeping up with the fancy food and gourmet food trends (being a great fan of the Fancy Food Show that is held several times a year), and she thinks she should tap into this sector by creating an online business that will complement her physical business. This would make her baskets available to a wider market. She is proud of the quality of her products and the customer loyalty that she has earned through her hard work and hopes she will be able to be just as successful in the e-commerce environment.

   Joan knows that she needs more information before proceeding further. She has asked you to prepare a report that answers the following questions: How will her physical business compare to her online business; that is, where will things be the same, and where will they be different? What business model should she use? What are the special challenges and obstacles she will face as she moves from traditional commerce to e-commerce? What is Web 2.0 all about and does she need to be concerned about it? She expects that you will do additional gourmet foods research to support your ideas.

2. E-COMMERCE OPERATIONS

LEARNING OBJECTIVES

1. Explain the issues associated with whether a small business should buy or build its website.
2. Explain some of the legal issues that are relevant to e-commerce.
3. Discuss the need for an ethical website, particularly in terms of security, privacy, and trust.
4. Explain why order fulfillment is such an important part of successful e-commerce.

There are multiple parts to the creation of an e-commerce website: the infrastructure (the nuts and bolts building of the site), the e-marketing side (the design and creation of a web presence, which is discussed in Chapter 7), and the operational side. The operational side is the focus of this section.

2.1 The Website: Buy or Build?

Unless a small business owner is technologically savvy or employs someone who is, building the company's website in-house from the ground up is not a particularly good idea. An effective website presence requires a good looking, professionally designed website. There are several approaches to having someone else build that website. Two are described here.

- **Full-service web developers** provide design, programming, support, hosting, search engine optimization, and more. Any combination of the services can be selected. Having the developer perform all the services would be the most expensive alternative. **Hosting** is the housing, serving, and maintaining of the files for one or more websites.[48] **Search engine optimization** refers to the strategies intended to position a website at the top of search engines such as Google, Yahoo!, and Bing.[49]

- A much lower-priced option is to select one of the many companies online that can help you to design your website. Typically these sites provide a choice of website design templates that can be easily edited; design services that are available if none of the templates meet your needs; hosting; **domain name selection** (your business address or name on the Internet, e.g., flatworldknowledge.com) and **domain name registration** (registering your domain name with a domain name registrar and paying a fee that must be renewed annually);[50] and **search engine placement** (submitting your website to specific search engines of your choice). Intuit.com and Webs.com are two companies that offer these and other services. The lowest level of services are often free.

 Video Clip 4.3

Domain Name Dollar Store
A humorous look at getting a URL for your website at a rock bottom price.

View the video online at: http://www.youtube.com/v/7FZ1M_UmQes

The ultimate cost for a website will be a function of its size, complexity, and the level of design. No two projects will cost the same. Part of the process of building a website, however, should be conducting some research and talking with website designers. The Internet offers a variety of sources on how to determine how much a website should cost. WebpageFX.com offers a historical perspective on website costs, a cost calculator to find out how much a web project would cost, and examples of specific web design and website development projects with cost figures.[51]

Consider the following two scenarios:

- "A small business needs a website for their business so they have a presence on the Internet. The site is simple—about 5 pages with information about the business, the services they provide, and a form that can be submitted and the information received via email. The budget isn't available for creating a graphic 'look,' and existing images will be used. A smaller, less experienced designer may take on a project like this for a few hundred dollars. A medium sized firm might quote $3000 to $4000 depending on variables. A larger firm would probably not take a project this small."[52]

- "A mail order company wants to get into online sales. They currently have no website. They have a narrow mix of about 200 products with a broad target market; it's also time to update their image. Depending on a wide range of variables, a project like this could start at about $7000 and go into six figures."[53]

There is no easy answer to the question of how much a website will cost. "A simple answer is that it will cost whatever a business is willing to spend—anywhere from free to millions of dollars."[54] A better way to address cost is to answer the following questions:[55]

- What are your needs, goals, and expectations?
- What are the needs and expectations of your visitors, customers, and clients?

- Is your business already established with its unique brand or identity?
- What is required in terms of the skills, experiences, and level of design?
- Do you want to hire a high-profile design shop, a medium-sized design studio, a small company, or a student?
- What can you afford to budget for your project?

2.2 Legal

There is nothing easy about the law. It is complex under the best of circumstances, but it is necessary to protect the rights and privileges of people and businesses. Companies that choose to engage in e-commerce must be aware of the legal environment because "a lack of awareness…can lead to missteps as well as missed opportunities…."[56] A summary of important legal issues for e-commerce is in Table 4.2. However, the focus here is on three areas: electronic transactions, intellectual property, and jurisdiction.

TABLE 4.2 Important Legal Issues for E-Commerce

Issue	Description
Jurisdiction	The ability to sue in other states or countries.
Electronic transactions	All transactions that take place online.
Liability	The use of multiple networks and trading partners makes documenting responsibility difficult. How can liability for errors, malfunctions, or fraudulent use of data be determined?
Identity fraud	The Identity, Theft, and Assumption Deterrence Act of 1998 makes identity fraud a federal felony carrying a three- to twenty-five-year prison sentence.
Defamation	Is the Internet service provider liable for material published on the Internet because of services it provides or supports? (Usually not.) Who else is liable for defamation? What if the publisher is in another country?
Intellectual property law	Protects creations of the human mind.
Digital signatures	Digital signatures are recognized as legal in the United States and some but not all other countries.
Regulation of consumer	The United States allows the compilation and sale of customer databases. The European Union does not.
Time and place	An electronic document signed in Japan on January 5 may have the date January 4 in Los Angeles. Which date is considered legal if a dispute arises?
Electronic contracts	If all the elements to establish a contract are present, an electronic contract is valid and enforceable.
Taxation	Taxation of sales transactions by states is on hold in the United States and some but not all other countries. Expect this issue to be revived because the potential for increased revenue to the states is significant.

Source: Efraim Turban et al., Electronic Commerce: A Managerial Perspective (Upper Saddle River, NJ: Pearson/Prentice Hall, 2008), 795.

Electronic transactions are the many kinds of transactions that take place online, including contractual dealings, buying and selling of goods and services, information exchange, financial transactions (credit card payments; payor services, such as PayPal; and money transfers), and communications. When developing a website, the small business owner must ensure that all online business transactions will be secure, particularly those involving money. This discussion must take place with whomever is developing your website.

Intellectual property is "a creation of the mind, such as inventions, literary and artistic works, and symbols, names, images, and designs, used in commerce."[57] Music, photos, videos, digital news, and artwork are forms of intellectual property that can be transmitted over the Internet. All small business owners need to be concerned about the theft of intellectual property. They are afforded multiple protections, which are summarized in Table 4.3.

electronic transactions

All transactions that take place online.

intellectual property

A creation of the mind—such as inventions; literary and artistic works; and symbols, names, images, and designs used in commerce.

TABLE 4.3 Intellectual Property Protections

Law	Protection Provided by the Law
Intellectual property law	Protects creations of the human mind
Patent law	Protects inventions and discoveries
Copyright law	Protects original works of authorship, such as music and literary works and computer programs
Trademark law	Protects brand names and other symbols that indicate source of goods and services
Trade secret law	Protects confidential business information
Law of licensing	Enables owners of patents, trademarks, copyrights, and trade secrets to share them with others on a mutually agreed-on basis
Law of unfair competition dealing with counterfeiting and piracy	Protects against those who try to take a free ride on the efforts and achievements of creative people

Source: Efraim Turban et al., Electronic Commerce: A Managerial Perspective (Upper Saddle River, NJ: Pearson/Prentice Hall, 2008), 779.

It is important to protect intellectual property because businesses will not realize the full benefits of their inventions and would be inclined to focus less on research and development. Additionally, without intellectual property protections, "exporters face unfair competition abroad, non-exporters face counterfeit imports at home, and all businesses face legal, health and safety risks from the threat of counterfeit goods entering their supply chains."[58] Unfortunately, US small businesses are at a disadvantage because[59]

- They may lack the knowledge, expertise, or resources necessary to prevent the theft of their ideas and products.

- Many small businesses do not have personnel and operators overseas, so they do not have the necessary eyes and ears needed to be vigilant. The theft of their ideas and products often goes undetected.

- Small businesses generally do not have the kinds of access and resources that are likely available to larger companies (e.g., specialized legal counsel).

Because of the complexities of intellectual property protections, this area requires the services of an attorney, preferably one experienced and knowledgeable in cyberlaw.

jurisdiction

The right and power that a court has to interpret and apply the law in a particular geographic location.

Jurisdiction refers to the right and power that a court has to interpret and apply the law in a particular geographic location.[60] "A court must have jurisdiction over the litigants and the claims before it entertains a lawsuit. In the context of Internet commerce, this issue erupts when a dispute arises between businesses from different states [or countries]."[61] Many small businesses will be selling products online in other states and in other countries, so it is important to understand the jurisdictions that might be applicable to any online transaction. "In many cases, laws from the customer's state are the ones that will apply in the event a problem arises. This is equally true regarding the laws of other countries."[62] From the perspective of any business, but particularly a small business, it would be much easier from both a time and a money perspective to have an issue litigated in the home state of a business. Although there are no guarantees, these steps can be taken to increase the chances of a dispute being settled in the home state of a business:[63]

1. If using a contract with another party, make sure the contract says that any dispute must be filed in your home state and that both parties to the contract agree to jurisdiction in that state.

2. When a customer is purchasing an item on the website of a business, one of the terms and conditions of the transaction should be that the customer agree to jurisdiction in the home state of that business. This can be done with a check box next to the statement. Make the customer check it off before completing the purchase.

3. A less effective way is to include a disclaimer on the website that any transaction will convey jurisdiction to the home state of a business, and any dispute must be heard by a court of competent jurisdiction in the home state of the business.

All these steps should also be considered when selling to other countries. However, the laws in other countries will undoubtedly introduce complications into protecting the US-based business. Take the example of Yahoo! and the sale of Nazi memorabilia on one of its auction websites. A French court ruled that such sales breached French law against the display of Nazi items. Yahoo! took steps to remove and ban all such hate paraphernalia from its auction sites, but it continued to fight jurisdiction of the French ruling in American courts.[64] It would be very easy for a small business to inadvertently find itself in a similar situation. That is why a business needs to be careful when selling outside its home country. Be familiar with foreign laws. This is not an easy task because the minute a business website goes live, the business goes global. The laws of the world suddenly become relevant.

2.3   Ethical Issues

It is known that "ethical factors do play a significant role in e-consumers' purchasing decisions."[65] Therefore, ethical factors should be of major concern in e-commerce and, accordingly, in the information and protections offered by an e-commerce website.

It has been observed that the "Internet represents a new environment for unethical behavior," and "ethical transgressions are more likely to happen in e-transactions as compared to face-to-face transactions."[66] To a large extent, this is due to the absence of physical and interpersonal cues that are present in traditional retailing or business settings. The implication is that e-commerce operations should focus more specifically and explicitly on the ethics messages that are being conveyed by the website. Thus the focus of this ethics discussion is on three major components of e-commerce ethics: security, privacy, and trust.

2.4   Security and Privacy

Website security (the protection of a company, its suppliers, its customers, and its employees from criminal activity) is a critical consideration for any small business engaged in e-commerce. The Internet is a global playground for criminals. It is less risky to steal online because "the potential for anonymity on the Internet cloaks many criminals in legitimate-looking identities, allowing them to place fraudulent orders with online merchants, steal information by intercepting e-mail,…shut down e-commerce sites by using software viruses,"[67] and steal financial information and money. This new type of crime is referred to as cybercrime, and it is a serious threat to e-commerce.

Cybercrime refers to any criminal activity that is done using computers and the Internet,[68] and it includes a wide range of offenses. Downloading illegal music, stealing from online bank accounts, stealing credit card numbers and personal information, stealing identities, posting confidential business information on the Internet, and creating and distributing viruses on other computers are only some of the thousands of crimes that are considered cybercrimes.[69] Cybercrimes can take place anytime and anyplace. It has cost American companies a median loss of $3.8 million a year, and data protection and information technology (IT) practitioners from 45 US organizations from various sectors reported that, across their companies, 50 successful attacks were experienced over a four-week period.[70]

> **website security**
>
> The protection of a company, its suppliers, its customers, and its employees from criminal activity.

> **cybercrime**
>
> Any criminal activity that is done using computers and the Internet.

Video Clip 4.4

The New Face of Cybercrime
Cybercrime today.

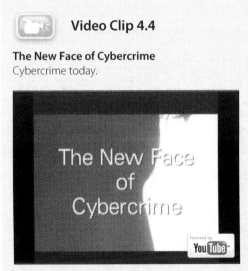

View the video online at: http://www.youtube.com/v/-5zxOLZ5jXM

Video Clip 4.5

The State of Cybercrime
Do not be fooled. Cybercrime is on the rise.

View the video online at: http://www.youtube.com/v/ZqxAk4tSBUM

Video Clip 4.6

Cybercrime Trailer
New cybercrime threats.

View the video online at: http://www.youtube.com/v/y9JMtExLZa4

Cybercrime is more profitable than the illegal drug trade (more than $100 billion globally per year). Every three seconds an identity is stolen, and without security, an unprotected PC can become infected within four minutes of connecting to the Internet.[71] A Microsoft security intelligence report maintains that cybercrime is fast maturing as a profession, with cybercriminals becoming more sophisticated and packaging online threats that can be sold to others.[72]

Examples of Cybercrimes[73]

The Computer Crime & Intellectual Property Section of the US Department of Justice keeps a running list of press releases related to cybercrimes. Here are three examples.

1. A Miami man pled guilty to one count of conspiracy to traffic in and possess unauthorized credit card numbers with intent to defraud, and one count of trafficking in unauthorized credit card numbers.
2. A Rhode Island man pleaded guilty to Internet sales of unregistered, unlabeled pesticides for cats and dogs while infringing on the trademark of two well-known national brand names, "Frontline" and "Frontline Plus." The man made more than 3,500 sales through eBay.
3. A Canadian man was sentenced to 33 years in prison for selling counterfeit cancer drugs using the Internet.

Cybercrime hurts the bottom line of any business, but small and medium-sized businesses are the new cybercrime target. "Hackers and computer criminals…are taking a new aim—directly at small and midsize businesses…Smaller businesses offer a much more attractive target than larger enterprises that have steeled themselves with years of security spending and compliance efforts."[74] Small businesses are potentially very lucrative targets for several reasons:

- Nearly one fifth of small businesses do not use antivirus software.
- Two thirds of small businesses do not have a security plan in place.
- Sixty percent of small businesses do not use encryption on their wireless links.
- Only about 60 percent of mom-and-pop shops have met the credit card industry's data security standards for protecting credit card data. Compliance at the smallest businesses is even worse.
- Two thirds of small and medium-sized businesses believe that large companies are the main target for cybercrime,…yet 85 percent of the fraud seen in business occurs in small and medium-sized businesses.[75]

The cybercriminal is looking to steal and disrupt. Securing a website should be a top priority for any company—small, medium, or large—that uses the Internet to conduct its business.

Video Clip 4.7

How SSL Security Works on E-Commerce Websites
How Amazon.com grew so fast by incorporating SSL security.

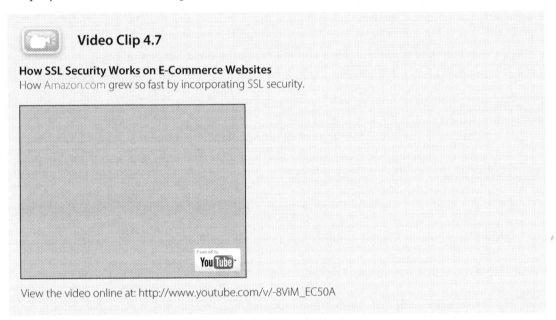

View the video online at: http://www.youtube.com/v/-8ViM_EC50A

Given the state of cybercrime, assuring the security and the **privacy** of e-consumers (the protection of the personal information of customers on the Internet) are necessary to build and maintain confidence in the e-market, particularly because the risk of privacy invasion and security flaws is significant.[76] Further, such assurances have been found to have a significant impact on the willingness to purchase.[77]

E-customers voice their privacy concerns in different ways. Here are some examples:[78]

- "I don't like websites that ask you for personal information that is not necessary for the purchase to be made."
- "All privacy notices contain the same information, and besides, how do I know that the website actually follows the privacy policy."
- "I'm not comfortable at all with the idea of the online retailer having my personal information and selling it to other companies for marketing purposes."

The scope of failure in protecting customers' personal information can be potentially devastating because of the global reach of the Internet; the effect can easily reach millions of people.[79] Heartland is a payment processor responsible for handling about 100 million credit card transactions every month. They disclosed in June 2009 that thieves had used malicious software in its network in 2008 to steal an unknown number of credit card numbers.[80]

Fortunately, the theft of credit card and other personal information originating from websites accounted for only about 11 percent of the identity theft or fraud that affected 11 million Americans in 2009.[81] This is why the act of providing credit card information on a website for a purchase is still considered by some people to be so risky that they refuse to conduct any Internet transactions. This has obvious implications for any small company that hopes to do business online.

privacy

The protection of personal information of customers on the Internet.

Secure Sockets Layer (SSL)

A security protocol that is used by web browsers and web servers to help users protect their data during transfer.

Fortunately, there is a very straightforward way to provide the security and privacy that online customers seek: the use of **Secure Sockets Layer (SSL)**, a security protocol that is used by web browsers and web servers to help users protect their data during transfer.[82] Companies like VeriSign offer SSL protection certificates, and the placement of its icon on a website can offer security and privacy assurances to online customers. The inclusion of SSL protection should be discussed with your website designer.

2.5 Trust

Trust is about believing—believing that someone will do what they say and that they will not intentionally do something to hurt you. Trust is an important part of all business relationships. Without trust, all e-commerce would come to a halt. "Trust is central to establishing successful e-commerce ventures and to ensure the continued success of this business paradigm into the future."[83] Trust will improve competitiveness, reduce the costs of doing business, build loyalty, and increase the effectiveness of websites. In short, trust can be an important source of competitive advantage. Trust is essential.

In the physical world, trust is much easier to develop. Physical cues from spaces and buildings, face-to-face voice and body language, and salesperson effectiveness can translate easily into trust relationships. In the online world, however, trust develops as a result of the complex interaction of multiple factors that have design implications for the website. Here are some examples of trust:[84]

- The customer observes the seller to be honest, fair, responsible, and benevolent.
- The customer expects that the company behind the website will not engage in opportunistic behavior.
- The customer is confident about the site's security and privacy protection (security and privacy having been shown to be an important determinant of a customer's willingness to buy online).
- The customer perceives the company's website as appealing (linked to layout, typography, font size, and color choices)—the belief being that an appealing website reflects a company has the capabilities and resources to fulfill its promises.
- The customer experiences a site that is easy to use (i.e., easy to navigate, easy to search, easy to gather information) and has relevant content, interactivity, site consistency, and site reliability.
- The customer perceives presentation flaws (e.g., poor style, incompleteness, language errors, conflicting colors, delay, and confusing terminology) as indicators of a low-quality, untrustworthy website.

order fulfillment

Meeting customer expectations with respect to processing the order and delivering of the product.

Another element of trust is **order fulfillment**. Order fulfillment is all about meeting expectations, and some argue that this is the most important element of trust.[85] Delays in the delivery of a product, the delivery of the wrong product, and the hassles of returning merchandise are stresses that can contribute to a less-than-satisfactory Internet buying experience. Such experiences contribute to a lack of trust. In contrast, satisfied consumers express themselves this way:[86]

- "Products at this site are a bit pricey, but it is worth purchasing from this site since you get what you order and within the promised delivery time."
- "I keep purchasing from this site because they always have the items I want in stock."

Buying some products online, such as clothing, furniture, and toys, does not offer buyers the opportunity to touch and feel the product before buying. As a result, order fulfillment becomes even more important to customer satisfaction.

product reliability

The accurate display and description of a product so that what customers receive is what they thought they ordered.

Linked closely to order fulfillment is **product reliability**. Product reliability refers to "the accurate display and description of a product so that what customers receive is what they thought they ordered."[87] Online retailers should provide a complete and realistic description of the product and its benefits—with high-quality pictures and perhaps even demonstration videos if possible, appropriate, and affordable—along with product availability and likely ship dates. Customers should be notified by e-mail of order acceptance, and the anticipated delivery date with phone and e-mail contacts for any needed assistance.

Video Link 4.1

Inflatable Fruitcake

Inflatable fruitcake with demonstration.

www.inflatablefruitcake.com/

What all this says is that website owners must proceed carefully to create their online presence in a way that will inspire trust. "If consumers trust online merchants and have confidence in the reliability and integrity of merchants, they will likely feel more at ease making purchases and disclosing sensitive information online. Therefore, the success of online merchants and the future of e-commerce may depend heavily on online trust."[88]

2.6 Payment Options

Nowhere are security, privacy, and trust more necessary than at the point of payment. Without this transaction, there is no e-commerce, so it is imperative that small businesses selling online take the necessary steps to reduce customer concerns about shopping online. A recent survey found that retailers operating online may have lost more than $44 billion dollars over a one-year period as a result of transaction problems on their websites; in addition, 27 percent of online shoppers would turn to an offline or online competitor if they encountered an online transaction issue.[89] More specifically, online shoppers who encountered a transaction problem would react as follows:[90]

- Sixty-six percent would contact customer service, including

    - Fifty-three percent calling customer service; and

    - Thirty-six percent e-mailing or logging a web complaint with customer service.

- Thirty-two percent would abandon the transaction entirely, including

    - Twenty-seven percent turning to an online or offline competitor.

To make matters even worse, the potential for lost revenue when customers have a negative online shopping experience is amplified by the rising use of social media like Facebook and Twitter; the voicing of displeasure on social networks can significantly damage a company's reputation.[91] The message is clear. Online transactions must run smoothly.

But there is another important issue: the number of payment options that are offered to the customer. Research shows that the more payment options customers have, the more likely they will complete their purchase.[92]

- Merchants offering multiple payment methods have lower cart abandonment rates.

- If you can afford it and maintain your profit margin, offering multiple payment options is a means to increase your sales by increasing customer confidence and convenience.

- North American online businesses with four or more options for payment see an average **sales conversion rate** of 72 percent. The sales conversion rate is the percentage of site visitors that make a purchase.

- Each new payment option added at the point of checkout results in a sales increase of 5–20 percent.

sales conversion rate

The percentage of site visitors who make a purchase.

Customers shopping online expect convenience and a variety of payment options. Credit cards are by far the most popular means for making an online payment, with one survey indicating that 70 percent of online consumers used this payment method.[93] Any small business that does not have its website set up to accept credit cards will lose 60–80 percent of its potential orders. Further, offering a credit card option will increase the number of orders, and those orders will be substantially larger because credit cards enable impulse buying, reassure customers of your legitimacy, and simplify your billing.[94]

Consistent with credit cards being the online payment method of choice, it has been reported that 99 percent of online businesses offer a general purpose credit card, which include Visa, MasterCard, American Express, and Discover.[95] However, debit cards are growing in popularity ahead of other payment alternatives.

TABLE 4.4 Payment Options Consumers Used to Make Online Purchases in 2009

Payment Option	% Used
Major credit card usable anywhere	70
Major debit card usable anywhere	55
Online payment service, such as PayPal or Google Checkout	51
Gift card good only at a specific merchant	41
Store-branded credit card good only at the merchant that issued the card	27
Prepaid card or payroll card usable anywhere	17
Online credit service such as BillMeLater	17
Store-branded debit card good only at merchant that issued the card	16

The implications of this for small business are that credit cards should be the first payment method that should be set up for online sales. Additional payment methods should be added as quickly as the budget allows because it is clear that more payment options translate into a greater likelihood of purchase. However, the choice of alternative payment methods should be in keeping with the growth strategy of the business. It may be that offering one method of payment provides a satisfactory level of sales, thereby eliminating the need for additional methods for sales growth.

KEY TAKEAWAYS

- It is important to protect intellectual property.
- Ethics influence consumer purchases.
- Small businesses are the new target for cybercrime. As a result, small businesses must pay attention to their website security because it will protect the business and influence customer trust.

EXERCISES

1. Find three small business websites. Analyze each website in terms of its trustworthiness. Discuss why you would or would not trust each site. Be specific.
2. Discuss whether you think an unintelligible privacy policy is ethical. Be specific in your arguments.

3. E-COMMERCE TECHNOLOGY

LEARNING OBJECTIVES

1. Explain what an e-commerce platform is.
2. Discuss the importance of a CRM solution to a small business.
3. Explain m-commerce and why small businesses should consider incorporating it into their e-commerce strategy.
4. Explain the significance of Web 2.0 to a small business.

As discussed in Chapter 1, digital technology has put small business on a more equal footing with its larger competitors. Although it is certainly true that a commitment to technology is not for every small business, it is also true that technology is transforming small business in important ways: (1) businesses are easier to find online than ever before; (2) communicating with customers is shifting to e-mail marketing and social media; (3) e-mail and mobile phones are improving productivity; (4) collaboration among employees who are working in multiple venues is easier; (5) outsourcing is easier; and (6) more companies are shifting their attention to how they can sell products and services online. Using technology well is proving to be one of the most prominent drivers of business success.[96]

Technology specifically related to e-commerce is a large umbrella. E-commerce platforms, customer relationship management (CRM), going mobile, and Web 2.0 will be discussed in this section.

3.1   E-Commerce Platforms

An **e-commerce platform** is the software that makes it possible for a business to sell online. In general, the core e-commerce platform should support basic requirements such as custom styling, **search engine optimization**, credit card processing, promotions, catalog management, analytics, product browsing, checkout, and order management. Additionally, e-commerce platforms should provide self-service content management systems (CMS), support multiple languages, and support multiple stores.[97] These requirements may vary slightly depending on which type of e-commerce is being conducted. **Analytics** refer to the tools that can track the different ways people use your website and then make sense of the data.[98] Analytics will be discussed in further detail in Chapter 8.

The **all-in-one e-commerce platform solution** has become more popular with online merchants. This solution provides everything: the core e-commerce platform plus hosting, accounting, analytics, and marketing tools such as e-mail management. Because all the tools are integrated, they work together.[99] It has also been reported that e-commerce platforms are now enabling online retailers to better reach consumers through mobile devices and social media sites.[100] This is great news for the small business that wants to tap into these growing markets.

The list of e-commerce software providers is always growing, but there are many products that are tailored specifically for small to medium-sized businesses. Some of the names that come up frequently for small business are BigCommerce, Magento, Affinity Internet, ProStores (for the smaller merchant), and Miva Merchant. However, this list is not exhaustive, and new products enter the marketplace all the time.

> **e-commerce platform**
>
> The software that makes it possible for a business to sell online.
>
> **analytics**
>
> The tools that can track the different ways people use a website and then make sense of the data.
>
> **all-in-one e-commerce platform solution**
>
> The core e-commerce platform plus hosting, accounting, analytics, and marketing tools such as e-mail management.

3.2   Customer Relationship Management

Customer relationship management, as mentioned in Chapter 2, refers to "a customer service approach that focuses on building long-term and sustainable customer relationships that add value for the customer and the company."[101] Some small businesses may wonder whether they really need the added complexity of a small business CRM solution. The answer will depend to a large extent on the size of the business and its growth objectives. However, it has been observed that there is no small business out there that, "sometimes in spite of themselves, didn't benefit from implementing a…CRM or its watered down equivalent—a simpler Contact Management software solution."[102] Recent studies have revealed that CRM applications account for the following:[103]

- Revenue increases of up to 41 percent per salesperson
- Decreased sales cycles of over 24 percent
- Lead conversion rate improvements of over 300 percent
- Customer retention improvements of 27 percent
- Decreased sales and marketing costs of 23 percent
- Improved profit margins of over 2 percent

It has also been noted that companies can boost their profits by almost 100 percent by retaining just 5 percent of their customers.[104] What does this mean for the small business that chooses to go with a CRM solution? As long as the solution is well implemented and actually used, there should be an immediate payoff and productivity improvement throughout the company. Additionally, choosing to engage in e-commerce makes the selection of a CRM solution even more important because the quality of customer relationships is so important to online success.

Although there was a time when CRM solutions were not feasible for small business, they are available today for even the smallest businesses. These CRM solutions are priced and designed with the small business in mind.

3.3   Going Mobile

As defined earlier in this chapter, **mobile e-commerce (m-commerce)** refers to the purchase of goods and services through wireless technology, such as cell phones and handheld devices. It consists of two primary components: "…the ability to use a wireless phone or other mobile device to conduct financial transactions and exchange payments over the Internet…and the ability to deliver information that can facilitate a transaction—from making it easy for your business to be 'found' via a mobile Web browser to creating mobile marketing campaigns such as text promotions and loyalty programs."[105] It is predicted that in 2015 m-commerce revenues will make up 8.5 percent of all US e-commerce revenue and 20 percent of global e-commerce revenue. In the United States, that will represent only one half of 1 percent of all retail revenues.[106] However, even though m-commerce is lagging behind other mobile uses, wireless devices and m-commerce are expected to create another revolution in e-commerce. The most important thing that online retailers can do is to "…take action soon because the mobile environment is adapting much more quickly than the web."[107]

Small businesses need to sort out the hype from what's real. What's real are the facts and the trends. [108]

1. From the second quarter 2009 through the second quarter 2010, Amazon's customers around the world used mobile devices to buy more than $1 billion in products. This is a trend that any small business with an e-commerce website should watch closely.

2. Mobile devices connected to the Internet are reshaping the way people are going about their personal and professional lives.

3. One of the fastest growth areas in e-commerce will be using mobile devices to make online purchases.

4. Close to 80 percent of organizations plan to have mobile websites by the end of 2011. Online retailers without an m-commerce strategy will be in the minority.

5. Handheld devices are increasingly being used to research products, compare prices, and buy online while shopping.

6. A central driver to m-commerce growth is **smartphone** ownership and the corresponding mobile Internet use.

7. Nearly 58 percent of Americans have researched a product or a service online.

8. Among cell phone owners, 11 percent purchased a product or a service using their phones.

  Video Clip 4.8

Mobile E-Commerce Capabilities
Gene Alvarez, Gartner Group, discusses m-commerce.

View the video online at: http://www.youtube.com/v/XSeWBz6gyvk

Major retailers have been able to easily offer remote access to customers who want to make purchases using mobile devices (e.g., Target and Nordstrom). Software is now available for small businesses to offer some of the same bells and whistles, giving their online customers the ability to shop via smartphones.[109]

Mobile e-commerce may not be for all small businesses, but a small business owner who is already in e-commerce or has plans to do so should give it consideration. Multichannel shoppers tend to purchase more, so small companies need to think of ways to "effectively engage customers by delivering consistent, rich experiences across all channels, including mobile, to maintain and fuel double-digit ecommerce industry growth rates."[110] Online customers are ready and increasingly interested in using mobile devices to make purchases.

3.4 Web 2.0

There is no agreement about an exact definition of **Web 2.0** but, in general, it refers to websites that are more interactive, engaging, and interesting than before. A Web 2.0 site is one where visitors can engage with you, your business, and your site by doing things like the following:[111]

- Posting comments on your blog or your articles or chatting in a forum
- Retweeting your content, sharing it on Facebook, or Digging it
- Watching a video, listening to a podcast, or participating in a webinar
- Taking a quiz or responding to a poll

Web 2.0 is about having a conversation with your customers. This is very different from **Web 1.0**, where websites were static and all you could do was read. Web 2.0 sites are collaborative and interactive. The small business that creates a site that engages and interacts with people, that makes people want to stick around, will be giving people more of a chance to create a connection with the business.[112] These closer ties will increase customer awareness and consideration of the company's products and services, improve customer satisfaction, increase the chances of loyalty, increase the chances for sales, and add to the bottom line. There will also be significant benefits realized between the small business and its suppliers and partners: lowering the costs of communication and doing business.

A much smaller percentage of small businesses have adopted elements of Web 2.0 as compared to large enterprises and midsize companies.[113] However, many small businesses are using Web 2.0 in a variety of positive ways.[114]

- One business owner operated a Facebook group, attracted interest in the business, and developed loyalty through the group.
- Another business routinely put press releases online and attested to their value at getting the company's website found in search engines.
- The owner of a product company reported good results with videos that were loaded on YouTube and on the company's website. The video attracted people to the site and also engaged existing visitors on the site.
- A small real-estate company has a Facebook page, a blog, and a property value calculator that allows homeowners to calculate an approximation of their home's value without having to speak with a realtor. The information is then sent via e-mail.

As Web 2.0 keeps evolving, the value and opportunities it will bring to small businesses will continue to grow. "The increased flow of two-way information between business and customer, the increase in information distribution through blogs and wikis, and the increased participation of customers in product improvement and even design will continue. By adopting Web 2.0 technologies and tools, small businesses can improve market share, profit, and reputation, now and in the future."[115]

Web 2.0

Websites that are more interactive, engaging, and interesting than available with Web 1.0.

Web 1.0

All websites were static, and all you could do was read.

 Video Clip 4.9

Web 2.0
Evolution of website technology to Web 2.0.

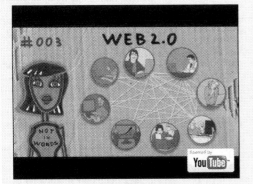

View the video online at: http://www.youtube.com/v/Bc0oDlEbYFc

4. THE THREE THREADS

4.1 Customer Value Implications

E-business in general and e-commerce in particular can both contribute to increased customer value. In the case of e-business, moving operations to digital technology can improve productivity, reduce or eliminate duplicative processes, streamline supply chain management and enterprise resource planning, improve customer and vendor relationships, improve business intelligence, increase and improve internal collaboration while doing the same with external business partners. In all instances, the customer, the vendor, and the business partner should realize increased value from doing business with the company in terms of greater efficiency, speed of information flows and transactions, and overall satisfaction.

In the case of e-commerce, customer value is provided via convenience, a greater selection of products, the ability to easily compare prices and services, 24/7 availability, privacy protection, multiple payment options, and reliable order fulfillment processes. Web 2.0, in particular, presents "consumers with a whole array of options in searching for value products and services and finding exactly what they need and want with minimum efforts, in line with the current customer desire for personalization, individual approach and empowerment."[116]

4.2 Cash-Flow Implications

The cash flow of a small business should benefit from all the sources of value just mentioned because they should result in lower operating costs, improved customer relationships, and higher sales. In particular, cash flow should increase as a result of the following:

- Prepaid purchases by business-to-business (B2B) customers. This may apply to other e-commerce customers as well.

- Multiple payment options. The greater the number of options, the higher the number of sales and the higher the average order size.

- Lower costs of sales as a result of the reduced need for telephone, travel expenses, and live salespeople.

- Eliminating many steps in business processes and cutting out the middlemen.[117]

- Saving money on employees and salaries because of **customer outsourcing** (i.e., anything that the customer does individually, things like searching for product or service information, entering his or her billing information, and signing up for an e-mail confirmation. These are things that customer service representatives do not have to do.[118]

- Increased sales as a result of selling niche products. "It turns out that most small businesses (and start-ups) have relatively niche-y products…The Internet disproportionately favors small businesses since it enables them to position their niche goods to people *shopping for* that particular niche good."[119]

This is not an exhaustive list. However, it is illustrative of the many ways in which e-business and e-commerce can impact the cash flow of a small business in a favorable way.

4.3   Digital Technology and E-Environment Implications

Although not all small businesses may choose to go the route of digital technology and the e-environment (e-business and e-commerce), it has been advised on many fronts that small businesses seriously consider creative ways in which to incorporate them all into their operations. Digital technology is difficult to avoid, whether it be computers, **smartphones**, or iPads (see the story of Lloyd's Construction in Chapter 1). Even on a small scale, digital technology can help improve business processes and keep costs down.

The importance of e-business and e-commerce to small business has been the focus of this chapter. Realistically, neither can be avoided by small businesses that want to grow. E-commerce in particular has opened up the world to small business. Websites have "created a flattening effect in the sense that small businesses and large businesses [are] suddenly on a level playing field…The web [allows] small companies to have the same reach as a large firm. A small company's web site [can] be viewed a million times just as easily as a large firm's web site, and that information [is] available worldwide, 24 hours a day. Small businesses [can] now have some of the same abilities as large companies to reach customers with rich content of information about their products nationally or internationally."[120] The small business that wants to grow will ignore e-business and e-commerce at its peril.

KEY TAKEAWAYS

- E-business and e-commerce both contribute to increased customer value.
- The cash flow of a small business should benefit from the customer value offered by e-business and e-commerce.
- Even though some small businesses may choose not to go the route of digital technology, e-business, or e-commerce, it has been suggested that small businesses seriously consider creative ways in which to incorporate them into all operations.

EXERCISES

1. Select three small businesses that engage in e-commerce. Interview the owners and ask them to describe (1) how e-commerce has added customer value and (2) the positive and negative impacts on cash flow.

2. Locate at least one small business that is a nonemployer (i.e., consists of only the owner). Interview the owner about the role that digital technology plays in the business and what his or her plans are, if any, to increase its incorporation. Find out if the business has a website. If it does, are there plans to engage in e-commerce? If the business does not have a website, find out why not and whether there are any plans to create one.

customer outsourcing

Anything that the customer does individually, such as searching for product or service information, entering billing information, and signing up for an e-mail confirmation.

Disaster Watch

I've Been Hacked!

Not discouraged by the bad economy, Marnie McCormick opened "The Country Store" in the local shopping center. McCormick had done her homework. She originally leased the store front for a temporary stint, selling a line of unique handcrafted products and locally made foods while asking people what sort of products they wished were available in the area. In this way, she was able to build the kind of store that was needed, using the existing demand to decide what kinds of products she would offer.

McCormick had a myriad of concerns at start-up—inventory, suppliers, marketing, outfitting the store, and administrative systems. What she did not know was that someone had hacked into her computer system. From somewhere unknown, the hard drive of her computer in the store had been hacked. The hackers had downloaded a key-logging program (a virus that makes it possible for the hacker to record all your keystrokes, gaining access to passwords and other sensitive information). The hackers were able to see everything that she typed into the computer: e-mails, communications with vendors and customers, passwords—everything. The hackers only had to wait until she logged into her online bank account before they had all the information they needed for the payoff. She soon discovered that someone had been in her bank account, transferring money at will. The hackers had changed the password. The system crashed immediately.

As soon as she had opened the doors to her new store, McCormick had to close them. What should she do to get her store up and running again? How can she prevent this from happening in the future?[121]

ENDNOTES

1. "The Vermont Teddy Bear Story," *Vermont Teddy Bear Company*, accessed March 24, 2012, www.vermontteddybear.com/Static/Our-Story.aspx; "Vermont Teddy Bear Company," *Score.org*, accessed March 24, 2012, www.score.org/success-stories/vermont-teddy-bear-company.

2. "The Vermont Teddy Bear Story," *Vermont Teddy Bear Company*, accessed March 24, 2012, www.vermontteddybear.com/Static/Our-Story.aspx.

3. Telephone interview with Jay Bruns, vice president of branding, Vermont Teddy Bear Company, March 9, 2012.

4. Portland Helmich, "Not Your Average Bear," *Business People Vermont*, 2002, accessed March 24, 2012, www.vermontguides.com/2002/2-feb/teddybear.htm.

5. Telephone interview with Victor Castro, director of e-commerce, Vermont Teddy Bear Company, March 9, 2012.

6. Kelly Wright, "E-Commerce vs. E-Business," *Poole College of Management*, November 27, 2002, accessed October 10, 2011, scm.ncsu.edu/scm-articles/article/e-commerce-vs-e-business.

7. Terri C. Albert and William B. Sanders, *e-Business Marketing* (Upper Saddle River, NJ: Prentice-Hall, 2003), 2–4; and Efraim Turban et al., *Electronic Commerce: A Managerial Perspective* (Upper Saddle River, NJ: Pearson/Prentice Hall, 2008), 4.

8. Lena L. West, "Business Intelligence: The Crystal Ball of Champions," *Small Business Computing.com*, April 11, 2006, accessed October 10, 2011, www.smallbusinesscomputing.com/biztools/article.php/3598131/Business-Intelligence-The-Crystal-Ball-of-Champions.htm.

9. Efraim Turban et al., *Electronic Commerce: A Managerial Perspective* (Upper Saddle River, NJ: Pearson/Prentice Hall, 2008), 759.

10. "What Is CRM?," cestinationCRM.com, February 19, 2010, accessed October 10, 2011, www.destinationcrm.com/Articles/CRM-News/Daily-News/What-is-CRM-46033.aspx.

11. Thomas Wailgum and Ben Worthen, "Supply Chain Management Definition and Solutions," *CIO*, November 20, 2008, accessed October 10, 2011, www.cio.com/article/40940/Supply_Chain_Management_Definition_and_Solutions.

12. Mary O. Foley, "ERP for Small Business: The Time is Ripe," *Inc.*, October 1, 2007, accessed October 10, 2011, technology.inc.com/2007/10/01/erp-for-small-business-the-time-is-ripe.

13. Dachary Carey, "What Is Intranet Technology Used For?," *Life123*, accessed October 10, 2011, www.life123.com/technology/internet/intranet/what-is-intranet.shtml.

14. Gerry Blackwell, "Altogether Now: Comparing Collaboration Software," *Small Business Computing.com*, January 28, 2008, accessed October 10, 2011, www.smallbusinesscomputing.com/buyersguide/article.php/10729_3724501_/Altogether-Now-Comparing-Collaboration-Software.htm.

15. "7 Things You Should Know about Wikis," *Educause Learning Initiative*, July 2005, accessed October 10, 2011, net.educause.edu/ir/library/pdf/ELI7004.pdf.

16. "Communicate Quickly and Efficiently Through Intranets, Extranets and Portals," *Gozapit Interactive*, 2009, accessed October 10, 2011, www.gozapit.com/intranet-extranet.htm.

17. "Communicate Quickly and Efficiently Through Intranets, Extranets and Portals," *Gozapit Interactive*, 2009, accessed October 10, 2011, www.gozapit.com/intranet-extranet.htm.

18. Elias M Awad, *Electronic Commerce: From Vision to Fulfillment* (Upper Saddle River, NJ: Pearson Education, 2005), 4.

19. "E-commerce: Small Businesses Become Virtual Giants on the Internet," accessed October 10, 2011, www.score.org/system/files/become_a_virtual_giant.pdf.

20. Sandeep Krishnamurthy, *E-Commerce Management: Text and Cases* (Mason, OH: South-Western, 2003), 73.

21. Efraim Turban et al., *Electronic Commerce: A Managerial Perspective* (Upper Saddle River, NJ: Pearson/Prentice Hall, 2008), 8.

22. Kenneth C. Laudon and Carol G. Traver, *E-commerce: Business, Technology, Society* (Upper Saddle River, NJ: Prentice Hall, 2007), 58; Turban et al., 2008, 8.

23. Zorayda Ruth Andam, "e-Commerce and e-Business," *Asia and Pacific Training Centre for Information and Communication Technology for Development*, May 2003, accessed June 21, 2012, http://www.unapcict.org/ecohub/resources/e-commerce-and-e-business/at_download/attachment1.

24. Efraim Turban et al., *Electronic Commerce: A Managerial Perspective* (Upper Saddle River, NJ: Pearson/Prentice Hall, 2008), 8.

25. "Ecommerce Definition and Types of Ecommerce," *DigitSmith*, accessed October 10, 2011, www.digitsmith.com/ecommerce-definition.html.

26. "Mobile Content Soars Thanks to Device and Network Advances," *eMarketer*, August 31, 2010, accessed October 10, 2011, www.emarketer.com/Articles/Print.aspx?1007899.

27. *Free Encyclopedia of Ecommerce*, "Peer-to-Peer Technology (P2P)," accessed June 1, 2012, http://ecommerce.hostip.info/pages/840/Peer-Peer-Technology-P2P.html.

28. "Tamago Launches First Peer-to-Peer eCommerce System," *PR Leap*, October 15, 2006, accessed October 10, 2011, www.prleap.com/pr/51931.

29. Michael Rappa, "Business Models on the Web," *DigitalEnterprise.org*, January 17, 2010, accessed October 10, 2011, digitalenterprise.org/models/models.html.

30. David J. Teece, "Business Models, Business Strategy and Innovation," *Long Range Planning* 43, no. 2–3 (2010): 172–94.

31. For additional discussions of business models, see Michael Rappa, "Business Models on the Web," *DigitalEnterprise.org*, January 17, 2010, accessed October 10, 2011, digitalenterprise.org/models/models.html; and Robert D. Atkinson et al., "The Internet Economy 25 Years After .Com: Transforming Commerce & Life," *Information Technology & Innovation Foundation*, March 2010, accessed October 10, 2011, www.itif.org/files/2010-25-years.pdf.

32. "About Supply Chain Connect," *Supply Chain Connect*, accessed October 10, 2011, www.supplychainconnect.com.

33. Michael Rappa, "Business Models on the Web," *DigitalEnterprise.org*, January 17, 2010, accessed October 10, 2011, digitalenterprise.org/models/models.html.

34. Kenneth C. Laudon and Carol G. Traver, *E-Commerce: Business, Technology, Society* (Upper Saddle River, NJ: Prentice Hall, 2007), 58; Efraim Turban et al., *Electronic Commerce: A Managerial Perspective* (Upper Saddle River, NJ: Pearson/Prentice Hall, 2008), 8.

35. Heather Green, "US Ecommerce Growth to Pick Up in 2010, But Hit Mature Stride," *Bloomberg BusinessWeek*, February 2, 2009, accessed October 10, 2011, www.BusinessWeek.com/the_thread/blogspotting/archives/2009/02/us_ecommerce_gr.html.

36. Geoffrey A. Fowler, "E-Commerce Growth Slows, But Still Out-Paces Retail," *Wall Street Journal*, March 8, 2010, accessed October 10, 2011, blogs.wsj.com/digits/2010/03/08/e-commerce-growth-slows-but-still-out-paces-retail.

37. Geoffrey A. Fowler, "E-Commerce Growth Slows, But Still Out-Paces Retail," *Wall Street Journal*, March 8, 2010, accessed October 10, 2011, blogs.wsj.com/digits/2010/03/08/e-commerce-growth-slows-but-still-out-paces-retail.

38. Frank Gruber, "Exploring the Latest E-Commerce Industry Trends," *Tech Cocktail*, June 3, 2010, accessed October 10, 2011, techcocktail.com/exploring-the-latest-e-commerce-industry-trends-2010-06.

39. "Recap of Ecommerce Trends from the Internet Retailer 2010 Conference," *Tealeaf*, June 22, 2010, accessed October 10, 2011, tealeaf.typepad.com/blog/2010/06/recap-of-ecommerce-trends.html.

40. "E-Commerce Industry," *QFinance*, accessed October 10, 2011, www.qfinance.com/sector-profiles/e-commerce.

41. John Tozzi, "Gov 2.0: The Next Internet Boom," *Bloomberg BusinessWeek*, May 27, 2010, accessed October 10, 2011, www.BusinessWeek.com/smallbiz/content/may2010/sb20100526_721134.htm.

42. Steve King et al., "INTUIT Future of Small Business Report: Technology Trends and Small Business," *Intuit*, June 2007, accessed October 10, 2011, http-download.intuit.com/http.intuit/CMO/intuit/futureofsmallbusiness/SR-1037B_intuit_tech_trends.pdf.

43. Secretary of Commerce Gary Locke, "Remarks at Organization for Economic Cooperation and Development (OECD) Conference," December 9, 2009, accessed October 10, 2011, www.commerce.gov/news/secretary-speeches/2009/12/09/remarks-organization-economic-cooperation-and-development-oecd-conference.html.

44. Steve King et al., "INTUIT Future of Small Business Report: Technology Trends and Small Business," *Intuit*, June 2007, accessed October 10, 2011, http-download.intuit.com/http.intuit/CMO/intuit/futureofsmallbusiness/SR-1037B_intuit_tech_trends.pdf.

45. Steve King et al., "INTUIT Future of Small Business Report: Technology Trends and Small Business," *Intuit*, June 2007, accessed October 10, 2011, http-download.intuit.com/http.intuit/CMO/intuit/futureofsmallbusiness/SR-1037B_intuit_tech_trends.pdf.

46. Abbey Klaasen, "Twitter Proves Its Worth as a Killer App for Local Businesses," *Advertising Age*, May 18, 2009, accessed October 10, 2011, adage.com/article/digital/twitter-proves-worth-a-killer-app-local-businesses/136662.

47. Beverly Kracher and Cynthia L. Corritore, "Is There a Special E-Commerce Ethics?," *Business Ethics Quarterly* 14, no. 1 (2004): 71–94.

48. "What Is Hosting (Web Site Hosting, Web Hosting, and Webhosting)?," accessed October 21, 2011, searchsoa.techtarget.com/definition/hosting.

49. Efraim Turban et al., *Electronic Commerce: A Managerial Perspective* (Upper Saddle River, NJ: Pearson/Prentice Hall, 2008), 758.

50. Christopher Heng, "How to Register Your Own Domain Name," *Thesitewizard.com*, 2010, accessed October 10, 2011, www.thesitewizard.com/archive/registerdomain.shtml.

51. "How Much Should a Web Site Cost?," 2010, accessed October 10, 2011, www.webpagefx.com/How-much-should-web-site-cost.html.

52. "How Much Does a Website Cost?," *Planetlink.com*, accessed October 10, 2011, www.planetlink.com/articles/how_much_does_website_cost.html.

53. "How Much Does a Website Cost?," *Planetlink.com*, accessed October 10, 2011, www.planetlink.com/articles/how_much_does_website_cost.html.

54. "How Much Does a Website Cost?," *Planetlink.com*, accessed October 10, 2011, www.planetlink.com/articles/how_much_does_website_cost.html.

55. "How Much Does a Website Cost?," *Planetlink.com*, accessed October 10, 2011, www.planetlink.com/articles/how_much_does_website_cost.html.

56. Kathleen Mykytn and Peter P. Mykytn, "The Importance of the Law for E-Commerce Strategies," *Information Systems Management* 22, no. 2 (2005): 50–56.

57. Efraim Turban et al., *Electronic Commerce: A Managerial Perspective* (Upper Saddle River, NJ: Pearson/Prentice Hall, 2008), 774.

58. "Why Protect Intellectual Property?," *StopFakes.gov*, accessed June 1, 2012, http://origin.www.stopfakes.gov/learn-about-ip/ip/why-should-i-protect-my-ip.

59. "Why Protect Intellectual Property?," *StopFakes.gov*, accessed June 1, 2012, http://origin.www.stopfakes.gov/learn-about-ip/ip/why-should-i-protect-my-ip.

60. Peter LaSorsa, "Selling Products Online: What Legal Jurisdiction," *Practical eCommerce*, November 5, 2008, accessed October 10, 2011, www.practicalecommerce.com/articles/860-Selling-Products-Online-What-Legal-Jurisdiction-Applies-.

61. Elias M. Awad, *Electronic Commerce: From Vision to Fulfillment* (Upper Saddle River, NJ: Prentice-Hall, 2005), 387.

62. Peter LaSorsa, "Selling Products Online: What Legal Jurisdiction," *Practical eCommerce*, November 5, 2008, accessed October 10, 2011, www.practicalecommerce.com/articles/860-Selling-Products-Online-What-Legal-Jurisdiction-Applies-.

63. Peter LaSorsa, "Selling Products Online: What Legal Jurisdiction," *Practical eCommerce*, November 5, 2008, accessed October 10, 2011, www.practicalecommerce.com/articles/860-Selling-Products-Online-What-Legal-Jurisdiction-Applies-.

64. Kathleen Mykytn and Peter Mykytn, "The Importance of the Law For E-Commerce Strategies," *Information Systems Management* 22, no. 2 (2005): 50–56.

65. Avshalom M. Adam, Avshalom Aderet, and Arik Sadeh, "Do Ethics Matter to E-Consumers?," *Journal of Internet Commerce* 6, no. 2 (2007): 19–34.

66. Sergio Roman, "The Ethics of Online Retailing: A Scale Development and Validation from the Consumer's Perspective," *Journal of Business Ethics*, 72 (2007): 131–48.

67. Kenneth C. Laudon and Carol G. Traver, *E-commerce: Business, Technology, Society* (Upper Saddle River, NJ: Prentice Hall, 2007), 248.

68. "Cybercrime," *TechTerms.com*, accessed October 10, 2011, www.techterms.com/definition/cybercrime.

69. "Cybercrime," *TechTerms.com*, accessed October 10, 2011, www.techterms.com/definition/cybercrime.

70. Alejandro Martinez-Cabrera, "Cybercrime Costs Firms $3.8 Million Yearly," *Computer Crime Research Center*, August 3, 2010, accessed October 10, 2011, www.crime-research.org/news/03.08.2010/3807.

71. "What Is Cybercrime?," *Symantec*, accessed October 10, 2011, us.norton.com/cybercrime/definition.jsp; and "Cyber Crime 'More Profitable Than Drugs'," *9News*, June 9, 2009, accessed October 10, 2011, news.smh.com.au/breaking-news-national/cyber-crime-more-profitable-than-drugs-20090609-c1qm.html.

72. Rudolph Muller, "Cybercrime Getting More Sophisticated," *Mybroadband*, June 24, 2010, accessed October 10, 2011, mybroadband.co.za/news/internet/13279-Cybercrime-getting-more-sophisticated.html.

73. "Computer Crime & Intellectual Property Section," US Department of Justice, accessed October 10, 2011, www.cybercrime.gov.

74. Tim Wilson, "Small Business: The New Black in Cybercrime Targets," *Dark Reading*, March 19, 2009, accessed October 10, 2011, www.darkreading.com/security/perimeter-security/215901301/small-business-the-new-black-in-cybercrime-targets.html.

75. Tim Wilson, "Small Business: The New Black in Cybercrime Targets," *Dark Reading*, March 19, 2009, accessed October 10, 2011, www.darkreading.com/security/perimeter-security/215901301/small-business-the-new-black-in-cybercrime-targets.html.

76. Avshalom M. Adam, Avshalom Aderet, and Arik Sadeh, "Do Ethics Matter to E-Consumers?," *Journal of Internet Commerce* 6, no.2 (2007): 19–34.

77. Naresh K. Malhotra, Sung S. Kim, and James Agarwal, "Internet Users' Information Privacy Concerns (IUIPC): The Construct, the Scale and a Causal Model," *Information Systems Research* 15, no. 4 (2004): 289–304, as cited in Avshalom M. Adam, Avshalom Aderet, and Arik Sadeh, "Do Ethics Matter to E-Consumers?," *Journal of Internet Commerce* 6, no.2 (2007): 19–34.

78. Sergio Roman, "The Ethics of Online Retailing: A Scale Development and Validation from the Consumer's Perspective," *Journal of Business Ethics*, 72 (2007): 131–48.

79. Beverly Kracher and Cynthia L. Corritore, "Is There a Special E-Commerce Ethics?," *Business Ethics Quarterly* 14, no. 1 (2004): 71–94.

80. Eric Larkin, "Massive Theft of Credit Card Numbers Reported," *PCWorld*, January 20, 2009, accessed October 10, 2011, www.pcworld.com/article/158003/massive_theft_of_credit_card_numbers_reported.html.

81. "Javelin Study Finds Identity Fraud Reached New High in 2008, but Consumers Are Fighting Back," *Javelin Strategy and Research*, February 10, 2010, accessed October 10, 2011, www.javelinstrategy.com/news/831/92/Javelin-Study-Finds-Identity-Fraud-Reached-New-High-but-Consumers-are-Fighting-Back/d.pressRoomDetail.

82. "FAQ: SSL Basics," *VeriSign Authentication Services*, 2011, accessed October 10, 2011, www.verisign.com/ssl/ssl-information-center/ssl-basics.

83. Albert J. Marcella, *Establishing Trust in Virtual Markets* (Altamonte Springs, FL: The Institute of Internal Auditors, 1999), as cited in Beverly Kracher and Corritore, "Is There A Special E-Commerce Ethics?," *Business Ethics Quarterly* 14, no. 1 (2004): 71–94.

84. Avshalom Adam, Avshalom Aderet, and Arik Sadeh, "Do Ethics Matter to E-Consumers?," *Journal of Internet Commerce* 6, no. 2 (2007): 19–34; and Andrea Everard and Dennis F. Galletta, "How Presentation Flaws Affect Perceived Site Quality, Trust, and Intention to Purchase from an Online Store," *Journal of Management Information Systems* 22, no. 3 (2005–6): 55–95; William Hampton-Sosa and Marios Koufaris, "The Effect of Web Site Perceptions on Initial Trust in the Owner Company," *International Journal of Electronic Commerce* 10, no. 1 (2005): 55–81; Beverly Kracher and Cynthia L. Corritore, "Is There a Special E-Commerce Ethics?," *Business Ethics Quarterly* 14, no. 1 (2004): 71–94; and Sergio Roman, "The Ethics of Online Retailing: A Scale Development and Validation from the Consumers' Perspective," *Journal of Business Ethics* 72 (2007): 131–48.

85. Terry Newholm et al., "Multi-Story Trust and Online Retailer Strategies," *International Review of Retail, Distribution and Consumer Research*, 14, no. 4 (2004): 437–56.

86. Sergio Roman, "The Ethics of Online Retailing: A Scale Development and Validation from the Consumers' Perspective," *Journal of Business Ethics* 72 (2007): 131–48.

87. Sergio Roman, "The Ethics of Online Retailing: A Scale Development and Validation from the Consumers' Perspective," *Journal of Business Ethics* 72 (2007): 131–48.

88. Ye Diana Wang and Henry H. Emurian, "Trust in E-Commerce: Consideration of Interface Design Factors," *Journal of Electronic Commerce in Organizations* 3, no. 4 (2005): 42–60.

89. "Tealeaf Survey Reveals That Online Retailers Potentially Lost More Than $44 Billion Due to Transaction Problems on Their Sites," *Tealeaf*, September 27, 2010, accessed October 10, 2011, www.tealeaf.com/news/news-releases/2010/Tealeaf-Survey-Reveals-Online-Retailers-Potentially-Lost.php.

90. "Tealeaf Survey Reveals That Online Retailers Potentially Lost More Than $44 Billion Due to Transaction Problems on Their Sites," *Tealeaf*, September 27, 2010, accessed October 10, 2011, www.tealeaf.com/news/news-releases/2010/Tealeaf-Survey-Reveals-Online-Retailers-Potentially-Lost.php.

91. "Tealeaf Survey Reveals That Online Retailers Potentially Lost More Than $44 Billion Due to Transaction Problems on Their Sites," *Tealeaf*, September 27, 2010, accessed October 10, 2011, www.tealeaf.com/news/news-releases/2010/Tealeaf-Survey-Reveals-Online-Retailers-Potentially-Lost.php.

92. Delilah Obie, "Choosing a Vendor to Process Your Online Transactions," *SCORE*, accessed October 10, 2011, www.score.org/resources/online-transactions-vendor; "How to Increase Sales with Online Payment Options," March 22, 2010, accessed October 10, 2011, www.openforum.com/idea-hub/topics/money/article/how-to-increase-sales-with-online-payment-options-thursday-bram; "More Payment Options Can Mean More Business," *MivaCentral*, 2009, accessed October 10, 2011, mivacentral.com/articles/payment.mv; T. Brandon, "Multiple Payment Processing Options Increase Sales," *eZine Articles*, October 21, 2007, accessed October 10, 2011, ezinearticles.com/?Multiple-Payment-Processing-Options-Increase-Sales&id=793303; and Efraim Turban et al., *Electronic Commerce: A Managerial Perspective* (Upper Saddle River, NJ: Pearson/Prentice Hall, 2008).

93. "Online Retail Payments Forecast 2010–2014: Alternative Payments Growth Strong but Credit Card Projected for Comeback," *Javelin Strategy and Research*, February 2010, accessed October 10, 2011, www.javelinstrategy.com/research/Brochure-171.

94. Delilah Obie, "Choosing a Vendor to Process Your Online Transactions," *SCORE*, accessed October 10, 2011, www.score.org/resources/online-transactions-vendor.

95. "More Payment Options Can Mean More Business," *MivaCentral*, 2009, accessed October 10, 2011, mivacentral.com/articles/payment.mv.

96. Ross Dawson, "Six Ways Technology Is Transforming Small Business," *Ross Dawson Blog*, November 18, 2009, accessed October 10, 2011, rossdawsonblog.com/weblog/archives/2009/11/six_ways_techno.html.

97. "Ecommerce Integration," *Treehouse Logic*, May 20, 2010, accessed October 10, 2011, blog.treehouselogic.com/2010/05/20/ecommerce-integration.

98. Justin Whitney, "What Is Web Analytics?," *AllBusiness.com*, 2010, accessed October 10, 2011, www.allbusiness.com/marketing-advertising/marketing-advertising/11382028-1.html.

99. James Macguire, "Starting Your Own E-Business, Pt 2: Choosing a Platform," *ecommerce-guide.com*, September 26, 2005, accessed October 10, 2011, www.ecommerce-guide.com/solutions/building/article.php/3551461.

100. "E-commerce Platforms Offer Retailers New Social and Mobile Features, *Internet Retailer*, April 22, 2010, accessed October 10, 2011, www.internetretailer.com/ECTR/article.asp?id=34549.

101. Efraim Turban et al., *Electronic Commerce: A Managerial Perspective* (Upper Saddle River, NJ: Pearson/Prentice Hall, 2008), 75.

102. Perry Norgarb, "Does Your Small Business Even Need a CRM Software Solution?," *SmallBizCRM*, accessed October 10, 2011, www.smallbizcrm.com/does-your-small-business-need-a-software-solution.html.

103. Peter Norgarb, "So Where Do You Start? How Do You Start?," 2010, www.smallbizcrm.com.

104. Peter Norgarb, "So Where Do You Start? How Do You Start?," 2010, www.smallbizcrm.com.

105. Laurie McCabe, "Mobile Commerce: Coming to Ecommerce Sites Near You," *ecommerce-guide.com*, September 14, 2010, accessed October 10, 2011, www.ecommerce-guide.com/news/trends/article.php/3903526/Mobile-Commerce-Coming-to-Ecommerce-Sites-Near-You.htm.

106. Ian Mansfield, "US Mobile Ecommerce Revenues Set to Rise to $23.8bn in 2015, *Cellular-News*, April 14, 2010, accessed October 10, 2011, www.cellular-news.com/story/42341.php.

107. Brendan Gibbons, "To Tap Mobile Buyers, First Determine Their Needs," *Practical eCommerce*, March 16, 2010, accessed October 10, 2011, www.practicalecommerce.com/articles/1732-To-Tap-Mobile-Buyers-First-Determine-Their-Needs.

108. Jim Jansen, "Online Product Research: 58% of Americans Have Researched a Product or Service Online," September 29, 2010, accessed October 10, 2011, http://pewinternet.org/Reports/2010/Online-Product-Research.aspx; "Majority of Online Retailers Plan to Have Mobile Ecommerce Websites by 2011," *Deluxe for Business*, August 20, 2010, accessed October 10, 2011, http://deluxesmallbizblog.com/web-design/search-marketing/majority-of-online-retailers-plan-to-have-mobile-ecommerce-websites-by-2011; Laurie McCabe, "Mobile Commerce: Coming to Ecommerce Sites Near You," *ecommerce-guide.com*, September 14, 2010, accessed October 10, 2011, www.ecommerce-guide.com/news/trends/article.php/3903526/Mobile-Commerce-Coming-to-Ecommerce-Sites-Near-You.htm; Ian Mansfield, "Mobile Internet Devices Expected to Surpass One Billion by 2013," *Cellular-News*, December 9, 2009, accessed October 10, 2011, www.cellular-news.com/story/40997.php; John Lawson, "75% of Online Retailers Are Ramping Up Mobile Strategies," *ColderICE*, accessed June 1,

2012, http://colderice.com/75-of-online-retailers-are-ramping-up-mobile-strategies/; Aaron Smith, "Mobile Access 2010," *Pew Internet & American Life Project*, July 7, 2010, accessed October 10, 2011, www.pewinternet.org/Reports/2010/Mobile-Access-2010.aspx; and Ian Mansfield, "US Mobile Ecommerce Revenues Set to Rise to $23.8bn in 2015, *Cellular-News*, April 14, 2010, accessed October 10, 2011, www.cellular-news.com/story/42841.php.

109. Stuart J. Johnston, "Small Business Ecommerce Trends: Shop by Smartphone," *Small Business Computing.com*, September 7, 2010, accessed October 10, 2011, www.smallbusinesscomputing.com/news/article.php/3902136/Small-Business-Ecommerce-Trends-Shop-by-Smartphone.html.

110. "Majority of Online Retailers Plan to Have Mobile Ecommerce Websites by 2011," *Deluxe for Business*, August 20, 2010, accessed October 10, 2011, deluxesmallbizblog.com/web-design/search-marketing/majority-of-online-retailers-plan-to-have-mobile-ecommerce-websites-by-2011.

111. Steve Strauss, "Maximizing Your Web Presence Is Key to Building Your Small Business," *USA Today*, April 11, 2010, accessed October 10, 2011, www.usatoday.com/money/smallbusiness/columnist/strauss/2010-04-11-building-web-presence_N.htm.

112. Steve Strauss, "Maximizing Your Web Presence Is Key to Building Your Small Business," *USA Today*, April 11, 2010, accessed October 10, 2011, www.usatoday.com/money/smallbusiness/columnist/strauss/2010-04-11-building-web-presence_N.htm.

113. Heather Claney, "Small Businesses Apparently Slow to Adopt Web 2.0 Philosophies," *IT Knowledge Exchange*, June 29, 2008, accessed October 10, 2011, itknowledgeexchange.techtarget.com/channel-marker/small-businesses-apparently-slow-to-adopt-web-20-philosophies.

114. Anita Campbell, "Real Life Examples of Business Owners Using Social Media," *Small Business Trends*, July 3, 2008, accessed October 10, 2011, smallbiztrends.com/2008/07/real-life-examples-of-business-owners-using-social-media.html.

115. Sang-Heui Lee, David DeWester, and So Ra Park, "Web 2.0 and Opportunities for Small Businesses," *Service Business* 2, no. 4 (2008): 335–45.

116. Efthymios Constantinides and Stefan J. Fountain, "Web 2.0: Conceptual Foundations and Marketing Issues," *Journal of Direct, Data and Digital Marketing Practice* 9, no. 3 (2008): 231–44.

117. Tamir Dotan, "How Can eBusiness Improve Customer Satisfaction? Case Studies in the Financial Service Industry," *University of Amsterdam*, accessed October 10, 2011, www.tamirdotan.com/e-business%20Article.html.

118. Dave Roos, "Advantages of E-commerce," *How Stuff Works*, 2010, accessed October 10, 2011, communication.howstuffworks.com/advantages-e-commerce.htm.

119. Brian Halligan, "Four Ways the Internet Is Transforming Small Business," *HubSpot Blog*, October 2, 2006, accessed October 10, 2011, blog.hubspot.com/blog/tabid/6307/bid/50/Four-Ways-the-Internet-Is-Transforming-Small-Business.aspx.

120. Sang-Heui Lee, David DeWester, and So Ra Park, "Web 2.0 and Opportunities for Small Businesses," *Service Business* 2, no. 4 (2008): 335–45.

121. Jake Lynch, "Hackers Set Sights on Small Businesses, Households," *Issaquah Reporter*, August 19, 2010, accessed October 10, 2011, www.pnwlocalnews.com/east_king/iss/news/101077494.html.

The Business Plan

Consolidated Industries' Hammer Forge

Source: Used with permission from Consolidated Industries.

Consolidated Industries represents one of the thousands of small manufacturers that exist throughout the United States. It has been in business for more than sixty years, specializing in the forging of ferrous, nonferrous, and exotic materials. Its prime customer base has been the aerospace industry, but it has also expanded into other industrial customers.

Originally a family business, Consolidated Industries was sold to new owners in 1999. Once the owner reached retirement age, his children, a brother and sister, found it difficult to agree on the future direction of the company. This period of confusion was made more difficult when the head of sales died. Competitors exploited this situation. The new CEO—John Wilbur—immediately recognized that there had been some complacency about generating new customers, and the firm would not be able to survive in the long run merely on its backlog of orders. Wilbur began to aggressively deal with the firm's problems and build its customer base. In ten years, he was able to take Consolidated Industries' sales from $8 million a year to $30 million a year. He attributes much of this success to the firm's commitment to business planning.

Soon after taking over the business, he started a comprehensive planning process. Given the pressing issues the firm was facing, the first plan had a one-year horizon. It was instrumental in gaining the support of Consolidated Industries' bankers, which carried it through those difficult years. In the intervening years, the plan's horizon was expanded to five years. Although Wilbur admitted that the projections may be "pipe dreams" after the first two years, he said it was important to maintain the five-year horizon to force the business to think about the future. The main goals of the plan had been to examine ways to lower costs and expand the customer base, particularly outside the aerospace industry.

The plan would be constantly evolving; detailed metrics would provide guidance to the various units throughout the firm. These metrics were broken down on a quarterly basis and were color coded to allow the various units to see how well they were progressing toward the achievement of the goals and the objectives. It had a detailed sales plan that emphasized developing new customers in new industries. To this end, it significantly focused on developing new products. In the past few years, the number of new products increased from six per year to seventy-seven per year. This meant an enlargement of the engineering staff, but it is also meant a much closer relationship with customers. Wilbur estimated that 50 percent of the new products were a codesign with customers. The planning process also enabled the business to incorporate technology in new ways. The firm used videoconferencing to communicate with both customers and sister units. Another important element of the plan was the concept of succession planning. As vital as the planning process was, Wilbur said that "it is all about people. Any plan to improve the firm has to bring people into the process and bring them together."

1. DEVELOPING YOUR STRATEGY

LEARNING OBJECTIVES

1. Understand the term *strategy* and why it is important for small business.
2. Define the four generic strategies identified by Porter.
3. Evaluate the ramifications of each generic strategy for the operations of a small business.

Without a strategy, the organization is like a ship without a rudder, going around in circles.

- *Joel Ross and Michael Kami*

As mentioned in Chapter 2, it is critically important for any business organization to be able to accurately understand and identify what constitutes customer value. To do this, one must have a clear idea of who your customers are or will be. However, simply identifying customer value is insufficient. An organization must be able to provide customer value within several important constraints. One of these constraints deals with the competition—what offerings are available and at what price. Also, what additional services might a company provide? A second critically important constraint is the availability of resources to the business organization. Resources consist of factors such as money, facilities, equipment, operational capability, and personnel.

Here is an example: a restaurant identified its prime customer base as being upscale clientele in the business section of a major city. The restaurant recognized that it has numerous competitors that are interested in providing the same clientele with an upscale dining experience. Our example restaurant might provide a five-course, five-star gourmet meal to its customers. It also provides superlative service. If a comparable restaurant failed to provide a comparable meal than the example restaurant, the example restaurant would have a competitive advantage. If the example restaurant offered these sumptuous meals for a relatively low price in comparison to its competitors, it would initially seem to have even more of an advantage. However, if the price charged is significantly less than the cost of providing the meal, the service in this situation could not be maintained. In fact, the restaurant inevitably would have to go out of business. Providing excellent customer service may be a necessary condition for business survival but, in and of itself, it is not a sufficient condition.

So how does one go about balancing the need to provide customer value within the resources available while always maintaining a watchful eye on competitors' actions? We are going to argue that what is required for that firm is to have a **strategy**.

strategy

The path by which a firm seeks to provide its customers with value, given the competitive environment and within the constraints of the resources available to the firm.

The word *strategy* is derived from the Greek word *strategos*, which roughly translates into the art of the general, namely a military leader. Generals are responsible for marshaling required resources and organizing the troops and the basic plan of attack. Much in the same way, executives as owners of businesses are expected to have a general idea of the desired outcomes, acquire resources, hire and train personnel, and generate plans to achieve those outcomes. In this sense, all businesses, large and small, have strategies, whether they are clearly written out in formal business plans or reside in the mind of the owner of the business.

There are many different formal definitions of strategy with respect to business. The following is a partial listing of some of the definitions given by key experts in the field:

A strategy is a pattern of objectives, purposes or goals and the major policies and plans for achieving these goals, stated in such a way as to define what business the company is in or is to be in and the kind of company it is or to be.[1]

- *Kenneth Arrow*

The determination of the long-run goals and objectives of an enterprise, and the adoption of courses of action and the allocation of resources necessary for carrying out these goals.[2]

- *Alfred Chandler*

What business strategy is all about, in a word, is competitive advantage.[3]

- *Kenichi Ohmae*

We define the strategy of a business as follows: *A firm's strategy is the path by which it seeks to provide its customers with value, given the competitive environment and within the constraints of the resources available to the firm.*

Whatever definition of strategy is used, it is often difficult to separate it from two other terms: strategic planning and strategic management. Both terms are often perceived as being in the domain of large corporations, not necessarily small to midsize businesses. This is somewhat understandable. The origin of strategic planning as a separate discipline occurred over fifty years ago. It was mainly concerned with assisting huge multidivisional or global businesses in coordinating their activities. In the intervening half-century, strategic planning has produced a vast quantity of literature. Mintzberg, Lampel, Ahlstrand, in a highly critical review of the field, identified ten separate schools associated with strategic planning.[4] With that number of different schools, it is clear that the discipline has not arrived at a common consensus. Strategic planning has been seen as a series of techniques and tools that would enable organizations to achieve their specified goals and objectives. Strategic management was seen as the organizational mechanisms by which you would implement the strategic plan. Some of the models and approaches associated with strategic planning and strategic management became quite complex and would prove to be fairly cumbersome to implement in all but the largest businesses. Further, strategic planning often became a bureaucratic exercise where people filled out forms, attended meetings, and went through the motions to produce a document known as the strategic plan. Sometimes what is missed in this discussion was a key element—strategic thinking. Strategic thinking is the creative analysis of the competitive landscape and a deep understanding of customer value. It should be the driver (see Figure 5.1) of the entire process. This concept is often forgotten in large bureaucratic organizations.

FIGURE 5.1 Strategy Troika

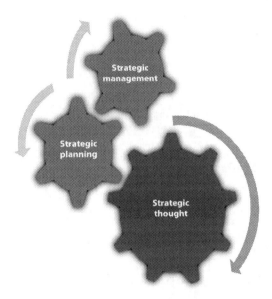

Strategic thinkers often break commonly understood principles to reach their goals. This is most clearly seen among military leaders, such as Alexander the Great or Hannibal. Robert E. Lee often violated basic military principles, such as dividing his forces. General Douglas MacArthur shocked the North Koreans with his bold landings behind enemy lines at Inchon. This mental flexibility also exists in great business leaders.

Solomon and Friedman recounted a prime example of true strategic thinking.[5] Wilson Harrell took a small, closely held, cleaning spray company known as Formula 409 to the point of having national distribution. In 1967, the position that Formula 409 held was threatened by the possible entry of Procter & Gamble into the same spray cleaning market. Procter & Gamble was a huge consumer products producer, noted for its marketing savvy. Procter & Gamble began a program of extensive market research to promote its comparable product they called Cinch. Clearly, the larger firm had a much greater advantage. Harrell knew that Procter & Gamble would perform test market research. He decided to do the unexpected. Rather than directly confront this much larger competitor, he began a program where he reduced advertising expenditures in Denver and stopped promoting his Formula 409. The outcome was that Procter & Gamble had spectacular results, and the company was extremely excited with the potential for Cinch. Procter & Gamble immediately begin a national sales campaign. However, before the company could begin, Harrell introduced a promotion of his own. He took the Formula 409 sixteen-ounce bottle and attached it to a half-gallon size bottle. He then sold both at a significant discount. This quantity of spray cleaner would last the average consumer six to nine months. The market for Procter & Gamble's Cinch was significantly reduced. Procter & Gamble was confused and confounded by its poor showing after the phenomenal showing in Denver. Confused and uncertain, the company chose to withdraw Cinch from the market. Wilson Harrell's display of brilliant strategic thinking had bested them. He leveraged his small company's creative thinking and flexibility against the tremendous resources of an international giant. Through superior strategic thinking, Harrell was able to best Procter & Gamble.

Video Clip 5.1

What Is Strategy?
Michael Porter of Harvard Business School provides a brief discussion of what strategy is.

View the video online at: http://www.youtube.com/v/ibrxlP0H84M

 Video Clip 5.2

Strategic Thinking and the Definition of Strategy
A Center for Management Organization and Effectiveness (CMOE) discussion of strategy; it leads to other similar videos.

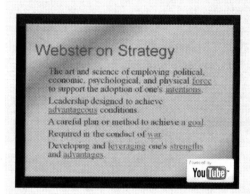

View the video online at: http://www.youtube.com/v/cgwDm_ABVA8

 Video Clip 5.3

Strategic Thinking—Develop Strategic Thinking Skills to Give Yourself a Competitive Edge
Follow-up CMOE video on strategic thinking.

View the video online at: http://www.youtube.com/v/R3Niq91bXqs

Video Clip 5.4

Strategic Thinking and Management for Competitive Advantage
Two Wharton professors discuss how strategic thinking is critical to the acquisition of competitive advantage.

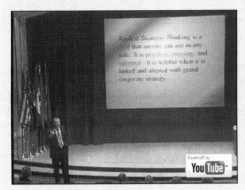

View the video online at: http://www.youtube.com/v/R3Niq91bXqs

Video Clip 5.5

Mastering Strategic Thinking Workshop
A professor discusses the importance of strategic thinking for leadership.

View the video online at: http://www.youtube.com/v/FbCOF1wl1dA

Video Clip 5.6

From Strategic Thinking to Planning
A speaker illustrates that successful plans are tied to strategic thinking.

View the video online at: http://www.youtube.com/v/3rsF6dOAth4

1.1 Do You Have a Strategy and What Is It?

We have argued that all businesses have strategies, whether they are explicitly articulated or not. Perry stated that "small business leaders seem to recognize that the ability to formulate and implement an effective strategy has a major influence on the survival and success of small business."[6]

The extent to which a strategy should be articulated in a formal manner, such as part of a business plan, is highly dependent on the type of business. One might not expect a formally drafted strategy statement for a nonemployee business funded singularly by the owner. One researcher found that formal plans are rare in businesses with fewer than five employees.[7] However, you should clearly have that expectation for any other type of small or midsize business.

Any business with employees should have an articulated strategy that can be conveyed to them so that they might better assist in implementing it. Curtis pointed out that in the absence of such communication, "employees make pragmatic short-term decisions that cumulatively form an ad-hoc strategy."[8] These ad hoc (realized) strategies may be at odds with the planned (intended) strategies to guide a firm.[9] However, any business that seeks external funding from bankers, venture capitalists, or "angels" must be able to specify its strategy in a formal business plan.

Clearly specifying your strategy should be seen as an end in itself. Requiring a company to specify its strategy forces that company to think about its core issues, such as the following:

- Who are your customers?
- How are you going to provide value to those customers?
- Who are your current and future competitors?
- What are your resources?
- How are you going to use these resources?

One commentator in a blog put it fairly well, "It never ceases to amaze me how many people will use GPS or Google maps for a trip somewhere but when it comes to starting a business they think that the can do it without any strategy, or without any guiding road-map."[10]

1.2 Types of Strategies

In 1980, Michael Porter a professor at Harvard Business School published a major work in the field of strategic analysis—*Competitive Strategy*.[11] To simplify Porter's thesis, while competition is beneficial to customers, it is not always beneficial to those who are competing. Competition may involve lowering prices, increasing research and development (R&D), and increasing advertising and other expenses and activities—all of which can lower profit margins. Porter suggested that firms should carefully examine the industry in which they are operating and apply what he calls the five forces model. These five forces are as follows: the power of suppliers, the power of buyers, the threat of substitution, the threat of new entrants, and rivalry within the industry. We do not need to cover these five forces in any great detail, other than to say that once the analysis has been conducted, a firm should look for ways to minimize the dysfunctional consequences of competition. Porter identified four generic strategies that firms may choose to implement to achieve that end. Actually, he initially identified three generic strategies, but one of them can be bifurcated. These four strategies are as follows (see Figure 5.2): cost leadership, differentiation, cost focus, and differentiation focus. These four generic strategies can be applied to small businesses. We will examine each strategy and then discuss what is required to successfully implement them.

FIGURE 5.2 Generic Strategies

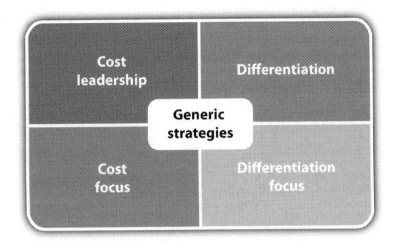

Low-Cost Advantage

A **cost leadership** strategy requires that a firm be in the position of being the lowest cost producer in its competitive environment. By being the lowest cost producer, a firm has several strategic options open to it. It can sell its product or service at a lower price than its competitors. If price is a major driver of customer value, then the firm with the lowest price should sell more. The low-cost producer also has the option of selling its products or services at prices that are comparable to its competitors. However, this would mean that the firm would have a much higher margin than its competitors.

Obviously, following a cost leadership strategy dictates that the business be good at curtailing costs. Perhaps the clearest example of a firm that employs a cost leadership strategy is Walmart. Walmart's investment in customer relations and inventory control systems plus its huge size enables it to secure the "best" deals from suppliers and drastically reduce costs. It might appear that cost leadership strategies are most suitable for large firms that can exploit economies of scale. This is not necessarily true. Smaller firms can compete on the basis of cost leadership. They can position themselves in low-cost areas, and they can exploit their lower overhead costs. Family businesses can use family members as employees, or they can use a web presence to market and sell their goods and services. A small family-run luncheonette that purchases used equipment and offers a limited menu of standard breakfast and lunch items while not offering dinner might be good example of a small business that has opted for a cost leadership strategy.

Differentiation

A **differentiation** strategy involves providing products or services that meet customer value in some unique way. This uniqueness may be derived in several ways. A firm may try to build a particular brand image that differentiates itself from its competitors. Many clothing lines, such as Tommy Hilfiger, opt for this approach. Other firms will try to differentiate themselves on the basis of the services that they provide. Dominoes began to distinguish itself from other pizza firms by emphasizing the speed of its delivery. Differentiation also can be achieved by offering a unique design or features in the product or the service. Apple products are known for their user-friendly design features. A firm may wish to differentiate itself on the basis of the quality of its product or service. Kogi barbecue trucks operating in Los Angeles represent such an approach. They offer high-quality food from mobile food trucks.[12] They further facilitate their differentiation by having their truck routes available on their website and on their Twitter account.

Adopting a differentiation strategy requires significantly different capabilities than those that were outlined for cost leadership. Firms that employ a differentiation strategy must have a complete understanding of what constitutes customer value. Further, they must be able to rapidly respond to changing customer needs. Often, a differentiation strategy involves offering these products and services at a premium price. A differentiation strategy may accept lower sales volumes because a firm is charging higher prices and obtaining higher profit margins. A danger in this approach is that customers may no longer place a premium value on the unique features or quality of the product or the service. This leaves the firm that offers a differentiation strategy open to competition from those that adopt a cost leadership strategy.

cost leadership

A firm is in the position of being the lowest cost producer in its competitive environment.

differentiation

A firm provides products or services that meet customer value in some unique way.

Focus—Low Cost or Differentiation

cost focus

A firm seeks to provide value through low cost for a *subset* of the market given the competitive environment and within the constraints of the resources available to the firm.

differentiation focus

A firm concentrates on providing a unique product or service to a segment of the market.

Porter identifies the third strategy—focus. He said that focus strategies can be segmented into a **cost focus** and a **differentiation focus**.

In a focus strategy, a firm concentrates on one or more segments of the overall market. Focus can also be described as a niche strategy. Focus strategy entails deciding to some extent that we do not want to have everyone as a customer. There are several ways that a firm can adopt a focus perspective:

- **Product line.** A firm limits its product line to specific items of only one or more product types. California Cart Builder produces only catering trucks and mobile kitchens.
- **Customer.** A firm concentrates on serving the needs of a particular type of customer. Weight Watchers concentrates on customers who wish to control their weight or lose weight.
- **Geographic area.** Many small firms, out of necessity, will limit themselves to a particular geographic region. Microbrewers generally serve a limited geographic region.
- **Particular distribution channel.** Firms may wish to limit themselves with respect to the means by which they sell their products and services. Amazon began and remains a firm that sells only through the Internet.

Firms adopting focus strategies look for distinct groups that may have been overlooked by their competitors. This group needs to be of sufficiently sustainable size to make it an economically defensible option. One might open a specialty restaurant in a particular geographic location—a small town. However, if the demand is not sufficiently large for this particular type of food, then the restaurant will probably fail. Companies that lack the resources to compete on either a national level or an industry-wide level may adopt focus strategies. Focus strategies enable firms to marshal their limited resources to best serve their customers.

As previously stated, focus strategies can be bifurcated into two directions—cost focus or differentiation focus. IKEA sells low-priced furniture to those customers who are willing to assemble the furniture. It cuts its costs by using a warehouse rather than showroom format and not providing home delivery. Michael Dell began his business out of his college dormitory. He took orders from fellow students and custom-built computers to their specifications. This was a cost focus strategy. By building to order, it almost totally eliminated the need for any incoming, work-in-process, or finished goods inventories.

A focus differentiation strategy concentrates on providing a unique product or service to a segment of the market. This strategy may be best represented by many specialty retail outlets. The Body Shop focuses on customers who want natural ingredients in their makeup. Max and Mina is a kosher specialty ice cream store in New York City. It provides a constantly rotating menu of more than 300 exotic flavors, such as Cajun, beer, lox, corn, and pizza. The store has been written up in the *New York Times* and *People* magazine. Given its odd flavors, Max and Mina's was voted the number one ice cream parlor in America in 2004.[13]

1.3   Evaluating Strategies

The selection of a generic strategy by a firm should not be seen as something to be done on a whim. Once a strategy is selected, all aspects of the business must be tied to implementing that strategy. As Porter stated, "Effectively implementing any of these generic strategies usually requires total commitment and supporting organizational arrangements."[14] The successful implementation of any generic strategy requires that a firm possess particular skills and resources. Further, it must impose particular requirements on its organization (see Table 5.1).

Even successful generic strategies must recognize that market and economic conditions change along with the needs of consumers. Henry Ford used a cost leadership strategy and was wildly successful until General Motors began to provide different types of automobiles to different customer segments. Likewise, those who follow a differentiation strategy must be cautious that customers may forgo "extras" in a downturn economy in favor of lower costs. This requires businesses to be vigilant, particularly with respect to customer value.

TABLE 5.1 Summary of Generic Strategies

Generic Strategy	Required Activities	Issues
Cost leadership	<ul><li>Economies of scale</li><li>Reduce overhead costs</li><li>Lower cost of supplies</li><li>Capital investment in technology to reduce cost</li><li>Labor cost reduction through supervision, outsourcing, and work design</li><li>Low-cost distribution</li><li>Reduce cost of manufacturing or providing service</li><li>Tight financial control</li><li>Operate in lower cost environments</li><li>Production-based incentives</li></ul>	<ul><li>Product or service becomes a commodity with no brand loyalty</li><li>Changing technology cuts your cost advantage</li><li>New entrants can produce at even lower costs (e.g., China)</li><li>Focus on cost reduction means that you miss changing customer tastes</li></ul>
Differentiation	<ul><li>Unique or highly improved products or services</li><li>Brand image</li><li>Creative approach to marketing</li><li>Reputation for quality and product or service innovation</li><li>Ability to attract creative personnel</li><li>Effective coordination among R&D, marketing, and operations</li></ul>	<ul><li>Qualitative difference between you and low-cost producer may not be enough to sustain sales</li><li>Differentiating factor may no longer be attractive to customers</li><li>Imitation narrows perceived differences</li></ul>
Focus—low cost	<ul><li>Reduce overhead costs</li><li>Lower cost of supplies</li><li>Labor cost reduction through supervision, outsourcing, and work design</li><li>Low-cost distribution</li><li>Tight financial control</li><li>Operate in lower cost environments</li><li>Production-based incentives</li></ul>	<ul><li>Cost advantage of focused firms is lost with respect to broader competitors</li><li>Differentiation advantage with a focused market is lost</li><li>Competitors find even smaller markets to focus on</li></ul>
Focus—differentiation	<ul><li>Unique or highly improved products or services</li><li>Creative approach to marketing</li><li>Reputation for quality and product/service innovation</li><li>Ability to attract creative personnel</li><li>Effective coordination among R&D, marketing, and operations</li></ul>	<ul><li>Cost advantage of focused firms is lost with respect to broader competitors</li><li>Differentiation advantage with a focused market is lost</li><li>Competitors find even smaller markets to focus on</li></ul>

Video Clip 5.7

Porter's Strategies—Generic Strategies
Examples of generic strategies.

View the video online at: http://www.youtube.com/v/ndARJzmKras

 Video Clip 5.8

The Five Competitive Forces That Shape Strategy
A long interview with Michael Porter discussing the five forces model.

View the video online at: http://www.youtube.com/v/mYF2_FBCvXw

KEY TAKEAWAYS

- Any firm, regardless of size, needs to know how it will compete; this is the firm's strategy.
- Strategy identifies how a firm will provide value to its customers within its operational constraints.
- Strategy can be reduced to four major approaches—cost leadership, differentiation, cost focus, and differentiation focus.
- Once a given strategy is selected, all of a firm's operations should be geared to implementing that strategy.
- No strategy will be successful forever and therefore needs to be constantly evaluated.

2.   THE NECESSITY FOR A BUSINESS PLAN

LEARNING OBJECTIVES

1. Understand that the probability of running a successful business is significantly increased with a formal business plan.
2. Understand that although many small business owners express reasons for not planning, they do themselves a great disservice by not having a formal plan.
3. Understand that businesses that seek to secure external funding must produce a formal plan.

An intelligent plan is the first step to success. The man who plans knows where he is going, knows what progress he is making and has a pretty good idea of when he will arrive. Planning is the open road to your destination. If you don't know where you're going, how can you expect to get there?
- *Basil Walsh*

In Chapter 1, we discussed the issue of failure and small businesses. Although research on small business failure has identified many factors, one reason that always appears at the top of any list is the failure to plan. Interestingly, some people argue that planning is not essential for a start-up business, but they are in a distinct minority.[15] The overwhelming consensus is that a well-developed plan is essential for the survival of any small (or large) business.[16],[17],[18],[19] Perry found that firms with more than five people benefit from having a well-developed business plan.[20]

A recent study found that there was a near doubling of successful growth for those businesses that completed business plans compared to those that did not create one. It must be pointed out that this study might be viewed as being biased because the founder of the software company whose main product is a program that builds business plans conducted the study. However, the results were examined by academics from the University of Oregon who validated the overall results. They found that "except in a small number of cases, business planning appeared to be positively correlated with business success as measured by our variables. While our analysis cannot say the completing of a business plan will lead to success, it does indicate that the type of entrepreneur who completes a business plan is also more likely to produce a successful business."[21]

Basically, there are two main reasons for developing a comprehensive business plan: (1) a plan will be extraordinarily useful in ensuring the successful operation of your business; and (2) if one is seeking to secure external funds from banks, venture capitalists, or other investors, it is essential that you be able to demonstrate to them that they will be recovering their money and making a profit. Let us examine each reason in detail.

Many small business owners operate under a mistaken belief that the only time that they need to create a business plan is at the birth of the company or when they are attempting to raise additional capital from external sources. They fail to realize that a business plan can be an important element in ensuring day-to-day success.

The initial planning process aids the operational success of a small business by allowing the owner a chance to review, in detail, the viability of the business idea. It forces one to rigorously consider some key questions:

- Is the business strategy feasible?
- What are the chances it will make money?
- Do I have the operational requirements for starting and running a successful business?
- Have I considered a well-thought-out marketing plan that clearly identifies who my customers will be?
- Do I clearly understand what value I will provide to these customers?

- What will be the means of distribution to provide the product or the service to my customers?
- Have I clarified to myself the financial issues associated with starting and operating the business?
- Do I have to reexamine these notions to ensure success?

Possessing an actual written plan enables you to have people outside the organization evaluate your business plan. Using friends, colleagues, partners, or even consultants may provide you with an unbiased evaluation of the assumptions.

It is not enough to create an initial business plan; you should anticipate making the planning process an annual activity. The Prussian military theorist von Moltke once argued that no military plan survives the first engagement with the enemy. Likewise, no company evolves in the same way as outlined in its initial business plan.

2.1 Overcoming the Reluctance to Formally Plan

By failing to prepare, you will prepare them to fail.
- *Benjamin Franklin*

Unfortunately, it appears that many small businesses do not make any effort to build even an initial business plan, let alone maintain a planning process as an ongoing operation, even though there is clear evidence that the failure to plan may have serious consequences for the future success of such firms. This unwillingness to plan may be understandable in nonemployee businesses, but it is inexcusable as a business grows in size. Why, therefore, do some businesses fail to begin the planning process?

- **We do not need to plan.** One of the prime reasons individuals fail to produce a business plan is that they believe that they do not have to plan. This may be attributable to the size of the firm; nonemployee firms that have no intention of seeking outside financing might sincerely believe that they have no need for a formal business plan. Others may believe that they so well understand the business and/or industry that they can survive and prosper without the *burdensome* process of a business plan. The author of *Business Plan for Dummies*, Paul Tiffany, once argued that if one feels lucky enough to operate a business successfully without resorting to a business plan, then he or she should forget about starting a business and head straight to Las Vegas.

- **I am too busy to plan.** Anyone who has ever run a business on his or her own can understand this argument. The day-to-day demands of operating a business may make it seem that there is insufficient time to engage in any ancillary activity or prepare a business plan. Individuals who accept this argument often fail to recognize that the seemingly endless buzz of activities, such as constantly putting out fires, may be the direct result of not having thought about the future and planned for it in the first place.

- **Plans do not produce results.** Small-business owners (entrepreneurs) are action- and results-oriented individuals. They want to see a tangible outcome for their efforts, and preferably they would like to see the results as soon as possible. The idea of sitting down and producing a large document based on assumptions that may not play out exactly as predicted is viewed as a futile exercise. However, those with broader experience understand that there will be no external funding for growth or the initial creation of the business without the existence of a well-thought-out plan. Although plans may not yield the specified results contained within them, the process of thinking about the plan and building it often yield results that the owner might not initially appreciate.

- **We are not familiar with the process of formal planning.** This argument might initially appear to have more validity than the others. Developing a comprehensive business plan is a daunting task. It might seem difficult if not impossible for someone with no experience with the concept. Several studies have indicated that small business owners are more likely to engage in the planning process if they have had prior experience with planning models in their prior work experience.[22] Fortunately, this situation has changed rather significantly in the last decade. As we will illustrate in Section 3, there are numerous tools that provide significant support for the development of business plans. We will see that software packages greatly facilitate the building of any business plan, including marketing plans and financial plans for small businesses. We also show that the Internet can provide an unbelievably rich source of data and information to assist in the building of these plans.

Although one could understand the reticence of someone new to small business (or in some cases even seasoned entrepreneurs), their arguments fall short with respect to the benefits that will be derived from conducting a structured and comprehensive business planning process.

2.2 Plans for Raising Capital

Every business plan should be written with a particular audience in mind. The annual business plan should be written with a management team and for the employees who have to implement the plan. However, one of the prime reasons for writing a business plan is to secure investment funds for the firm. Of course, funding the business could be done by an individual using his or her own personal wealth, personal loans, or extending credit cards. Individuals also can seek investments from family and friends. The focus here will be on three other possible sources of capital—banks, venture capitalists, and angel investors. It is important to understand what they look for in a business plan. Remember that these three groups are investors, so they will be anticipating, at the very least, the ability to recover their initial investment if not earn a significant return.

Bankers

Bankers, like all businesspeople, are interested in earning a profit; they want to see a return on their investment. However, unlike other investors, bankers are under a legal obligation to ensure that the borrower pledge some form of collateral to secure the loan.[23] This often means that banks are unwilling to fund a start-up business unless the owner is willing to pledge some form of collateral, such as a second mortgage on his or her home. Many first-time business owners are not in a position to do that; securing money from a bank occurs most frequently for an existing business that is looking to expand or for covering a short-term cash-flow need. Banks may lend to small business owners who are opening a second business provided that they can prove a record of success and profitability.

Banks will require a business plan. It should be understood that bank loan officers will initially focus on the financial components of that client, namely, the income statement, balance sheet, and the cash-flow statement. The bank will examine your projections with respect to known industry standards. Therefore, the business plan should not project a 75 percent profit margin when the industry standard is 15 percent, unless the author of the plan can clearly document why he or she will be earning such a high return.

Some businesses may raise funds with the assistance of a Small Business Administration (SBA) loan. These loans are always arranged through a commercial bank. With these loans, the SBA will pledge up to 70 percent of the total value of the loan. This means that the owner still must provide, at the very least, 30 percent of the total collateral. The ability to secure one of these loans is clearly tied to the adequacy of the business plan.

Venture Capitalists

Another possible source of funding is **venture capitalists**. The first thing that one should realize about venture capitalists is that they are not in it just to make a profit; they want to make returns that are substantially above those to be found in the market. For some, this translates into the ability to secure five to ten times their initial investment and recapture their investment in a relatively short period of time—often less than five years. It has been reported that some venture capitalists are looking for returns in the order of twenty-five times their original investment.[24]

The financial statement, particularly the profit margin, is obviously important to venture capitalists, but they will also be looking at other factors. The quality of the management team identified in the business plan will be examined. They will be looking at the team's experience and track record. Other factors needed by venture capitalists may include the projected growth rate of the market, the extent to which the product or the service being offered is unique, the overall size of the market, and the probability of producing a highly successful product or service.

Businesses that are seeking financing from banks know that they must go to loan officers who will review the plan, even though a computerized loan assessment program may make the final decision. With venture capitalists, on the other hand, you often need to have a personal introduction to have your plan considered. You should also anticipate that you will have to make a presentation to venture capitalists. This means that you have to understand your plan and be able to present it in a dynamic fashion.

venture capitalists

Individuals who provide money for start-up businesses or additional capital for a business to grow. They invest to make not only a profit but also returns that are substantially above those found in the market.

Angel Investors

angel investors

Individuals who initially invested in Broadway shows and films. As with venture capitalists, they are looking for returns higher than they can normally find in the market; however, they often are expecting returns lower than those anticipated by the venture capitalist.

The third type of investors is referred to as **angel investors**, a term that originally came from those individuals who invested in Broadway shows and films. Many angel investors are themselves successful entrepreneurs. As with venture capitalists, they are looking for returns higher than they can normally find in the market; however, they often expect returns lower than those anticipated by venture capitalist. They may be attracted to business plans because of an innovative concept or the excitement of entering a new type of business. Being successful small business owners, many angel investors will not only provide capital to fund the business but also bring their own expertise and experience to help the business grow. It has been estimated that these angel investors provide between three and ten times as much money as venture capitalists for the development of small businesses.[25]

Angel investors will pay careful attention to all aspects of the proposed business plan. They expect a comprehensive business plan—one that clearly specifies the future direction of the firm. They also will look at the management team not only for its track record and experience but also their (the angel investor's) ability to work with this team. Angel investors may take a much more active role in the management of the business, asking for positions on the board of directors, taking an equity position in the firm, demanding quarterly reports, or demanding that the business not take certain actions unless it has the approval of these angel investors. These investors will take a much more hands-on approach to the operations of a firm.

KEY TAKEAWAYS

- Planning is a critical and important component of ensuring the success of a small business.
- Some form of formal planning should not only accompany the start-up of a business but also be a regular (annual) activity that guides the future direction of the business.
- Many small business owners are reluctant to formally plan. They can produce many excuses for not planning.
- Businesses may have to raise capital from external sources—bankers, venture capitalists, or angel investors. Each type of investor will expect a business plan. Each type of investor will be more or less interested in different parts of the plan. Business owners should be aware of what parts of the plan each type of investor will focus on.

EXERCISE

1. In Exercise 2 in Section 1, you were asked to interview five local business owners. In addition to asking them questions about strategy, ask them the following questions about planning: (a) When you began the business, did you have a formal plan? (b) If not, why not? (c) Do you conduct some form of planning regularly?

3. BUILDING A PLAN

LEARNING OBJECTIVES

1. Understand that before starting a business and before writing a formal plan, individuals should ask themselves some specific questions to see if they are ready for the challenges of small business ownership.
2. Understand that any solidly written plan will require information about the competitive environment. There are many publicly available sources of such information.
3. Understand that plans are future-oriented documents that require forecasts. Forecasting can be done through a variety of methods. Planners should be familiar with a variety of forecasting methods.
4. Understand that formal business plans should contain specific sections.
5. Know that scenario planning should help businesses prepare for low-probability events that might have a significant impact on the firm.
6. Know that there are many computer software packages that can assist in building a formal business plan.

Before talking about writing a formal business plan, someone interested in starting a business might want to think about doing some personal planning before drafting the business plan. Some of the questions that he or she might want to answer before drafting a full business plan are as follows:

- Why am I going into this business?
- What skills and resources do I possess that will help make the business a success?
- What passion do I bring to this business?
- What is my risk tolerance?
- Exactly how hard do I intend to work? How many hours per week?
- What impact will the business have on my family life?
- What do I really wish from this business?
    - Am I interested in financial independence?
    - What level of profits will be required to maintain my personal and/or family's lifestyle?
    - Am I interested in independence of action (no boss but myself)?
    - Am I interested in personal satisfaction?
- Will my family be working in this business?
- What other employees might I need?[26]

Having addressed these questions, one will be in a much better position to craft a formal business plan.

 Video Clip 5.9

How to Write a Business Plan
Cartoon introduction to building a business plan.

View the video online at: http://www.youtube.com/v/3sNDdEMHoYw

Video Clip 5.10

How to Write a Business Plan in 6 Minutes—Template
Voiceover PowerPoint video.

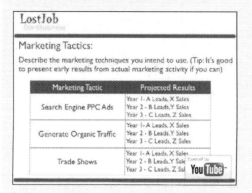

View the video online at: http://www.youtube.com/v/x9B3Ubl61CM

Video Link 5.1

Writing a Business Plan—Bloomberg: Your Money

A brief video from Bloomberg's Business of Life program.

www.videopediaworld.com/video/45083/Writing-a-Business-Plan—Bloomberg-Your-Money

 Video Clip 5.11

How to Start a Business: How to Write a Business Plan
A video from Startupdaddy.com that emphasizes the need for a business plan.

View the video online at: http://www.youtube.com/v/x0y3VgjhGw0

3.1 Gathering Information

Building a solid business plan requires knowing the economic, market, and competitive environments. Such knowledge transcends "gut feelings" and is based on data and evidence. Fortunately, much of the required information is available through library resources, Internet sources, and government agencies and, for a fee, from commercial sources. Comprehensive business plans may draw from all these sources.

Public libraries and those at educational institutions provide a rich resource base that can be used at no cost. Some basic research sources that can be found at libraries are given in this section—*be aware that the reference numbers provided may differ from library to library.*

Library Sources

Background Sources

- Berinstein, Paula. *Business Statistics on the Web: Find Them Fast—At Little or No Cost* (Ref HF1016 .B47 2003).
- *The Core Business Web: A Guide to Information Resources* (Ref HD30.37 .C67 2003).
- Frumkin, Norman. *Guide to Economic Indicators*, 4th ed. (Ref HC103 .F9 2006). This book explains the meanings and uses of the economic indicators.
- Solie-Johnson, Kris. *How to Set Up Your Own Small Business*, 2 volumes (Ref HD62.7 .S85 2005). Published by the American Institute of Small Business.

Company and Industry Sources

- *North American Industry Classification System, United States* (NAICS), 2007 (Ref HF1042 .N6 2007). The NAICS is a numeric industry classification system that replaced the Standard Industrial Classification (SIC) system. An electronic version is available from the US Census Bureau.
- *Standard Industrial Classification Manual* (Ref HA40 .I6U63 1987). The industry classification system that preceded the NAICS.
- *Value Line Investment Survey* (Ref HG4751 .V18). Concise company and industry profiles are updated every thirteen weeks.

Statistical Sources

- *Almanac of Business and Industrial Financial Ratios* (Ref HF5681 .R25A45 2010).
- *Business Statistics of the United States* (Ref HC101 .A13123 2009). This publication provides recent and historical information about the US economy.
- *Economic Indicators* (1971–present). The Council of Economic Advisers for the Joint Economic Committee of Congress publishes this monthly periodical; recent years are in electronic format only. Ten years of data are presented. Electronic versions are available in ABI/INFORM and ProQuest from September 1994 to present and Academic OneFile from October 1, 1991.
- *Industry Norms and Key Business Ratios* (Dun & Bradstreet; Ref HF5681 .R25I532 through Ref HF5681 .I572 [2000–2001 through 2008–2009]).
- *Rma Annual Statement Studies* (Ref HF5681 .B2R6 2009–2010). This publication provides annual financial data and ratios by industry.
- *Statistical Abstract of the United States* (Ref HA202 .S72 2010). This is the basic annual source for statistics collected by the government. Electronic version is available at www.census.gov/compendia/statab.
- *Survey of Current Business* (1956–present). The Bureau of Economic Analysis publishes this monthly periodical; recent years are in electronic format only.

At some libraries, you may find access to the following resources online:

- Mergent Webreports. Mergent (formerly Moody's) corporate manuals are in digitized format. Beginning with the early 1900s, the reports include corporate history, business descriptions, and in-depth financial statements. The collection is searchable by company name, year, or manual type.
- ProQuest Direct is a database of general, trade, and scholarly periodicals, with many articles in full text. Many business journals and other resources are available.
- Standard and Poor's Netadvantage is a database that includes company and industry information.

Internet Resources

In addition to government databases and other free sources, the Internet provides an unbelievably rich storehouse of information that can be incorporated into any business plan. It is not feasible to provide a truly comprehensive list of useful websites; this section provides a highly selective list of government sites and other sites that provide free information.

Government Sites

- US Small Business Administration (SBA). This is an excellent site to begin researching a business plan. It covers writing a plan, financing a start-up, selecting a location, managing employees, and insurance and legal issues. A follow-up page at http://www.sba.gov provides access to publications, statistics, video tutorials, podcasts, business forms, and chat rooms. Another page—http://www.sba.gov/about-offices-list/2—provides access to localized resources.

- SCORE Program. The SCORE program is a partner of the SBA. It provides a variety of services to small business owners, ranging from online (and in-person) mentoring, workshops, free computer templates, and advice on a wide range of small business issues.

In developing a business plan, it is necessary to anticipate the future economic environment. The government provides extensive statistics online.

- Consumer Price Index. This index provides information on the direction of prices for industries and geographic areas.
- Producer Price Index. Businesses that provide services or are focused on business-to-business (B2B) operations may find these data more appropriate for estimating future prices.
- National Wage Data. This site provides information on prevailing wages and can be broken down by occupation and location down to the metropolitan area.
- Consumer Expenditures Survey. This database provides information on expenditures and income. It allows for a remarkable level of refinement by occupation, age, or race.
- State and Local Personal Income and Employment. These databases provide a breakdown of personal income by state and metropolitan area.
- GDP by State and Metropolitan Region. This will provide an accurate guide to the overall economic health of a region or a city.
- US Census. This is a huge site with databases on population, income, foreign trade, economic indicators, and business ownership.

There are nongovernment websites, either free or charging a fee, that can provide assistance in building a business plan. A simple Google search for the phrase *small business plan* yields more than 67 million results. Various sites will either help with writing the plan, offer to write the plan for a fee, produce reports on industries, or assist small businesses by providing a variety of support services. The Internet offers a veritable cornucopia of information and support for those working on their business plans.

3.2 Forecasting for the Plan

Prediction is very difficult, especially about the future.
  - *Nils Bohr, Nobel Prize winner*

Any business plan is a future-oriented document. Business plans are required to look between three and five years into the future. To produce them and accurately forecast sales, you will need estimates of expenses and other items, such as the required number of employees, interest rates, and general economic conditions. There are many different techniques and tools that can be used to forecast these items. The type of techniques used will be influenced by many factors, such as the following:

- **The size of the business.** Smaller businesses may have fewer resources to apply a wide variety of forecasting techniques.
- **The analytical sophistication of people who will be conducting the forecast.** The owner of a home business may have no prior experience with forecasting techniques.
- **The type of the organization.** A manufacturing concern that sells to a stable and relatively predictable environment that has been in existence for years might be able to employ a variety of standard statistical forecasting techniques; however, a small firm operating in a new or a chaotic environment might have to rely on significantly different techniques.
- **Historical records.** Does the firm have historical records for sales that can be used to project into the future?

There is no universal set of forecasting techniques that can be used for all types of small and midsize businesses. Forecasting can fall into a fairly comprehensive range of techniques with respect to level of sophistication. Some forecasting can be done on an intuitive basis (e.g., back-of-the-envelope calculations); others can be done with standard computer programs (e.g., Excel) or programs that are specifically dedicated to forecasting in a variety of environments.

A brief review of basic forecasting techniques shows that they can be divided into two broad classes: **qualitative forecasting methods** and **quantitative forecasting methods**. Actually, these terms can be somewhat misleading because qualitative forecasting methods do not imply that no numbers will be involved. The two techniques are separated by the following concept: qualitative forecasting methods assume that one either does not have historical data or that one cannot rely on past historical data. A start-up business has no past sales that can be used to project future sales. Likewise, if there is a significant change in the environment, one may feel uncomfortable using past data to project into the future. A restaurant operates in a small town that contains a large automobile factory. After the factory closes, the restaurant owner should anticipate that past sales will no longer be a useful guideline for projecting what sales might be in the next year or two because the owner has lost a number of customers who worked at the factory. Quantitative forecasting, on the other hand, consists of techniques and methods that assume you can use past data to make projections into the future.

Table 5.2 provides examples of both qualitative forecasting methods and quantitative forecasting methods for sales forecasting. Each method is described, and their strengths and weaknesses are given.

qualitative forecasting methods

Methods that assume that one does not have historical data or cannot rely on past historical data.

quantitative forecasting methods

Methods that consist of techniques that assume you can use past data to make projections of the future.

TABLE 5.2 Overview of Forecasting Methods

Technique	Description	Strength	Weakness
Qualitative Sales Forecasting Methods			
Simple extrapolation	This approach uses some data and simply makes a projection based on these data. The data might indicate that a particular section of town has many people walk through the section each day. Knowing that number, a store might make a simple estimate of what sales might be.	An extremely simple technique that requires only the most basic analytical capabilities.	Its success depends on the "correctness" of the assumptions and the ability to carry them over to reality. You might have the correct number of people passing your store, but that does not mean that they will buy anything.
Sales force	In firms with dedicated sales forces, you would ask them to estimate what future sales might be. These values would be pieced together with a forecast for next year.	The sales force should have the pulse of your customers and a solid idea of their intentions to buy. Its greatest strength is in the B2B environment.	Difficult to use in some business-to-customer (B2C) environments. Sales force members are compensated when they meet their quotas, but this might be an incentive to "low-ball" their estimates.
Expert opinion	Similar to sales force approach, this technique ask experts within the company to produce estimates of future sales. These experts may come from marketing, R&D, or top-level management.	Coalescing sales forecasts of experts should lead to better forecasts.	Teams can produce biased estimates and can be influenced by particular members of the team (i.e., the CEO).
Delphi	A panel of outside experts would be asked to estimate sales for a particular product or service. The results would be summarized in a report and given to the same panel of experts. They would then be asked to read their forecast. This might go through several iterations.	Best used for entirely new product service categories.	One has to be able to identify and recruit "experts" from outside the organization.
Historical analogy	With this technique, one finds a similar product's or service's past sales (life cycle) and extrapolates to your product or service. A new start-up has developed an innovative home entertainment product, but nothing like it has been seen in the market. You might examine past sales of CD players to get a sense of what future sales of the new product might be like.	One can acquire a sense of what factors might affect future sales. It is relatively easy and quick to develop.	One can select the wrong past industry to compare, and the future may not unfold in a similar manner.
Market research	The use of questionnaires and surveys to evaluate customer attitudes toward a product or a service.	One gains very useful insights into the stated desires and interests of consumers. Can be highly accurate in the short term.	Experienced individuals should do these. They can take time to conduct and are relatively expensive.
Quantitative Sales Forecasting Methods			
Trend analysis	This forecasting technique assumes that sales will follow some form of pattern. For example, sales are projected to increase at 15 percent a year for the next five years.	Extremely simple to calculate.	Sales seldom follow the same growth rate over any length of time.
Moving average	This technique takes recent class data for N number of periods, adds them together, and divides by the number N to produce a forecast.	Easy to calculate.	The basic use of this type of model fails to consider the existence of trends or seasonality in the data.

Technique	Description	Strength	Weakness
Seasonality analysis	Many products and services do not have uniform sales throughout the year. They exhibit seasonality. This technique attempts to identify the proportion of annual sales sold for any given time. The sales of swimming pool supplies in the Northeast, for example, would be much higher in the spring and summer than in the fall and winter.	Many products and services have seasonal demand patterns. By considering such patterns, forecasts can be improved.	Requires several years of past data and careful analysis. Useful for quarterly or monthly forecasts.
Exponential smoothing	This analytical technique attempts to correct forecasts by some proportion of the past forecast error.	Incorporates and weighs most recent data. Attempts to factor in recent fluctuations.	Several types of this model exist, and users must be familiar with their strengths and weaknesses. Requires extensive data, computer software, and a degree of expertise to use and interpret results.
Causal models—regression analysis	Causal models, of which there are many, attempt to identify why sales are increasing or decreasing. Regression is a specific statistical technique that relates the value of the dependent variable to one or more independent variables. The dependent variable sales might be affected by price and advertising expenditures, which are independent variables.	Can be used to forecast and examine the possible validity of relationships, such as the impact on sales by advertising or price.	Requires extensive data, computer software, and a high degree of expertise to use and interpret results.

Forecasting key items such as sales is crucial in developing a good business plan. However, forecasting is a very challenging activity. The further out the forecast, the less likely it will be accurate. Everyone recognizes this fact. Therefore, it is useful to draw on a variety of forecasting techniques to develop your final forecast for the business plan. To do that, you should have a fairly solid understanding of the strengths and weaknesses of the various approaches. There are many books, websites, and articles that could assist you in understanding these techniques and when they should or should not be used. In addition, one should be open to gathering additional information to assist in building a forecast. Some possible sources of such information would be associations, trade publications, and business groups. Regardless of what technique is used or the data source employed in building a forecast for business plan, one should be prepared to justify why you are employing these forecasting models.

 Video Clip 5.12

Ask Tim Berry—How Do I Start a Sales Forecast?
Provides useful insights on how to start forecasting in the small business environment.

View the video online at: http://www.youtube.com/v/E78j9AsE7lk

Video Clip 5.13

Sales Forecast, Part 1: Structure

Tim Berry starts a discussion about using spreadsheets for forecasting.

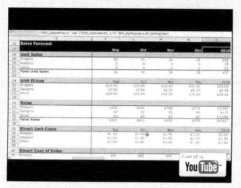

View the video online at: http://www.youtube.com/v/f8uEp_eg2kE

 Video Clip 5.14

Sales Forecast, Part 2: Logic

This module discusses how to explain the logic behind a forecast.

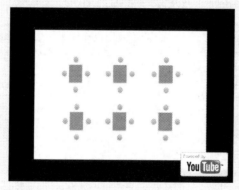

View the video online at: http://www.youtube.com/v/nMkUL6jdlrl

 Video Clip 5.15

Sales Forecast, Part 3: Back to the Spreadsheet

This module continues by explaining how to use spreadsheets in forecasting.

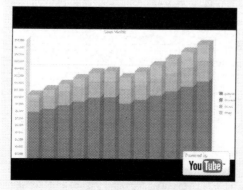

View the video online at: http://www.youtube.com/v/YKKXG2BFBO4

Web Resources for Forecasting

- **Three methods of sales forecasting** (sbinfocanada.about.com/od/cashflowmgt/a/salesforecast.htm). This site provides three simplified approaches to sales forecasting.
- **Forecasting in business** (www.enotes.com/business-finance-encyclopedia/forecasting-business). This is a relatively comprehensive overview of forecasting techniques in nontechnical terms.
- **Sales forecasting techniques** (www.statisticalforecasting.com/sales-forecasting-techniques.php). This page provides insights into how to begin a sales forecast. It has excellent links to more advanced topics.
- **Time-critical decision making for business administration** (home.ubalt.edu/ntsbarsh/stat-data/forecast.htm). This site has an e-book format with several chapters devoted to analytical forecasting techniques.

3.3 Building a Plan

Building your first business plan may seem extremely formidable. This may explain why there are so many software packages available to assist in this task. After building your first business plan, that steep learning curve should make subsequent plans for the business or other businesses significantly easier.

In preparing to build a business plan, there are some problem areas or mistakes that you should be on guard to avoid. Some may be technical in nature, while others relate to content issues. For the technical side, first and foremost, one should make sure that there are no misspellings or punctuation errors. The business plan should follow a logical structure. No ideal business plan clearly specifies the exact sections that need to be included nor is there an ideal length. Literature concerning business plans indicates that the appropriate length of the body of a business plan line should be between twenty and forty pages. This does not include appendixes that might provide critical data for the reader.

In developing a lengthy report, sometimes it is easy to fall into clichés or overused expressions. These should be avoided. Consider the visuals in the report. Data should be placed in either clearly mapped-out tables or well-designed graphs. The report should be as professional looking as possible. Anticipate the audience that will be reading the report and write in a way that easily reaches them; avoid using too much jargon or technical terms.

The content in any business plan centers on two areas: realism and accuracy.

Components of the Plan

There is no idealized structure for a business plan or a definitive number of sections that it must contain. The following subsections discuss the outline of a plan for a business start-up and identify some of the major sections that should be part of the plan.

Cover Page

The cover page provides the reader with information about either the author of the plan or the person to contact concerning the business plan. It should contain all the pertinent information to enable the reader to contact the author, such as the name of the business, the business logo, and the contact person's address, telephone number, and e-mail address.

The table of contents enables the reader to find the major sections and components of the plan. It should identify the key sections and subsections and on which pages those sections begin. This enables the reader to turn to sections that might be of particular importance.

Executive Summary

The **executive summary** is a section of critical importance and is perhaps the single most important section of the entire business plan. Quite often, it is the first section that a reader will turn to, and sometimes it may be the only section of the business plan that he or she will read. Chronologically, it should probably be the last section written.[27] The executive summary should provide an accurate overview of the entire document, which cannot be done until the whole document is prepared.

If the executive summary fails to adequately describe the idea behind the business or if it fails to do so in a captivating way, some readers may discard the entire business plan. As one author put it, the purpose of the executive summary is to convince the reader to "read on."[28] The executive summary should contain the following pieces of information:

- What is the company's business?
- Who are its intended customers?
- What will be its legal structure?

executive summary

The introduction to the business plan that describes the company's business, the intended customers, the legal structure, the type and amount of funding that will requested, and the capabilities of the key executives.

- What has been its history (where one exists)?
- What type of funding will be requested?
- What is the amount of that funding?
- What are the capabilities of the key executives?

All this must be done in an interesting and captivating way. The great challenge is that executive summaries should be relatively short—between one and three pages. For many businesspeople, this is the great challenge—being able to compress the required information in an engaging format that has significant size limitations.

Business Section

Goals. These are broad statements about what you would like to achieve some point in the near future. Your goals might focus on your human resource policies ("We wish to have productive, happy employees"), on what you see as the source of your competitive advantage ("We will be best in service"), or on financial outcomes ("We will produce above average return to our investors.") Goals are useful, but they can mean anything to anyone. It is therefore necessary to translate the goals into objectives to bring about real meaning so that they can guide the organization. Ideally, objectives should be **SMART**—specific, measurable, achievable, realistic, and have a specific timeline for completion. Here is an example: one organizational goal may be a significant rise in sales and profits. When translating that goal into an objective, you might word the objectives as follows: a 15 percent increase in sales for the next three years followed by a 10 percent increase in sales for the following two years and a 12.5 percent increase in profits in each of the next five years. These objectives are quite specific and measurable. It is up to the decision maker to determine if they are achievable and realistic. These objectives—sales and profits—clearly specify the time horizon. In developing the plan, owners are often very happy to develop goals because they are open to interpretation, but they will avoid objectives. Goals are sufficiently ambiguous, whereas objectives tie you to particular values that you will have to hit in the future. People may be concerned that they will be weighed on a scale and found wanting for failing to achieved their objectives. However, it is critical that your plan contains both goals and objectives. Objectives allow investors and your employees to clearly see where the firm intends to go. They produce targeted values to aim for and, therefore, are critical for the control of the firm's operations.

vision statement

A document that articulates the long-term purpose and idealized notion of what the business wishes to become.

mission statement

A document that articulates the fundamental nature of the business. It should address what business the company is in, the company's potential customers, and how customer value will be provided.

Vision and Mission Statements. To many, there is some degree of confusion concerning the difference between a vision statement and a mission statement. **Vision statements** articulate the long-term purpose and idealized notion of what a business wishes to become. In the earliest days of Microsoft, when it was a small business, its version of a vision statement was as follows: "A computer on every desk and in every home." In the early 1980s, this was truly a revolutionary concept. Yet it gave Microsoft's employees a clear idea (vision) that to bring that vision into being, the software being developed would have to be very "user-friendly" in comparison to the software of that day. **Mission statements**, which are much more common in small business plans, articulate the fundamental nature of the business. This means identifying the type of business, how it will leverage its competencies, and possibly the values that drive the business. Put simply, a mission statement should address the following questions:

- Who are we? What business are we in?
- Who do we see as our customers?
- How do we provide value for those customers?

Sometimes vision and mission statements are singularly written for external audiences, such as investors or shareholders. They are not written for the audience for whom it would have the greatest meaning—the management team and the employees of the business. Unfortunately, many recognize that both statements can become exercises of stringing together a series of essentially meaningless phrases into something that appears to sound *right* or *professional*. You can find software on the web to automatically generate such vacuous and meaningless statements.

Sometimes a firm will write a mission statement that provides customers, investors, and employees with a clear sense of purpose of that company. Zappos has the following as its mission statement: "Our goal is to position Zappos as an online service leader. If we can get customers to associate Zappos as the absolute best in service, then we can expand beyond shoes."[29] The mission statement of Ben & Jerry's Ice Cream focuses both on defining their product and their values: "To make, distribute and sell the finest quality all-natural ice cream and euphoric concoctions with a continued commitment to incorporating wholesome, natural ingredients and promoting business practices that respect the Earth and the Environment."[30]

Keys to Success. This section identifies those specific elements of your firm that you believe will ensure success. It is important for you to be able to define the competencies that you intend to leverage to ensure success. What makes your product or service unique? What specific set of capabilities do you bring to the competitive scene? These might include the makeup of and the experience of your management team; your operational capabilities (e.g., unique skills in design, manufacturing, or delivery); your marketing skill sets: your financial capabilities (e.g., the ability to control costs); or the personnel that make up the company.

Industry Review

In this section, you want to provide a fairly comprehensive overview of the industry. A thorough understanding of the industry that you will be operating in is essential to understand the possible returns that your company will earn within that industry. Investors want to know if they will recover their initial investment. When will they see a profit? Remember, investors often carefully track industries and are well aware of the strengths and limitations within a particular industry. Investors are looking for industries that can demonstrate growth. They also want to see if the industry is structurally attractive. This might entail conducting Porter's five forces analysis; however, this is not required in all cases. If there appear to be some issues or problems with industry level growth, then you might want to be able to identify some segments of the industry where growth is viable.

Products or Services

This section should be an in-depth discussion of what you are offering to customers. It should provide a complete and clear statement of the products or the services that you are offering. It should also discuss the core competencies of your business. You should highlight what is unique, such as a novel product or service concept or the possession of patents. You need to show how your product or service specifically meets particular market needs. You must identify how the product or the service will satisfy specific customers' needs. If you are dealing with a new product or service, you need to demonstrate what previously unidentified needs it will meet and how it will do so. At its birth, Amazon had to demonstrate that an online bookstore would be preferable to the standard bookstore by offering the customer a much wider selection of books than would be available at an on-site location.

This section could include a discussion of technical issues. If the business is based on a technological innovation—such as a new type of software or an invention—then it is necessary to provide an adequate discussion of the specific nature of the technology. One should take care to always remember the audience for whom you are writing the plan. Do not make this portion too technical in nature. This section also might discuss the future direction of the product or service—namely, where will you be taking (changing) the product or the service after the end of the current planning horizon? This may require a discussion of future investment requirements or the required time to develop new products and services. This section may also include a discussion of pricing the product or the service, although a more detailed discussion of the issue of pricing might be found in the marketing plan section. If you plan to include the issue of pricing here, you should discuss how the pricing of the product or the service was determined. The more detailed you are in this description, the more realistic it will appear to the readers of the business plan. You may wish to discuss relationships that you have with vendors that might have an impact on reducing cost and therefore an impact on price. It is important to discuss how your pricing scheme will compare with competitors. Will it be higher than average or below the average price? How does the pricing fit in with the overall strategy of the firm?

This section must have a high degree of honesty. Investors will know much about the industry and its limitations. You need to identify any areas that might be possible sources of problems, such as government regulations, issues with new product development, securing distribution channels, and informing the market of your existence. Further, it is important to identify the current competitors in the industry and possible future competitors.

Marketing Plan

An introductory marketing course always introduces the four Ps: product, price, place, and promotion. The marketing section of the business plan might provide more in-depth coverage of how the product or the service better meets customer value than that of competitors. It should identify your target customers and include coverage of who your competitors are and what they provide. The comparison between your firm and its competitors should highlight differences and point to why you are providing superior value. Pricing issues, if not covered in the previous section, could be discussed or discussed in more detail.

The issue of location, particularly in retail, should be covered in detail. Perhaps one of the most important elements of the marketing plan section is to specify how you intend to attract customers, inform them of the benefits of using your product or service, and retain customers. Initially, customers are attracted through advertising. This section should delineate the advertising plan. What media will be used—flyers, newspapers, magazines, radio, television, web presence, direct marketing, and/or social media campaigns? This section should cover any promotional campaigns that might be used.

The Management Team

Physical resources are not the only determinant of business success. The human resources available to a firm will play a critical role in determining its success. Readers of your business plan and potential investors should have a clear sense of the management team that will be running a business. They should know the team with respect to the team's knowledge of the business, their experience and capabilities, and their drive to succeed. Arthur Rock, a venture capitalist, was once quoted as saying, "I invest in people, not the idea."[31]

This section of the business plan has several elements. It should contain an organizational chart that will delineate the responsibilities and the chain of command for the business. It should specify who will occupy each major position of the business. You might want to explain who is doing what job and why. For every member of the management team, you should have a complete résumé. This should include educational background (both formal and informal) and past work experience, including the jobs they have held, responsibilities, and accomplishments. You might want to include some other biographical data such as age, although that is not required.

If you plan to use specific advisers or consultants, you should mention the names and backgrounds of these people in this section of the plan. You should also specify why these people are being used.

An additional element of your discussion of the management team will be the intended compensation schemes. You should specify the intended salaries for the management team while also including issues of their benefits and bonuses or any stock position that they may take in the company. This section should also identify any gaps in the management team and how you intend to fill these positions.

Depending on the nature of the business, you might wish to include in this section the personnel (employees) that will be required. You should identify the number of people that are currently working for the firm or that will have to be hired; you should also identify the skills that they need to possess. Further discussion should include the pay that will be provided: whether they will be paid a flat salary or paid hourly, if and when you intend to use overtime, and what benefits you intend to provide. In addition, you should discuss any training requirements or training programs that you will have to implement.

Financial Statements

The financial statements section of the business plan should be broken down into three key subsections: the income statement, the balance sheet, and the cash-flow statement. Before proceeding with these sections, we discuss the assumptions used to build these sections. The opening section of the financial statements section should also include, in summary format, projections of sales, the sales growth rate, key expenses and their growth rates, net income across the forecasting horizon, and assets and liabilities.[32]

As previously discussed, bankers—and to lesser extent venture capitalists—will be primarily concerned with this section of the business plan. It is vital that this section—whether you are an existing business seeking more funding or a start-up—have realistic financial projections. The business plan should contain clear statements of the underlying assumptions that were used to make these financial projections. The clearer the statements and the more realistic the assumptions behind these statements, then the greater the confidence the reader will have in these projections. Few businesspeople have a thorough understanding of these financial statements; therefore, it is advisable that someone with an accounting or a financial background review these statements before they are included in the report. We will have a much more in-depth discussion of these statements in Chapter 9.

The future planning horizon for financial projections is normally between three and five years. The duration that you will use will depend on the amount of capital that the business is seeking to raise, the type of industry the business is in, and the forecasting issues associated with making projections. Also, the detail required in these financial statements will be directly tied to the type and size of the business.

Income Statement

income statement

A report that provides an examination of the overall profitability of a firm over a particular period of time.

The **income statement** examines the overall profitability of a firm over a particular period of time. As such, it is also known as a profit-and-loss statement. It identifies all sources of revenues generated and expenses incurred by the business. For the business plan, one should generate annual plans for the first three to five years. Some suggest that the planner develop more "granulated" income statements for the first two years. By granulated, we mean that the first year income statement should be broken down on a monthly basis, while the second year should be broken down on a quarterly basis.

Some of the key terms (they will be reviewed in much greater detail in Chapter 10) found in the income statement are as follows:

- **Income.** All revenues and additional incomes produced by the business during the designated period.
- **Cost of goods sold.** Costs associated with producing products, such as raw materials and costs associated directly with production.
- **Gross profit margin.** Income minus the cost of goods sold.
- **Operating expenses.** Costs in doing business, such as expenses associated with selling the product or the service, plus general administration expenses.

- **Depreciation.** This is a special form of expense that may be included in operating expenses. Long-term assets—those whose useful life is longer than one year—decline in value over time. Depreciation takes this fact into consideration. There are several ways in which this declining value can be determined. It is a noncash expenditure expense.
- **Total expenses.** The cost of goods sold plus operating expenses and depreciation.
- **Net profit before interest and taxes.** This is the gross profit minus operating expenses; another way of stating net profit is income minus total expenses.
- **Interest.** The required payment on all debt for the period.
- **Taxes.** Federal, state, and local tax payments for the firm.
- **Net profit.** This is the net profit after interest and taxes. This is the term that many will look at to determine the potential success of business operations.

Balance Sheet

The **balance sheet** examines the assets and liabilities and owner's equity of the business at some particular point in time. It is divided into two sections—the credit component (the assets of the business) and the debit component (liabilities and equity). These two components must equal each other. The business plan should have annual balance sheet for the three- or five-year planning horizon. The elements of the credit component are as follows:

- **Current assets.** These are the assets that will be held for less than one year, including cash, marketable securities, accounts receivable, notes receivable, inventory, and prepaid expenses.
- **Fixed assets.** These assets are not going to be turned into cash within the next year; these include plants, equipment, and land. It may also include intangible assets, such as patents, franchises, copyrights, and goodwill.
- **Total assets.** This is the sum of current assets and fixed assets.

Liabilities consist of the following:

- **Current liabilities.** These are debts that are to be paid within the year, such as lines of credit, accounts payable, other items payable (including taxes, wages, and rents), short-term loans, dividends payable, and current portion of long-term debt.
- **Long-term liabilities.** These are debts payable over a period greater than one year, such as notes payable, long-term debt, pension fund liability, and long-term lease obligations.
- **Total liabilities.** This is the sum of current liabilities and long-term liabilities.
- **Owner's equity.** This represents the value of the shareholders' ownership in the business. It is sometimes referred to as net worth. It may be composed of items such as preferred stock, common stock, and retained earnings.

> **balance sheet**
>
> A report that examines the assets, liabilities, and owner's equity of the business at some particular point in time.

Cash-Flow Statement

From a practical and survival standpoint, the **cash-flow statement** may be the most important component of the financial statements. The cash-flow statement maps out where cash is flowing into the firm and where it flows out. It recognizes that there may be a significant difference between profits and cash flow. It will indicate if a business can generate enough cash to continue operations, whether it has sufficient cash for new investments, and whether it can pay its obligations. Businesspeople soon realize that profits are nice, but cash is king.

Cash flows can be divided into three areas of analysis: cash flow from operations, cash flow from investing, and cash flow from financing. Cash flow from operations examines the cash inflows from revenues and interest and dividends from investments held by the business. It then identifies the cash outflows for paying suppliers, employees, taxes, and other expenses. Cash flow from investing examines the impact of selling or acquiring current and fixed assets. Cash flow from financing examines the impact on the cash position from the changes in the number of shares and changes in the short- and long-term debt position of the firm. Given the critical importance of cash flow to the survival of the small business, it will be covered in much more detail in Chapter 10.

> **cash-flow statement**
>
> A document that maps out where cash is flowing into a firm and where it flows out. It recognizes that there may be a significant difference between profits and cash flow.

Additional Information

Depending on the nature of the business and the amount of funding that is being sought, the plan might include more materials. For an existing business, you may wish to include past tax statements and/or personal financial statements. If the business is a franchise, you should include all legal contracts and documents. The same should be done for any leasing, licensing, or rent agreements. This section should be seen as a catchall incorporating any materials that would support the plan. One does not want to be in the position of being asked by readers of the plan—"Where are these documents?"

Appendixes

The financial section of the business plan should include summaries of the three key financial elements. The details behind the financial statements should be included as an appendix along with clear statements concerning the assumptions that were used to build them. The appendixes may also include different scenarios that were considered in building the plan, such as alternative market growth assumptions or alternative competitive environments. Demonstrating that the author(s) considered "what-if" situations tells potential investors that the business is prepared to handle changing conditions. It should include items such as logos, diagrams, ads, and organizational charts.

3.4 Developing Scenarios

Change is constant.

- *Benjamin Disraeli*

Business plans are analyses of the future; they can err on the side of either optimistic projections or conservative projections. From the standpoint of the potential investor, it is always better to err on the side of conservatism. Regardless of either bias, business plans are generally built on the basis of expected futures and past experience. Unfortunately, the future does not always emerge in a clearly predicated manner. One can have a dramatic change that can have significant impact on the business. Often such changes occur in the external environment and are beyond the control of the business management team. These external changes can occur within the technical environment; it can be based on changes in customer needs, changes with respect to the suppliers, changes in the economic environment—at the local, national, or global level. Dramatic change can also occur within the organization itself—the death of the owner or members of the management team.[33]

scenario planning

A process that examines the impact and possible responses to events that may be unlikely but that would have significant impact on a business.

One way for an organization to deal with significant changes is a process known as **scenario planning**. The real origins of scenario planning can be traced back to the early nineteenth century activity known as Kreigsspiel—war gaming—a system for training officers developed by the Prussian command. This process of looking at future wars was adopted by many militaries in the later nineteenth century. In the 1950s, a more formal format was used at the RAND Institute for examining possible future changes in the military and geopolitical environments. The early 1980s saw it applied to industrial settings. Royal Dutch Shell examined the question of what would happen if there were a significant drop in the price of oil. This was after two oil crises that pushed the price of oil up significantly. The notion that oil prices would drop was considered to be an extremely unlikely event, but it did occur. Royal Dutch Shell was one of the few oil companies that did not suffer because its scenario analyses enabled them to be ready to deal with that situation.[34]

What could be the possible use of scenario planning for small businesses? There are several areas in which small businesses should apply scenario planning to be better prepared for future disruptions.

Identify Significant Changes That Might Impact the Business

Consider major shifts in the customer's notion of value. As mentioned in Chapter 2, the firm should always be examining what constitutes value in the eyes of the consumer and how that might shift. Henry Ford's model T car was a global success because customers initially valued a reliable vehicle at a low price. Ford Motor Company continued to meet the customer's notion of value by constantly driving down the unit cost. However, by the mid-1920s, customers' notion of value included not only price but also issues such as styling and improved technologies. General Motors was able to recognize that there were changes in the customer's value notion and provided them with a range of vehicles. Ford failed to recognize that change and suffered a significant drop in sales.

Shifts in the economic environment. The recent recession clearly indicates that economies can suffer significant shifts in a short period of time. These shifts can have dramatic impact on all business operations. Small-business owners have seen significant tightening of bank credit and changes with respect to the requirements for using credit cards. One could easily imagine the critical importance for small businesses to consider the impacts that would follow significant changes in interest rates. Southwest Airlines, in anticipation of possible fluctuations in oil prices, used futures contracts to deal with dramatic shifts in the price of oil. When oil prices rose significantly, they were in a much better position than their competitors.

The entrance of new competitors. Small businesses should always be ready to consider the impact of facing new competitors and new types of competition. Consider the case of small local retail outlets when a Walmart superstore opens in the area.

Consideration of Disasters

The best way to deal with any potential disaster is not while it is occurring or after it has happened but before it occurs. Small businesses should anticipate what they will do in the case of physical disasters, such as fire, earthquakes, or floods. Other disasters might involve the bankruptcy or loss of a major supplier or a major customer. A restaurant or a food market should have a contingency plan in the case of a power failure that might lead to food spoilage. Such a business might also want to conduct a scenario planning exercise to see what its responses would be in the case of a customer complaining of food poisoning. Other disaster scenarios that should be considered by small businesses include the impact and ramifications of having the computer system crash; having the service for the website crash; or having the website hacked, with the possible loss of customer information.

New Opportunities

Almost all businesses, large and small, must be prepared to seize new opportunities. This may mean that they have to consider the impact of technological change on the business or how technology can offer them new business opportunities. The technology of stereo lithography, a process by which three-dimensional objects are built layer by layer, has been available for more than a decade. Bespoke Innovations saw the potential for using this technology. Bespoke Innovations can develop, in a short period of time, custom artificial legs for a price of $5,000–$6,000 and with features that are not found in $60,000 prostheses.[35]

Scenario planning should be a periodic exercise, but it should be conducted no more than once a year. The actual frequency might be dependent on the perceived rate of change for the industry or the presence of storm clouds on the horizon. Scenario planning has several distinct activities, which may be as follows:

- **Pick one area that might occur in the future that would have significant impact on the business.** What if the national joblessness rate remains at over 9 percent for the next three to five years? What if a major customer decides to buy from a competitor or that customer is in financial trouble? What if there are changes in the national defense budget? A luncheonette in New London, Connecticut, where Electric Boat builds nuclear submarines, wants to consider the impact of changes in the defense budget. A decrease in the budget for building nuclear submarines would reduce the number of subs made in New London, which might lead to layoffs at Electric Boat and fewer customers for the luncheonette.

- **Identify factors that might impact that issue.** This sometimes is referred to as a PEST analysis, where the P stands for political issues, E stands for economic issues, S stands for sociocultural issues, and T stands for technology issues. Each factor would be analyzed to see how it might impact the scenario. In our previous luncheonette example, the restaurant might want to consider an upcoming election to see how each party would support defense appropriations, and it might look at the overall economy to determine whether a downturn in the economy might lead to a cut in defense appropriations. It is unlikely that sociocultural issues would impact defense appropriations. Technology issues, whether a breakthrough in some design by the United States or by some other country, might determine the number and location of submarines built in the United States.

- **Rank the relative importance of the previous factors.** Not all factors under consideration can be considered equally important. It is critical in a scenario planning exercise to see which factors are most important so that decision makers can focus on the ramifications of those factors in the analysis.

- **Develop scenarios.** Having identified the relative importance of the factors, the next stage would be to develop a limited number of possible scenarios (no more than two or three). Each scenario would map out possible outcomes for each key factor. Based on these values, the group conducting the scenario planning exercise would develop insights into this possible future world.

- **How do the scenarios impact your business?** For each future scenario, the team should examine how that possible future state would impact the operation of the business. Continuing with the luncheonette example, the owner might see that a particular political party would be elected in the next election and the economy will still be in the doldrums. Together, this might indicate a cut in the naval building budget. This will translate into a reduced number of submarines built in New London and a reduction in employment at Electric Boat. The luncheonette's sales will obviously drop off. Now the owner must consider what it might do in that situation.

Scenario planning offers the opportunity for small business owners to examine the future on a long-term basis. It should force them to look at external environments and conditions that can have a dramatic impact on the survival of their firm. It broadens their thinking and creates an environment of increased flexibility. It enables a business to respond to those sudden shocks that might destroy other firms.

3.5 Computer Aids

Business plans can be built using a combination of word-processing and spreadsheet programs by those who are adept at using them. However, the entire process of constructing a comprehensive business plan can be greatly simplified by using a dedicated business plan software package. These packages are designed to produce reports that have all the required sections for a business plan, they greatly facilitate the creation of the financial statements with charts, and they often allow for the inclusion of materials from other programs. Most of them are fairly reasonably priced from $50 to $150.

There are many such packages on the market, and they range from those designed for novices to those that can generate annual plans by easily incorporating data from external sources, such as the accounting programs of a business. When evaluating competing programs, there are some primary and secondary factors that should be considered.[36] The primary factors are as follows:

- **Ease of building the report.** The various sections of the report should be clearly identified, and the authors should be able to work on each section independent of their sequence within the report. Text and data entry should be simple and allow for easy corrections or revisions.
- **Financial statements.** The software should facilitate building the income statement, the balance sheet, and the cash-flow statement. For multiyear projections, the software should support the forecasting process.
- **Import from other programs.** The software should be able to incorporate data from a variety of programs, such as Word and Excel. Ideally, it should be able to import data from a variety of accounting programs.
- **Support services.** The software company should bundle a variety of support services, including clear instructions, tutorials, and access to Internet or call-number support. Many packages provide sample business plans for different industries.

The secondary factors are as follows:

- **Access to research support.** Some software packages include access to business publications and databases to aid with market research.
- **Export options.** These packages allow for the report or parts of the report to be exported to different formats—Word, Excel, PowerPoint, HTML, or PDF.
- **Ancillary analysis tools.** Some packages either directly include or offer additional programs for market planning, budgeting, or valuation.

The following is a partial listing of companies that have business planning software:

- **Small Business Point.** This company offers business planning software and the opportunity for them to build your plan for you.
- **Business Plan Pro.** This company provides business planning software with sample plans for a wide number of industries plus options for acquiring industry data at national, state, or local levels. The company also has programs for marketing planning and legal issues advice.
- **Business Plan Software.** This company offers a number of products, including business planning software, a strategic planning program, financial projection and cash-flow forecasting programs, and marketing planning software.
- **JIAN Biz Plan.** This company's products include business planning programs, software for human resources, marketing planning programs, and contract development software.
- **PlanWrite.** In addition to offering programs for business, strategic, and marketing planning, this company has products that provide advice in the area of sales strategy and pricing.
- **Plan Magic.** This company offers a suite of planning products ranging from particular industries to financial and marketing planning software.

EXERCISES

1. In Exercise 2 of Section 1, you were asked to interview five local business owners. In addition to asking them questions about strategy, please ask them the following questions: (a) How do they forecast their sales? (b) Inventory? (c) Economic conditions? (d) Have they ever conducted anything like a scenario analysis or formally considered what they would do if an emergency struck—fire, flood, death of a business partner, and so forth?

2. Go to the Appendix (Chapter 16), which contains Robert Rainsford's business plan. (You will be asked to examine portions of this report throughout the text to evaluate different sections.)

    a. Read his executive summary and critique it. How would you improve it?

    b. Evaluate the document's vision and mission statements. Are there any major problems? How would you improve them?

    c. Evaluate the industry analysis section of the report. What additional data could be used in this section of the report? Where would you suggest that Robert go to get the data?

3. Imagine that you are going to start a business and that you want a great looking plan. Evaluate three of the business plan software packages. Based on your evaluation, write a report that describes their strengths and weaknesses. Which would you select and why?

4. THE THREE THREADS

LEARNING OBJECTIVES

1. Learn that the planning process can add significantly to the delivery of customer value.
2. Understand that the proper management of the cash flow of a business can occur only in an environment of comprehensive planning.
3. Understand that although not all businesses will rely on e-business or e-commerce, they should carefully plan their inclusion into a firm's operations.

The business plan is the backbone of both start-up and existing businesses. The initial business plan forces one to consider the core issues in detail. These issues directly relate to the themes that are stressed throughout this text: customer value; cash flow; and digital technologies, e-commerce, and e-business. Building a good initial business plan requires the author(s) to seriously consider these three themes. It must be pointed out that these themes *must* be reviewed regularly as part of a continuous planning process. A great mistake of many small businesses is that they may begin with a formal plan, but they abandon the concept after receiving initial funding. Regardless of the industry or the business size, formally thinking about these themes in the context of planning is essential.

4.1 Customer Value

Businesses survive because they provide value to customers. To begin a business, one should have a clear vision as to what constitutes value to the targeted customers. The initial business plan must be able to articulate this vision. However, that notion of value can change over time. Customers' perceptions of value can evolve or change radically. Competitors can change what they offer customers, and the firm itself can acquire or lose capabilities that were used to provide value. This shifting value landscape does not allow any business to adhere to its initial plan as though it were dogma. Evaluations of customer value must be conducted regularly as part of an annual planning process.

4.2 Cash-Flow Implications

It cannot be repeated too often nor overemphasized: the survival of a small business often hinges on its ability to successfully manage its cash flow. Balancing cash inflows with outflows is not something that can be done in an ad hoc fashion. It requires a plan. Because one cannot count on accuracy in long-range forecasts, or even short-range forecasts, examining your cash flow must become part of an ongoing planning process. The text has promoted the idea of small businesses having annually updated plans. In the case of cash-flow calculations, it might be advisable for small firms to update their cash-flow analyses monthly.

4.3 The Influence of E-Commerce and E-Business

Not all firms will have the same commitment to e-commerce or e-business options. The level of commitment will be determined not so much by size, but by the nature of the business, the knowledge and experience of the owner(s) and the management team, and the firm's growth objectives. However, given the declining costs for website development and hosting, and the increasing ease of using tools such as social media, web store sales management, and **customer relationship management**,[37] it would be odd if these options were not considered in the planning process. This is not to say that all small businesses must include them in their initial business plan, but the integration of e-commerce or e-business can be an evolutionary process that can be made much easier by thoughtful planning.

KEY TAKEAWAYS

- The planning process for a small business must always incorporate the notion of customer value and recognize that this notion can change over time.
- The proper management of a firm's cash flow requires a commitment to planning the management of one's cash flow.
- Although e-business and e-commerce options may not be considered in the original plan for a business, if they are eventually considered, their successful implementation will require a detailed plan.

EXERCISES

1. In Question 2 of Exercise 5.1, you were asked to interview five local business owners. Ask them how they manage to identify how customer needs might change over time and how they would plan on responding to such changes.
2. While interviewing them, ask how they go about managing their cash flow. Ask how far ahead they plan their cash-flow management.
3. If they have a website, ask how they planned for its creation and use.

Disaster Watch

The man who is prepared has his battle half won.
- *Miguel de Cervantes*

When failure is not an option, then planning is a necessity. A well-built plan enables the management team of a business to fully anticipate what problems they may encounter and what will be required of them to make the firm successful. There are an almost innumerable number of factors that can become a disaster for a business, but solid planning can significantly reduce that number. A good plan should also force the owner and the management team to anticipate major areas of concern that can become disasters, such as the following:

- **Are the participants ready?** For the prospective first-time business owner, the task of building a business plan should provide valuable insights into what will be required to make the business function. The plan should indicate the necessary initial funding and the work commitment necessary for success.

- **Unrealistic expectations.** A thoughtful plan should eliminate assumptions or outcomes that cannot be supported after careful consideration or analysis. It may be sound that your sales will grow by 100 percent every year for five years or that you will recoup your investment in six months, but some simple running of numbers might show that those are impossible outcomes. Simply "forcing" someone to articulate such assumptions can help return him or her to a more realistic vision of the world. Better yet, have some outside sets of "eyes"—friends, other businesspeople, your lawyer, or your accountant—review the plan.

- **Determining whether the business will be profitable.** The financial analysis section of your plan should indicate when a start-up will become profitable or how much profit a business will make. This is of great importance to potential investors and to the owner.

- **Not truly understanding the market by failing to know how customers determine value.** The business plan requires that one clearly identifies who the targeted customers are and how the business will provide greater value than its competitors. Plans force owners and managers to specifically articulate how they will serve their customer base. Without clearly stating these key points, any business is headed for disaster because having some sort of "hunch" or "idea" about your customers and their needs is not enough.

- **Failure to adequately capitalize the business.** The overwhelming consensus is that small businesses "fail" for two main reasons: inadequate management (often attributed to a failure to plan) and insufficient capitalization. Start-ups often underestimate the required capital to begin operations and continue operations for the foreseeable horizon. A structured plan requires them to consider what will be needed during the next few years.

- **Not determining the cash flow.** The lifeblood of any business is its cash flow. This is particularly true for small businesses. Anticipating a firm's cash inflows and outflows is not something that can be handled in an intuitive fashion. It requires analysis. Misjudging these two flows is, perhaps, the surest recipe for disaster.

- **Failure to create the appropriate management structure.** Small-business owners are often accused of wanting complete control of all aspects of their firm's operations. For microsized small businesses, this may be feasible, but as the firm's size increases, it is critical that lines of responsibility be clearly drawn. Managers and employees must know what is expected of them and their responsibilities. A failure to do so produces confusion and conflict—another good recipe for disaster. If the formal delineation of the management structure is not part of a plan, then it is highly unlikely that necessary clarity will arise spontaneously.

Managers in businesses both small and large often complain of "firefighting" problems; unfortunately, many of these problems are a result of inadequate or nonexistent planning. In the case of the smaller enterprise, a small blaze can rapidly become an inferno that can lead to disaster. According to a report released by the Epicurus Institute, "when a business starts or operates without a plan, the principles are not prepared to deal with the slightest problem that can affect their business."

ENDNOTES

1. Kenneth Arrow, *The Concept of Corporate Strategy* (Homewood, IL: Irwin, 1971), 28.

2. Alfred Chandler, *Strategy and Structure* (Cambridge, MA: MIT Press, 1962), 13.

3. Kenichi Ohmae, *The Mind of the Strategist* (Harmondsworth, UK: Penguin Books, 1983), 6.

4. Henry Mintzberg, Joseph Lampel, and Bruce Ahlstrand, *Strategic Safari: A Guided Tour through the Wilds of Strategic Management* (New York: Free Press, 1998).

5. Paul Solman and Thomas Friedman, *Life and Death on the Corporate Battlefield: How Companies Win, Lose, Survive* (New York: Simon and Schuster, 1982), 24–27.

6. Stephen C. Perry, "A Comparison of Failed and Non-Failed Small Businesses in the United States: Do Men and Women Use Different Planning and Decision Making Strategies?," *Journal of Developmental Entrepreneurship* 7, no. 4 (2002): 415.

7. Stephen C. Perry, "An Exploratory Study of U.S. Business Failures and the Influence of Relevant Experience and Planning," (PhD diss., George Washington University, 1998; dissertation available through UMI Dissertation Services, Ann Arbor, MI), 42.

8. David A. Curtis, *Strategic Planning for Smaller Businesses: Improving Corporate Performance and Personal Reward* (Cambridge, MA: Lexington Books, 1983), 29.

9. Henry Mintzberg, *The Rise and Fall of Strategic Planning* (New York: Free Press, 1994), 46.

10. Harry Tucci, comment posted to the following blog: Rieva Lesonsky, "A Small Business Plan Doubles Your Chances for Success, Says a New Survey, *Small Business Trends*, June 20, 2010, accessed October 10, 2011, smallbiztrends.com/2010/06/business-plan-success-twice-as-likely.html.

11. Michael Porter, *Competitive Strategy: Techniques for Analyzing Industries and Competitors* (New York: Free Press, 1980), 21.

12. "Kogi Truck Schedule," *Kogi BBQ*, accessed October 10, 2011, kogibbq.com.

13. *Max and Mina's Ice Cream*, accessed October 10, 2011, www.maxandminasicecream.com.

14. Michael Porter, *Competitive Strategy: Techniques for Analyzing Industries and Competitors* (New York: Free Press, 1980), 21.

15. Jason Cohen, "Don't Write a Business Plan," *Building43*, January 27, 2010, accessed October 10, 2011, www.building43.com/blogs/2010/01/27/dont-write-a-business-plan.

16. T. C. Carbone, "Four Common Management Failures and How to Avoid Them," *Management World* 10, no. 8 (1981): 38.

17. Patricia Schaeffer, "The Seven Pitfalls of Business Failure and How to Avoid Them," *Business Know-How*, 2011, accessed October 10, 2011, www.businessknowhow.com/startup/business-failure.htm.

18. Isabel M. Isodoro, "10 Rules for Small Business Success," *PowerHomeBiz.com*, 2011, www.powerhomebiz.com/vol19/rules.htm.

19. Rubik Atamian and Neal R. VanZante, "Continuing Education: A Vital Ingredient of the 'Success Plan' for Small Business," *Journal of Business and Economic Research* 8, no. 3 (2010): 37.

20. Stephen C. Perry, "A Comparison of Failed and Non-Failed Small Businesses in the United States: Do Men and Women Use Different Planning and Decision Making Strategies?," *Journal of Developmental Entrepreneurship* 7, no. 4 (2002): 415.

21. Rieva Lesonsky, "A Small Business Plan Doubles Your Chances for Success, Says a New Survey," *Small Business Trends*, June 20, 2010, accessed October 10, 2011, smallbiztrends.com/2010/06/business-plan-success-twice-as-likely.html.

22. H. Hodges and T. Kent, "Impact of Planning and Control Sophistication in Small Business," *Journal of Small Business Strategy* 17, no. 2 (2006–7): 75.

23. Tim Berry, "What Bankers Look for in a Business Plan…and What You Should Expect When Taking Your Business Plan to a Bank," *AllBusiness.com*, November 7, 2006, accessed October 10, 2011, www.allbusiness.com/business-planning-structures/business-plans/3878953-1.html.

24. Marc Mays, "Small Business Venture Capital Strategies," *eZine Articles*, 2010, accessed October 10, 2011, ezinearticles.com/?Small-Business-Venture-Capital-Strategies&id=4714691.

25. "The Importance of Angel Investing in Financing the Growth of Entrepreneurial Ventures," *Small Business Notes*, September 2008, accessed October 10, 2011, www.smallbusinessnotes.com/aboutsb/rs331.html.

26. Melinda Emerson, "Life Plan before Business Plan," *Small Business Trends*, March 22, 2010, accessed October 10, 2011, smallbiztrends.com/2010/03/life-plan-before-business-plan.html.

27. Jeffry Timmons, Andrew Zachary, and Stephen Spinelli, *Business Plans That Work—A Guide for Small Business* (New York: McGraw-Hill, 2004), 113.

28. Carolyn Brown, "The Dos and Don'ts of Writing a Winning Business Plan," *Black Enterprise*, April 1996, 114–122.

29. "Inc. 500 Mission Statements," *MissionStatements.com*, accessed October 10, 2011, www.missionstatements.com/inc_500_mission_statements.html.

30. "Mission Statement," *Ben & Jerry's*, accessed October 10, 2011, www.benjerry.com/activism/mission-statement.

31. "Invest in People, Not Ideas," *Michael Karnjanaprakorn*, January 15, 2009, accessed October 10, 2011, www.mikekarnj.com/blog/2009/01/15/invest-in-people-not-ideas.

32. Amir M Hormozi, Gail S. Sutton, Robert D. McMinn, Wendy Lucio, "Business Plans for New or Small Businesses: Paving the Path to Success," *Management Decision* 40, no. 8 (2002): 755.

33. "Workshops and Events," *SCORE*, accessed October 10, 2011, www.score.org/events/workshops.

34. P. McNamee, *Tools and Techniques for Strategic Management* (New York: Pergamon Press, 1985), 187.

35. Ashlee Vance, "A Technology Sets Inventors Free to Dream," *New York Times*, September 14, 2010.

36. "2012 Business Plan Software Product Comparisons," *TopTenReviews.com*, accessed October 10, 2011, business-plan-software-review.toptenreviews.com.

37. Efraim Turban et al., *Electronic Commerce: A Managerial Perspective* (Upper Saddle River, NJ: Pearson/Prentice Hall, 2008), 759.

CHAPTER 6
Marketing Basics

Max and Mina's Homemade Ice Cream and Ices

Source: Used with permission from Max and Mina's Ice Cream.

Growing up in the 1970s, Bruce and Mark Becker loved ice cream. Their Grandpa Max used to create all different kinds of ice cream for Grandma Mina and the boys to try. Grandpa was an organic chemist and loved to create some interesting flavors. Years later, after Grandpa Max passed away, Bruce was cleaning out his grandpa's house and discovered his secret book of recipes.

And so it began.

In the 1980s, Bruce started on his journey and traveled throughout Europe and the United States doing gourmet ice cream research. With all the new information gathered and the treasure trove of Grandpa Max's secret recipes, Bruce and Mark opened Max and Mina's Ice Cream in 1997 in a shopping center next to Shimon's Pizza Falafel Dairy Restaurant in Flushing, Queens, New York. They test marketed their recipes directly to the public. The public loved it—and so did the local restaurants and party planners.

Max and Mina's Ice Cream revolutionized America's favorite dessert with daring ingredients and bold innovation. Their unique ability to intrigue and challenge old notions of mundane flavors draws unbelievable attention at home in New York and around the globe. The most distant customer of note was from Australia, someone who insisted on going to Max and Mina's right off the plane at Kennedy Airport.

The Beckers make their ice cream products with at least 16 percent butterfat, putting them into the gourmet category. All their ice creams are kosher, but some products adhere to even stricter dairy guidelines. The shop itself features an array of posters, a display of Wacky Packages bubblegum stickers, candy wrappers, a Jerry Garcia etching, and old-fashioned signs.

A visit to Max and Mina's will be an unusual ice cream experience (see "Video Clip 6.1"). If you dare to take the plunge, why not try unforgettable flavors like beer, lox, babka, corn-on-the-cob, ketchup, garlic, or merlot—just to mention a few? There are also many of the more traditional flavors that you know and love. There is a rotating menu of one thousand flavors, but only about forty ice cream flavors and eight to ten sorbets are available at any one time. Bruce and Mark constantly encourage their patrons to be vocal in brainstorming new flavors, especially flavors that compliment events. Turkey ice cream, anyone? Have an idea? Stop by and give Max and Mina's a try.[1]

Video Clip 6.1

Max and Mina's Ice Cream
An ice cream revolution.

View the video online at: http://www.youtube.com/v/aBr7qEB7N1M

1. WHAT MARKETING IS ALL ABOUT

LEARNING OBJECTIVES

1. Define marketing.
2. Explain why marketing is so important to small business.
3. Explain the marketing concept, the societal marketing concept, and the holistic marketing concept.
4. Define customer value and discuss the role of marketing and delivering it.
5. Explain market segmentation, target market, marketing mix, differentiation, positioning, marketing environment, marketing management, and marketing strategy.

Because the purpose of business is to create a customer, the business enterprise has two—and only two—basic functions: marketing and innovation. Marketing and innovation produce results; all the rest are costs. Marketing is the distinguishing, unique function of the business.[2]
  - *Peter Drucker*

marketing

The activity, set of institutions, and processes for creating, communicating, and exchanging offerings that have value for customers, clients, partners, and society at large. It is a unique, distinguishing function of a business.

Marketing is defined by the American Marketing Association as "the activity, set of institutions, and processes for creating, communicating, and exchanging offerings that have value for customers, clients, partners, and society at large."[3] Putting this formality aside, marketing is about delivering value and benefits: creating products and services that will meet the needs and wants of customers (perhaps even delighting them) at a price they are willing to pay and in places where they are willing to buy them. Marketing is also about promotional activities such as advertising and sales that let customers know about the goods and services that are available for purchase. Successful marketing generates revenue that pays for all other company operations. Without marketing, no business can last very long. It is that important and that simple—and it applies to small business.

Marketing is applicable to goods, services, events, experiences, people, places, properties, organizations, businesses, ideas, and information.[4]

There are several concepts that are basic to an understanding of marketing: the marketing concept, customer value, the marketing mix, segmentation, target market, the marketing environment, marketing management, and marketing strategy.

1.1   The Marketing Concept…and Beyond

The **marketing concept** has guided marketing practice since the mid-1950s.[5] The concept holds that the focus of all company operations should be meeting the customer's needs and wants in ways that distinguish a company from its competition. However, company efforts should be integrated and co-ordinated in such a way to meet organizational objectives and achieve profitability. Perhaps not sur-prisingly, successful implementation of the marketing concept has been shown to lead to superior com-pany performance.[6] "The marketing concept recognizes that there is no reason why customers should buy one organization's offerings unless it is in some way better at serving the customers' wants and needs than those offered by competing organizations. Customers have higher expectations and more choices than ever before. This means that marketers have to listen more closely than ever before."[7]

Sam Walton, the founder of Walmart, put it best when he said, "There is only one boss: the cus-tomer. And he can fire everybody in the company, from the chairman on down, simply by spending his money somewhere else."[8] Small businesses are particularly suited to abiding by the marketing concept because they are more nimble and closer to the customer than are large companies. Changes can be made more quickly in response to customer wants and needs.

The **societal marketing concept** emerged in the 1980s and 1990s, adding to the traditional mar-keting concept. It assumes that a "company will have an advantage over competitors if it applies the marketing concept in a manner that maximizes society's well-being"[9] and requires companies to bal-ance customer satisfaction, company profits, and the long-term welfare of society. Although the expect-ation of ethical and responsible behavior is implicit in the marketing concept, the societal marketing concept makes these expectations explicit.

Small business is in a very strong position in keeping with the societal marketing concept. Al-though small businesses do not have the financial resources to create or support large philanthropic causes, they do have the ability to help protect the environment through **green business practices** such as reducing consumption and waste, reusing what they have, and recycling everything they can. Small businesses also have a strong record of supporting local causes. They sponsor local sports teams, donate to fund-raising events with food and goods or services, and post flyers for promoting local events. The ways of contributing are virtually limitless.

Video Link 6.1

Do Well While Doing Good

Small business sustainability practices.

www.startupnation.com/podcasts/episodes/9564/creating-sustainable-business-practices.htm

The **holistic marketing concept** is a further iteration of the marketing concept and is thought to be more in keeping with the trends and forces that are defining the twenty-first century. Today's mar-keters recognize that they must have a complete, comprehensive, and cohesive approach that goes bey-ond the traditional applications of the marketing concept.[10] A company's "sales and revenues are in-extricably tied to the quality of each of its products, services, and modes of delivery and to its image and reputation among its constituencies. [The company] markets itself through everything it does, its substance as well as its style. It is that all-encompassing package that the organization then sells."[11] What we see in the holistic marketing concept is the traditional marketing concept on steroids. Small businesses are natural for the holistic marketing concept because the bureaucracy of large corporations does not burden them. The size of small businesses makes it possible, perhaps imperative, to have fluid and well-integrated operations.

---

marketing concept

The focus of all company operations should be meeting the customer's needs and wants in ways that distinguish a company from its competition but yet allow a company to meet organizational objectives and achieve profitability.

societal marketing concept

A company will have an advantage over its competitors if it applies the marketing concept in a manner that maximizes society's well-being, which requires balancing customer satisfaction, company profits, and the long-term welfare of society.

green business practice

A business practice that contributes to protecting the environment.

holistic marketing concept

Developing, designing, and implementing marketing programs, processes, and activities that recognize breadth and interdependence.

1.2 Customer Value

customer value

The difference between the benefits a customer receives from a product or a service and the costs associated with obtaining the product or the service.

functional value

A product or a service performs a utilitarian purpose.

social value

A sense of relationship with other groups through images or symbols.

emotional value

The ability to evoke an emotional or an affective response.

epistemic value

Offering novelty or fun.

conditional value

Derived from a particular context or a sociocultural setting, such as shared holidays.

market segmentation

Dividing the market into several portions that are different from each other. It involves recognizing that the market at large is not homogeneous.

The definition of **marketing** specifically includes the notion that offerings must have value to customers, clients, partners, and society at large. This necessarily implies an understanding of what customer value is. **Customer value** is discussed at length in Chapter 2, but we can define it simply as the difference between perceived benefits and perceived costs. Such a simple definition can be misleading, however, because the creation of customer value will always be a challenge—most notably because a company must know its customers extremely well to offer them what they need and want. This is complicated because customers could be seeking **functional value** (a product or a service performs a utilitarian purpose), **social value** (a sense of relationship with other groups through images or symbols), **emotional value** (the ability to evoke an emotional or an affective response), **epistemic value** (offering novelty or fun), or **conditional value** (derived from a particular context or a sociocultural setting, such as shared holidays)—or some combination of these types of value. (See Chapter 2 for a detailed discussion of the types of value.)

Marketing plays a key role in creating and delivering value to a customer. Customer value can be offered in a myriad of ways. In addition to superlative ice cream, for example, the local ice cream shop can offer a frequent purchase card that allows for a free ice cream cone after the purchase of fifteen ice cream products at the regular price. Your favorite website can offer free shipping for Christmas purchases and/or pay for returns. Zappos.com offers free shipping both ways for its shoes. The key is for a company to know its consumers so well that it can provide the value that will be of interest to them.

1.3 Market Segmentation

The purpose of segmenting a market is to focus the marketing and sales efforts of a business on those prospects who are most likely to purchase the company's product(s) or service(s), thereby helping the company (if done properly) earn the greatest return on those marketing and sales expenditures.[12] **Market segmentation** maintains two very important things: (1) there are *relatively* homogeneous subgroups (no subgroup will ever be exactly alike) of the total population that will behave the same way in the marketplace, and (2) these subgroups will behave differently from each other. Market segmentation is particularly important for small businesses because they do not have the resources to serve large aggregate markets or maintain a wide range of different products for varied markets.

The marketplace can be segmented along a multitude of dimensions, and there are distinct differences between consumer and business markets. Some examples of those dimensions are presented in Table 6.1.

LifeLock, a small business that offers identity theft protection services, practices customer type segmentation by separating its market into business and individual consumer segments.

TABLE 6.1 Market Segmentation

Consumer Segmentation Examples	Business Segmentation Examples
Geographic Segmentation ■ Region (e.g., Northeast or Southwest) ■ City or metro size (small, medium, or large) ■ Density (urban, suburban, or rural) ■ Climate (northern or southern)	**Demographic Segmentation** ■ The industry or industries to be served ■ The company sizes to be served (revenue, number of employees, and number of locations)
Demographic Segmentation ■ Age ■ Family size ■ Family life cycle (e.g., single or married without kids) ■ Gender ■ Income ■ Occupation ■ Education ■ Religion ■ Race/ethnicity ■ Generation ■ Nationality ■ Social class	**Operating Variables** ■ The customer technologies to be focused on ■ The users that should be served (heavy, light, medium, or nonusers) ■ Whether customers needing many or few services should be served
Psychographic Segmentation ■ Personality ■ Lifestyle ■ Behavioral occasions (regular or special occasion) ■ Values	**Purchasing Approaches: Which to Choose?** ■ Highly centralized versus decentralized purchasing ■ Engineering dominated, financially dominated, and so forth ■ Companies with whom a strong relationship exists or the most desirable companies ■ Companies that prefer leasing, service contracts, systems purchases, or sealed bidding ■ Companies seeking quality, service, and price
Behavioral Segmentation ■ Benefits of the product (e.g., toothpaste with tartar control) ■ User status (nonuser, regular user, or first-time user) ■ Usage rate (light user, medium user, or heavy user) ■ Loyalty status (none, medium, or absolute) ■ Attitude toward the product (e.g., enthusiastic or hostile)	**Situational Factors: Which to Choose?** ■ Companies that need quick and sudden delivery or service ■ Certain application of the product instead of all applications ■ Large or small orders or something in-between
Personal Characteristics: Which to Choose? ■ Companies with similar people and values ■ Risk-taking or risk-aversive customers ■ Companies that show high loyalty to their suppliers	**Other Characteristics** ■ Status in industry (technology or revenue leader) ■ Need for customization (specialized computer systems)

Source: Adapted from "Market Segmentation," Business Resource Software, Inc., accessed December 2, 2011, http://www.businessplans.org/ segment.html; adapted from Philip Kotler and Kevin Lane Keller, Marketing Management (Upper Saddle River, NJ: Pearson Prentice Hall, 2009), 214, 227.

Market segmentation requires some marketing research. The marketing research process is discussed in Section 3.

1.4   Target Market

Market segmentation should always precede the selection of a **target market**. A target market is one or more segments (e.g., income or income + gender + occupation) that have been chosen as the focus for business operations. The selection of a target market is important to any small business because it enables the business to be more precise with its marketing efforts, thereby being more cost-effective. This will increase the chances for success. The idea behind a target market is that it will be the best match for a company's products and services. This, in turn, will help maximize the efficiency and effectiveness of a company's marketing efforts:

> It is not feasible to go after all customers, because customers have different wants, needs and tastes. Some customers want to be style leaders. They will always buy certain styles and usually pay a high price for them. Other customers are bargain hunters. They try to find the lowest price. Obviously, a company would have difficulty targeting both of these market segments simultaneously with one type of product. For example, a company with premium products would not appeal to bargain shoppers…
>
> Hypothetically, a certain new radio station may discover that their music appeals more to 34–54-year-old women who earn over $50,000 per year. The station would then target these women in their marketing efforts.[13]

Target markets can be further divided into niche markets. A **niche market** is a small, more narrowly defined market that is not being served well or at all by mainstream product or service marketers. People are looking for something specific, so target markets can present special opportunities for small businesses. They fill needs and wants that would not be of interest to larger companies. Niche products would include such things as wigs for dogs, clubs for left-handed golfers, losing weight with apple cider vinegar, paint that transforms any smooth surface into a high performance dry-erase writing surface, and 3D printers. These niche products are provided by small businesses. Niche ideas can come from anywhere.

1.5   Marketing Mix

Marketing mix is easily one of the most well-known marketing terms. More commonly known as "the four Ps," the traditional marketing mix refers to the combination of product, price, promotion, and place (distribution). Each component is controlled by the company, but they are all affected by factors both internal and external to the company. Additionally, each element of the marketing mix is impacted by decisions made for the other elements. What this means is that an alteration of one element in the marketing mix will likely alter the other elements as well. They are inextricably interrelated. No matter the size of the business or organization, there will always be a marketing mix. The marketing mix is discussed in more detail in Chapter 7. A brief overview is presented here.

FIGURE 6.1 The Marketing Mix

Product

Product refers to tangible, physical products as well as to intangible services. Examples of product decisions include design and styling, sizes, variety, packaging, warranties and guarantees, ingredients, quality, safety, brand name and image, brand logo, and support services. In the case of a services business, product decisions also include the design and delivery of the service, with delivery including such things as congeniality, promptness, and efficiency. Without the product, nothing else happens. Product also includes a company's website.

Price

Price is what it will cost for someone to buy the product. Although the exchange of money is what we traditionally consider as price, time and convenience should also be considered. Examples of pricing decisions include pricing strategy selection (e.g., **channel pricing** and **customer segment pricing**), retail versus wholesale pricing, credit terms, discounts, and the means of making online payments. Channel pricing occurs when different prices are charged depending on where the customer purchases the product. A paper manufacturer may charge different prices for paper purchased by businesses, school bookstores, and local stationery stores. Customer segment pricing refers to charging different prices for different groups. A local museum may charge students and senior citizens less for admission.[14]

channel pricing

Different prices are charged depending on where a customer purchases a product.

customer segment pricing

Different prices for different groups.

Promotion

Having the best product in the world is not worth much if people do not know about it. This is the role of *promotion*—getting the word out. Examples of promotional activities include advertising (including on the Internet), sales promotion (e.g., coupons, sweepstakes, and 2-for-1 sales), personal sales, public relations, trade shows, webinars, videos on company websites and YouTube, publicity, social media such as Facebook and Twitter, and the company website itself. **Word-of-mouth communication**, where people talk to each other about their experiences with goods and services, is the most powerful promotion of all because the people who talk about products and services do not have any commercial interest.

word-of-mouth communication

People talk to each other about their experiences with goods and services.

Place

Place is another word for distribution. The objective is to have products and services available where customers want them when they want them. Examples of decisions made for place include inventory, transportation arrangements, channel decisions (e.g., making the product available to customers in retail stores only), order processing, warehousing, and whether the product will be available on a very limited (few retailers or wholesalers) or extensive (many retailers or wholesalers) basis. A company's website is also part of the distribution domain.

Two Marketing Mixes

No matter what the business or organization, there will be a marketing mix. The business owner may not think about it in these specific terms, but it is there nonetheless. Here is an example of how the marketing mix can be configured for a local Italian restaurant (consumer market).

- **Product.** Extensive selection of pizza, hot and cold sub sandwiches, pasta and meat dinners, salads, soft drinks and wine, homemade ice cream and bakery products; the best service in town; and free delivery.
- **Price.** Moderate; the same price is charged to all customer segments.
- **Promotion.** Ads on local radio stations, websites, and local newspaper; flyers posted around town; coupons in ValPak booklets that are mailed to the local area; a sponsor of the local little league teams; ads and coupons in the high school newspaper; and a Facebook presence.
- **Place.** One restaurant is located conveniently near the center of town with plenty of off-street parking. It is open until 10:00 p.m. on weekdays and 11:30 p.m. on Fridays and Saturdays. There is a drive-through for takeout orders, and they have a special arrangement with a local parochial school to provide pizza for lunch one day per week.

Here is an example of how the marketing mix could be configured for a green cleaning services business (business market).

- **Product.** Wide range of cleaning services for businesses and organizations. Services can be weekly or biweekly, and they can be scheduled during the day, evening, weekends, or some combination thereof. Only green cleaning products and processes are used.
- **Price.** Moderate to high depending on the services requested. Some price discounting is offered for long-term contracts.
- **Promotion.** Ads on local radio stations, website with video presentation, business cards that are left in the offices of local businesses and medical offices, local newspaper advertising, Facebook and Twitter presence, trade show attendance (under consideration but very expensive), and direct mail marketing (when an offer, announcement, reminder, or other item is sent to an existing or prospective customer).
- **Place.** Services are provided at the client's business site. The cleaning staff is radio dispatched.

1.6 The Marketing Environment

The **marketing environment** includes all the factors that affect a small business. The **internal marketing environment** refers to the company: its existing products and strategies; culture; strengths and weaknesses; internal resources; capabilities with respect to marketing, manufacturing, and distribution; and relationships with stakeholders (e.g., owners, employees, intermediaries, and suppliers). This environment is controllable by management, and it will present both threats and opportunities.

marketing environment

The factors that affect a small business.

internal marketing environment

A company's existing products and strategies; culture; strengths and weaknesses; internal resources; capabilities with respect to marketing, manufacturing, and distribution; and relationships with stakeholders.

The **external marketing environment** must be understood by the business if it hopes to plan intelligently for the future. This environment, not controllable by management, consists of the following components:

- **Social factors.** For example, cultural and subcultural values, attitudes, beliefs, norms, customs, and lifestyles.
- **Demographics.** For example, population growth, age, gender, ethnicity, race, education, and marital status.
- **Economic environment.** For example, income distribution, buying power and willingness to spend, economic conditions, trading blocs, and the availability of natural resources.
- **Political and legal factors.** For example, regulatory environment, regulatory agencies, and self-regulation.
- **Technology.** For example, the nature and rate of technological change.
- **Competition.** For example, existing firms, potential competitors, bargaining power of buyers and suppliers, and substitutes.[15]
- **Ethics.** For example, appropriate corporate and employee behavior.

external marketing environment

Social factors, demographics, economic environment, political and legal factors, technology, competition, and ethics.

FIGURE 6.2 The Marketing Environment

Small businesses are particularly vulnerable to changes in the external marketing environment because they do not have multiple product and service offerings and/or financial resources to insulate them. However, this vulnerability is offset to some degree by small businesses being in a strong position to make quick adjustments to their strategies if the need arises. Small businesses are also ideally suited to take advantage of opportunities in a changing external environment because they are more nimble than large corporations that can get bogged down in the lethargy and inertia of their bureaucracies.

1.7   Marketing Strategy versus Marketing Management

marketing strategy

Selecting one or more target markets, making differentiation and positioning decisions, and creating and maintaining a marketing mix—all within the context of marketing objectives.

The difference between marketing strategy and marketing management is an important one. **Marketing strategy** involves selecting one or more target markets, deciding how to differentiate and position the product or the service, and creating and maintaining a marketing mix that will hopefully prove successful with the selected target market(s)—all within the context of marketing objectives. **Differentiation** involves a company's efforts to set its product or service apart from the competition. **Positioning** "entails placing the brand [whether store, product, or service] in the consumer's mind in relation to other competing products, based on product traits and benefits that are relevant to the consumer."[16] Segmentation, target market, differentiation, and positioning are discussed in greater detail in Chapter 7.

differentiation

A company's efforts to set its product or service apart from the competition.

positioning

Placing the brand (whether store, product, or service) in the consumer's mind in relation to other competing products, based on product traits and benefits that are relevant to the consumer.

Video Link 6.2

Custom Suit Business Gets Makeover

A change in marketing strategy: the name of the business.

money.cnn.com/video/smallbusiness/2010/10/21/sbiz_turnaround_balani.cnnmoney

Video Link 6.3

Sock Business Comes Home

A change in marketing strategy: the product.

money.cnn.com/video/smallbusiness/2010/11/17/sbiz_turnaround_darn_tough_vermont.smb

marketing management

The day-to-day tactical decisions, resource allocations, and carrying out of tasks that implement a marketing strategy.

Marketing management, by contrast, involves the day-to-day tactical decisions, resource allocations (funds and people), and carrying out of tasks that implement the marketing strategy. It is the responsibility of marketing management to focus on quality and develop the marketing plan, which is discussed in Chapter 8.

 ### Video Clip 6.2

Marketing Concepts in Two Minutes
A humorous definition of key marketing concepts.

View the video online at: http://www.youtube.com/v/l4seWLW2KhQ

KEY TAKEAWAYS

- Marketing is a distinguishing, unique function of a business.
- Marketing is about delivering value and benefits, creating products and services that will meet the needs and wants of customers (perhaps even delighting them) at a price they are willing to pay and in places where they are willing to buy them. It is also about promotion, getting the word out that the product or the service exists.
- The marketing concept has guided business practice since the 1950s.
- Customer value is the difference between perceived benefits and perceived costs. There are different types of customer value: functional, social, epistemic, emotional, and conditional.
- Marketing plays a key role is delivering value to the customer.
- Market segmentation, target market, niche market, marketing mix, marketing environment, marketing management, and marketing strategy are key marketing concepts.
- The marketing mix, also known as the four Ps, consists of product, price, promotion, and place.

EXERCISE

1. Select two different kinds of local small businesses. Ask the owners how they segment the market, who they target, and how they define their marketing mix. Compare the answers that you get. Do you notice any similarities?

2. THE CUSTOMER

LEARNING OBJECTIVES

1. Explain the difference between a customer and a consumer.
2. Understand the relationship between the customer/consumer and the marketing mix.
3. Define the two types of customer markets.
4. Understand the factors that contribute to consumer behavior.
5. Describe the B2C and B2B buying processes.
6. Understand the differences between B2C and B2B buying behavior.
7. Define customer experience and explain its role in small business marketing.
8. Explain the importance of customer loyalty to small business.

It is very important in marketing to distinguish between the customer and the consumer. The **customer**, the person or the business that actually buys a product or a service, will determine whether a business succeeds or fails. It is that simple. It does not matter one iota if a business thinks its product or service is the greatest thing since sliced bread if no one wants to buy it. This is why customers play such a central role in marketing, with everything revolving around their needs, wants, and desires. We see the customer focus in the marketing concept, and we see it in the marketing mix.

customer

The person or the business that actually buys a product or a service.

FIGURE 6.3 The Customer and the Marketing Mix

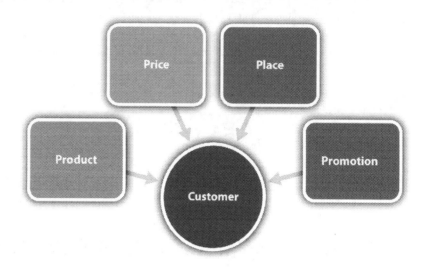

The marketing mix should follow the determination of customer needs, wants, and desires. However, there are instances in which a product is created before the target market is selected and before the rest of the marketing mix is designed. One well-known example is Ivory Soap. This product was created by accident. Air was allowed to work its way into the white soap mixture that was being cooked. The result was Ivory Soap, a new and extraordinarily successful product for Procter & Gamble.[17] Most companies do not have this kind of luck, though, so a more deliberate approach to understanding the customer is critical to designing the right marketing mix.

consumer

The person or the company that uses or consumes a product.

The **consumer** is the person or the company that uses or consumes a product. For example, the customer of a dry cleaning service is the person who drops off clothes, picks them up, and pays for the service. The consumer is the person who wears the clothes. Another example is a food service that caters business events. The person who orders lunch on behalf of the company is the customer. The people who eat the lunch are the consumers. The person who selects the catering service could be either or both. It is common for the customer and the consumer to be the same person, but this should not be assumed for all instances. The challenge is deciding whether to market to the customer or the consumer—or perhaps both.

2.1 Customer Markets

business-to-business (B2B)

Organizations such as corporations; small businesses; government agencies; wholesalers; retailers; and nonprofit organizations, such as hospitals, universities, and museums.

There are two major types of customer markets: **business-to-business (B2B)** customers and **individual consumers or end users (business-to-consumer [B2C])**. B2B customers are organizations such as corporations; small businesses; government agencies; wholesalers; retailers; and nonprofit organizations, such as hospitals, universities, and museums. In terms of dollar volume, the B2B market is where the action is. More dollars and products change hands in sales to business buyers than to individual consumers or end users.[18] The B2B market offers many opportunities for the small business. Examples of B2B products include office supplies and furniture, machinery, ingredients for food preparation, telephone and cell phone service, and delivery services such as FedEx or UPS.

individual consumers or end users (business-to-consumer [B2C])

People who buy for themselves, their households, friends, coworkers, or for other non-business-related purposes.

The B2C market consists of people who buy for themselves, their households, friends, coworkers, or other non-business-related purposes. Examples of B2C products include cars, houses, clothing, food, telephone and cell phone service, cable television service, and medical services. Opportunities in this market are plentiful for small businesses. A walk down Main Street and a visit to the Internet are testaments to this fact.

2.2 Understanding the Customer

The better a small business understands its customers, the better off it will be. It is not easy, and it takes time, but knowing who the customers are, where they come from, what they like and dislike, and what makes them tick will be of immeasurable value in designing a successful marketing mix. Being intuitive can and does work...but not for everyone and not all the time. A more systematic and thorough approach to understanding the customer makes much more sense. The problem is that many if not most small businesses probably do not take the time to do what it takes to understand their customers. This is an important part of the reason why so many small businesses fail.

Video Clip 6.3

Consumer Behavior Matters
Understanding a customer's behavior will increase sales.

View the video online at: http://www.youtube.com/v/1C73fHAdAUM

Consumer Behavior

Consumer behavior—"how individuals, groups, and organizations select, buy, use, and dispose of goods, services, ideas, or experiences to satisfy their needs and wants"[19] —is the result of a complex interplay of factors, none of which a small business can control. These factors can be grouped into four categories: **personal factors**, **social factors**, **psychological or individual factors**, and **situational factors**. It is important that small-business owners and managers learn what these factors are.

consumer behavior

How individuals, groups, and organizations select, buy, use, and dispose of goods, services, ideas, or experiences to satisfy their needs and wants.

personal factors

Age, gender, race, ethnicity, occupation, income, and life-cycle stage.

social factors

Culture, subculture, social class, family, and reference groups.

psychological or individual factors

Motivation, perception, learning, attitudes, personality, and self-concept.

situational factors

The reason for purchase, the time we have available to shop and buy, our mood, and the shopping environment.

life-cycle stage

Where an individual is with respect to passage through the different phases of life (e.g., single, married without children, empty nester, and widow or widower).

reference group

A group that has a direct or indirect influence on a person's attitudes and behavior.

perception

How each person sees, hears, touches, and smells and then interprets the world around him or her.

self-concept

How we see ourselves and how we would like others to see us.

shopping environment

The physical and sensory environment that characterizes all shopping venues.

- **Personal factors.** Age, gender, race, ethnicity, occupation, income, and **life-cycle stage** (where an individual is with respect to passage through the different phases of life, e.g., single, married without children, empty nester, and widow or widower). For example, a 14-year-old girl will have different purchasing habits compared to a 40-year-old married career woman.

- **Social factors.** Culture, subculture, social class, family, and **reference groups** (any and all groups that have a direct [face-to-face] or indirect influence on a person's attitudes and behavior, e.g., family, friends, neighbors, professional groups [including online groups such as LinkedIn], coworkers, and social media such as Facebook and Twitter).[20] For example, it is common for us to use the same brands of products that we grew up with, and friends (especially when we are younger) have a strong influence on what and where we buy. This reflects the powerful influence that family has on consumer behavior.

- **Psychological or individual factors.** Motivation, **perception** (how each person sees, hears, touches, and smells and then interprets the world around him or her), learning, attitudes, personality, and **self-concept** (how we see ourselves and how we would like others to see us). When shopping for a car, the "thud" sound of a door is perceived as high quality whereas a "tinny" sound is not.

- **Situational factors.** The reason for purchase, the time we have available to shop and buy, our mood (a person in a good mood will shop and buy differently compared to a person in a bad mood), and the **shopping environment** (e.g., loud or soft music, cluttered or neat merchandise displays, lighting quality, and friendly or rude help). A shopper might buy a higher quality box of candy as a gift for her best friend than she would buy for herself. A rude sales clerk might result in a shopper walking away without making a purchase.

These factors all work together to influence a five-stage buying-decision process (Table 6.2), the specific workings of which are unique to each individual. This is a generalized process. Not all consumers will go through each stage for every purchase, and some stages may take more time and effort than others depending on the type of purchase decision that is involved.[21] Knowing and understanding the consumer decision process provides a small business with better tools for designing and implementing its marketing mix.

TABLE 6.2 Five Stages of the Consumer Buying Process

	Stage	Description	Example
1.	**Problem recognition**	Buyer recognizes a problem or need.	Joanne's laptop just crashed, but she thinks it can be fixed. She needs it quickly.
2.	**Information search**	Buyer searches for extensive or limited information depending on the requirements of the situation. The sources may be personal (e.g., family or friends), commercial (e.g., advertising or websites), public (e.g., mass media or consumer rating organizations), or experiential (e.g., handling or examining the product).	Joanne is very knowledgeable about computers, but she cannot fix them. She needs to find out about the computer repair options in her area. She asks friends for recommendations, checks out the yellow pages, does a Google search, draws on her own experience, and asks her husband.
3.	**Evaluation of alternatives**	Buyer compares different brands, services, and retailers. There is no universal process that everyone uses.	Joanne knows that computer repair services are available at the nearby Circuit Place and Computer City stores. Unfortunately, she has had bad experiences at both. Her husband, David, recently took his laptop to a small computer repair shop in town that has been in business for less than a year. He was very pleased. Joanne checks out their website and is impressed by the very positive reviews. None of her friends could recommend anyone.
4.	**Purchase decision**	Buyer makes a choice.	Joanne decides to take her computer to the small repair shop in town.
5.	**Postpurchase behavior**	How the buyer feels about the purchase and what he or she does or does not do after the purchase.	Joanne's laptop was fixed quickly, and the cost was very reasonable. She feels very good about the experience, so she posts a glowing review on the company's website, recommends the shop to everyone she knows, and plans to go back should the need arise. Had she been unhappy with her experience, she would have posted a negative review on the company's website, told everyone she knows not to go there, and refuse to go there again. It is this latter scenario that should be every small business's nightmare.

Source: Philip Kotler and Kevin Lane Keller, *Marketing Management* (Upper Saddle River, NJ: Pearson Prentice Hall, 2009), 168; Dana-Nicoleta Lascu and Kenneth E. Clow, *Essentials of Marketing* (Mason, OH: Atomic Dog Publishing, 2007), 112–17.

Video Link 6.4

California's Bargain Wine Boom

Consumers are shifting to less expensive wines from small winemakers.

www.time.com/time/video/player/0,32068,101527510001_1997358,00.html

Business Buying Behavior

Understanding how businesses make their purchasing decisions is critical to small businesses that market to the business sector. Purchases by a business are more complicated than purchases by someone making a personal purchase (B2C). B2B purchases vary according to dollar amount, the people involved in the decision process, and the amount of time needed to make the decision,[22] and they involve "a much more complex web of interactions between prospects and vendors in which the actual transaction represents only a small part of the entire purchase process."[23]

The individual or the group that makes the B2B buying decisions is referred to as the **buying center**. The buying center consists of "all those individuals and groups who participate in the purchasing decision-making process, who share some common goals and the risks arising from the decision."[24] The buying center in a small business could be as small as one person versus the twenty or more people in the buying center of a large corporation. Regardless of the size of the buying center, however, there are seven distinct roles: initiator, gatekeeper, user, purchaser or buyer, decider, approver, and influencer.[25] One person could play multiple roles, there could be multiple people in a single role, and the roles could change over time and across different purchase situations.

1. **Initiator**. The person who requests that something be purchased.
2. **Gatekeeper**. The person responsible for the flow of information to the buying center. This could be the secretary or the receptionist that screens calls and prevents salespeople from accessing users or deciders. By having control over information, the gatekeeper has a major impact on the purchasing process.
3. **User**. The person in a company who uses a product or takes advantage of a service.
4. **Purchaser or buyer**. The person who makes the actual purchase.
5. **Decider**. The person who decides on product requirements, suppliers, or both.
6. **Approver**. The person who authorizes the proposed actions of the decider or the buyer.
7. **Influencer**. The person who influences the buying decision but does not necessarily use the product or the service. The influencer may assist in the preparation of product or service specifications, provide vendor ideas, and suggest criteria for evaluating vendors.

buying center

Individuals and groups who participate in the purchasing decision-making process and who share some common goals and the risks arising from the decision.

FIGURE 6.4 The B2B Buying Process

Identification of Needs

These needs are usually a direct result of the company's operations. For example,
the local deli needs bread, rolls, meats, cheese, and other ingredients.
When supplies run low, it's time to reorder.

Establishment of Specifications

The business spells out what is needed and hopefully develops decision criteria on which
to make a vendor choice. If the current vendor is satisfactory, it becomes a simple rebuy
situation. If the current vendor is not satisfactory, it becomes a new buy situation.
A local deli owner likes all of her current vendors, so she just reorders.

Identification of Feasible Solutions

There may be different ways to handle a particular purchasing need—most commonly
purchasing from an external business, producing the product yourself, or leasing it.
In the case of the local deli owner, she will purchase from external businesses.

Identification of Feasible Vendors

If external sources will be used, they need to be contacted to determine their interest.
All those who are interested must submit a bid or price quote. The formality of the
process will be determined by the size of the small business and the nature of
the product. Buying deli ingredients should be simple and straightforward.

Evaluation of Vendors

Each vendor's proposal, bid, or price quotation must be evaluated for acceptability.
The decision criteria can be simple or complicated depending on the nature of
the product and business. If the owner of the local deli were looking to change
vegetable vendors, she would have to compare quality, price, and service.

Vendor Selection

The choice is made. The local deli owner will buy her vegetables from Veggies 'R Us.

Negotiation of Purchase Terms

This last step tends to be a formality because most of the purchase terms have already
been worked out. The buyer will have to work out any terms that still remain. The local
deli is all set. Everything, including the delivery schedule, has been agreed upon.

Source: Adapted from Dana-Nicoleta Lascu and Kenneth E. Clow, Essentials of Marketing (Mason, OH: Atomic Dog Publishing, 2007), 148–55.

The B2B purchasing process for any small business will be some variation of the process described in Figure 6.4. The specifics of the process will depend on the nature of product, the simplicity of the decision to be made, and the number of people involved. Clearly the purchasing process for a single-person business will be much simpler than for a multiproduct business of 400 employees.

2.3   The Customer Experience

Customer experience is one of the great frontiers for innovation.[26]

- *Jeneanne Rae*

Customer experience refers to a customer's entire interaction with a company or an organization. The experience will range from positive to negative, and it begins when any potential customer has contact with any aspect of a business's persona—the company's marketing, all representations of the total brand, and what others say about the experience of working with the business.[27]

Customer Experience in the B2C Market

Customers will experience multiple **touch points** (i.e., all the communication, human, and physical interactions that customers experience during their relationship life cycle with a small business)[28] during their visit. In a retail situation, a customer will experience the store design and layout; the merchandise that is carried and how it is displayed; the colors, sounds, and scents in the store; the cleanliness of the store; the lighting; the music; the helpfulness of the staff; and the prices. In a business situation, a customer will experience the design and layout of the reception and office areas, the colors chosen for carpeting and furniture, the friendliness and helpfulness of the reception staff, and the demeanor of the person or people to be seen. The experience also occurs when a customer communicates with a company via telephone; e-mail; the company website; and Facebook, Twitter, or other social media.

> ### The Role of Store Design in Customer Experience
>
> Store design plays a very important role in a customer's experience. Check out the following three examples of small business store redesigns that have contributed to increased profitability:
>
> 1. Fine Wine & Good Spirits, Philadelphia
>   www.retailcustomerexperience.com/slideshow.php?ssn=273
> 2. The Diamond Cellar, Dublin, Ohio
>   www.retailcustomerexperience.com/slideshow.php?ssn=145
> 3. Roche Bros. Supermarkets
>   www.retailcustomerexperience.com/slideshow.php?ssn=261

Good customer experiences "*from the perspective of the customer*…are useful (deliver value), usable (make it easy to find and engage with the value), and enjoyable (emotionally engaging so that people want to use them)."[29] A customer experience can be a one-time occurrence with a particular company, but experiences are more likely to happen across many time frames.[30] The experience begins at the point of need awareness and ends at need extinction.[31]

> ### Video Link 6.5
>
> #### Exploring Consumer Behavior Online and Offline
>
> Consumers are willing to pay more for products they can touch. "Touching" is an important part of the customer experience.
>
> videos.smallbusinessnewz.com/2010/09/16/exploring-consumer-behavior-online-and-offline

B2C customer experiences also involve emotional connections. When small businesses make emotional connections with customers and prospects, there is a much greater chance to forge bonds that will lead to repeat and referral business. When a business does not make those emotional connections, a customer may go elsewhere or may work with the business for the moment—but never come back and not refer other customers or clients to the business.[32]

Many businesses may not appreciate that 50 percent of a customer's experience is about how a customer feels. Emotions can drive or destroy value.[33] "Customers will gladly pay more for an experience that is not only functional but emotionally rewarding. Companies skilled at unlocking emotional issues and building products and services around them can widen their profit margins…Great customer experiences are full of surprising 'wow' moments."[34]

Small businesses should learn and think about how to market a great B2C customer experience, not just a product or a service.[35] Design an experience that is emotionally engaging by mapping the

customer experience

A customer's entire interaction with a company or an organization.

touch points

All the communication, human, and physical interactions that customers experience during their relationship life cycle with a small business.

customer's journey[36] —and then think of ways to please, perhaps even delight, the customer along that journey. A history of sustained positive customer experiences will increase the chances that a business will be chosen over its competition.[37]

> *Meaningful, memorable, fun, unusual and unexpected experiences influence the way customers perceive you in general and feel about you in particular. These little details are so easy to overlook, so tempting to brush off as unimportant. But add a number of seemingly minor details together, and you end up with something of far more value than you would without them.*
>
> *It's the little details that keep a customer coming back over and over, it's the little details that cause a customer to rationalize paying more because she feels she is getting more, it's the little details that keep people talking about you and recommending everyone they know to you.*
>
> *Anyone can do the big things right; it's the little things that differentiate one business from another and that influence customers to choose one over the other. Often, small-business owners cut out the little details when times get tough, and this is a big mistake.[38]*

There is, however, no one-size-fits-all design for customer experience in the B2C market. Small businesses vary in terms of the size, industry, and nature of the business, so customer experience planning and design will necessarily differ in accordance with these factors. The customer experience for a 1-person business will be very different from an experience with a 400-employee company.

 Video Clip 6.4

How to Hire the Right Customer Service Person For Your Small Business

View the video online at: http://www.youtube.com/v/ToP37pi5NIQ

Customer Experience in the B2B Market

Talk to customer experience executives in a B2B environment about emotional engagement and you will see their eyes roll. Ask them if they would consider designing retail stores with customized smell and music to reinforce the customer experience and you will most likely be ushered out of their offices. Mention the iPod or MySpace experience and you will likely face a torrent of sighs and frowns.[39]
  - Lior Arussy

Creating customer relationships in the B2B environment is radically different from the B2C environment because customers face different challenges, resources, and suppliers.[40] In the B2B world, there will almost always be "multiple people across multiple functions who play major roles in evaluating, selecting, managing, paying for and using the products and services their company buys…So, unlike the B2C company, if you are a B2B supplier there will be a host of individual 'customers' in engineering, purchasing, quality, manufacturing, etc. with different needs and expectations whose individual experiences you must address to make any given sale."[41] This is offset, however, by the fact that a B2B company probably has a substantially smaller number of potential customers in a given target market, so it is often possible to actually get to know them personally. Smart B2B firms can tailor their products or services specifically to deliver the experiences wanted by people they know directly.[42]

Video Clip 6.5

How Customer Experience Applies in the B2B Sector
Customer experience concerns are relevant in the B2B environment.

View the video online at: http://www.youtube.com/v/Zb0iXDyiHdY

Despite the challenges, customer experience is relevant in the B2B environment. However, because "the buy decision-making processes in most companies are typically fully structured and quantitative criteria-based...the explicitly emotional experience laden sales pitch that drives consumer buying is not a fit in the B2B world."[43] The products that often represent B2B business's sole value proposition are rarely emotionally engaging or visually appealing. Think bolts, wires, copy paper, shredding machines, bread for a restaurant, and machinery. How engaging can these items be?

There are touch points in B2B processes[44] before and after the sale (e.g., information gathering, website visits and inquiries, delivery of spare parts, service calls on machinery and office equipment, and telephone interactions) that can be identified and improved. However, the inherent differences between B2B and B2C environments must be clearly understood so that the B2C customer experience models do not become the paradigm for B2B customer experience designs. As is the case in the B2C market, there is no universal approach to customer experience in the B2B market. Small B2B companies also vary in terms of the products and the services offered and the size, industry, and nature of the business, so customer experience planning and design will necessarily differ in accordance with these factors.

The greatest challenge in delighting B2B customers is adding unique and differentiating value that solves customer problems. When defining the customer experience, recognize that this value should extend to the entire customer and business life cycle—presale engagement, the sales process, and post-sale interactions. Experiences at every stage of the customer life cycle should be customized to each individual customer.[45]

Video Link 6.6

Customer Experience Differentiation

Customer experience in the B2C and B2B environments.

www.clearaction.biz/differentiation.html

2.4 Customer Loyalty

Customer loyalty is "all about attracting the right customers, getting them to buy, buy often, buy in higher quantities and bring [the business] even more customers."[46] It involves an emotional commitment to a brand or a business ("We love doing business with your company."), an attitude component ("I feel better about this brand or this business."), and a behavior component ("I'll keep buying this brand or patronizing that business, regardless."). Attitudes are important because repeat purchases alone do not always mean that a customer is emotionally invested.[47] Think about the thrill of buying car insurance. We may keep buying from the same company, but we rarely have an emotional commitment to that company. Emotional commitment is key in customer loyalty.

The benefits of loyal customers are numerous:[48]

customer loyalty

Attracting the right customers, getting them to buy, buy often, buy in higher quantities, and bring the business even more customers.

fixed costs

Costs that remain the same regardless of the amount of sales (e.g., rent).

- They buy more and are often willing to pay more. This creates a steadier cash flow for a business.
- Loyal customers will refer other customers to a company, saving the marketing and advertising costs of acquiring customers.
- They are more forgiving when you make mistakes—even serious ones—especially if you have a system in place that empowers employees to correct errors on the spot. Then loyal customers become even more loyal.
- A loyal customer's endorsement can outstrip the most extravagant marketing efforts. The word on the street is usually more powerful.
- Thriving companies with high customer loyalty usually have loyal employees who are genuinely engaged.
- Thriving companies with high customer and employee loyalty are generally known to outpace their competition in innovation.
- Loyal customers understand a company's processes and can offer suggestions for improvement.
- An increase in customer retention can boost a company's bottom-line profit by 25–100 percent, depending on **fixed costs**—costs that remain the same regardless of the amount of sales (e.g., rent).

Customer loyalty begins with the customer experience and is built over time through the collection of positive experiences.[49] This will be true no matter the size, industry, and nature of the small business. Customers' experiences will influence how much they will buy, whether they switch to a competitor, and whether they will recommend the brand or the business to someone else.[50] Small businesses cannot rely on the loyalty that comes from convenience (e.g., using the car dealer close to home for repairs instead of the one farther away that provides better service). Loyalty is about making a customer feel special. This is the dream of all small businesses—which is something that small businesses are particularly well suited to create. Because of their size, it is easier for small businesses to have closer relationships with their customers, create a more personal shopping environment, and, in general, create great customer experiences. Think back to Bob Brown of the Cheshire Package Store (Chapter 2). He prides himself on the kind of shopping environment and customer relationships that lead to loyalty.

Grounds for Loyalty

How do people make choices about which pharmacy to go to? Paul Gauvreau decided to find out by asking customers why they were shopping in one particular store.

- "I shop here because it's close to where I live." (The convenience shopper.)
- "I like the pharmacist, I trust him/her." (This customer has a good relationship with their pharmacist.)
- "The staff makes me feel like part of the family."
- "I feel like they care about my health."
- "The entire atmosphere in this store reminds me of home, where I felt welcome."
- "I don't feel like another number here or just another patient. They really care about me."

Paul concluded that this pharmacy succeeded in differentiating itself from the competition in a unique way: by how they made their customers feel—and this is what will generate the most intimate loyalty in a customer.[51]

Video Link 6.7

Listening to Customers Leads to Loyalty

All customers really want is for the companies they do business with to listen to them.

www.1to1media.com/video/watch.aspx?v=HXkpCS3dYz8&playlist=Search-Results&query=listening

Video Link 6.8

Is There a Right Kind of Customer Loyalty?

Behavioral, emotional, and profitable customer loyalty. What they are, and what companies can do to create and improve them.

www.1to1media.com/video/watch.aspx?v=wLbyc2uOY0c

Small businesses that are operating in the B2B sector might wonder whether there are major differences between B2B and B2C models of customer loyalty. Michael Lowenstein, vice president and senior consultant in customer loyalty management at Harris Interactive says that "except for the specific supplier decision criteria, which varies from situation to situation, there is [sic] more similarities than differences between B2C and B2B in what drives customer loyalty behavior."[52] What can be concluded in either case is that achieving and retaining loyal customers should be an important goal for any company—small or large.

KEY TAKEAWAYS

- The customer and the consumer are not necessarily the same person…but they can be.
- The customer and the consumer should be the focus of the marketing mix.
- B2C and B2B are the two types of customer markets. The B2B market dwarfs the B2C market in terms of sales.
- It is critical for a small business to understand its customers.
- Customer experience is a person's entire interaction with a small business. It involves emotional connections to the business.
- There is no one-size-fits-all customer experience for a B2C or a B2B small business. The customer's journey should be mapped and changes made to improve the experience.
- There are big differences between the customer experiences for B2C and B2B businesses.
- There are multiple benefits to customer loyalty. It is important to small business success. A positive customer experience drives loyalty.

EXERCISES

1. Visit a small business that you patronize often. Plan to make a purchase. Describe your experience from the time you enter the store to the time you leave (the touch points) as specifically as possible. What surprised you the most? Were you disappointed at all? Please explain. What recommendations would you make to the owner? Do you plan on going back to this store?
2. Identify a small business to which you are loyal. Why are you loyal to that business? What in particular does the business do that you like? Have you told them?

3. MARKETING RESEARCH

LEARNING OBJECTIVES

1. Understand and be able to explain what marketing research is all about.
2. Explain why a small business should conduct marketing research and why many small businesses do not do it.
3. Define and give examples of the two types of marketing research.
4. Understand the marketing research process.
5. Understand the costs of marketing research.

Not everyone can be like Steve Jobs of Apple. Jobs was famous for saying that he did not pay too much attention to customer research, particularly with respect to what customers say they want. Instead, he was very "adept at seeing under the surface of what customers want now; they just don't realize it until they see it. This ability is best expressed by the German word 'zeitgeist'—the emerging spirit of the age or mood of the moment. It probably best translates as market readiness or customer readiness. People like Jobs can see what the market is ready for before the market knows itself."[53] Most small businesses will not find themselves in this enviable position. However, this does not mean that all small businesses take a methodical approach to studying the marketplace and their prospective as well as current consumers. Marketing research among small businesses ranges along a continuum from no research at all to the hiring of a professional research firm. Along the way, there will be both formal and informal approaches, the differences again being attributable to the size, industry, and nature of the business along with the personal predispositions of the small-business owners or managers. Nonetheless, it is important for small-business owners and managers to understand what marketing research is all about and how it can be helpful to their businesses. It is also important to understand that marketing research must take the cultures of different communities into consideration because the target market might not be the same—even in relatively close localities.

3.1 What Is Marketing Research?

Marketing research is about gathering the information that is needed to make decisions about a business. As an important precursor to the development of a marketing strategy, marketing research "involves the systematic design, collection, recording, analysis, interpretation, and reporting of information pertinent to a particular marketing decision facing a company."[54] Marketing research is not a perfect science because much of it deals with people and their constantly changing feelings and behaviors—which are all influenced by countless subjective factors. What this means is that facts and opinions must be gathered in an orderly and objective way to find out what people want to buy, not just what the business wants to sell them.[55] It also means that information relevant to the market, the competition, and the marketing environment should be gathered and analyzed in an orderly and objective way.

3.2 Why Do It?

The simple truth is that a small business cannot sell products or services—at least not for long—if customers do not want to buy them. Consider the following true scenario:[56] A local small business that specialized in underground sprinkling systems and hot tubs for years decided to start selling go-carts. Not long after they introduced them, they had a fleet of go-carts lined up outside their business with a huge "Must go; prices slashed" banner over them. This was not a surprise to anyone else. Go-carts had nothing to do with their usual products, so why would their regular customers be interested in them? Also, a quick look at the demographics of the area would have revealed that the majority of the consumers in the retirement town were elderly. There would likely be little interest in go-carts. It is clear that the business owner would have benefitted from some marketing research.

Marketing research for small business offers many benefits. For example, companies can find hidden niches, design customer experiences, build customer loyalty, identify new business opportunities, design promotional materials, select channels of distribution, find out which customers are profitable and which are not, determine what areas of the company's website are generating the most revenue, and identify market trends that are likely to have the greatest impact on the business. Answers can be found for the important questions that all small businesses face, such as the following:[57]

- How are market trends impacting my business?
- How does our target market make buying decisions?
- What is our market share and how can we increase it?
- How does customer satisfaction with our products or services measure up to that of the competition?
- How will our existing customers respond to a new product or service?

In many ways, small businesses have a marketing research advantage over large businesses. The small business is close to its customers and is able to learn much more quickly about their buying habits, what they like, and what they do not like. However, even though "small business owners have a sense [of] their customers' needs from years of experience…this informal information may not be timely or relevant to the current market."[58]

It therefore behooves a small business to think seriously in terms of a marketing research effort—even a very small one—that is more focused and structured. This will increase the chances that the results will be timely and will enable the small-business owner or manager "to reduce business risks, spot current and upcoming problems in the current market, identify sales opportunities, and develop plans of actions."[59] The specific nature and extent of any marketing research effort will, however, be a function of the product, the size and nature of the business, the industry, and the small-business owner or manager. There is no approach that is right for all situations and all small businesses.

3.3   Types of Marketing Research

Small businesses can conduct primary or secondary marketing research or a combination of the two. **Primary marketing research** involves the collection of data for a specific purpose or project.[60] For example, asking existing customers why they purchase from the business and how they heard about it would be considered primary research. Another example would be conducting a study of specific competitors with respect to products and services offered and their price levels. These would be simple marketing research projects for a small business, either business-to-consumer (B2C) or business-to-business (B2B), and would not require the services of a professional research company. Such companies would be able to provide more sophisticated marketing research, but the cost might be too high for the many small businesses that are operating on a shoestring budget.

Data gathering techniques in primary marketing research can include observation, surveys, interviews, questionnaires, and **focus groups**. A focus group is six to ten people carefully selected by a researcher and brought together to discuss various aspects of interest at length.[61] Focus groups are not likely to be chosen by small businesses because they are costly. However, the other techniques would be well within the means of most small businesses—and each can be conducted online (except for observation), by mail, in person, or by telephone. SurveyMonkey is a popular and very inexpensive online survey provider. Its available plans run from free to less than $20 per month for unlimited questions and unlimited responses. They also provide excellent tutorials. SurveyMonkey, used by many large companies, would be an excellent choice for any small business.

Secondary marketing research is based on information that has already been gathered and published. Some of the information may be free—as in the case of the US Census, public library databases and collections, certain websites, company information, and some trade associations to which the company belongs—or it can be bought. Purchased sources of information (not an exhaustive list) include newspapers,[62] magazines, trade association reports, and **proprietary research reports** (i.e., reports from organizations that conduct original research and then sell it). eMarketer is a company that provides excellent marketing articles for free but also sells its more comprehensive reports. The reports are excellent, providing analysis and in-depth data that cannot be found elsewhere, but they are pricey.

If a small business was looking to introduce a new product to an entirely different market, secondary research could be conducted to find out where customer prospects live and whether the potential market is big enough to make the investment in the new product worthwhile.[63] Secondary research would also be appropriate when looking for things such as economic trends, online consumer purchasing habits, and competitor identification.

primary marketing research

The collection of data for a specific purpose or project.

focus group

Six to ten people carefully selected by the researcher(s) and brought together to discuss various aspects of interest at length.

secondary marketing research

Information that has already been gathered and published.

proprietary research report

A report from an organization that conducts original research and then sells the results.

TABLE 6.3   Types of Marketing Research

Primary Marketing Research	Secondary Marketing Research
Data for a specific purpose or for a specific project	Information that has already been gathered and published
Tends to be more expensive	Tends to be lower cost
Customized to meet a company's needs	May not meet a company's needs
Fresh, new data	Data are frequently outdated (e.g., using US 2000 census data in 2011)
Proprietary—no one else has it	Available to competitors
Examples: in-person surveys, customer comments, observation, and SurveyMonkey online survey	**Examples:** *Wall Street Journal*, *Bloomberg BusinessWeek*, US Census 2010, Bureau of Labor Statistics, FedStats, MarketingSherpa, ResearchInfo, and eMarketer

Source: Adapted from Marcella Kelly and Jim McGowen, BUSN (Mason, OH: South-Western, 2008), 147.

The Marketing Research Process

Most small-business owners do marketing research every day—without being aware of it. They analyze returned items, ask former customers why they switched to another company, and look at a competitor's prices. Formal marketing research simply makes this familiar process orderly by providing the appropriate framework.[64] Effective marketing research follows the following six steps:[65]

1. **Define the problem and the research objectives.** Care must be taken not to define the problem too broadly or too narrowly—and not to identify a symptom as the problem. The research objectives should flow from the problem definition.

2. **Develop the research plan.** This is a plan for gathering the needed information, part of which will include cost. Also to be determined is the following: whether primary research, secondary research, or some combination of the two will be used. The specific techniques will be identified, and a timetable will be established.

3. **Collect the information.** This phase is typically the most expensive and the most error prone.

4. **Analyze the information.** Analysis involves extracting meaning from the raw data. It can involve simple tabulations or very sophisticated statistical techniques. The objective is to convert the raw data into actionable information.

5. **Present the findings.** The findings are presented to the decision maker(s). In many small businesses, the owner or the manager may conduct the research, so the findings are presented in a format that will make sense for the owner and other members of the decision-making team.

6. **Make the decision.** The owner or manager must consider the information and decide how to act on it. One possible result is that the information gathered is not sufficient for making a decision. The problem may be a flawed marketing research process or problems obtaining access to appropriate data. The question becomes whether the situation is important enough to warrant additional research.

3.4 What Does It Cost?

A popular approach with small-business owners is to allocate a small percentage of gross sales for the most recent year for marketing research. This usually amounts to about 2 percent for an existing business. It has been suggested, however, that as much as 10 percent of gross sales should be allocated to marketing research if the business is planning to launch a new product.[66]

There are several things that small businesses can do to keep the costs down. They can do the research on their own; work with local colleges and universities to engage business students in research projects; conduct online surveys using companies such as SurveyMonkey and Zoomerang; and create an online community with forums, blogs, and chat sessions that reveal customers' experiences with a company's product or the perception of a company's brand.[67] The latter two options, of course, presume the existence of an e-commerce operation. Even given the inexpensive options that are available, however, hiring a professional research firm can be worth the price. The specific marketing research choice(s) made will depend, as always, on the size and the nature of the business, the industry, and the individual B2C or B2B small-business owner or manager.

3.5 When Should Marketing Research Be Done?

There is no precise answer to this question. As a general rule, marketing research should be done when important marketing decisions must be made. It should be done at times when customers may be easily accessible (e.g., a gift shop may want to conduct research before the holiday season when customers are more likely to be thinking about buying gifts for friends and loved ones), when you are thinking about adding a new product or service to the business, or when a competitor seems to be taking away market share. The trick, though, "is not to wait very long, because your competitors can start getting the answers before you do."[68]

3.6 Common Marketing Research Mistakes

Before deciding on a marketing research path, it is important for a small-business owner or manager to be aware of the following common pitfalls that small businesses encounter:[69]

- **Thinking the research will cost too much.** Small businesses definitely face a challenge to afford the costs of marketing research. However, marketing research costs range from free to several thousands of dollars.

- **Using only secondary research.** The published work of others is a great place to start, but it is often outdated and provides only broad knowledge. More specific knowledge can be obtained from purchasing proprietary reports, but this can be pricey, and the focus may not be quite right. Primary research should also be considered.

- **Using only web resources.** Data available on the Internet are available to everyone who can find it. It may not be fully accurate, and its accuracy may be difficult to evaluate. Deeper searches can be conducted at the local library, college campus, or small business center.

- **Surveying only the people you know.** This will not get you the most useful, accurate, and objective information. You must talk to actual customers to find out about their needs, wants, and expectations.
- **Hitting a wall.** Any research project has its ups and downs. It is easy to lose motivation and shorten the project. Persistence must be maintained because it will all come together in the end. It is important to talk to actual or potential customers early.

KEY TAKEAWAYS

- Many small businesses do not conduct any marketing research.
- Marketing research is about gathering the information that is needed to make decisions about the business.
- Marketing research is important because businesses cannot sell products or services that people do not want to buy.
- Small businesses can conduct primary or secondary research or a combination of the two. They can also buy proprietary reports that have been prepared by other companies.
- It is common for small businesses to allocate 2 percent of their gross sales to marketing research. Several things can be done to keep marketing research costs down.
- Marketing research should be done when key decisions must be made.
- Small-business owners should be aware of several common marketing research pitfalls that small businesses encounter.

EXERCISE

1. A small-business owner has an idea for a new product that may be a big hit with current customers and bring in new customers as well. The owner has not done much marketing research in the past, but with the lagging economy, the owner wants to be sure that the right steps are being taken. What would you advise the owner concerning the importance of marketing research and how to proceed? Be specific.

FRANK'S BARBEQUE: A MARKETING QUESTION

One night after the restaurant had closed, Frank Rainsford sat down with his son, Robert. Frank had finished reading his son's business plan for a third time. Robert sensed that his father had some sort of reservations. "What's the matter, Dad? Didn't you like the plan?" Frank paused and said, "Bobby, from a technical standpoint I think you have done a very, very credible job, but you are right. I do have some concerns." Disappointed, Robert asked his father to lay out his concerns.

Frank told him that opening another restaurant was a huge and expensive undertaking. He knew that Robert understood the financial risks, but he was not sure that his son understood the problems associated with getting people to come to a new restaurant. Frank was straightforward and told his son, "I have been at this for thirty-plus years. It took me years to build up my client base. I really know my customers and what they like. Up until this year the only marketing I did was flyers and a few ads in the local paper and the church bulletin. How are we going to understand our customers at the new location? We are going to have to fill it up quickly if we are to pay the bills. I know I've had some good success with selling the sauces during the last few years, but remember that I'm selling them from Harry's grocery store. His customers already know me and my product. Your plans for ramping up sauce sales are great, but again, how are we going to get people to know who we are and interested enough to by a six dollar bottle of barbecue sauce?" Frank went on to tell his son that he knew that Robert was extremely knowledgeable about marketing and the use of the Internet. He reminded Robert that he had given him a greatly enlarged marketing budget in 2010.

If you were Robert, how would you go about alleviating your father's concerns? (You may want to consult Chapter 16 and review Robert's business plan for a new restaurant.) Answer the question from a marketing perspective.

4. THE THREE THREADS

LEARNING OBJECTIVES

1. Understand how marketing contributes to customer value.
2. Explain how marketing can positively and negatively impact cash flow.
3. Explain how digital technology and the e-environment impact marketing.

4.1 Customer Value Implications

It is the customer who decides whether to buy a small business's products or services. The customer decides whether the appropriate value is present, and that value will always be as he or she perceives it. "The decision to buy and the price that customers are willing to pay is dependent on their assessment of the value they will receive from one product relative to the known alternatives."[70] Marketing plays a key role in creating and delivering value to the customer, but it is the establishment of a strong link between customer value requirements and the major value-producing activities of the firm that is the foundation on which the delivery of superior customer value is based.[71]

The creation of customer value begins with a company commitment to the customer. Marketing has the responsibility for researching the current or prospective customer base, selecting a target market, and then developing a marketing mix that will hopefully meet the value expectations of customers. Product comes first, followed by price, promotion, and place. Delivering customer value should be the key consideration in all marketing mix decisions, with all four Ps working together. A small business needs to be aware, however, that customer value can and does change. What is considered as providing appropriate value one day may change the next day. It is marketing's responsibility to keep on top of such value migrations so that the marketing mix can be changed accordingly. Fortunately, small businesses are in a stronger position to make marketing mix changes because they are generally more nimble and are closer to the customer.

4.2 Cash-Flow Implications

Because sales are the only generator of revenue in most small businesses, marketing decisions play a major role in the health of a company's cash flow. A product or a service that does not sell will have a negative impact on cash flow, whereas a winner can result in a cash-flow bonanza. However, a product or a service that generates major cash can actually send the business into failure if the appropriate cash-flow mechanisms are not in place. The timely collection of money owed and being able to pay for the products and the services needed to run the business are critical to a positive cash flow. Providing extended terms for vendor accounts to be paid, delayed payments from credit cards used by customers for their purchases (something that is expected by most customers as part of the value they receive), the costs associated with an over ambitious expansion, money-losing customer promotions, a product or a service that is priced too low (unable to cover costs), and a distribution approach that does not work well will all have a negative impact on cash flow.

Video Clip 6.6

Cash Flow and the Marketing Budget
Why cash flow is relevant to marketing.

View the video online at: http://www.youtube.com/v/0gYdhI7_qhM

4.3 Digital Technology and E-Environment Implications

The integration, acceptance, and popularity of technology in the current marketplace and workplace are widespread, particularly with respect to marketing. Marketing opportunities have exploded with the rise of digital technology and the Internet, and with those opportunities have come new ways to make marketing decisions and interact with customers.

As do all businesses, small businesses should be concerned about the customer experience. Emerging mobile technologies make it possible "to elevate the classic brick-and-mortar shopper experience."[72] But there is a cautionary note. A **mobile shopping solution** (i.e., a way for shoppers to engage with their favorite retail brand or store using their mobile phones) can be cost-prohibitive for many retailers or B2B businesses, especially small ones. Nonetheless, it is a technology that small retail businesses should keep their eye on. One retail shopping solution is being developed by ARS Interactive and CellPoint Mobile. It will be "the only fully integrated mobile retail shopping solution in the United States that combines product information, coupons, customer loyalty and mobile payment into one experience. This will give customers complete shopping control directly from their mobile phones, while providing retailers with a constant customer touch-point inside and outside the store."[73]

mobile shopping solution

A way for shoppers to engage with their favorite retail brand or store using their mobile phones.

 Video Clip 6.7

Mobile Marketing Solutions for Retail
An example of a mobile-assisted shopping solution offered by 2ergo.

View the video online at: http://www.youtube.com/v/P6IVuUuTC0U

Technology is also available to help in customer value analysis. New in 2010, the Value-Strategy Tool Kit helps a company[74]

- understand the true strengths and weaknesses of a product offer and identify opportunities that can make a product more competitive,
- look at a product head-to-head against each competitor to think through the selling strategy,
- set prices based on what a product is truly worth,
- hone the marketing message, and
- align the management team around a plan to serve customers better.

The target for this software is the larger business, but the principles remain the same. Because the price is based on the number of users, a small business with only one or two users may find it affordable.

Social media also needs to be seriously considered in small business marketing efforts. Social media "generally refers to websites featuring user-generated content or material created by visitors rather than the website publishers. In turn, these sites encourage visitors to read and respond to that material."[75] Popular social media sites include Facebook and Twitter. These channels are being used by a wide range of small businesses to market their businesses via interaction with their customers.

As has been said in the past, small businesses will have different technology needs and desires. However, given the pervasiveness of technology in marketing, it is in the best interests of any small business to consider how technology could improve marketing effectiveness.

KEY TAKEAWAYS

- Marketing plays a key role in delivering customer value.
- Marketing decisions play a major role in the health of a company's cash flow.
- Small businesses of any size should consider how technology could improve marketing effectiveness.

EXERCISE

1. Assume that you have a friend who owns a small office-supply business. Your friend is doing fairly well, but you are convinced that integrating more technology into his marketing efforts would increase sales. What would you recommend to your friend? How might technology add to customer value and a positive cash flow?

Disaster Watch

Customer Experience

You are the owner of the local BMW dealer. A customer has just taken delivery of a new BMW 1 Series. Within a couple of weeks, the customer was in an accident with the car. Another driver had driven into her shiny new car—her pride and joy. It was a disaster for the customer. Her dream of owning a BMW had been shattered by the accident happening when the car was only a few days old.[76] It is now your responsibility to manage the repairs and deal with a customer whose car ownership experience is now in disaster territory. The customer knows that when she gets the car back, it will no longer be new. What could you do to turn this disaster into a great customer experience?

ENDNOTES

1. "About Us," *Max and Mina's Ice Cream*, accessed December 2, 2011, www.maxandminasicecream.com/about.html; Miriam Hill, "1000 Flavors and a Little Romance," *Philadelphia Inquirer*, accessed December 2, 2011, www.maxandminasicecream.com/images/articles/4.jpg; John Hyland, "Lox in a Cone: Sliced Thin It's Not," *New York Times*, August 16, 2000, accessed December 2, 2011, www.maxandminasicecream.com/images/articles/1.jpg.

2. Jack Trout, "Peter Drucker on Marketing," *Forbes*, July 3, 2006, accessed January 19, 2012, www.forbes.com/2006/06/30/jack-trout-on-marketing-cx_jt_0703drucker .html.

3. "AMA Definition of Marketing," *American Marketing Association*, December 17, 2007, accessed December 1, 2011, www.marketingpower.com/Community/ARC/Pages/ Additional/Definition/default.aspx.

4. Adapted from Philip Kotler and Kevin Lane Keller, *Marketing Management* (Upper Saddle River, NJ: Pearson Prentice Hall, 2009), 6–7.

5. Philip Kotler and Kevin Lane Keller, *Marketing Management* (Upper Saddle River, NJ: Pearson Prentice Hall, 2009), 19.

6. Rohit Deshpande and John U. Farley, "Measuring Market Orientation: Generalization and Synthesis," *Journal of Market-Focused Management* 2 (1998): 213–32; Ajay K. Kohli and Bernard J. Jaworski, "Market Orientation: The Construct, Research Propositions, and Managerial Implications," *Journal of Marketing* 54 (1990): 1–18; and John C. Narver and Stanley F. Slater, "The Effect of a Market Orientation on Business Profitability," *Journal of Marketing* 54 (1990): 20–35—all as cited in Philip Kotler and Kevin Lane Keller, *Marketing Management* (Upper Saddle River, NJ: Pearson Prentice Hall, 2009), 19.

7. Charles W. Lamb, Joseph F. Hair, and Carl McDaniel, *Essentials of Marketing* (Mason, OH: South-Western, 2004), 8.

8. "You Don't Say?," *Sales and Marketing Management*, October 1994, 111–12.

9. Dana-Nicoleta Lascu and Kenneth E. Clow, *Essentials of Marketing* (Mason, OH: Atomic Dog Publishing, 2007), 12.

10. Philip Kotler and Kevin Lane Keller, *Marketing Management* (Upper Saddle River, NJ: Pearson Prentice Hall, 2009), 19.

11. Charles S. Mack, "Holistic Marketing," *Association Management*, February 1, 1999, accessed January 19, 2012, www.asaecenter.org/Resources/ AMMagArticleDetail.cfm?ItemNumber=880.

12. Center for Business Planning, "Market Segmentation," *Business Resource Software, Inc.*, accessed December 1, 2011, www.businessplans.org/segment.html.

13. Rick Suttle, "Define Market Segmentation & Targeting," *Chron.com*, accessed December 1, 2011, smallbusiness.chron.com/define-market-segmentation-targeting-3253 .html.

14. Philip Kotler and Kevin Lane Keller, *Marketing Management* (Upper Saddle River, NJ: Pearson Prentice Hall, 2009), 401.

15. Philip Kotler and Kevin Lane Keller, *Marketing Management* (Upper Saddle River, NJ: Pearson Prentice Hall, 2009), 294–95.

16. Dana-Nicoleta Lascu and Kenneth E. Clow, *Essentials of Marketing* (Mason, OH: Atomic Dog Publishing, 2007), 170.

17. "History of Ivory Soap," *Essortment.com*, accessed December 1, 2011, www.essortment.com/history-ivory-soap-21051.html.

18. Philip Kotler and Kevin Lane Keller, *Marketing Management* (Upper Saddle River, NJ: Pearson Prentice Hall, 2009), 182.

19. Philip Kotler and Kevin Lane Keller, *Marketing Management* (Upper Saddle River, NJ: Pearson Prentice Hall, 2009), 182.

20. Adapted from Philip Kotler and Kevin Lane Keller, *Marketing Management* (Upper Saddle River, NJ: Pearson Prentice Hall, 2009), 155.

21. Dana-Nicoleta Lascu and Kenneth E. Clow, *Essentials of Marketing* (Mason, OH: Atomic Dog Publishing, 2007), 112.

22. Dana-Nicoleta Lascu and Kenneth E. Clow, *Essentials of Marketing* (Mason, OH: Atomic Dog Publishing, 2007), 137.

23. Bill Furlong, "How the Internet Is Transforming B2B Marketing," *BrandNewBusi-nesses.com*, accessed December 1, 2011, www.brandnewbusinesses.com/ NewsletterAugust2003A1.aspx.

24. Frederick E. Webster Jr. and Yoram Wind, *Organizational Buying Behavior* (Upper Saddle River, NJ: Prentice-Hall, 1972), 2, as cited in Philip Kotler and Kevin Lane Keller, *Marketing Management* (Upper Saddle River, NJ: Pearson Prentice Hall, 2009), 188.

25. Philip Kotler and Kevin Lane Keller, *Marketing Management* (Upper Saddle River, NJ: Pearson Prentice Hall, 2009), 188; Dana-Nicoleta Lascu and Kenneth E. Clow, *Essentials of Marketing* (Mason, OH: Atomic Dog Publishing, 2007), 139.

26. Jeneanne Rae, "The Importance of Great Customer Experiences…And the Best Ways to Deliver Them," *Bloomberg BusinessWeek*, November 27, 2006, accessed December 1, 2011, www.BusinessWeek.com/magazine/content/06_48/b4011429.htm?chan =search.

27. Fran ONeal, "'Customer Experience' for Small Business: When Does It Start?," *Small Business Growing*, August 23, 2010, accessed December 1, 2011, smallbusinessgrowing.com/2010/08/23/what-is-the-customer-experience-for-small -business.

28. Eric Brown, "Engage Emotion and Shape the Customer Experience," *Small Business Answers*, December 14, 2010, accessed December 1, 2011, www.smallbusinessanswers.com/eric-brown/engage-emotion-and-shape-the -customer-ex.php.

29. Harley Manning, "Customer Experience Defined," *Forrester's Blogs*, November 23, 2010, accessed December 1, 2011, blogs.forrester.com/harley_manning ?page=1&10-11-23-customer_experience_defined=.

30. Harley Manning, "Customer Experience Defined," *Forrester's Blogs*, November 23, 2010, accessed December 1, 2011, blogs.forrester.com/harley_manning ?page=1&10-11-23-customer_experience_defined=.

31. Lynn Hunsaker, *Innovating Superior Customer Experience* (Sunnyvale, CA: ClearAction, 2009), e-book, accessed December 1, 2011, www.clearaction.biz/innovation.

32. "Grow Customers and Referrals!" *Small Business Growing*, accessed December 1, 2011, smallbusinessgrowing.com/grow-customers-and-referrals.

33. Colin Shaw, "Engage Your Customers Emotionally to Create Advocates," *Customer-Think*, September 17, 2007, accessed December 1, 2011, www.customerthink.com/ article/engage_your_customers_emotionally.

34. Jeneanne Rae, "The Importance of Great Customer Experiences…And the Best Ways to Deliver Them," *Bloomberg BusinessWeek*, November 27, 2006, accessed December 1, 2011, www.BusinessWeek.com/magazine/content/06_48/b4011429.htm?chan =search.

35. Shaun Smith, "When Is a Store Not a Store—The Next Stage of the Retail Customer Experience," *shaunsmith+co Ltd*, March 29, 2010, accessed December 1, 2011, www.smithcoconsultancy.com/2010/03/when-is-a-store-not-a-store-%E2%80%93 -the-next-stage-of-the-retail-customer-experience.

36. Colin Shaw, "Engage Your Customers Emotionally to Create Advocates," *Customer-Think*, September 17, 2007, accessed December 1, 2011, www.customerthink.com/ article/engage_your_customers_emotionally.

37. Jeneanne Rae, "The Importance of Great Customer Experiences…And the Best Ways to Deliver Them," *Bloomberg BusinessWeek*, November 27, 2006, accessed December 1, 2011, www.BusinessWeek.com/magazine/content/06_48/b4011429.htm?chan =search.

38. Sydney Barrows, "6 Ways to Create a Memorable Customer Experience," *Entrepreneur*, May 19, 2010, accessed December 1, 2011, www.entrepreneur.com/article/206760.

39. Lior Arussy, "Creating Customer Experience in B2B Relationships: Managing 'Multiple Customers' Is the Key," *G-CEM*, accessed December 28, 2011, www.g-cem.org/eng/ content_details.jsp?contentid=2203&subjectid=107.

40. Lior Arussy, "Creating Customer Experience in B2B Relationships: Managing 'Multiple Customers' Is the Key," *G-CEM*, accessed December 28, 2011, www.g-cem.org/eng/ content_details.jsp?contentid=2203&subjectid=107.

41. Richard Tait, "What's Different about the B2B Customer Experience," *Winning Customer Experiences*, August 16, 2010, accessed December 1, 2011, winningcustomerexperiences.wordpress.com/2010/08/16/whats-different-about -the-b2b-customer-experience.

42. Richard Tait, "What's Different about the B2B Customer Experience," *Winning Customer Experiences*, August 16, 2010, accessed December 1, 2011, winningcustomerexperiences.wordpress.com/2010/08/16/whats-different-about -the-b2b-customer-experience.

43. Richard Tait, "What's Different about the B2B Customer Experience," *Winning Customer Experiences*, August 16, 2010, accessed December 1, 2011, winningcustomerexperiences.wordpress.com/2010/08/16/whats-different-about -the-b2b-customer-experience.

44. Adapted from Pawan Singh, "The 9 Drivers of B2B Customer Centricity," *Destination CRM.com*, December 11, 2010, accessed December 1, 2011, www.destinationcrm.com/Articles/Web-Exclusives/Viewpoints/The-9-Drivers-of -B2B-Customer-Centricity-72672.aspx.

45. Lior Arussy, "Creating Customer Experience in B2B Relationships: Managing 'Multiple Customers' Is the Key," *G-CEM*, accessed December 28, 2011, www.g-cem.org/eng/ content_details.jsp?contentid=2203&subjectid=107.

46. "What Is Customer Loyalty?," *Customer Loyalty Institute*, accessed December 1, 2011, www.customerloyalty.org/what-is-customer-loyalty.

47. Adapted from "Why Measure—What Is Loyalty?," *Mindshare Technologies*, accessed December 1, 2011, www.mshare.net/why/what-is-loyalty.html.

48. Adapted from Rama Ramaswami, "Eight Reasons to Keep Your Customers Loyal," *Multichannel Merchant*, January 12, 2005, accessed December 1, 2011, multichannelmerchant.com/opsandfulfillment/advisor/Brand1-custloyal/.

49. Jeffrey Gangemi, "Customer Loyalty: Dos and Don'ts," *BusinessWeek*, June 29, 2010, accessed December 1, 2011, www.BusinessWeek.com/smallbiz/tipsheet/06/29.htm.

50. Bruce Temkin, "The Four Customer Experience Core Competencies," *Temkin Group*, June 2010, accessed December 1, 2011, experiencematters.files.wordpress.com/ 2010/06/1006_thefourcustomerexperiencecorecompetencies_v2.pdf.

51. Paul Gauvreau, "Making Customers Feel Special Brings Loyalty," *Pharmacy Post* 11, no. 10 (2003): 40.

52. Michael Lowenstein, "Customer Loyalty Behavior in B2B vs. B2C Scenarios," *SearchCRM*, January 31, 2007, accessed December 1, 2011, searchcrm.techtarget.com/answer/Customer-loyalty-behavior-in-B2B-vs-B2C -scenarios.

53. Shaun Smith, "Why Steve Jobs Doesn't Listen to Customers," *Customer Think*, February 8, 2010, accessed December 1, 2011, www.customerthink.com/blog/ why_steve_jobs_doesnt_listen_to_customers.

54. Dana-Nicoleta Lascu and Kenneth E. Clow, *Essentials of Marketing* (Mason, Ohio: Atomic Dog Publishing, 2007), 191.

55. "Market Research Basics," *SmallBusiness.com*, October 26, 2009, accessed December 1, 2011, smallbusiness.com/wiki/Market_research_basics.

56. Susan Ward, "Do-It-Yourself Market Research—Part 1: You Need Market Research," *About.com*, accessed December 1, 2011, sbinfocanada.about.com/cs/marketing/a/marketresearch.htm.

57. Jesse Hopps, "Market Research Best Practices," *EvanCarmichael.com*, accessed December 1, 2011, www.evancarmichael.com/Marketing/5604/Market-Research-Best-Practices.html; adapted from Joy Levin, "How Marketing Research Can Benefit a Small Business," *Small Business Trends*, January 26, 2006, accessed December 1, 2011, smallbiztrends.com/2006/01/how-marketing-research-can-benefit-a-small-business.html.

58. "Market Research Basics," *SmallBusiness.com*, October 26, 2009, accessed December 1, 2011, smallbusiness.com/wiki/Market_research_basics.

59. "Market Research Basics," *SmallBusiness.com*, October 26, 2009, accessed December 1, 2011, smallbusiness.com/wiki/Market_research_basics.

60. Philip Kotler and Kevin Lane Keller, *Marketing Management* (Upper Saddle River, NJ: Pearson Prentice Hall, 2009), 91.

61. Philip Kotler and Kevin Lane Keller, *Marketing Management* (Upper Saddle River, NJ: Pearson, Prentice Hall, 2009), 93.

62. Patricia Faulhaber, "Today's Headlines Provide Market Research," *Marketing and PR @ Suite101*, May 14, 2009, accessed December 1, 2011, patricia-faulhaber.suite101.com/todays-healines-provide-market-research-a117653.

63. Joy Levin, "How Marketing Research Can Benefit a Small Business," *Small Business Trends*, January 26, 2006, accessed December 1, 2011, smallbiztrends.com/2006/01/how-marketing-research-can-benefit-a-small-business.html.

64. "Market Research Basics," *SmallBusiness.com*, October 26, 2009, accessed December 1, 2011, smallbusiness.com/wiki/Market_research_basics.

65. Adapted from Philip Kotler and Kevin Lane Keller, *Marketing Management* (Upper Saddle River, NJ: Pearson Prentice Hall, 2009), 91–103.

66. "Market Research Basics," *SmallBusiness.com*, October 26, 2009, accessed December 1, 2011, smallbusiness.com/wiki/Market_research_basics.

67. John Tozzi, "Market Research on the Cheap," *Bloomberg BusinessWeek*, January 9, 2008, accessed December 1, 2011, www.BusinessWeek.com/smallbiz/content/jan2008/sb2008019_352779.htm.

68. Joy Levin, "How Marketing Research Can Benefit a Small Business," *Small Business Trends*, January 26, 2006, accessed December 1, 2011, smallbiztrends.com/2006/01/how-marketing-research-can-benefit-a-small-business.html.

69. Darrell Zahorsky, "6 Common Market Research Mistakes of Small Business," *About.com*, accessed December 1, 2011, sbinformation.about.com/od/marketresearch/a/marketresearch.htm; Lesley Spencer Pyle, "How to Do Market Research—The Basics," *Entrepreneur*, September 23, 2010, accessed December 1, 2011, www.entrepreneur.com/article/217345.

70. Robert R. Harmon and Greg Laird, "Linking Marketing Strategy to Customer Value: Implications for Technology Marketers," *IEEEXplore Digital Library*, July 31, 1997, accessed December 1, 2011, ieeexplore.ieee.org/xpl/freeabs_all.jsp?arnumber=653700.

71. Robert R. Harmon and Greg Laird, "Linking Marketing Strategy to Customer Value: Implications for Technology Marketers," *IEEEXplore Digital Library*, July 31, 1997, accessed December 1, 2011, ieeexplore.ieee.org/xpl/freeabs_all.jsp?arnumber=653700.

72. Nathan Pettyjohn, "Evolving the Customer Experience with Mobile Technology," *MarketingProfs*, December 28, 2010, accessed December 1, 2011, www.marketingprofs.com/articles/2010/4134/evolving-the-customer-experience-with-mobile-technology.

73. "Mobile Retail Shopping Solution Featuring Near Field Communication Technology," *PRWeb*, January 6, 2011, accessed December 1, 2011, www.prweb.com/releases/2011/ARSMOBILE/prweb4946004.htm.

74. Bradley T. Gale, "Webinar on Customer Value Mapping," *Customer Value, Inc.*, accessed December 1, 2011, www.cval.com.

75. Robbin Block, *Social Persuasion: Making Sense of Social Media for Small Business* (Breinigsville, PA: Block Media, 2010), 2.

76. The Customer's Shoes, "How to Turn a Disaster into a Great Customer Experience," *The Customer's Shoes Ltd.*, December 6, 2010, accessed December 1, 2011, www.thecustomersshoes.com/2010/12/how-to-turn-a-disaster-into-a-great-customer-experience.

CHAPTER 7
Marketing Strategy

Elegant Touch

Source: Used with permission from Anita Bruscino.

Anita Bruscino, the sole proprietor of Elegant Touch, began her career as a mechanical engineer. She worked in her family's manufacturing business until she and her father left because of too many factions in the company. This provided her with the opportunity to start her own business, something she had always known in her heart that she wanted to do.

Anita was inspired to open a gift shop by a family friend who had owned her own gift shop. She gave Anita advice on starting her own business, and Elegant Touch opened in 1994. Anita has since expanded the business and is celebrating the shop's eighteenth anniversary, with the last six years in its larger location. The shop is warm, lovely, and comfortable, featuring unique gifts for all occasions and specializing in American handcrafted gift items and gift baskets. Shoppers will also find maternity gifts, items for the sweet tooth, specialty foods, special seasonal sections[1] —and a friendly smile from Anita. One thing that you will not find at Elegant Touch is what you find in other gift shops in her market area. When selecting products for her shop, Anita asks vendors whether other stores in the area carry the gift line she is considering. She will not carry duplicates. She likes to see new things and follows the trade magazines to help her do that. When asked how she chooses the products to carry, she described the process as instinctive—"from the gut."

Anita describes her customer demographics as mostly women, between thirty and seventy years old, married, and established with a home. Because many of her customers are repeat customers, the reason for fresh products is clear. A stale product line is not something that she can afford. Her pricing strategy is consistent with common practice in the industry, but many of her customers have commented that she delivers very high value for the prices she charges. She is not interested in selling online because she does not want to expand any further. She is at a nice comfort level and does not want to deal with the additional inventory implications or the need to hire additional employees. As a result, the Elegant Touch website is for basic information only. In promoting Elegant Touch, Anita says that word of mouth works the best. She advertises in the local paper occasionally, supports local events, and is preparing for her first e-mail blast. She is exploring a Facebook presence but is not yet convinced that it will be of much value to her business.

Like all small businesses, Elegant Touch has been impacted by the ups and downs in the economy, with some times being tougher than others. Because Anita has only two part-time employees, however, she has not been faced with the employee layoffs that have hit other small companies. When asked what keeps her going in the rough times, she answered, "You have to love it." Just walk into her gift shop, and you will see clearly that she does.[2]

1. THE IMPORTANCE OF A MARKETING STRATEGY

LEARNING OBJECTIVES

1. Understand how marketing for small businesses differs from marketing for big businesses.
2. Understand the most significant risk factor facing small businesses.
3. Explain marketing strategy and why it is so important for small businesses.

Small-business marketing and big business marketing are not the same. The basic marketing principles that guide both are the same, but there are important differences with respect to scope, budget, risk factors, and areas of opportunity.[3] (See Chapter 6 for a discussion of marketing principles.) Small businesses cannot compete with the marketing budgets of big companies. As a result, small businesses do not have the luxury of large staffs and the staying power that comes with high profits. There is little room for error. Failed strategies can lead to ruin.

The scope of small business marketing does not extend across the same level of multiple products and services that characterize most big businesses. Combined with having few if any products in the pipeline, this significantly reduces the insulation that small businesses have against ups and downs in the marketplace or strategic failures. "Small business marketing strategies have to be more targeted, cost-effective and more elaborately planned [s]o as to minimize the losses in case the strategy fails."[4]

Competition is the most significant risk factor facing small businesses. Trying to eliminate an established brand takes a lot of work, but it is an overnight job to wipe out a small business. Competition is a huge threat for small businesses.[5] This means that small businesses should be very knowledgeable about their competition to deal effectively with them.

Opportunity areas for small businesses are also very different from those of big businesses. The small business can take advantage of niche markets and local needs and wants. They are much better able to emphasize personal, one-to-one interactions and can market real time in ways that cannot be matched by big businesses. Smaller can actually end up being more powerful.[6]

Given the special marketing vulnerabilities of small businesses, the importance of understanding the components of a **marketing strategy** should be clear. A marketing strategy involves selecting one or more target markets, deciding how to differentiate and position the product or the service, and creating and maintaining a marketing mix that will hopefully prove successful with the selected target market(s)—all within the context of **marketing objectives**. Marketing objectives are what a company wants to accomplish with its marketing strategy: "Strategy is not a wish list, set of goals, mission statement, or litany of objectives…A marketing strategy is a clear explanation of how you're going to get there, not where or what there is. An effective marketing strategy is a concise explanation of your stated plan of execution to reach your objectives…Marketing without strategy is the noise before failure."[7]

marketing strategy

Selecting one or more target markets, making differentiation and positioning decisions, and creating and maintaining a marketing mix—all within the context of marketing objectives.

marketing objectives

What a company wants to accomplish with its marketing strategy.

KEY TAKEAWAYS

- Small-business marketing and big business marketing are not the same.
- The most significant risk factor facing small businesses is competition.
- It is important for a small business to have a marketing strategy so that it is better positioned to choose among options.
- An effective marketing strategy is a concise explanation of a business's stated plan of execution to reach its objectives.
- Marketing without strategy is the noise before the failure.

EXERCISE

1. You just started a new job with a twenty-five-employee small business. By accident, you found out that the company does not have a clear marketing strategy. So far, the company has been lucky with its product sales, but you have a feeling that things will not continue at the same pace for much longer because a competitor has entered the marketplace. Assuming that you had the opportunity, how would you go about convincing the owner that the smart thing to do right now is to create a marketing strategy? Make the case to the owner.

2. THE MARKETING STRATEGY PROCESS

LEARNING OBJECTIVES

1. Describe the marketing strategy process.
2. Explain why segmentation, target market, differentiation, positioning, and website decisions are so important for the small business.
3. Describe the marketing strategy decision areas for each element of the marketing mix.

The focus of this text is on the management of the small business that is up and running as opposed to a start-up operation. As a result, the considerations of marketing strategy are twofold: (1) to modify or tweak marketing efforts already in place and (2) to add products or services as the business evolves. In some instances, it may be appropriate and desirable for a small business to backfit its marketing activities into a complete marketing strategy framework.

The marketing strategy process consists of several components (Figure 7.1). Each component should be considered and designed carefully: company vision, company mission, marketing objectives, and the marketing strategy itself.

FIGURE 7.1 Marketing Strategy Process

- Company vision — Where do we see the business going?
- Company mission — Why does our business exist?
- Marketing objectives — What do we want to accomplish with our marketing strategy?
- Marketing strategies — How will we accomplish our marketing objectives?

Source: Susan I. Reid, "How to Write a Great Business Vision Statement," Alkamae, February 23, 2009, accessed December 2, 2011, http://alkamae.com/content.php?id=285; "Marketing Plan: Marketing Objectives and Strategies," Small Business Notes, accessed December 2, 2011, http://www.smallbusinessnotes.com/starting-a-business/marketing-plan-marketing-objectives-and-strategies.html.

2.1 Vision and Mission

It is awfully important to know what is and what is not your business.[8]
   - *Gertrude Stein*

vision statement

A document that articulates
the long-term purpose and
idealized notion of what the
business wishes to become.

mission statement

A document that articulates
the fundamental nature of
the business. It should
address what business the
company is in, the company's
potential customers, and how
customer value will be
provided.

The **vision statement** tries to articulate the long-term purpose and idealized notion of what a business hopes to become. (Where do we see the business going?) It should coincide with the founder's goals for the business, stating what the founder ultimately envisions the business to be.[9] The **mission statement** looks to articulate the more fundamental nature of a business (i.e., why the business exists). It should be developed from the customer's perspective, be consistent with the vision, and answer three questions: What do we do? How do we do it? And for whom do we do it?

Both the vision statement and the mission statement must be developed carefully because they "provide direction for a new or small firm, without which it is difficult to develop a cohesive plan. In turn, this allows the firm to pursue activities that lead the organization forward and avoid devoting resources to activities that do not."[10] Although input may be sought from others, the ultimate responsibility for the company vision and mission statements rests with the small business owner. The following are examples of both statements:

- **Vision statement.** "Within the next five years, Metromanage.com will become a leading provider of management software to North American small businesses by providing customizable, user-friendly software scaled to small business needs."[11]
- **Mission statement.** "Studio67 is a great place to eat, combining an intriguing atmosphere with excellent, interesting food that is also very good for the people who eat there. We want fair profit for the owners and a rewarding place to work for the employees."[12]

2.2 Marketing Objectives

Marketing objectives are what a company wants to accomplish with its marketing. They lay the groundwork for formulating the marketing strategy. Although formulated in a variety of ways, their achievement should lead to sales. The creation of marketing objectives is one of the most critical steps a business will take. The company needs to know, as precisely as possible, what it wants to achieve before allocating any resources to the marketing effort.

Marketing objectives should be SMART: specific, measurable, achievable, realistic, and time-based (i.e., have a stated time frame for achievement). It has been recommended that small businesses limit the number of objectives to a maximum of three or four. If you have fewer than two objectives, you aren't growing your business like you should be in order to keep up with the market. Having more than four objectives will divide your attention, and this may result in a lackluster showing on each objective and no big successes.[13] If a small business has multiple marketing objectives, they will have to be evaluated to ensure that they do not conflict with each other. The company should also determine if it has the resources necessary to accomplish all its objectives.[14]

e-marketing

Information technology
applied to traditional
marketing.

For small businesses that already have, or are looking to have, a web presence and sell their products or services online, **e-marketing** objectives must be included with all other marketing objectives. E-marketing is defined as "the result of information technology applied to traditional marketing."[15] The issues of concern and focus will be the same as for traditional marketing objectives. The difference is in the venue (i.e., online versus onground). Examples of e-marketing objectives are as follows: to establish a direct source of revenue from orders or advertising space; improve sales by building an image for the company's product, brand, and/or company; lower operating costs;[16] provide a strong positive customer experience; and contribute to brand loyalty. The ultimate objective, however, will be "the comprehensive integration of e-marketing and traditional marketing to create seamless strategies and tactics."[17]

2.3 The Marketing Strategy

With its focus being on achieving the marketing objectives, marketing strategy involves segmenting the market and selecting a target or targets, making differentiation and positioning decisions, and designing the marketing mix. The design of the product (one of the four Ps) will include design of the company website. Differentiation refers to a company's efforts to set its product or service apart from the competition, and positioning is placing the brand (whether store, product, or service) in the consumer's mind in relation to other competing products based on product traits and benefits that are relevant to the consumer.[18] These steps are discussed in Section 3 through Section 8. It has been said that "in some cases strategy just happens because a market and a product find each other and grow organically. However, small businesses that understand the power of an overarching marketing strategy, filtered and infused in every tactical process, will usually enjoy greater success."[19]

3. SEGMENTATION AND THE TARGET MARKET

Whether market segments and target markets are selected on the basis of intuition, marketing research, or a combination of the two, they are the basis for creating an effective marketing mix for any small business. Segmentation and target market decisions must be made for both onground and online customers.

3.1 Segmentation

Market segmentation, dividing a market into relatively homogeneous subgroups that behave much the same way in the marketplace, is the necessary precursor to selecting a target market or target markets. The extensive bases on which a company is able to segment a market are presented in Table 6.1. The challenge is knowing which group(s) to select. Many small business owners have a good intuitive sense of the segments that make sense for the business, and they choose to go with that intuition in devising their marketing strategy. However, that intuition may not be precise or current enough to be of the most help in planning a marketing strategy. Marketing research can be of help here, even to the smallest of businesses.

market segmentation

Dividing the market into several portions that are different from each other. It involves recognizing that the market at large is not homogeneous.

measurability

The ease with which a segment can be identified and how easily the size of the segment be estimated.

substantiality

The segment is large and profitable enough to justify an investment.

stability

Whether consumer preferences are stable over time.

accessibility

Being able to communicate with and reach the segment.

actionability

Whether a small business is capable of designing an effective marketing program that can serve the chosen market segment.

differential response

The extent to which market segments are easily distinguishable from each other and respond differently to company marketing strategies.

Marketing research can help the small business identify and refine the segments that offer the greatest opportunities. Part of that process will be to identify segments that meet the requirements of **measurability**, **substantiality**, **stability**, **accessibility**, **actionability**, and **differential response**.[20] Meeting these requirements will increase the chances for successful segmentation.

- **Measurability.** Is it easy to identify and estimate the size of a segment? A small business that moves forward without a clear definition of its market segments is working blind. Intuition can only go so far. Are there people who are interested in freshly baked cookies for dogs (it would seem so), and how many of these people are there? (Check out Happy Hearts Dog Cookies.)

- **Substantiality.** Is the segment large and profitable enough to justify an investment? A small business may not require a huge number of customers to be profitable, but there should be enough people interested in the product or the service being offered to make operating the business worthwhile. Fancy designer clothes for dogs, for example, is a business that can survive—but not everywhere (see www.ralphlauren.com/search/index.jsp?kw=pup&f=Home).

- **Stability.** Stability has to do with consumer preferences. Are they stable over time? Although segments will change over time, a small business needs to be aware of preferences that are continuously changing. Small businesses can be more nimble at adapting their businesses to change, but too much volatility can be damaging to a business's operations.

- **Accessibility.** Can a business communicate with and reach the segment? A small business interested in women who work outside the home will present greater communication challenges than will stay-at-home wives and mothers.

- **Actionability.** Is a small business capable of designing an effective marketing program that can serve the chosen market segment? There was a small manufacturer of low-priced cigarettes in Virginia that found it difficult to compete with the big brands and other established lower-priced brands such as Bailey's. The manufacturer's solution was to sell to Russia where "Made in Virginia, USA" worked very well with customers and retailers.[21]

- **Differential response.** The extent to which market segments are easily distinguishable from each other and respond differently to company marketing strategies.[22] For the small business that chooses only one segment, this is not an issue. However, the small manufacturer of ramen noodles in New York City needs to know whether there are different segments for the product and whether the marketing strategy will appeal to those segments in the same positive way.

Once multiple segments have been identified, it is necessary to select a target market or target markets. If only a single segment has been identified, it becomes the target market.

3.2 Target Market

target market

One or more segments that have been chosen as the focus for business operations.

The selection of a **target market** or target markets will be based on the segments that have been identified as having the greatest potential for the business. (In Chapter 6, a target market refers to one or more segments that have been chosen as the focus for business operations.) Only some of the people in the marketplace will be interested in buying and/or using a company's product or service, and no company has the resources to be all things to all people. Resources are always finite, but this will especially be the case for the small business, so all marketing efforts should be directed as precisely as possible.

Selecting the target market should be guided by several considerations:[23]

- **Financial condition of the firm.** Limited resources may dictate the selection of only one target market.

- **Whether the competition is ignoring smaller segments.** If yes, this may be a ready-made target market.

- **Is the market new to the firm?** If yes, concentrating on one target market may make the most sense.

- **Specific need or want.** Does the proposed target market have a specific need or want for the product or the service?

- **Ability to buy.** Does the proposed target market have the resources to buy the product or the service?

- **Willingness to buy.** Is the proposed target market willing to buy the product or the service?

- **Will this target market be profitable?** There needs to be enough demand to make money.

Choosing the right target market is a critical part of the marketing strategy of a small business. The target market should be the best match for a company's products and services, thus helping to maximize the efficiency and effectiveness of its marketing efforts.

If a small business wants to go with a **niche market**, the same considerations apply. A niche market is a small, more narrowly defined market that is not being served well or at all by mainstream product or service marketers. The great advantage of pursuing a niche market is that you are likely to be alone there: "other small businesses may not be aware of your particular niche market, and large businesses won't want to bother with it."[24] Ideally, a small business marketing to a niche market will be the only one doing so. Niches are very important to small businesses that want to sell pricey chocolates (see, for example, www.cocoadolce.com/about.php). They focus on niches such as weddings, seasonal offerings, and specialty items. They also sell online in order to reach a broader market.

niche market

A small, more narrowly defined market that is not being served well or at all by mainstream product or service marketers.

KEY TAKEAWAYS

- Market segments and target markets are the basis for creating an effective marketing mix.
- Segmentation and target market decisions must be made for both onground and online customers.
- Market segmentation precedes the selection of a target market.
- There are many ways to segment a market.
- Segments must be measurable, substantial, stable, accessible, actionable, and easily distinguishable from other segments.
- The target market should be the segment or segments that show the greatest profit potential for a small business.
- A niche market is a small, more narrowly defined target market that is not being served well or at all by other businesses.

EXERCISES

1. How should the market for Frank's All-American BarBeQue be segmented for his new restaurant in Darien, Connecticut? How should Frank decide on a target market or target market(s)? Be specific. Do not assume that the Darien market is the same as the Fairfield market.
2. Assume that you work for a small manufacturer of children's hair-care products. What criteria would you use for effective segmentation? How would you then decide on a target market or target markets? Be specific.[25]

4. DIFFERENTIATION AND POSITIONING

LEARNING OBJECTIVES

1. Explain differentiation and positioning.
2. Explain why differentiation and positioning are so important for an online marketing strategy and an onground marketing strategy.
3. Understand that a successful differentiation strategy cannot be copied by competitors.
4. Understand that there are many ways to differentiate a product or a service.
5. Understand that successful positioning of a small business or its brand is built on a well-defined target market combined with solid points of differentiation.

Differentiation and positioning considerations are relevant to each element of the marketing mix as well as to onground and online marketplaces. The small business should be working toward a **competitive advantage**—"the ability to perform in one or more ways that competitors cannot or will not match."[26]

competitive advantage

The ability to perform in one or more ways that competitors cannot or will not match.

4.1 Differentiation

Differentiation, setting yourself apart from the competition, is one of the most important and effective marketing tools available to small business owners.[27] Effective differentiation can put a business (or a brand) in the top position among the competition, but an ineffective differentiation strategy can leave a business buried in the middle or at the bottom of the pack.[28] A successful differentiation strategy cannot be imitated by competitors—but it can bring you great success with consumers.[29]

 Video Clip 7.1

Business Differentiation: Showing Up Differently
Differentiation is everyone's goal, but few are able to achieve it.

View the video online at: http://www.youtube.com/v/a3LEhiK2uGA

Small businesses, whether business-to-consumer (B2C) or business-to-business (B2B), can differentiate their companies or brands in many different ways: quality, service, price, distribution, perceived customer value, durability, convenience, warranty, financing, range of products/services offered, accessibility, production method(s), reliability, familiarity, product ingredients, and company image are all differentiation possibilities.[30] There are others as well, limited only by the imagination. One way to uncover differentiation possibilities is to examine customer experience with a product or a service by asking the following questions:[31]

- How do people become aware of their needs for a product or a service?
- How do customers find a company's offering?
- How do customers make their final selection?
- How do consumers order and purchase the product or the service?
- What happens when the product or the service is delivered?
- How is the product installed?
- How is the product or the service paid for?
- How is the product stored?
- How is the product moved around?
- What is the consumer really using the product for?
- What do consumers need help with when they use the product?
- What about returns or exchanges?
- How is the product repaired or serviced?
- What happens when the product is disposed of or no longer used?

No matter what the bases are for differentiating a company or a product, the decision should be made carefully with the expectation that the difference cannot be imitated. When customers are asked whether they can tell the difference between a particular small business and its closest competitors, the answer will hopefully be yes.

Video Clip 7.2

The "Murals Your Way" Advantage
How Murals Your Way sets itself apart from other wall mural companies.

View the video online at: http://www.youtube.com/v/FfyX6EJGphA

Video Link 7.1

Bedbug Dog Sniffs Up Profits

An unusual means of differentiation.

money.cnn.com/video/smallbusiness/2010/08/13/sbiz_bedbug_canine.cnnmoney

4.2 Positioning

Positioning is about the mind of the consumer: placing a company or a brand (sometimes they are the same, e.g., Carbonite, CakeLove, and Sugar Bakery & Sweet Shop) in the consumer's mind in relation to the competition.[32]

The positioning decision is often the critical strategic decision for a company or a brand because the position can be central to customers' perception and choice decisions. Further, because all elements of the marketing program can potentially affect the position, it is usually necessary to use a positioning strategy as a focus for developing the marketing program. A clear positioning strategy can ensure that the elements of the marketing program are consistent and supportive.[33]

Both big and small businesses practice positioning, but small businesses may not know it as positioning. The small business owner thinks about positioning intuitively, does not use the terminology, and does not always know how to promote the position. Additionally, in many if not most small businesses, "the positioning of products is based on the opinions of the business owner, his or her family, and selected friends and family."[34] This notwithstanding, an understanding of positioning should be in every small business owner's tool kit.

Video Clip 7.3

Small-Business Market Position
Small-business owners must figure out how the company should be positioned.

View the video online at: http://www.youtube.com/v/Ct3VR_RKbu8

 Video Clip 7.4

What Is Market Positioning?
A discussion of positioning.

View the video online at: http://www.youtube.com/v/4Vxl85DvQjM

Successful positioning of a small business or its brand is built on a well-defined target market combined with solid points of differentiation. There are six approaches to positioning that the small business owner should consider:[35]

1. **Positioning by attribute.** The most frequent positioning strategy. The focus is on a particular attribute, a product feature, or customer benefit. CakeLove in Maryland positions itself as "cakes from scratch" with natural ingredients (not the least of which is butter, lots of it).

Video Link 7.2

Welcome to CakeLove

An introduction to CakeLove bakery.

vimeo.com/8942129

2. **Positioning by price/quality.** A very pervasive approach to positioning. Some small companies and brands offer more in terms of service, features, or performance, and a higher price serves to signal this higher quality to the customer. As an example, Derry Church Artisan Chocolates are very expensive, but they position themselves as having the very high quality that justifies a high price.[36]

3. **Positioning by use or application.** Focuses on how a product is used or different applications of the product. A solitary custom tailoring shop located in a downtown professional office area could position itself as the only tailor where you can conveniently go "for lunch."

4. **Positioning by product user.** The focus shifts from the product to the user. KIND Snacks are cereal bars positioned as a snack bar for those who are interested in a snack that is wholesome, convenient, tasty, healthy, and "economically sustainable and socially impactful."[37] It is a great snack for hikers and campers.

5. **Positioning by product class.** Focuses on product-class associations. A cleaning service that uses only green products and processes can position itself as the green choice in cleaning services. Healthy Homes Cleaning is an example of a green cleaning business.

6. **Positioning with respect to a competitor.** Comparing a small business brand to its competitors. Some comparisons will be very direct; others will be subtle.[38] A small manufacturer that does not miss delivery times and makes products that are free of flaws can position itself on the basis of timely delivery and manufacturing excellence.[39]

Joe's Redhots' Business Positioning Strategy

Joe's Redhots will sell premium-quality hot dogs and other ready-to-eat luncheon products to upscale business people in high-traffic urban locations. *Joe's Redhots* will be positioned versus other luncheon street vendors as "the best place to have a quick lunch." The reasons are that *Joe's Redhots* have the cleanest carts; the most hygienic servers; the purest, freshest products; and the best value. Prices will be at a slight premium to reflect this superior vending service. *Joe's Redhots* will also be known for its fun and promotional personality, offering consumers something special every week for monetary savings and fun.[40]

The challenge for a small business is to decide which approach to positioning a company or a brand is the best fit. This decision "often means selecting those associations which are to be built upon and emphasized and those associations which are to be removed or de-emphasized."[41] In the process of writing a positioning statement, something that is encouraged as a way to keep the business on track, be aware of the difference between a broad positioning statement and a narrow positioning statement. A broad statement should encompass enough to allow a company to add products without the need to create a new positioning statement on a frequent basis; a narrow positioning statement puts a company in a "specialist" position in its market.[42] The following are some examples:

- **Broad position statement.** "Professional money management services for discerning investors"
- **Narrow position statement.** "Equity strategies for low risk investors"
- **Broad position statement.** "Elegant home furnishings at affordable prices"
- **Narrow position statement.** "Oak furniture for every room in your house"[43]

KEY TAKEAWAYS

- Differentiation and positioning considerations are relevant to each element of the marketing mix as well as the onground and online marketplaces.
- Differentiation and positioning can contribute to the competitive advantage of a small business.
- Differentiation is one of the most important and effective marketing tools available to a small business owner.
- Small businesses, both B2B and B2C, can differentiate their companies or brands in many different ways.
- Ideally, differentiation should be done in a way that cannot be imitated by the competition.
- Positioning is about placing a company or a brand in the mind of the consumer in relation to the competition. It is always comparative.
- Small businesses practice positioning as much as larger companies do, but they may not use the terminology.
- All small business owners should understand what positioning is and how they can use it to their advantage.

EXERCISES

1. Although Frank's All-American BarBeQue has a very loyal following in Fairfield, Connecticut, developing a marketing plan and strategy for the Darien store will require specific statements of differentiation and positioning. What should they be? Remember that the Darien market may be similar to the Fairfield market, but the two markets should not be seen as identical.

2. Continuing with the scenario about the small manufacturer of hair-care products for children, how would you differentiate and position the product for competitive advantage?

5. MARKETING STRATEGY AND PRODUCT

LEARNING OBJECTIVES

1. Understand why product is the key element in the marketing mix.
2. Identify the multiple decisions and considerations that factor into product or service development.
3. Describe the three product layers and explain why small businesses should pay attention to them.
4. Explain the importance of product design to marketing strategy.
5. Understand the role of packaging to product success.
6. Explain what a brand is and why it is probably a company's most important asset.
7. Explain the implications of the product life cycle for the marketing mix.
8. Understand that a company's website is part of its product or service, whether or not the company sells anything online.
9. Explain the decision areas for the company website.

The key element in the marketing mix is the product. Without it, price, promotion, and place are moot. The same is true for marketing strategy. Fulfilling a company's vision and mission and achieving its marketing objectives must be led by the product.

There are multiple decisions and considerations that factor into product or service development: features and benefits, product mix, design, brand, the product life cycle, and the company website. Knowing product development issues can be very helpful for even the smallest business that is looking to keep its current product line responsive to the customers while also looking to expand its product line as the company grows (if growth is desired).

FIGURE 7.2 Factors in Product or Service Decisions

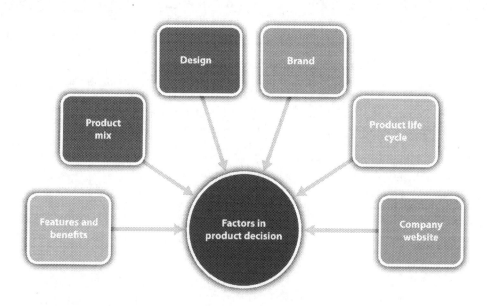

5.1   Product Features and Benefits

A product has multiple layers: core, augmented, and symbolic. These three layers can help a small business owner understand the product features and benefits that will best deliver value to current and prospective customers. These layers also provide the bases for differentiating and positioning the product. The product layers refer to both products and services and business-to-consumer (B2C) or business-to-business (B2B) customers.

FIGURE 7.3 The Product Layers

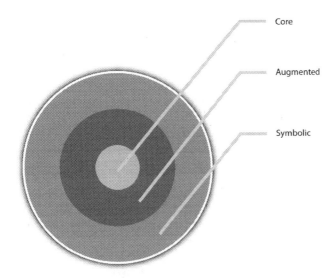

The **core layer** is the nuts and bolts of a product, its physical anatomy, and its basic features. It is also the basic benefit or problem solution that B2C or B2B customers are looking for. Someone buying an airline ticket, for example, is buying transportation.[44] Someone buying an ice cream cone is buying a delicious and fun treat. The core layer is also where considerations of **quality** begin. Quality "refers to overall product quality, reliability, and the extent to which [the product or the service] meets consumers' needs," and the perception of quality has the greatest impact on customer satisfaction.[45] Decisions about design, manufacturing, preparation, ingredients, service delivery, component parts, and process materials all reflect a business's philosophy about quality. The **augmented layer** is where additional value is added via things such as packaging, promotion, warranties, guarantees, brand name, design, financing opportunities where appropriate, prompt and on-time service, and additional services that may enhance a product. The augmented layer for Southwest Airlines is its well-known brand name, its packaging and promotion as a "fun" flying experience, and its "bags fly free" policy. The ice cream cone that is purchased in an old-fashioned ice cream parlor will likely be considered of greater value to many customers than the ice cream cone purchased at a Dairy Queen. It is this layer where many marketing mistakes are made because opportunities are missed. The **symbolic layer** captures the meaning of a product to a consumer—its emotional and psychological connections. There are many loyal customers of Southwest Airlines because they really enjoy flying with them. It is inexpensive, convenient, and fun. The old-fashioned ice cream parlor will engender nostalgia and create powerful emotional ties. The most serious marketing errors are made when the symbolic product layer is either ignored or not understood. The power of symbolism should never be underestimated.

Every small business should look at its products within the context of the product layers. It is the creativity and imagination of the small business owner with the product layers that can set a business apart. They provide an excellent basis for dissecting an existing product to see where opportunities may have been missed, features could be added or changed, and features or enhancements could be explained more effectively in promotional activities. The product layers should also be used to develop new products that the business plans to introduce.

5.2   Product Mix

All small businesses have a product mix, the selection of products or services that is offered to the marketplace. With respect to the product mix for small companies, a company will usually start out with a limited product mix. However, over time, a company may want to differentiate products or acquire

core layer

The nuts and bolts of a product, its physical anatomy, and its basic features.

quality

Overall product quality, reliability, and the extent to which a product or a service meets consumers' needs.

augmented layer

Where additional value is added via things such as packaging, promotion, warranties, guarantees, brand name, design, financing opportunities where appropriate, prompt and on-time service, and additional services that may enhance a product.

symbolic layer

The meaning of a product to a consumer—its emotional and psychological connections.

new ones to enter new markets. A company can also sell existing products to new markets by coming up with new uses for its products.[46] No matter the approach, the product mix needs to be created so that it is responsive to the needs, wants, and desires of the small business's target market.

For small businesses engaged in e-marketing, product selection is a key element for online success. Part of the challenge is deciding which products to market online because some products sell better online than others.[47] If a business has a brick-and-mortar presence, a decision must be made whether all the inventory or only part of it will be sold online. Items that sell well online change over time, so it is important to keep up to date on the changes.[48] A second decision to be made is the number of items in the catalog (i.e., the number of items you will sell). Given intense online competition and shoppers' desires for good selections, there needs to be a critical mass of products and choices—unless a company is lucky enough to have a very narrow niche with high demand. If a company has only one or two products to sell, the situation should be evaluated to determine whether selling online will be profitable.[49]

5.3   Product Design

In his book, *Re-imagine! Business Excellence in a Disruptive Age*,[50] Tom Peters devotes two chapters to the importance of design to business success. He says that design is "the principal reason for emotional attachment (or detachment) relative to a product service or experience"—and he quotes Apple's CEO, Steve Jobs, in saying that design is the "fundamental soul of a man-made creation."[51] This is true whether the product comes from a big business or a small business.

Product design involves aesthetic properties such as color, shape, texture, and entire form, but it also includes a consideration of function, ergonomics, technology, and usability[52] as well as touch, taste, smell, sight, and sound. The pulling together of these things, as appropriate to the specific product or service being designed, should result in a design that matches customer expectations. "Design represents a basic, intrinsic value in all products and services."[53]

Design offers a powerful way to differentiate and position a company's products and services, often giving company a competitive edge.[54] Improved profit margins from increased sales and increased market share are often the result. It is essential to get the visual design of a product right for the market you are appealing to. It can make the difference between selling a product—or not.[55]

Design is particularly important in making and marketing retail services, apparel, packaged goods, and durable equipment. The designer must figure out how much to invest in form, feature development, performance, conformance, durability, reliability, repairability, and style. To the company, a well-designed product is one that is easy to manufacture and distribute. To the customer, a well-designed product is one that is pleasant to look at and easy to open, install, use, repair, and dispose of. The designer must take all these factors into account.

The arguments for good design are particularly compelling for smaller consumer products companies and start-ups that do not have big advertising dollars.[56]

Quirky.com is a small business that has taken product design to a whole new level: collaboration. First seen as a "bold but ultimately wild-eyed idea,"[57] Quirky recently secured $6 million in venture financing. Check out how they operate in "Video Clip 7.5". A company like this could be very helpful to a small business that is looking to introduce a new product.

product design

Aesthetic properties such as color, shape, texture, and entire form plus a consideration of ergonomics, technology, and usability as well as touch, taste, smell, sight, and sound.

Video Clip 7.5

Quirky's Ben Kaufman on Innovation
An innovative approach to product design: collaboration.

View the video online at: http://www.youtube.com/v/FFOvzxxQx8c

Design issues also apply to services. Some of the design issues for services that are delivered in a store (e.g., dry cleaning, repair, and restaurant) are the same as for any retail store: the design of the physical space, the appearance of the personnel, the helpfulness of the personnel, the ease of ordering, and the quality of service delivery. For services that are performed at a customer's home or at a business site, the design issues include timeliness; the appearance and helpfulness of personnel; the quality of install-ation, service, and repair; and the ease of ordering the service. The special characteristics of services (i.e., **intangibility**, **perishability**, **inseparability**, and **variability**, as defined in Figure 7.4) present design challenges that are different from those faced by physical products.

intangibility

A service cannot be seen, smelled, heard, tasted, or touched prior to purchase.

perishability

A service cannot be stored like a physical good.

inseparability

A service is performed and consumed at the same time.

variability

Each time a service is performed, it will be performed in a different way.

FIGURE 7.4 The Characteristics of Services

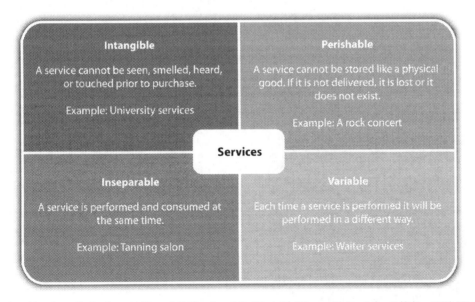

Source: *Adapted from Dana-Nicoleta Lascu and Kenneth E. Clow, Essentials of Marketing (Mason, OH: Atomic Dog Publishing, 2007), 264–68.*

Whether a small business is offering a product, a service, or a combination of the two to either the B2C or B2B marketplace, there is no question that excellent product design is a gateway to business success.

5.4 Packaging Design

packaging

All the activities of designing and producing the container for a product.

The design of the product or the service package is another decision component of the product. **Packaging** can be defined as "all the activities of designing and producing the container for a product."[58] Packages "engage us consciously and unconsciously. They are physical structures but at the same time they are very much about illusion. They appeal to our emotions as well as to our reason."[59] Thus the package communicates both emotional and functional benefits to the buyer, and it can be a powerful means of product differentiation. A well-designed package can build brand equity and drive sales.[60] A poorly designed package can turn the customer off and can lead to wrap rage—the anger and frustration that results from not being able to readily access a product, which often leads to injuries (see "Video Clip 7.6"). Although difficult-to-open packaging may be seen as necessary by the manufacturers and retailers, it does not do much for a positive customer experience.

 Video Clip 7.6

Wrap Rage
Wrap rage: what it is about, with examples.

View the video online at: http://www.youtube.com/v/qxlDdfhyTzY

 Video Clip 7.7

Opening Plastic Clamshells with a Can Opener
Plastic clamshell packages inspire wrap rage. They are easier to open if you start with a can opener.

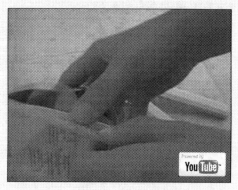

View the video online at: http://www.youtube.com/v/uyw2AxcC9xE

5.5 Brand

A **brand** is defined by the American Marketing Association as "a name, term, sign, symbol, or design, or a combination of them, intended to identify the goods or services of one seller or group of sellers and to differentiate them from those of competitors…A brand may identify one item, a family of items, or all items of that seller. If used for the firm as a whole, the preferred term is trade name."[61] A brand is a promise to the consumer that certain expectations will be met, a promise that—if broken—may result in the loss of that customer. A company's brand is probably its most important asset.

Video Clip 7.8

A Brand Is More Than a Logo
What a brand is all about.

View the video online at: http://www.youtube.com/v/WTeO0lf_CV0

Building a brand is an ongoing process for a small business because it wants a memorable identity. It is important for the business to constantly monitor its brand to ensure that it represents the core values and needs of its existing and potential customers.[62] The brand needs to reach people on an emotional level[63] because customers ultimately make decisions on an emotional level, not a logical level. For this reason, a small business should think in terms of tapping into as many senses as possible with its brand. "Almost our entire understanding of the world is experienced through our senses. Our senses are our link to memory and can tap right into emotion."[64] Scenting the air of a store with a fresh fragrance could be a powerful contributor to the store's brand.

Whether a small business wants to keep its brand (but may be monitoring it) or is looking to **rebrand** (changing the brand), there are four fundamental qualities of great brands that should be kept in mind:[65]

1. They offer and communicate a clear, relevant *customer promise*, such as fun, speedy delivery, or superior taste.
2. They *build trust* by delivering on that promise. Keeping a customer informed when something goes wrong can help build and retain trust.
3. They drive the market by *continually improving* the promise. A small business should always be looking to make things better for its customers. Think in terms of the total customer experience.
4. They seek further advantage by *innovating beyond the familiar*. If a small business focuses on the customer experience, there are undoubtedly ways to improve the brand by adding the unexpected.

The ultimate objective is to have a brand that delivers a clear message, is easy to pronounce, confirms a company's credibility, makes an emotional connection with the target market, motivates the buyer, and solidifies customer loyalty.[66]

Video Clip 7.9

Good Branding Will Build a Company
A strong branding and marketing strategy is an investment that will pay dividends for years to come.

View the video online at: http://www.youtube.com/v/zicXpZDG7HM

 Video Clip 7.10

Small Business Branding Tips
A small business owner talks about the importance and mechanisms of creating a strong and memorable company brand.

View the video online at: http://www.youtube.com/v/aMYoquJOugQ

5.6 Product Life Cycle

Every product has a life span. Some are longer than others. The pet rock had a very short life span. The automobile is still going strong. Some products or services experience an early death, not able to make it very far out the door. Take, for example, Colgate Kitchen Entrees (yes, as in the toothpaste); Cosmopolitan Yogurt (off the shelves in eighteen months); and Ben-Gay Aspirin (the idea of swallowing Ben-Gay was not a winner).[67]

product life cycle (PLC)

The performance of a product in terms of sales and profits over time.

Even the big guys make mistakes, so small businesses are not immune from product goofs. The products that do make it, however, go through what is known as the **product life cycle (PLC)**, defined as "the performance of the product in terms of sales and profits over time."[68] The traditional PLC is shown in Figure 7.5.

FIGURE 7.5 The Traditional Product Life Cycle

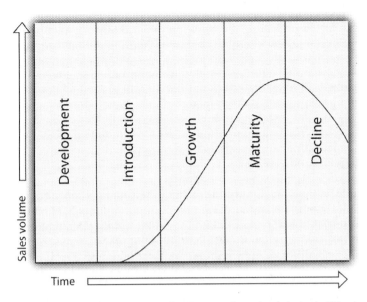

Source: "The Product Life Cycle," NetMBA, accessed December 2, 2011, http://www.netmba.com/marketing/product/lifecycle.

Small-business owners should understand the PLC because there are specific implications for marketing strategy. The **product development (incubation) stage** is when a product is being prepared for sale. There are costs but no sales. The **product introduction stage** is when a product is available to buy for the first time. Sales will generally be low but increasing, marketing expenses will be high, and profits will be typically low or nonexistent. The focus of the marketing strategy will be to create awareness, establish a market, and create demand for the product.[69] The **product growth stage** is when sales grow rapidly as the target market adopts a product and competition enters the marketplace once it observes the success. Marketing strategy should focus on differentiation and building a brand preference. There is substantial profit improvement.[70] Rapid growth must be managed carefully so that the company does not succeed into failure. The **product maturity stage** is characterized by slow growth because most of the buyers interested in a product have bought it. Sales may increase but slowly due to intense price competition. Profits stabilize or decline. The marketing strategy must focus on getting people to switch brands by using special promotions and incentives.[71] The **product decline stage** is when sales decline and profits erode. A product has become obsolete because of an innovation (think VHS to DVD to Blu-Ray) or the tastes of the target market have changed. The marketing strategy works to reinforce the brand image of the product. The product may be dropped from the product line or rejuvenated if possible and practical.

There are many small business owners who may not see the PLC as applying to their products or services. After all, accounting services are accounting services, a luncheonette is a luncheonette, and hardware is hardware. Thinking this way would be a mistake. Accounting practices change, people's tastes change, hardware solutions change, and government regulation inserts itself. What is successful today may not be successful tomorrow. The PLC provides guidance for watching how a product or a service progresses in the marketplace so that the necessary marketing strategy steps can be taken.

product development (incubation) stage

When a product is being prepared for sale.

product introduction stage

When a product is available to buy for the first time.

product growth stage

When sales grow rapidly as the target market adopts a product and competition enters the marketplace once it observes the success.

product maturity stage

Characterized by slow growth because most of the buyers interested in a product have bought it.

product decline stage

When sales decline and profits erode.

The New Product Development Process

If the development of a new product is being considered, the following steps are suggested as guidance:

- **Generate new product ideas.** Search for ideas for new products.
- **Screen new product ideas.** Make sure the product fits the target market and the overall mission of the business.
- **Develop and evaluate new product concepts.** Develop product concepts and determine how consumers will view and use the product.
- **Perform a product business analysis.** Calculate projected business costs, return on investment, cash flow, and the long-term fixed and variable costs. Long-term fixed costs are production costs that do not vary with the number of units produced (e.g., annual rent). Long-term variable costs are production costs that vary with the number of units produced (e.g., selling more hot dogs will require more hot dogs, ketchup, mustard, and relish).

- **Design and develop the product.** Develop a product prototype. A product prototype is an exact match to the product description developed in the concept development and evaluation stages. It is a sample.
- **Test market the product.** Introduce the product to a market to find out how the product will be received when it is introduced for real. The test market should be as close as possible in terms of characteristics (e.g., demographics) as the target market. For a small business, an appropriate test market might be a few select customers.
- **Launch the product or the service.** The product is introduced to the full marketplace.[72]

5.7 The Company Website

A company's website is part of its product or service. The conventional wisdom is that all businesses should have a website. The reality is that there are many small businesses that do very well for themselves without a web presence. The small local deli, accounting or insurance services, a legal firm, a liquor store, or a dental office may not see the need for a website. At the same time, customers are increasingly expecting a web presence, so any small business that does not have a website runs the risk of losing sales because of it. The time may also be approaching when not having a website will be perceived as odd, with questions raised as to the seriousness of the business. Every small business without a website should determine whether this matters to them or not.

This section about the company website is targeted to the small business that has a web presence already or is planning to have one. A small business owner should have a basic understanding of website design to contribute to the discussion and communicate effectively when working with professionals[73]—as well as to organize the owner's visceral reaction when it is time to evaluate other websites, plan the company's website, or revise the company's current website.[74] In addition, any commitment to e-marketing requires a website.

Stanford University's Persuasive Technology Lab found that people quickly evaluate a website by visual design alone, with the visual design setting the tone for the user's experience.[75] "Image is everything online. Good design evokes trust, makes navigation clear, establishes branding, appeals to target customers, and makes them feel good about doing business with the website they are on. Design does not have to be expensive for it to work. It does, however, need to represent an organization and appeal to a visitor. Professional design is not something organizations spend money on; it is something *they invest in to support trust, positioning, and long-term marketing*" (emphasis added).[76]

This section of the chapter discusses website objectives and the fundamental design elements: layout, color, typography, graphics, interactivity, navigation, usability, content, and performance. User experience is also discussed.

 Video Clip 7.11

Top Web Design Mistakes Small and Large Businesses Make
Four mistakes that small businesses should watch for when designing their websites.

View the video online at: http://www.youtube.com/v/022tMCnizgQ

Website Objectives

"The goal of any Web site is to deliver quality content to its intended audience and to do so with an elegant design."[77] **Website objectives** define what a company wants its website to do. For example, a website can build awareness of the business; build awareness of particular brands or services; distribute information to supporters, customers, and stakeholders on products or issues; sell products or services; build relationships with customers; develop a new marketing strategy or reinforce an existing strategy; manage an event (e.g., online registration and payment); build the company image; and gather marketing research by collecting data from users or conducting online surveys.[78] Whichever objective or combination of objectives is chosen, each objective should meet the criteria discussed in Section 2. Clear-cut objectives will increase the chances that a company's website design and content will work to achieve those objectives.[79]

website objectives

What a company wants its website to do.

Website Layout

Layout refers to the positioning of the various elements that comprise a web page: where each text object will be positioned on each page or screen, the width and length of columns, the amount of space that will be placed between the lines of text, the alignment to be used (e.g., left or right), whether the page will be text only or use more advanced designs (e.g., multiple columns),[80] and the placement of graphics. Layout is important because it is one of the first things a visitor perceives when landing on a website. Research shows that "web users spend 69% of their time viewing the left half of the page and 30% viewing the right half, [so] a conventional layout is thus more likely to make sites profitable."[81]

layout

The positioning of the various elements that comprise a web page.

Color

Color is a powerful component of design. It affects mood and emotion, and it evokes associations with time and place. For example, psychedelic color combinations take us back to the 1960s, and turquoise and yellow combinations remind us of art deco in the 1950s. For websites, color is important in defining a site's environment because "people see color before they absorb content."[82] A lasting color impression occurs within ninety seconds and accounts for 60 percent of acceptance. What are the implications for website design? Decisions regarding color can be highly important to success.

The key to the effective use of color in website design is "to match the expectations of the target audience. Financial services sites tend to use formal colors (e.g., green or blue) with simple charts to illustrate the text but not many pictures. Sites directed at a female audience tend to feature lighter colors, usually pastels, with many pictures and an open design featuring lots of white space. Game sites are one type of site that can get away with in-your-face colors, Flash effects, and highly animated graphics."[83]

Colors should be selected that reflect the purpose of the site and enhance the design. Understanding the meaning of color and the cultural use of color and how colors interact is important in website design to convey the right tone and message and evoke the desired response to the site.[84] The wrong choice could adversely affect a visitor's experience at the site,[85] which could adversely affect a company's sales and image.

 Video Clip 7.12

Color Psychology in Web Design
Insights into color and its importance in website design.

View the video online at: http://www.youtube.com/v/7aiaPxdGXMw

Color Perceptions for Business

"The following list provides the traditional meanings of common colors and suggests compatible business usage:

- **Pink.** Romance, love, friendship, delicacy, feminine; ideal for relationship coaches, florists, and breast cancer awareness sites.
- **Purple.** Royalty, spiritual, transformation, creativity, new age; ideal for spirituality-based or new age businesses and businesses in the creative realm.
- **Blue.** Solid, communication, calm, wisdom, trust, reassuring; ideal for financial businesses, insurance companies, and lawyers.
- **Green.** Growth, money, abundance, fertility, freshness, health, environment; ideal for grocers, environmental businesses, therapists, healthcare businesses.
- **Red.** Energy, strength, passion; ideal for bold businesses based on power and for professionals; use in combination with black.
- **Black.** Power, sophisticated, elegant, formal, style, dramatic, serious; ideal for fine dining establishments; commonly used as an accent color.
- **Gold and yellow.** Wealth, wisdom, prestige, power, energy, joy, clarity, light, intelligence, optimism; ideal for the construction industry.
- **White.** Purity, goodness, simplicity, clean; ideal for almost every business.
- **Brown.** Friendship, earthy, comfort, content, reliable, sturdy; ideal for businesses involved in administrative support.
- **Orange.** Vibrant, enthusiasm, energy, warmth; ideal for creative businesses and teachers.
- **Gray.** Security, staid, quality, professional, stable; ideal for the legal industry."[86]

Typography

typography

The use of typefaces (or fonts) in a design.

typeface

A specific type or font.

"**Typography** is the art of designing a communication by using the printed word."[87] More specifically, it is the use of **typefaces (or fonts)** in a design. Typeface refers to a particular type or font (e.g., Times New Roman and Arial). Typography is an integral part of web design and plays a role in the aesthetics of the website.[88] About 95 percent of the information on the web is written language, so it is only logical that a web designer should understand the shaping of written information (i.e., typography).[89] It is possible to blow away more than 50 percent of website visitors and readers by choosing the wrong typeface.[90]

Graphics

graphics

Pictures, artwork, animations, or videos.

browser safe colors

Colors that look the same on PC and Macintosh operating systems.

Graphics, defined as pictures, artwork, animations, or videos, can be very effective if used correctly. Graphics can provide interest, information, fun, and aesthetics, but they can also take forever to load, be meaningless or useless, not fit on the screen, and use colors that are not **browser safe colors** (i.e., colors that look the same on PC and Macintosh operating systems). Images enhance a web page, but they should be selected and placed carefully.

Graphics should be used to "convey the appropriate tone of your message. As the old saying goes, a picture is worth a thousand words. Make sure your images correspond to the text and are appropriate to the business you offer. For example, an audiologist shouldn't use a picture of a woman holding her glasses because the spotlight should be on hearing."[91] Graphics should also help create a mood, or a sense of place. The use of the graphics has to be thoroughly considered because they slow the loading of a website.[92]

It has been shown that quality images boost sales and enhance the visitor experience. "Consumers who browse products on websites want to see the products they're considering for purchase represented by the highest quality image possible…People do not buy what they cannot see, so the higher the quality and resolution of [the] imagery, the better [the] results will be."[93] The key for any small business that wants graphics on its website is to consider how the graphics will add value to the user experience. The graphics should be for the direct benefit of the user, not the business. Do not get carried away with lots of images and animations because they can make a web page very hard to read. Graphics are a major part of the design, not just afterthoughts.[94]

Site Navigation

People will not use a website if they cannot find their way around it. If web users cannot find what they are looking for or figure out how the site is organized, they are not likely to stay long—or come back.[95] "The purpose of **site navigation** is to help visitors quickly and easily find the information they need on a website. Among the questions considered in site navigation are, How will visitors enter a site? How will visitors use the site? How will they find out what is available at the site? How will they get from one page to another and from one section to another? How will visitors find what they are looking for?"[96]

Site navigation must be easy, predictable, consistent, and intuitive enough so that visitors do not have to think about it.[97] "Designing effective navigation can also entice your visitors to try out the other things you offer on your site."[98] The key to understanding navigation is to realize that if it is too hard to use or figure out, web visitors will be gone in a nanosecond, perhaps never to be seen again. What does this mean to a small business? Lost sales and lost opportunities.

site navigation
The design to help visitors quickly and easily find the information they need on a website.

Site Usability

A website's **usability**, or ease of use, "can make or break an online experience, and it is directly correlated to the success of the site."[99] Website usability measures the quality of a user's experience when interacting with a website,[100] and it works hand in hand with site navigation. According to usability.gov, usability is a combination of five factors:[101]

1. **Ease of learning.** How fast can a user who has never seen the **user interface** before learn it sufficiently well to accomplish basic tasks? The user interface is the way a person interacts with a website.[102]
2. **Efficiency of use.** Once an experienced user has learned to use the website, how fast can he or she accomplish tasks?
3. **Memorability.** If a user has used the website before, can he or she remember enough to use it effectively the next time or does the user have to start over again learning everything?
4. **Error frequency.** How often do users make errors while using the website, how serious are these errors, and how do users recover from these errors?
5. **Subjective satisfaction.** How much does the user like using the website?

Usability is necessary for survival on the Internet. If a website is difficult to use, people will leave,[103] and they may be inclined to tell everyone they know on Facebook and Twitter about their negative experiences. It is as simple—and as serious—as that. Small-business owners should consider postlaunch usability testing to help ensure the best user experience. Three free tools are HubSpot's Website Grader, SiteTuners, and Google Analytics.

usability
A website's ease of use.

user interface
The way a person interacts with a website.

Site Interactivity

Site interactivity is about things on a company's website site that prompt some kind of action from visitors.[104] Visitors become engaged with the site, they stay longer, they look deeper into the site to see what the company is offering, they are less likely to jump to another site, and they feel that they are part of a community and connected. This will keep them coming back to the site.[105]

There are many ways in which a small business can provide interactivity on its site. The following are some examples:[106]

- Free calculators for calculating payments when something is being financed
- Surveys, polls, or quizzes
- Blogs, bulletin boards, and discussion forums
- Facebook and Twitter links
- Searchable database of frequently asked questions
- Site search engine
- Interactive games, puzzles, and contests
- Articles that engage visitors, allowing them to add comments or opinions
- Three-dimensional flip-books (e.g., Gorenje Kitchens showcase a range of products, thus engaging the visitor while flipping through the book.)

site interactivity
Things on a company's website site that prompt some kind of action from visitors.

The sources of interactivity on a website are limited only by a small business owner's creativity and, of course, budget. However, it should never be a question of saying yes or no to interactivity. It is a matter of how much, what kind, and where. Remember that when customers feel compelled to do something, they are that much closer to buying.[107]

Content

Content refers to all the words, images, products, sound, video, interactive features, and any other material that a business puts on its website.[108] It is the content that visitors are looking for, and it is what will keep them on the site. High-quality content will also keep people interested so that they come back for more. "A poorly and ineffectively 'written' website has an adverse impact on the efficiency of the website. Moreover, it also gives a negative impression of the brand [or company] behind it. Without good 'content' a website is an empty box."[109]

Good content is relevant, customer-centric (i.e., it is written in the language and words of the target audience(s) that visit the website), and complies with what we know about how people read online content. They don't. They scan it—because it takes 25 percent longer to read the same material online than it does to read it on paper.[110] If a company's content does not fit its target audience(s), the website will not generate good results.[111]

Most small businesses may think that they must generate all website content. However, some of the best and most successful content may be the easiest to create: the content generated by website users. Interestingly, it is not uncommon for user-generated content to get higher search engine rankings than a business's home page, not an insignificant fact.[112] User-generated content includes the following:[113]

- Message boards
- Product reviews
- New uses for a company's products (e.g., using a dishwasher to cook a whole salmon)
- Testimonials or case studies (how users solved problems)
- Social media pages
- Twitter feeds
- Video contest submissions
- Interviews with users
- Online groups or communities such as LinkedIn or Ning

The gold standard of user-generated content is customer reviews. Customer reviews can increase site traffic by as much as 80 percent, overall conversions by 60 percent, and the average order value by 40 percent. With respect to the posting of both positive and negative reviews, it has been shown that "users trust organizations that post both negative and positive reviews of their product *if* organizations address the feedback constructively."[114]

There are many factors that will contribute to the success of a small business website. However, the website will not do as well as it should, and it will not reach its full potential, without good quality content.[115]

Video Link 7.3

The Value of the About Page

Why the "About" page is so important to a business website.

videos.smallbusinessnewz.com/2011/01/26/the-value-of-the-about-page

Product Display

How a website displays products will impact the success of the website. As a result, product display should be seen as a website design issue. Key decisions that should be made for each category of product that is available on the website include the choice of which products to feature, how to provide product detail pages (an individual page for each product is preferable because there is more room for product details), the sort options that will be available to the shopper (e.g., price), and where items on special will be placed on the page (the upper right corner is recommended).[116]

Performance

No matter how well designed a website is, and no matter how high the quality of content, a website that takes too long to load will lose visitors. A website's **loading speed** determines how fast the pages respond to a user request. Faster site speed is preferred by the users who want an optimal browsing experience, and the small business that wants increasing incoming connections and high sales. Users want faster speeds.[117]

Visiting a fast-loading site is a pleasant experience. Visiting a slow-loading site is not. Surveys now show that a person will wait less than three seconds (perhaps even less) for a webpage to load before leaving, with a one-second delay possibly meaning a 7 percent reduction in sales.[118] Google claims that the amount of site traffic drops by 20 percent for every 0.5 seconds of load time.[119]

There are several factors that slow down the loading time for a website, not the least of which is the connection speed of the user's computer. This is out of the control of the web designer and the site owner (the small business). The biggest culprit, however, is a large graphic or several small graphics on a single page.[120] There are ways around this, known by any credible website designer. The impact of "slow down" features should be tested before the site launches and monitored afterwards.[121] The small business owner can take advantage of some of the popular tools that are available, usually for free, to measure a company's website speed: YSlow (a Firefox extension); Google Page Speed (a Firefox add-on); or Webmaster Tools.[122] Once the problem areas have been identified, steps can be taken to make improvements. The goal is to have an interesting and speedy site.

loading speed

How fast the pages respond to a user request.

KEY TAKEAWAYS

- The key element in the marketing mix is the product. Without it, price, promotion, and place are moot.
- All products and services have three layers: core, augmented, and symbolic.
- All small businesses have a product mix, the selection of products or services that is offered to the marketplace.
- Product selection is a key element for online success because some products will sell better online than others.
- Product design is the principal reason for emotional attachment or detachment relative to a product, a service, or an experience. It presents a powerful way to differentiate and position a company's products and services.
- The product or service package communicates both emotional and functional benefits to the buyer, and it can be an important means of product differentiation.
- A company's brand is probably its most important asset.
- The product life cycle refers to a product's life span.
- A company's website is part of its product or service. Website objectives must be developed and decisions must be made about the fundamental design elements of layout, color, typography, graphics, interactivity, usability, content, product display, and performance.

EXERCISES

1. Go to "How to Rate a Web Site" at www.newentrepreneur.com/Resources/Articles/Rate_a_Web_Site/rate_a_web_site.html and download the Web Site Scorecard. Select two small business websites or use the websites specified by your professor. Working with the "How to Rate a Web Site" article and the Web Site Scorecard, evaluate the two sites. Be sure to note your impressions about the site's performance in each area.

2. Frank's All-American BarBeQue has a very basic website: the store's location, hours, and some of the menu. Frank's son, Robert, has extensive experience with website design. How do you think he would advise his father on fully using the website for competitive advantage?

3. For each of the following, describe the core, augmented, and symbolic layers.

   a. a gift shop
   b. a dry cleaner
   c. a dance studio
   d. highway paving materials

4. Some marketers believe that product performance (functions) makes the most difference when consumers evaluate products. Other marketers maintain that the looks, feel, and other design elements of products (form) are what really make the difference. *Make the case*: Product functionality is the key to brand success OR product design is the key to product success.[123]

---

6. MARKETING STRATEGY AND PRICE

LEARNING OBJECTIVES

1. Understand the role of price in the marketing mix and to a company.
2. Understand the different pricing strategies that a small business can follow.
3. Understand price-quality signaling and its importance to the pricing decision.
4. Understand that the price of a product or a service lets customers know what to expect from a business.

price

The amount of money charged for a product or a service. It is the sum of all values that buyers exchange for the benefits of having or using a good or a service.

price transparency

Where buyers and sellers can view and compare prices for products sold online.

dynamic pricing

Prices are varied for individual consumers.

price-quality signaling

When the cost of a good or a service reflects the perceived quality of that product or service.

Marketing, whether online or onground, is the only activity that generates revenue for most small businesses, and the price element in the marketing mix accounts for that. **Price** can be defined very narrowly as the amount of money charged for a product or a service. However, price is really more than that. It is "the sum of all values (such as money, time, energy, and psychic cost) that buyers exchange for the benefits of having or using a good or service."[124] Ultimately, the meaning of price will depend on the viewpoints of the buyer and the seller.[125]

Deciding on a price for its products or services is one of the most important decisions that a small business will make. The price of a product or a service must be a price that the company's target market is willing to pay and a price that generates a profit for the company. If this is not the case, the business will not be around for long.[126]

Choosing the right pricing strategy is not an easy thing to do because there are so many factors involved. For example, competition, suppliers, the availability of substitute products or services, the target market, the image and reputation of a business, cost and profit objectives, operating costs, government regulation, and differentiation and positioning decisions will all impact price. Pricing is a complex activity, often seen as an art rather than a science. For small businesses that are marketing or want to market online, pricing strategies are even more complicated. For example, online buyers have increasing power that leads to control over pricing in some instances (e.g., online bidding on eBay). There is also **price transparency** where buyers and sellers can easily and quickly view and compare prices for products sold online, and some companies use **dynamic pricing** by varying prices for individual customers.[127]

There are several pricing strategies available to the small business owner. However, having the lowest price is not typically a strong position for small businesses because larger competitors can easily destroy any small business that is trying to compete on price alone.[128] Think Walmart. The best choice for a small business will be the strategy that helps the business reach its sales and profit objectives, enhances the reputation of the company, satisfies the target market, and sends the correct price-quality signal. **Price-quality signaling** occurs when the cost of a good or a service reflects the perceived quality of that product or service.[129] However, pricing objectives must be formulated before a pricing strategy can be selected.

6.1   Pricing Objectives

Pricing objectives (i.e., what the company wants to accomplish with its pricing strategy) should be related to a company's objectives and should follow the decision about where a company wants to position its products or services.[130] Different small businesses in the same industry may have different pricing objectives based on size of the business; in-house capabilities; and whether the focus is on profit, sales, or government action.[131]

- **Sales-based objectives.** Increasing sales volume and market share relative to the competition may involve **penetration pricing**, where a business prices a new product below that of the competition to quickly penetrate the market at the competitor's expense, acquire a large market share, and then gradually raise the price. This objective might be appropriate for a small business that is introducing a new product or service to a very competitive marketplace.

- **Profit-maximization objectives.** Quickly recovering the costs of product development while providing customer value may involve **price skimming**, where a new product is priced higher than that of the competition to maximize profit. This objective would work for a small business with customers who are more concerned with quality, uniqueness, and status rather than price. However, a product's image and quality must warrant the high price.

- **Status-quo-based objectives.** Used to minimize the impact of competitors, government, or channel members and to avoid a sales decline, these objectives are reactive rather than proactive, so they should be adopted for the short term only. Small businesses must be able to meet the needs of their target market.

6.2   Pricing Strategy

Once the pricing objectives are set, a small business must determine a pricing strategy. The small business owner can consider a variety of approaches. Discount pricing, cost-based pricing, prestige pricing, even-odd pricing, and geographic pricing are discussed here. In general, traditional pricing strategies can also be applied to the online environment.[132] How goods and services are priced tells consumers a lot about what to expect from a small business.

Discount Pricing

A small business might choose a **discount pricing** strategy[133] if it is looking to drive traffic and sales short term or if it wants to be permanently seen as the value leader in an industry.[134] Discount pricing is used with customers who buy in large quantities, customers who buy during off-peak times (seasonal), promotions used to increase traffic, and **loss leaders** (products that are discounted to get customers in the door in the hope that they will also buy more profitable products). Discount pricing can be used in the online environment in ways similar to brick-and-mortar stores. If the discounting is short term, inventory can be reduced, and revenues are increased temporarily.[135] An important disadvantage, however, is that customers often associate low price with low quality, particularly if a brand name is unfamiliar. A discount pricing strategy could lead to a product or a service being perceived as low quality. Also, price reductions can be easily matched by the competition, eliminating any but the earliest advantage.[136]

Cost-Based Pricing

Cost-based pricing is a very simple approach. A company figures out how much it costs to make a product or deliver a service and then sets the price by adding a profit to the cost.[137] For example, if it costs a small toy manufacturer $10 to make its signature stuffed animal (taking into account fixed and variable costs) and the company wants a 20 percent profit per unit, the price to the retailer will be $12.[138]

Cost-based pricing is very easy to use. It is flexible (allowing different profit percentages to be added to different product lines), allows for easy price adjustments if costs go up or down, and is simple to calculate. On the downside, cost-based pricing ignores product demand, what the competition is doing with pricing, and positioning, and it provides no incentive for cost efficiencies.[139]

---

pricing objectives

What a company wants to accomplish with its pricing strategy.

penetration pricing

A business prices a product below that of the competition to quickly penetrate the market at the competitor's expense, acquire a large market share, and then gradually raise the price.

price skimming

A product is priced over that of the competition to maximize profit.

discount pricing

Offering quantity discounts to customers who buy in large quantities.

loss leader

A product that is discounted to get customers in the door in the hope that they will also buy more profitable products.

cost-based pricing

A company figures out how much it costs to make a product or deliver a service and then sets the price by adding a profit to the cost.

Prestige Pricing

prestige pricing (or premium pricing)

Based on the premise that consumers will feel that products below a particular price will have inferior quality and will not convey a desired status and image.

Prestige pricing (or premium pricing) taps into the belief that a high price means high quality. Although this relationship exists in many instances, it is not true in all cases. Nonetheless, prestige pricing is "a strategy based on the premise that consumers will feel that products below a particular price will have inferior quality and will not convey a desired status and image."[140] A small children's clothing store that carries only top-of-the-line merchandise would use a prestige pricing strategy. Clothing from this store would be seen as having a higher perceived value than clothing from Macy's but perhaps comparable in value to clothing from Bloomingdale's, Nordstrom, or Neiman-Marcus.

Prestige pricing can be very effective at improving brand identity in a particular market. However, it is not typically used when there is direct competition because such competition tends to have a downward effect on pricing. Unique products usually have the best chance of succeeding with prestige pricing.[141]

Even-Odd Pricing

even-odd pricing

Used to communicate quality (even-numbered price) or value (odd-numbered price).

Also known as the "nine and zero effect,"[142] **even-odd pricing** can be used to communicate quality or value. It assumes that consumers are not perfectly rational, which is true. Emotion plays a much larger role in consumer behavior than rationality.

Even-numbered pricing, or setting selling prices in whole numbers (e.g., $20), conveys a higher-quality image. A small, high-end gift shop, for example, would use even pricing for most if not all its products, with odd-numbered prices (e.g., $18.97) used for products that are on sale. Odd-numbered prices give consumers the impression that they are getting a great value. It is a psychological effect with no basis in logic. But it does work in practice.

Geographic Pricing

geographic pricing

A pricing strategy that takes the geographic location of a customer into consideration.

Some small companies will use a **geographic pricing** strategy. This pricing strategy takes the geographic location of a customer into consideration, the rationale being that distribution can increase product delivery costs and thus the cost of the product.[143] Taxes, the cost of advertising, competitors who benefit from government subsidies, consumer demand, differences in costs of living, and the general cost of doing business are other factors that enter into the decision to use geographic pricing. Small businesses that sell outside the United States would likely encounter the need for geographic pricing. This strategy might also be appropriate when selling in different states.

KEY TAKEAWAYS

- Marketing is the only activity that generates revenue for most small businesses.
- Price accounts for revenue.
- Determining a price for its products or services is one of the most important decisions that a small business will make.
- There are many factors involved in choosing the right pricing strategy.
- Having the lowest price is not typically a strong position for small businesses.
- Pricing objectives should be created before a pricing strategy is selected.
- In general, traditional pricing strategies can be applied to the online environment.
- Discount pricing, cost-based pricing, prestige pricing, even-odd pricing, and geographic pricing are pricing strategies that can be considered by a small business.
- How goods and services are priced tells consumers a lot about what to expect from a small business.

1. Frank's All-American BarBeQue is planning to significantly expand its takeout business. Currently, customers come into the restaurant and order from the menu. With the new Darien facility and website, customers will be able to order online or fax an order to the restaurant. Frank and Robert have been arguing over how to structure the takeout portion of their operations. Frank wants to maintain the approach where customers order items from the menu. Robert believes that in today's world, it would be more convenient for customers to order complete prepackaged meals. Father and son have argued about the nature of these meals. Frank has suggests a limited number of standard meals that could be prepared during the day and sold in the evening when commuters are returning home. However, this might mean that excess inventory would be built up on unwanted items. Robert wants to offer greater variety. These would include a main course, two side dishes, and a dessert. Because there could be a large number of combinations, most would have to be made after the receipt of an order. The "rush" to make these meals would drive up costs. How would you go about pricing these two types of meals?

2. Visit two small businesses—one that you think would use even-numbered pricing and one that you think would use odd-numbered pricing. Were you right? If not, how would you describe their pricing strategies? Be as specific as you can.

3. Visit NapaStyle, and analyze its pricing strategy.

4. Select a product or a service that you purchased recently from an onground small business and an online small business. The two businesses should be different. Evaluate the price that you paid. What appears to be the pricing strategy of each business? Do you think the price was fair? Why or why not? How would you assess the value that you received for the price you paid?[144] *Tip*: If you are not sure whether an online business can be considered a small business, type in the name of the business plus "corporate HQ" into Google or your preferred search engine. The search should return results that include the number of employees. As long as the company has fewer than five hundred employees, you are all set.

7. MARKETING STRATEGY AND PLACE

LEARNING OBJECTIVES

1. Understand the role of place in the marketing mix and the importance of place to a company.
2. Understand the different distribution strategies that a small business can follow.
3. Explain the importance of logistics to small businesses.

No matter how great a product or a service may be, customers cannot buy it unless it is made available to them onground or online or both. This is the role of the **place** P in the marketing mix—to get a product or a service to the target market at a reasonable cost and at the right time. Channels of distribution must be selected, and the physical distribution of goods must be managed.[145]

place

Getting a product or a service to the target customer at a reasonable cost and at the right time.

7.1 Channels of Distribution

A small business may choose the direct, retail, wholesale, service, or hybrid channels. In general, business-to-business (B2B) distribution channels parallel those of business-to-consumer (B2C) businesses.

FIGURE 7.6 Channels of Distribution

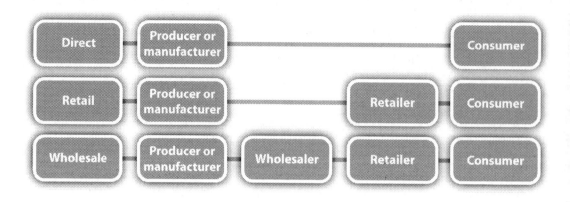

Direct Channel

Many small businesses use the **direct channel**. The direct channel involves selling directly to the final consumer with no **intermediaries** (retailers and wholesalers, also known as middlemen) in the process. The direct channel provides close contact with the customer and full control of all aspects related to the marketing of a company's products.[146] The Sugar Bakery & Sweet Shop in East Haven, Connecticut (winner of the Food Network's 2010 "Cupcake Wars"), uses the direct channel, as does the local farmer when selling fruits and vegetables to the local population. Michael Dell started out by selling computers from his dorm room, and the founders of Nantucket Nectars began their business by selling their home-brewed fruit drinks to boaters in Nantucket Harbor.[147] Many B2B sellers also use the direct channel. Consolidated Industries, Inc., for example, sells helicopter parts directly to Sikorsky Aircraft and airline parts directly to Boeing. (See Chapter 5 for more information on Consolidated Industries, Inc.)

 Video Clip 7.13

Sugar Bakery & Sweet Shop
The story of the winner of the Food Network's 2010 "Cupcake Wars."

View the video online at: http://www.youtube.com/v/Hpsol0zYjnA

Video Link 7.4

iPhone App Beefs Up Sausage Sales

How an iPhone app has made business easier and better for a mobile sausage vendor.

money.cnn.com/video/technology/2010/09/16/t_turnaround_lets_be_frank_square.cnnmoney

Service businesses use the direct channel because there is no way to do otherwise. Services are performed and consumed at the same time, so there is no role for intermediaries. Tanning salons, home repair services, legal services, real estate services, and medical services all deliver directly to the consumer. Online services are also delivered directly to the final consumer, such as Carbonite and Legal Zoom.

The Internet has increased the opportunities for small businesses to use the direct channel as the only means of distribution or as an additional sales channel.[148] For example, Vermont Teddy Bear in Shelburne, Vermont, uses the Internet as its primary sales channel. Its only other channel is its on-ground factory tours that are offered year-round.

 Video Clip 7.14

Vermont Teddy Bear Company
How the company started and how it has grown. It now makes 5,000 bears a day.

View the video online at: http://www.youtube.com/v/6_xpWdb7SvE

Retail Channel

Many small businesses may choose to produce or manufacture products and distribute them to retailers for sale. This is considered an **indirect channel** because the retailer is an **intermediary** between the producer or manufacturer and the final consumer. If a small business that makes one-of-a-kind, handcrafted picture frames sells its frames to a picture-framing business that in turn sells the frames to its customers, this would be an example of using the retail channel. An online business that sells products made by several producers or manufacturers would also be using the retail channel—and would be called an e-tailer.

indirect channel

When a retailer and/or a wholesaler is an intermediary between the producer or the manufacturer and the final consumer.

 Video Clip 7.15

Future Vision of Retailing
Microsoft's vision of future retailing.

View the video online at: http://www.youtube.com/v/J7CVUw13eqw

Video Clip 7.16

YOUReality Retail Visualization Product
A new software product that enables customers to interact with products in their own space—really, really cool.

View the video online at: http://www.youtube.com/v/JlmdZ9QbMjc

Although selling through retailers may expand the distribution coverage to a small business's target market, the business must give up some control over pricing and promotion. In addition, the business should expect to get a wholesale price from the retailer that is significantly lower than what it would get if it sold directly to the final consumer.[149]

Wholesale Channel

wholesalers

A (large or small) business that sells to retailers, contractors, or other types of businesses but not to the general public.

Wholesalers are also **intermediaries**. A wholesaler is "a [large or small] business that sells to retailers, contractors, or other types of businesses (excluding farms), but not to the general public (or at least not in any significant amount)."[150] A small business that chooses to use wholesalers is also using an **indirect channel** of distribution. Using a wholesaler makes sense when a business makes a product that it wants to sell in many stores that would not be easily or conveniently reachable through the direct channel or the retail channel. For example, Kathleen King's small gourmet baked goods company (now known as Tate's Bake Shop) earns much of its annual revenue from the wholesale distribution of its baked goods to approximately one hundred gourmet shops on Long Island, in New York City, and in other states.[151] Her products can be viewed online at www.tatesbakeshop.com, and her story—including some valuable business lessons that she learned along the way—can be viewed in "Video Clip 7.17".

Video Clip 7.17

Tate's Bake Shop
The story of Kathleen King's gourmet baked goods business—and some important business lessons learned.

View the video online at: http://www.youtube.com/v/xSW_tBG_Clo

Although any small business that uses wholesalers will see a reduction in profit, there are several advantages to wholesaling. For example, wholesalers are able to sell and promote to more customers at a reduced cost, they can deliver more quickly to buyers because wholesalers are closer to them, and wholesalers can inventory products, thereby reducing inventory costs and risks to their suppliers and customers.[152] Small businesses that produce only one or a few products commonly use the wholesale channel of distribution. Retail outlets may not be placing orders from the small business because it is not known. The wholesaler can put the product in front of them.[153]

Multichannel Distribution

A small business may choose a **multichannel distribution system (or hybrid channel)**. This channel option uses two or more channels of distribution to reach one or more customer segments, offering customers multiple purchase and communication options.[154] The multichannel approach offers three important advantages:[155]

1. **Increased market coverage.** More customers are able to shop for a company's product in more places, and customers who buy in more than one channel are often more profitable than one-channel customers.

2. **Lower channel cost.** Selling by phone or online is cheaper than selling via personal visits to small customers.

3. **More customized selling.** A technical sales force could be added to sell more complex equipment.

The hybrid approach works well for small businesses. Tate's Bake Shop sells directly through its store in Southampton, New York, and online. It sells indirectly to gourmet retailers such as Sugar and Spice in Chappaqua, New York, through its wholesalers. Local restaurants also use the multichannel approach when customers can order online or by phone and then pick up the food at the restaurant.

7.2 Physical Distribution (Logistics)

Physical distribution (logistics) involves "all the activities involved in the physical flow and storage of materials, semifinished goods, and finished goods to customers in a manner that is efficient and cost effective."[156] Logistics can be performed by the producer or the manufacturer, intermediaries, or the customer. Deciding on the right logistics solution may be the differentiator that puts a company ahead of its competition.[157] Logistics are relevant to both online and onground companies.

The costs of logistics can account for as much as 10–35 percent of a company's gross revenues, so any money that can be saved can lead to more affordable products for consumers and increased profitability. The costs will vary by several factors (e.g., industry sector, company location, and company size). Retailers that offer a wide assortment of products will spend more on logistics because transportation and storage costs will increase as the number of carried products increases.[158]

> **multichannel distribution system (or hybrid channel)**
>
> Two or more channels of distribution to reach one or more customer segments that offers customers multiple purchase and communication options.

> **physical distribution (logistics)**
>
> All the activities involved in the physical flow and storage of materials, semifinished goods, and finished goods to customers in a manner that is efficient and cost-effective.

Video Clip 7.18

Logistics

UPS Commercial: We Love Logistics. A fun insight into what logistics are all about.

View the video online at: http://www.youtube.com/v/mRAHa_Po0Kg

Logistics involve the following four primary functions: transportation, warehousing, inventory control, and order processing.[159]

1. **Transportation.** The transportation choices for a small business will determine whether products will arrive at their destination in good condition and on time. Transportation costs will increase

product price. The choices include truck, rail, air, water, and pipeline. Table 7.1 compares these choices. The selection of the best mode or combination of transportation modes depends on a variety of factors, including cost, speed, appropriateness for the type of good, dependability, and accessibility.[160] All these things will affect customer value and customer satisfaction.

TABLE 7.1 Characteristics of Different Modes of Transportation

Mode	Percentage of Total Transportation	Cost	Speed	Product Examples*
Rail	42	Medium	Lower	Coal, stone, cement, oil, grain, lumber, and cars
Truck	28	Higher	Higher	Perishables, clothing, furniture, and appliances
Pipeline	16	Lower	Low	Oil, gas, chemicals, and coal as a semifluid
Water	13	High	Low	Coal, stone, cement, oil, grain, and cars
Air	0.4	High	High	Jewelry, perishables, electronics, wine, and spirits
*Small businesses are represented in each of the product examples given.				

Source: Adapted from Dana-Nicoleta Lascu and Kenneth E. Clow, Essentials of Marketing (Mason, OH: Atomic Dog Publishing, 2007), 308.

inventory control

Ensuring that goods are where customers want them when they want them.

2. **Warehousing.**[161] Producers and manufacturers must store goods before they are sold because production and consumption rarely match. Some inventory may be kept at or near the point of production or manufacture, but the rest is located in warehouses. Some warehouses also provide assembly, packaging, and promotional display construction services…all for a fee, of course.

3. **Inventory control. Inventory control** is about ensuring that goods are where customers want them when they want them. In other words, it is about avoiding the "out of stock" situation that irritates customers. Small-business owners must understand how much inventory will be needed to address their customers' needs on a timely basis and at the appropriate cost (think pricing strategy). High inventories are undesirable because they may lead to obsolete products, depressed sales of new models, and liquidation prices that may change customer expectations in the future.[162] Small businesses should think of inventory as a wasting asset: it does not improve with time and, in fact, becomes less valuable with every day that passes—taking up space and incurring heat, light, power, handling, and interest charges. Every day that shows inventory and no sales will also show no profit. The goal is to keep inventory as low as possible.[163]

4. **Order processing.**[164] Every small business should want to shorten the elapsed time between an order's receipt, delivery, and payment. Although there are typically multiple steps involved, the reality is that the longer the cycle, the lower the customer's satisfaction, the higher the company's costs, and the lower the company's profits. Streamlining the process should be a priority.

There are several things that small businesses can do to increase the efficiency and the effectiveness of their logistics.[165] For example, a business can select a logistics company that is industry specific (e.g., wine or clothing) because that company will understand the shipping needs of the products or use small business logistics services from UPS or FedEx.

Logistics management also includes supply chain management. This is the focus of Chapter 11.

7.3 Place and the Website

For small businesses that sell online or hope to sell online, the company website "places" the product or the service in the hands of the customer. As a result, there are several decisions that must be made to facilitate the process so that customers can have a good online experience[166] and be less inclined to abandon their shopping carts and leave the site without making a purchase.

- **Better sorting and searching.** Make it easier for shoppers to find what they are looking for.
- **Multibrand combinations in a single cart.** If multiple brands are carried, make it possible to combine shopping carts across brands and apply promotions on the entire cart.
- **Clarity on price and delivery rate.** Prices and delivery rates should be marked clearly, with no ambiguity.
- **Multiple payment options.** Offer more than credit cards. (See Chapter 4 for a discussion of payment options.)
- **Check-out options.** Do not require a customer to register before completing checkout.

- **Provide a product search engine.** The larger and more complex the product selection, the more a product search engine is needed. Shoppers can search by product name; product type; price; product attributes, such as color, size, or material; or brand either alone or in combination.
- **Two clicks to buy.** The fewer the number of clicks to buy, the greater the chances that a shopper will do just that.
- **Customer support.** Offer customer support throughout the buying process. Make it easy to communicate with a real person; spell out the company's warranty, refund, and return policies; ensure privacy and security; and let shoppers know if you put cookies on their computers.
- **Fulfilling orders.** Ideally, send each customer an e-mail confirming when the order is completed, remind the shopper to print the order details, and provide a tracking number with a direct link to the carrier's website so that the shopper can follow the progress of shipment.

Shopping cart abandonment, or leaving a website without buying any of the items in the shopping cart, is something that affects almost every Internet retailer, including small businesses. Cart abandonment estimates range from 20 percent to 60 percent.[167] An understanding of why shoppers are abandoning their carts should lead to some serious thinking during website design and operation. Table 7.2 gives examples of why shoppers abandon a purchase. Because shipping is the number one reason why shoppers abandon their shopping carts, think very carefully about what the shipping charges will be.[168]

> **shopping cart abandonment**
>
> Leaving a website without buying any of the items in the shopping cart.

TABLE 7.2 Why Online Shoppers Abandon Their Shopping Carts

High shipping charges	46%
Wanted to comparison shop	37%
Lack of money	36%
Wanted to look for a coupon	27%
Wanted to shop offline	26%
Could not find preferred payment option	24%
Item was unavailable at checkout	23%
Could not find customer support	22%
Concerned about security of credit card data	21%[169]

KEY TAKEAWAYS

- Understand that place is about getting the product or the service to the target market where customers want it, when they want it, and at a reasonable cost.
- A small business may choose the direct, retail, wholesale, service, or hybrid channels or some combination of these channels.
- In general, B2B distribution channels parallel those of B2C businesses.
- The direct channel involves selling to the final customer with no intermediaries involved.
- Service businesses use the direct channel only because services are performed and consumed at the same time.
- The retail channel is considered indirect because the retailer is an intermediary between the producer or manufacturer and the final customer.
- The wholesale channel is also an indirect channel. The wholesaler is placed between the producer or manufacturer and the retailer.
- The multichannel distribution system (hybrid channel) uses two or more channels to reach one or more customer segments.
- Logistics are about getting materials, semifinished goods, and finished goods to customers efficiently and cost effectively. They can be handled by the producer or the manufacturer, intermediaries, or the customer.
- Logistics include decisions related to warehousing, transportation, inventory control, and order processing. These decisions are relevant to both online and onground companies.
- Websites play an important role in "placing" goods and services into the hands of customers.
- It is important to reduce the number of customers who abandon their shopping carts (i.e., leave the website without purchasing the items in their shopping carts).
- Shopping cart abandonment is common among online retailers. Shoppers abandon their carts for a variety of reasons, the most important one being high shipping charges.

EXERCISES

1. In the Appendix (Chapter 16), you will find the business plan for Frank's All-American BarBeQue. This plan examined several possible locations for a second restaurant. Frank and Robert considered several factors when evaluating alternative towns as possible locations. Some of these included population size, average income, travel times, and percentage of population. Based on the data, they selected Darien, Connecticut. Do you agree with the decision? Why or why not? Do you think other factors should have been considered? If yes, what would you recommend?

2. Assume that you own a small business that specializes in gift baskets for children. You have been satisfied with your success so far but are anxious to spread your wings. You sell online as well as onground and have received several notes from potential online customers expressing their disappointment that you distribute the gift baskets only in the New England area. You have decided to find out what logistics would be involved in shipping to San Francisco, California; Dallas, Texas; Chicago, Illinois; and Anchorage, Alaska. Discuss the transportation mode(s) that would best fit your company for each area.

3. Visit Levenger, Carbonite, and ZipCar. How do these small businesses get their products or services "into the hands" of the customer? Think broadly and creatively.

---

8. MARKETING STRATEGY AND PROMOTION

LEARNING OBJECTIVES

1. Understand the role of promotion in the marketing mix and its importance to a company.
2. Understand the different ways that a small business can promote its products or services.
3. Explain the differences and similarities in the marketing communications mix of online and onground businesses.

Promotion, the fourth P in the marketing mix, is now more commonly referred to as **marketing communications**. Marketing communications can be defined as "the means by which firms attempt to inform, persuade, and remind customers—directly or indirectly—about the products and brands they sell. In a sense, marketing communications represent the 'voice' of the company and its brands and are a means by which it can establish a dialogue and build relationships with consumers."[170] Marketing communications are all about getting the word out about a company's products and services because customers cannot buy what they do not know about, and, in the process, creating more of a two-way relationship with customers than was typical of the more traditional notion of promotion. A further conceptual iteration is the term **integrated marketing communications (IMC)**, which is "the coordination and integration of all marketing communication tools, avenues, and sources within a company into a seamless program designed to maximize the communication impact on consumers, businesses, and other constituencies of an organization."[171] Small-business owners should be familiar and comfortable with all three terms because at least one of them will be the basis of conversations with vendors, employees, and other businesses. However, from a small business management perspective, IMC should be the guiding philosophy for a company.

Prior to selecting and designing any communications, however, objectives must be established for the marketing communications program.

8.1 IMC Objectives

Every small business must decide what it wants to accomplish with its IMC plan. Although many IMC plans may be oriented toward a single objective, it is possible for a program to accomplish more than one objective at a time. The problem is that this may be confusing to potential customers.[172] IMC objectives can fall into seven major categories: increase demand, differentiate a product (stressing benefits and features not available from competitors), provide more information about the product or the service (more information seen as being correlated with greater likelihood of purchase), build **brand equity** (the value added to a brand by customer perceptions of quality and customer awareness of the brand), reduce purchase risk (important for new products and gaining new customers of current products), stimulate trial (to build new brands and rejuvenate stagnant brands),[173] and brand recognition. As with all objectives, IMC objectives must meet the SMART (specific, measurable, achievable, realistic, and time-based) criteria that are described in Section 2.

8.2   Marketing Communications Mix

The **marketing communications mix** for a small business, either pure-play or brick-and-click, will consist of some combination of the following major modes of communication: advertising, sales promotion, events and experiences, public relations (PR) and publicity, direct marketing, interactive marketing, word-of-mouth communication, and personal selling.[174] Each mode of communication has its own advantages and disadvantages, which should all be considered carefully before any final selections should be made.

marketing communications mix

Advertising, sales promotion, events and experiences, PR and publicity, direct marketing, interactive marketing, word-of-mouth communication, and personal selling.

FIGURE 7.7 The Marketing Communications Mix

Source: Philip Kotler and David Lane Keller, Marketing Management (Upper Saddle River, NJ: Pearson Prentice Hall, 2009), 473.

Advertising

Advertising is "any paid form of nonpersonal presentation and promotion of ideas, goods, or services by an identified sponsor."[175] Advertising is around us all the time—for example, ads are on television and radio, in newspapers and magazines, in train stations and on trains, on the sides and inside of buses, in public restrooms, in taxis, on websites, and on billboards. Ads can also be found in other places, and the locations are limited only by the creativity of the company placing the ads.

Small businesses must choose **advertising media** (e.g., radio, television, newspapers, billboards, the Internet, and magazines) based on its product, target audience, and budget. A local travel agency selling spring getaways to college students, for example, might post flyers on campus bulletin boards, run ads in the campus newspaper (for the students) and local newspapers (for the parents), and run ads on the college radio station.[176] Examples of tried and true advertising media for small businesses include the yellow pages, newspaper and magazine advertising, direct mail, business cards, vehicle advertising, radio and cable television advertising, bench/bus stop advertising, local website advertising, e-mail advertising, eBay listings, community involvement, and cross-promotion (joining forces with other businesses).[177] Even advertising in the big leagues is not out of the question for a small business. Salesgenie.com decided to advertise during Super Bowl XLII in February 2008, choosing to risk major capital to connect with the huge Super Bowl customer base.[178]

advertising

Any paid form of nonpersonal presentation and promotion of ideas, goods, or services by an identified sponsor.

advertising media

Radio, television, newspapers, billboards, the Internet, and magazines.

banner ads

Image ads that range in size and technical capability.

e-mail advertising

Ads in newsletters, an ad in another company's e-mail, e-mailing a list with a dedicated message, or a company advertising to its own customers with its own e-mail list.

news site advertising

Placing ads on news, opinion, entertainment, and other sites that the audience frequents.

blog advertising

Buying ads directly on popular blogs.

social media advertising

Advertising on sites such as Twitter, Facebook, and LinkedIn.

affiliate marketing

Company A places an ad for its product on the site of company B.

Advertising on the Internet is also a consideration for the marketing communications mix of any business with a web presence. According to Lorrie Thomas, author of *Online Marketing*,[179] online advertising "can rocket your web marketing into the stratosphere" if it is done correctly. If not done correctly, however, it will "blast a giant crater in your budget." Online advertising includes the following entities: **banner ads** (image ads that range in size and technical capability); **e-mail advertising** (ads in newsletters, an ad in another company's e-mail, e-mailing a list with a dedicated message, or a company advertising to its own customers with its own e-mail list); **news site advertising** (placing ads on news, opinion, entertainment, and other sites that the audience frequents); **blog advertising** (buying ads directly on popular blogs); **social media advertising** (advertising on sites such as Twitter, Facebook, and LinkedIn); and **affiliate marketing** (company A places an ad for its product on the site of company B; company A then pays company B an agreed-on fee when a customer clicks on the ad and buys something.)[180] Another possibility is Google AdWords. A small business can promote itself alongside relevant Google search results and on Google's advertising network. This allows a business to reach people who are already looking online for information about the products and services that a business offers.[181]

Video Link 7.5

Attracting Consumer Attention through Advertising

Relating ads to the target market, making ads appealing, and including the element of surprise.

videos.smallbusinessnewz.com/2011/01/31/attracting-consumer-attention-through-advertising

Advertising offers several advantages to the small business. For example, advertising is able to reach a diverse and geographically dispersed audience; it allows the seller to repeat a message many times; and it provides the opportunity for dramatizing the company and its products through the artful use of print, color, and sound. However, the audience does not feel obligated to pay attention or respond to an ad.[182] Whether the advantages of advertising outweigh the costs and disadvantages is something that must be decided by each small business.

Sales Promotion

sales promotion

The variety of short-term incentives to encourage trial or purchase of a product or a service.

Given the expense of advertising and the fact that consumers are exposed to so many advertising messages every day, many companies correctly believe that advertising alone is not enough to get people to try a product a product or a service. Enter lower-cost sales promotion techniques. **Sales promotion** refers to the variety of short-term incentives to encourage trial or purchase of a product or a service. Examples of commonly used sales promotions include contests, sweepstakes, coupons, premiums and gifts, product samples, rebates, low-interest financing, price discounting, point-of-sale displays, and frequent user or loyalty programs.[183] These promotions can be used by and offer several advantages to small businesses:[184]

webinars or webcasts

Seminars or presentations that are delivered online and that are typically an hour in length.

- **Attracting new customers with price.** A reduced price could lure customers away from the competition. For example, a small electronics store that is competing with a large retailer could offer a discounted price on a popular cell phone for a limited time.
- **Gain community favor.** By offering a promotion that helps a worthy cause, you can create a good name for the business. Donate a portion of sales to the local food bank, buy clothing for the homeless, or donate to the local animal shelter to help pay veterinarian bills.
- **Encourage repeat purchases.** Rewards and loyalty programs can be very successful for small businesses. Coffee clubs are popular (buy so many coffees at the regular price and you get one cup free), but this approach can work for sandwiches at a deli, bags of bird food or dog food at the local pet store, shoe repairs at the local cobbler, dry cleaning services, and virtually any other kind of business.
- **Entice reluctant customers.** Giving away a free product or service is usually a good way to get people to try a product or a service for the first time, the hope being that it will lead to a purchase. However, the product or the service has to be good enough to stand on its own so that when the "free" unit is gone, the person will come back to buy.
- **Providing information.** It can be very effective if you run a promotion that helps provide information to potential customers to help them make a decision. This works especially well for products or services that are complicated or unfamiliar to customers, for example, software or product usage (particularly for business-to-business [B2B] customers), financial services, investment services, or estate planning. Free onground seminars or **webinars or webcasts**

(seminars or presentations that are delivered online and that are typically an hour in length) can be very effective at gaining new customers or clients.

Sales promotions can be delivered to the customer in a variety of ways, such as snail mail (US Postal Service), in person, in local new newspapers and regional editions of national magazines, on television and radio, in e-mail, on websites, and in electronic coupons that are sent to a customer's mobile device. Groupon (see "Video Clip 7.19"), which is described as the hottest thing in retail marketing right now, offers customers coupons at local businesses: everything from restaurants to spas to painting lessons to sleigh rides.

Video Clip 7.19

Learn How Groupon Works!
A hot new source of coupons for local businesses.

View the video online at: http://www.youtube.com/v/_xgPtqT0XBY

Events and Experiences

Events and experiences are "company-sponsored activities and programs designed to create daily or special brand interactions."[185] A small business could choose to sponsor a Halloween costume event for pets[186] or an entertainment event, such as a battle of the bands, to raise money for local scholarships. Participation in a local business fair could provide exposure for a product or a service and the opportunity to experience the product if that is possible. A local restaurant could participate in a chili competition. Factory tours and company museums, both of which can also be virtual, can offer great experiences for customers.

There are several advantages to events and experiences:[187] (1) A well-chosen event or experience can be very effective because the consumer gets personally involved. (2) Experiences are more actively involving for consumers because they are real time. (3) Events are not hard sell, and most consumers will appreciate the softer sell situation.

Events and experiences also tap into the importance of the customer experience, discussed in Chapter 6. Today, customers "want products, communications, and marketing campaigns to deliver experiences. The degree to which a company is able to deliver a desirable customer experience—and to use information technology, brands, and integrated communications and entertainment to do so—will largely determine its success."[188] By having special events, a small business will stand out from the rest,[189] and they will create desirable publicity for the company.

Public Relations and Publicity

Public relations (PR) and **publicity** are designed to promote a company's image or its individual products.[190] A small business can also use PR to clarify information in response to negative publicity. (Publicity usually being "an outcome of PR that is produced by the news media and is not paid for or sponsored by the business involved.")[191] Traditional PR tools include press releases and press kits that are sent to the media to generate positive press on behalf of the business. A press kit, the most widely used PR tool, pulls together company and product information to make a good, solid first impression.[192] (Be sure to print the company's website address on everything.) A press kit can be particularly useful for small businesses, although the smallest of businesses may not see the need. Other common platforms include speeches, seminars (online and offline), brochures, newsletters, annual reports, charitable donations, community relations, and company magazines.[193] Increasingly, companies are using

public relations (PR)

Designed to promote a company's image or its individual products.

publicity

An outcome of PR that is produced by the news media and not paid for or sponsored by the business involved.

the Internet: interactive social media, such as blogs, Twitter, and Facebook; home-page announcements for specific occasions (e.g., messages of sympathy for the victims of a disaster); and e-mail.

Social media services such as Google Alerts and TweetBeep can be very helpful for managing a company's reputation. **Reputation management** "is the process of tracking other's opinions and comments about a company's actions and products, and reacting to those opinions and comments to protect and enhance the company's reputation."[194] Both services notify the business when the company name is mentioned. Addressing extremely negative comments immediately is very important for any small business with a web presence.

Most small businesses are not likely to have PR departments. Instead, there will be one person whose job includes—among many other things—PR and publicity. The key is for PR and marketing to work closely together so that "every piece of communication produced by the company speaks with one voice."[195]

Getting publicity for a small business is usually free. Stories about events and experiences might be of interest to the media. One great idea is to have a group of people outside the business with positive picketing, holding signs such as "Low prices" or "Beware of friendly employees." This was actually done by a small business, and it resulted in the business being on the front page of the local paper.[196]

reputation management

The process of tracking opinions and comments about a company's actions and products and reacting to those opinions and comments to protect and enhance the company's reputation.

Video Link 7.6

Obtaining Publicity for a Business

Information and tips for small businesses.

videos.smallbusinessnewz.com/2009/08/28/obtaining-publicity-for-your-business

PR and publicity tend to be underused by all businesses. However, PR and publicity should be particularly appealing to the small business because of the following three distinct qualities:[197]

- **High credibility.** News stories and features are more authentic and credible to readers.
- **Ability to catch buyers off guard.** PR can reach prospects who prefer to avoid salespeople and advertisements.
- **Dramatization.** PR has the potential for dramatizing a company or a product.

Direct Marketing

direct marketing

The promotion of a product from the producer directly to the consumer or business user without using any type of channel members.

Direct marketing is the "promotion of a product from the producer directly to the consumer or business user without the use of any type of channel members."[198] Common direct marketing platforms include catalogs; direct mailing; telemarketing; television shopping; electronic shopping; fax mail; voice mail; blogs; websites;[199] e-mail; direct response radio, television, and Internet;[200] social media, such as Facebook and Twitter; and mobile devices. Because channel members are bypassed, direct marketing normally allows for greater profitability; perhaps more importantly, however, it can develop stronger brand loyalty with customers.[201]

Video Link 7.7

What Is Direct Marketing?

A brief explanation of direct marketing.

www.videojug.com/expertanswer/small-business-advertising/what-is-direct-marketing

Direct marketing is about using information to educate, establish trust, and build a company (or someone in it) as an authority. This can be accomplished in multiple ways, such as website copy, a one-time piece of direct mail, a series of articles that build on one another,[202] a webcast or webinar, or a blog. There is no one more qualified to educate the market about a need than a small business owner: "They're the ones who will know their audience and what they'll find unique, irresistible and compelling. They're the best people to craft the message. Everything else in the organization can be outsourced, but the knowledge that a small business owner has about the people they serve, that can't be replicated."[203]

Direct marketing offers several advantages to both the business-to-consumer (B2C) and B2B small businesses:[204]

- **Flexible targeting.** A business can identify, isolate, and "talk" with well-defined target markets. This can translate into a higher conversion and success rate than if you tried to communicate with everyone in the mass market.

- **Customized messages.** Can be prepared to appeal to the addressed individual.

- **Up-to-date.** Messages can be prepared quickly.

- **Multiple uses.** Direct marketing can be used to sell, but it can also be used to test new markets, trial new products or customers, reward existing customers to reward loyalty, collect information for future campaigns, or segment a customer base.

- **Lower cost per customer acquisition.** The cost can be significantly less than other marketing methods.

- **Control and accountability.** Direct marketing offers great control and accountability than other marketing methods.

- **Swift and flexible.** Direct marketing is swift and flexible in achieving results.

Interactive Marketing

Interactive marketing refers to "online activities and programs designed to engage customers or prospects and directly or indirectly raise awareness, improve image, or elicit sales of products and services."[205] Everything is personalized and individualized—from the website content to the products being promoted.[206] The audience is engaged with the brand, with customers getting the chance to reshape and market it in their own unique way.[207] Forrester Research forecasts that interactive marketing expenditures will reach $55 billion by 2015, accounting for 21 percent of all expenditures on marketing. The greatest growth is projected to come from social media, with the next biggest growth sector being mobile marketing.[208]

Common interactive marketing tools include e-mail, websites, online shopping, videos, webinars and webcasts, blogs, and social media such as Facebook and Twitter. Because e-mail, websites, online shopping, webinars and webcasts have been mentioned previously, the focus here will be on videos, blogs, and social media. Using online videos has become an increasingly popular strategy in small business marketing. Consumers are much more likely to visit a company after viewing its video, and they can be up to 40 percent more likely to make some sort of contact.[209] Online video content is becoming increasingly popular with avid Internet users, so a small business should consider creating a video for its website. The content can be created easily, and it can be posted on the company's website as well as in other locations on the Internet (YouTube or on the company's blog, for instance) to get more page views.[210] According to Ad-ology's 2011 Small Business Marketing Forecast, 45 percent of US small businesses with fewer than 100 employees plan to use online video. This reflects the fact that small businesses are becoming increasingly savvy about how to use the Internet to market their products and services.[211] Paul Bond Boots, a small US maker of custom-made cowboy boots that are individually handmade to fit, features five really cool videos on its website. Recently, the company has turned to the Internet for most of its sales.

A **blog** "is a web page made up of usually short, frequently updated posts that are arranged chronologically—like a what's new page or a journal." Business blogs, as opposed to personal blogs, are used as a company communication tool to share a company's knowledge and expertise, build additional web traffic, connect with potential customers, develop niche markets, give the business a human face, help reputation management, and provide a free avenue for press releases.[212] For an example, visit Michael Chiarello's blog at www.michaelchiarello.com. If his name is not familiar, he is the founder of NapaStyle, a high-end small business retailer with both an onground and online presence.

Blogs are fairly simple to set up, and they are a great way to keep website content fresh. However, even though small businesses hear much about blogs these days, creating one must be considered carefully. Blogs today "have evolved into multimedia communities where bloggers (and the blogging community) have grown in size, stature, and impact to eclipse all but the largest media outlets."[213] But this does not mean that it is essential for every small business to have a blog. Maintaining a blog takes a lot of time and energy—and then there need to be people to read it. After careful consideration, it may be better to focus a company's promotional efforts elsewhere.

interactive marketing

Online activities and programs designed to engage customers or prospects and directly or indirectly raise awareness, improve image, or elicit sales of products and services.

blog

A web page made up of usually short, frequently updated posts that are arranged chronologically.

social media

Websites that feature
user-generated content or
material created by visitors
rather than the website
publishers and encourage
visitors to read and respond
to that material.

Social media "generally refers to websites featuring user-generated content or material created by visitors rather than the website publishers. In turn, these sites encourage visitors to read and respond to that material."[214] Social media is changing the way that people communicate and behave. Social media outlets such as Facebook, LinkedIn, and Twitter are, among other things, driving purchases—and they should be seen "like a virtual cocktail party where all attendees can discuss [a company's] products, services, experiences, and new ideas."[215]

The top four social media networks are Twitter, Facebook, LinkedIn, and YouTube. This is true in general and for small businesses in particular.[216] Overall, small businesses use social media sites for lead generation, monitoring what is being said about their businesses, keeping up with the industry, improving the customer experience, and competitive intelligence.[217] Many small businesses in the B2B sector are already using social media for business as a resource, to engage in initiatives, or both. However, companies with more than one hundred employees are more active than smaller companies.[218]

Despite the hype surrounding social media, and the fact that many small businesses are already connected, small businesses must still consider the use of social media just as carefully as the other modes of marketing communications. Social media has not worked out well for some small businesses that have used it, so each business must decide what social media is expected to do for the company, and then it must be used well and strategically. When considering whether or how to factor social media into an IMC strategy, consider these words from Lisa Barone, cofounder and chief branding officer at *Outspoken Media*, "In 2011, if you're not using social media to gain attention over your competitors, you can bet they're using it to gain attention over you."[219] This will undoubtedly continue to be the case.

Video Clip 7.20

Social Media

The top five things you should know about social media.

View the video online at: http://www.youtube.com/v/lvbs-oQr5ms

Personal Selling

personal selling

The process of
communicating with a
potential buyer (or buyers)
face-to-face with the purpose
of selling a product or a
service.

A small business owner needs to connect with customers before a sale can take place. Sometimes personal selling is the best way to do that. **Personal selling**, "the process of communicating with a potential buyer (or buyers) face-to-face with the purpose of selling a product or service,"[220] is absolutely essential in the marketing communications mix of a small business. History has shown that the most successful entrepreneurs have been skilled salespeople who were able to represent and promote their companies and products in the marketplace.[221] It stands to reason that successful small business owners should have the same sales skills.

Although personal selling plays an important role in the sale of consumer products, it is even more important in the sale of industrial and business products. More than four times as many personal selling activities are directed toward industrial and business customers than toward consumers.[222] Regardless of the type of customer or consumer, however, the objectives of personal selling are the same:[223]

- **Building product awareness.** A salesperson should educate customers and consumers on new product offerings.

- ▪ **Creating interest.** Because personal selling is a person-to-person, and often a face-to-face, communication, it is a natural way for getting customers and consumers to experience a product for the first time. Creating interest goes hand-in-hand with building product awareness.
- ▪ **Providing information.** A large part of the conversation with the customer focuses on product information.
- ▪ **Stimulating demand.** The most important objective of personal selling by far is persuading customers and consumers to make a purchase.
- ▪ **Reinforcing the brand.** Most personal selling focuses on building long-term relationships with customers and consumers. However, strong relationships can be built only over time, and they require regular communication.

Like all other forms of marketing communications, personal selling offers both advantages and disadvantages. On the plus side, personal selling is flexible and dynamic, providing companies with the best opportunity to tailor a message to satisfy customers' needs. Personal selling's interactive nature also makes it the most effective promotional method for building relationships with customers, particularly in the B2B market, and it is the most practical promotional method for reaching customers who are not easily reached through other methods.[224] Personal selling can help a small business build strong, loyal relationships with customers and consumers.

On the minus side, the biggest disadvantage may be the negative perceptions that many people have of salespeople: pushy, annoying, slippery, and willing to do anything for the sale—whether legal or not. The reality, of course, is that most salespeople (unfortunately, not all) do not fit this stereotype. The successful salesperson is the person who focuses his or her efforts on satisfying customers over the long term as opposed to his or her own selfish interests. Also on the negative side is the high cost of personal selling. Personal sales contacts are very expensive, with the costs incurred (compensation plus sales support) whether the sale is made or not.[225] Then there are the costs of training the sales staff on product knowledge, industry information, and perhaps selling skills.[226] Depending on the size of the company, small businesses will have varying numbers of salespeople, so some of the costs will vary as well.

The traditional sales process is typically seen as a series of six steps:[227]

1. **Prospecting and qualifying.** Locating potential customers who have a need for a product and the ability to pay for it. For example, prospects for a small electric motor company would be all the businesses that use small electric motors. Prospects can be found through a variety of sources, including current customers, trade directories, business associates, and newspaper or magazine articles.

2. **Preapproach.** It is important to learn as much about a prospect as you can. For example, you want to know about the prospect's needs, attitudes about available products and brands, critical product attributes and benefits desired, and current vendor(s).

3. **Presentation and demonstration.** This is where the salesperson tells the product "story" to the buyer: the product's features, advantages, benefits, and value. It is important not to spend too much time on product features because benefits and value will most directly influence the purchase decision. It is also important to ask questions and listen carefully to a prospect's answers because they will provide valuable insights into the prospect's needs.

4. **Overcoming objections.** You should expect customers to pose objections. The key to overcoming these objections is to maintain a positive approach, ask the prospect to clarify the objections, and respond to the objections by reiterating the major benefits of the product or the service and pointing out additional features, guarantees, service, and anything else that would address the objections.

5. **Closing.** This is when the salesperson asks the prospect to buy the product. The request can be direct, or the salesperson can encourage the purchase by using a trial closing approach like asking, "Would you like us to finance product A for you?" Closing the sale is understandably the most difficult step for many salespeople because of the fear that the prospect will say no.

6. **Follow-up and maintenance.** These activities are necessary for customer satisfaction and repeat business. They are key to establishing the strong long-term relationships that every small business desires and needs. The salesperson should schedule a follow-up call to ensure proper installation, instruction, servicing, and troubleshooting and resolution should any problems be detected. Always remember that unhappy customers will defect to competition—and they will spread negative comments about the company. Because it is much cheaper to retain an old customer than to obtain new ones, it is in a company's best interests to provide good follow-up and maintenance services.

Although these steps are helpful as a way to summarize the kinds of things that are relevant to personal selling, the Internet has revolutionized the selling process.[228] The traditional process just described has become largely obsolete, with roles changing. Web searches and online content help prospective customers or clients do their own prospecting and qualifying. This eliminates the most time-consuming part of the traditional sales process. A company's website becomes the first sales presentation and, as a result, is critical in moving a prospect toward a sale. In short, all employees must be fully integrated into web marketing because web marketing is the primary driver of the sales process. The more web-savvy you are, the greater the chances that your selling will beat the competition.[229]

Video Link 7.8

Small Business Selling

An overview of personal selling.

www.videojug.com/interview/small-business-selling

KEY TAKEAWAYS

- Promotion and marketing communications are relatively synonymous terms.
- IMC is about pulling all the marketing communications together to convey a consistent message.
- Small-business owners should be familiar and comfortable with the terms *promotion, marketing communications*, and *integrated marketing communications (IMC)*.
- There are multiple categories of IMC objectives.
- The marketing communications mix for a small business will consist of some combination of advertising, sales promotion, events and experiences, PR and publicity, direct marketing, interactive marketing, and personal selling. This mix is applicable to both pure-play and brick-and-click businesses.
- There is a lot of hype about blogs and social media. They can be very effective, but they have not worked well for all small businesses that have used them. They should be considered carefully before inclusion in a company's IMC strategy.

EXERCISES

1. Frank's All-American BarBeQue has historically taken a very low-key approach to promoting the business, choosing to rely on word-of-mouth communication. Robert believes that Frank needs to increase the sophistication of the marketing communications. Design an IMC plan for Frank's BarBeQue. Keep the following in mind: (1) Frank's is a small business with a very limited IMC budget; (2) advertising in prime time and national television are not options; and (3) Frank's is selling both food and its BBQ sauces.

2. Choose two products or services that you purchased recently from small businesses, one from an online business and one from an onground business. The products should be different from those chosen for price. For each product or service, identify the various media that were used to promote the product or the service and analyze the marketing communications mix. Do you agree with the marketing communications mix that was used? What recommendations would you make for change?[230] *Tip*: If you are not sure whether an online business can be considered a small business, type in the name of the business plus "corporate HQ" into Google or your preferred search engine. The search should return results that include the number of employees. As long as the company has fewer than five hundred employees, you are all set.

9. THE THREE THREADS

LEARNING OBJECTIVES

1. Understand the role of marketing strategy in delivering customer value.
2. Explain how marketing strategy can positively and negatively impact cash flow.
3. Explain how digital technology and the e-environment are impacting marketing strategy.

9.1 Customer Value Implications

As stated in Chapter 6, marketing plays a key role in creating and delivering value to the customer, but it is the establishment of a strong link between customer value requirements and the major value-producing activities of a firm that is the foundation on which the delivery of superior customer value is based.[231] Marketing strategy provides that strong link.

A customer's decision to buy will always be contingent on the strategic effectiveness of the marketing mix: the ability of the product or the service to meet the needs, wants, and desires of the customer; a price that is attractive when compared with possible alternatives; the availability of the product or the service in an onground or online place that is in sync with the customer's needs; and an integrated marketing communications (IMC) program that creates awareness, provides information, and persuades. Although the different elements of the marketing mix will be of differing importance depending on the customer and the situation, it all begins with the product. Well-designed and well-made products will usually come out ahead on the customer value scale. Innovative channels of distribution, such as Redbox for DVDs, gourmet and ethnic food carts, kiosks in airports for selling small electronics products, and conducting financial transactions on a smartphone, can all add to customer value. Social media as a part of the IMC mix can be a particularly great way to create customer value because a consumer's social network can be used as a communication channel to spread the word about a product's characteristics, quality, benefits, and value.[232] Salespeople also create value for customers by helping to identify creative and cost-effective solutions to customer problems, making the customer buying process easier, and creating a positive customer experience. Pricing is always tricky, but there should be a clear and positive link between the price that customers pay and what customers see as the value received in return.

9.2 Cash-Flow Implications

An efficient and effective marketing strategy will keep costs down and stimulate sales. A small business owner could not ask for more as a way to realize a positive cash flow. However, the reality is that things will not go as planned most of the time, and this will wreak havoc with cash flow. This means that the marketing strategy should be developed and implemented within the context of a cash-flow strategy so that when things do not go as planned, you can make appropriate adjustments.

One of the biggest temptations for creating cash flow when money is tight is cutting the price as a way to stimulate sales. Think very carefully before doing this. The price reduction may generate more sales, but you may send unintended negative signals to customers about quality and value. You may also trigger a price cut by competitors that eliminates the benefits of your own price cut. A better strategy would be to maintain the price and offer the customer more value—as long as that additional value does not end up costing you more in money in the long run.[233]

9.3 Digital Technology and E-Environment Implications

The opportunities for using digital technology and the e-environment in marketing strategy have exploded as the technologies continue to develop and become more sophisticated. Strategic decisions can be made more quickly, with information that can be compiled and analyzed more completely and faster than ever before. The Internet offers an information bonanza and myriad opportunities for implementing the marketing strategy.

Mobile commerce continues to be one of the biggest trends to affect small business owners. More than 48 percent of Americans who own smartphones use them for shopping, so integrating mobile commerce into the marketing strategy should be strongly considered. Many small businesses that already use mobile commerce are seeing positive results. Aaron Maxwell, founder of Mobile Web Up, reported that one client has already seen 10 percent growth per month.[234] Since early 2011, small

quick-response (QR) code

A high-tech bar code.

companies have increasingly been drawn to **quick-response (QR) codes** to target customers on the go. These high-tech bar codes are scanned with smartphone cameras, after which company and/or product content pops up on the screen. The customer then chooses to act or not act based on the content. The Ethical Bean Coffee Company in Vancouver, British Colombia, uses this technology in its train ads. Customers scan the code in an ad, a coffee menu pops up on their screens, and they can order a cup of coffee to be picked up at one of the Ethical Bean coffee shops. There are some challenges with using this technology, including cost,[235] but it is worth considering for the marketing communications strategy.

Mobile technologies, such as wireless Internet and cellular Internet access, have significantly impacted personal selling, making it possible for salespeople to access needed information at any time. Key business applications are increasingly being made available through a browser rather than being loaded on a salesperson's computer—again being accessible anywhere or anytime. Online video conferencing and web or phone conferencing allow for electronic presentations in lieu of face-to-face meetings. Sales training can be delivered over the Internet, and RSS feeds or e-mail enable salespeople to be notified quickly when new training material is available. See "Trends in Selling."

crowdfunding

Securing small amounts of money from multiple contributors online.

The marketing strategy of a small bank could include targeting the increasing number of small business owners that are starting to do their banking on the go. Customers can check balances, transfer funds, and take and send pictures of checks for remote deposit. It has been estimated that at least 50 percent of small businesses will do their banking through mobile devices by the end of 2013.[236] For the very small business, raising cash to proceed with the marketing strategy can actually be done through **crowdfunding**, the practice of securing small amounts of money from multiple contributors online. Margaret Broom of New Haven, Connecticut, used Peerbackers.com to raise money for renovating a new space for a yoga studio. In 45 days she raised $10,000 from more than 100 contributors, with average contributions of $15 to $20. The funds do not need to be paid back because they are contributions. However, some businesses give their contributors products or services from the business as an appreciation.[237]

 Video Clip 7.21

Susie's Lemonade Stand
How wireless technology can provide communication and distribution support.

View the video online at: http://www.youtube.com/v/KQnDK9tvb-Y

KEY TAKEAWAYS

- Marketing strategy plays a key role in delivering customer value.
- Marketing strategy should be developed within the context of a cash-flow strategy.
- Digital technology and the e-environment continue to offer significant opportunities for small businesses.

You run a small, specialized electronics firm that produces unique and highly sophisticated products. Your sales are evenly split between military contracts and commercial aviation. Two years ago, during a recent economic downturn, your business was under considerable cost pressure. To reduce costs, you switched from two American-based suppliers to a Taiwanese manufacturer. Last week, a national newspaper released a story that revealed that this Taiwanese manufacturer was using counterfeit chips produced in mainland China. This is clearly illegal, but things were made even worse by the speculation that the Chinese-made chips might be mechanisms that could be used in cyber warfare. It looks as though there will be at least one congressional investigation that will examine the national security issues associated with the counterfeit chips. Unfortunately, your firm was prominently mentioned in the article as one of the firms that had purchased a large number of these chips. This could have a major impact on a firm of your size.

1. What should you do?
2. How would you develop a marketing communications plan to deal with this crisis?
3. How would you deal with the anticipated cash-flow crisis?
4. How should you handle the issue of customer value?

Disaster Watch

Robert has spent the last year building his Internet business. He registered his domain name shortly after developing his idea. Three months were then spent waiting for his web developer to create a custom website built to his specifications. Just when Robert thought his online venture was going to die on the vine, his web guru called to ask if Robert wanted to see the site.

Robert quickly typed in the URL of his domain. There, for all to see, was his website. The online catalog was complete, the merchant account had been set up—and has been for two weeks because he has been paying the monthly fees in anticipation of the site launch date. The e-mail at the domain is configured, and Robert's online business is underway.

Search engine optimization helps to drive traffic to Robert's site. He sends out e-mail messages to everyone on his mailing list to let them know that his online venture is now open for business. Sales started slowly, as expected, but they grew steadily. The twenty-third sale was as exciting as the first.

On the morning of the business's one-year anniversary since buying his domain name, Robert goes to the office and turns on his computer with thoughts of checking his e-mail. His e-mail program announces an error. Something about "could not connect to server."

Robert's first thought was that perhaps the hosting company was having a network issue. He decides to wait for half an hour…but gets the same error. He decides to wait another ten minutes and try again. If it still does not work then, he plans to call his hosting company.

Ten minutes go by. The error keeps showing up. One more try. The error pops up again. Robert picks up the phone and calls the hosting company. Once he gets a tech on the phone, he explains the situation, saying that he needs his e-mail up and running so that he can follow up on the orders that came into the store last night. The next ten minutes are spent double-checking settings on the e-mail program. Still nothing works.

Eventually, someone at the hosting company thinks to check the domain name. **DISASTER!** The domain name had expired at midnight. No business can be conducted, and some people may think he has gone out of business.

What does Robert have to do now?[238]

ENDNOTES

1. Leslie Hutchison, "Elegant Touch Fine Gifts," *CheshirePatch*, accessed March 24, 2012, cheshire.patch.com/listings/elegant-touch-fine-gifts.

2. Except for the content from CheshirePatch.com, all information herein is based on an interview with Anita Bruscino, owner of Elegant Touch, March 2, 2012.

3. Lynne Saarte, "Small Business Marketing Is Different from Big Business Marketing," *Articlecity*, accessed December 1, 2011, www.articlecity.com/articles/marketing/article_4959.shtml; Lyndon David, "Small Business Marketing Strategy: How Different Is It from Larger Businesses?," *Slideshare*, accessed December 1, 2011, www.slideshare.net/lyndondavid/small-business-marketing-strategy-how-different-is-it-from-larger-businesses.

4. Lyndon David, "Small Business Marketing Strategy: How Different Is It from Larger Businesses?," *Slideshare*, accessed December 1, 2011, www.slideshare.net/lyndondavid/small-business-marketing-strategy-how-different-is-it-from-larger-businesses.

5. Lyndon David, "Small Business Marketing Strategy: How Different Is It from Larger Businesses?," *Slideshare*, accessed December 1, 2011, www.slideshare.net/lyndondavid/small-business-marketing-strategy-how-different-is-it-from-larger-businesses.

6. Ann Handley, "Act Your Shoe Size, Not Your Age: 3 Ways to Market Smaller in 2011," *MarketingProfs*, January 3, 2011, accessed December 1, 2011, www.mpdailyfix.com/3-ways-to-market-smaller-in-2011.

7. John Jantsch, "Marketing without Strategy Is the Noise before Failure," *Duct Tape Marketing*, November 29, 2010, accessed December 1, 2011, www.ducttapemarketing.com/blog/2010/11/29/marketing-without-strategy-is-the-noise-before-failure.

8. Jay Ebben, "Developing Effective Vision and Mission Statements," *Inc.*, February 1, 2005, accessed December 1, 2011, www.inc.com/resources/startup/articles/20050201/missionstatement.html.

9. Jay Ebben, "Developing Effective Vision and Mission Statements," *Inc.*, February 1, 2005, accessed December 1, 2011, www.inc.com/resources/startup/articles/20050201/missionstatement.html.

10. Jay Ebben, "Developing Effective Vision and Mission Statements," *Inc.*, February 1, 2005, accessed December 1, 2011, www.inc.com/resources/startup/articles/20050201/missionstatement.html.

11. Susan Ward, "Sample Vision Statements," *About.com*, accessed December 1, 2011, sbinfocanada.about.com/od/businessplanning/a/sampievisions.htm.

12. "Organic Restaurant Business Plan: Studio67," *Bplans*, accessed December 1, 2011, www.bplans.com/organic_restaurant_business_plan/executive_summary_fc.cfm.

13. "How to Choose Marketing Plan Objectives," accessed January 24, 2012, www.hellomarketing.biz/planning-strategy/marketing-plan-objectives.php.

14. Adapted from "Marketing Plan: Marketing Objectives and Strategies," *Small Business Notes*, accessed December 1, 2011, www.smallbusinessnotes.com/starting-a-business/marketing-plan-marketing-objectives-and-strategies.html.

15. Judy Strauss and Raymond Frost, *E-Marketing* (Upper Saddle River, NJ: Pearson Prentice Hall, 2009), 6.

16. Bobette Kyle, "Marketing Objectives for Your Website," *WebSiteMarketingPlan.com*, December 10, 2010, accessed December 1, 2011, www.websitemarketingplan.com/marketing_management/marketingobjectivesarticle.htm.

17. Judy Strauss and Raymond Frost, *E-Marketing* (Upper Saddle River, NJ: Pearson Prentice Hall, 2009), 5.

18. Dana-Nicoleta Lascu and Kenneth E. Clow, *Essentials of Marketing* (Mason, OH: Atomic Dog Publishing, 2007), 179.

19. John Jantsch, "The Cycle of Strategy," *Duct Tape Marketing*, March 29, 2010, accessed December 1, 2011, www.ducttapemarketing.com/blog/2010/03/29/the-cycle-of-strategy.

20. Dana-Nicoleta Lascu and Kenneth E. Clow, *Essentials of Marketing* (Mason, OH: Atomic Dog Publishing, 2007), 175–76.

21. Dana-Nicoleta Lascu and Kenneth E. Clow, *Essentials of Marketing* (Mason, OH: Atomic Dog Publishing, 2007), 176.

22. Dana-Nicoleta Lascu and Kenneth E. Clow, *Essentials of Marketing* (Mason, OH: Atomic Dog Publishing, 2007), 176.

23. Susan MaGee, "How to Identify a Target Market and Prepare a Customer Profile," accessed January 24, 2012, http://edwardlowe.org/erc/?ercID=6373; Adapted from "3 Reasons to Choose a Target Market," *Morningstar Marketing Coach*, December 16, 2008, accessed December 1, 2011, www.morningstarmultimedia.com/3-reasons-to-choose-a-target-market.

24. Susan Ward, "Niche Market," *About.com*, accessed December 1, 2011, sbinfocanada.about.com/cs/marketing/g/nichemarket.htm.

25. Adapted from Dana-Nicoleta Lascu and Kenneth E. Clow, *Essentials of Marketing* (Mason, OH: Atomic Dog Publishing, 2007), 185.

26. Philip Kotler and Kevin Lane Keller, *Marketing Management* (Upper Saddle River, NJ: Pearson Prentice Hall, 2009), 276.

27. Bonny Albo, "Making a Business Stand Out from Its Competitors," *Entrepreneurs @ Suite 101*, August 9, 2009, accessed December 1, 2011, bonny-albo.suite101.com/marketing-strategy-differentiation-a136498.

28. Kim T. Gordon, "Dare to Be Different," April 1, 2005, accessed December 1, 2011, www.entrepreneur.com/article/76736.

29. Dan Herman, "The Surprising Secret of Successful Differentiation," *Fast Company*, June 7, 2008, accessed December 1, 2011, www.fastcompany.com/blog/dan-herman/outsmart-mba-clones/surprising-secret-successful-differentiation?.

30. Bonny Albo, "Making a Business Stand Out from Its Competitors," *Entrepreneurs @ Suite 101*, August 9, 2009, accessed December 1, 2011, bonny-albo.suite101.com/marketing-strategy-differentiation-a136498.

31. Ian C. MacMillan and Rita Gunther McGrath, "Discovering New Points of Differentiation," *Harvard Business Review*, July–August 1997, 133–145, as cited in Philip Kotler and Kevin Lane Keller, *Marketing Management* (Upper Saddle River, NJ: Pearson Prentice Hall, 2009), 277.

32. Al Ries and Jack Trout, *Positioning: The Battle for Your Mind* (New York: McGraw-Hill, 2001), 3.

33. David A. Aaker and Gary Shansby, "Positioning Your Product," *Business Horizons*, May–June 1982, 56–62.

34. "Product Positioning," *Inc.*, accessed December 1, 2011, www.inc.com/encyclopedia/product-positioning.html.

35. David A. Aaker and Gary Shansby, "Positioning Your Product," *Business Horizons*, May–June 1982, 56–62.

36. Jim T. Ryan, "Sweet Strategy: Artisan Chocolatier Eyes Internet, Corporate Giving for Growth," *Central Penn Business Journal*, November 26, 2010, 3–6.

37. "Our Story," *KIND Healthy Snacks*, accessed December 8, 2011, www.kindsnacks.com/our-story.

38. Dana-Nicoleta Lascu and Kenneth E. Clow, *Essentials of Marketing* (Mason, OH: Atomic Dog Publishing, 2007), 181.

39. Lisa Nielsen, "Product Positioning and Differentiation Strategy," *Chron.com*, accessed June 1, 2012, http://smallbusiness.chron.com/product-positioning-strategy-3350.html.

40. "Positioning Strategy Statement," *Business Owner's Toolkit*, accessed December 1, 2011, www.toolkit.com/small_business_guide/sbg.aspx?nid=P03_7003.

41. David A. Aaker and Gary Shansby, "Positioning Your Product," *Business Horizons*, May–June 1982, 56–62.

42. Andy LaPointe, "Is Your Positioning Statement Confusing Your Customers?," *Small Business Branding*, May 13, 2007, accessed December 1, 2011, www.smallbusinessbranding.com/714/is-your-positioning-statement-confusing-your-customers.

43. Andy LaPointe, "Is Your Positioning Statement Confusing Your Customers?," *Small Business Branding*, May 13, 2007, accessed December 1, 2011, www.smallbusinessbranding.com/714/is-your-positioning-statement-confusing-your-customers.

44. Dana-Nicoleta Lascu and Kenneth E. Clow, *Essentials of Marketing* (Mason, OH: Atomic Dog Publishing, 2007), 226.

45. Dana-Nicoleta Lascu and Kenneth E. Clow, *Essentials of Marketing* (Mason, OH: Atomic Dog Publishing, 2007), 117.

46. Rick Suttle, "What Is a Product Mix?," *Chron.com*, accessed December 1, 2011, smallbusiness.chron.com/product-mix-639.html.

47. Jan Zimmerman, *Web Marketing for Dummies*, 2nd ed. (Hoboken, NJ: Wiley, 2009), 101.

48. Jan Zimmerman, *Web Marketing for Dummies*, 2nd ed. (Hoboken, NJ: Wiley, 2009), 101.

49. Jan Zimmerman, *Web Marketing for Dummies*, 2nd ed. (Hoboken, NJ: Wiley, 2009), 101–2.

50. Tom Peters, *Re-imagine! Business Excellence in a Disruptive Age* (London: Dorling Kindersley Limited, 2003), 132–46.

51. Tom Peters, *Re-imagine! Business Excellence in a Disruptive Age* (London: Dorling Kindersley Limited, 2003), 132–146, as cited in Bob Lamons, "Strong Image Design Creates Passion for Firm, Its Products," *Marketing News*, April 15, 2005, 7.

52. Dana-Nicoleta Lascu and Kenneth E. Clow, *Essentials of Marketing* (Mason, OH: Atomic Dog Publishing, 2007), 242; Dominic Donaldson, "The Importance of Good Product Design," *Artipot*, December 8, 2008, accessed December 1, 2011, www.artipot.com/articles/246078/the-importance-of-good-product-design.htm.

53. Ted Mininni, "Design: The New Corporate Marketing Strategy," *MarketingProfs*, November 5, 2005, accessed December 1, 2011, www.marketingprofs.com/articles/2005/1670/design-the-new-corporate-marketing-strategy.

54. Philip Kotler and Kevin Lane Keller, *Marketing Management* (Upper Saddle River, NJ: Pearson Prentice Hall, 2009), 325.

55. Dominic Donaldson, "The Importance of Good Product Design," *Artipot*, December 8, 2008, accessed December 1, 2011, www.artipot.com/articles/246078/the-importance-of-good-product-design.htm.

56. Philip Kotler and Kevin Lane Keller, *Marketing Management* (Upper Saddle River, NJ: Pearson Prentice Hall, 2009), 325.

57. Cliff Kuang, "Product-Design Startup Quirky Gets $6 Million in VC Funding," *Fast Company*, April 7, 2010, accessed December 1, 2011, www.fastcompany.com/1609737/product-design-startup-quirky-gets-6-million-in-vc-funding.

58. Philip Kotler and Kevin Lane Keller, *Marketing Management* (Upper Saddle River, NJ: Pearson Prentice Hall, 2009), 239.

59. Randall Frost, "Packaging Your Brand's Personality," *Brandchannel*, October 3, 2005, accessed December 1, 2011, www.brandchannel.com/features_effect.asp?pf_id=283.

60. Philip Kotler and Kevin Lane Keller, *Marketing Management* (Upper Saddle River, NJ: Pearson Prentice Hall, 2009), 339.

61. "Brand," *American Marketing Association*, accessed December 1, 2011, www.marketingpower.com/_layouts/Dictionary.aspx?dLetter=B.

62. Miranda Brookins, "How to Brand a Business," *Chron.com*, accessed December 1, 2011, smallbusiness.chron.com/brand-business-211.html.

63. Marc Gobe, *Emotional Branding: The New Paradigm for Connecting Brands to People* (New York: Allworth Press, 2001), xv.

64. Martin Lindstrom, *Brand Sense: Build Powerful Brands through Touch, Taste, Smell, Sight, and Sound* (New York: Free Press, 2005), 10.

65. Adapted from Patrick Barwise and Sean Meehan, "The One Thing You Must Get Right When Building a Brand," *Harvard Business Review*, December 2010, 80–84.

66. Laura Lake, "What Is Branding and How Important Is It to Your Marketing Strategy?," *About.com*, accessed December 1, 2011, marketing.about.com/cs/brandmktg/a/whatisbranding.htm; Dana-Nicoleta Lascu and Kenneth E. Clow, *Essentials of Marketing* (Mason, OH: Atomic Dog Publishing, 2007), 230.

67. "Top 25 Biggest Product Flops of All Time," *Daily Finance*, accessed December 1, 2011, www.dailyfinance.com/photos/top-25-biggest-product-flops-of-all-time.

68. Dana-Nicoleta Lascu and Kenneth E. Clow, *Essentials of Marketing* (Mason, OH: Atomic Dog Publishing, 2007), 244.

69. Philip Kotler and Kevin Lane Keller, *Marketing Management* (Upper Saddle River, NJ: Pearson Prentice Hall, 2009), 339; Dana-Nicoleta Lascu and Kenneth E. Clow, *Essentials of Marketing* (Mason, OH: Atomic Dog Publishing, 2007), 244; Kristie Lorette, "How Would the Marketing Mix Change at Different Stages of the Product Life Cycle?," *Chron.com*, accessed December 1, 2011, smallbusiness.chron.com/would-marketing-mix-change-different-stages-product-life-cycle-3283.html.

70. Philip Kotler and Kevin Lane Keller, *Marketing Management* (Upper Saddle River, NJ: Pearson Prentice Hall, 2009), 339; Dana-Nicoleta Lascu and Kenneth E. Clow, *Essentials of Marketing* (Mason, OH: Atomic Dog Publishing, 2007), 244; Kristie Lorette, "How Would the Marketing Mix Change at Different Stages of the Product Life Cycle?," *Chron.com*, accessed December 1, 2011, smallbusiness.chron.com/would-marketing-mix-change-different-stages-product-life-cycle-3283.html.

71. Philip Kotler and Kevin Lane Keller, *Marketing Management* (Upper Saddle River, NJ: Pearson Prentice Hall, 2009), 339; Dana-Nicoleta Lascu and Kenneth E. Clow, *Essentials of Marketing* (Mason, OH: Atomic Dog Publishing, 2007), 244; Kristie Lorette, "How Would the Marketing Mix Change at Different Stages of the Product Life Cycle?," *Chron.com*, accessed December 1, 2011, smallbusiness.chron.com/would-marketing-mix-change-different-stages-product-life-cycle-3283.html.

72. Dana-Nicoleta Lascu and Kenneth E. Clow, *Essentials of Marketing* (Mason, OH: Atomic Dog Publishing, 2007), 239–43.

73. Efraim Turban et al., *Electronic Commerce: A Managerial Perspective* (Upper Saddle River, NJ: Pearson Prentice Hall, 2008), 751.

74. Jan Zimmerman, *Web Marketing for Dummies*, 2nd ed. (Hoboken, NJ: Wiley, 2009), 67.

75. Lorrie Thomas, *Online Marketing* (New York: McGraw-Hill, 2011), 22–23.

76. Lorrie Thomas, *Online Marketing* (New York: McGraw-Hill, 2011), 23.

77. Efraim Turban et al., *Electronic Commerce: A Managerial Perspective* (Upper Saddle River, NJ: Pearson Prentice Hall, 2008), 751.

78. "What Are the Objectives of Your Web Site?," *3w designs*, accessed December 1, 2011, www.3w-designs.co.uk/textonly/new-web-site-aims.html.

79. Ottavio Storace, "How to Build a Web Site That Achieves Objectives," *Webmaster Resources @ Suite 101*, July 13, 2009, accessed December 1, 2011.

80. "Glossary of Web Terminology: Website Layout," April 5, 2010, accessed January 24, 2012, www.azurewebdesign.com/glossary-of-web-terminology; Sue A. Conger and Richard O. Mason, *Planning and Designing Effective Web Sites* (Cambridge, MA: Course Technology, 1998), 96.

81. Jakob Nielsen, "Horizontal Attention Leans Left," *Useit.com*, April 6, 2010, accessed December 1, 2011, www.useit.com/alertbox/horizontal-attention.html.

82. "Welcome to Color Voodoo Publications," *Color Voodoo*, accessed December 1, 2011, www.colorvoodoo.com.

83. Efraim Turban et al., *Electronic Commerce: A Managerial Perspective* (Upper Saddle River, NJ: Pearson Prentice Hall, 2008), 751.

84. Jacci Howard Bear, "The Meaning of Color," *About.com*, accessed December 1, 2011, desktoppub.about.com/od/choosingcolors/p/color_meanings.htm?p=1.

85. Joanne Glasspoole, "Choosing a Color Scheme," *Metamorphosis Design*, accessed December 1, 2011, www.metamorphozis.com/content_articles/web_design/Choosing_A_Color_Scheme.php.

86. Lena Claxton and Alison Woo, *How to Say It: Marketing with New Media* (New York: Prentice Hall, 2008), 34.

87. Colin Wheildon, *Type & Layout: How Typography and Design Can Get Your Message Across—or Get in the Way* (Berkeley, CA: Strathmoor Press, 1996), 19.

88. Shannon Noack, "Basic Look at Typography in Web Design," *Six Revisions*, April 7, 2010, accessed December 1, 2011, sixrevisions.com/web_design/a-basic-look-at-typography-in-web-design.

89. Oliver Reichenstein, "Web Design Is 95% Typography," *Information Architects, Inc.*, October 19, 2006, accessed December 1, 2011, www.informationarchitects.jp/en/the-web-is-all-about-typography-period.

90. Colin Wheildon, *Type & Layout: How Typography and Design Can Get Your Message Across—or Get in the Way* (Berkeley, CA: Strathmoor Press, 1996), 19.

91. Lena Claxton and Alison Woo, *How to Say It: Marketing with New Media* (New York: Prentice Hall, 2008), 35.

92. "When to Use Graphics on Your Website," *Improve the Web*, May 9, 2007, accessed December 1, 2011, www.improvetheweb.com/when-use-graphics-your-site.

93. Dave Young, "Quality Images Boost Sales," *Practical eCommerce*, March 14, 2007, accessed December 1, 2011, www.practicalecommerce.com/articles/436-Quality-Images-Boost-Sales.

94. Jennifer Kyrnin, "Basics of Web Layout," *About.com*, accessed December 1, 2011, webdesign.about.com/od/layout/a/aa062104.htm.

95. Steve Krug, *Don't Make Me Think: A Common Sense Approach to Web Usability* (Berkeley, CA: New Riders Publishing, 2000), 51.

96. Efraim Turban et al., *Electronic Commerce: A Managerial Perspective* (Upper Saddle River, NJ: Pearson Prentice Hall, 2008), 754.

97. Efraim Turban et al., *Electronic Commerce: A Managerial Perspective* (Upper Saddle River, NJ: Pearson Prentice Hall, 2008), 754.

98. "Website Navigation Tips," *Entheos*, accessed December 1, 2011, www.entheosweb.com/website_design/website_navigation_tips.asp.

99. Lorrie Thomas, *Online Marketing* (New York: McGraw-Hill, 2011), 38.

100. "Usability Basics," *Usability.gov*, accessed December 1, 2011, www.usability.gov/basics/index.html.

101. "Usability Basics," *Usability.gov*, accessed December 1, 2011, www.usability.gov/basics/index.html.

102. "Definition of User Interface," accessed December 1, 2011, www.pcmag.com/encyclopedia_term/0,2542,t=user+interface&i=53558,00.asp.

103. Efraim Turban et al., *Electronic Commerce: A Managerial Perspective* (Upper Saddle River, NJ: Pearson Prentice Hall, 2008), 756.

104. "Web Development Glossary for Small Businesses," *Lightwave Communications*, accessed December 1, 2011, www.lightwavewebdesign.com/web-development-glossary/website-glossary-g-i.html.

105. Folusho Orokunie, "Do Not Make Your Website Visitors Yawn! Make Your Site Interactive," accessed December 1, 2011, folusho.com/do-not-make-your-website-visitors-yawn-make-your-site-interactive.

106. "Examples of Possible Interactive Features on Your Website," *Zamba*, accessed December 1, 2011, www.zambagrafix.com/interact.htm; "Importance of Web Interactivity: Tips and Examples, *Hongkiat*, accessed December 1, 2011, www.hongkiat.com/blog/importance-of-web-interactivity-tips-and-examples.

107. "Importance of Interactive Websites," *Thunder Data Systems*, accessed December 1, 2011, www.thunderdata.com/thunder_bits/importance_of_interactive_websites.html.

108. Efraim Turban et al., *Electronic Commerce: A Managerial Perspective* (Upper Saddle River, NJ: Pearson Prentice Hall, 2008), 744; Jan Zimmerman, *Web Marketing for Dummies*, 2nd ed. (Hoboken, NJ: Wiley, 2009), 67.

109. JPDC, "The Importance of Visitor-Oriented Online Content on Your Website," *Mycustomer.com*, June 12, 2009, accessed December 1, 2011, www.mycustomer.com/blogs/marketingadvisor/marketing-advisor/importance-visitor-oriented-online-content-your-website.

110. Jan Zimmerman, *Web Marketing for Dummies*, 2nd ed. (Hoboken, NJ: Wiley, 2009), 73.

111. JPDC, "The Importance of Visitor-Oriented Online Content on Your Website," *Mycustomer.com*, June 12, 2009, accessed December 1, 2011, www.mycustomer.com/blogs/marketingadvisor/marketing-advisor/importance-visitor-oriented-online-content-your-website.

112. Lorrie Thomas, *Online Marketing* (New York: McGraw-Hill, 2011), 55.

113. Lorrie Thomas, *Online Marketing* (New York: McGraw-Hill, 2011), 55.

114. Lorrie Thomas, *Online Marketing* (New York: McGraw-Hill, 2011), 56.

115. "Content Is King—Good Content Holy Grail of Successful Web Publishing," *The Media Pro*, August 14, 2010, accessed December 1, 2011, www.themediapro.com/earn-sleeping/content-is-king-holy-grail-of-successful-web-publishing.

116. Jan Zimmerman, *Web Marketing for Dummies*, 2nd ed. (Hoboken, NJ: Wiley, 2009), 103.

117. "Google Finally Sets the Record Straight: Website Speed Is a Legit Search Ranking Factor," *Linkbuilding.net*, June 13, 2010, accessed December 1, 2011, linkbuilding.net/2010/06/13/google-finally-sets-the-record-straight-website-speed-is-a-legit-search-ranking-factor.

118. Imad Mouline, "Is Your Website Fast Enough for Your Customers?," *CNN Money*, August 27, 2010, accessed June 1, 2012, http://tech.fortune.cnn.com/2010/04/27/is-your-website-fast-enough-for-your-customers/#more-24083.

119. "Improving Site Speed and Load Times," *Optimum7.com*, April 6, 2010, accessed December 1, 2011, www.optimum7.com/internet-marketing/website-speed/improving-site-speed-and-load-time.html.

120. Efraim Turban et al., *Electronic Commerce: A Managerial Perspective* (Upper Saddle River, NJ: Pearson Prentice Hall, 2008), 755.

121. Imad Mouline, "Is Your Website Fast Enough for Your Customers?," *CNN Money*, August 27, 2010, accessed June 1, 2012, http://tech.fortune.cnn.com/2010/04/27/is-your-website-fast-enough-for-your-customers/#more-24083.

122. "Google Finally Sets the Record Straight: Website Speed Is a Legit Search Ranking Factor," *Linkbuilding.net*, June 13, 2010, accessed December 1, 2011, linkbuilding.net/

2010/06/13/google-finally-sets-the-record-straight-website-speed-is-a-legit-search-ranking-factor; "Improving Site Speed and Load Times," *Optimum7.com*, April 6, 2010, December 7, 2011, www.optimum7.com/internet-marketing/website-speed/improving-site-speed-and-load-time.html.

123. Philip Kotler and Kevin Lane Kotler, *Marketing Management* (Upper Saddle River, NJ: Pearson Prentice Hall, 2009), 343.

124. Judy Strauss and Raymond Frost, *E-Marketing* (Upper Saddle River, NJ: Pearson Prentice Hall, 2009), 233.

125. Judy Strauss and Raymond Frost, *E-Marketing* (Upper Saddle River, NJ: Pearson Prentice Hall, 2009), 233.

126. "Pricing a Product or Service," *Small Business Notes*, accessed June 1, 2012, http://www.smallbusinessnotes.com/marketing-your-business/pricing-a-product-or-service.html.

127. Judy Strauss and Raymond Frost, *E-Marketing* (Upper Saddle River, NJ: Pearson Prentice Hall, 2009), 233.

128. Darrell Zahorsky, "Pricing Strategies for Small Business," *About.com*, accessed December 1, 2011, sbinformation.about.com/cs/bestpractices/a/aa112402a.htm.

129. Dana Griffin, "Pricing Strategy Theory," *Chron.com*, accessed December 1, 2011, smallbusiness.chron.com/pricing-strategy-theory-1106.html.

130. Philip Kotler and Kevin Lane Keller, *Marketing Management* (Upper Saddle River, NJ: Pearson Prentice Hall, 2009), 383.

131. Dana-Nicoleta Lascu and Kenneth E. Clow, *Essentials of Marketing* (Mason, OH: Atomic Dog Publishing, 2007), 358–59.

132. Judy Strauss and Raymond Frost, *E-Marketing* (Upper Saddle River, NJ: Pearson Prentice Hall, 2009), 247.

133. Diane Watkins, "What Is Discount Pricing Strategy?," *Chron.com*, accessed December 1, 2011, smallbusiness.chron.com/discount-pricing-strategy-794.html.

134. Rick Suttle, "Industry Pricing Strategy," *Chron.com*, accessed December 1, 2011, smallbusiness.chron.com/industry-pricing-strategy-4684.html.

135. Diane Watkins, "What Is Discount Pricing Strategy?," *Chron.com*, accessed December 1, 2011, smallbusiness.chron.com/discount-pricing-strategy-794.html.

136. Diane Watkins, "What Is Discount Pricing Strategy?," *Chron.com*, accessed December 1, 2011, smallbusiness.chron.com/discount-pricing-strategy-794.html.

137. Karen Collins, *Exploring Business* (Irvington, NY: Flat World Knowledge, 2009), 237.

138. "Cost-Based Pricing," *Small Business Notes*, accessed December 1, 2011, www.smallbusinessnotes.com/marketing-your-business/cost-based-pricing.html.

139. "The Highs And Lows of Cost-Based Pricing," *Fiona Mackenzie*, August 26, 2009, December 1, 2011, fionamackenzie.com.au/pricing-strategy/the-highs-and-lows-of-cost-based-pricing.html.

140. Dana-Nicoleta Lascu and Kenneth E. Clow, *Essentials of Marketing* (Mason, OH: Atomic Dog Publishing), 358–59.

141. Lisa Magloff, "What Is Premium Pricing Strategy?," *Chron.com*, accessed December 1, 2011, smallbusiness.chron.com/premium-pricing-strategy-1107.html.

142. Ivana Taylor, "8 Pricing Strategies You Can Implement Right Now," August 19, 2008, accessed December 1, 2011, *Small Business Trends*, smallbiztrends.com/2008/08/8-pricing-strategies-you-can-implement-right-now.html.

143. Dana-Nicoleta Lascu and Kenneth E. Clow, *Essentials of Marketing* (Mason, OH: Atomic Dog Publishing, 2007), 369.

144. Adapted from David L. Kurtz, *Contemporary Business* (Hoboken, NJ: John Wiley & Sons, 2011), 488.

145. Karen Collins, *Exploring Business* (Irvington, NY: Flat World Knowledge, 2009), 297.

146. Dana-Nicoleta Lascu and Kenneth E. Clow, *Essentials of Marketing* (Mason, OH: Atomic Dog Publishing, 2007), 300.

147. Karen Collins, *Exploring Business* (Irvington, NY: Flat World Knowledge, 2009), 239.

148. Karen Collins, *Exploring Business* (Irvington, NY: Flat World Knowledge, 2009), 239.

149. Karen Collins, *Exploring Business* (Irvington, NY: Flat World Knowledge, 2009), 240.

150. "Monthly & Annual Wholesale Trade Definitions," *US Census Bureau*, October 22, 2010, accessed December 1, 2011, www.census.gov/wholesale/definitions.html.

151. Dana-Nicoleta Lascu and Kenneth E. Clow, *Essentials of Marketing* (Mason, OH: Atomic Dog Publishing, 2007), 300.

152. Philip Kotler and Kevin Keller, *Marketing Management* (Upper Saddle River, NJ: Pearson Prentice Hall, 2009), 458–59.

153. Jeff Madura, *Introduction to Business* (St. Paul, MN: Paradigm Publishing, 2010), 445.

154. Philip Kotler and Kevin Keller, *Marketing Management* (Upper Saddle River, NJ: Pearson Prentice Hall, 2009), 429; Dana-Nicoleta Lascu and Kenneth E. Clow, *Essentials of Marketing* (Mason, OH: Atomic Dog Publishing, 2007), 303.

155. Philip Kotler and Kevin Keller, *Marketing Management* (Upper Saddle River, NJ: Pearson Prentice Hall, 2009), 429.

156. Dana-Nicoleta Lascu and Kenneth E. Clow, *Essentials of Marketing* (Mason, OH: Atomic Dog Publishing, 2007), 306.

157. Jennifer Nichols, "Guide to Transportation and Logistics Companies for Small Business," *Business.com*, accessed December 1, 2011, www.business.com/guides/logistics-management-for-small-business-175.

158. Dana-Nicoleta Lascu and Kenneth E. Clow, *Essentials of Marketing* (Mason, OH: Atomic Dog Publishing, 2007), 307.

159. Dana-Nicoleta Lascu and Kenneth E. Clow, *Essentials of Marketing* (Mason, OH: Atomic Dog Publishing, 2007), 307.

160. Karen Collins, *Exploring Business* (Irvington, NY: Flat World Knowledge, 2009), 241.

161. Philip Kotler and Kevin Keller, *Marketing Management* (Upper Saddle River, NJ: Pearson Prentice Hall, 2009), 464.

162. Dana-Nicoleta Lascu and Kenneth E. Clow, *Essentials of Marketing* (Mason, OH: Atomic Dog Publishing, 2007), 312.

163. "How to Run a Small Business: Inventory Management," *StartupNation LLC*, accessed December 1, 2011, www.startupnation.com/business-articles/899/1/AT_InventoryMgt.asp.

164. Philip Kotler and Kevin Keller, *Marketing Management* (Upper Saddle River, NJ: Pearson Prentice Hall, 2009), 464.

165. Jennifer Nichols, "Guide to Transportation and Logistics Companies for Small Business," *Business.com*, accessed December 1, 2011, www.business.com/guides/logistics-management-for-small-business-175.

166. Adapted from Sharad Singh, "Five Retail IT Trends to Watch in 2011," *RetailCustomerExperience.com*, December 10, 2010, accessed December 1, 2011, www.retailcustomerexperience.com/article/178220/Five-retail-IT-trends-to-watch-in-2011; Jan Zimmerman, *Web Marketing for Dummies*, 2nd ed. (Hoboken, NJ: Wiley, 2009), 111–19.

167. "Digital Window Shopping: The Long Journey to 'Buy'" *McAfee, Inc.*, accessed December 1, 2011, www.mcafeesecure.com/us/resources/whitepapers/digital_window_shopping.jsp.

168. Jan Zimmerman, *Web Marketing for Dummies*, 2nd ed. (Hoboken, NJ: Wiley, 2009), 118.

169. "Digital Window Shopping: The Long Journey to 'Buy'" *McAfee, Inc.*, accessed December 1, 2011, www.mcafeesecure.com/us/resources/whitepapers/digital_window_shopping.jsp.

170. Philip Kotler and David Lane Keller, *Marketing Management* (Upper Saddle River, NJ: Pearson Prentice Hall, 2009), 470.

171. Dana-Nicoleta Lascu and Kenneth E. Clow, *Essentials of Marketing* (Mason, OH: Atomic Dog Publishing, 2007), 380.

172. Dana-Nicoleta Lascu and Kenneth E. Clow, *Essentials of Marketing* (Mason, OH: Atomic Dog Publishing, 2007), 393.

173. Adapted from Dana-Nicoleta Lascu and Kenneth E. Clow, *Essentials of Marketing* (Mason, OH: Atomic Dog Publishing, 2007), 393–96.

174. Philip Kotler and David Lane Keller, *Marketing Management* (Upper Saddle River, NJ: Pearson Prentice Hall, 2009), 470.

175. Philip Kotler and David Lane Keller, *Marketing Management* (Upper Saddle River, NJ: Pearson Prentice Hall, 2009), 472.

176. Karen Collins, *Exploring Business* (Irvington, NY: Flat World Knowledge, 2009), 245.

177. Susan Ward, "17 Advertising Ideas for Small Businesses," *About.com*, accessed December 1, 2011, sbinfocanada.about.com/od/advertising/a/17adideas.htm. Lanee Blunt, "Small Business Advertising: Low Cost Flyers," *Advertising @ Suite 101*, February 11, 2011, accessed December 1, 2011, lanee-blunt.suite101.com/small-business-advertising-low-cost-flyers-a346278.

178. The Street, "Small Shops Aim for Super Bowl Edge," *MSN Money*, February 1, 2011, accessed December 1, 2011, money.msn.com/how-to-invest/small-shops-aim-for-a-super-edge-thestreet.aspx.

179. Lorrie Thomas, *Online Marketing* (New York: McGraw-Hill, 2011), 157.

180. Lorrie Thomas, *Online Marketing* (New York: McGraw-Hill, 2011), 159–61.

181. "Google AdWords: Advertise Your Business on Google," accessed January 24, 2012, accounts.google.com/ServiceLogin?service=adwords&hl=en&ltmpl=regionalc&passive=true&ifi=false&alwf=true&continue=https://adwords.google.com/um/gaiaauth?apt%3DNone%26ltmpl%3Dregionalc&sacu=1&sarp=1&sourceid=awo&subid=us-en-et-bizsol.

182. Philip Kotler and David Lane Keller, *Marketing Management* (Upper Saddle River, NJ: Pearson Prentice Hall, 2009), 487.

183. Philip Kotler and David Lane Keller, *Marketing Management* (Upper Saddle River, NJ: Pearson Prentice Hall, 2009), 472; "Sales Promotion Strategy," *Small Business Bible*, accessed December 1, 2011, www.smallbusinessbible.org/salespromotionstrategy.html.

184. Chris Joseph, "Sales Promotion Advantages," *Chron.com*, accessed December 1, 2011, smallbusiness.chron.com/sales-promotion-advantages-1059.html.

185. Philip Kotler and David Lane Keller, *Marketing Management* (Upper Saddle River, NJ: Pearson Prentice Hall, 2009), 472.

186. Jerry Robertson, "Secrets to Low Cost PR for Small Businesses," *Yahoo! Voices*, February 14, 2007, accessed December 1, 2011, voices.yahoo.com/secrets-low-cost-pr-small-businesses-193968.html.

187. Philip Kotler and David Lane Keller, *Marketing Management* (Upper Saddle River, NJ: Pearson Prentice Hall, 2009), 489.

188. Bernd H. Schmitt, *Experiential Marketing* (New York: The Free Press, 1999), 22, 24.

189. Jerry Robertson, "Secrets to Low Cost PR for Small Businesses," *Yahoo! Voices*, February 14, 2007, accessed December 1, 2011, voices.yahoo.com/secrets-low-cost-pr-small-businesses-193968.html.

190. Philip Kotler and David Lane Keller, *Marketing Management* (Upper Saddle River, NJ: Pearson Prentice Hall, 2009), 472.

191. Dana-Nicoleta Lascu and Kenneth E. Clow, *Essentials of Marketing* (Mason, OH: Atomic Dog Publishing, 2007), 382.

192. "Developing a Press Kit for Your Small Business," *AllBusiness*, accessed December 1, 2011, www.allbusiness.com/print/445-1-22eeq.html.

193. Philip Kotler and David Lane Keller, *Marketing Management* (Upper Saddle River, NJ: Pearson Prentice Hall, 2009), 472.

194. Erica DeWolf, "Social Media Tools Should Be Used for PR," *eMarketing & New Media*, May 4, 2009, accessed December 1, 2011, ericadewolf.wordpress.com/2009/05/04/social-media-tools-should-be-used-for-pr.

195. Dana-Nicoleta Lascu and Kenneth E. Clow, *Essentials of Marketing* (Mason, OH: Atomic Dog Publishing, 2007), 444.

196. Jerry Robertson, "Secrets to Low Cost PR for Small Businesses," *Yahoo! Voices*, February 14, 2007, accessed December 1, 2011, voices.yahoo.com/secrets-low-cost-pr-small-businesses-193969.html.

197. Philip Kotler and David Lane Keller, *Marketing Management* (Upper Saddle River, NJ: Pearson Prentice Hall, 2009), 488–489.

198. Erica DeWolf, "Social Media Tools Should Be Used for PR," *eMarketing & New Media*, May 4, 2009, accessed December 1, 2011, ericadewolf.wordpress.com/2009/05/04/social-media-tools-should-be-used-for-pr.

199. Philip Kotler and David Lane Keller, *Marketing Management* (Upper Saddle River, NJ: Pearson Prentice Hall, 2009), 473.

200. Dana-Nicoleta Lascu and Kenneth E. Clow, *Essentials of Marketing* (Mason, OH: Atomic Dog Publishing, 2007), 505.

201. Dana-Nicoleta Lascu and Kenneth E. Clow, *Essentials of Marketing* (Mason, OH: Atomic Dog Publishing, 2007), 504.

202. Lisa Barone, "Webcast: Direct Marketing for Small Businesses," *Outspoken Media*, April 16, 2009, accessed December 1, 2011, outspokenmedia.com/online-marketing/webcast-direct-marketing-for-small-businesses.

203. Lisa Barone, "Webcast: Direct Marketing for Small Businesses," *Outspoken Media*, April 16, 2009, accessed December 1, 2011, outspokenmedia.com/online-marketing/webcast-direct-marketing-for-small-businesses.

204. Kris Carrie, "Advantages of Direct Marketing," Article Dashboard, accessed December 1, 2011, www.articledashboard.com/Article/Advantages-of-Direct-Marketing/587894.

205. Philip Kotler and David Lane Keller, *Marketing Management* (Upper Saddle River, NJ: Pearson Prentice Hall, 2009), 472.

206. Dana-Nicoleta Lascu and Kenneth E. Clow, *Essentials of Marketing* (Mason, OH: Atomic Dog Publishing, 2007), 558.

207. Mike Yapp, "10 Best Interactive Marketing Practices," *iMedia Connection*, January 9, 2006, accessed December 1, 2011, www.imediaconnection.com/content/7764.asp.

208. Joe Mandese, "Forrester Revises Interactive Outlook, Will Account for 21% of Marketing by 2014," *MediaPost News*, July 8, 2009, accessed December 1, 2011, www.mediapost.com/publications/?fa=Articles.showArticle&art_aid=109381.

209. Karen Scharf, "Small Business Marketing with Video," *Business Know-How*, accessed December 1, 2011, www.businessknowhow.com/internet/videomarketing.htm.

210. Sean Rasmussen, "Using Online Videos to Increase Popularity," *Aussie Internet Marketing Blog*, July 30, 2009, accessed December 1, 2011, seanseo.com/internet-marketing/using-online-videos.

211. Mike Sachoff, "Small Businesses Plan to Focus on Mobile Marketing and Online Video in 2011," *SmallBusinessNewz*, January 18, 2011, accessed December 1, 2011, www.smallbusinessnewz.com/topnews/2011/01/18/small-businesses-plan-to-focus-on-mobile-marketing-and-online-video-in-2011.

212. Lorrie Thomas, *Online Marketing* (New York: McGraw-Hill, 2011), 73–74.

213. Lorrie Thomas, *Online Marketing* (New York: McGraw-Hill, 2011), 72.

214. Robbin Block, *Social Persuasion: Making Sense of Social Media for Small Business* (Breinigsville, PA: Block Media, December 2010), 2.

215. Lorrie Thomas, *Online Marketing* (New York: McGraw-Hill, 2011), 99.

216. Lisa Barone, "Which Social Media Sites Are Most Beneficial?," *Small Business Trends*, January 26, 2011, accessed December 1, 2011, smallbiztrends.com/2011/01/which-social-media-site-most-beneficial%E2%80%99.html.

217. Lisa Barone, "Which Social Media Sites Are Most Beneficial?," *Small Business Trends*, January 26, 2011, accessed December 1, 2011, smallbiztrends.com/2011/01/which-social-media-site-most-beneficial%E2%80%99.html.

218. Lisa Barone, "Study: How Are B2Bs Using Social Media," *Small Business Trends*, November 25, 2009, accessed December 1, 2011, smallbiztrends.com/2009/11/b2bs-social-media-study.html.

219. Lisa Barone, "Which Social Media Sites Are Most Beneficial?," *Small Business Trends*, January 26, 2011, accessed December 1, 2011, smallbiztrends.com/2011/01/which-social-media-site-most-beneficial%E2%80%99.html.

220. "Personal Selling," *eNotes*, accessed December 1, 2011, www.enotes.com/personal-selling-reference/personal-selling-178681.

221. "Personal Selling," *eNotes*, accessed December 1, 2011, enotes.com/personal-selling-reference/personal-selling-178681.

222. John M. Ivancevich and Thomas N. Duening, *Business Principles, Guidelines, and Practices* (Mason, OH: Thomson Learning, 2007), 431.

223. "Objectives of Personal Selling," *KnowThis.com*, accessed December 1, 2011, www.knowthis.com/principles-of-marketing-tutorials/personal-selling/objectives-of-personal-selling.

224. "Advantages of Personal Selling," *KnowThis.com*, accessed December 1, 2011, www.knowthis.com/principles-of-marketing-tutorials/personal-selling/advantages-of-personal-selling.

225. "Disadvantages of Personal Selling," *KnowThis.com*, accessed December 1, 2011, www.knowthis.com/principles-of-marketing-tutorials/personal-selling/disadvantages-of-personal-selling.

226. "Disadvantages of Personal Selling," *KnowThis.com*, accessed December 1, 2011, www.knowthis.com/principles-of-marketing-tutorials/personal-selling/disadvantages-of-personal-selling.

227. John M. Ivancevich and Thomas N. Duening, *Business Principles, Guidelines, and Practices* (Mason, OH: Thomson Learning, 2007), 435; Philip Kotler and Kevin Lane Keller, *Marketing Management* (Upper Saddle River, NJ: Pearson Prentice Hall, 2009), 560–561; Dana-Nicoleta Lascu and Kenneth E. Clow, *Essentials of Marketing* (Mason, OH: Atomic Dog Publishing, 2007), 489–98.

228. Thomas Young, "A Selling Revolution: How the Internet Changed Personal Selling (Part 1)," *Executive Street*, accessed December 1, 2011, blog.vistage.com/marketing/a-selling-revolution-how-the-internet-changed-personal-selling.

229. Thomas Young, "A Selling Revolution: How the Internet Changed Personal Selling (Part 1)," *Executive Street*, accessed December 1, 2011, blog.vistage.com/marketing/a-selling-revolution-how-the-internet-changed-personal-selling.

230. Adapted from David L. Kurtz, *Contemporary Business* (Hoboken, NJ: John Wiley & Sons, 2011), 488.

231. Robert R. Harmon and Greg Laird, "Linking Marketing Strategy to Customer Value: Implications for Technology Marketers," *PDFCast.org*, accessed December 1, 2011, pdfcast.org/pdf/linking-marketing-strategy-to-customer-value-implications-for-technology-marketers.

232. Angela Hausman, "Marketing Strategy: Using Social Media to Create Customer Value," *Hausman Marketing Letter*, October 25, 2010, accessed June 1, 2012, http://www.hausmanmarketingletter.com/marketing-strategy-using-social-media-to-create-customer-value.

233. Mark Hunter, "Discounting to Create Cash Flow? Be Careful," *PowerHomeBiz.com*, May 19, 2011, accessed December 1, 2011, www.powerhomebiz.com/blog/2011/05/discounting-to-create-cash-flow-be-careful.

234. Lauren Simonds, "Mobile Commerce Experts Talk Small Business," *Small Business Computing.com*, May 3, 2011, accessed December 1, 2011, www.smallbusinesscomputing.com/emarketing/article.php/3932506/Mobile-Commerce-Experts-Talk-Small-Business.htm.

235. Emily Glazer, "Target: Customers on the Go," *Wall Street Journal*, May 16, 2011, accessed December 1, 2011, online.wsj.com/article/SB10001424052748704132204576285631212564952.html.

236. Javier Espinoza, "Need to Bank? Phone It In," *Wall Street Journal*, November 14, 2011, accessed December 1, 2011, online.wsj.com/article/SB10001424052970204485304576644853956740860.html.

237. Sarah E. Needleman, "Raise Cash on Crowdfunding Sites," *Wall Street Journal*, November 27, 2011, accessed December 1, 2011, online.wsj.com/article/SB10001424052970204443404577052013654406558.html?mod=googlenews_ws.

238. Michael Raymond, "Costly Small Business Marketing Mistakes Every Entrepreneur Must Avoid," *Helium*, accessed December 1, 2011, www.helium.com/items/1644285-current-domain-registration-expired-domain-names.

CHAPTER 8
The Marketing Plan

The New Britain Rock Cats

Source: Reprinted with permission from the New Britain Rock Cats official website: http://web.minorleaguebaseball.com/index.jsp?sid=t538.

The New Britain Rock Cats were founded in 1983 in New Britain, Connecticut. They are the double-A minor league baseball affiliate of the Minnesota Twins major league baseball club, competing in the Eastern League. The 2011 season marked the 29th anniversary of Eastern League Baseball in New Britain.

There is a rich history of baseball in New Britain, and the Rock Cats are the Nutmeg State's oldest, continuously operating professional sports franchise. From Cy Young Award–winners to most valuable players (MVPs) and batting champions to rookie of the year award winners and all-stars, New Britain has been an enormously productive foundation for major league baseball. Over four million fans have seen professional baseball in New Britain over the years. The Rock Cats have many notable alumni, including MVPs Jeff Bagwell (third baseman) and Mo Vaughn (first baseman). All-stars include Brady Anderson (outfielder), Ellis Burks (outfielder), Aaron Sele (right-handed pitcher), John Valentin (shortstop), and Cy Young Award winner Roger Clemens.

In 2000, the club was sold to a group of investors headed by a local attorney, Coleman Levy, and William Dowling, a former New York Yankees executive vice president. Dowling is the president and CEO of the club, and Levy is the vice president. With a substantially new front office and new increased promotions, the club saw every attendance record fall, passing the 300,000 mark for the past 3 years.

The Rock Cats see themselves as selling affordable family entertainment, not baseball. They target women and children. They integrated the Internet into their marketing activities three years ago and have found it very useful for selling tickets. They also have a Facebook and Twitter presence. About 3 years ago, they spent $5,000 for a professionally prepared marketing research report. As Dowling commented, "It made the company more sophisticated."

The marketing planning process is relatively informal, with everyone participating. There is no formal document. Dowling's philosophy is that if something costs less than $1,000, "go do it." If it costs more than $1,000, "justify it." The Rock Cats are run out of a small office in New Britain. The communication among the staff is regular and effective. Here is an instance in which a formal marketing plan does not seem necessary. Whatever they are doing, it is working just fine.[1]

Video Clip 8.1

Rock Cats Baseball
A fun look at what the Rock Cats offer to fans.

View the video online at: http://www.youtube.com/v/QzbmFKHIWws

1. THE NEED FOR A MARKETING PLAN

LEARNING OBJECTIVES

1. Understand why a small business should have a marketing plan.
2. Understand the implications of not having a marketing plan.

Let's face it, as a small business owner, you are really in the business of marketing.[2]
  - *John Jantsch*

Many small businesses do not have a marketing plan, choosing instead to market their products and services on an intuitive, sometimes seat-of-the-pants basis. As long as there is regular and effective communication with the rest of the people in the organization, a formal written plan may not be necessary. However, as the business grows and regular and effective communication becomes more difficult, a written marketing plan should be seriously considered. For the small businesses that do have a marketing plan, few actually use it.[3]

There are many reasons why so many small businesses do not have marketing plans. Among the reasons are the following:[4]

- They do not have enough knowledge of marketing.
- They take a scatter-gun approach to marketing.
- They do not know how to go about developing a marketing plan.
- They do not have enough money to do marketing properly.
- They do not have enough time to do marketing properly.
- They do not have good people or resources to help them with marketing.

This tells us that understanding what a marketing plan is all about and how a marketing plan can be put together simply and inexpensively are invaluable parts of a small business owner's tool kit.

1.1 What Is a Marketing Plan?

A **marketing plan** "is a written document that summarizes what the marketer has learned about the marketplace and indicates how the firm plans to reach its marketing objectives. It contains tactical guidelines for the marketing programs and financial allocations over the planning period."[5] A marketing plan provides a specific marketing direction for a small business and is a very valuable tool if it is done correctly. Because the ultimate purpose of the plan is to generate efficient, profitable action, the marketing plan should consist of usable, practical instructions that are designed to ensure that resources are properly applied.[6]

Marketing plans can range from a one-page summary to more than one hundred pages. Although it is said by some that the ideal marketing plan length for a stand-alone document (i.e., a document that is not part of the total business plan for a company) is twenty to fifty pages,[7] the length of a marketing plan for a small business can be any length that will satisfy the needs of the business. The page count of the plan may not be a good way to measure the adequacy of the plan. The marketing plan should be measured by readability and summarization. A good marketing plan will provide the reader with a good general idea of its main contents even after only a quick skim in fifteen minutes or less.[8] No matter the length, the plan should be practical, to the point, with useful graphics as appropriate, and worded clearly with no flowery or legalistic language.[9]

The plan should cover one year, which is often the best way to think about marketing for the small company. This is not to say that you should not also think about the long term. It just means that things change more rapidly in the short term. People leave, markets evolve, and customers come and go. Consideration should be given to two to four years down the road.[10]

Because small business owners have very little time to spend on writing an elaborate marketing plan, it is worth considering using software or online templates to put the plan together. One software program is Marketing Plan Pro, which is now included as part of Sales and Marketing Pro. The number one best-selling marketing plan software tool for building small business marketing plans for several years, Marketing Plan Pro provides step-by-step guidance, easy forecasts and budgets, customization options, execution guidance, and several sample plans across a wide variety of business types. Marketing plan assistance is also available through the Small Business Administration (SBA) and the Service Corps of Retired Executives (SCORE) program. SCORE—a nonprofit association dedicated to educating entrepreneurs and helping small businesses start, grow, and succeed—is an SBA resource partner that has been mentoring small business owners for more than forty years.[11]

marketing plan

A written document that summarizes what the marketer has learned about the marketplace and indicates how the firm plans to reach its marketing objectives.

1.2 Why Have a Marketing Plan?

A marketing plan is a very important part of the small business roadmap to success. The plan drives action and points the way.[12] There are many good reasons for developing a marketing plan, including the following:[13]

- It forces you to identify the target market. A company's best customers, and hopefully the ideal customer, should be in the target market.
- You get a higher return on investment (ROI). Every dollar will work harder when it is focused.
- It forces you to think about both short- and long-term marketing strategies. Focusing only on the short term can be devastating to the future of the company.
- It provides a basis on which to evaluate a company against its industry or market in terms of strengths, weaknesses, opportunities, and threats.
- You can eliminate waste by building efficiency. Limited resources can be allocated to create the greatest return.
- It will be easier to see where past decisions have helped or hindered the growth of a business. The plan will provide a guide for measuring progress and outcomes.
- It will help you to minimize risk, mistakes, and failures.
- It helps you to establish a timeline, keeping people accountable for the growth and success of operation.
- It gives clarity to who does what, when, and with what marketing tools.
- It lays out a company's game plan. If people leave, if new people arrive, if memories falter, if events bring pressure to alter the givens, the information in the written marketing plan is a reminder of what you agreed on.

1.3 What If There Is No Marketing Plan?

In *Alice in Wonderland*, Alice encounters the Cheshire cat. He asks her where she is going. She answers that she does not know. The Cheshire cat answers that any road will take her there. It is clear that Alice did not have a marketing plan. David Campbell has a similar philosophy as reflected in the title of his book: *If You Don't Know Where You're Going, You'll Probably End Up Somewhere Else.*[14] Without a marketing plan, a small business could be moving at great speed…but in the entirely wrong direction.

Because many small businesses seem to operate successfully without a marketing plan, depending on how you want to define successfully, the absence of a marketing plan does not mean automatic failure. However, there are some distinct disadvantages to not having a marketing plan. The following are some examples:

- Not having a marketing plan, whether it be a stand-alone document or a section in the business plan, will put you at a significant disadvantage when trying to get any type of business loan.
- Not having a marketing plan can push a business into a meandering mode that could result in slowed growth, missed opportunities, and ignored threats.
- The target market may not be defined correctly.
- Not having a marketing plan may force you to focus on the short term with little or no attention to the long term. This can be devastating to the future of a company.
- Potential efficiencies will not be realized.
- Risk will likely increase.

In short, not having a marketing plan means that you will not realize the advantages of having one. Even if you are an owner-only business, a marketing plan can provide a discipline and a structure for growing the business—if that is desired. On the other hand, if an owner is perfectly satisfied with where and how things are, a marketing plan will most likely not be helpful. Just remember that change is constant. Without a marketing plan, a business may not be ready for change.

KEY TAKEAWAYS

- Many small businesses do not have a marketing plan.
- There are many reasons why small businesses do not have a marketing plan. One very important reason is that they do not know how to develop a plan.
- A marketing plan provides a specific marketing direction for a small business. The ultimate purpose of the plan is to generate efficient, profitable action.
- Although a marketing plan should cover one year in detail, this does not mean that a business should ignore the longer term.
- There are many reasons why small businesses should have a marketing plan, not the least of which is that a marketing plan can help the business minimize risk, mistakes, and failures.
- Without a marketing plan, a small business could be moving at great speed…but in the wrong direction.
- Not having a marketing plan means that the business cannot realize the many benefits of having one.
- A marketing plan may not be for all businesses. If one is happy with where and how a business is, one may think that a marketing plan is not needed. Remember, though, that change will happen, and a business may not be ready for it without a marketing plan.

EXERCISE

1. At Frank's All-American BarBeQue, Frank is pleased with the profitability of the business and the standing that the company has in the local community. Not as pleased is Frank's son, Robert, who thinks that the business can be bigger and better. The new store that is opening in neighboring Darien, Connecticut, is a good start, but Robert still thinks that the business is not realizing its full potential. A business plan has been prepared except for the marketing plan section. Robert wants to develop the marketing plan for Frank's, but his father is balking at the idea. His father's position is, "If it ain't broke, why fix it?" Taking the position of Robert, make the case for preparing a marketing plan for Frank's. Think critically when developing your argument, integrating specifics from Frank's business. Resist the temptation to simply list the advantages of having a plan versus the disadvantages of not having a plan. Frank will need to see something much more persuasive than this.

2. THE MARKETING PLAN

Although there is no universally accepted format for a marketing plan, the requirements can be grouped into the seven sections identified in Figure 8.1. The marketing plan can be a stand-alone document or a section of the business plan. If it is part of the business plan, it will duplicate information that is presented in other sections of the business plan.

A solid marketing strategy is the foundation of a well-written marketing plan,[15] and the marketing strategy should have onground and online components if the small business has or wants to have a web presence. The online portion of the marketing plan should be a plan that can be implemented easily, be changed rapidly as appropriate, and show results quickly.[16]

FIGURE 8.1 The Marketing Plan

2.1 Executive Summary

The executive summary is a one- to two-page synopsis of a company's marketing plan. The summary gives a quick overview of the main points of the plan, a synopsis of what a company has done, what it plans to do, and how it plans to get there.[17] The executive summary is for the people who lack the time and interest to read the entire marketing plan but who need a good basic understanding of what it is about.[18]

Executive Summary Example

Sigmund's Gourmet Pasta

Note: The marketing plan for Sigmund's Gourmet Pasta is a sample small business marketing plan provided by and copyrighted by Palo Alto Software. Permission has been given to the authors to use this plan as the basis for this chapter. This plan will be used throughout this chapter to illustrate marketing plan concepts. Additional complete sample marketing plans for small businesses are available at http://www.mplans.com.

Sigmund's Gourmet Pasta will be the leading pasta restaurant in Eugene, Oregon, with a rapidly developing consumer brand and growing customer base. The signature line of innovative, premium pasta dishes include pesto with smoked salmon, pancetta and peas linguine in an Alfredo sauce, lobster ravioli in a lobster sauce, and fresh mussels and clams in a marinara sauce. Sigmund's Gourmet Pasta also serves distinct salads, desserts, and beverages. All desserts are made on-site.

Sigmund's Gourmet Pasta will reinvent the pasta experience for individuals, families, and takeout customers with discretionary income by selling high-quality, innovative products at a reasonable price; designing tasteful, convenient locations; and providing industry-benchmark customer service. Our web presence enhances our brand.

To grow at a rate consistent with our objectives, Sigmund's is offering an additional $500,000 in equity. Existing members will be given the first option to subscribe to the additional equity to allow each of them to maintain their percentage of ownership. The portion not subscribed by existing members will be available to prospective new investors.[19]

2.2 Vision and Mission

vision statement

A document that articulates the long-term purpose and idealized notion of what the business wishes to become.

The **vision statement** tries to articulate the long-term purpose and idealized notion of what the business hopes to be in terms of growth, values, employees, contributions to society, and so forth—that is, where the owner sees the business going. Self-reflection by the business founder is a vital activity if a meaningful vision is to be developed.[20]

Vision Statement Examples

Mobile News Games: Developer of Mobile Games Relating to Current News Events

"Our vision is to provide people with a brief escape of fun over the course of their normal day. We do this by providing them with timely interactive games that they can access on their mobile devices—games that are easy to play and have some connection with current pop culture news."[21]

Neon Memories Diner

"Neon Memories Diner is a place for family togetherness organized around a common love of the traditional American diner and the simpler times of the '50s and '60s. Neon Memories Diner transcends a typical theme restaurant by putting real heart into customer service and the quality of its food so that its unique presentation and references to times past are just part of the picture."[22]

mission statement

A document that articulates the fundamental nature of the business. It should address what business the company is in, the company's potential customers, and how customer value will be provided.

By contrast, the **mission statement** for the marketing plan looks to articulate the more fundamental nature of the business (i.e., why the business exists). A company's mission is its sense of purpose—the reason why the owner gets up every day and does what he or she does. It captures the owner's values and visions, along with that of the employees (if applicable) and community plus suppliers and stakeholders. It literally is the foundation of a company's future.[23] As such, the mission statement is an important foundation of a business's marketing plan. It is common for the mission statement to appear in the marketing strategy section of the marketing plan. It is also common for the plan to include either a vision statement or a mission statement but not both.

Mission Statement Examples

Disney

"To make people happy."[24]

Coca-Cola

"To Refresh the World…in body, mind, and spirit."[25]

Organic Body Products, Inc. (Small Business)

"To provide high-quality skincare and body care products to women who want what goes on their bodies to have as high a quality as what goes in their bodies."[26]

Sigmund's Gourmet Pasta (Small Business)

"Sigmund's Gourmet Pasta's mission is to provide the customer the finest pasta meal and dining experience. We exist to attract and maintain customers. When we adhere to this maxim, everything else will fall into place. Our services will exceed the expectations of customers."[27]

2.3 Situation Analysis

The **situation analysis** gives a picture of where a company is now in the market and details the context for its marketing efforts (see Figure 8.2). Although individual analyses will vary, the contents will generally include relevant information about current products or services, sales, the market (defining it and determining how big it is and how fast it is growing), competition, target market(s), trends, and keys to success. These factors can be combined to develop a **SWOT analysis**—an identification of a company's strengths, weaknesses, opportunities, and threats—to help a company differentiate itself from its competitors.

situation analysis

A picture of where a business is now in the market, detailing the context for its marketing efforts.

SWOT analysis

An identification of a company's strengths, weaknesses, opportunities, and threats.

FIGURE 8.2 Situation Analysis

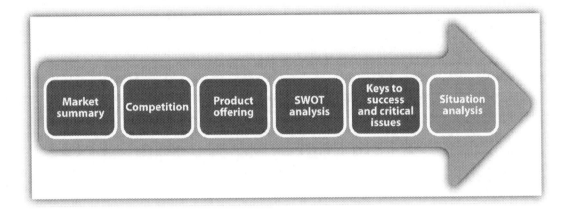

Market Summary

As the title implies, the **market summary** summarizes what is known about the market in which a company competes, plans to compete, or both. This summary may be all that is read, so it must be short and concise. The market summary should include a description of the market and its attributes, market needs, market trends, and market growth. See Figure 8.3.

market summary

What is known about the market in which a company competes, plans to compete, or both.

FIGURE 8.3 Market Summary

Market Summary Example

Introductory Paragraph: Sigmund's Gourmet Pasta

Sigmund's Gourmet Pasta possesses good information about the market and knows a great deal about the common attributes of our most prized and loyal customers. Sigmund's Gourmet Pasta will leverage this information to better understand who is served, their specific needs, and how Sigmund's can better communicate with them.[28]

The Market and Its Attributes

This section of the marketing plan is where a company's customers are identified. If a business has an online presence or wants to have one, information needs to be generated for online customers as well. Some, perhaps most but not all, of a company's online customers will come from the company's on-ground customers. This depends on the company's marketing strategy. However, a web presence can considerably expand a company's market.

The information that should be provided about customers is as follows:[29]

1. All relevant demographic (e.g., age and gender) and lifestyle or behavior (e.g., activities, interests, and spending patterns) information. This information can be linked to important differences in buyer behavior.

Demographics for Sigmund's Gourmet Pasta

- Male and female
- Ages 25–50, this segment makes up 53 percent of the Eugene market according to the Eugene Chamber of Commerce
- Young professionals who work close to the location
- Yuppies
- Have attended college and/or graduate school
- Income over $40,000[30]

Behavior and Lifestyle Factors for Sigmund's Gourmet Pasta

- Eat out several times a week
- Tend to patronize higher-quality restaurants
- Are cognizant about their health
- Enjoy a high-quality meal without the mess of making it themselves
- When ordering, health concerns in regard to foods are taken into account
- There is a value attributed to the appearance or the presentation of food[31]

2. The location of the customers (local, regional, national, or international). There are often distinct differences in buyer behavior based on geographic location, so it is important to know what those differences are to tap into them. For example, grits are a common breakfast item in the South, but they are not a menu staple anywhere else in the United States.

Geographics for Sigmund's Gourmet Pasta

- Sigmund's immediate geographic target is the city of Eugene with a population of 130,000.
- A 15-mile geographic area is in need of Sigmund's services.[32]

3. An assessment of the size of the market and its estimated growth. There should be enough of a market to justify a business's existence in the first place. Even a niche market must be large enough to offer profitability potential. At the same time, a company will want the market to grow so that the business can grow (assuming growth is desired). If, on the other hand, a company wants to remain small, market growth is not as important—except that it may present opportunities for new competitors to enter the marketplace.

Market Size for Sigmund's Gourmet Pasta

- The total targeted population is estimated at 46,000.
- The target markets are individuals, families, and takeout.[33]

Target Markets—Sigmund's Gourmet Pasta

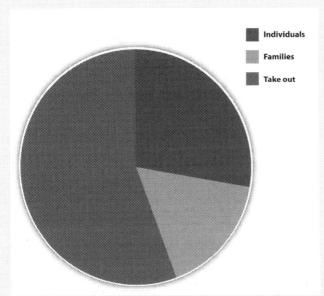

Source: "Pasta Restaurant Marketing Plan: Sigmund's Gourmet Pasta: Situation Analysis," Mplans.com, accessed December 2, 2011, http://www.mplans.com/pasta_restaurant_marketing_plan/situation_analysis_fc.php. Reprinted by permission of Palo Alto Software.

Estimated Market Growth for Sigmund's Gourmet Pasta

In 2010, the global pasta market reached $8 billion. Pasta sales are estimated to grow by at least 10 percent for the next few years. This growth can be attributed to several different factors. The first factor is an appreciation for health-conscious food. Although not all pasta is "good for you," particularly cream-based sauces, pasta can be very tasty yet health conscious at the same time. Pasta is seen as a healthy food because of its high percentage of carbohydrates relative to fat.

Another variable that contributes to market growth is an increase in the number of hours our demographic is working. Over the last five years, the number of hours spent at work of our archetype customer has significantly increased. As the number of work hours increases, there is a high correlation of people who eat out at restaurants. This is intuitively explained by the fact that with a limited number of hours available each day, people have less time to prepare their meals, and eating out is one way to maximize their time.[34]

Projected Market Growth—Sigmund's Gourmet Pasta*

Potential Customers	Growth (%)	2011	2012	2013	2014	2015	CAGR (%)**
Individuals	8	12,457	13,454	14,530	15,692	16,947	8.00
Families	9	8,974	9,782	10,662	11,622	12,668	9.00
Takeout	10	24,574	27,031	29,734	32,707	35,978	10.00
TOTAL	9.27	46,005	50,267	54,926	60,021	65,593	9.27
*All numbers are hypothetical.							
** Compound annual growth rate.							

Source: Adapted from "Pasta Restaurant Marketing Plan: Sigmund's Gourmet Pasta," Mplans.com, accessed December 1, 2011, http://www.mplans.com/pasta_restaurant_marketing_plan/marketing_strategy_fc.php.

4. An identification of market needs and how a business plans to meet them.[35] Without knowing and understanding market needs, it is extremely difficult to create a marketing mix that will successfully meet those needs. There are instances of small businesses that are successful because

of an intuitive sense for what the market needs, but these businesses may eventually experience limited growth opportunities because their intuition can take them only so far. Market needs change, so small businesses must adapt quickly to those changes. They cannot adapt to changes they do not know about.

Identifying and Meeting Market Needs for Sigmund's Gourmet Pasta

Sigmund's Gourmet Pasta is providing its customers with a wide selection of high-quality pasta dishes and salads that are unique and pleasing in presentation, offering a wide selection of health-conscious choices, and using top-shelf ingredients. Sigmund's Gourmet Pasta seeks to fulfill the following benefits that are important to their customers:

- **Selection.** There is a wide choice of pasta and salad options.
- **Accessibility.** The patron can gain access to the restaurant with minimal waits and can choose the option of dine in or takeout.
- **Customer service.** Patrons will be impressed with the level of attention that they receive.
- **Competitive pricing.** All products/services will be competitively priced relative to comparable high-end pasta and Italian restaurants.

5. An identification of market trends.[36] Just as it is important to understand market needs, a small business should be able to identify where the market is going so that its marketing mix can be adjusted accordingly. Capitalizing on market trends early in the game can offer a powerful competitive advantage.

Identifying Market Trends for Sigmund's Gourmet Pasta

The market trend for restaurants is headed toward a more sophisticated customer. The restaurant patron today relative to yesterday is more sophisticated in several different ways.

- **Food quality.** The preference for high-quality ingredients is increasing as customers learn to appreciate the qualitative difference.
- **Presentation/appearance.** As presentation of an element of the culinary experience becomes more pervasive, patrons are learning to appreciate this aspect of the industry.
- **Health consciousness.** As Americans in general are more cognizant of their health, evidenced by the increase in individuals exercising and health-club memberships, patrons are requesting more healthy alternatives when they eat out. They recognize that an entrée can be both quite tasty and reasonably good for you.
- **Selection.** People are demanding a larger selection of foods. They no longer accept a limited menu.

The reason for this trend is that within the last few years, restaurant offerings have increased, providing customers with new choices. Restaurant patrons no longer need to accept a limited number of options. With more choices, patrons have become more sophisticated. This trend is intuitive as you can observe a more sophisticated patron in larger city markets such as Seattle, Portland, or New York, where there are more choices. People are also increasingly expecting a web presence for restaurants. This presence includes a website, a membership on Facebook, and oftentimes a Twitter presence. The importance of a website and the use of social media cannot be underestimated.

Competition

Every marketing plan should include an assessment of the competition: who they are, what they offer, their growth rates (if known), and their market share (if known). Market share is defined as the percentage of total sales volume in a market that is captured by a brand, a product, or a company.[37] Think of the market as a pie, with each slice being a "share" of that pie. The larger the slice, the larger the percentage of sales volume captured by a brand, a product, or a company. With all this knowledge, a business will be in the best position to differentiate itself in the marketplace. However, while the sales figures of a business are easily accessible, it is not likely that the owner will have either total market sales figures or growth rate, sales figures, and market share information for the competition. This information, if available at all, is usually available from trade associations and market research firms,[38] with the likelihood being even less if the information desired is about other small businesses. Competitor websites and Internet searches may prove helpful, but because most small businesses are privately held, the information available online will be limited. As a result, you will be restricted in the information that you can collect about the competition to things that can easily be observed in person or are available on company websites. Examples include product selection, price points, service quality, and product quality.

Competition should be addressed in terms of being direct or indirect. **Direct competition** refers to competition from similar businesses or products, whereas **indirect competition** refers to competition from alternative, substitutable businesses or products. In the case of Sigmund's Gourmet Pasta, direct competition would come from other restaurants that serve pasta. Indirect competition would come from other types of full-service restaurants, fast food, the freezer- or prepared-foods areas in the grocery store, delis, preparation services that target the home, and even online businesses that sell prepared foods (DineWise). Many if not most small business marketing plans address only direct competition.

Direct Competition for Sigmund's Gourmet Pasta

1. **National Competition**
   - **Pastabilities.** Offers consumers their choice of noodles, sauces, and ingredients, allowing customers to assemble their dishes as they wish. Food quality is average.
   - **PastaFresh.** Has a limited selection, but the dishes are assembled with high-quality ingredients. The price point is high, but the food is quite good.
   - **Pasta Works.** Offers pasta that is reasonably fresh, reasonably innovative, and at a lower price point. The company was sold a few years ago, and consequently the direction of management has been stagnant lately, which has resulted in excessive employee turnover.
   - **Perfect Pasta.** Offers medium-priced pasta dishes that use average ingredients, no creativity, and a less than average store atmosphere. Sigmund's is not sure how this company has been able to grow in size as their whole product is mediocre at best.

2. **Local Competition**
   - **Restaurant A.** This is an upscale Italian restaurant with a limited selection of pasta dishes. Although the selection is limited and pricey, the dishes are quite good.
   - **Restaurant B.** An Italian restaurant with a decent pasta selection; however, the quality is inconsistent.
   - **Restaurant C.** An upscale restaurant with a large wine selection and good salads. Everything else is mediocre at best and overpriced. Service can often be poor.[39]

Product or Service Offering

The marketing plan must be very clear about the product or the service that is being offered to the marketplace because the product drives the creation of the marketing mix and the marketing strategy. An error in product identification and definition can wreak havoc in the company and in the marketplace because misdirected marketing actions can occur. The responsibility for the product definitions rests squarely with the owner. For example, if a business is a live theater that features very sophisticated plays, would you define the product as entertainment or art? The answer to this question will have major implications for a company's marketing strategy.

The product or the service offering must also consider a company's website because a web presence will be an important part of what is offered to customers.

Service Offering for Sigmund's Gourmet Pasta

Sigmund's has created gourmet pastas and salads that are differentiated and superior to competitors. Customers can taste the quality and freshness of the product in every bite. The following are the characteristics of the product:

- Sigmund's pasta dough is made with Italian semolina flour.
- All cheeses are imported.
- Vegetables are organic and fresh with three shipments a week.
- Meats are all top-shelf varieties and organic when possible.
- Wines are personally selected by the owner.[40]

At Sigmund's, food is not a product; the experience of dining is a service. Sigmund's prides itself on providing service that is on par with fine dining. This is accomplished through an extensive training program and hiring only experienced employees.[41]

At a Glance—The Prototype Sigmund's Store

- Location: an upscale mall, a suburban neighborhood, or an urban retail district
- Design: bright, hip, clean
- Size: 1,200–1,700 square feet
- For people who dine in, an interactive dining experience will be available through the iPad. A virtual wine cellar application will allow diners to flip through Sigmund's assortment of wines and make an educated decision. Diners will be able to spin the bottles around to view the back label, read reviews, view the vineyard on Google maps, search wine by price and region, and see information about food pairings.[42]
- Employees: six to seven full time
- Seating: 35–45
- Types of transactions: 80 percent dine in, 20 percent takeout

Sigmund's website[43] will educate prospects with an eye toward encouraging them to try the restaurant and then return. Site visitors will be informed about the menu and the restaurant's commitment to quality in using homemade pasta made with Italian semolina flour, imported cheeses, organic vegetables that are delivered three times a week, and top-shelf meats. The website will not sell things directly.

Prospective customers will be encouraged through the warm and friendly atmosphere of the website. A photo gallery will provide a visual tour of the restaurant to demonstrate its décor and atmosphere. The pages of the website will include the following:

- The mission and vision of the restaurant, including a profile of the founder, emphasizing wine expertise
- A discussion of the commitment to top-quality ingredients and a top-quality customer dining experience
- A slide show virtual tour of the restaurant
- Dining-in and takeout menus
- Directions, hours, and contact information (both telephone and e-mail)
- Links to Facebook and Twitter
- Customer comments

SWOT Analysis

A **SWOT analysis** combines the key strengths and weaknesses within a company with an assessment of the opportunities and threats that are external to the company. This analysis can provide powerful insights into the potential and critical issues affecting a business.[44] A strength is an asset or a resource, tangible or intangible, internal to a company that is within its control. What does the company do well? What advantages does the company have over its competition? You should look to identify the positive aspects internal to a business that add value or offer a competitive advantage.[45] Examples of strengths are the quality of employees, company reputation, available capital and credit, established customers, unique channels of distribution, intellectual property, location, and facilities.

Strengths for Sigmund's Gourmet Pasta

- Strong relationships with vendors that offer high-quality ingredients and fast/frequent delivery schedules
- Excellent staff who are highly trained and very customer attentive
- Great retail space that is bright, hip, clean, and located in an upscale mall, a suburban neighborhood, or an urban retail district
- High customer loyalty among repeat customers
- High-quality food offerings that exceed competitors' offerings in quality, presentation, and price[46]

Video Link 8.1

Rebirth of the American-Made Baseball Mitt

The strengths of the Insignia company.

money.cnn.com/video/smallbusiness/2011/05/05/sbiz_baseball_mitt.cnnmoney

A weakness is a factor internal to a company that may cause it to have a less competitive position in the marketplace. A company can have control over this factor and should look to improve or remove it to successfully accomplish its marketing objectives. Weaknesses detract from the value of a business. Examples of weaknesses are lack of expertise, limited resources, bad location, poor facilities, inferior customer service and customer experience, difficulty in hiring and retaining good people, and weak brand recognition.

Weaknesses for Sigmund's Gourmet Pasta

- Sigmund's name lacks **brand equity**. Brand equity is the commercial value of all associations and expectations (positive and negative) that people have of a brand based on all the experiences they have had with the brand over time.[47] The greater the positive brand equity, the more power in the marketplace.
- A limited marketing budget to develop brand awareness.
- The struggle to continually appear to be cutting edge.[48]

> **brand equity**
>
> The commercial value of all associations and expectations that people have of a brand based on all the experiences they have had with the brand over time.

An opportunity is an attractive external factor that represents the reason a business exists and prospers. You have no control over opportunities, but you can take advantage of them to benefit the business. Opportunities will come from the market, the environment, or the competition, and they reflect the potential that can be realized through marketing strategies.[49] Examples of opportunities include market growth, a competitor going out of business, lifestyle changes, demographic changes, and an increased demand for a product or a service.

Opportunities for Sigmund's Gourmet Pasta

- Growing market with a significant percentage of the target market still not aware that Sigmund's Gourmet Pasta exists.
- Increasing sales opportunities in takeout business that can be enhanced even further by our web presence.
- The ability to spread overhead over multiple revenue centers. Sigmund's will be able to spread the management overhead costs among multiple stores, decreasing the fixed costs per store.[50]

Video Link 8.2

Vinyl Makes a Comeback

A small company in Brooklyn, New York, takes advantage of the opportunity presented by the surging interest in vinyl records.

money.cnn.com/video/smallbusiness/2011/04/15/sbiz_vinyl_comeback.cnnmoney

A threat is an external factor beyond a company's control that could place a marketing strategy, or the business itself, at risk. Threats come from an unfavorable trend or development that could lead to deteriorating revenues or profits (such as high gasoline prices); a new competitor that enters the market; a public relations (PR) nightmare that leads to devastating media coverage; a gender discrimination lawsuit; a shift in consumer tastes and behavior that reduces sales; government regulation; an economic slump; or the introduction of a "leap frog" technology that may make a company's products, equipment, or services obsolete.[51] Threats come from anywhere and at any time, and a small business may be particularly vulnerable because of its size. At the same time, a small business may be nimble enough to effectively deal with threats because of its small size.

Threats for Sigmund's Gourmet Pasta

- Competition from local restaurants that respond to Sigmund's Gourmet Pasta's superior offerings

- Gourmet pasta restaurant chains found in other markets coming to Eugene
- A slump in the economy reducing the customer's disposable income for eating out[52]

Video Link 8.3

Historic Paper Company Thrives

Surviving threats and taking advantage of opportunities.

money.cnn.com/video/smallbusiness/2010/08/06/sbiz_hwgs_crane.cnnmoney

Performing a SWOT analysis is a valuable exercise. It might help an owner identify the most promising customers, perhaps even the ideal customer. The analysis is meant to improve a customer's experience with a company, so the person who will benefit most from a SWOT analysis is the customer.[53]

Keys to Success and Critical Issues

keys to success

The factors that, if achieved, will lead to a profitable and a sustainable business.

The **keys to success** are those factors that, if achieved, will lead to a profitable and a sustainable business. Identifying these factors should be based on an understanding of the industry or the market in which a small business is competing because these things play a critical role in success and failure.

Focusing on three to five of the most important success factors makes sense for a small business. However, the actual number will be a function of the business. Whatever the number, the keys to success may change from time to time or year to year as the industry or the market changes.[54] Examples of key success factors include the hiring and retention of excellent employees, successful new product introductions, a strong supplier network, a low-cost structure, retaining existing customers, a strong distribution network or channel,[55] a cutting edge manufacturing process, and customer service.

Keys to Success for Sigmund's Gourmet Pasta

Location, location, location.

Sigmund's site selection criteria are critical to its success. Arthur Johnson, the former vice president of real estate for Starbucks, helped us identify the following site selection criteria:

- Daytime and evening populations
- Shopping patterns
- Car counts
- Household income levels[56]

Critical Issues for Sigmund's Gourmet Pasta

Sigmund's Gourmet Pasta is still in the speculative stage as a retail restaurant. Its critical issues are as follows:

- Continue to take a modest fiscal approach; expand at a reasonable rate, not for the sake of expansion in itself but because it is economically wise to do so
- Continue to build brand awareness that will drive customers to existing stores as well as ease the marketing efforts of future stores[57]

2.4 Marketing Strategy

The marketing strategy section of the marketing plan involves selecting one or more target markets, deciding how to differentiate and position the product or the service, and creating and maintaining a marketing mix that will hopefully prove successful with the selected target market(s)—all within the context of the marketing objectives. It also includes a web strategy for the small businesses that have or want to have a web presence. By aligning online marketing with onground efforts, a company will be in a much stronger position to accomplish marketing and overall company objectives. It will also be presenting a consistent style and message across all points of contact with its target audience.[58]

Introduction to Marketing Strategy for Sigmund's Gourmet Pasta

Sigmund's advertising budget is very limited, so the advertising program is simple. Sigmund's will do direct mail, banner ads, and inserts in the *Register Guard*, which are likely to be the most successful of the campaigns. (We will also use our website and social media to promote the business.) Lastly, Sigmund's will leverage personal relationships to get articles about Sigmund's in the *Register Guard*. Friends who have had their restaurants featured in the *Register Guard* have seen a dramatic increase of sales immediately after the article was published.[59]

Marketing Objectives

Marketing objectives are what a company wants to accomplish with its marketing strategy. They lay the groundwork for formulating the marketing strategy, and although formulated in a variety of ways, their achievement should lead to sales. The creation of marketing objectives is one of the most critical steps a business will take. Both online and onground objectives must be included. A business must know, as precisely as possible, what it wants to achieve before allocating any resources to the marketing effort.

marketing objectives

What a company wants to accomplish with its marketing strategy.

Marketing Objectives for Sigmund's Gourmet Pasta

1. Maintain positive, steady growth each month.
2. Generate at least $40,000 in sales each month.
3. Experience an increase in new customers who become long-term customers.
4. Realize a growth strategy of one store per year.[60]
5. Achieve one thousand Facebook fans in six months.[61]
6. Achieve a Twitter follower base of five hundred people in six months.[62]

You should note that the first and third objectives in this sample marketing plan do not meet some of the SMART criteria—specific, measurable, achievable, realistic, and time-based (a stated time frame for achievement). These two objectives are not specific enough to be measurable, and they may not be realistic. This will make it difficult to determine the extent to which they have been or can be accomplished.

Target Market

The target market is the segment that has been identified as having the greatest potential for a business. A segment is a relatively homogeneous subgroup that behaves much the same way in the marketplace. The identification of segments is a necessary precursor to selecting a target market. The more precise the target market is, the easier it will be to create a marketing mix that will appeal to the target market.

Target Markets for Sigmund's Gourmet Pasta

The market can be segmented into three target populations.

1. **Individuals.** People who dine by themselves.
2. **Families.** A group of people, either friends or a group of nuclear relatives, dining together.
3. **Takeout.** People who prefer to eat Sigmund's food in their own homes or at a location other than the actual restaurant.

Sigmund's customers are hungry individuals between the ages of 25 and 50, making up 53 percent of Eugene (according to the Eugene Chamber of Commerce). Age is not the most defined demographic of this customer base, as all age groups enjoy pasta. The most defined characteristic of the target market is income. Gourmet pasta stores have been very successful in high-rent, mixed-use urban areas, such as Northwest 23rd Street in Portland. These areas have a large day and night population consisting of businesspeople and families who have household disposable incomes over $40,000.

Combining several key demographic factors, Sigmund's profile of the primary customer is as follows:

- Sophisticated families who live nearby

- ◼ Young professionals who work close to the location
- ◼ Shoppers who patronize high-rent stores[63]

Positioning

positioning

Placing the brand (whether store, product, or service) in the consumer's mind in relation to other competing products, based on product traits and benefits that are relevant to the consumer.

The **positioning** section of the marketing plan reflects the decisions that have been made about how a company plans to "place" its business in a consumer's mind *in relation to* the competition. Is a particular business seen as a high-priced or a low-priced alternative? Is a business considered a high-quality or a medium-quality alternative? Is the delivery time to customers better, worse, or the same as that of the competition? There are many different approaches to positioning that the small business owner should consider, but the selected approach should be the one that puts the company or the brand in the best light. Keep in mind that a good positioning strategy will come from a solid understanding of the market, the customer, and the competition because this knowledge will provide a basis for comparing one business with others.

Positioning for Sigmund's Gourmet Pasta

Sigmund's Gourmet Pasta will position itself as a reasonably priced, upscale, gourmet pasta restaurant. Eugene consumers who appreciate high-quality food will recognize the value and unique offerings of Sigmund's Gourmet Pasta. Patrons will be singles and families, ages twenty-five to fifty.

Sigmund's Gourmet Pasta positioning will leverage its product and service competitive edge:

- ◼ **Product.** The product will have the freshest ingredients, including homemade pasta, imported cheeses, organic vegetables, and top-shelf meats. The product will also be developed to enhance presentation. Everything will be aesthetically pleasing.
- ◼ **Service.** Customer service will be the priority. All employees will ensure that customers are having the most pleasant dining experience. All employees will go through an extensive training program, and only experienced people will be hired.

By offering a superior product, coupled with superior service, Sigmund's will excel relative to the competition.[64]

 ### Video Clip 8.2

Small Business Market Position
Market position refers to how the general public views the business or the product.

View the video online at: http://www.youtube.com/v/Ct3VR_RKbu8

Video Clip 8.3

Small Business Market Position Tips
Choose a unique position for a business or a product.

View the video online at: http://www.youtube.com/v/-tANM6ETl_M

 Video Clip 8.4

Choosing a Small Business Market Position
Look ten to fifteen years into the future when thinking about positioning.

View the video online at: http://www.youtube.com/v/guphP399LNs

Marketing Strategy Pyramid

The **marketing strategy pyramid** assumes that the marketing strategy is built on concrete tactics that are built on specific, measurable marketing programs—activities with budgeted expenses, well-defined responsibilities, deadlines, and measurable results.[65]

marketing strategy pyramid

Assumes that the marketing strategy is built on concrete tactics that are specific, measurable marketing programs—activities with budgeted expenses, well-defined responsibilities, deadlines, and measurable results.

FIGURE 8.5 Marketing Strategy Pyramid

Source: Tim Berry, "What Is the Marketing Strategy Pyramid, Where Did It Come From?," BPlans, accessed December 2, 2011,
http://www.bplans.com/ask-bplans/640/what-is-the-marketing-strategy-pyramid-where-did-it-come-from.

The strategy at the top of Figure 8.5 focuses on well-defined markets and user needs. The second level consists of the tactics that you use to satisfy user needs and communicate with the target market. The third level is where specific programs are defined.[66] It is this framework that is built into the sample marketing plans that are available through Palo Alto Software in Sales and Marketing Pro and at www.mplans.com. However, it is a solid approach that can be used in any marketing planning situation.

Strategy Pyramid for Sigmund's Gourmet Pasta

The single objective is to position Sigmund's as the premier gourmet pasta restaurant in the Eugene, Oregon, area, commanding a majority of the market share within five years. The marketing strategy will seek to first create customer awareness regarding the services offered, develop that customer base, and work toward building customer loyalty and referrals.

The message that Sigmund's will seek to communicate is that Sigmund's offers the freshest, most creative, health-conscious, reasonably priced, gourmet pasta in Eugene. This message will be communicated through a variety of methods. The first will be direct mail. The direct mail campaign will be a way to communicate directly with the consumer. Sigmund's will also use banner ads and inserts in the *Register Guard*. This will be particularly effective because the *Register Guard* is a popular local paper that is consulted when people are looking for things to do in Eugene. The restaurant's website will also encourage patronage because the warm and friendly atmosphere of the site will reflect the atmosphere of the actual restaurant. Facebook and Twitter followers along with customer comments will also add to brand awareness.[67]

The last method for communicating Sigmund's message is through a grassroots PR campaign. This campaign will leverage personal relationships with people on the staff of the *Register Guard* to get a couple of articles written about Sigmund's. One will be from the business point of view, talking about the opening of the restaurant and the people behind the venture. This is likely to be run in the business section. The second article will be a food review. In speaking with many different retailers and restaurateurs, significant increases of traffic have followed articles in the *Register Guard*. Because of this level of effectiveness and low/zero cost, Sigmund's will work hard to get press in the *Register Guard*.[68]

Marketing Mix

A company's marketing mix is its unique approach to product, price, promotion, and place (distribution)—the four Ps. The marketing mix is the central activity in the implementation of a company's marketing strategy, so the decisions must be made carefully. It is through the marketing mix that marketing objectives will be achieved. The final determination of the marketing mix requires inputs from other areas, such as purchasing, manufacturing, sales, human resources, and finance.[69]

Marketing Mix for Sigmund's Gourmet Pasta

Sigmund's marketing mix consists of the following approaches to pricing, distribution, advertising and promotion, and customer service.

- **Pricing.** Sigmund's pricing scheme is that the product cost is 45 percent of the total retail price.
- **Distribution.** Sigmund's food will be distributed through a model in which customers can either call in their orders or place them online[70] and come to the restaurant to pick them up or come into the restaurant, place their orders, and wait for them to be completed.
- **Advertising and promotion.** The most successful advertising will be banner ads and inserts in the *Register Guard* as well as a PR campaign of informational articles and reviews within the *Register Guard* and coupons available on the website. The first-timer discount coupon and code will be prominently displayed on the website's home page to encourage prospects to become customers. Coupons will also be available for repeat customers once per month.[71] Holiday specials will be offered on Valentine's Day, Easter, Mother's Day, and Father's Day.
- **Social media.** Sigmund's Gourmet Pasta will establish a Facebook page that will allow users to engage directly with the company by posting likes, dislikes, and ideas to the Wall, which will be answered directly by management. Customers will be encouraged to become fans of the Facebook page and then share the page with their friends.[72] Sigmund's will also establish a Twitter presence.[73]

 ### Video Clip 8.5

How To Use Twitter For Business
A tutorial about using Twitter for business.

View the video online at: http://www.youtube.com/v/JXPmI4YaOpM

 ### Video Clip 8.6

What a Business Needs to Do to Connect More on Twitter
A humorous look at why a business should use a picture, not its business logo, on Twitter.

View the video online at: http://www.youtube.com/v/D3FDywzDDeI

Marketing Research

Marketing research is about gathering the information that is needed to make business decisions, which should be an ongoing process. A marketing plan should be based on marketing research. The research can range from something very simple conducted by the owner or an employee to a more sophisticated study that is prepared by a marketing research firm. The overall goal of the research, however, is to help a company offer products that people will want, at an appealing price, in the place where they want to buy them. The research should also help a company decide how to promote its products so that people will be aware of them. People cannot buy what they do not know about.

Marketing Research for Sigmund's Gourmet Pasta

During the initial phases of developing the marketing plan, several focus groups were held to gain insight into a variety of patrons of restaurants. These focus groups provided useful insight into the decisions and decision-making processes of consumers.

An additional source of dynamic market research is a feedback mechanism based on a suggestion card system. The suggestion card system has several statements that patrons are asked to rate in terms of a given scale. There are also several open-ended questions that allow the customer to freely offer constructive criticism or praise. Sigmund's will work hard to implement reasonable suggestions to improve its service offerings as well as show its commitment to customers that their suggestions are valued. This suggestion system will also be incorporated into our website so that customers can provide feedback online.[74]

The last source of market research is competitive analysis and appreciation. Sigmund's will continually patronize local restaurants for two reasons. The first is for competitive analysis, providing Sigmund's with timely information regarding the service offerings of other restaurants. The second reason is that local business owners, particularly restaurant owners, are often part of an informal fraternal organization where they support each other.[75]

2.5 Financials

The financials section of the marketing plan should provide a financial overview of the company as it relates to the marketing activities. Typically addressed in this section are the breakeven analysis, a sales forecast, and an expense forecast and how they link to the marketing strategy.[76]

Breakeven Analysis

breakeven analysis

Used to determine the amount of sales volume a company needs to start making a profit: when its total sales or revenues equal its total expenses.

fixed costs

Costs that remain the same regardless of the amount of sales (e.g., rent).

variable costs

Costs that vary directly with the number of units of product or the amount of service provided.

A **breakeven analysis** is used to determine the amount of sales volume a company needs to start making a profit.[77] A company has broken even when its total sales or revenues equal its total expenses. However, a breakeven analysis is not a predictor of demand, so if a company goes into the marketplace with the wrong product or the wrong price, it may never reach the break-even point.[78]

The most relevant types of costs that must be considered when preparing a breakeven analysis are **fixed costs** and **variable costs**. Fixed costs are costs that must be paid whether or not any units are produced or any services are delivered. They are "fixed" over a specified period of time or range of production. Rent, insurance, and computers would be considered fixed costs because they are outlays that must occur before a company makes its first sale.[79]

Variable costs are recurring costs that must be absorbed with each unit or service sold. These costs vary directly with the number of units of product or the amount of service provided.[80] Labor costs and the cost of materials are examples of variable costs.

Breakeven Analysis for Sigmund's Gourmet Pasta

Sigmund's Breakeven Analysis

Break-even point = where line intersects with 0

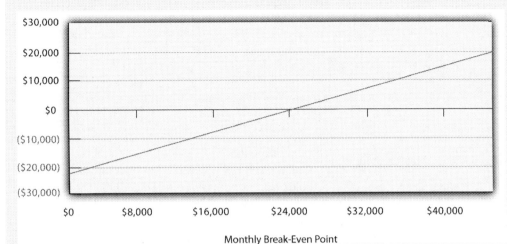

Monthly Break-Even Point

Source: "Pasta Restaurant Marketing Plan: Sigmund's Gourmet Pasta: Situation Analysis," Mplans.com, accessed December 2, 2011, http://www.mplans.com/pasta_restaurant_marketing_plan/situation_analysis_fc.php. Reprinted by permission of Palo Alto Software.

The breakeven analysis indicates that $23,037 in monthly revenue will be required to reach the break-even point. The analysis assumes a 45 percent annual variable cost and a $22,000 estimated monthly fixed cost.[81]

Sales Forecast

A company's **sales forecast** is the level of sales that a company expects based on a chosen marketing plan and an assumed marketing environment. The sales forecast does not establish a basis on which to decide how much should be spent on marketing. Rather, it is the result of an assumed marketing expenditure plan.[82] A sales forecast can be very helpful in creating important milestones for a business. However, it is still an educated guess. No matter what a company forecasts, it will typically make less than expected.[83]

sales forecast

The level of sales expected based on a chosen marketing plan and an assumed marketing environment.

Sales Forecast for Sigmund's Gourmet Pasta

The first two months will be used to get the restaurant up and running. By the third month, things will get busier. Sales will gradually increase, with profitability being achieved by the beginning of the new year.[84]

Sigmund's Sales Forecast

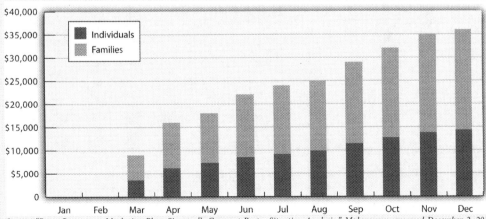

Source: "Pasta Restaurant Marketing Plan: Sigmund's Gourmet Pasta: Situation Analysis," Mplans.com, accessed December 2, 2011, http://www.mplans.com/pasta_restaurant_marketing_plan/situation_analysis_fc.php. Reprinted by permission of Palo Alto Software.

Sigmund's Forecast of Sales and Direct Cost of Sales

Category	2011	2012	2013
Sales			
Individuals	$103,710	$262,527	$327,424
Families	$150,304	$380,474	$474,528
Total sales	$254,014	$643,001	$801,952
Direct Cost of Sales			
Individuals	$46,669	$118,137	$147,341
Families	$67,637	$171,213	$213,538
Total direct cost of sales	$114,306	$289,350	$360,879
Note: Sigmund's separated sales on the basis of its target market, but it did not include a separate sales forecast for takeout. It should have.			

Source: "Pasta Restaurant Marketing Plan: Sigmund's Gourmet Pasta: Situation Analysis," Mplans.com, accessed December 1, 2011, http://www.mplans.com/pasta_restaurant_marketing_plan/situation_analysis_fc.php.

Expense Forecast

expense forecast

A tool that can be used to keep operations on target.

A company's **expense forecast** is a tool that can be used to keep its operations on target. The forecast will provide indicators when corrections or modifications are needed for the proper implementation of the marketing plan. An expense forecast is vital for a company and its sales goals because it will keep the company on track and keep costs down; however, a company will typically spend much more than expected.[85] If a company is not sure what to include in its expense forecast, there are online templates that can provide assistance (see www.chic-ceo.com/userfiles/ExpenseForecast.pdf for sample templates).

Expense Forecast for Sigmund's Gourmet Pasta

Marketing expenses are to be budgeted so that they are ramped up for months two through four and then lower and plateau from month five to month ten. Restaurants typically have increased business in the fall. This generally occurs because during the summer, when the weather is nice and it does not get dark until late, people tend to eat out less. From month ten to month twelve, the marketing costs will increase again.[86]

Sigmund's Expense Forecast

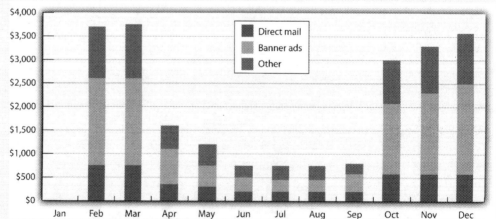

Source: "Pasta Restaurant Marketing Plan: Sigmund's Gourmet Pasta: Situation Analysis," Mplans.com, accessed December 2, 2011, http://www.mplans.com/pasta_restaurant_marketing_plan/situation_analysis_fc.php. Reprinted by permission of Palo Alto Software.

Sigmund's Marketing Expense Budget

Category	2011	2012	2013
Direct mail	$5,267	$5,605	$5,421
Banner ads	$11,704	$12,455	$12,047
Other	$7,022	$7,473	$7,228
Total sales and marketing expenses	**$23,993**	**$25,533**	**$24,696**
Percentage of sales	9.45%	3.97%	3.08%

Note: These marketing expenses do not account for website, social media, or coupon redemption expenses, and they do not reflect the cost of preparing marketing materials (e.g., the direct mail pieces, the coupons, and the banner ads). For the sake of convenience, we can include these expenses in the "Other" category. However, there should be separate figures for these expenses. Also, it should be made clear what kinds of expenses are included as "Other."

Source: *"Pasta Restaurant Marketing Plan: Sigmund's Gourmet Pasta: Situation Analysis," Mplans.com, accessed December 1, 2011, http://www.mplans.com/pasta_restaurant_marketing_plan/situation_analysis_fc.php.*

2.6   Implementation, Evaluation, and Control

This last section of a marketing plan outlines what a company will do to implement the plan, evaluate its performance, and monitor and adjust plan implementation through controls. In other words, this section of the plan is all about numbers, results, and timelines.[87]

Implementation

Implementation is about the day-to-day activities that effectively put a marketing plan into action and focuses on who, where, when, and how: Who will do that? Where to start and when? When to do that? How to do that?[88] Effective implementation can give a business the edge in a market with similar marketing plans simply because any company that is better and faster at execution is sure to have the advantage in terms of market share.[89] This will be true for a small business of any size. There is, however, no such thing as a one-time implementation of a marketing plan. Rather, it is a process that evolves with the product or the service.[90]

   Several steps are recommended for the proper implementation of a marketing plan. Examples include the following:[91]

1. **Be sure to always check progress.** Know what is working and what is not working. Doing so will help you stay on top of programs that need work and can build on programs that are working.

2. **Be sure to reward employees for jobs well done.** When goals are met, deadlines are met, and so forth, make sure to congratulate the people responsible for these goals and deadlines.

3. **Always try new things.** A company should never sit on its hands. The market is always changing, so a company should also change. Learn to adapt.

4. **Don't jump ship too soon.** Give the plan time to work. If it is not working, do not give up. Work with the team. Let them help the company succeed.

5. **Be open to ideas.** Some employees may have a better idea about the reality of the market than the owner has. Listen to them. Hear what they have to say.

Implementation Milestones for Sigmund's Gourmet Pasta

The following milestones identify the key marketing programs. It is important to accomplish each one on time and on budget.[92]

Sigmund's Implementation Milestones

Milestones	Start Date	End Date	Budget	Manager	Department
Advertising					
Marketing plan completion	1/1/2011	2/1/2011	$0	Kevin	Marketing
Banner ad campaign #1	2/1/2011	4/1/2011	$3,754	Kevin	Marketing
Banner ad campaign #2	10/1/2011	1/1/2011	$4,900	Kevin	Marketing
Total advertising budget			**$8,654**		
Direct Marketing					
Direct mail campaign #1	2/1/2011	4/1/2011	$1,689	Kevin	Marketing
Insert campaign #1	2/1/2011	4/1/2011	$2,252	Kevin	Marketing
Direct mail campaign #2	10/1/2011	1/1/2011	$2,205	Kevin	Marketing
Insert campaign #2	10/1/2011	1/1/2011	$2,940	Kevin	Marketing
Total direct marketing budget			**$9,086**		
Web development				Outside firm	Marketing
Totals			**$17,741**		

Note: The authors of this textbook added the web development milestone to acknowledge that this activity still needs to be scheduled and budgeted. It was not part of the original sample marketing plan. Under normal conditions, the dates and numbers for web development would also be included.

Source: "*Pasta Restaurant Marketing Plan: Sigmund's Gourmet Pasta: Situation Analysis*," Mplans.com, accessed December 1, 2011, http://www.mplans.com/pasta_restaurant_marketing_plan/situation_analysis_fc.php.

Evaluation

You can't manage what you don't measure.[93]

- *Peter Drucker*

The evaluation section of the marketing plan is about assessing the strengths and weaknesses of a marketing plan to improve its effectiveness.[94] Without an evaluation process, a company will not know whether its marketing campaign is effective or whether it is spending too much or too little money to achieve its goals. The evaluation process, if done correctly, will allow a company to continually improve its tactics and assess the results of its marketing efforts. Thus it is important to set up a timely process to track, capture, and analyze collected data as it is collected. If this is done on a regular basis, a marketing activity (e.g., banner advertising) that doesn't work can be changed to more effective tactics (e.g., advertising in the local paper) that do work.[95]

There are many ways to evaluate how well a company is doing. The following are some of the ways:[96]

1. **Look at sales (or fee) income.** Sales or fee income should be increasing. However, some small businesses will have longer sales cycles than others, so it might be better to measure the number of new leads generated, or the number of appointments, or the number of billable hours achieved. Also remember that discounts, variances in fees, and promotional pricing will affect total sales volume. If a company is selling online and onground, look at the path of both income streams.

2. **Ask clients or customers.** Find out where and how clients and customers heard about the business. Most businesses never ask this question, so they miss out on valuable insights into how clients and customers pick a product or a service.

3. **Does advertising and/or promotional activity produce direct responses?** It should. If not, a company should work to find out why not. This is also relevant for a web presence. A company should want to know how site visitors found out about the company.

4. **Check the conversion rate.** How successful is a business at closing the sale? Has it improved? If a company is selling online, how many site visitors are actually buying something?

5. **Does the plan have a positive return on investment (ROI)?** Does it bring in enough new or repeat business to justify the expense? A company should evaluate the cost-effectiveness of each specific online and onground marketing activity so that it can change or eliminate unproductive

activities. There are online tools available to help companies with this evaluation. As an example, a free ROI calculator is available at www.cymbic.com/tools/roi_calc.php.

To best evaluate the effectiveness of a marketing plan, it will be necessary to track each type of marketing activity in the plan. The data and techniques will vary widely depending on product type and market—and whether a company has an online presence only or both an onground presence and an online presence. However, most small businesses should select the simplest route possible because of the lower costs and the limited need for very sophisticated tracking. The following are some common and very doable tracking techniques for the small business:

- **Advertising efficiency.** The number of inquiries generated by an advertisement and the cost per inquiry. This applies to both online and traditional advertising.[97]
- **Sales promotion efficiency.** The number of inquiries generated by a promotion (e.g., a coupon or a banner ad) and the percentage of coupons or vouchers redeemed. This also applies to online and traditional sales promotion activities.[98]
- **Sales closure rate.** The number of sales closed compared to sales leads. Collect data for both online and onground sales.
- **Direct marketing.** The number of inquiries or customers generated by a direct marketing activity. Direct marketing uses a variety of channels, such as direct mail, telemarketing, e-mail, interactive television, websites, mobile devices, door-to-door leaflet marketing, broadcast faxing, voicemail marketing, and coupons.
- **Web analytics.** One of the big benefits of having a web presence is that there is a vast amount of tracking and statistics available to the site owner. Small-business owners will want to know things such as where site traffic comes from, how they got to the site, what search words or phrases were used, how many people are viewing the site, how many people are buying if you are selling something, the geographic location of site visitors, and the time each visitor spends on the site. Website analysis tools can track the ways people use a website while helping the owner make sense of the mountain of data that a site generates.[99]

Video Link 8.4

Using Web Analytics Tools

How analytics tools can help you make informed decisions about online endeavors.

www.entrepreneur.com/video/217594

Small-business owners may choose to have the web analytics performed by an outside vendor or use inexpensive analytics tools such as Google Analytics.

Video Clip 8.7

Three Important Questions to Ask Google Analytics
How Google Analytics helps to answer the three most important questions about a website.

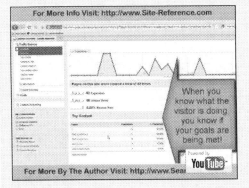

View the video online at: http://www.youtube.com/v/ecm6j9hVn_Y

- **Social media metrics.** If social media is part of a company's marketing plan, the owner will want to find out whether it is worth all the time and effort involved. The goal is to be able to draw lines and connect the dots between social media participation and sales or perhaps something else like brand recognition.[100] Twitter metrics are fairly simple, beginning with the number of followers you have. However, it is the number of retweets you get that will be an indication of the messages that are actually resonating with customers. This is a measure of social influence. Klout is a free tool that measures your online influence on a scale of 1 to 100. This information can guide you to identifying strengths and weaknesses.[101] It is also important to tap into the analytics provided by LinkedIn and Facebook.[102] Perhaps the best approach for a small business to measure its social media effectiveness is to choose an easy-to-understand and easy-to-use web analytics package. Google Analytics was mentioned previously. Another good choice would be the software available from HubSpot because this company focuses specifically on the needs of small and medium-sized businesses.

Marketing Calculators

The Internet is a wonderful place. You can find most anything there. The following are three free marketing calculators that you might find useful in measuring the effectiveness of marketing:[103]

1. Pay-per-click ROI calculator. This calculator determines the ROI for pay-per-click advertising campaigns. Based on a campaign's results and costs, the ROI can be calculated.

2. Conversion rate calculator. Even the most successful websites convert only a fraction of their visitors into paying customers. A company can increase its sales by upping its conversion rate, attracting more traffic to the site, or encouraging buyers to spend more money. This handy calculator experiments with these variables. Enter the number of visitors and total orders and see what an increase in conversion can do.

3. E-mail marketing ROI calculator. E-mail marketing campaigns to interested prospects who have opted to receive a company's e-mail messages is a great way to increase direct sales. This simple calculator makes it easy to see the ROI from various campaigns, based on expected costs and response levels. It can be used to test different scenarios and test results.

Evaluation for Sigmund's Gourmet Pasta

Unfortunately, the marketing plan for Sigmund's Gourmet Pasta does not address the evaluation of its marketing activities. They should have provided information about the plans for measuring and evaluating the effectiveness of its banner ads, direct mail, and insert campaigns. The website and social media activities added by the authors of this textbook would have to be measured and evaluated for their effectiveness as well.[104]

Controls

There is no planning without control, the process of monitoring a proposed plan as it proceeds and adjusting it when necessary.[105] Every business needs someone to take responsibility for pushing things along. A good schedule and budget should make it easy to monitor progress, but when things fall behind schedule or there are cost overruns, you must be ready to do something about it and adapt the plan accordingly. From time to time, the owner must step back and ask whether the plan is working. What can you learn from mistakes, and how can you use what you know to make a better marketing plan for the future?[106]

In addition to setting a schedule and measuring and evaluating the effectiveness of marketing activities, a marketing plan needs to say how it will be controlled. Although there are many approaches to control, the small business owner will likely look to activities such as sales analysis (monthly and annual revenue), expense analysis (monthly and annual expenses), feedback from customer satisfaction surveys, and the observation of competitor activities in response to the marketing plan (marketing research). The organization of the marketing function itself can also be seen as a means of control.

contingency planning

A formal process to manage a crisis, whether it comes from inside or outside a company.

Marketing Plan Control for Sigmund's Gourmet Pasta

The marketing plan for Sigmund's Gourmet Pasta includes implementation milestones, the marketing organization, and **contingency planning** as controls for their marketing plan. Implementation was discussed previously. Contingency planning is a formal process to manage a crisis, whether it comes from inside or outside a company. A contingency plan involves potential problem identification, prioritizing the problems in a list of most probable, and developing planned steps to limit the harm to a company if the potential problem becomes real.[107] It would have been helpful if Sigmund's marketing plan had included other controls as well. The more specific a marketing plan is about its controls, the better the chances that those controls will be carried out successfully.

Marketing Organization

Kevin Lewis, the owner, is primarily responsible for marketing activities. This is in addition to his other responsibilities, and he depends on some outside resources for graphic design work and creativity.

Contingency Planning

Difficulties and risks include the following:

- Problems generating visibility
- Overly aggressive and debilitating actions by competitors
- An entry into the Eugene market of an already existing, franchised gourmet pasta restaurant

Worst-case risks may include the following:

- Determining that the business cannot support itself on an ongoing basis
- Having to liquidate equipment or intellectual property to cover liabilities[108]

KEY TAKEAWAYS

- There is no universally accepted format for a marketing plan. The plan can be a stand-alone document or a section of the business plan.
- A marketing plan has several critical sections: executive summary; vision and mission; situation analysis; marketing objectives; marketing strategy; financials; and implementation, evaluation, and control.
- The executive summary is a one- to two-page synopsis of the marketing plan.
- The vision statement tries to articulate the long-term purpose and idealized notion of what a business hopes to be—that is, where the owner sees the business going.
- The mission statement looks to articulate the more fundamental nature of a business—that is, why the business exists.
- The situation analysis gives a picture of where a business is now in the market and provides the context for marketing efforts. This analysis includes a market summary, competition, product offerings, the SWOT analysis, keys to success, and critical issues.
- The marketing strategy section of the plan involves selecting one or more target markets, deciding how to differentiate and position a product or a service, and creating and maintaining a marketing mix that will hopefully prove successful with the selected target market(s)—all within the context of marketing objectives. It also includes a web strategy for small businesses that have or want to have a web presence.
- The financials section of the marketing plan should provide a financial overview of a company as it relates to its marketing activities. For the small business, this should typically include a breakeven analysis, a sales and direct cost of sales forecast, and a forecast of marketing expenses.
- The implementation, evaluation, and control section of the marketing plan should include how a company will put the plan into action, evaluate whether the plan is working, and monitor and adjust implementation of the plan through marketing plan controls.

EXERCISE

1. In a group of four or five students, develop a marketing plan for Frank's All-American BarBeQue. Be sure to draw from the business plan in the Appendix (Chapter 16).

3. THE THREE THREADS

L E A R N I N G   O B J E C T I V E S

1. Understand how having a marketing plan contributes to customer value.
2. Understand how having a marketing plan can impact cash flow.
3. Understand how digital technology and the e-environment impact the marketing plan.

3.1 Customer Value Implications

customer value proposition

The whole cluster of benefits a business is promising to deliver to a customer.

Marketing is all about ascertaining and providing customer value, so it should be no surprise that there needs to be a strong linkage between a small business marketing plan and customer value. **Customer value** is the amount of benefits that a customer realizes from a product or a service as compared to the costs associated with acquiring those benefits. Because a marketing plan provides a specific marketing direction for a small business, the plan necessarily captures how it plans to deliver value to customers. The specific consideration of product, price, place, and promotion should all be geared to appealing to the target market or markets. This "appeal" must be based on understanding the value that customers are seeking—as the business understands it. The product should also be positioned in a way that reflects value by setting it apart from the competition for easy recognition and comparison. In short, the marketing plan should be the embodiment of a business's **customer value proposition**—that is, the whole cluster of benefits a business is promising to deliver to a customer.[109]

3.2 Cash-Flow Implications

It is not uncommon for a business to spend three times as much as expected and make three times less than expected.[110] This combination is not good for any company's cash flow. It is, therefore, critical that marketing plan expenses be as tight as possible without sacrificing quality (as defined by the business), with every effort being made to keep costs low. This implies the efficient use of employee time on marketing activities, competitive bidding for outside vendors, very careful attention paid to the costs of media and their effectiveness so that promotional campaigns that are not working are replaced with campaigns that look more promising and more cost-effective, and web presence measurement and evaluation to ascertain what efforts are not working so that the costs of those efforts can be replaced with something more cost-effective.

3.3 Digital Technology and E-Environment Implications

Digital technology and the e-environment are becoming more important to the small business every day. With specific respect to the marketing plan, **technology** can enter the process at multiple points. The following are a few examples:

- Digital technology makes it easy to develop a plan that is responsive to the needs of any size small business. Sales and Marketing Pro from Palo Alto Software is specifically geared to the needs of small business. The templates can be edited to fit the needs of the business, and both companies provide excellent customer support.
- When implementing the plan, digital technology makes it possible for salespeople to have quick access to the right information about inventory and pricing through a company's website, smartphones, and iPads.[111]
- Technology can help a company quickly customize offers for top-tier customers or personalize discounts for those who buy a specific product.[112]
- New technology tools and document management services can now analyze customer preferences, niche markets, regional buying habits, and more to help small businesses focus efforts and resources. The possible result is a more focused marketing plan.[113]
- Software solutions are also available for managing sales (e.g., Salesforce). These solutions are typically very inexpensive.

The **e-environment** has also had an impact on developing the marketing plan. The following are some examples:

- Online options provide new channels for small businesses to communicate and market their products and services and also offer the capability to deliver customized, one-to-one messages.[114]

- Small businesses can now plan to reach out to their target markets for little to no cost due to several new options for promotion that previously did not exist (e.g., e-mail, blog postings, podcasting, and online community forums).[115]

- SurveyMonkey, a do-it-yourself survey program, can be used to find out customer likes, dislikes, and demographic profiles.[116]

- A multitude of online tools are available to measure online and onground marketing activities. This includes the all-important measurement of website activity. Examples include free web analytics tools, such as Google Analytics and HubSpot, and free marketing calculators.

KEY TAKEAWAYS

- The marketing plan should be an embodiment of the customer value proposition of a business.
- The marketing plan should represent a commitment to keeping costs as low as possible without sacrificing quality. This will help the company's cash flow.
- Both digital technology and the e-environment can make important contributions to the development, implementation, evaluation, and control of the marketing plan.

EXERCISE

1. Your boss is struggling with the company's marketing plan. He knows that a plan is needed, but he is really crunched for time—as usual. You have suggested to him that there is a much easier and cost-effective way to develop the plan by using digital technology and the Internet. He agrees but does not have the time to check into the options. He has asked you to do it for him. Prepare a list of options that includes an explanation of each option and a discussion of how each option will contribute to customer value and keep costs down. Be as specific as possible but do not overwhelm him with paper. He will not have the time to read it.

Disaster Watch

What Now?

MaryAnn has always wanted her own real estate office. She earned her real estate license as soon as she was eligible and was able to land a position with the top realtor in the area. As she gained sales experience, she studied for her broker's license and obtained it on the "fast track." Her plan was to open her own office as soon as she felt confident that she had enough experience under her belt.

Her office, Power Real Estate, is now open, and MaryAnn has done well in building a business and establishing a good reputation for results. One of the things she noticed in her years of real estate experience was that many people were wary of letting real estate agents sell their homes because they did not believe the agents would aggressively try to sell them fast enough.[117] In response to this reluctance, MaryAnn developed and aggressively marketed a "Twenty-Point Power Marketing Plan" that would result in a client's house being sold in thirty days or less.[118] She knew it was risky, but so far things have worked out well.

Then the housing collapse occurred. MaryAnn found herself swamped with homeowners anxious to sell before being hit with foreclosure. She quickly found out that she could no longer sell homes in thirty days or less because there was a housing glut. She now sees her reputation at risk because of the housing glut. Her marketing plan is down the drain. What should she do? She does not see closing her office as an option she wants to consider.

ENDNOTES

1. William Dowling (Rock Cats president and CEO), personal interview, March 15, 2011; "Rock Cats History," *Minor League Baseball*, accessed December 2, 2011, web.minorleaguebaseball.com/team5/page.jsp?ymd=20100316&content_id =8806396&vkey=team5_t538&text=.jsp&sid=t538; "New Britain Rock Cats," *Wikipedia*, accessed December 2, 2011, en.wikipedia.org/wiki/New_Britain_Rock_Cats.

2. John Jantsch, *Duct Tape Marketing: The World's Most Practical Small Business Marketing Guide* (Nashville, TN: Thomas Nelson, Inc., 2006), back cover copy.

3. Becky McCray, "Simplify Your Small Business Marketing Plan," *Small Biz Survival*, February 12, 2010, accessed December 2, 2011, www.smallbizsurvival.com/2010/02/ simplify-your-small-business-marketing.html.

4. Adapted from Danielle MacInnis, "74% of Small Business [sic] Have No Marketing Plan!" *Marketing Blog for Small Businesses*, February 7, 2011, accessed December 2, 2011, www.daniellemacinnis.com/small-business-marketing/74-of-small-business -have-no-marketing-plan.

5. Philip Kotler and Kevin Lane Keller, *Marketing Management* (Upper Saddle River, NJ: Pearson Prentice Hall, 2009), 56.

6. "How to Write Small Business Marketing Plans," *SmallBusiness-Marketing-Plans.com*, accessed December 2, 2011, www.smallbusiness-marketing-plans.com.

7. "How to Write Small Business Marketing Plans," *SmallBusiness-Marketing-Plans.com*, accessed December 2, 2011, www.smallbusiness-marketing-plans.com.

8. Tim Berry, "How Long Should a Business Plan Be?," *BPlans*, accessed December 2, 2011, articles.bplans.com/writing-a-business-plan/how-long-should-a-business -plan-be/49.

9. "How to Write Small Business Marketing Plans," *SmallBusiness-Marketing-Plans.com*, accessed December 2, 2011, www.smallbusiness-marketing-plans.com.

10. "How to Create a Marketing Plan," *Entrepreneur*, August 7, 2001, accessed June 1, 2012, http://www.entrepreneur.com/article/186830.

11. "About SCORE," *Score.org*, accessed December 1, 2011, www.score.org/about-score.

12. Joanna L. Krotz, "5 Easy Steps to Create a Marketing Plan," *Microsoft*, accessed December 2, 2011, www.microsoft.com/business/en-us/resources/marketing/ market-research/5-easy-steps-to-create-a-marketing-plan.aspx?fbid=WTbndqFrlI.

13. "Marketing," *University of Missouri*, January 2010, accessed December 2, 2011, www.missouribusiness.net/sbtdc/docs/marketing.pdf; Entrepreneur, "How to Create a Marketing Plan," *Entrepreneur*, August 7, 2001, accessed December 2, 2011, www.entrepreneur.com/article/43018; Joanna L. Krotz, "5 Easy Steps to Create a Marketing Plan," *Microsoft*, accessed December 2, 2011, www.microsoft.com/business/ en-us/resources/marketing/market-research/5-easy-steps-to-create-a-marketing -plan.aspx?fbid=WTbndqFrlI; Emily Suess, "Marketing Plan Basics for Small Business," *Small Business Bonfire*, April 13, 2011, accessed December 2, 2011, smallbusinessbonfire.com/marketing-plan-basics-for-small-business-owners; "How to Write Small Business Marketing Plans," *SmallBusiness-Marketing-Plans.com*, accessed December 2, 2011, www.smallbusiness-marketing-plans.com.

14. David Campbell, *If You Don't Know Where You're Going, You'll Probably End Up Some-where Else* (Allen, TX: Thomas Moore Publishing, 1974).

15. Cash Miller, "Why Does Your Business Need a Good Marketing Plan?," *Yesformn*, October 27, 2010, accessed December 2, 2011, www.yesformn.org/why-does-your -business-need-a-good-marketing-plan.php.

16. "An Online Marketing Plan for the Small Business Owner," *WebMarketingNow*, accessed December 1, 2011, www.webmarketingnow.com/who/who_business _owner.html.

17. "How to Write a Marketing Plan," *Arizona Office of Tourism*, accessed December 1, 2011, www.azot.gov/documents/Marketing_Tool_Kit.pdf.

18. "Marketing Plan: The Executive Summary," *Small Business Notes*, accessed December 1, 2011, www.smallbusinessnotes.com/starting-a-business/marketing-plan-the -executive-summary.html.

19. Adapted from "Pasta Restaurant Marketing Plan: Sigmund's Gourmet Pasta," *Mplans.com*, accessed December 1, 2011, www.mplans.com/pasta_restaurant _marketing_plan/executive_summary_fc.php.

20. Jay Ebben, "Developing Effective Vision and Mission Statements," *Inc.*, February 1, 2005, accessed December 2, 2011, www.inc.com/resources/startup/articles/ 20050201/missionstatement.html.

21. "Sample Marketing Plan," *MoreBusiness.com*, accessed December 1, 2011, www.morebusiness.com/templates_worksheets/bplans/printpre.brc.

22. "Restaurant Marketing Plan: Neon Memories Diner," *MPlans.com*, accessed December 2, 2011, www.mplans.com/restaurant_marketing_plan/marketing_vision_fc.php.

23. Corte Swearingen, "Writing a Mission Statement," *SmallBiz Marketing Tips*, accessed December 2, 2011, www.small-biz-marketing-tips.com/writing-a-mission-statement.html.

24. Corte Swearingen, "Writing a Mission Statement," *SmallBiz Marketing Tips*, accessed December 2, 2011, www.small-biz-marketing-tips.com/writing-a-mission -statement.html.

25. Corte Swearingen, "Writing a Mission Statement," *SmallBiz Marketing Tips*, accessed December 2, 2011, www.small-biz-marketing-tips.com/writing-a-mission -statement.html.

26. Kristie Lorette, "Examples of How to Write a Marketing Plan," *Chron.com*, accessed December 2, 2011, smallbusiness.chron.com/examples-write-marketing-plan -1689.html.

27. "Pasta Restaurant Marketing Plan: Sigmund's Gourmet Pasta," *Mplans.com*, accessed December 1, 2011, www.mplans.com/pasta_restaurant_marketing_plan/ marketing_strategy_fc.php.

28. "Pasta Restaurant Marketing Plan: Sigmund's Gourmet Pasta," *Mplans.com*, accessed December 1, 2011, www.mplans.com/pasta_restaurant_marketing_plan/ marketing_strategy_fc.php.

29. Adapted from "Marketing," *University of Missouri*, January 2010, accessed December 2, 2011, www.missouribusiness.net/sbtdc/docs/marketing.pdf.

30. "Pasta Restaurant Marketing Plan: Sigmund's Gourmet Pasta," *Mplans.com*, accessed December 1, 2011, www.mplans.com/pasta_restaurant_marketing_plan/ marketing_strategy_fc.php.

31. "Pasta Restaurant Marketing Plan: Sigmund's Gourmet Pasta," *Mplans.com*, accessed December 1, 2011, www.mplans.com/pasta_restaurant_marketing_plan/ marketing_strategy_fc.php.

32. "Pasta Restaurant Marketing Plan: Sigmund's Gourmet Pasta," *Mplans.com*, accessed December 1, 2011, www.mplans.com/pasta_restaurant_marketing_plan/ marketing_strategy_fc.php.

33. "Pasta Restaurant Marketing Plan: Sigmund's Gourmet Pasta," *Mplans.com*, accessed December 1, 2011, www.mplans.com/pasta_restaurant_marketing_plan/ marketing_strategy_fc.php.

34. Adapted from "Pasta Restaurant Marketing Plan: Sigmund's Gourmet Pasta," *Mplans.com*, accessed December 1, 2011, www.mplans.com/pasta _restaurant_marketing_plan/marketing_strategy_fc.php.

35. "Pasta Restaurant Marketing Plan: Sigmund's Gourmet Pasta," *Mplans.com*, accessed December 1, 2011, www.mplans.com/pasta_restaurant_marketing_plan/ marketing_strategy_fc.php.

36. Adapted from "Pasta Restaurant Marketing Plan: Sigmund's Gourmet Pasta," *Mplans.com*, accessed December 1, 2011, www.mplans.com/pasta _restaurant_marketing_plan/marketing_strategy_fc.php.

37. "Market Share," *BusinessDictionary.com*, accessed December 1, 2011, www.businessdictionary.com/definition/market-share.html.

38. "Market Share," *QuickMBA*, accessed December 1, 2011, www.quickmba.com/ marketing/market-share.

39. "Pasta Restaurant Marketing Plan: Sigmund's Gourmet Pasta," *Mplans.com*, accessed December 1, 2011, www.mplans.com/pasta_restaurant_marketing_plan/ marketing_strategy_fc.php.

40. The authors of this textbook added this product characteristic.

41. "Pasta Restaurant Marketing Plan: Sigmund's Gourmet Pasta," *Mplans.com*, accessed December 1, 2011, www.mplans.com/pasta_restaurant_marketing_plan/ marketing_strategy_fc.php.

42. The authors of this textbook added this dimension of Sigmund's Prototype Store, drawing from the following two articles: Brodie Beta, "How Restaurants Are Using the iPad," *The Next Web*, May 1, 2011, accessed December 2, 2011, thenextweb.com/ apple/2011/01/05/how-restaurants-are-using-the-ipad/; "Apple iPad Restaurant Menus: The New Way to Order Food," *QuickOnlineTips*, June 6, 2010, accessed December 2, 2011, www.quickonlinetips.com/archives/2010/06/apple-ipad -restaurant-menus.

43. This information about the Sigmund's website is a combination of the ideas of the authors of this textbook and the following two sample marketing plans: "Locally Produced Clothing Retailer Marketing Plan: Local Threads," *MPlans.com*, accessed December 2, 2011, www.mplans.com/locally_produced_clothing_retailer _marketing_plan/marketing_vision_fc.php; "Restaurant Marketing Plan: Neon Memories Diner," *MPlans.com*, accessed December 2, 2011, www.mplans.com/ restaurant_marketing_plan/marketing_vision_fc.php.

44. Tim Berry, "How to Perform a SWOT Analysis," *MPlans.com*, accessed December 2, 2011, articles.mplans.com/how-to-perform-a-swot-analysis.

45. "How to Write a Marketing Plan," *Arizona Office of Tourism*, accessed December 1, 2011, www.azot.gov/documents/Marketing_Tool_Kit.pdf; Tim Berry, "How to Perform a SWOT Analysis," *MPlans.com*, accessed December 2, 2011, articles.mplans.com/how-to-perform-a-swot-analysis.

46. "Pasta Restaurant Marketing Plan: Sigmund's Gourmet Pasta," *Mplans.com*, accessed December 1, 2011, www.mplans.com/pasta_restaurant_marketing_plan/ marketing_strategy_fc.php.

47. "The Language of Branding: Brand Equity," *Branding Strategy Insider*, January 20, 2008, accessed December 2, 2011, www.brandingstrategyinsider.com/brand_equity.

48. "Pasta Restaurant Marketing Plan: Sigmund's Gourmet Pasta," *Mplans.com*, accessed December 1, 2011, www.mplans.com/pasta_restaurant_marketing_plan/ marketing_strategy_fc.php.

49. Tim Berry, "How to Perform a SWOT Analysis," *MPlans.com*, accessed December 2, 2011, articles.mplans.com/how-to-perform-a-swot-analysis.

50. "Pasta Restaurant Marketing Plan: Sigmund's Gourmet Pasta," *Mplans.com*, accessed December 1, 2011, www.mplans.com/pasta_restaurant_marketing_plan/ marketing_strategy_fc.php.

51. Tim Berry, "How to Perform a SWOT Analysis," *MPlans.com*, accessed December 2, 2011, articles.mplans.com/how-to-perform-a-swot-analysis.

52. "Pasta Restaurant Marketing Plan: Sigmund's Gourmet Pasta," *Mplans.com*, accessed December 1, 2011, www.mplans.com/pasta_restaurant_marketing_plan/ marketing_strategy_fc.php.

53. Corte Swearingen, "Marketing SWOT Analysis," *SmallBiz Marketing Tips*, accessed December 2, 2011, www.small-biz-marketing-tips.com/marketing-swot-analysis .html.

54. Kris Bovay, "Build a Successful Marketing Plan—15 Key Business Success Factors," *eZine @rticles*, accessed December 2, 2011, ezinearticles.com/?Build-a-Successful-Marketing-Plan—15-Key-Business-Success-Factors&id=2156709.

55. Kris Bovay, "Build a Successful Marketing Plan—15 Key Business Success Factors," *eZine @rticles*, accessed December 2, 2011, ezinearticles.com/?Build-a-Successful-Marketing-Plan—15-Key-Business-Success-Factors&id=2156709.

56. "Pasta Restaurant Marketing Plan: Sigmund's Gourmet Pasta," *Mplans.com*, accessed December 1, 2011, www.mplans.com/pasta_restaurant_marketing_plan/marketing_strategy_fc.php.

57. "Pasta Restaurant Marketing Plan: Sigmund's Gourmet Pasta," *Mplans.com*, accessed December 1, 2011, www.mplans.com/pasta_restaurant_marketing_plan/marketing_strategy_fc.php.

58. Bobette Kyle, "Internet Marketing Strategy: Developing a Website Marketing Plan," *WebSiteMarketingPlan.com*, accessed December 1, 2011, www.websitemarketingplan.com/marketing_management/MarketingPlanningArticle.htm.

59. Adapted from "Pasta Restaurant Marketing Plan: Sigmund's Gourmet Pasta," *Mplans.com*, accessed December 1, 2011, www.mplans.com/pasta_restaurant_marketing_plan/marketing_strategy_fc.php.

60. Adapted from "Pasta Restaurant Marketing Plan: Sigmund's Gourmet Pasta," *Mplans.com*, accessed December 1, 2011, www.mplans.com/pasta_restaurant_marketing_plan/marketing_strategy_fc.php.

61. This is an addition to "Pasta Restaurant Marketing Plan: Sigmund's Gourmet Pasta," *Mplans.com*, accessed December 1, 2011, www.mplans.com/pasta_restaurant_marketing_plan/marketing_strategy_fc.php.

62. This is an addition to "Pasta Restaurant Marketing Plan: Sigmund's Gourmet Pasta," *Mplans.com*, accessed December 1, 2011, www.mplans.com/pasta_restaurant_marketing_plan/marketing_strategy_fc.php.

63. "Pasta Restaurant Marketing Plan: Sigmund's Gourmet Pasta," *Mplans.com*, accessed December 1, 2011, www.mplans.com/pasta_restaurant_marketing_plan/marketing_strategy_fc.php.

64. "Pasta Restaurant Marketing Plan: Sigmund's Gourmet Pasta," *Mplans.com*, accessed December 1, 2011, www.mplans.com/pasta_restaurant_marketing_plan/marketing_strategy_fc.php.

65. Tim Berry, "What Is the Marketing Strategy Pyramid, Where Did It Come From?," *BPlans*, accessed June 1, 2012, http://www.bplans.com/ask-bplans/640/what-is-the-marketing-strategy-pyramid-where-did-it-come-from.

66. Tim Berry, "What Is the Marketing Strategy Pyramid, Where Did It Come From?," *BPlans*, accessed June 1, 2012, http://www.bplans.com/ask-bplans/640/what-is-the-marketing-strategy-pyramid-where-did-it-come-from.

67. The website and social media are additions to "Pasta Restaurant Marketing Plan: Sigmund's Gourmet Pasta," *Mplans.com*, accessed December 1, 2011, www.mplans.com/pasta_restaurant_marketing_plan/marketing_strategy_fc.php.

68. "Pasta Restaurant Marketing Plan: Sigmund's Gourmet Pasta," *Mplans.com*, accessed December 1, 2011, www.mplans.com/pasta_restaurant_marketing_plan/marketing_strategy_fc.php.

69. Philip Kotler and Kevin Lane Keller, *Marketing Management* (Upper Saddle River, NJ: Pearson Prentice Hall, 2009), 57.

70. The authors of this textbook added the capability to place an order online.

71. The addition of coupons is a combination of ideas from the authors of this textbook and the following sample marketing plan: "Restaurant Marketing Plan: Neon Memories Diner," *MPlans.com*, accessed June 1, 2012, http://www.mplans.com/restaurant_marketing_plan/marketing_vision_fc.php.

72. The Facebook plan was drawn from the following two sample marketing plans: "Locally Produced Clothing Retailer Marketing Plan: Local Threads," *MPlans.com*, accessed December 2, 2011, www.mplans.com/locally_produced_clothing_retailer_marketing_plan/marketing_vision_fc.php; "Restaurant Marketing Plan: Neon Memories Diner," *MPlans.com*, accessed December 2, 2011, http://www.mplans.com/restaurant_marketing_plan/marketing_vision_fc.php.

73. "Pasta Restaurant Marketing Plan: Sigmund's Gourmet Pasta," *Mplans.com*, accessed December 1, 2011, www.mplans.com/pasta_restaurant_marketing_plan/marketing_strategy_fc.php. The authors of this textbook added Twitter to the social media plan.

74. The authors of this textbook added the online suggestion system.

75. "Pasta Restaurant Marketing Plan: Sigmund's Gourmet Pasta," *Mplans.com*, accessed December 1, 2011, www.mplans.com/pasta_restaurant_marketing_plan/marketing_strategy_fc.php.

76. "Pasta Restaurant Marketing Plan: Sigmund's Gourmet Pasta," *Mplans.com*, accessed December 1, 2011, www.mplans.com/pasta_restaurant_marketing_plan/marketing_strategy_fc.php.

77. Susan Ward, "Breakeven Analysis," *About.com*, accessed December 1, 2011, sbinfocanada.about.com/cs/startup/g/breakevenanal.htm.

78. Daniel Richards, "How to Do a Breakeven Analysis," *About.com*, accessed December 1, 2011, entrepreneurs.about.com/od/businessplan/a/breakeven.htm.

79. Daniel Richards, "How to Do a Breakeven Analysis," *About.com*, accessed December 1, 2011, entrepreneurs.about.com/od/businessplan/a/breakeven.htm; Susan Ward, "Breakeven Analysis," *About.com*, accessed December 1, 2011, sbinfocanada.about.com/cs/startup/g/breakevenanal.htm.

80. Daniel Richards, "How to Do a Breakeven Analysis," *About.com*, accessed December 1, 2011, entrepreneurs.about.com/od/businessplan/a/breakeven.htm; Susan Ward, "Breakeven Analysis," *About.com*, accessed December 1, 2011, sbinfocanada.about.com/cs/startup/g/breakevenanal.htm.

81. "Pasta Restaurant Marketing Plan: Sigmund's Gourmet Pasta," *Mplans.com*, accessed December 1, 2011, www.mplans.com/pasta_restaurant_marketing_plan/marketing_strategy_fc.php.

82. Philip Kotler and Kevin Lane Keller, *Marketing Management* (Upper Saddle River, NJ: Pearson Prentice Hall, 2009), 112.

83. "Expense and Sales Forecasting," *Chic-CEO.com*, accessed December 2, 2011, www.chic-ceo.com/expense-and-sales-forecasting.

84. "Pasta Restaurant Marketing Plan: Sigmund's Gourmet Pasta," *Mplans.com*, accessed December 1, 2011, www.mplans.com/pasta_restaurant_marketing_plan/marketing_strategy_fc.php.

85. "Expense and Sales Forecasting," *Chic-CEO.com*, accessed December 2, 2011, www.chic-ceo.com/expense-and-sales-forecasting.

86. "Pasta Restaurant Marketing Plan: Sigmund's Gourmet Pasta," *Mplans.com*, accessed December 1, 2011, www.mplans.com/pasta_restaurant_marketing_plan/marketing_strategy_fc.php.

87. Philip Kotler and Kevin Lane Keller, *Marketing Management* (Upper Saddle River, NJ: Pearson Prentice Hall, 2009), 57; Emily Suess, "Marketing Plan Basics for Small Business," *Small Business Bonfire*, April 13, 2011, accessed December 2, 2011, smallbusinessbonfire.com/marketing-plan-basics-for-small-business-owners.

88. Steve Arun, "How to Successfully Implement Your Marketing Plan," *VA4Business*, March 14, 2010, accessed December 2, 2011, www.va4business.com/business/428/how-to-successfully-implement-your-marketing-plan.

89. "Implementing Your Marketing Plan," *Marketing Plan Success*, accessed December 2, 2011, www.marketing-plan-success.com/articles/controls-implementation.php.

90. Steve Arun, "How to Successfully Implement Your Marketing Plan," *VA4Business*, March 14, 2010, accessed December 2, 2011, www.va4business.com/business/428/how-to-successfully-implement-your-marketing-plan.

91. "Implementing Your Marketing Plan," *Marketing Plan Success*, accessed December 2, 2011, www.marketing-plan-success.com/articles/controls-implementation.php; Steve Arun, "How to Successfully Implement Your Marketing Plan," *VA4Business*, March 14, 2010, accessed December 2, 2011, www.va4business.com/business/428/how-to-successfully-implement-your-marketing-plan.

92. "Pasta Restaurant Marketing Plan: Sigmund's Gourmet Pasta," *Mplans.com*, accessed December 1, 2011, www.mplans.com/pasta_restaurant_marketing_plan/marketing_strategy_fc.php.

93. "Measuring Brand Performance," *Branding Strategy Insider*, February 22, 2011, accessed December 2, 2011, www.brandingstrategyinsider.com/brand_equity.

94. "About Us," *American Evaluation Association*, accessed December 2, 2011, www.eval.org/aboutus/organization/aboutus.asp.

95. "Marketing Plan: Evaluation," *Will It Fly*, accessed December 1, 2011, www.willitfly.com/wif/educelbrief.jsp?briefId=93&sponsorId=61&modId=241&modNm=Marketing%2BPlan&sectionNm=Evaluation.

96. Adapted from Stuart Ayling, "7 Ways to Evaluate Your Marketing Plan," *WebSiteMarketingPlan.com*, accessed December 2, 2011, www.websitemarketingplan.com/mplan/evaluateplan.htm.

97. John Vencil, "The Marketing Plan VII—Evaluation," *VPI Strategies*, 2003, accessed December 2, 2011, www.vpistrategies.com/articles_pdf/Mktg7_Eval.pdf.

98. John Vencil, "The Marketing Plan VII—Evaluation," *VPI Strategies*, 2003, accessed December 2, 2011, www.vpistrategies.com/articles_pdf/Mktg7_Eval.pdf.

99. Justin Whitney, "What Is Web Analytics," *AllBusiness.com*, accessed December 2, 2011, www.allbusiness.com/marketing-advertising/marketing-advertising/11382028-1.html.

100. Community eBook, *Practical Social Media Measurement & Analysis* (Fredericton, New Brunswick, Canada: Radian6, 2010), 9, accessed December 2, 2011, www.radian6.com/wp-content/uploads/2010/03/Radian6_eBook_March2010.pdf.

101. Anoop George Joseph, "Twitter Metrics," *Web Technology and Softwares—A Technical Blog*, December 16, 2011, accessed June 1, 2012, http://webtechsoftwares.wordpress.com/2011/12/16/twitter-metrics/; "The Klout Score," accessed June 1, 2012, http://klout.com/understand/score.

102. Viveka Von Rosen, "ROI and Measuring your LinkedIn Presence," *#LinkedInChat*, February 21, 2012, accessed May 30, 2012, http://linkedintobusiness.com/roi-and-measuring-your-linkedin-presence/; Jenn Deering Davis, Ph.D., "5 Most Essential Facebook Marketing Metrics," *AllFacebook*, April 17, 2012, accessed May 30, 2012, http://allfacebook.com/facebook-metrics-essentials_b86156.

103. These calculators were obtained from and self-described at www.mplans.com/marketing_calculators.

104. "Pasta Restaurant Marketing Plan: Sigmund's Gourmet Pasta," *Mplans.com*, accessed December 1, 2011, www.mplans.com/pasta_restaurant_marketing_plan/marketing_strategy_fc.php.

105. "Marketing Controls," *MarketingTeacher.com*, accessed December 2, 2011, www.marketingteacher.com/lesson-store/lesson-control.html.

106. "How to Write a Marketing Plan," *Arizona Office of Tourism*, accessed December 1, 2011, www.azot.gov/documents/Marketing_Tool_Kit.pdf.

107. Larry A. Bauman, "Contingency Planning Occurs before the Crisis Begins," *Small Business Success*, accessed December 1, 2011, www.smallbusinesssuccess.biz/articles_week/business_contingency_planning.htm.

108. "Pasta Restaurant Marketing Plan: Sigmund's Gourmet Pasta," *Mplans.com*, accessed December 1, 2011, www.mplans.com/pasta_restaurant_marketing_plan/marketing_strategy_fc.php.

109. Philip Kotler and Kevin Lane Keller, *Marketing Management* (Upper Saddle River, NJ: Pearson Prentice Hall, 2009), 123.

110. "Expense and Sales Forecasting," *Chic-CEO.com*, accessed December 2, 2011, www.chic-ceo.com/expense-and-sales-forecasting.

111. Adapted from "Use of Technology in Marketing," *Microsoft Business*, accessed December 2, 2011, www.microsoft.com/business/en-us/resources/ArticleReader/website/default.aspx?Print=1&ArticleId=techstrategiestopoweryourmarketingmuscleanddollars&fbid=knBWf5av0wR.

112. Adapted from "Use of Technology in Marketing," *Microsoft Business*, accessed December 2, 2011, www.microsoft.com/business/en-us/resources/ArticleReader/website/default.aspx?Print=1&ArticleId=techstrategiestopoweryourmarketingmuscleanddollars&fbid=knBWf5av0wR.

113. Adapted from "Use of Technology in Marketing," *Microsoft Business*, accessed December 2, 2011, www.microsoft.com/business/en-us/resources/ArticleReader/website/default.aspx?Print=1&ArticleId=techstrategiestopoweryourmarketingmuscleanddollars&fbid=knBWf5av0wR.

114. "How Has Online Technology Changed Small Business Marketing and Advertising?," *Torian Group.com*, accessed December 1, 2011, www.toriangroup.com/Portals/0/Documents/How%20Has%20Online%20Technology%20Changed%20Small%20Business%20Marketing%20and%20Advertising.pdf.

115. "How Has Online Technology Changed Small Business Marketing and Advertising?," *Torian Group.com*, accessed December 1, 2011, www.toriangroup.com/Portals/0/Documents/How%20Has%20Online%20Technology%20Changed%20Small%20Business%20Marketing%20and%20Advertising.pdf.

116. "How Has Online Technology Changed Small Business Marketing and Advertising?," *Torian Group.com*, accessed December 1, 2011, www.toriangroup.com/Portals/0/Documents/How%20Has%20Online%20Technology%20Changed%20Small%20Business%20Marketing%20and%20Advertising.pdf.

117. David Frey, "6 Deadly Small Business Marketing Mistakes," accessed June 21, 2012, http://www.onyxwebsolutions.com.au/resources/Six_Marketing_Mistakes.pdf.

118. David Frey, "6 Deadly Small Business Marketing Mistakes," accessed June 21, 2012, http://www.onyxwebsolutions.com.au/resources/Six_Marketing_Mistakes.pdf.

CHAPTER 9
Accounting and Cash Flow

Simione Consultants LLC

Source: Used with permission from Simione Consultants LLC.

Health care is the largest single industry in the US economy. Currently, health care represents nearly 17 percent of the gross domestic product, encompassing nearly 600,000 establishments and employing more than 14 million people. The health-care industry covers an extraordinary wide range of businesses and operations. It includes large hospitals, diagnostic laboratories, nursing care facilities, and the offices of doctors and dentists. Each establishment has individuals that possess considerable expertise in their respective disciplines. However, they may not possess the knowledge or the expertise that would enable them to manage their establishments in the most efficient manner. That is where firms like Simione Consultants LLC play a vital role.

Simione Consultants LLC represents the evolution of consulting companies that have spun off from many accounting firms. Accountants are no longer merely reconciling accounts or preparing tax returns for their clients. They are now offering a broad range of consulting services. Simione Consultants LLC provides expert assistance to hospital-based and hospital-affiliated home health and hospice agencies, visiting nurse associations, small proprietary agencies, and large national chains. They provide services that one might expect from a firm whose origins were in a standard accounting practice—such as assisting in accounts receivables and cash-flow management. Other accounting services that they provide include financial analysis reports and the preparation of cost reports for the federal government. They can conduct in-depth cost analyses at a detailed and a granular level so that clients can improve their operational efficiencies. The compliance division consulting services include working with health-care attorneys, corporate compliance and audit departments, and government agencies such as the Office of the Inspector General. Its clinical operations division works closely with financial consultants to improve the financial health of its clients.

What makes Simione Consultants LLC distinct is its ability to go beyond these basic accounting tasks and provide vital ancillary support for its clients in this niche market. They are in a position to conduct the valuation of businesses or assist in mergers and acquisitions. They help clients with preparing a prospectus or assisting with negotiations. Their consulting services can advise on how a client can maximize its return on an information management system by identifying system requirements and specifying possible solutions. In addition, the company has developed a software product—"The Financial Monitor"—that provides quarterly home health and hospice reports with multiple valuable benchmarks, including national, state, and profit-status norms, to help their clients and the industry make informed financial decisions.

A measure of how firms such as Simione Consultants LLC have moved beyond balance accounts is the company's ability to support a client's marketing function. The firm can help build comprehensive marketing plans and assist clients in developing and improving sales materials and training.

Simione Consultants LLC began its work in the home health-care industry more than forty years ago with an agency in Hamden, Connecticut. It was the vision of William J. Simione Jr., the founding member, who saw an opportunity. With his brother Robert J. Simione, the managing principal, and a dedicated team of principals, management, and staff, William Simione has helped Simione Consulting LLC become one of the leading home health and hospice consulting companies in the United States with over a thousand clients. Robert Simione says that a company is only as good as the people who work for it, and Simione Consultants LLC has the best home health and hospice consultants in the country.

1. UNDERSTANDING THE NEED FOR ACCOUNTING SYSTEMS

LEARNING OBJECTIVES

1. Understand why a basic knowledge of accounting is important for a small business.
2. Understand the importance of selecting an accountant to enhance the overall operation of a business.
3. Define the two major approaches to accounting systems: cash versus accruals.

The older I get, the more interesting I find lawyers and accountants.[1]
- Alex James

Imagine that you invite a friend from China, who is visiting the United States for the first time, to a baseball game. Your friend has never been to a baseball game before and knows nothing of the game's rules. He might notice on the scoreboard listings for runs, hits, and errors. Your friend might also see notations on the number of strikes and balls. He does not know exactly what any of those terms mean, but he notices that some people in the stands applaud when the number of runs increases. Your friend might be amused by seeing individuals periodically running from one base to another; however, without knowing the basic rules of baseball, he cannot possibly understand what is actually occurring. He certainly could not comment on how well the game is going or provide suggestions about what one of the teams should do next. Most Americans would be in the same position if they were watching a cricket match. In both cases, you and your friend are in the same position of someone who wishes to run a business without having a fundamental understanding of accounting systems.

Warren Buffett has said that accounting is, to put it simply, the language of business. Without a fundamental understanding of this language of accounting and its set of rules, you are in the same position as your Chinese friend—you really do not know what is going on with a business. If someone is considering starting a business, he or she should possess some degree of fluency in this language. One does not expect this businessperson to be as knowledgeable as a certified public accountant (CPA) or an expert in tax issues. However, such businesspeople should have a clear expectation that they will be able to look at the key elements of an accounting system and interpret how well their businesses are doing. They should be able to track some of the key tasks and elements associated with a comprehensive accounting system. As we will see in Section 4, computerized accounting programs for small businesses have greatly simplified this responsibility.

accounting

The art of recording, classifying, and summarizing in a significant manner and in terms of money, transactions and events which are, in part at least, of a financial character, and interpreting the results thereof.

Accounting is defined by the American Institute of Certified Public Accountants (AICPA) as "the art of recording, classifying, and summarizing in a significant manner and in terms of money, transactions and events which are, in part at least, of a financial character, and interpreting the results thereof."[2] Put more simply, it is essentially an information system. Accounting provides critical information to potential investors and businesses managers. Accounting may, in fact, be one of the oldest information systems known to humans. Some have argued that accounting systems were the impetus for the development of writing systems in Mesopotamia.[3] Archaeologists have discovered clay tokens, dating back 10,000 years ago, which functioned as part of the inventory system measuring agricultural goods, such as grains and domesticated animals. By 3500 BC, these tokens were being stored in containers—known as *bullae*. Notations on the surface of these containers indicated the type and quantity of the tokens held within; for many, this system was the basis of an abstract system of written communication.[4]

Other ancient societies recognized the importance of carefully monitoring and recording economic transactions. The Roman Empire needed to finance its operations and employed the familiar concept of an annual budget to coordinate expenditures and taxation. It had treasury managers, known as *questors*, who were subject to periodic audits.[5] The most famous monograph on accounting dates to Renaissance Italy. Luca Pacioli, a Franciscan friar and polymath, wrote *Summa de Arithmetica, Geometria, Proportioni et Proportionalita* in 1494. Essentially this was a math textbook, but it included a section on double-entry bookkeeping. This approach to accounting had been covered by Beredetto Cotrugli a century earlier.[6] The text was immediately recognized as an important contribution and was one of the first books produced by Gutenberg. On a first reading, Pacioli's coverage appears to be remarkably "modern." It described how merchants should identify their assets and liabilities, note transitions as they occur, and identify them as either debits or credits. He pointed out that the total of debits and credits must be equal, thus his model became the basis of the balance sheet. In the intervening five hundred years, business has essentially adapted Pacioli's approach. Obvious, over the last five centuries, businesses have grown both in size and in complexity, and accounting systems have grown with them.

Therefore, it is important for any business regardless of size to be able to "count" on solid accounting information.

The exact nature of accounting support will be greatly determined by the type and size of the small business. The level of accounting support required by the nonemployer business will obviously differ significantly from the level required by a business generating tens of millions of dollars of revenue and employing hundreds of workers. The level of support will also be influenced by the business owner's familiarity with accounting and the type of accounting information systems that have been determined as appropriate. Regardless of size or type, small businesses should plan on eventually acquiring the talents of an accountant. Preferably, the decision to use an accountant should occur with the creation of the business.

Hiring an accountant or an accounting firm is an important decision for a small business. Employing an accountant does not translate into this individual being a full-time employee of the business. At the start, most small businesses will use the accountant as a consultant or a contract employee. As they grow, some small businesses might benefit from acquiring the services of full-service accounting firm. Although some start-ups, particularly those that might be cash-strapped, use the services of the book-keeper only, but this is ill-advised. Most small businesses will need the services of a CPA. Another type of accountant a small business might employ is known as an enrolled agent. These are accountants who have passed a tax test from the Internal Revenue Service (IRS).

When looking for an accountant, there are some issues that you should consider. Try to find an accountant who has some working familiarity with a particular type of business or industry. Hopefully, you will be able to find an accountant with whom you have some rapport. This is important because a good accountant is more than simply someone who balances the books. You should consult an accountant before determining what type of accounting system you intend to employ—cash versus accrual (see Section 1). Remember that an accountant will play an important role in assisting you in the creation, purchase, and development of an accounting information system for the business. This system is important in providing the appropriate information to the external community (for this audience the term **financial accounting** is often used)—bankers, angel investors, venture capitalists, and/or the government. The same accounting information system will also be an important component of internal controls (in this case the term **managerial accounting** is used)—the systems and policies by which you make a firm more efficient. In this role, an accountant can help develop appropriate policies with respect to cash control and inventory control. An accountant can play a critical role in developing business plans, particularly with respect to budgets and financial statements. As highlighted in Section 3, you should consult an accountant before selecting an accounting software package. Quite often, an accountant can be extremely useful in training people to use such a software package.[7]

financial accounting

An accounting system that provides the appropriate information to the external community—bankers, angel investors, venture capitalists, and/or the government.

managerial accounting

An accounting system that provides information to the management of a business and aids in internal controls—systems and policies that make a firm more efficient.

Video Clip 9.1

Why Warren Buffett Said Accounting Is the Language of Business
This video introduces the importance of accounting.

View the video online at: http://www.youtube.com/v/Z6YEsyO0eOo

Video Clip 9.2

Why You Need an Accountant
This video explains why a small business needs the services of a professional accountant.

View the video online at: http://www.youtube.com/v/DAT4NY9iQTQ

 Video Clip 9.3

What CPAs Wish Every Small Business Knew
This video approaches small business's need for accounting from the accountant's perspective.

View the video online at: http://www.youtube.com/v/R_FcOu2_SoA

1.1 Alternative Approaches to Accounting Systems

The system of double-entry bookkeeping is, perhaps, the most beautiful one in the wide domain of literature or science. If it were less known, it would be the admiration of the learned world.[8]
- *Edwin T. Freedley*

The evolution of accounting has led to two major systems: the cash basis model and the accrual basis model. Before describing the two systems, we must identify a very important term—accounting transactions. When in business, we either receive money from a sale or spend money, such as in buying a piece of equipment. We can define these as transactions. The manner in which we record transactions defines the difference between a cash basis accounting system or an accrual accounting system.

In most cases, either system can be used by a business (there are situations under which a cash-based accounting system cannot be used, the details of which are discussed later), but regardless of the system used, a business must clearly specify which method is being employed.

In the **cash-based accounting** system, a transaction is recorded when money is either received or spent. As an example, a business has three sales on June 29 of a particular year. The first sale is for $500, the second is for $1,000, and the third is for $300. However, the three customers use different methods of payment. The first customer pays for the product in cash, the second customer writes a personal check, and the third customer pays by credit card. The second customer's personal check clears on July 5, while the credit card company transfers the $300 into the business's account on July 3. Under the

cash-based accounting

An accounting system where transactions are recorded when money is either received or spent.

cash basis accounting system, the business would list the first sale of $500 as a June transaction, but it would list the second and third sales (totaling $1,300) as July transactions. The same logic is used with respect to expenditures. If the same firm purchased a laptop computer in July but did not have to pay for two months, then the transaction would be recorded in September.

Under the **accrual accounting** system, transactions are recorded when they occur. If the aforementioned business was functioning under the accrual basis accounting system, then all three sales (totaling $1,800) would be recorded as June transactions, and the purchase of the laptop would be designated as a July transaction.

Generally, though, with some few exceptions, businesses must use the accrual basis accounting method if they have inventory of any component of items that they sell to the public and if the sales are more than $5 million per year. Other conditions under which the cash basis accounting system may not be used include C corporations, partnerships with at least one C corporation partner, and tax shelters.[9] The major benefit of cash basis accounting is its simplicity. It greatly reduces the demand on bookkeeping. The cash basis system also provides a much more accurate indication of a company's current cash position. This approach may be used to affect taxable income, which can be done by deferring billing so that payments are received in the next year.[10] However, there are drawbacks to the cash basis approach—the most serious being that it may provide a distorted or an inaccurate indication of profitability. The reality is that cash basis accounting systems are really only appropriate for businesses with sales under $1 million and that function basically on a cash basis.

Accrual basis accounting is in conformance with IRS and generally accepted accounting principles (GAAP) regulations. Although more complex and generally requiring greater bookkeeping with a more sophisticated approach to accounting, the accrual basis provides a more accurate indication of the profitability of a business. The major drawback of the accrual basis system comes with respect to understanding the business's cash position. A firm may look profitable under this system, but if customers have not paid for the goods and services, the cash position might be dire.[11] A summary of the pros and cons of the two systems is provided in Figure 9.1.

accrual accounting

An accounting system where transactions are recorded when they occur.

FIGURE 9.1 Comparative Accounting Systems

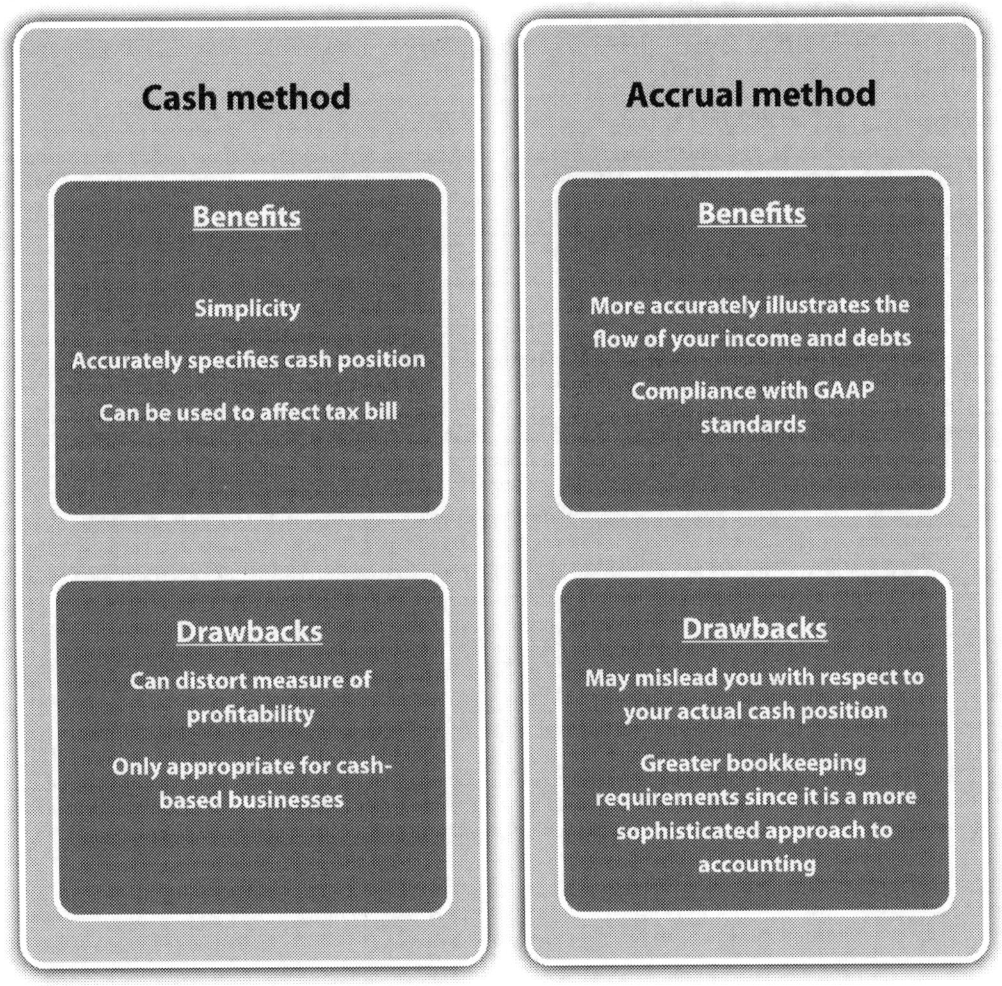

Video Clip 9.4

Accrual versus Cash-Basis Accounting Video Presentation
A lecture on the two accounting systems.

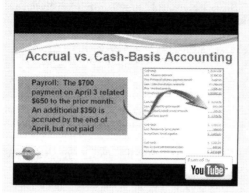

View the video online at: http://www.youtube.com/v/mAEscMr5IMA

 Video Clip 9.5

Accrual Basis versus Cash Basis Accounting Power
A video with voice-over of a PowerPoint presentation.

View the video online at: http://www.youtube.com/v/3RxJFyUPu_o

KEY TAKEAWAYS

- Accounting is one of the oldest activities of human civilizations and dates back over five thousand years.
- Small businesses require accounting capabilities, which must be done either in-house or through an external service.
- The selection process for an accounting service should be carefully considered. The evaluation process should consider the following: expertise in a particular type of business or industry, rapport, availability of additional consulting services, and the ability to support computerized accounting systems.
- Accounting systems may be divided into two major types: cash basis and accrual basis.
- Cash basis systems count a transaction when the cash is received. Such systems are used by smaller businesses that have no appreciable inventory.
- Accrual basis systems count transactions when they occur. Although this system may require additional analysis to determine a business's actual cash position, it provides a more accurate measure of profitability.

2.   FINANCIAL ACCOUNTING STATEMENTS

LEARNING OBJECTIVES

1. Understand what is measured on a balance sheet.
2. Understand the term *depreciation*.
3. Understand what goes on an income statement.
4. Understand what is measured in a cash-flow statement.
5. Appreciate the importance of forecasting when developing a cash-flow projection statement.

It sounds extraordinary, but it's a fact that balance sheets can make fascinating reading.[12]
- *Mary, Lady Archer of Weston*

As discussed in Chapter 5, all business plans should contain sets of financial statements. However, even after the initial business plan is created, these financial statements provide critical information that will be required for the successful operation of the business. They not only are necessary for tax purposes but also provide critical insights for managing the firm and addressing issues such as the following:

- Are we profitable?
- Are we operating efficiently?
- Are we too heavily in debt or could we acquire more debt?
- Do we have enough cash to continue operations?
- What is this business worth?

There are three key financial statements: the balance sheet, the income statement, and the cash-flow statement. Every business owner or manager needs to be able to correctly interpret these statements if he or she expects to continue successful operations. It should be pointed out that all three financial statements follow general formats. The degree of detail or in some cases terminology may differ slightly from one business to another; as an example, some firms may wish to have an extensive list of operational expenses on their income statements, while others would group them under broad categories. Likewise, privately held businesses would not use the term *shareholders' equity* but rather use *owner's equity* in their balance sheet, and they would not list dividends. This aim of this chapter is to provide the reader with a broad overview of accounting concepts as they apply to managing small and mid-sized businesses.

2.1   The Balance Sheet Statement

One should think of the **balance sheet** statement as a photograph, taken at a particular point in time, which images the financial position of a firm. The balance sheet is dominated by what is known as the accounting equation. Put simply, the accounting equation separates what is owned from who owns it. Formally, the accounting equation states the following:

$$\text{assets} = \text{liabilities} + \text{owner's equity}.$$

balance sheet

A report that examines a business's assets, liabilities, and owner's equity at some particular point in time.

assets

Economic resources that are expected to produce a benefit in the future.

liabilities

The amount of money owed to outside claims—people outside of a business.

owner's equity

The claims on a business by those who own the business.

current assets

Assets that will be held for less than one year.

cash

The most liquid of all assets.

marketable securities

Stocks and bonds that a business may hold in the hope that they will provide a greater return to the business rather than just letting cash "sit" in a bank account.

accounts receivables

The amount of money due to a business from prior credit sales.

notes receivable

A formal debt instrument that will be paid to the company within a year.

prepaid expenses

An accrual accounting term that represents payments in advance of their actual occurrence.

inventory

Tangible goods, categorized as raw materials, WIP, and finished goods, held by a business for the production of goods and services.

long-term assets

Assets that will not be turned into cash within the next year.

fixed assets

Long-term assets generally valued at their original cost.

depreciation

A noncash expense that specifically recognizes that assets decline in value over time.

Assets are "economic resources that are expected to produce a benefit in the future."[13] **Liabilities** are the amount of money owed to outside claims (i.e., money owed to people outside the business). **Owner's equity**—also known as stockholders' equity—represents the claims on the business by those who own the business. As specified in the accounting equation, the dollar value of assets must equal the dollar value of the business's liabilities plus the owner's equity. Before proceeding with any numerical example, let us define some important terms.

Current assets are assets that will be held for less than one year. They include **cash**, **marketable securities**, **accounts receivables**, **notes receivable**, **prepaid expenses**, and **inventory**. These are listed in a specific order. The order is based on the degree of liquidity of each asset. *Liquidity* measures the ease in which an asset can be converted into cash. Naturally, cash is the most liquid of all assets. All firms should have cash readily available. The exact amount of the desirable amount of cash to be held at hand will be determined by the sales level of the anticipated cash receipts and the cash needs of the business.

Marketable securities are stocks and bonds that a business may hold in the hope that they would provide a greater return to the business rather than just letting cash "sit" in a bank account. Most of these securities can be easily turned into cash—should the need arise.

Accounts receivables represent the amount of money due to a business from prior credit sales. Not all firms operate on a strictly cash sales basis. Many firms will offer customers the opportunity to purchase on a credit basis. As an example, a furniture store sells a bedroom set worth $6,000 to a newlywed couple. The couple puts down $2,500 to fix the sale and then signs a contract to pay the remaining $3,500 within the next year. That $3,500 would be listed as accounts receivable for the furniture firm.

Prepaid expense is an accrual accounting term that represents a payment that is made in advance of their actual occurrence. Insurance would be an example of a prepaid expense because a company is paying premiums to cover damages that might occur in the near future. If a year's worth of rent were paid at one time, it too would be viewed as a prepaid expense.

Inventory is the tangible goods held by a business for the production of goods and services. Inventory can fall into three categories: raw materials, work-in-process (WIP), and finished goods. Raw materials inventory represents items or commodities purchased by a firm to create products and services. WIP inventory represents "partially completed goods, part or subassemblies that are no longer part of the raw materials inventory and not yet finished goods."[14] The valuation of WIP should include the cost of direct material, direct labor, and overhead put into the WIP inventory. Finished inventory represents products that are ready for sale. Generally accepted accounting principles (GAAP) require that a business value its inventory on either the cost price or the market price—whichever is lowest. This inherent conservative approach to valuation is due to the desire to prevent the overestimation of inventory during inflationary periods.

Total current assets are the summation of the aforementioned items and are defined as follows:

$$\text{total current assets} = \text{cash} + \text{marketable securities} + \text{accounts receivable} + \text{prepaid expenses} + \text{inventory}.$$

The next set of items in the asset section of the balance sheet is long-term assets. **Long-term assets** are those assets that will not be turned into cash within the next year. Long-term assets may include a category known as investments. These are items that management holds for investment purposes, and they do not intend to "cash in" within the upcoming year. They might consist of other companies' stock, notes, or bonds. In some cases, they may represent specialized forms—money put away for pension funds. The next major category of long-term assets is fixed assets. **Fixed assets** include plant, equipment, and land. Generally, these are valued at their original cost. The value of these assets will decline over time. As an example, you purchase a new car for $25,000. If you were to sell the same car one, two, or five years later, its value would be less than the original purchase price. This recognition is known as **depreciation**, which is a noncash expense that specifically recognizes that assets decline in value over time. Accumulated depreciation is a running total of all depreciation on assets. Depreciation is also found on the income statement. Its presence in that financial statement enables a business to reduce its taxable income. There are many methods by which you can compute the depreciation value on fixed assets. These methods can be split into two broad categories: straight-line depreciation and accelerated depreciation. Straight-line depreciation is fairly easy to illustrate. In the example of the car, assume you purchased this car for company use. You intend to use it for five years, and at the end of the five years, you plan on scrapping the car and expect that its salvage value will be zero. This is illustrated in Table 9.1.

TABLE 9.1 Depreciation Calculations

	Year 0	Year 1	Year 2	Year 3	Year 4	Year 5
Depreciation	$0	$5,000	$5,000	$5,000	$5,000	$5,000
Accumulated depreciation	$0	$5,000	$10,000	$15,000	$20,000	$25,000
Net asset value	$25,000	$20,000	$15,000	$10,000	$5,000	$0

Because the useful lifetime of the vehicle was five years, the original value of the vehicle was divided by five; therefore, the annual depreciation would equal $5,000 ($25,000/5 = $5,000 per year). The accumulated depreciation simply sums up the prior years' depreciation for that particular asset.

Accelerated depreciation methods attempt to recapture a major portion of the depreciation earlier in the life of an asset. Accelerated depreciation yields tax-saving benefits earlier in the life of any particular fixed asset. The appropriate method of depreciating an asset for tax purposes is dictated by the Internal Revenue Service (IRS). One should look at the IRS publication 946—*How to Depreciate Property*—to get a better understanding of the concept of depreciation and how to properly compute it.

The last category of long-term assets is **intangible assets**—assets that provide economic value to a business but do not have a tangible, physical presence. Intangible assets include items such as patents, franchises, copyrights, and goodwill. Thus the value of long-term assets can be calculated as follows:

long-term assets = investments + fixed assets − accumulated depreciation + intangible assets.

The last element on the asset side of the balance sheet is the total assets. This is the summation of current assets and long-term assets.

On the other side of the balance sheet, we have liabilities plus owner's equity. The elements of liabilities consist of current liabilities and long-term liabilities. These represent what a business owes to others. **Current liabilities** are debts and obligations that are to be paid within a year. These include **notes payable**, **accounts payable**, other items payable (e.g., taxes, wages, and rents), dividends payable, and the current portion of long-term debt. In equation form,

current liabilities = notes payable + accounts payable + other items payable + dividends payable + the current portion of long-term debt.

Notes payable represents money that is owed and which must be repaid within a year. It is fairly inclusive because it may include lines of credit from banks that have been used, short-term bank loans, mortgage obligations, or payments on specific assets that are due within a year.

Accounts payable are short-term obligations that a business owes to suppliers, vendors, and other creditors. It may consist of all the supplies and materials that were purchased on credit.

Other items payable can include items such as the payroll and tax withholdings owed to employees or the government but which have not as of yet been paid.

Dividends payable is a term that is appropriate for businesses structured as corporations. This category represents the amount that a business plans to pay its shareholders.

The current portion of long-term debt represents how much of the long-term debt must be repaid within the upcoming fiscal year. This would include the portion of the principal that is due in this fiscal year.

The other portion of liabilities is represented by long-term liabilities. These are debts payable over a period greater than one year and include long-term debt, pension fund liability, and long-term lease obligations. In equation form,

long-term liabilities = long-term debt + pension fund liabilities + long-term lease obligations.

Total liabilities is the sum of current liabilities and long-term liabilities.

The other major component of the right-side of the balance sheet is owner's (or stockholders') equity. Owner's equity represents the value of the shareholders' ownership in a business. It is sometimes referred to as net worth. It may be composed of items such as paid in capital and retained earnings. Paid in capital is the amount of money provided by investors through the issuance of common or preferred stock.[15] **Retained earnings** is the cumulative net income that has been reinvested in a business and which has not been paid out to shareholders as dividends.[16]

The entire balance sheet and its calculations are summarized in Figure 9.2.

intangible assets

Assets that provide economic value to a business but do not have a tangible, physical presence.

current liabilities

Debts and obligations that are to be paid within the year.

notes payable

Money, such as lines of credit from banks, short-term bank loans, mortgage obligations, or payments on specific assets, that is owed and must be repaid within the year.

accounts payable

Short-term obligations that a business owes to suppliers, vendors, and other creditors.

retained earnings

The cumulative net income that has been reinvested in a business and not paid out to shareholders as dividends.

FIGURE 9.2 The Balance Sheet

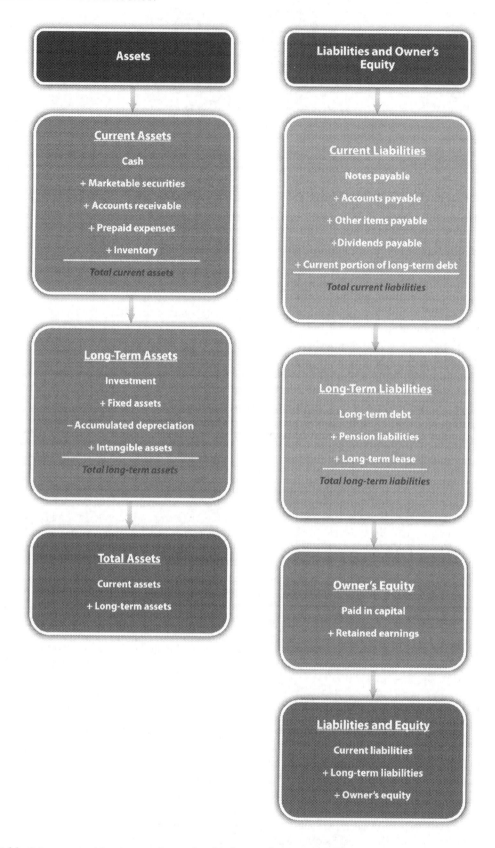

In Table 9.2, we provide six years' worth of balance sheet statements for a hypothetical small business—Acme Enterprises. It is obviously important to have such information, but what exactly might this tell us in terms of the overall success and operation of the business? We will return to these statements in Section 3 to show how those questions can be addressed with ratio analysis.

TABLE 9.2 Acme Enterprises' Balance Sheet, 2005–2010 ($ Thousands)

	December 31					
Assets	**2005**	**2006**	**2007**	**2008**	**2009**	**2010**
Cash and marketable securities	$30.0	$32.3	$34.7	$37.3	$40.1	$43.1
Accounts receivable	$100.0	$107.5	$115.6	$124.2	$133.5	$143.6
Inventories	$70.0	$75.3	$80.9	$87.0	$93.5	$100.5
Other current assets	$90.0	$96.8	$104.0	$111.8	$120.2	$129.2
Total current assets	$290.0	$311.8	$335.1	$360.3	$387.3	$416.3
Property, plant, and equipment—gross	$950.0	$1,154.5	$1,387.2	$1,654.6	$1,958.1	$2,306.2
Accumulated depreciation	$600.0	$695.0	$810.5	$949.2	$1,114.6	$1,310.4
Property, plant, and equipment—net	$350.0	$459.5	$576.7	$705.4	$843.5	$995.7
Other noncurrent assets	$160.0	$176.0	$193.6	$213.0	$234.3	$257.7
Total assets	$800.0	$947.3	$1,105.5	$1,278.6	$1,465.1	$1,669.7
Liabilities						
Accounts payable	$91.0	$97.8	$105.2	$113.0	$121.5	$130.6
Short-term debt	$150.0	$177.5	$216.3	$264.2	$328.1	$406.0
Other current liabilities	$110.0	$118.3	$127.1	$136.7	$146.9	$157.9
Total current liabilities	$351.0	$393.6	$448.6	$513.9	$596.5	$694.6
Long-term debt	$211.0	$211.0	$211.0	$211.0	$211.0	$211.0
Deferred income taxes	$50.0	$53.8	$57.8	$62.1	$66.8	$71.8
Other noncurrent liabilities	$76.0	$81.7	$87.8	$94.4	$101.5	$109.1
Total liabilities	$688.0	$740.0	$805.2	$881.4	$975.8	$1,086.5
Paid in capital	$—	$—	$—	$—	$—	$—
Retained earnings	$112.0	$207.3	$300.3	$397.2	$489.3	$583.3
Total owner's equity	$112.0	$207.3	$300.3	$397.2	$489.3	$583.3
Total liabilities + owner's equity	$800.0	$947.3	$1,105.5	$1,278.6	$1,465.1	$1,669.7

 Video Clip 9.6

Beginner's Guide to Financial Statements: Balance Sheets
An introduction to the balance sheet.

View the video online at: http://www.youtube.com/v/Nu6sCQ91HUc

Video Clip 9.7

What Is the Balance Sheet?
A voice-over PowerPoint presentation describing the balance sheet. Be aware that this is seven minutes long.

View the video online at: http://www.youtube.com/v/LOOkN14L4_c

 Video Clip 9.8

Balance Sheet: How to Explain How a Balance Sheet Works
Another description of the balance sheet.

View the video online at: http://www.youtube.com/v/KKXuDV4PdGw

2.2 The Income Statement

income statement

A report that examines the overall profitability of a firm over a particular period of time.

cost of goods sold (COGS)

All the costs associated with the direct production of goods and services that were sold during the time period.

gross profit

Income minus COGS.

Whereas the balance sheet looks at a firm at a particular point (date) in time, the **income statement** examines the overall profitability of a firm over a particular length or period of time. Normally, there are several time periods that may be used: fiscal year, fiscal quarter, or monthly. The income statement is also known as a *profit and loss statement*. It identifies all sources of revenues generated by a business and all the expenses incurred. The income statement provides the best insight into whether a business is profitable.

The income statement begins by identifying the sales or income for the designated period of time. Sales would be all the revenues derived from all the products and services sold during that time. The term *income* is sometimes used and represents all revenues and additional incomes produced by a business during the designated period. The next item in the income statement is the **cost of goods sold (COGS)**, which is composed of all costs associated with the direct production of goods and services that were sold during the time period. It would include the costs of the raw materials used to produce the goods and those costs associated with production, such as direct labor. With these two values, the first measure of profit—**gross profit**—can be calculated:

$$\text{gross profit} = \text{income} - \text{COGS}.$$

The next element in the income statement is **operating expenses**—expenses that are incurred during the normal operation of a business. Operating expenses can be broken down into four broad categories: selling expenses, general and administrative expenses, depreciation, and other overhead expenses. Selling expenses would include all salaries and commissions paid to the business's sales staff. It would also include the cost of promotions, advertising expenses, and other sales expenditures. Promotion costs might consist of costs associated with samples or giveaways. Advertising expenses would include all expenditures for print, radio, television, or Internet ads. Other sales expenditures would include money spent on meals, travel, meetings, or presentations by the sales staff. General and administrative expenses are those associated with the operation of a business beyond COGS and direct-selling expenses. Expenditures in this category would include salaries of office personnel, rent, and utilities. Depreciation was covered in the previous subsection. The balance sheet has a component designated accumulated depreciation. This is the summation of several years' worth of depreciation on assets. In the income statement, depreciation is the value for a particular time period. If you look back in Table 9.1, the annual depreciation on the vehicle was $5,000. If a business was developing an income statement for one particular year, then the depreciation would be listed as $5,000. It is a noncash expenditure expense. The last component of operating expenses would be other overhead costs—a fairly generic category that may include items such as office supplies, insurance, or a variety of services a business might use. Having identified all the components of operating expenses, one is now in a position to compute a second measure of profitability—**operating profit**, which is sometimes referred to as earnings before interest and taxes (EBIT):

$$\text{operating profit (EBIT)} = \text{gross profit} - \text{operating expenses.}$$

The next section of the income statement is designated **other revenues and expenses**. This segment would include other nonoperational revenues (such as interest on cash or investments) and interest payments on loans and other debt instruments. When the other revenues and expenses are subtracted from the operating profit, one is left with **earnings before taxes (EBT)**:

$$\text{EBT} = \text{operating profit} - \text{other revenues and expenses.}$$

Taxes are then computed on the EBT and then subtracted. This includes all federal, state, and local tax payments that a business is obligated to pay. This brings us to our last measure of profitability—**net profit**:

$$\text{net profit} = \text{EBT} - \text{taxes.}$$

If a business does not pay out dividends, the net profit becomes an addition to retained earnings. The format of the income statement is summarized in Figure 9.3. The income statement is the item that most individuals look at to determine the success of business operations. In Table 9.3, the income statements for Acme Enterprises are given for the period 2005 to 2010.

operating expenses

Expenses that are incurred during the normal operation of a business.

operating profit

Gross profit minus operating expenses.

other revenues and expenses

Other nonoperational revenues and interest payments on loans and other debt instruments.

earnings before taxes (EBT)

Operating profit minus other revenue and expenses.

net profit

EBT minus taxes.

FIGURE 9.3   The Income Statement

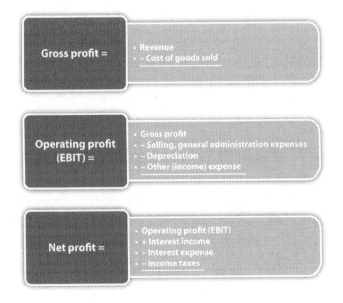

TABLE 9.3 Acme Enterprises' Income Statement, 2005–10 ($ Thousands)

	2005	2006	2007	2008	2009	2010
Sales	$1,000.0	$1,075.0	$1,155.6	$1,242.3	$1,335.5	$1,435.6
COGS	$500.0	$537.5	$566.3	$608.7	$641.0	$689.1
Gross operating profit	$500.0	$537.5	$589.4	$633.6	$694.4	$746.5
Selling and general administrative expenses	$250.0	$268.8	$288.9	$310.6	$333.9	$358.9
Depreciation	$95.0	$115.5	$138.7	$165.5	$195.8	$230.6
Other net (income)/expenses	$0.0	$0.0	$0.0	$0.0	$0.0	$0.0
EBIT	$155.0	$153.3	$161.7	$157.5	$164.8	$157.0
Interest income	$2.1	$2.3	$2.4	$2.6	$2.8	$3.0
Interest expense	$10.5	$12.4	$15.1	$18.5	$23.0	$28.4
Pretax income	$146.6	$143.1	$149.0	$141.7	$144.6	$131.6
Income taxes	$51.31	$50.10	$52.16	$49.58	$50.61	$46.06
Net income	$95.29	$93.04	$96.87	$92.08	$93.99	$85.54
Dividends	$—	$—	$—	$—	$—	$—
Addition to retained earnings	$95.29	$93.04	$96.87	$92.08	$93.99	$85.54

 Video Clip 9.9

What Is the Income Statement?

A basic introduction to income statements.

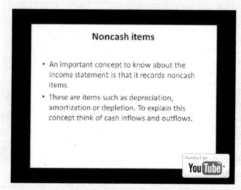

View the video online at: http://www.youtube.com/v/tDc3KulcE9Q

 Video Clip 9.10

Income Statement

A further description of an income statement.

View the video online at: http://www.youtube.com/v/Bpcn7QYOTx0

2.3 The Cash-Flow Statement

Customer satisfaction, employee satisfaction and cash flow the three most important indicators for business.[17]

  - *Jack Welch*

The third component of financial statements is the **cash-flow statement**. There are two types of cash-flow statements—one examines cash flows for a given period (historic), and the other is a projection of future cash flows. The **historic cash-flow statement** is similar to the income statement in that it looks at cash inflows and cash outflows for a business during a specified period of time. Like the income statement, these periods of time can be the fiscal year, the fiscal quarter, or a month. The **cash-flow projections statement** attempts to identify cash flows into a firm and cash flows from a firm for some future period. This projection is extremely important because it may identify future subperiods in which a firm is producing a negative cash flow—where cash outflows exceed cash inflows.

From the standpoint of a small business owner, cash-flow statements provide insight into where cash flows are coming and going. The cash-flow projections statement may be the most important component of all the financial statements. Its importance stems from the fact that the flow of cash into a firm may not be synchronized with its cash outflows. Should there be a significant mismatch with cash outflows being significantly higher than cash inflows, a business may be in great difficulty with respect to meeting its current obligations, such as payroll, paying suppliers, and meeting short-term creditors. As we will see, cash-flow projection statements require several forecasts. These are discussed later in this section.

At some point, many businesses will experience negative cash flow. In fact, a negative cash flow is quite common in start-up operations and high-growth businesses where there is a pressing need for capital expenditures, research and development expenditures, and other significant cash outflows. One can also see the recurring presence of negative cash flows in businesses with seasonal sales. Negative cash flows can be covered by short-term borrowing. However, this type of borrowing brings up two important issues. First, any type of borrowing raises the overall debt level of a business, which might have an impact on the interest rate on the debt. Second, when a negative cash flow exists either because of an unforeseen exigency or because a business owner has failed to properly conduct a cash-flow projection analysis, a lender might look at a business in a jaundiced manner, which could have long-term consequences for a business.

A careful examination of the cash-flow statement could illustrate a point that has been mentioned several times in this book: there can be a significant difference between positive cash flow and profit. In looking at the income statement, one could find a positive net income (profit) and then examine the cash-flow statement and discover that a business has a significant negative cash flow. The cash-flow statement specifically maps out where cash is flowing into a firm and where it flows out. A properly developed cash-flow statement will show if a business will be generating enough cash to continue operations, whether it has sufficient cash for new investments, and whether it can pay its obligations. As previously stated, many of the uninitiated will look singularly at profits, while those who have greater expertise in business will always believe that cash is king.

As a way of visualization, the cash-flow statement bears some similarity to the bank statement you may receive at the end of the month. A bank statement shows the beginning cash balance, deposits (cash inflows), and checks you have written (cash outflows) for that month. Hopefully, you have a positive cash flow—cash inflows are greater than cash outflows—and you have not bounced any checks. Unlike the bank statement, the cash-flow statement is broken into three major categories: operations, financing, and investing. Cash flow from operations examines the cash inflows from all revenues, plus interest and dividend payments from investments held by a business. It then identifies the cash outflows for paying suppliers, employees, taxes, and other expenses. Cash flow from investing examines the impact of selling or acquiring current and fixed assets. Cash flow from financing examines the impact on the cash position from the changes in the number of shares and changes in the short and long-term debt position of a firm.

Cash inflows from operating activities consist of the following:

- Cash derived from the sale of goods or services
- Cash derived from accounts receivable
- Any cash derived from interest or dividends
- Any other cash derived that is not identified with financing or investments

The cash outflows from operating activities consist of the following:

- Cash outlays for goods purchased in the creation of goods and services
- Cash outlays for payment to suppliers

cash-flow statement

Maps out where cash is flowing into a firm and where it flows out and recognizes that there may be a significant difference between profits and cash flow.

historic cash-flow statement

A statement similar to the income statement in that it looks at cash inflows and cash outflows for a business during a specified period of time.

cash-flow projections statement

A statement that attempts to identify cash flows into a firm and cash flows from a firm for some future period. It recognizes that there may be a significant difference between profits and cash flow.

- Cash outlays to employees
- Cash paid for taxes or interest paid to creditors

Financing focuses on the cash flows associated with debt or equity. Some of the cash inflows associated with financing activities consist of the following:

- Cash from the sale of a company's stock
- Cash received from borrowing (debt)

Cash outflows associated with financing consist of the following:

- Cash outlays to repay principal on long- and short-term debt
- Cash outlays to repurchase preferred stocks
- Cash outlays to pay for dividends on either common or preferred stock

The third category is investing. The sources of cash flow from investing activities consist of the following:

- Cash received from the sale of assets
- Cash received from the sale of equity investments
- Cash received from collections on a debt instrument

Cash outflows associated with investing activities consist of the following:

- Cash outlays to acquire a debt instrument of another business
- Cash payments to buy equity interest in other businesses
- Cash outlays to purchase a productive asset

A schematic of the cash-flow statement's three areas of analysis is presented in Figure 9.4.

FIGURE 9.4 Cash Flow Breakdown

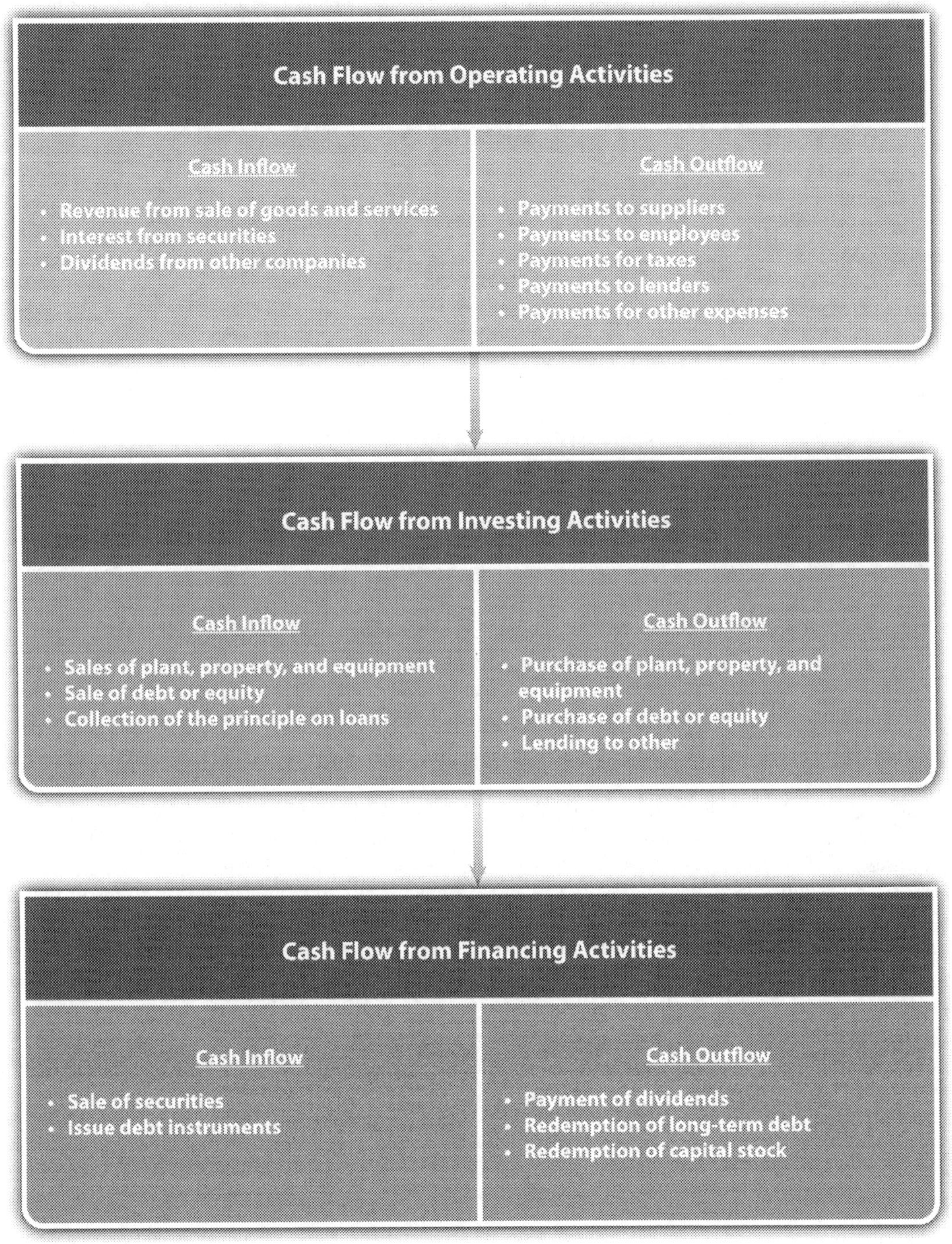

Cash Flow from Operating Activities	
Cash Inflow	**Cash Outflow**
• Revenue from sale of goods and services • Interest from securities • Dividends from other companies	• Payments to suppliers • Payments to employees • Payments for taxes • Payments to lenders • Payments for other expenses

Cash Flow from Investing Activities	
Cash Inflow	**Cash Outflow**
• Sales of plant, property, and equipment • Sale of debt or equity • Collection of the principle on loans	• Purchase of plant, property, and equipment • Purchase of debt or equity • Lending to other

Cash Flow from Financing Activities	
Cash Inflow	**Cash Outflow**
• Sale of securities • Issue debt instruments	• Payment of dividends • Redemption of long-term debt • Redemption of capital stock

Cash-flow projection statements are about the state of future cash flows, which means they require forecasts. This translates into multiple forecasts—sales forecasts, forecasts of expenses, forecasts for necessary investments, and forecasts for a business's financing requirements. The importance of forecasts for planning is discussed in Chapter 5.

The most common approach for cash-flow forecasting in small businesses centers on projections of cash receipts and disbursements. These projections are often based on recent past data. We will demonstrate—shortly—this approach through an extensive example. This approach is generally limited to short and midterm forecasts (i.e., three to twelve months). There are other approaches to cash-flow forecasting; however, given the relative complexity of these approaches, they are often used only by larger and more sophisticated businesses. These other approaches include the adjusted net income method, the pro forma balance sheet method, and the accrual reversal method.[18]

The concept of cash-flow projection forecasting can be illustrated by using an example. Alex McLellan runs Soft Serve Services—a business that repairs and services soft-serve ice cream machines.

His clients include ice cream parlors, resorts, and outlets at malls. Alex is a former engineer and somewhat methodical in developing his calculations for future budgets. He will be operating on the assumption that his business will be limited to his current locale. Alex has followed the same pattern for forecasting cash flows for years. First, he gathers together from his records his monthly and annual sales for the last five years, which are provided in Table 9.4.

TABLE 9.4 Sales Data for Soft Serve Services

	2006	2007	2008	2009	2010
January	$20,135	$20,562	$21,131	$22,657	$23,602
February	$19,545	$19,739	$19,852	$22,154	$22,307
March	$24,451	$24,360	$24,594	$26,361	$27,590
April	$22,789	$23,374	$24,000	$26,220	$32,968
May	$25,986	$28,531	$27,099	$30,057	$34,834
June	$28,357	$30,468	$32,893	$34,168	$37,078
July	$32,650	$35,307	$36,830	$40,321	$46,899
August	$34,488	$37,480	$40,202	$44,890	$52,042
September	$26,356	$27,909	$29,317	$32,917	$33,309
October	$24,211	$22,795	$23,719	$24,339	$25,691
November	$21,722	$22,272	$22,147	$23,080	$23,466
December	$22,017	$22,454	$28,321	$30,468	$33,583
Annual sales	$302,706	$315,252	$330,105	$357,631	$393,368

Using these data, Alex was able to calculate the growth rate in sales for the last four of the five years. As an example:

growth rate 2007 = (sales 2007 − sales 2006) / (sales 2006) = ($315,252 − $302,706) / ($302,706) = ($12,546) / ($302,706) = 4.14 percent.

Although the average of the four annual growth rates was 6.8 percent (the annual growth rates were 4.14 percent in 2007, 4.71 percent in 2008, 8.34 percent in 2009, and 9.99 percent in 2010, thus having an average of 6.8 percent), Alex believes that the last two years were unusually good, and the growth rate for 2011 would be slightly lower at a rate of 6.5 percent. This rate of growth would mean that his estimate for sales in 2011 would be $418,937, which comes from the following:

annual sales 2011 = annual sales 2010 × (1 + growth rate 2011) = $393,368 × (1.065).

He knows from experience that his sales are quite seasonal, as illustrated in Figure 9.5. Alex believes that there is a high degree of consistency in this seasonality of sales across the years. So he computes (using a spreadsheet program) what percentage of annual sales occurs in each month. This calculation for January 2006 would be given as follows:

percentage of annual sales for January 2006 = (January 2006 sales) / (annual sales 2006) = ($20,135) / ($302,706) = 6.65 percent.

His analysis for each month in each of the five years is provided in Table 9.5, as are the averages for each month.

FIGURE 9.5 Seasonality in Sales

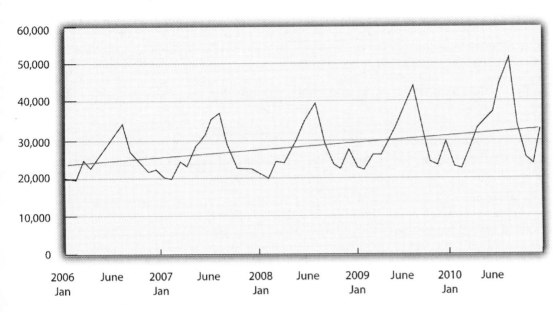

TABLE 9.5 Monthly Sales as a Percentage of Annual Sales

	2006 (%)	2007 (%)	2008 (%)	2009 (%)	2010 (%)	Average (%)
January	6.65	6.52	6.40	6.34	6.00	6.38
February	6.46	6.26	6.01	6.19	5.67	6.12
March	8.08	7.73	7.45	7.37	7.01	7.53
April	7.53	7.41	7.27	7.33	8.38	7.59
May	8.58	9.05	8.21	8.40	8.86	8.62
June	9.37	9.66	9.96	9.55	9.43	9.60
July	10.79	11.20	11.16	11.27	11.92	11.27
August	11.39	11.89	12.18	12.55	13.23	12.25
September	8.71	8.85	8.88	9.20	8.47	8.82
October	8.00	7.23	7.19	6.81	6.53	7.15
November	7.18	7.06	6.71	6.45	5.97	6.67
December	7.27	7.12	8.58	8.52	8.54	8.01

Alex was the able to estimate sales for January 2011 in the following manner:[19]

January 2011 sales = annual sales 2011 × January percentage = ($418,937) × (6.38 percent) = $26,737.

Using the same approach, he was able to compute forecasted sales for February and March. To maintain sales, Alex offers his customers a rather generous credit policy. He asks them to pay 50 percent of the bill in the month in which the work is done; another 35 percent of the bill in the following month, and the remaining 15 percent of the bill two months after the work has been completed. For Alex to project cash inflows for January, he would need to consider sales from the two prior months—December and November. His projected cash inflows for January would be determined as follows:[20]

November 2010 sales = $23,466

December 2010 sales = $33,583

January 2011 sales = $26,737

cash inflow from November 2010 sales = ($23,466) × 15 percent = $3,520

cash inflow from December 2010 sales = ($33,583) × 35 percent = $11,754

cash inflow from January 2011 sales = ($26,737) × 50 percent = $13,368 total cash inflows from operations = sum of cash inflows for three months = $28,642.

Alex then estimates his cash outflows from operations. From past experience, he knows that the purchases of parts and materials run approximately 50 percent of the dollar value of his sales. However, because of delays in acquiring parts and materials, he must order them in advance. He has to anticipate what sales would be the following month and has to place a purchase order predicated on that value. Further, 60 percent of that dollar value is in that month and the remaining 40 percent is in the following month. This can be illustrated for January 2011. To determine the purchases of parts and materials in January, he begins with his forecast for sales in February 2011.

February 2011 sales = $25,637

parts and materials purchases in January 2011 = 50 percent of February 2011 sales = 50 percent × $25,637 = $12,819.

He is obligated to pay 60 percent of this amount in January 2011 and the remaining 40 percent in February 2011. This also means that his cash outlay in January 2011 must include a payment for 40 percent of December's purchases.

parts and materials purchases in December 2011 = 50 percent of January 2011 sales = 50 percent × $26,737 = $13,369

parts and materials cash outlay in January 2011 = 60 percent of purchases January 2011 + 40 percent of purchases December 2010

parts and materials cash outlay in January 2011 = (60 percent × $12,819) + (40 percent × $13,369) = $13,038.

In addition to purchasing parts and materials, Alex has to consider his operational expenses, which include wages, payroll taxes, office supplies, repairs, advertising, and expenses related to automobiles, phone bills, rent, utilities, expenses associated with accounting services, and taxes. These are itemized in Table 9.6. Adding in these expenses brings his total cash outflow $19,864.

For January 2001, he has no cash inflows or cash outflows with respect to either investment activities or financing activities. This means that his total cash flow for January 2011 represents the difference between cash inflows and outflows for operational activities. His cash flow for January 2011 was a positive value of $8,778. Because he ended December 2010 with a cash position of $3,177, the addition of this $8,778 brings his cash position at the end of January 2011 to $11,955. His bank, with which he has an open line of credit, requires that he maintain a minimum of $2,500 in his cash account each month. Should Alex drop below this amount, his bank will lend him—automatically—up to $5,000.

It is useful to examine the rest of his projections (see Table 9.6). February 2011 follows much as January 2011. Alex was able to produce a positive net cash flow in February of $5,669, which brought his ending cash position at the end of February 2011 to $17,624.

Unlike the other months of 2011, Alex planned on producing cash flows with respect to investment activities in March 2011. He planned on selling an asset to a friend and anticipated a positive cash flow of $500 from this sale. He also planned on purchasing a used van in March 2011 and estimated that the price would be $21,000. His intention was to pay for the van from his cash account and not take out a car loan. His cash outflows for March 2011 were a negative $16,075. With the bank's requirement of maintaining a $2,500 minimum balance, this meant that Alex activated the automatic borrowing option from his bank to the amount of $950. It required some effort on Alex's part to build the cash-flow spreadsheet, but it enabled him to examine various options, such as the impact of deferring the purchase of the van until May 2011. Although any cash-flow spreadsheet is dependent on the accuracy of forecasts, it is a mechanism by which a small business owner can examine various scenarios and determine the possible impact of those scenarios on his or her overall cash flow.

TABLE 9.6 Cash-Flow Projections for the First Quarter of 2011

	November	December	January	February	March
Cash Flow from Operating Activities					
Cash on hand at end of month		$3,177	$11,955	$17,624	$1,550
Cash Inflow from Operations					
Sales	$23,466	$33,583	$26,737	$25,637	$31,537
Cash flow from month of sales			$13,369	$12,818	$15,769
Cash flow from prior month's sales			$11,754	$9,358	$8,973
Cash flow from two month's prior sales			$3,520	$5,037	$4,011
Total cash inflow from operations			$28,642	$27,214	$28,752
Parts Purchases					
Cash outflow for this month's purchases			$7,691	$9,461	$9,533
Cash outflow for prior month's purchases			$5,347	$5,127	$6,307
Gross wages (excludes withdrawals)			$4,000	$4,000	$4,000
Payroll expenses (taxes, etc.)			$150	$150	$150
Outside services			$—	$—	$—
Supplies (office and operating)			$50	$50	$50
Repairs and maintenance			$—	$—	$450
Advertising			$100	$200	$250
Auto, delivery, and travel			$120	$150	$180
Accounting and legal			$200	$200	$200
Rent			$1,650	$1,650	$1,650
Telephone			$65	$65	$65
Utilities			$325	$325	$325
Insurance			$166	$166	$166
Taxes (real estate, etc.)			$—	$—	$1,000
Interest			$—		
Other expenses			$—	$—	$—
Total cash outflows from operations			$19,864	$21,544	$24,327
Sale of asset			$—	$—	$500
Sale of debt or equity			$—	$—	$—
Collection of principal on a loan			$—	$—	$—
Total cash flow from investing activities			$—	$—	$500
Purchase of plant, property, and equipment			$—	$—	$21,000
Purchase of debt			$—	$—	$—
Total cash outflows from investing			$—	$—	$21,000
Sales of securities or equity			$—	$—	$—
Issue of debt instruments			$—	$—	$—
Total cash inflow from financing activities			$—	$—	$—
Payment of dividends			$—	$—	$—
Redemption of long-term debt			$—	$—	$—
Total cash outflows from financing			$—	$—	$—
Net cash flow			$8,778	$5,669	$(16,075)
Required cash balance	$2,500	$2,500	$2,500	$2,500	$2,500
Required borrowing			$—	$—	$(950)

Video Clip 9.11

Cash-Flow Analysis
A discussion of cash flow.

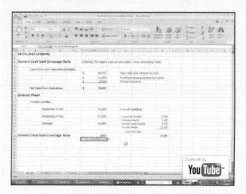

View the video online at: http://www.youtube.com/v/H_9tRSgSnCg

KEY TAKEAWAYS

- To truly understand how well a business is doing requires an ability to understand the financial statements of the business.
- The balance sheet shows what a business owns and what claims are on the business.
- The income statement shows how profitable a business is and identifies the expenses of the business.
- Cash flow is the lifeblood of a business's operation.
- Cash-flow projections are vital for any business.

EXERCISES

Edwina Haskell was an accomplished high school student who looked forward to attending Southern New England University (SNEU). SNEU was unique in that it operated on a trimester basis, its policy was to actively foster independent development among the students. Edwina's mother and father each own their own small businesses. Soon after freshman orientation at SNEU, Edwina recognized a need among the students that could be the basis for developing a small business. Freshman students could not bring their cars on the campus. In effect, they were confined to the dorm; if they wished to travel, they had to take school-provided buses that operated on a fixed schedule. Further, the university's cafeteria closed at eight in the evening. Students who wanted to have some food or snacks after 8:00 p.m. had to call local restaurants that delivered. The few restaurants in the neighborhood around SNEU that had delivery services often were late in their deliveries, and hot food, such as pizza, was frequently delivered cold.

Edwina felt that there was a niche market on the campus. She believed that students would be interested in ordering sandwiches, snacks, and sodas from a fellow student provided that the food could be delivered in a timely fashion. After talking with several students in her dorm complex, she believed that offering a package of a sandwich, a soda, and a small snack, such as potato chips, for $5 and a guaranteed delivery of 15 minutes or less would be a winner. Because her dorm complex consisted of four large adjoining buildings that house nearly 1,600 students, she felt that there would be sufficient demand to make the concept profitable. She talked about this concept with her roommates and with her parents. Her roommates were willing to help prepare the sandwiches and deliver them. She planned on paying each of them $250 per trimester for taking orders, making sandwiches, and delivering them. All three roommates, whom she knew from high school, were willing to be paid at the end of the trimester.

Edwina recognized that for this business plan to work, she would have to have a sufficient inventory of cold cuts, lettuce, tomatoes, soda, chips, and condiments to be able to meet student demands. The small refrigerators in the dorm rooms would not be sufficient. After talking to her parents, they were willing to help her set up her business. They would lend her $1,000 to buy a larger refrigerator to place in her dorm room. She did not have to repay this loan until she graduated in four years, but her parents wanted her to appreciate the challenges of operating a small business. They set up several conditions. First, although she did not have to pay back the $1,000 for the refrigerator for four years, she had to pay interest on this "loan." She had to repay 3 percent of this loan each trimester. Further, they reminded her that although she could pay her friends at the end of the semester, she would need funds to buy the cold cuts, bread, rolls, soda, snacks, condiments, and supplies such as foil to wrap the sandwiches, plus plates and paper bags. Although Edwina was putting $500 of her own money into her business, her parents felt that she might need an infusion of cash during the first year (i.e., the first three trimesters). They were willing to operate as her bank—lending her money, if needed, during the trimesters. However, she had to pay the loan(s) back by the end of the year. They also agreed that the loan(s) would be at a rate of 2 percent per trimester.

Within the first three weeks of her first trimester at SNEU, Edwina purchased the $1,000 refrigerator with the money provided by her parents and installed it in her dorm. She also went out and purchased $180 worth of supplies consisting of paper bags; paper plates; and plastic knives, spoons, and forks. She paid for these supplies out of her original $500 personal investment. She and her roommates would go out once or twice a week, using the SNEU bus system to buy what they thought would be the required amount of cold cuts, bread, rolls, and condiments. The first few weeks' worth of supplies were purchased out of the remainder of the $500. Students paid in cash for the sandwiches. After the first two weeks, Edwina would pay for the food supplies out of the cash from sales.

In the first trimester, Edwina and her roommates sold 640 sandwich packages, generating revenue of $3,200. During this first trimester, she purchased $1,710 worth of food supplies. She used $1,660 to make the 640 sandwich packages. Fortunately, the $50 of supplies were condiments and therefore would last during the two-week break between the trimesters. Only $80 worth of the paper products were used for the 640 sandwich packages. Edwina spent $75 putting up posters and flyers around the campus promoting her new business. She anticipated that the tax rate would be approximately 35 percent of her earnings before taxes. She estimated this number at the end of the first trimester and put that money away so as to be able to pay her tax bill.

During the two weeks off between the first and second trimester, Edwina and her roommates talked about how they could improve business operations. Several students had asked about the possibility of having warm sandwiches. Edwina decided that she would purchase two Panini makers. So at the beginning of the second trimester, she tapped into her parents' line of credit for two Panini grills, which in total cost $150. To make sure that the sandwiches would be delivered warm, she and her roommates spent $100 on insulated wrappings. The $100 came from cash. The second trimester proved to be even more successful. The business sold 808 sandwiches, generating revenue of $4,040. During this second trimester, the business purchased $2,100 worth of food supplies, using $2,020 of that to actually create the 808 sandwich packages. They estimated that during the second trimester, they used $101 worth of supplies in creating the sandwich packages.

There was only a one-week break between the second and third trimesters, and the young women were quite busy in developing ideas on how to further expand the business. One of the first decisions was to raise the semester salary of each roommate to $300 apiece. More and more students had been asking for a greater selection of warm sandwiches. Edwina and her roommates decided to do some cooking in the dorms so as to be able to provide meatball and sausage sandwiches. Edwina once again tapped into her parents' line of credit to purchase $275 worth of cooking supplies. One of the problems they noticed was that sometimes students would place calls to order a sandwich package, but the phones were busy. Edwina hired a fellow student to develop a website where students could place an order and select the time that they would like a sandwich package to be delivered. The cost of creating and operating this website for this third trimester was $300.

This last semester of Edwina's freshman year proved to be the most successful in terms of sales. They were able to fulfill orders for 1,105 sandwich packages, generating revenue of $5,525. Edwina determined that the direct cost of food for these sandwich packages came out to be $2,928.25. The direct cost of paper supplies was $165.75. At the end of her freshman year, Edwina repaid her parents the $425 that came from her credit line that was used to purchase the Panini makers and the cooking utensils.

1. Prepare a beginning balance sheet for the first day of Edwina's business.
2. Prepare income statements for the end of each trimester.
3. Prepare balance sheets for the end of each semester.

3. FINANCIAL RATIO ANALYSIS

LEARNING OBJECTIVES

1. Understand why the numbers found on a balance sheet and an income statement may not be enough to properly evaluate the performance of a business.
2. Understand the concept of financial ratios and the different categories of financial ratios.
3. Acquire the ability to calculate financial ratios and interpret their meaning.

One can say that figures lie. But figures, when used in financial arguments, seem to have the bad habit of expressing a small part of the truth forcibly, and neglecting the other, as do some people we know.[21]
- *Fred Schwed*

Section 1 discusses the differences between managerial accounting and financial accounting. Managerial accounting focuses on providing information that is useful for the managers of a firm. Financial accounting provides information to interested external constituencies. Both use information derived from financial statements. These numbers, however, may not provide a singular insight into the overall economic effectiveness of any particular business. These numbers must be placed in some form of context. As an example, suppose you are told that a particular business earned $2 million worth of profit last year. Obviously, earning a $2 million profit is better than a $1 million profit and certainly better than a $2 million loss. However, you are still left with the question of exactly how good that $2 million profit is. After all, if you were told that Walmart made only $2 million profit last year, you would likely be concerned with respect to the management capability and performance of Walmart. Making only $2 million profit on revenues in excess of $400 billion worth of sales would not be at all impressive. However, if you were told that a mom-and-pop grocery store made $2 million profit last year based on $4 million of sales, you would be amazed at that mom-and-pop store and hold them in considerable esteem for their management capability.

One way of putting financial data into a comparative context is known as financial ratio analysis. From a financial accounting standpoint, ratio analysis enables external constituencies to evaluate the performance of a firm with respect to other firms in that particular industry. This is sometimes referred to as comparative ratio analysis. From a managerial accounting standpoint, ratio analysis can assist a management team to identify areas that might be of concern. The management team can track the performance on these ratios across time to determine whether the indicators are improving or declining. This is referred to as trend ratio analysis. There are literally scores of financial ratios that can be calculated to evaluate a firm's performance.

Financial ratios can be grouped into five categories: **liquidity ratios**, **financial leverage ratios**, **profitability ratios**, **asset management or efficiency ratios**, and **market value ratios**. Because many small businesses are not publicly held and have no publicly traded stock, market ratios play no role in analyzing a small firm's performance. This section will review some of the most commonly used ratios in each category.

Liquidity ratios provide insight into a firm's ability to meet its short-term debt obligations. It draws information from a business's current assets and current liabilities that are found on the balance sheet. The most commonly used liquidity ratio is the current ratio given by the formula

$$\text{current assets / current liabilities.}$$

The normal rule of thumb is that the current ratio should be greater than one if a firm is to remain solvent. The greater this ratio is above one, the greater its ability to meet short-term obligations. As with all ratios, any value needs to be placed in context. This is often done by looking at standard ratio values for the same industry. These ratios are provided by Dun and Bradstreet; these data are also available on websites, such as Bizstats.com.

Another ratio used to evaluate a business's ability to meet in short-term debt obligations is the quick ratio—also known as the acid test. It is a more stringent version of the current ratio that recognizes that inventory is the least liquid of all current assets. A firm might find it impossible to immediately transfer the dollar value of inventory into cash to meet short-term obligations. Thus the quick ratio, in effect, values the inventory dollar value at zero. The quick ratio is given by the following formula:

$$\text{current assets} - \text{inventory / current liabilities.}$$

Using the data provided in the balance sheet for Acme Enterprises (Table 9.2), we can compute the current ratio and the quick ratio. The results for Acme Enterprises and its industry's means are provided in Table 9.7.

TABLE 9.7 Liquidity Ratio Results

	2005 (%)	2006 (%)	2007 (%)	2008 (%)	2009(%)	2010 (%)
Acme's current ratio	0.83	0.79	0.75	0.70	0.65	0.60
Industry's current ratio	1.15	1.08	1.04	1.02	1.03	1.01
Acme's quick ratio	0.63	0.60	0.57	0.53	0.49	0.45
Industry's quick ratio	1.04	1.02	0.98	0.95	0.94	0.91

One should immediately notice that this business appears to be in serious trouble. None of the current ratios are above of value of 1.0, which indicates that the business would be unable to meet short-term obligations to its creditors should they have to be paid. Acme's current ratios are below the industry's average values; however, it should be noted that the industry's values are quite close to one. Further, the current ratio values for Acme and the industry are declining, but Acme's are declining quite significantly. This indicates the financially precarious position of the firm is growing steadily worse. The quick ratio shows an even direr situation should the firm not be able to sell off its inventory at market value. Acme's quick ratio values are well below the industry's average. Without these two ratios, a quick perusal of the total current assets of Acme Enterprises would result in a false impression that the firm is growing in a healthy fashion and current assets are rising.

Financial leverage ratios provide information on a firm's ability to meet its total and long-term debt obligations. It draws on information from both the balance sheet and the income statement. The first of these ratios—the debt ratio—illustrates the extent to which a business's assets are financed with debt. The formula for the debt ratio is as follows:

$$\text{total debt / total assets.}$$

A variation on the debt ratio is the ratio of debt to the total owner's equity (the debt-to-equity ratio). As with the other ratios, one cannot target a specific, desirable value for the debt-to-equity ratio. Median values will vary significantly across different industries. The automobile industry, which is rather capital intensive, has debt-to-equity ratios above two. Other industries, such as personal computers, may have debt-to-equity ratios under 0.5.[22] The formula for the debt-to-equity ratio is as follows:

$$\text{total debt / total owner's equity.}$$

One can refine this ratio by examining only the long-term portion of total debt to the owner's equity. Comparing these two debt-to-equity ratios gives insight into the extent to which a firm is using long-term debt versus short-term debt. The formula for the long-term debt-to-owner's equity ratio is as follows:

long-term debt / total owner's equity.

The interest coverage ratio examines the ability of a firm to cover or meet the interest payments that are due in a designated period. The formula for the interest coverage ratio is as follows:

EBIT / total interest charges.

times interest earned ratio

A highly effective measure to determine a business's ability to meet it debt obligations. It is given by times interest earned = earnings before interest and taxes (EBIT) / interest charges.

The financial leverage ratios for Acme and its industry are provided in Table 9.8. Interestingly, Acme's debt-to-total-assets ratio has declined over the last six years. Further, its ratio has always been lower than the industry average in every year. This stands in contrast to the liquidity ratios. The business's debt-to-equity ratio has declined precipitously over the last six years and was significantly lower than the industry averages. The same is true for the long-term debt-to-equity ratios. These ratios have declined for several reasons. The total assets of the firm have doubled over the last six years, and equity has grown by a factor of five while the long-term debt has remained constant. It would appear that the firm has been financing its growth with short-term debt and its own profits. However, one should note that the **times interest earned ratio** has declined dramatically, falling to approximately half the level of the industry average in 2010. This indicates that the firm has less ability to meet its debt obligations. In conjunction with the results of the other ratios, one would say that Acme has relied, excessively, on its short-term debt and should take actions to return to a firmer financial footing.

TABLE 9.8 Financial Leverage Ratios Results

	2005 (%)	2006 (%)	2007 (%)	2008 (%)	2009 (%)	2010 (%)
Acme's debt-to-total assets ratio	0.86	0.78	0.73	0.69	0.67	0.65
Industry's debt-to-total assets ratio	1.01	0.97	0.95	0.92	0.89	0.86
Acme's debt-to-equity ratio	6.14	3.57	2.68	2.22	1.99	1.86
Industry's debt-to-equity ratio	3.31	3.25	3.67	3.11	2.96	2.65
Acme's long-term debt-to-equity ratio	1.88	1.02	0.70	0.53	0.43	0.36
Industry's long-term debt-to-equity ratio	1.52	1.54	1.42	1.32	1.27	1.12
Acme's times interest earned ratio	14.76	12.34	10.68	8.52	7.17	5.52
Industry's times interest earned ratio	11.55	11.61	10.95	10.65	10.43	10.01

The next grouping of ratios is the profitability ratios. Essentially, these ratios look at the amount of profit that is being generated by each dollar of sales (revenue). Remember, from the review of the income statement, we can identify three different measures of profit: gross profit, operating profit, and net profit. Each measure of profit can be examined with respect to the net sales of a business, and each can give us a different insight into the overall efficiency of a firm in generating profit.

The first profitability ratio examines how much gross profit is generated by each dollar of revenue and is given by the following formula:

gross profit margin = gross profit / revenue.

The next examines operating profit per dollar of sales and is calculated in the following manner:

operating profit margin = operating profit / revenue.

Lastly, the net profit margin is the one that is mostly used to evaluate the overall profitability of a business. It is determined as follows:

net profit margin = net profit / revenue.

The profitability ratios for Acme and its industry are provided in Table 9.9. Acme has seen a slight increase in its gross profit margin over the last six years, which indicates a reduction in either direct labor or direct materials costs. Acme's gross profit margin is slightly lower, across the six years, than the industry's mean values. Acme's operating profit margins have declined, particularly since 2008. This would indicate, in light of an increasing gross profit margin, that its operating expenses have increased proportionately. Acme's operating profit margins had parity with its industry until 2008. The most troublesome results may be the net profit margins, which experienced a one-third decline over the last six years. Although the industry's net profit margins have declined, they have not done so at the same rate as those for Acme. These results indicate that Acme needs to carefully review its operational expenses with a clear intention to reduce them.

CHAPTER 9 ACCOUNTING AND CASH FLOW

TABLE 9.9 Profitability Ratios Results

	2005 (%)	2006 (%)	2007 (%)	2008 (%)	2009 (%)	2010 (%)
Acme's gross profit margin	50.0	50.0	51.0	51.0	52.0	52.0
Industry's gross profit margin	51.2	51.3	51.6	51.5	53.2	53.1
Acme's operating profit margin	15.5	14.3	14.0	12.7	12.3	10.9
Industry's operating profit margin	14.7	14.1	14.2	13.2	13.0	13.2
Acme's net profit margin	9.5	8.7	8.4	7.4	7.0	6.0
Industry's net profit margin	9.2	8.9	8.5	8.4	8.1	7.9

The last category of financial ratios is the asset management or efficiency ratios. These ratios are designed to show how well a business is using its assets. These ratios are extremely important for management to determine its own efficiency. There are many different activity or efficiency ratios. Here we will examine just a few. The sales-to-inventory ratio computes the number of dollars of sales generated by each dollar of inventory. Firms that are able to generate greater sales volume for a given level of inventory are perceived as being more efficient. This ratio is determined as follows:

$$\text{sales to inventory} = \text{sales} / \text{inventory}.$$

There are other efficiency ratios that look at how well a business is managing its inventory. Some look at the number of days of inventory on hand; others look at the number of times inventory is turned over during the year. Both can be used to measure the overall efficiency of the inventory policy of a firm. For simplicity's sake, these ratios will not be reviewed in this text.

The sales-to-fixed-asset ratio is another efficiency measure that looks at the number of dollars of sales generated by a business's fixed assets. Again, one is looking for a larger value than the industry average because this would indicate that a business is more efficient in using its fixed assets. This ratio is determined as follows:

$$\text{sales to fixed assets} = \text{sales} / \text{fixed assets}.$$

Another commonly used efficiency ratio is the days-in-receivables ratio. This ratio shows the average number of days it takes to collect accounts receivables. The desired trend for this ratio is a reduction, indicating that a firm is being paid more quickly by its customers. This ratio is determined as follows:

$$\text{days in receivables} = \text{accounts receivable} / (\text{sales} / 365).$$

The 365 in the denominator represents the number of days in a year. A summary of the activity ratios for Acme and the industry is provided in Table 9.10.

TABLE 9.10 Efficiency Ratios Results

	2005 (%)	2006 (%)	2007 (%)	2008 (%)	2009 (%)	2010 (%)
Acme's sales to inventory	14.3	14.3	14.3	14.3	14.3	14.3
Industry's sales to inventory	16.2	15.7	15.3	14.9	14.3	13.7
Acme's sales to fixed assets	8.57	7.02	6.01	5.28	4.75	4.33
Industry's sales to fixed assets	7.64	7.12	6.78	6.55	6.71	6.34
Acme's days in receivables	36.5	36.5	36.5	36.5	36.5	36.5
Industry's days in receivables	33.2	34.6	38.2	37.4	33.9	35.1

Almost immediately one should notice several interesting sets of value. Acme's sales-to-inventory ratios for the period 2005 to 2010 and its days in receivables for the same time frame are constant. This is not true for the industry values. This might indicate that Acme has a rigorous policy of tying its inventory level to sales. Likewise, it would appear that Acme has some formal policy to explicitly link accounts receivable to sales volume. Industry values for both ratios fluctuated across the time span; however, it should be noted that the industry's days in receivables fluctuated across a rather narrow band. Acme's sales to fixed assets have been declining from 2005 to 2010. In fact, it has dropped almost in half. This is a sign that Acme's ability to manage its assets vis-à-vis sales has declined significantly and should be a source of considerable worry for the management team.

Financial ratios serve an extremely useful purpose for small business owners who are attempting to identify trends in their own operations and see how well their business's stand up against its competitors. As such, owners should periodically review their financial ratios to get a better understanding of the current position of their firms.

Video Clip 9.12

Financial Ratios: Debt Management
Basic coverage for calculating debt ratios.

View the video online at: http://www.youtube.com/v/KjXn8qAG8vY

 Video Clip 9.13

Financial Ratios: Profitability
Basic coverage for calculating profitability ratios.

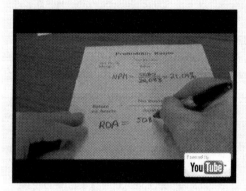

View the video online at: http://www.youtube.com/v/EVSGhWbe30c

 Video Clip 9.14

Financial Ratios: Asset Management
Basic coverage for calculating asset management ratios.

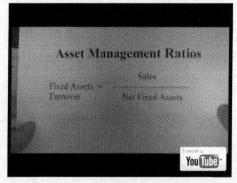

View the video online at: http://www.youtube.com/v/wcr7gWV10SQ

KEY TAKEAWAYS

- ■ Financial ratios enable external constituencies to evaluate the performance of a firm with respect to other firms in a particular industry.
- ■ Ratio analysis can help a management team identify areas that might be of concern.
- ■ The management team can track the performance on these ratios across time to determine whether the indicators are improving or declining.
- ■ Financial ratios can be grouped into five categories: liquidity ratios, financial leverage ratios, asset management or efficiency ratios, profitability ratios, and market value ratios.

EXERCISES

1. In the Appendix (Chapter 16), you will find the income statements and balance sheets for Frank's All-American BarBeQue for the years 2006 to 2010. Compute some of the key financial ratios for this business and discuss the meanings of any trends.
2. Locate the average values of these values for the restaurant industry and comment on how well or poorly Frank's All-American BarBeQue appears to be doing with respect to the industry.
3. Frank's business plan in the Appendix (Chapter 16) provides projected income statements and balance sheets for a five-year forecast horizon. Compute the same ratios as in Exercise 1 and comment on your results.

4. THE THREE THREADS

LEARNING OBJECTIVES

1. To understand that a functioning accounting system can provide customer value through accurate billings and records.
2. To understand that there are several techniques that can help a small business maintain a positive cash flow.
3. To appreciate that small businesses can use sophisticated, low-cost computer accounting systems to manage their accounting and operational operations.

4.1 Customer Value

One might find at first consideration a tenuous link between a business's accounting system and the concept of customer value. However, if looked at from the customer's perspective, a business that provides accurate and prompt billings is a business that can control its costs, which can result in lower prices. A business that improves its overall efficiency because it can accurately monitor and track its operations provides far greater value than a business with a haphazard approach to accounting controls.

The ability to tailor a business's operations to better meet customer needs is the key to providing value. As a business acquires a better appreciation of its capabilities, it can then make improvements that will better meet customer needs and outperform competitors.[23]

As a business grows more confident in its ability to handle accounting issues, it may wish to look at more sophisticated techniques that can better serve the business and the customer. As Andrew Hereth puts it, "An accounting process needs to be established that accounts for the cost of each customer, for each market and for each channel."[24]

4.2 Cash-Flow Implications

Like good health, positive cash flow is something you're most aware of when you haven't got it. That's one of the most profound truths in life.[25]

- *Robert Heller*

Creating a positive cash flow or at least reducing a negative cash flow should be of central interest to all small businesses. Unlike the example of Alex's Soft Serve Services, not all small businesses can anticipate that they will be able to cover a negative cash flow simply by borrowing. That means that businesses must be much more proactive in attempting to eliminate or reduce negative cash flows. Therefore it is important to examine some ways in which a small business can increase its cash inflows.

- **Restrict credit and credit terms.** Many small businesses, but not all, offer credit terms and policies for current and potential customers. The easier the credit, the more likely a business will be able to generate a sale; however, easy credit terms generally mean that it will take a longer period of time for the business to receive the total cash payment from a sale. Thus many businesses accept only cash or debit and credit cards. Restricting the credit terms may simply mean that credit is provided only to particular customers or the terms of the credit are tightened—for example, 60 percent of the sale price is due the day of the sale, and the remaining 40 percent would be due in thirty days.

- **Conduct credit checks.** Businesses that plan to offer credit to customers, particularly customers who will be making large purchases, may find that it pays to spend money to conduct a credit check on these customers. Again, the use of credit checks is very much a function of the type and size of the business and the potential sales that may be involved.

- **Make credit terms explicit.** For businesses that provide credit to their customers, it is critical to make sure the customer has an explicit idea of what the exact credit terms are. In the long run, it will pay to clearly indicate on the invoice the exact payment schedule.

- **Provide incentives to expedite customer payment.** It is often worth to knock off several percentage points on a sale to speed up a customer's payment. The exact size of the discount will have to be determined by the business owner.

- **Request partial payment in advance.** When providing credit terms, small businesses should consider the requirement of a deposit or a retainer up front. Hopefully, this should not deter many customers from purchasing particularly high-priced items. The request for payment in advance assures that a business will receive some cash inflow even if the customer defaults.

One of the best ways to maintain a positive cash flow is to reduce the size of the negative cash flow, which can be done by conducting cash-flow analyses on a regular basis. Throughout this chapter, the time frame most commonly used has been the fiscal year or a fiscal month. In the case of rigorously monitoring cash flow, it is strongly suggested that one consider using even smaller time units, namely a weekly analysis or even a daily analysis.

4.3 Digital Technology and E-Environment Implications

Computer-based accounting systems have much to offer the owner of a small business. Most small businesses would find that a computerized accounting system has the following advantages over a manual system:

- **Accuracy.** In computerized systems, data entry can be structured so as to preclude the input of wrong information. Further, transactions are entered only once in computerized systems, whereas they may require several entries in a manual system.

- **Speed.** Data entry and data retrieval can occur on a real-time basis. Calculations are done instantly in a computerized system. For businesses with multiple locations, data can be instantly coordinated rather than waiting for the collection of data from diverse locations as would occur with manual systems.

- **Report generation.** Computerized systems can provide real-time generation of a variety of reports that can enable owners or operators to improve their decision making.

- **Cost reduction.** Although small businesses may be required to expend money on the initial purchase (and maintenance) of computerized accounting system, these systems often provide significant savings in terms of reducing the amount of time required for bookkeepers and accountants to track businesses records.[26]

- **Backup.** The records in a computerized system can be backed up at a variety of locations. This minimizes the chance that all records would be destroyed in some form of accident, such as a fire or a flood, as might be the case with paper records in a manual system.[27]

Computer-based accounting packages that have been designed for small to midsize businesses have been available for more than a quarter of a century. Many of the packages that existed twenty-five years ago are no longer available. Some have argued that a natural selection process exists for computerized accounting system so that today's survivors represent the best qualities required of such systems.[28] In recent years, a whole new category of accounting software has been developed—cloud-based software.

This software resides on the web and does not require a software package to be downloaded on small business owner's computer. Such programs are accessible from any computer.

Selecting a new computer accounting system or changing from a manual system to a computer-based system is a major step for any small business. It should be conducted with careful consideration and treated as a major project. Prior to starting the project, it is highly advisable to sit down with one's accountant and consider the options. Some of the first steps in starting this project involve specifying the budget and the required attributes of the software package. In developing the budget, one should consider the initial acquisition price of the software, training costs, and maintenance costs. If one is planning to move from one computerized accounting system to another, the cost of transferring operations should also be considered in the overall budgeting process. With regard to the initial purchase price, these packages can range from being free to costing thousands of dollars depending on the number of modules required. Some systems use a fee structure that is based on the number of users. This would allow a business owner to get some sense of the look and the feel of the software package.

The second initial phase of the acquisition process centers on identifying what is needed in the accounting package. This relates to the elements (support services) or modules that are absolutely required. One should also identify what modules might be of benefit at some point in the future. To assist an owner in identifying what modules are required or may be required in the future, the information that flows into the accounting system must be specified. In Section 1, we refer to the idea of accounting transactions, which fall into several categories. A business needs to identify all the required categories, particularly if it is transitioning from a manual system to a computerized system. A business also needs to identify the accounting reports that are required throughout the business. It is important to consider if the software is compatible with e-business, e-commerce, and Internet capabilities.

Another issue is to consider how many people will have to access the system throughout the entire business. This number will have a dramatic impact on the training requirements. Recognize that the business will have to provide manuals that must be accessible to all who will be using the accounting system. This also brings up the issue of the necessity of employee training programs. Consider the relative ease of use of any computerized accounting system—not only for yourself but also for the employees. This is where an understanding of the learning curve of using the system will be extremely important. Again, a business's accountant can play a critical role not only in determining the selection of the system but also in developing training programs for the employees and showing them how to use the system. Having generated this list of the required components of the accounting system, one should identify competing software products (along with their costs) and prioritize them, as shown in Figure 9.6. In addition to consulting with an accountant, a business owner should review the various accounting software packages by talking to other business owners, reading evaluations in the business and computer press, and exploring software packages on a trial basis.[29] Many accounting software packages allow users to try out the system with no initial charge. After a fixed period of time, usually thirty days, the program becomes inoperative. This allows you to become familiar with the look and the feel of the software.

FIGURE 9.6 Evaluation of Computer Accounting Systems

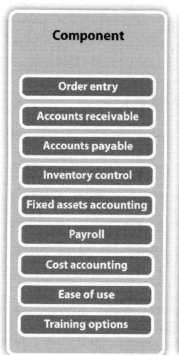
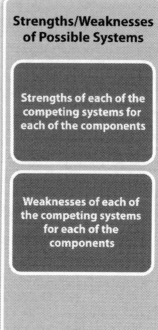
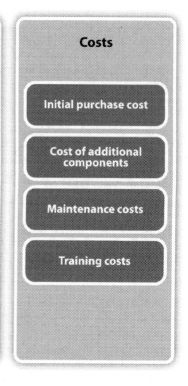

The third preliminary step is the creation of a timeline that would determine when you must successfully implement the accounting package into the actual operations of the business. This timeline should consider the time required to conduct test runs of the software. Tests should be conducted with only one or two modules. They should be operated for a sufficient period of time (at least a month) to examine if the system works as well as the manual system or the current computerized system. A timeline should also be created for training the personnel who will be using the software.

Moving to a computerized accounting system or a new system means that you should be ready for any disaster. To prepare for such disasters, there should be a formal policy of backing up all data on a regular basis. The backed up data should be at another locale other than the main storage site. Portable hard drives for off-site data storage site serve this purpose well. Some software packages perform their own backup procedures.

Several factors may need to be considered when examining accounting software for small businesses, including the followinging: will the software run on computers that a business currently uses, how often should the company provide updates of the software, and are there specific versions of the accounting software for the industry in which a business operates. Small businesses should also consider cloud computing options with regard to accounting software. **Cloud computing** refers to the fact that programs and data are stored off-site at another location. This means that accounting transactions can be entered from any computer, in some cases from smartphones, and are accessible anywhere in the world. Although for start-up businesses and the very smallest of businesses the adoption of a computerized accounting system appears to be a daunting task, in the long run, it is a key element for the long-term survival of the business.

Video Link 9.1

Evaluating Accounting Software

Video that discusses ways to determine what software is best.

www.ehow.com/video_5103398_evaluating-accounting-software.html

- Good accounting systems can help a firm provide value to its customers through better billing and increased efficiency.
- Small businesses can be proactive in preserving cash flow through a variety of simple actions.
- Small businesses today can acquire very powerful computer accounting software packages. These packages are affordable and relatively easy to use.

EXERCISES

1. Besides the suggestions provided, what other approaches might a small business use to preserve cash flow?
2. Select five or six computerized accounting packages (including one of the cloud variety) that might be used by a start-up restaurant, and prepare a rigorous analysis of which should be selected and why.

Disaster Watch

Sales and cash-flow forecasting can often prove to be a significant challenge to small business owners. Assumptions have to be made, forecasting models must be selected, and calculations have to be made. In many cases, the forecasts will not be exact. This can be profoundly frustrating. Yet one of the great benefits of forecasting is that it may force a small business owner to think about what the future may hold. However, neither small businesses nor large businesses can predict or plan for all events. Certain events just happen. Given this element of unpredictable chance, businesses should think about how they might protect and conserve their cash flow should the "unthinkable" occur.

Yankee Gas had a project that involved installing a pipeline from Waterbury, Connecticut, to Wallingford, Connecticut.[30] The original intent according to Yankee Gas was that all work on the pipeline would occur during the night to minimize customer disruptions. Or at least, this was what the storeowners along the line of the work were told. During one phase of the project, the company altered the schedule and began working during daytime hours. Installation involved digging a trench into which the pipeline was laid. This produced a major disruption that required that traffic be diverted away from several businesses' main entrances and their parking lots. Multiple businesses found their customers had to be "forceful" with the local police to enter areas near the businesses. One of the businesses was a deli that focused on preparing fresh food on a daily basis. Food that was not sold during the day had to be discarded that night. This occurred during the summer months, which were the best times for this deli. A local gas station saw sales drop so precipitously that the owner was unable to meet the rent.

One of the responses on the part of many of the business owners was to seek compensation. Unfortunately, they found that no one was willing to accept responsibility for the detour policy. As an owner of a travel agency put it, "The Town said it was the State, the State said it was the (local) police and the police said it was Yankee Gas."[31] While the owners await the resolution of responsibility, they have to consider the possibility of more street work during the following summer.

ENDNOTES

1. *Independent* (London), April 21, 2010, quoted in "Accounting Quotes," *Qfinance*, accessed February 14, 2012, www.qfinance.com/finance-and-business-quotes/accounting.

2. Ramnik Singh Wahla, *Accounting Terminology Bulletin No. 1: Review and Résumé*, 1953, accessed February 14, 2012, c0403731.cdn.cloudfiles.rackspacecloud.com/collection/papers/1950/1953_0101_AccountingReview.pdf.

3. Denise Schmandt-Besseart, "An Ancient Token System: The Precursor to Numerals and Writing," *Archaeology* 39 (1986): 32–39; Richard Mattessich, "Prehistoric Accounting and the Problem of Representation: On Recent Archeological Evidence of Middle East from 8000 B.C. to 3000 B.C.," *Accounting Historians Journal* 14, no. 2 (1987): 71–91.

4. Salvador Carmona and Mahmoud Ezzamel, "Accounting and Forms of Accountability in Major Civilizations: Mesopotamia and Ancient Egypt" (working paper, Instituto de Empresa Business School, Madrid, Spain, and Cardiff University, Cardiff, UK, 2005), accessed December 2, 2011, latienda.ie.edu/working_papers_economia/WP05-21.pdf.

5. John R. Alexander, *History of Accounting* (Princeville, HI: Association of Chartered Accountants in the United States, 2002), 4.

6. John R. Alexander, *History of Accounting* (Princeville, HI: Association of Chartered Accountants in the United States, 2002), 9.

7. Jean Murray, "Finding Help with Bookkeeping and Accounting Tasks," *About.com*, accessed December 2, 2011, biztaxlaw.about.com/od/businessaccountingrecords/a/findacpa.htm.

8. "Edwin T. Freedley," *Cyber Nation*, accessed February 14, 2012, www.cybernation.com/victory/quotations/authors/quotes_freedley_edwint.html.

9. "Comparison of Cash and Accrual Methods of Accounting," *Wikipedia*, accessed December 2, 2011, en.wikipedia.org/wiki/comparison_of_cash_method_and_accrual_method_of_accounting.

10. Melissa Bushman, "Cash Basis versus Accrual Accounting," *Yahoo! Voices*, accessed December 2, 2011, voices.yahoo.com/cash-basis-versus-accrual-basis-accounting-147864.html?cat=3.

11. "Cash vs. Accrual Accounting," *Nolo.com*, accessed December 2, 2011, www.nolo.com/legal-encyclopedia/cash-vs-accrual-accounting-29513.html.

12. "Accounting Quotes," *Qfinance*, accessed February 14, 2012, www.qfinance.com/finance-and-business-quotes/accounting.

13. Walter Harrison, Charles Lungren, and Bill Thomas, *Financial Accounting*, 8th ed. (Boston, MA: Prentice Hall, 2010), 63.

14. "Work in Process," *BusinessDictionary.com*, accessed December 2, 2011, www.businessdictionary.com/definition/work-in-process.html.

15. "Paid in Capital," *Investopedia*, accessed December 2, 2011, www.investopedia.com/terms/p/paidincapital.asp.

16. "Retained Earnings," *The Free Dictionary*, accessed December 2, 2011, financial-dictionary.thefreedictionary.com/Retained+Earnings.

17. Jack Welch, "A Healthy Company?," *Business Week*, May 3, 2006.

18. Richard Bort, "Medium-Term Funds Flow Forecasting," in *Corporate Cash Management Handbook*, ed. Richard Bort (New York: Warren Gorham & Lamont, 1990), 125.

19. Because Alex was using spreadsheet software, the monthly averages were computed out to more than two decimal places. This explains why the calculations are not exact. As in the case of January, the actual monthly percentage was closer to 6.3821 percent, which provides the monthly forecast of $26,737.

20. These calculations have been rounded to the nearest dollar. This is also true for the values in Table 9.6.

21. "Accounting Quotes," *Qfinance*, accessed February 14, 2012, www.qfinance.com/finance-and-business-quotes/accounting.

22. "Debt/Equity Ratio," *Investopedia*, accessed December 2, 2011, www.investopedia.com/terms/D/debtequityratio.asp.

23. "Customer Value Analysis," *Quality Solutions, Inc.*, accessed December 2, 2011, www.qualitysolutions.com/customer_value_analysis.htm.

24. Andrew Hereth, "Accounting for Superior Customer Service," *Andrew M. Hereth Blog*, accessed December 2, 2011, andrewmhereth.com/blog/accounting-for-superior-customer-service.

25. "The Importance of Cash Flow Management—Entrepreneur University," *Young Entrepreneur Blog*, February 9, 2009, accessed February 14, 2012, www.youngentrepreneur.com/blog/entrepreneur-university/the-importance-of-cash-flow-management-entrepreneur-university.

26. "The Advantages of Using a Computerized Accounting Package such as MYOB Accounting Software," *ITS Tutorial School*, accessed December 2, 2011, www.tuition.com.hk/computerized-accounting.htm.

27. Sheila Shanker, "Differences between Manual and Computerized Accounting Systems," *Chron.com*, accessed January 31, 2012, smallbusiness.chron.com/differences-between-manual-computerized-accounting-systems-3764.html.

28. John Hedtke, "Natural Selection of Low-Cost Accounting," *Accounting Technology* 22, no. 5 (2006): 34–38.

29. "Top 15 Accounting Software Vendors Revealed," *Business-Software.com*, accessed December 2, 2011, www.business-software.com/erp/about-erp-financial-accounting.php.

30. Josh Morgan, "Yankee Gas Work Upsets Local Businessowners," *The Cheshire Herald* (Cheshire, Connecticut), October 21, 2010.

31. Josh Morgan, "Yankee Gas Work Upsets Local Businessowners," *The Cheshire Herald* (Cheshire, Connecticut), October 21, 2010.

CHAPTER 10
Financial Management

The Notch Store

Source: Used with permission from Frank Salvatore.

No small business, or for that matter no large business, becomes a landmark and community-gathering place overnight. It takes time along with some very sharp management skills. In the case of the Notch Store, a local legend in Cheshire, Connecticut, it took ninety years and three generations of family members.

The business began in 1921 when Pauline Salvatore recognized a business opportunity. Her husband Mike worked in the nearby quarry, and she recognized that the employees needed a location where they could buy groceries for their lunch or to bring home for dinner. She began to sell them from her living room. Soon the business located to a facility next to her home. The name Notch Store came from its use in the quarry.

A few years later, Mike left the quarry and began to work with Pauline. Over the years, the Notch Store evolved as customer needs changed. They began to expand their offerings. The physical store was enlarged. A gasoline pump was installed, and for several years, one wall of the store carried auto parts.

In 1967, Mike and Pauline's son Frank and his wife Josephine took over the operation of the business. In the 1970s, the Notch Store extended its offerings to include deli items and lunches. It even offered a homemade cider every fall. The business grew and included its third generation of Salvatores—Frank Jr.

In the early 1990s, Frank Jr. was in charge of operations. Like any business man, he was open to suggestions from others, including his employees. One woman who worked for Frank Jr. suggested that he add breakfast sandwiches to the menu. To make these sandwiches, Frank Jr. needed a restaurant-quality stove. In one of those strange twists of life, Frank Jr. had a friend who knew Joe Namath and his wife. The Namaths were building a new home, and Joe's wife did not like the stove in the home. Frank Jr. acquired it, and since then, the breakfast sandwich offerings have become a major staple in the Notch Store.

No business develops without encountering problems, and the Notch Store was no exception. Several years ago, a number of customers complained that they had become ill from the Notch's cider. This was followed by several lawsuits. For most businesses, this might have been a fatal crisis and financial ruin. Fortunately, years before, Frank Jr. had listened to his brother Robert's advice (Robert was in the insurance industry). The Notch Store had $2.3 million in insurance coverage, which was more than enough to ensure its survival. For several reasons, including recognition of the risk of serving food to the public, the Notch Store has adopted a limited liability corporation format. Even with the best of financial planning and risk reduction strategies, many businesses have to deal with factors beyond their control. The recent economic downturn has meant that there is a significant reduction in new homes being built in Cheshire. This means that there are far fewer builders buying breakfasts and lunches, but Frank Jr. is coping with a small line of credit at a local bank. The future is still bright for the Notch Store and so is the possibility of it continuing into a fourth generation.[1]

1. THE IMPORTANCE OF FINANCIAL MANAGEMENT IN SMALL BUSINESS

LEARNING OBJECTIVES

1. Understand the difference between accounting and finance for small businesses.
2. Understand the major activities of finance.
3. Understand how finance can affect the selection of a business form.
4. Understand the various sources that can be used to finance the start-up operations of a business.
5. Understand what factors might affect the extent to which a firm is financed by either debt or equity.

finance

The science of money management that consists of financial planning, financial control, and financial decision making.

Chapter 9 discusses the critical importance of a small business owner understanding the fundamentals of accounting—"the language of business." This chapter examines finance and argues that the small business owner should acquire a basic understanding of some key principles in this discipline. One question that might come to someone's mind immediately is as follows: "What is the difference between accounting and finance?" As an academic discipline, finance began in the early decades of the twentieth century. We have already seen that accounting predates the formal study of finance by millennia.[2] Yet some have argued that accounting should be seen as a subset of finance.[3] Others have argued that both accounting and finance should be seen as subdisciplines of economics. Not surprisingly, others have argued in favor of the primacy of accounting. If we get beyond this debate, we can see that accounting is involved with the precise reporting of the financial position of a firm through the financial statements, which is presented in Chapter 9. The accounting function is expected to collect, organize, and present financial information in a systematic fashion. **Finance** can be seen as "the science of money management" and consists of three major activities: financial planning, financial control, and financial decision making. Financial planning deals with the acquisition of adequate funds to maintain the operations of a business and making sure that funds are available when needed. Control seeks to assure that assets are being efficiently used. Decision making is associated with determining how to acquire funds, where to acquire funds, and how those funds should be used and within the context of the risk assessment of the aforementioned decisions. As an academic discipline, finance has grown tremendously over the last four decades.

Much of the work produced during this period possessed both an esoteric analytical quality and profound practical consequences. One only has to look at newspapers and the business press, during the last few years, to see how financial theory (efficient market hypothesis) and financial models (options pricing, derivatives, and arbitrage models) have played a dominant role in the global economy. Fortunately, most small businesses have no need to directly involve themselves with these analytical abstractions. But this does not mean that small business owners do not need to concern themselves with fundamental issues of financing their firms.

1.1 Impact of Organization Type on Finance Decisions

Selecting the form of business organization that is adopted by a business depends on many factors. One could begin by anticipating the eventual size and nature of the business.[4] The complexity of a business may dictate the type of business organization that is adopted. However, many of the factors that go into this determination are either directly or indirectly financial in nature. The indirect factors are as follows: the extent to which a business owner wishes to attain control of the business, the relationship that the owner would have with partners or investors, and the perceived risk associated with the business. This last factor is tied to the question of the extent to which the owner will invest his or her own money and assets. The direct financial factors that go into selecting the type of the business organization include the following: expected profits or losses, tax issues, the vulnerability and threat from lawsuits, and the ability to extract profits from the business for the owner's use. The federal government recognizes six forms of business organizations for tax purposes: **sole proprietorship**, partnership, **C-corporation**, **S-corporation**, trust, and nonprofit. The last two are unlikely to be adopted by small businesses. It is useful to examine the financial implications of organizing along the remaining four basic formats.

Sole Proprietorship

Many small businesses operated by a single individual adopt sole proprietorship format of business organization. It is the most basic type of business organization. It is also the least expensive to create and the easiest to operate and dissolve. Sole proprietorships can be incorporated if the owner so desires. Not being a legal entity, single scratch sole proprietorships disappear after the death of the owner. This type of business is essentially a format for a single-person business (although many have between one and ten employees), where the owner makes *all* the decisions related to the business's operations. The owner can extract all profits from the business for his or her personal use, or the owner can decide to reinvest any portion of the profits back into the business. It is interesting to know that 70 percent of all businesses in the United States are sole proprietorships yet they only produce 20 percent of all the nation's profits.[5] Because a single proprietorship is not a legal entity, any income generated by the business goes directly on the owner's personal tax return. However, the single owner is also personally responsible for any debts that the business acquires. This means that the owner may put his or her own personal assets at risk. In addition, this business organization means unlimited liability for its owner. The format means that there is very little opportunity to raise funds from sources other than the owner's own capital or consumer loans.

Partnerships

Partnerships generally are unincorporated businesses. From a financial standpoint, partnerships offer a few advantages over sole proprietorship. By having more than one owner (investor), it is often easier to raise additional capital. In some businesses, such as law firms and accounting firms, the prospect of becoming a partner may be an attractive inducement to gain employees. There are several versions of partnerships.

The **general partnership** is composed of two or more owners who contribute the initial capital of the business and share in the profits and any losses. It is similar to a sole proprietorship in that all partners are personally responsible for all the debts and the liabilities of the business. A general partnership is comparable to a sole proprietorship in that neither is a taxable entity; therefore, the partners' profits are taxed as personal income. They can deduct any business losses from their personal income taxes. The exact proportion of ownership of the firm is generally found in a written document known as the partnership agreement.

A **limited partnership** is a business that may have several general partners and several more limited partners. The major difference with a general partnership is that the limited partners do not have unlimited liability. Their losses are limited to their original investment in the business. Common practice means that these limited partners do not play a major decision-making role in the life of the business.

C-Corporations

Selecting a C-corporation form of business entails more effort and expense in creating this format. Corporations must be chartered by the state in which they are headquartered. Corporations are viewed as legal entities, meaning that they can enter into legal agreements with individuals and other corporations. They are also subject to numerous local and state regulations. This often results in extensive paperwork that can be costly. Corporations are owned by their shareholders. The shareholders are liable only for their original investment in the business. They cannot be sued for more than that amount. One of the major advantages of adopting a corporate format is that in this type of business, it is sometimes much easier to raise capital through either debt or the issuance of stock. Profits derived from this type

sole proprietorship

The most basic type of business organization in which there is only one owner.

C-corporation

A legal entity that must be chartered by the state in which it is headquartered, giving it the capability to enter into legal agreements with individuals and other corporations.

S-corporation

A special format designed to eliminate the problem of double taxation that one might find with a C-corporation format.

general partnership

A business composed of two or more owners who contribute the initial capital of the business and share in the profits and the losses.

limited partnership

A business format that may have several general partners and several more limited partners who do not have unlimited liability.

of business are taxed at the corporate rate. It is important to note that dividends paid to shareholders, unlike interest expenses, are not deductible. So in a real sense, this form of income is doubly taxed.

S-Corporations

The S-corporation is a special format designed to eliminate the problem of double taxation that one might find with a C-corporation format. It first differs from a C-corporation in that it is limited to a hundred shareholders, although it can be created with just one shareholder. If a shareholder is an employee of the business and contributes any service to the business, then the corporation is required to pay that individual a salary. The term that is used is "reasonable" salary. This definition may vary under several conditions. A failure to comply with this ambiguous definition of "reasonable" salary means that the IRS can reclassify the profits as wages and tax the amount at the personal income rate.

Limited Liability Company

limited liability company

An organizational form that can be limited to a single individual or several other owners or shareholders.

A **limited liability company** is an organizational form that can be limited to a single individual or several other owners or shareholders. Like a general partnership, there is a requirement for documents that define the distribution of responsibilities, profits, or losses. Generally, the members of a limited liability company are liable for the debts of the company. This format may provide tax and financial benefits for the participants. This format cannot be used in the banking or insurance industries.

1.2　Acquisition of Funds

Capital is the lifeblood of all businesses. It is needed to start, operate, and expand a business. Capital comes from several sources: equity, debt, internally generated funds, and trade credits (see Figure 10.1).

FIGURE 10.1　Sources of Capital

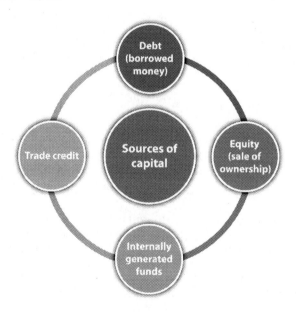

Equity financing raises money by selling a certain share of the ownership of the business. It involves no explicit obligation or expectation, on the part of the investors, to be repaid their investment. The value of equity financing lies in the partial ownership of the business.

Perhaps the major source of equity financing for most small start-up businesses comes from personal savings. The term *bootstrapping* refers to using personal, family, or friends' money to start a business.[6] The use of one's own money (or that of family and friends) is a strong indicator that a business owner has a strong commitment to and belief in the success of the business. If a business is financed totally from one's personal savings, that means the owner or the operator has total control of the business.

If a business is structured as a corporation, it may issue stock. Generally, two major types of stock may be issued: common stock and preferred stock. It should be noted that in most cases, owners of common stock have what are known as voting rights. They have a proportional vote (directly related to the number of shares they own) for members of the board of directors. Preferred stock does not carry with it voting rights, but it has a form of guaranteed dividend.

Corporations that issue stock must comply with several steps to meet both federal and state statutes, including the following: outlines to issue stock to shareholders, determining the price and number of shares to be issued, creating stock certificates; developing a record to record all stock transactions; and meeting all federal and state securities requirements.[7] Smaller businesses may choose to issue stock only to those who were involved in the initial investment of the business. In such cases, one generally does not have to register these securities with state or federal agencies. However, one may be required to fill out all the forms.[8]

Chapter 5 discusses two sources of capital investment: venture capitalist and angel investors. Venture capitalists are looking for substantial returns on their initial investment—five, ten, sometimes even twenty-five times their original investment. They will be looking for firms that can rapidly generate significant profits or significant growth in sales. Angel investors may be more attracted to their interest in the small business concept than in reaping significant returns. This is not to say that they are not interested in recouping their original investment with some type of significant return. It is much more likely that angel investors, as compared to venture capitalists, will play a much more active role in the decision-making process of the small business.

One area for possible capital infusion into a small business may come from a surprising source. Many students (and some adults) may find funding to start up a business through business plan competitions. These competitions are often hosted by colleges and universities or small business associations. The capital investment may not be large, but it might be enough to start very small businesses.

Debt financing represents a legal obligation to repay the original debt plus interest. Most debt financing involves a fixed payment schedule to repay both principal and interest. A failure to meet the schedule has serious consequences, which might include the bankruptcy of the business. Those who provide debt financing expect that the principal will be repaid with interest, but they are not formal investors in the business.

There are numerous sources for debt financing. Some small businesses begin with financing by borrowing from friends and family. Some firms may choose to finance business operations by using either personal or corporate credit cards. This approach to financing can be extraordinarily expensive given the interest rates charged on credit cards and the possibility that the credit card companies may change (by a significant amount) the credit limit associated with the credit card.

The largest source of debt financing for small businesses in the United States comes from commercial banks.[9] Bank lending can take many forms. The most common loan specifies the amount of money to be repaid within a specific time frame for a specific interest rate. These loans can be either secured or unsecured. Secured loans involve pledging some assets—such as a home, real estate, machinery, and plant—as collateral. Unsecured loans provide no such collateral. Because they are riskier for the bank, they generally have higher interest rates. For a more comprehensive discussion of bank loans, see Section 2.

The Small Business Administration (SBA) has a large number of programs designed to help small businesses. These include the business loan programs, investment programs, and bonding programs. The SBA operates three different loan programs. It should be understood that the SBA does not make the loan itself to a small business but rather guarantees a portion of the loan to its partners that include private lenders, microlending institutions, and community development organizations. To secure one of these loans, the borrower must meet criteria set forth by the SBA. It should be recognized that these SBA loan rules and guidelines can be altered by the US Congress and are dependent on prevailing economic and political conditions. The following subsections briefly describe some of the loan programs used by the SBA.

(a) Loan Programs

This class of loans may be used for a variety of reasons, including the purchase of land, buildings, equipment, machinery, supplies, or materials. It may also be used for long-term working capital (paying accounts payable or the purchase of inventory). It may even be used to purchase an existing business. This class of loans cannot, however, be used to refinance existing debt, to pay delinquent taxes, or to change business ownership.

- **Special-purpose loans program.** These loans are designed to assist small businesses for specific purposes. They have been used to help small businesses purchase and incorporate pollution control systems, develop employee stock ownership plans, and aid companies negatively impacted by the North American Free Trade Agreement (NAFTA). It includes programs such as the CAPLines, which provide assistance to businesses for meeting their short-term working capital needs. There is also the Community Adjustment and Investment Program. This program is designed to assist businesses that might have been adversely impacted by NAFTA.

- **Express and pilot programs.** These loan programs are designed to accelerate the process of providing loans. SBA Express can respond to a loan application within thirty-six hours while also providing lower interest rates.

- **Community express programs.** These programs are designed to assist borrowers whose businesses are located in economically depressed regions of the country.
- **Patriot express loans.** These loans are designed to assist members of the US military who wish to create or expand a small business. These loans have lower interest rates and can be used for starting a business, real estate purchases, working capital, expansions, and helping the business if the owner should be deployed.
- **Export loan programs.** Given the remarkable fact that 70 percent of American exporters have less than twenty employees, it is not surprising that the SBA makes a special effort to support these businesses by providing specialized loan programs. These programs include the following:
  - **Export Express Program.** This program has a rapid turnaround time to support export-based activities. It can provide for funds up to $500,000 worth of financing. Financing can be either a term loan or a line of credit.
  - **Export Working Capital Program.** A major challenge that small exporters face is the fact that many American banks will not provide working capital advances on orders, receivables, or even letters of credit. This SBA program assures up to the 90 percent of a loan so as to enhance a business's export working capital.
  - **SBA and Ex-Im Bank Coguarantee Program.** This is an extension of the Export Working Capital Program and deals with expanding a business's export working capital lines up to $2 million.
  - **International Trade Loan Program.** This program, with a maximum guarantee of $1.75 million, enables small businesses to start an exporting program, enlarge an exporting program, or deal with the consequences of competition from overseas imports.

Another source of debt financing is the issuance of bonds. Bonds are promissory notes. There are many forms of bonds, and here we discuss only the most basic type. The fundamental format of the bond is that it is a debt instrument that promises to repay a fixed amount of money within a given time frame while providing interest payments on a regular basis. The issuance of bonds is generally an option available to businesses with a corporation format. It also requires extensive legal and financial preparations.

Another source of capital is the generation of internal funding. This simply means that a business plows its retained earnings back into the business. This is a viable source of capital when a business is highly profitable.

The last source of capital is trade credit. Trade credit involves purchasing supplies or equipment through financing made available by vendors. This approach may allow someone to acquire inventory of materials and supplies without having the full price at the time of purchase. Some analysts say that trade credit is the second largest source of financing for small businesses after borrowing from banks.[10] Trade credit is often a vital way of securing supplies.

Trade credit is often expressed in terms of three important numbers—a discount rate, the number of days for one to pay to qualify for the discount, and the number of days on which the bill must be paid. As an example, a trade credit offered by a supplier might be listed as 5/5/30. This translates into a 5 percent discount if the bill is paid within five days of the issuance. The third number means that the bill must be paid *in full* within thirty days.

Video Clip 10.1

How to Raise Capital: The #1 Skill of an Entrepreneur
Describes what an entrepreneur needs to do in order to acquire capital for the firm.

View the video online at: http://www.youtube.com/v/yQLhWtgAT0A

 Video Clip 10.2

Pat Gage: Getting Business Financing for a Small Business
Voice-over PowerPoint identifies where a small business owner can acquire funding.

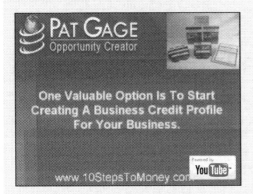

View the video online at: http://www.youtube.com/v/bgpjEAPHSjs

 Video Clip 10.3

How to Finance a Business: How to Get Start-Up Business Financing
Examines the use of bank financing for the small business.

View the video online at: http://www.youtube.com/v/Jsek3PQypzw

Video Clip 10.4

Financing a New Business: How to Find Government Small Business Grants
Locate places to find small business grants through search engines with ideas from a certified public accountant in this free video on new business financing.

View the video online at: http://www.youtube.com/v/I_Cz4Kf-4w0

 Video Clip 10.5

The Role of Credit Cards in Small Business Financing
Congressional testimony that warns of the use of using credit cards to finance small businesses.

View the video online at: http://www.youtube.com/v/havCohM8EbE

Video Clip 10.6

Financial Analysis for Small-Business Owners
This excerpt from the popular video learning series at BusinessBuffet.com introduces the core concepts behind financial analysis for small business.

View the video online at: http://www.youtube.com/v/OoQvgDBUNNc

Web Resources

Financing Small Business Portal

Discusses financing opportunities.

www.businessfinance.com/

Credit Loans for Small Businesses

The Chase portal—one provider of loans for small businesses.

www.chase.com/index.jsp?pg_name=ccpmapp/smallbusiness/credit_loans/page/bb_lending

Five Ways to Finance a Business in Difficult Financial Times

Alternative ways of financing when banks are not lending.

biztaxlaw.about.com/od/financingyourstartup/tp/financingsmallbiz.htm

1.3 Capital Structure: Debt versus Equity

A critical component of financial planning for any business is determining the extent to which a firm will be financed by debt and by equity. This decision determines the **financial leverage** of a business. Many factors enter into this decision, particularly for the small business. From the classic economic and finance perspective, one should evaluate the cost of both debt and equity. Debt's cost centers largely on the interest rate associated with a specific debt. Equity's cost includes ceding control to other equity partners, the cost of issuing stock, and dividend payments. One should also consider the fact that the interest payment on debt is deductible and therefore will lower a business's tax bill.[11] Neither the cost of issuing stock nor dividend payments is tax deductible.

Larger businesses have many more options available to them than smaller enterprises. Although this is not always true, larger businesses can often arrange for larger loans at more favorable rates than smaller businesses.[12] Larger businesses often find it easier to raise capital through the issuance of stock (equity).

By increasing a business's proportion of debt, its financial leverage can be increased. There are many reasons for attempting to increase a business's financial leverage. First, one is growing the business with someone else's money. Second, there is the deductible nature of interest on debt. Third, as more clearly shown in Section 3, increasing one's financial leverage can have a positive impact on the business's return on equity. For all these benefits, however, there is the inescapable fact that increasing a business's debt level also increases a business's overall risk. The term *financial leverage* can be seen as being comparable to the base word—lever. Levers are tools that can amplify an individual's power. A certain level of debt can amplify the "lifting" power of a business (see the upper portion of Figure 10.2). However, beyond a certain point, the debt may be out of reach, and therefore the entire lifting power of financial leverage may be lost (see the lower portion of Figure 10.2). Beyond the loss of lifting power,

financial leverage

The proportion of a firm that is financed by debt and by equity.

the assumption of too much debt may lead to an inability to pay the interest on the debt. This situation becomes the classic case of filing for Chapter 11 bankruptcy.

FIGURE 10.2 Acceptable and Unacceptable Levels of Leverage

Acceptable level of leverage   **Unacceptably high level of leverage**

This major issue for small businesses—determining how to raise funds through either debt or equity—often transcends economic or financial decisions. For many small business owners, the ideal way of financing business growth is through generating internal funds. This means that a business does not have to acquire debt but has generated sufficient profits from its operations. Unfortunately, many small businesses, particularly at the beginning, cannot generate sufficient internal funds to finance areas such as product development, the acquisition of new machinery, or market expansions. These businesses have to rely on securing additional capital debt, equity, or some combination of both.

Many individuals start small businesses with the express purpose of finding independence and control over their own economic and business lives. This desire for independence may make many small business owners averse to the idea of equity financing because that might mean ceding business control to equity partners.[13] Another issue that makes some small business owners averse to acquiring additional equity partners is the simple fact that the acquisition of these partners means less profit to the business owner. This factor in the control issue must be considered when the small business owner is looking to raise additional capital through venture capitalist and angel investors.[14]

A recent research paper[15] examined the relationship between profitability and sources of financing for firms that had fewer than twenty-five employees. It found several rather interesting results:

- Firms that use only equity have a low probability of being profitable compared to firms that use only business or personal debt.
- Firms owned by females and minority members relied less on personal debt than male and minority owners.
- Female owners will be more likely to rely on equity from friends and family than their male counterparts.
- Firms that rely exclusively on personal savings to finance business operations will more likely be profitable than firms using equity forms of debt.

Web Resources

Capital Structure

Definition and explanation of capital structure.

www.enotes.com/capital-structure-reference/capital-structure-178334

Capital Structure from an Investor's Perspective

This reviews how an investor would interpret a business's capital structure.

beginnersinvest.about.com/od/financialratio/a/capital-structure.htm

EXERCISES

1. Interview the owners of five local businesses and ask them what business organizational format they use and why they adopted that form.
2. Ask them how they initially financed the start-up of their businesses.
3. Ask these same owners how they prefer to finance the firm. (Note that most owners will probably not want to go into any detail about the financial operations of their businesses.)
4. Ask them if they have had any experience with any SBA loan program and if they have any reactions to these programs.

2. FINANCIAL CONTROL

LEARNING OBJECTIVES

1. Learn about the importance of cultivating a relationship with a banker.
2. Understand the elements of the CAMPARI approach to evaluating a loan.

2.1 Relationships with Bank and Bankers

One often hears the following standard complaint of small businesses: bankers lend money only to those businesses that do not need the money. The inverse of this complaint from the bank's standpoint might be that small businesses request money only when they are least likely to be able to repay it. The conflict between small businesses and bankers may stem from a misunderstanding of the respective roles of both groups. At face value, it might appear—particularly to small businesses—that bankers are investing in their companies.

Under normal conditions, bankers are extremely risk averse. This means they are not investors anticipating a substantial return predicated on the risks associated with a particular business. Bankers lend money with the clear expectation that they will be repaid both principal and interest. It is in the interest of both parties to transcend these two conflicting perceptions of the role of bankers in the life of a small business. The key way is for the small business owner to try to foster improved communications with a banker. This communication promoted by the small business owner should become the basis of a solid working relationship with the bank. Most often, this means developing a personal relationship with the loan officer of the bank, which is sometimes a problematic proposition. Bank loan officers are often moved to different branches, or they may change jobs and work for different banks. It should be the responsibility of the small business owner to maintain frequent contact with whoever is representing the bank. This should involve more than just providing quarterly statements. It should include face-to-face discussions and even asking the officer to tour a business's facilities. The point is to personalize the working relationship between the two parties. "Ideally, it's a human relationship as well as a business relationship," says Bill Byne, an entrepreneur and author of *Habits of Wealth*.[16]

Although bankers and loan officers will rely heavily on data related to the creditworthiness of a small business, they will also consider the trustworthiness and integrity of the business owner. This intangible sense that a business owner is a worthy credit risk may play a determinant role in whether a loan is approved with the extension of a credit line. This notion of integrity has to be built over time. It is predicated on projecting an image that you can be counted on to honor what you say, know the right thing to do to make the business a success, and be able to execute the correct decisions.

CAMPARI

An acronym used by bankers to describe factors that they consider when evaluating a loan: character, ability, means, purpose, amount, repayment, and insurance.

It is sometimes said that bankers, when reviewing a perspective loan applicant, think of the drink "**CAMPARI**," which stands for the following:

- **Character.** As previously stated, bankers will consider the issue of personal integrity. Part of that definition of integrity will include a sense of professionalism, which can be reflected in one's attitude and dress. Bankers will also review one's history as a business leader, namely one's track record of success. This notion of character may also be extended to the upper echelon of the management team of a small business.

- **Ability.** The bank's prime concern is with repayment of the principal and the interest of a loan. The loan application should clearly demonstrate a business's ability to repay the loan. All support materials should be brought to bear to prove to the banker that the loan will not be defaulted on and will be paid in a timely fashion.

- **Means.** This refers to a business's ability to function in a way so that it can repay the loan. Bankers must be convinced of this crucial point. The best way to do this is by providing a comprehensive business plan with detailed numbers that indicate the business's ability to repay the loan. The business plan should also include the business strategy and the business model that will be employed to convince the banker of the validity of the overall plan.

- **Purpose.** Bankers want to know for what purpose the borrowed money will be used. You should never request a loan with the argument that having more money is better for the business than having less money. You should clearly identify how the money will be used, such as purchasing a piece of capital equipment. Having done that, you should also indicate how the acquisition of the capital equipment will positively affect the bottom line of the business.

- **Amount.** It would be extraordinarily inadvisable to begin a request for a business loan by saying "I need some money." It is very important that you specify the exact amount of the loan and also justify how you determined this amount of money. As an example, you might want to identify a particular piece of capital equipment that you plan to acquire. How did you determine its price? You should be able to address what additional expenditures might be required—such as training on the use of the equipment. The greater the degree of precision that is brought to this proposal, the greater the confidence the bank might have in granting the loan.

- **Repayment.** This refers to demonstrating an ability to repay both the interest and the principal. Again, detailed documentation, such as sales projections, profit margins, and projected cash flows, is essential if you wish to secure the loan. It is important when generating these data that you try to be as honest as possible. Extremely positive projections may be misleading. Worse still, if they are misleading and inaccurate, it may result in the business defaulting on the loan and perhaps losing the business.

- **Insurance.** Even the most scrupulously developed sales and profit projections might not pan out. It would be extraordinarily useful to show contingency plans to the bank that would indicate how you would repay the loan in the event that the scenarios that you have identified do not come to fruition.

One should recognize that a good relationship with the bank can yield benefits above and beyond credit lines and business loans. Bankers can serve as interlocutors, connecting you to potential customers, suppliers, and other investors. A good working relationship with a bank can be the best reference a business could have. This is particularly true in the current business climate where bankers have significantly restricted lending to small businesses.

KEY TAKEAWAYS

- Any business owner must be aware that bankers consider several factors when considering a loan decision.
- Business owners should be aware of their own and their business's creditworthiness.
- Business owners should be aware that bankers appreciate precision, particularly when it comes to the exact size of the loan, its purpose, and how it will be repaid.

EXERCISES

1. Arrange an interview with a loan officer at a local bank. Ask him or her what factors are considered when evaluating a small business loan for

   a. a start-up business
   b. a line-of-credit
   c. an equipment purchase
   d. a real estate purchase

2. Ask him or her how the bank evaluates the risk associated with these loans.

3. Ask the loan officer what might constitute a "red flag" that would mean that the loan would not be approved.

---

3. FINANCIAL DECISION MAKING

LEARNING OBJECTIVES

1. Learn the importance of a breakeven analysis.
2. Understand how to conduct a breakeven analysis.
3. Understand the potential power and danger of financial leverage.
4. Learn how changing financial leverage can affect measures of profitability, such as ROA and ROE.
5. Learn how to use scenarios to evaluate the impact of various levels of financial leverage.

3.1 Breakeven Analysis

A **breakeven analysis** is remarkably useful to someone considering starting up a business. It examines a business's potential costs—both fixed and variable—and then determines the sales volume necessary to produce a profit for given selling price.[17] This information enables one to determine if the entire concept is feasible. After all, if one has to sell five million shoes in a small town to turn a profit, one would immediately recognize that there may be a severe problem with the proposed business model.

A breakeven analysis begins with several simplifying assumptions. In its most basic form, it assumes that you are selling only one product at a particular price, and the production cost per unit is constant over a wide range of values. The purpose of a breakeven analysis is to determine the sales volume that is required so that you neither lose money nor make a profit. This translates into a situation in which the profit level is zero. Put in equation form, this simply means

$$\text{total revenue} - \text{total costs} = \$0.$$

By moving terms, we can see that the break-even point occurs when total revenues equal total costs:

$$\text{total revenue} = \text{total costs}.$$

We can define total revenue as the selling price of the product times the number of units sold, which can be represented as follows:

$$\text{total revenue (TR)} = \text{selling price (SP)} \times \text{sales volume (Q)}$$

$$\text{TR} = \text{SP} \times \text{Q}.$$

Total costs are seen as being composed of two parts: fixed costs and total variable costs. Fixed costs exist whether or not a firm produces any product or has any sales and consist of rent, insurance, property taxes, administrative salaries, and depreciation. Total variable costs are those costs that change across the volume of production. As part of the simplifying assumptions of the breakeven analysis, it is assumed that there is a constant unit cost of production. This would be based on the labor input and the amount of materials required to make one unit of product. As production increases, the total variable cost will likewise increase, which can be represented as follows:

breakeven analysis

Used to determine the amount of sales volume a company needs to start making a profit: when its total sales or revenues equal its total expenses.

total variable costs (TVC) = variable cost per unit (VC) × sales quantity (Q)

$$TVC = VC \times Q.$$

Total costs are simply the summation of fixed costs plus the total variable costs:

total costs (TC) = [fixed costs (FC) + total variable cost (TVC)]

$$TC = FC + TVC.$$

The original equation for the break-even point can now be rewritten as follows:

[selling price (SP) × sales volume (Q)] − total costs (TC) = $0

$$(SP \times Q) - TC = \$0.$$

At the break-even point, revenues equal total costs, so this equation can be rewritten as

$$SP \times Q = TC.$$

Given that the total costs equal the fixed costs plus the total variable costs, this equation can now be extended as follows:

selling price (SP) × sales volume (Q) = [fixed costs (FC) + total variable costs (TVC)]

$$SP \times Q = FC + TVC.$$

This equation can be expanded by incorporating the definition of total variable costs as a function of sales volume:

$$SP \times Q = FC + (VC \times Q).$$

This equation can now be rewritten to solve for the sales value:

$$(SP \times Q) - (VC \times Q) = FC.$$

Because the term *sales volume* is present in both terms on the left-hand side of the equation, it can be factored to produce

$$Q \times (SP - VC) = FC.$$

The sales value to produce the break-even point can now be solved for in the following equation:

$$Q = FC / (SP - VC).$$

The utility of the concept of break-even point can be illustrated with the following example.

Carl Jacobs, a retired engineer, was a lifelong enthusiast of making plastic aircraft models. Over thirty years, he entered many regional and national competitions and received many awards for the quality of his model building. Part of this success was due to his ability to cast precision resin parts to enhance the look of his aircraft models. During the last ten years, he acquired a reputation as being an expert in this field of creating these resin parts. A friend of his, who started several businesses, suggested that Carl look at turning this hobby into a small business opportunity in his retirement. This opportunity stemmed from the fact that Carl had created a mold into which he could cast the resin part for a particular aircraft model; this same mold could be used to produce several hundred or several thousand copies of the part, all at relatively low cost.

Carl had experience only with sculpturing and casting parts in extremely low volumes—one to five parts at a time. If he were to create a business format for this hobby, he would have to have a significant investment in equipment. There would be a need to create multiple metal molds of the same part so that they could be cast in volume. In addition, there would be a need for equipment for mixing and melting the chemicals that are required to produce the resin. After researching, he could buy top-of-the-line equipment for a total of $33,000. He also found secondhand but somewhat less efficient equipment. Carl estimated that the total cost of acquiring all the necessary secondhand equipment would be close to $15,000. After reviewing the equipment specifications, he concluded that with new equipment, the unit cost of producing a set of resin parts for a model would run $9.25, whereas the unit cost for using the secondhand equipment would be $11.00. After doing some market research, Carl determined that the maximum price he could set for his resin sets would be $23.00. This would be true whether the resin sets were produced with new or secondhand equipment.

Carl wanted to determine how many resin sets would have to be sold to break even with each set of equipment. For simplicity's sake, he assumed that the initial purchase price of both options would be his fixed cost. His analysis is presented in Table 10.1.

TABLE 10.1 break-even point Analysis

Option	Fixed Costs	Variable Cost	Selling Price	break-even point
New equipment	$33,000	$9.25/unit	$23.00	Q = $33,000 / ($23.00 − $9.25) Q = $33,000 / $13.75 Q = 2,400 units
Secondhand equipment	$15.000	$11.00/unit	$23.00	Q = $15,000 / ($23.00 − $11.00) Q = $15,000 / $12.00 Q = 1,250 units

From this analysis, he could see that although the secondhand equipment is not as efficient (hence the higher variable cost per unit), it will break even at a significantly lower level of sales than the new equipment. Carl was still curious about the profitability of the two sets of equipment at different levels of sales. So he ran the numbers to calculate the profitability for both sets of equipment at sales levels of 1,000 units, 3,000 units, 5,000 units, 7,500 units, and 10,000 units. The results are presented in Table 10.2.

TABLE 10.2 Sales Level versus Profit Breakdown

Sales Level	Secondhand Equipment				New Equipment			
	Revenue	Fixed Cost	Total Variable Costs	Profit	Revenue	Fixed Cost	Total Variable Costs	Profit
1,000	$23,000	$15,000	$11,000	$(3,000)	$23,000	$33,000	$9,250	$(19,250)
3,000	$69,000	$15,000	$33,000	$21,000	$69,000	$33,000	$27,750	$8,250
5,000	$115,000	$15,000	$55,000	$45,000	$115,000	$33,000	$46,250	$35,750
7,500	$172,500	$15,000	$82,500	$75,000	$172,500	$33,000	$69,375	$70,125
10,000	$230,000	$15,000	$110,000	$105,000	$230,000	$33,000	$92,500	$104,500

From these results, it is clear that the secondhand equipment is preferable to the new equipment. At 10,000 units, the highest annual sales that Carl anticipated, the overall profits would be greater with secondhand equipment.

Video Clip 10.7

Breakeven Analysis: Economics for Managers
A slide show showing breakeven calculations.

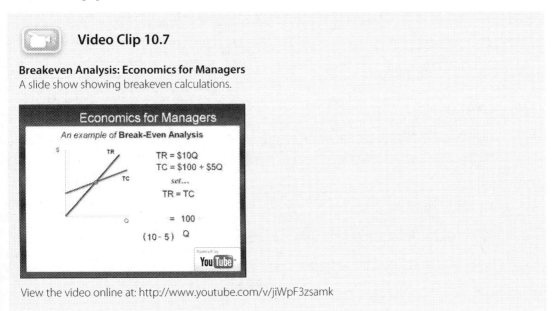

View the video online at: http://www.youtube.com/v/jiWpF3zsamk

Video Clip 10.8

Breakeven Analysis

A breakeven tutorial with voice-over.

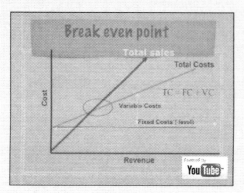

View the video online at: http://www.youtube.com/v/rQLBGmiAD3c

 Video Clip 10.9

Perform a Breakeven Analysis with Excel's Goal Seek Tool

Shows how Excel can be used to conduct sophisticated breakeven analyses.

Change Price		Change Units Sold	
Selling Price	$2.25	Selling Price	$2.25
Units Sold	15,000	Units Sold	15,000
Revenue	$33,750.00	Revenue	$33,750.00
Cost per Unit	$1.00	Cost per Unit	$1.00
Variable Costs	$15,000.00	Variable Costs	$15,000.00
Fixed Costs	$20,000.00	Fixed Costs	$20,000.00
Profit	($1,250.00)	Profit	($1,250.00)

View the video online at: http://www.youtube.com/v/1N6p3OxJxrQ

Breakeven Analysis

This site provides a straightforward description of breakeven analysis with an example.

www.businesstown.com/accounting/projections-breakeven.asp

3.2 Capital Structure Issues in Practice

In Section 2, the need to balance debt and equity, with respect to financing a firm's operations, is briefly discussed. A critical financial decision for any business owner is determining the extent of financial leverage a firm should acquire. Building a firm using debt amplifies a return of equity to the owners; however, the acquisition of too much debt, which cannot be repaid, may lead to a Chapter 11 bankruptcy, which represents a complete failure of the firm.

In the early 1950s, the field of finance tried to describe the effect of financial leverage on the valuation of a firm and its cost of capital.[18] A major breakthrough occurred with the works of Franco Modigliani and Merton Miller.[19] Reduced to simplest form, their works hypothesized that the valuation of a firm increases as the financial leverage increases. This is true but only *up to a point*. When a firm exceeds a particular value of financial leverage—namely, it has assumed too much debt—the overall value of the firm begins to decline. The point at which the valuation of a firm is maximized

cost of capital

The weighted average of a firm's debt and equity, where equity is directly related to the firm's stock.

determines the optimal capital structure of the business. The model defined valuation as a firm's earnings before interest and taxes (EBIT) divided by its cost of capital. **Cost of capital** is a weighted average of a firm's debt and equity, where equity directly relates to a firm's stock. The reality is that this model is far more closely attuned, from a mathematical standpoint, to the corporate entity. It cannot be directly applied to most small businesses. However, the basic notion that there is some desired level of debt to equity, a level that yields maximum economic benefit, is germane, as we will now illustrate.

Let us envision a small family-based manufacturing firm that until now has been able to grow through the generation of internal funds and the equity that has been invested by the original owners. Presently, the firm has no long-term debt. It has a revolving line of credit, but in the last few years, it has not had to tap into this line of credit to any great extent. The income statement for the year 2010 and the projected income statement for 2011 are given in Table 10.3. In preparing the projected income statement for 2011, the firm assumed that sales would grow by 7.5 percent due to a rapidly rising market. In fact, the sales force indicated that sales could grow at a much higher rate if the firm can significantly increase its productive capacity. The projected income statement estimates the cost of goods sold to be 65 percent of the firm's revenue. This estimate is predicated on the past five years' worth of data. Table 10.4 shows an abbreviated balance sheet for 2010 and a projection for 2011. The return on assets (ROA) and the return on equity (ROE) for 2010 and the projected values for 2011 are provided in Table 10.5.

TABLE 10.3 Income Statement for 2010 and Projections for 2011

	2010	2011
Revenue	$475,000	$510,625
Cost of goods sold	$308,750	$331,906
Gross profit	$166,250	$178,719
General sales and administrative	$95,000	$102,125
EBIT	$71,250	$76,594
Interest	$—	$—
Taxes	$21,375	$22,978
Net profit	$49,875	$53,616

TABLE 10.4 Abbreviated Balance Sheet

	2010	2011
Total assets	$750,000	$765,000
Long-term debt	$—	$—
Owners' equity	$750,000	$765,000
Total debt and equity	$750,000	$765,000

TABLE 10.5 ROA and ROE Values for 2010 and Projections for 2011

	2010 (%)	2011 (%)
Return on assets	6.65	7.01
Return on equity	6.65	7.01

After preparing these projections, the owners were approached by a company that manufactures computer-controlled machinery. The owners were presented with a series of machines that will not significantly raise the productive capacity of their business while also reducing the unit cost of production. The owners examined in detail the productive increase in improved efficiency that this computer-controlled machinery would provide. They estimated that demand in the market would increase if they had this new equipment, and sales could increase by 25 percent in 2011, rather than 7.5 percent as they had originally estimated. Further, the efficiencies brought about by the computer-controlled equipment would significantly reduce their operating costs. A rough estimate indicated that with this new equipment the cost of goods sold would decrease from 65 percent of revenue to 55 percent of revenue. These were remarkably attractive figures. The only reservation that the owners had was the cost of this new equipment. The sales price was $200,000, but the business did not have this amount of cash available. To raise this amount of money, they would either have to bring in a new equity partner who would supply the entire amount, borrow the $200,000 as a long-term loan, or have some combination of equity partnership and debt. They first approached a distant relative who has successfully invested in several businesses. This individual was willing to invest $50,000, $100,000, $150,000, or the entire $200,000 for taking an equity position in the firm. The owners also went to the bank where they had line of credit and asked about their lending options. The bank was impressed with the improved productivity and efficiency of the proposed new machinery. The bank was also willing to lend the business $50,000, $100,000, $150,000, or the entire $200,000 to purchase the computer-controlled equipment. The bank, however, stipulated that the lending rate would depend on the amount that was borrowed. If the firm borrowed $50,000, the interest rate would be 7.5 percent; if the amount borrowed was $100,000, the interest rate would increase to 10 percent; if $150,000 was the amount of the loan, the interest rate would be 12.5 percent; and if the firm borrowed the entire $200,000, the bank would charge an interest rate of 15 percent.

net present value (NPV)

A financial model that examines future cash flows from an investment and discounts the value of those investments by a specified interest rate. It then subtracts this discounted cash flow from the original value of the investment to determine whether or not a business should make an investment.

To correctly analyze this investment opportunity, the owners could employ several financial tools and methods, such as **net present value (NPV)**. This approach examines a lifetime stream of additional earnings and cost savings for an investment. The cash flow that might exist is then discounted by the cost of borrowing that money. If the NPV is positive, then the firm should undertake the investment; if it is negative, the firm should not undertake the investment. This approach is too complex—for the needs of this text—to be examined in any detail. For the purpose of illustration, it will be assumed that the owners began by looking at the impact of alternative investment schemes on the projected results for 2011. Obviously, any in-depth analysis of this investment would have to entail multi-year projections.

They examined five scenarios:

1. Their relative provides the entire $200,000 for an equity position in the business.

2. They borrow $50,000 from the bank at an interest rate of 7.5 percent, and their relative provides the remaining $150,000 for a smaller equity position in the business.

3. They borrow $100,000 from the bank at an interest rate of 10 percent, and their relative provides the remaining $100,000 for a smaller equity position in the business.

4. They borrow $150,000 from the bank at an interest rate of 12.5 percent, and their relative provides the remaining $50,000 for an even smaller equity position in the business.

5. They borrow the entire $200,000 from the bank at an interest rate of 15 percent.

Table 10.6 presents the income statement for these five scenarios. (An abbreviated balance sheet for the five scenarios is given in Table 10.7.) All five scenarios begin with the assumption that the new equipment would improve productive capacity and allow sales to increase, in 2011, by 25 percent, rather than the 7.5 percent that had been previously forecasted. Likewise, all five scenarios have the same cost of goods sold, which in this case is 55 percent of the revenues rather than the anticipated 65 percent if the new equipment is not purchased. All five scenarios have the same EBIT. The scenarios differ, however, in the interest payments. The first scenario assumes that all $200,000 would be provided by a relative who is taking an equity position in the firm. This is not a loan, so there are no interest payments. In the remaining four scenarios, the interest payments are a function of the amount borrowed and the corresponding interest rate. The payment of interest obviously impacts the earnings before taxes (EBT) and the amount of taxes that have to be paid. Although the tax bill for those scenarios where money has been borrowed is less than the scenario where the $200,000 is provided by equity, the net profit also declines as the amount borrowed increases.

TABLE 10.6 Income Statement for the Five Scenarios

	Borrow $0	Borrow $50,000	Borrow $100,000	Borrow $150,000	Borrow $200,000
Revenue	$593,750	$593,750	$593,750	$593,750	$593,750
Cost of goods sold	$326,563	$326,563	$326,563	$326,563	$326,563
Gross profit	$267,188	$267,188	$267,188	$267,188	$267,188
General sales and administrative	$118,750	$118,750	$118,750	$118,750	$118,750
EBIT	$148,438	$148,438	$148,438	$148,438	$148,438
Interest	$—	$3,750	$10,000	$18,750	$30,000
Taxes	$44,531	$43,406	$41,531	$38,906	$35,531
Net profit	$103,906	$101,281	$96,906	$90,781	$82,906

TABLE 10.7   Abbreviated Balance Sheet for the Five Scenarios

	Borrow $0	Borrow $50,000	Borrow $100,000	Borrow $150,000	Borrow $200,000
Total assets	$965,000	$965,000	$965,000	$965,000	$965,000
Long-term debt	$—	$50,000	$100,000	$150,000	$200,000
Owners' equity	$965,000	$915,000	$865,000	$815,000	$765,000
Total debt and equity	$965,000	$965,000	$965,000	$965,000	$965,000

The owners then calculated the ROA and the ROE for the five scenarios (see Table 10.8). When they examined these results, they noticed that the greatest ROA occurred when the new machinery was financed exclusively by equity capital. The ROA declined as they began to fund new machinery with debt: the greater the debt, the lower the ROA. However, they saw a different situation when they looked at the ROE for each scenario. The ROE was greater in each scenario where the machinery was financed either exclusively or to some extent by debt. In fact, the lowest ROE (the firm borrowed the entire $200,000) was 50 percent higher than if the firm did not acquire the new equipment. A further examination of the ROE results provides a very interesting insight. The ROE increases as the firm borrows up to $100,000 of debt. When the firm borrows more money ($150,000 or $200,000), the ROE declines (see Figure 10.3). This is a highly simplified example of optimal capital structure. There is a level of debt beyond which the benefits measured by ROE begins to decline. Small businesses must be able to identify their "ideal" debt-to-equity ratio.

TABLE 10.8   ROA and ROE for the Five Scenarios

	Borrow $0	Borrow $50,000	Borrow $100,000	Borrow $150,000	Borrow $200,000
ROA	10.77%	10.50%	10.04%	9.41%	8.59%
ROE	10.77%	11.07%	11.20%	11.14%	10.84%

FIGURE 10.3   ROE for the Five Scenarios

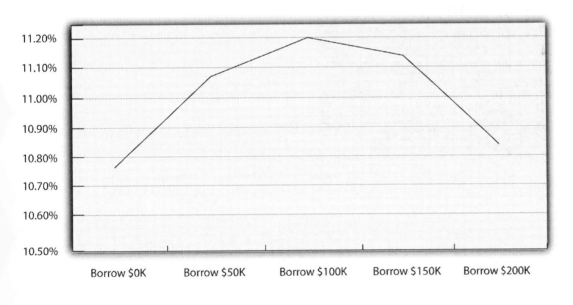

———— Return on equity

The owners decided to carry their analysis one step further; they wondered if the sales projections were too enthusiastic. They were concerned about the firm's ability to repay any loan should there be a drop in sales. Therefore, they decided to examine a worst-case scenario. Such analyses are absolutely critical if one is to fully evaluate the risk of undertaking debt. They ran the numbers to see what the results would be if there was a 25 percent decrease in sales in 2011 rather than a 25 percent increase in sales compared to 2010. The results of this set of analyses are in Table 10.9. Even with a heavy debt burden for the five scenarios, the firm is able to generate a profit, although it is a substantially lower profit compared to if sales increased by 25 percent. They examined the impact of this proposed declining sales on ROA and ROE. These results are found in Table 10.10.

TABLE 10.9 Income Statement for the Five Scenarios Assuming a 25 Percent Decrease in Sales

	Borrow $0	Borrow $50,000	Borrow $100,000	Borrow $150,000	Borrow $200,000
Revenue	$356,250	$356,250	$356,250	$356,250	$356,250
Cost of goods sold	$195,938	$195,938	$195,938	$195,938	$195,938
Gross profit	$160,313	$160,313	$160,313	$160,313	$160,313
General sales and administrative	$71,250	$71,250	$71,250	$71,250	$71,250
EBIT	$89,063	$89,063	$89,063	$89,063	$89,063
Interest	$—	$3,750	$10,000	$18,750	$30,000
Taxes	$26,719	$25,594	$23,719	$21,094	$17,719
Net profit	$62,344	$59,719	$55,344	$49,219	$41,344

TABLE 10.10 ROA and ROE for the Five Scenarios under the Condition of Declining Sales

	Borrow $0	Borrow $50,000	Borrow $100,000	Borrow $150,000	Borrow $200,000
ROA	6.46%	6.19%	5.74%	5.10%	4.28%
ROE	6.46%	6.53%	6.40%	6.04%	5.40%

 Video Clip 10.10

Debt Financing versus Equity Financing: Which Is Best for Us?
Overview of the benefits and dangers associated with debt financing and equity financing.

View the video online at: http://www.youtube.com/v/revyx4o390s

 Video Clip 10.11

Capital Structure
Compares capital structure to a commercial aircraft.

View the video online at: http://www.youtube.com/v/6uB1eWJz9jI

Video Clip 10.12

Lecture in Capital Structure
Explains why capital structure matters.

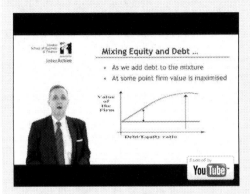

View the video online at: http://www.youtube.com/v/1W-Oa7IkdHA

 Video Clip 10.13

The Capital Structure of a Company
Discusses the issue of long-term and short-term debt in capital structure.

View the video online at: http://www.youtube.com/v/uPY5-gtkgL4

KEY TAKEAWAYS

- A relatively simply model—breakeven analysis—can indicate what sales level is required to start making a profit.
- Financial leverage—the ratio of debt to equity—can improve the economic performance of a business as measured by ROE.
- Excessive financial leverage—too much debt—can begin to reduce the economic performance of a business.
- There is an ideal level of debt for a firm, which is its optimal capital structure.

EXERCISES

1. A new start-up business will have fixed costs of $750,000 per year. It plans on selling one product that will have a variable cost of $20 per unit. What is the product's selling price to break even?

2. Using data from the business in Exercise 1, in its second year of operation, it adds a second selling facility, which increases the fixed cost by $250,000. The variable cost has now decreased by $2.50 per unit. What is the new selling price to break even?

3. Using the example in Section 3, how would the ROA and the ROE change if economic conditions made borrowing money more expensive? Specifically, what would be the impact if the interest rate on $50,000 was 10 percent; $100,000, 15 percent; $150,000, 17.5 percent; and $200,000, 20 percent?

4. Again using the example in Section 3, how much would sales have to decrease to threaten the business's ability to repay its interest on a $100,000 loan?

---

4. THE THREE THREADS

LEARNING OBJECTIVES

1. Understand that effective and efficient financial management can enhance value provided to customers.
2. Appreciate that effective financial management can improve the firm's cash-flow position.
3. Understand that the use of technologies can significantly reduce cost of operations and improve profitability.

4.1 Customer Value

activity-based costing system

An accounting system where costs are assigned due to the cause-and-effect relationship between costs and the activity that drives the cost.

In Chapter 2, Chapter 6, and Chapter 7, there has been extensive discussion of the notion of market segmentation. By segmenting the market, one improves the probability that a business will be able to better serve particular customers' needs and thus provide better customer value. From a financial perspective, there may be an equivalent notion of segmentation. Earlier discussions on market segmentation were centered on how a business could provide value to particular sets of customers. A subsequent stage of this analysis would be to examine how and if these customers can provide value to a business. No one is served if the business provides significant value to its customers but the business goes broke in the process. The financial equivalent of customer segmentation examines the profitability of different groups of customers. Some customer groups may be extremely profitable to a firm, while others produce nothing but losses. Identifying these different groups requires a commitment to accounting and a financial analysis of each customer base. The first step is to determine the margin provided by each customer group. In many cases, this is a bit of a challenge. It may require more extensive record keeping. The business may have to use **activity-based costing systems**. (Activity-based costing systems were developed in the late 1970s and the early 1980s.) This approach to accounting "is a process where costs are assigned due to the cause and effect relationship between costs and the activity that drives the cost."[20]

Done properly, activity-based accounting can help a business identify the true costs for serving particular customer groups and therefore identify their real profit margins. A business may discover that some customer groups are actually a source of losses for the firm.

It should be pointed out that activity-based accounting is complex, difficult to implement, and, in some instances, does not conform to the requirements of generally accepted accounting principles. This might mean that a business would have to have two coexisting accounting systems, which may be too much of a burden for the small business.

4.2   Cash-Flow Implications

It should not be too surprising to find that good financial management can benefit tremendously when a firm's cash flow is improved. Two areas where good financial management can help would be e-procurement and factoring. **E-procurement** involves managing the timing of invoices to customers and from suppliers to improve the cash flow of the firm.[21] The electronic handling of orders and their associated invoices assures that customers will receive their orders in a more timely fashion. E-procurement means that fewer personnel are required to take and handle orders. This can be a tremendous source of cash saving in and of itself. E-procurement should be on any supply chain management program of a business. We discuss supply chain management in Chapter 12.

Another area where good financial management can improve cash flow is factoring. The most common form of factoring is associated with a business's accounts receivable. Trade credits involve purchasing and taking delivery of supplies now while planning to pay for it later. (See Section 1 for a discussion of trade credits.) Three key numbers often identify trade credits: a discount rate for early payment, the time to pay to take advantage of the discount rate, and the date by which the entire bill must be paid. We underscore the kinds of the factoring with the following example.

A firm makes a large sale of supplies—$200,000. The trade credit program is 2/10/60. This means that the firm will give a 2 percent discount if the customer pays the entire $200,000 within 10 days and expects the payment of the entire $200,000 within the next 60 days. The firm knows that its customer never exercises the discount opportunity and always pays on the last possible date. Further, let us assume that this firm is having a problem with its cash flow. It would like to expedite payment as quickly as possible but does not expect that the customer will obtain a 2 percent discount by paying within 10 days. This firm could exercise the factoring option. This business goes to another firm that would provide as much as 80 percent of the cash receivable invoice immediately for small fee. In other words, the firm would receive $160,000 immediately rather than waiting 60 days. When its customer pays the bill, the firm would receive, in total, slightly less than the $200,000 but would have expedited the payment and thus aided its cash flow. Factoring can be an important element in improving the overall cash flow of any firm.

4.3   Digital Technology and E-Environment Implications

We identify four sources of capital in Section 1, one of which is internally generated funds. Businesses can increase the supply of capital money by becoming more operationally efficient. Improved operational efficiency can save any organization considerable amounts of money. Many start-ups, particularly those with some technological savvy, use technology to produce significant cost savings. This recognition of the vital role of technology as a cost-saving tool came to the forefront at a recent GeeknRolla conference in London. This conference brings together new business start-ups and potential investors. There is a heavy emphasis on how new businesses (and established businesses) can successfully integrate a variety of technologies and improve their operational efficiencies. As one participant in the conference, Michael Jackson, an investor, said, "Companies that are cottoning on quickly to these tools are doing very well, and they are taking business away from those who are too slow to adapt."[22]

The 2011 conference paid special attention to the concept of **cloud computing**. This term refers to having software programs and databases located on an outsourced site. As an example, rather than buying Microsoft's Office Suite for every computer in a business, one could access a word-processing program, a spreadsheet program, or a database as needed. The firm would be charged for each use or a monthly fee rather than having to purchase an entire package. Chapter 9, Section 4 mentions that one can even access an entire accounting system as a part of a cloud computing option. As Sharif Sakr said, "In addition to being 'pay-as-you-go,' cloud computing has the advantage of reducing the number of computers, servers and network connections that a small business needs."[23]

In addition to reducing a small business's initial commitment to an information technology (IT) infrastructure—computers, software, network systems, and IT staff—cloud computing provides some of the following additional benefits:

- **Scalability.** Many cloud applications allow for the growth of a business. As an example, some cloud accounting packages charge on the basis of the number of users; therefore, a company could purchase as much capability as it needed.

- **Updates.** Businesses do not have to worry about purchasing the latest version of the software, uninstalling the old version, and installing the latest version. This is done automatically by the vendor.

- **Access.** Cloud programs can be accessed wherever one has a connection to the Internet. A business is not tied to its own computer or the network where the software resides. This results in

e-procurement

The purchasing of supplies through the Internet and the timing of invoices to customers and from suppliers to improve the cash flow of a firm.

cloud computing

The situation in which vendor software does not reside on the computer system of a small business.

tremendous flexibility; as an example, one can access the program and the data while on the road with a client.

- **Integration.** Having programs and databases on the cloud facilitates multiple members of an organization successfully working together. No one has to worry whether he or she is working with the latest version of the spreadsheet or the client list.

- **Security.** Cloud providers recognize that securing their client's data is a core issue for business survival. They will bring into play the required technology to ensure that every one's data are secure and safe. They have much greater capability of assuring this than almost any small business.

- **Customization.** Businesses can acquire the software that they need.

- **Extensions into the world of social media.** More and more businesses are using various forms of social media—Facebook, Twitter, LinkedIn, and so forth—yet many small businesses lack the technological savvy to fully exploit these new avenues of marketing. Cloud providers can assist these businesses in this vital area.[24]

So how can smaller businesses aspire to efficiencies that much larger organizations have achieved through the use of IT while achieving it at a fraction of the cost? Entire accounting systems can be placed on the cloud. FreshBooks, which is free for solo location businesses, provides an accounting system that can be extended to allow business operators to submit invoices via the iPhone. Shoeboxed, another cloud-based company, allows small businesses to take digitalized receipts and turn them into invoices.

Owners and employees can more productively manage their time by using a variety of scheduling programs. TimeTrade is an effective personal scheduling assistant. It can show prospective clients available times and assist in arranging a scheduled appointment. Major companies, such as Microsoft and Google, provide cloud-based applications that can be employed by both large corporations and the smallest of businesses. Microsoft has an e-mail system—Exchange—that can be used by smaller businesses for fees as low as $50 per month. Google Voice can translate voice mail and e-mail messages and forward them anywhere in the world. Programs such as Mail-Chimp can send information packages to any or all of a business's clients and then automatically post the same information on the company's Facebook and Twitter sites.

KEY TAKEAWAYS

- Just as a business must identify what is of value to its customers, it should also determine how valuable its customers are to the business.
- It may not "pay" to attract and keep all customers.
- Techniques such as factoring accounts receivable may improve the cash flow of a firm.
- The use of cloud computing can significantly reduce costs and improve the financial position of a firm.
- Local, national, and international economic conditions can affect any firm. Businesses should plan on how to deal with major economic upheavals.

EXERCISES

1. Search the Internet to find out about the availability and price of activity-based accounting software.
2. Imagine your boss has asked you to prepare a small report on using factoring as an option in her auto parts business. Search the Internet to find out about the economics of factoring.
3. Prepare a report on accounting and finance software packages available through cloud computing. Discuss their pros, cons, and pricing structures.

Disaster Watch

At the beginning of Chapter 10, it was stated that a major cause of failure in small businesses is inadequate financial management. If one looks at that statement at face value, the only conclusion one can come to is that failure solely rests on the shoulders of the small business owner. This is far from the full story. Small businesses can face disastrous financial situations over which they have absolutely no control. This simple fact has been brought to the forefront in the last few years with the economic downturn.

For most small businesses, the major source of external financing comes from banks. Anything that affects the banks' ability or desire to lend to small businesses can have a profound effect. One of the first responses on the part of commercial banks to the crisis of 2008 was a severe restriction of credit. At the height of the crisis in October 2008, nearly 72 percent of large banks and 78 percent of small banks stated that they were tightening their credit standards for small businesses.[25] This slightly more restrictive approach on the part of smaller banks represented a change from some prior recessions. Berger and Udell (1994) found that during the credit crunch of 1990–92 smaller banks were more willing to lend than larger banks.[26]

The current credit crunch has even more significance for small businesses. The originator of current economic difficulties was in the US real estate industry. The result has been a significantly depressed real estate market. Many small businesses use either personal residences or business property (real estate) as the basis for collateral to secure loans. A depressed real estate market reduces the viability of this option. Other negative consequences for small businesses in this current economic environment revolve around its impact on alternatives of raising capital via commercial bank loans. In earlier credit crunches, many small businesses turned to commercial finance companies. These types of companies would lend money to small businesses that pledged assets as collateral.[27] Since the early 1990s, many of these firms either disappeared or have been absorbed by larger commercial banking institutions. Today, many of the largest firms in the United States are holding onto cash (some estimate it in the neighborhood of $2 trillion to $3 trillion). Their unwillingness to spend or invest is impacting smaller businesses that operate further down the supply chain. Another impact of the current economic crisis has been that many banks have changed their lending practices for credit cards. They have raised rates, raised fees, and lowered credit limits. Many small businesses are sometimes reduced to using credit cards as a basis for attaining short-term financing for purchases or meeting bills. This sudden change in the "rules of the game" for credit cards has presented many small businesses with an unexpected challenge.

None of these changes in the financial landscape were brought about by the decision making or the knowledge of entrepreneurs and small business operators. Only an extraordinarily small number of financial experts saw the crisis coming. Nonetheless, entrepreneurs and small business owners have found that they must learn to rapidly adapt to what is simply a disastrous situation. The financial lesson to be learned from the current crisis is that any business, particularly small businesses, must prepare to have alternative sources of financing available for the continued operations.

ENDNOTES

1. Frank Salvatore (owner), in discussion with the authors.

2. "Difference between Accounting and Finance," *DifferenceBetween.net*, accessed February 1, 2012, www.differencebetween.net/business/difference-between -accounting-and-finance.

3. "Difference between Accounting and Finance," *DifferenceBetween.net*, accessed February 1, 2012, www.differencebetween.net/business/difference-between -accounting-and-finance.

4. "Types of Business Organizations," *BusinessFinance.com*, accessed December 2, 2011, www.businessfinance.com/books/startabusiness/startabusinessworkbook010.htm.

5. "Business Finance—by Category," *About.com*, accessed December 2, 2011, bizfinance.about.com/od/income tax/a/busorgs.htm.

6. "Financing," *Small Business Notes*, accessed December 2, 2011, www.smallbusinessnotes.com/business-finances/financing.

7. "Checklist: Issuing Stock," *San Francisco Chronicle*, accessed December 2, 2011, allbusiness.sfgate.com/10809-1.html.

8. "How to Form a Corporation," *Yahoo! Small Business Advisor*, April 26, 2011, accessed February 1, 2012, smallbusiness.yahoo.com/advisor/how-to-form-a-corporation -201616320.html.

9. "How Will a Credit Crunch Affect Small Business Finance?," *Federal Reserve Bank of San Francisco*, March 6, 2009, accessed December 2, 2011, www.frbsf.org/publications/ economics/letter/2009/el2009-09.html.

10. Anita Campbell, "Trade Credit: What It Is and Why You Should Pay Attention," *Small Business Trends*, May 11, 2009, accessed December 2, 2011, smallbiztrends.com/2009/ 05/trade-credit-what-it-is-and-why-you-should-pay-attention.html.

11. Gavin Cassar, "The Financing of Business Startups," *Journal of Business Venturing* 19 (2004): 261–83.

12. Lola Fabowale, Barbara Orse, and Alan Riding, "Gender, Structural Factors, and Credit Terms between Canadian Small Businesses and Financial Institutions," *Entrepreneurship Theory and Practice* 19 (1995): 41–65.

13. Harry Sapienza, M. Audrey Korsgaard, and Daniel Forbes, "The Self-Determination Mode of an Entrepreneur's Choice of Financing," in *Advances in Entrepreneurship, Firm Emergence, and Growth: Cognitive Approaches to Entrepreneurship Research*, ed. Jerome A. Katz and Dean Shepherd (Oxford: Elsevier JAI, 2003) 6:105–38.

14. Allen N. Berger and Gregory F. Udell, "The Economics of Small Business Finance: The Roles of Private Equity and Debt Markets in the Financial Growth Cycle," *Journal of Banking and Finance* 22, no. 6–8 (1998): 613–73.

15. Rowena Ortiz-Walters and Mark Gius, "Performance of Newly Formed Micro Firms: The Role of Capital Financing Structure and Entrepreneurs' Personal Characteristics" (unpublished manuscript), 2011.

16. "The Benefits of Making Your Banker Your Friend," *Small Business Administration*, accessed December 2, 2011, www.sbaonline.sba.gov./smallbusinessplanner/start/ financestartup/SERV_BANKERFRIEND.html.

17. "Breakeven Analysis: Know When You Can Expect a Profit," *Small Business Administration*, accessed December 2, 2011, www.sba.gov/content/breakeven-analysis -know-when-you-can-expect-profit.

18. David Durand, "Cost of Debt and Equity Funds for Business: Trends and Problems of Measurement," *Conference on Research in Business Finance* (New York: National Bureau of Economic Research, 1952), 220.

19. Franco Modigliani and Merton Miller, "The Cost of Capital, Corporation Finance and the Theory of Investment," *American Economic Review* 48, no. 3 (1958): 261–97; Franco Modigliani and Merton Miller, "Taxes and the Cost of Capital: A Correction," *American Economic Review* 53 (1963): 433–43.

20. Tiffany Bradford, "Activity-Based Costing," *Accounting @ Suite 101*, accessed December 2, 2011, tiffany-bradford.suite101.com/activitybased-costing-abc-a52148.

21. Peter Robbins, "E-Procurement—Making Cash Flow King," *Credit Control* 26, no. 2 (2005): 23–26.

22. Sharif Sakr, "GeeknRolla: Tech Start-Ups Reveal Cost-Cutting Tips," *BBC Business*, accessed December 2, 2011, www.bbc.co.uk/news/business-12962023.

23. Sharif Sakr, "GeeknRolla: Tech Start-Ups Reveal Cost-Cutting Tips," *BBC Business*, accessed December 2, 2011, www.bbc.co.uk/news/business-12962023.

24. Eilene Zimmerman, "A Small Business Made to Seem Bigger," *New York Times*, March 2, 2011, accessed December 2, 2011, www.nytimes.com/2011/03/03/business/ smallbusiness/03sbiz.html?_r=1.

25. "How Will a Credit Crunch Affect Small Business Finance?," *Federal Reserve Bank of San Francisco*, March 6, 2009, accessed December 2, 2011, www.frbsf.org/publications/ economics/letter/2009/el2009-09.html.

26. Allen N. Berger and Gregory F. Udell, "Did Risk-Based Capital Allocate Bank Credit and Cause a Credit Crunch in the US?," *Journal of Money, Credit and Banking* 26 (1994): 585–628.

27. Gregory F. Udell, *Asset-Based Finance: Proven Disciplines for Prudent Lending* (New York: Commercial Finance Association, 2004), 16.

CHAPTER 11
Supply Chain Management: You Better Get It Right

R. W. Hine

Source: Used with permission from R. W. Hine.

No business—small, midsize, or large—survives for more than a century without successfully identifying changing customer needs and adapting its processes and technologies. The adoption of new technologies is not limited to advanced manufacturing or web-based business. New technologies can be crucial to any business, even a business as seemingly prosaic as the local hardware store. However, successfully running a business with an inventory between twenty-five thousand and thirty thousand different items is anything but prosaic.

R. W. Hine has been a central fixture in Cheshire, Connecticut, since it was established in 1910. For the last quarter century, it has been owned and managed by Pat Bowman.

It is obvious that any local hardware store, which must carry an extremely large number of different products, faces a considerable challenge when competing with big box stores such as Home Depot or Lowe's. Hine is a relatively small enterprise with approximately twenty-five employees, many of whom are high school or college students working part time. Hine is able to effectively compete because of two main factors. The first is an edge seen in many small businesses—a clear focus on identifying and meeting what constitutes customer value and meeting it rapidly. A typical example is as follows: in anticipation of a major winter storm, Hine quickly stocked up on roof rakes—a tool that is used to remove heavy snow from roofs. Hine has had a tremendous success meeting the special needs of its customers. The second factor is Hine's membership in the ACE Hardware Cooperative. ACE Hardware was founded in 1924 to centralize purchasing for member stores. In 1973, ACE Hardware became a cooperative. Today, it consists of nearly 4,500 member hardware stores. The cooperative centralizes purchasing for all members. It provides all members with the benefit of volume purchasing, which significantly reduces costs. The cooperative also simplifies inventory maintenance issues for its member stores. A member store can either order items directly from a participating supplier or have items shipped from an ACE Hardware warehouse. Shipments are generally done on a weekly or a semiweekly basis. Such rapid turnaround allows member stores, such as Hine, to respond to customer demand. Hine also uses Epicor enterprise resource planning (ERP) software. It enables Hine to monitor its historic sales information, set targeted inventory levels, and suggest reorder times. The juxtaposition of a commitment to giving customers value and the effective use of supply chain management techniques appear to prove that this local hardware store will succeed in its second century of operation.

1. THE SUPPLY CHAIN AND A FIRM'S ROLE IN IT

LEARNING OBJECTIVES

1. Understand what is meant by the term *supply chain management*.
2. Understand the four components of supply chain management.
3. Understand the "bullwhip" phenomenon.
4. Recognize the benefits for a small business in adopting supply chain management.

No man is an island, entire of itself.[1]
  - *John Donne*

management by objectives

A program in which the supervisor and the subordinate sit down and map out the objectives for the subordinate to accomplish in the upcoming year.

business process reengineering

A management program that analyzes the processes of a business and tries to redesign them so that all non-value-added activities are eliminated.

learning organization

An organization that is able to adapt to changing situations and pressures. It places a premium on organizations and individuals that can learn from the environment.

benchmarking

A program where a business looks at the world leaders in particular processes and attempts to emulate them.

Given the almost daily exposure and coverage of modern business theories or concepts in the popular press, one of the great challenges for both small business owners and corporate executives is the need to separate the wheat from the chaff. In the last four or five decades, businesspeople have heard and read about the next great idea that will revolutionize business as we know it. One almost feels obligated to run out and buy a book that lays out the general principles of concepts such as **management by objectives**, **business process reengineering**, transactional versus transformational leadership, management by walking around, the **learning organization**, matrix management, **benchmarking**, lean methodologies, and several quality systems—total quality management, the Deming method, and Six Sigma. Some of these have proven to be business fads and have run their course—sometimes with poisonous effects.[2] Others, such as lean methodologies and some quality systems, have proven to be solid bases on which to improve an organization's efficiency and effectiveness.

A modern concept that has been popularized over the last two decades is that of supply chain management. In one sense, supply chain management is as old as business itself. One has to look only at the traffic along antiquity's Silk Road trade route. This route was used to move goods across Asia's vast steppes between China and the Middle East and as far west as ancient Rome. It possessed most of the fundamental elements of today's supply chain: goods were produced (make), transported (move), deposited in warehouses (store), purchased by merchants (buy), and sold to customers (sell; see Figure 11.2). As will be seen, these five activities are the core of any supply chain.[3] If these activities have been universal dimensions of business, then what is different about supply chain management? That question will now be addressed.

FIGURE 11.1   Material Flows in a Supply Chain

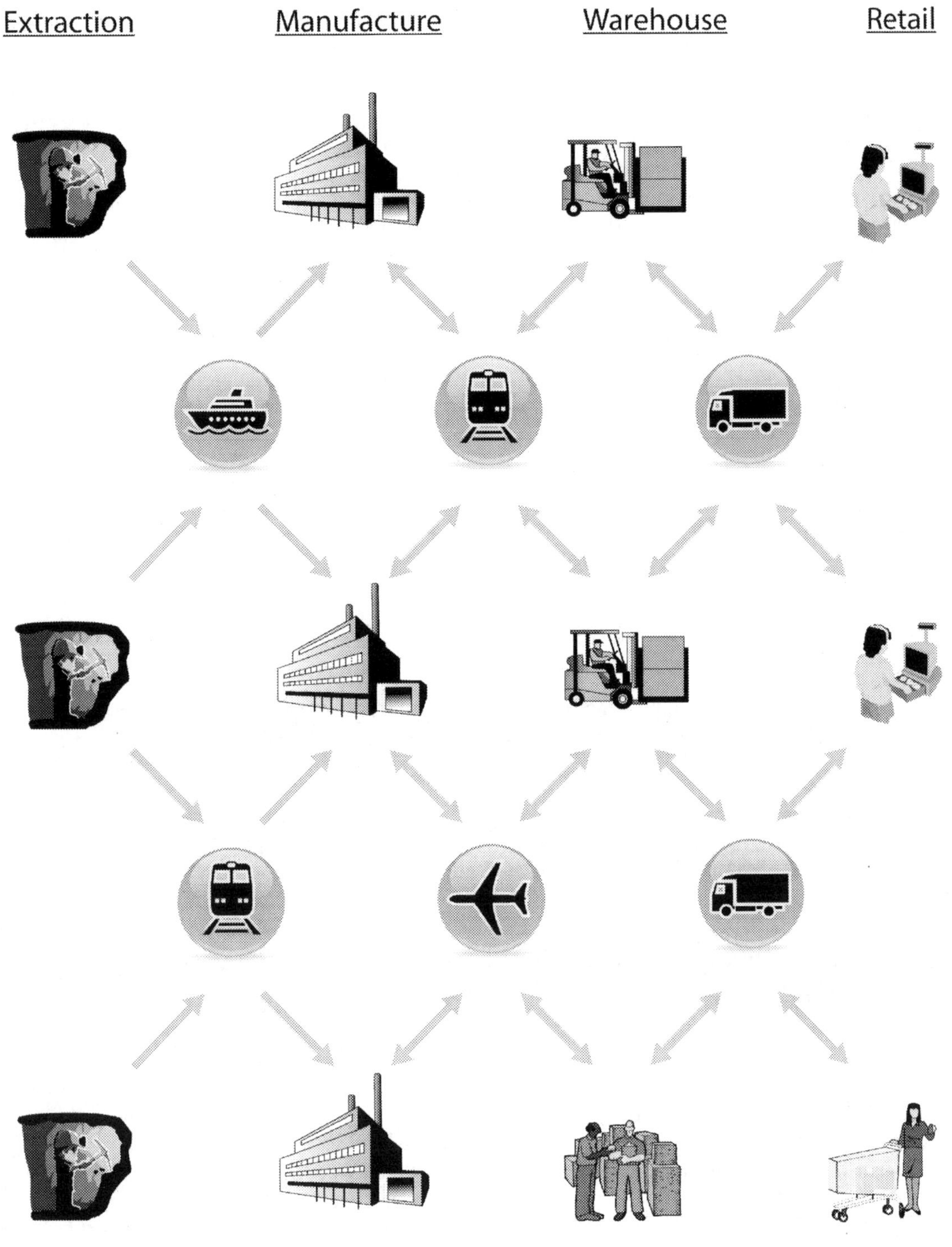

Extraction   Manufacture   Warehouse   Retail

1.1   What Is a Supply Chain?

The owners of many small businesses may pride themselves on knowing many—if not all—of their employees. Other small businesses may have some degree of familiarity with most of their customers. They may have professional contacts with someone at the office of their immediate suppliers. Beyond those contacts, the daily demands of operations may mean that they have failed to see their firm's position in the larger context known as the supply chain. What precisely do we mean when we use the term **supply chain management**? Industrial organizations and academics provide several different definitions of supply chain management.

The Council of Supply Chain Management Professionals provides the following definition: "Supply chain management encompasses the planning and management of all activities involved in sourcing and procurement, conversion, and all logistics management activities. Importantly, it also includes coordination and collaboration with channel partners, which can be suppliers, intermediaries,

supply chain management

A systematic and integrated flow of materials, information, and money from the initial raw material supplier through fabricators, manufacturers, warehouses, distribution centers, retailers, and the final customer.

third party service providers, and customers. In essence, supply chain management integrates supply and demand management within and across companies."[4]

The Association for Operations Management (APICS) defines a supply chain as "a total systems approach to designing and managing the entire flow of information, materials, and services—from raw material suppliers, through factories and warehouses, and finally to the customer…The chain comprises many links, such as links between suppliers that provide inputs, links to manufacturing and service support operations that transform the input into products and services, and links to the distribution and local service providers that localized the product."[5]

In a seminal article on the subject, supply chain management was defined as follows: "Supply chain management is the systemic, strategic coordination of the traditional business functions and the tactics across these business functions within a particular company and across businesses within the supply chain, for the purposes of improving the long-term performance of the individual companies and the supply chain as a whole."[6]

For our purpose, we define the supply chain as follows: "It is a systematic and integrated flow of materials, information, and money from the initial raw material supplier through fabricators, manufacturers, warehouses, distribution centers, retailers, and the final customer. Its ultimate objective is the improvement of the entire process, which means an increase of economic performance of all participants and an increase in value for the end customer."

If we examine these definitions, several common themes stand out. Supply chain management is not limited to the flow of goods and materials. The successful supply chain requires a consideration of both financial flows and information flows across the entire chain (see Figure 11.2). A second theme is that organizations must overcome myopia of just being concerned with their immediate suppliers and customers. They must take into consideration their suppliers' suppliers and their customers' customers. To be able to do this, organizations must expand the flow of communication and information.

FIGURE 11.2 Additional Flows in a Supply Chain

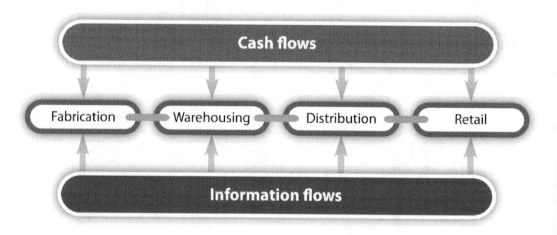

One might easily pose the following question: How has the concept of supply chain management taken off in the last twenty years? The proliferation of supply chain management is a core concept for businesses that can be attributed to several major factors, including the following:

- **The increasing importance of globalization.** Global trade has seen a spectacular increase in the last half century. It is estimated that international trade has increased by 100 percent increase since 1955.[7] The end of the Cold War in the early 1990s produced a political environment conducive to the promotion of the notion of free trade. Free trade advocates that nations lower or eliminate trade barriers and tariffs so that countries might develop some particular competencies so that they can participate in the global economy. Several trading blocs have been built during the last three decades that facilitate trade among their partners, including the European Union, which currently consists of twenty-seven countries with a total population in excess of five hundred million and a gross domestic product (GDP) greater than that of the United States. The European Union shares a common currency, and there are no trade barriers among its member states. NAFTA stands for the North American Free Trade Agreement and encompasses Canada, the United States, and Mexico. With respect to the combined GDP of these three countries, NAFTA represents the largest trading bloc in the world. Two other trading blocs in the Western Hemisphere are the Dominican Republic-Central American Free Trade Agreement and MERCOSUR (Common Southern Agreement), which promotes trade among Argentina, Brazil, Paraguay, and Uruguay. The spectacular growth of international finance should also be considered when examining the growth of globalism in recent history.

- **Changes in consumer demands.** Across the world, consumers are becoming progressively more demanding. They expect better quality products with more options and at a lower cost. One has to look only at the global market for cell phones for an example. Even in countries that might be classified as Third World countries, consumers expect to be able to buy cell phones with cutting-edge capability at reasonable prices. This results in a great need for new products, which in turn requires a reduction in life cycle development times. Normally, increasing the product development time would generally result in higher cost, something that is unacceptable today. To meet increasing and often conflicting demands, businesses find that they must work closely with members of their supply chain.

- **Organizations that have recognized the need to change.** Increasingly, more and more businesses recognize that old models may no longer function. In the past, many businesses strove to be vertically integrated. This meant that they wanted to control as many aspects of their operations as possible. Large oil companies exhibit vertical, industry-wide integration. A firm such as Exxon-Mobil has the capacity to carry out almost all the functions associated with the petroleum industry. Exxon-Mobil has units that can explore for oil, drill for oil, transport oil, refine oil into gasoline, and sell it directly to consumers. In this way, it has almost complete control over the entire supply chain. This approach—total vertical integration—may work in some industries where firms recognize that it is economically advantageous to outsource noncore activities. Firms are making the decision whether to make or buy, and they are finding it financially attractive to have other businesses make components or products for them. As outsourcing became more popular, there was immediate recognition that businesses had to pay careful attention to all the elements of their supply chains. They had to develop working relationships with their suppliers and their customers. As will be highlighted in Section 2, successful supply chain management requires new approaches for dealing with suppliers. Those businesses that have successfully made this transition can fully exploit the benefits of supply chain management.

  Another area where businesses have learned to change, which has greatly impacted the acceptance of supply chain management, is the change from a push philosophy to a pull philosophy. A push philosophy means that a business produces goods and services and pushes it into the marketplace. A push-based system will forecast demand in the market, produce the required amount, push the product out the door, and hope that the forecast was correct. In contrast, a pull philosophy means that the production of goods and services is initiated only when the marketplace or the consumer demands it. Production is initiated by actual demand.

- **Technical innovations.** Today's approach to supply chain management would be impossible without technological revolutions in the fields of communication and computer software. It would be impossible to operate in a global supply chain without the Internet. As will be discussed in Section 4, software packages for customer relationship management (CRM), warehousing control, inventory management, and supply chain relationship software are vital to the growth of supply chains.

 Video Clip 11.1

What Is a Supply Chain?
A brief explanation of the supply chain.

View the video online at: http://www.youtube.com/v/NudCAtI2bBE

Video Clip 11.2

Supply Chain: Three Key Things to Know
Rob O'Byrne of the Logistics Bureau talks about three key concepts for a supply chain.

View the video online at: http://www.youtube.com/v/OaxJ4oEuBO8

 Video Clip 11.3

What Is Supply Chain Management?
The first of a series of twelve videos on supply chain management, providing an excellent overview of the subject.

View the video online at: http://www.youtube.com/v/Mi1QBxVjZAw

1.2 Key Elements of a Supply Chain

What precisely makes up a supply chain management system? Various authors identify the different components or elements of such a system.[8] The simple list would include four core elements: procurement, operations, distribution, and integration.

FIGURE 11.3 The Core Elements of a Supply Chain Management System

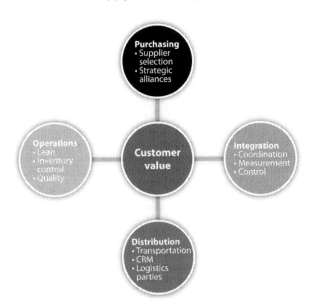

The first of the four elements—**procurement**—begins with the purchasing of parts, components, or services. However, it does not end with the purchase. Procurement must ensure that the right items are delivered in the exact quantities at the correct location on the specified time schedule at minimal cost. This means that procurement must concern itself with the determination of who should supply the parts, the components, or the services. It must address the question of assurance that these suppliers will deliver as promised. The opening phrase of this question is often as follows: should the business make or buy a particular part or service? The make-or-buy question can have both strategic significance and economic significance. Some businesses will choose not to have others make or provide services because they believe they may lose control over particular technologies or skill sets. Will it benefit a business to have lower cost in the short run yet lose its source of competitive advantage in the long run to another competitor? Overseas outsourcing may pose difficulties with respect to communication difficulties, extended transportation distances, and timelines. The inability to ensure the overall quality of the outsourced item may be a deciding factor in not having another business make the part or provide the service. Recent difficulties with the quality assurance of products made in China have given many American manufacturers second thoughts about outsourcing.

There are, however, reasons for businesses to outsource production or services. The most obvious reason is associated with lower costs. Read the business press and discover the phrase *the China price*. This refers to the low cost of products produced in China given its low wages. One should not think that outsourcing is associated only with overseas manufacturing. Many firms will domestically outsource certain in-house service activities. The firm ADP specializes in preparing businesses payrolls, employee benefits, and tax compliance. ADP has been successful because it is able to provide a high-quality product at lower cost than many firms could produce in-house. Another reason why a business may outsource production or other activities is that the business is currently unable to meet particular demand levels.

If one were to exclude strategic considerations and merely look at economic issues, many make-or-buy decisions could be fairly straightforward variations of breakeven analysis. Imagine a firm is thinking about outsourcing the manufacture of a particular part to a Chinese firm. The plot is not unique from a technical standpoint, so outsourcing would have no strategic significance. The firm has gathered the data in Table 11.1 for its own operations and that of the Chinese firm.

procurement

A process that not only involves the purchasing of parts, components, or services but also considers that the right parts are delivered in the exact quantities at the correct location on the specified time schedule at minimal cost.

TABLE 11.1 Data for Domestic Production versus Chinese Outsourcing Option

Costs	Domestic Production ($)	Outsourcing to China ($)
Fixed costs	40,000	4,000
Labor cost per unit	9.90	4.25
Material cost per unit	7.20	7.20
Transportation cost per unit	0.40	3.80
Tariff duty per unit	0.00	1.50
Total cost per unit	17.50	16.75

With these figures, there is no need to conduct a breakeven analysis. Outsourcing to China produces a lower total unit cost, and the fixed costs are significantly lower. The total cost reduction would dictate that China is the preferred location to produce the part. But now envision another scenario, one in which the transportation cost increases by $2.55 (increasing the transportation cost per unit to $6.35) and the tariff duty per unit increases by $1 per unit. These results are presented in Table 11.2.

TABLE 11.2 Revised Data for Domestic Production versus Chinese Outsourcing Option

Costs	Domestic Production ($)	Outsourcing to China ($)
Fixed costs	40,000	4,000
Labor cost per unit	9.90	4.25
Material cost per unit	7.20	7.20
Transportation cost per unit	0.40	6.35
Tariff duty per unit	0.00	2.50
Total cost per unit	17.50	19.30

Given these changes, we can now conduct a breakeven analysis.

Domestic Production Total Costs		Outsourced to China Total Costs
Fixed costs + total variable costs	=	Fixed costs + total variable costs
$40,000 + $17.50 * Q	=	$4,000 + $19.30 * Q
($40,000 − $4,000)	=	($19.30 − $17.50) * Q
$36,000	=	$1.80 * Q
break-even point Q	=	20,000 units
Q = Quantity		

This simply means that if the demand for the part is fewer than 20,000 units, then it is cheaper to produce the part in China; however, if the demand is greater than 20,000 units, it is cheaper to produce the part domestically.

The key issue in procurement is how one goes about selecting and maintaining a supplier, which can be approached from two directions. The first centers on how a firm might evaluate a potential supplier. The second is how a firm evaluates those businesses that are already suppliers to an operation. When looking at the potential suppliers of a business, a firm may be aided by examining those suppliers with some form of certification. Perhaps the most globally recognized certification program is ISO 9000, a program designed to ensure that suppliers are certified and fully committed to quality production. A supplier that is ISO 9000 certified may mean that incoming goods need not be tested. In examining suppliers, one might also look at the number of employees of the potential supplier who have received certification in the area of supply chain management. The Association for Operations Management, formerly known as the American Production and Inventory Control Society (APICS), has a program to certify professionals in supply chain management. After selecting a supplier, one must have a program that continuously evaluates the capability of the supplier. Some of the capabilities that may be considered include on-time delivery, the accuracy of delivery (i.e., correct items in the correct quantities are shipped), the ability to handle fluctuations in demand, and the ability to hold inventory until needed by the customer. One needs a comprehensive set of metrics to perform such an analysis. One set of metrics will be discussed in Section 2. In addition, one must think about developing a new type of relationship with suppliers, one that is not adversarial but develops a close working relationship bordering on being an alliance.

The second major element of supply chain management system is **operations**. Having received raw materials, parts, components, assemblies, or services from suppliers, the firm now must transform them and produce the products or the services that meet the needs of its consumers. It must conduct this transformation in an efficient and effective manner for the benefit of the supply chain management system. We will briefly overview those operational activities that most directly relate to supply chain management.

operations

The activities and tasks associated with turning a firm's inputs (materials, capital, and labor) into goods and services.

One element is demand management. This involves attempting to match demand with capacity. In a manufacturing environment, this may entail a better and more detailed production schedule. In a service environment, it may entail rescheduling customer appointments to better match service provider availability. A key element is improvements in inventory control, which may be done by using **materials requirement planning** software or instituting a **just-in-time** program. Just-in-time attempts to create an inventory system where the inventory arrives exactly when it is needed. Another way of achieving operational efficiency to improve the supply chain management system is by adopting **lean methodologies**. The essence of lean is attempting to eliminate all forms of waste from a production or service system.

The third element of the supply chain management system is **distribution**. Distribution involves several activities—transportation (**logistics**), warehousing, and **customer relationship management (CRM)**. The first and most obvious is logistics—the transportation of goods across the entire supply chain. The need to efficiently transport goods has led to a hierarchy of logistics providers. Some argue that it now consists of a four-party hierarchy. First-party logistics providers are those who wish to ship goods to a particular location. Second-party logistics providers are those businesses that provide the means of transportation, including shipping freight by air, rail, or truck. Second-party logistics providers may also offer warehousing services to temporarily store goods. Third-party logistics providers specialize in offering an array of services to simplify transportation. They offer services that synthesize a variety of services, including the shipping of goods, warehousing, inventory management, and packaging. They also may offer services associated with facilitating customs operation and the resolution of problems associated with international transportation. The range of services can be so extensive that the literature segments third-party logistics providers into four groups.[9] They range from those businesses that pick up and deliver goods to those businesses that essentially perform the entire logistics function for a customer. In the last fifteen years, a fourth level of logistics providers was added to this hierarchy. Although there is some argument as to what distinguishes sophisticated third-party logistics providers from fourth-party logistics providers, the essential distinction is that fourth-party logistics providers function as consultants for supply chain management logistics issues. They are non-asset-based integrators[10] —firms do not own shipping assets or warehouses; they simply provide consulting services.

The CRM component of the distribution element represents an attempt to automate interactions with customers and facilitate the development of sales prospects through software packages. Most small businesses will start using CRM as a means of contacting current customers and future prospective customers. They then move on to software that automates the entire sales process. The ultimate goal of CRM is the greater connection with customers, thus providing them with greater value.

The last element of supply chain management is the need for **integration**. At the beginning of this chapter, we mentioned that many small businesses are unfamiliar with their immediate customers and their immediate suppliers; however, they may be part of a much larger chain. It is critical that all participants in the service chain recognize the entirety of the service chain. A failure to overcome the myopia of just being concerned with the immediate customer and the immediate supplier can produce significant disruptions in the entire chain. These disruptions can significantly increase costs and destroy value.

The impact of the failure to adopt a system-wide perspective—that is, examining the totality of the chain—is most clearly seen in what is known as the "bullwhip" effect. This effect illustrates how a narrow perspective can produce unexpected consequences. Envision a classic supply chain composed of a retailer—who is supplied by a wholesaler—who in turn is supplied by a distributor with a product coming from the manufacturer. Each element of this chain must forecast its anticipated demand and determine the appropriate levels of inventory. Because no element of this chain wishes to "stock out"—having insufficient inventory to meet a customer's demand—each element will carry what is known as safety stock. In many cases, the more certain the demand, the greater the need for such safety stock. If demand at the retail level increases, then it follows that demand will also increase at each level further up the supply chain. If demand decreases at the retail level, the demand will likewise decrease further up the chain. The rate at which demand and inventory levels fluctuate is dependent on the lead time at each level in the chain. The delay between an increase for the retail level and the corresponding increase or decrease at the manufacturing level will be a function of this lead time. The bullwhip effect recognizes that the amplitude of inventory swings increases as one travels up the supply chain because each element of the supply chain is a relatively narrow focus of just trying to meet the needs of their customers. If the forecast for "shared" demand across the entire chain could be made simultaneously or if the lead time could be significantly reduced, then this phenomenon would not be quite as dramatic or problematic. The bullwhip effect calls for integrating information across the entire supply chain.

materials requirement planning

A computerized inventory control system that schedules the production of goods and takes into consideration the available and the required inventory.

just-in-time

An approach to inventory that seeks to eliminate excess waste and reduce inventory to a minimal level.

lean methodologies

A series of techniques designed to eliminate waste from manufacturing and service processes and provide greater customer value.

distribution

A process that involves several activities: transportation (logistics), warehousing, and CRM.

logistics

The active management of the distribution of materials throughout a system.

customer relationship management (CRM)

A service approach that hopes to build a long-term and sustainable relationship with customers that has value for both the customer and the company.

integration

The coordination of all activities across the entire supply chain.

enterprise resource planning (ERP)

A system that integrates multiple business functions from purchasing to sales, billings, accounting records, and payroll.

An **enterprise resource planning (ERP)** system can successfully integrate information across the entire supply chain. An ERP system is an integrated set of computer programs that brings information about a firm's accounting, financial, sales, and operations into a common database.[11] One also needs a series of metrics that would indicate the overall performance of the supply chain. This should also be part of the integration process. We discuss such metrics in Section 2.

 Video Clip 11.4

Module 2: Buy It: Managing Supply
An introduction to purchasing.

View the video online at: http://www.youtube.com/v/zYbtZ0x9_SA

 Video Clip 11.5

Module 3: Make It: Manufacturing and Operations
Manufacturing and supply chain management in local firms operations.

View the video online at: http://www.youtube.com/v/ncli94xodm8

Video Clip 11.6

Module 4: Move It: Transportation and Logistics
Discussion of the difference between transportation and logistics.

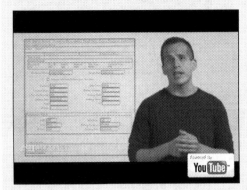

View the video online at: http://www.youtube.com/v/-ZpHiMTwOdM

 ### Video Clip 11.7

Module 5: Sell it and Service It: Retail Considerations
Discussion of supply chains in the retail environment.

View the video online at: http://www.youtube.com/v/ZUO2EaJnb-w

Web Resources

Supply Chain Management Description

An introduction to the topic.

www.eil.utoronto.ca/profiles/rune/node5.html

About.com Introduction to Supply Chain Management

Brief coverage of supply chain management for small businesses with additional links.

logistics.about.com/od/forsmallbusinesses/For_the_Small_Business.htm

Big Business Supply Chain Management: A Small Business Option?

Looks at the benefits of supply chain management for smaller businesses.

smallbiztrends.com/2006/05/big-business-supply-chain-management-a-small-business-option.html

2. A FIRM'S ROLE IN THE SUPPLY CHAIN

2.1 Developing New Relationships

game theory

A branch of mathematics that examines competitive situations in which one's outcomes may be influenced or dictated by the decisions of other players.

zero-sum game

A game in which the total benefits for all participants total zero.

non-zero-sum game

A game that potentially has net results other than zero.

Game theory is a branch of mathematics. Broadly stated, game theory examines competitive situations in which one's outcomes may be influenced or dictated by the decisions of other players. It has been applied to a variety of worldwide domains, including economics, military operations, political science, and business strategy. It has its own very large literature base, and work in this field has been recognized by several Nobel prizes in economics. To better understand some of the risk associated for small businesses participating in supply chain management, we will briefly look at two types of games: zero-sum games and non-zero-sum games.

Zero-sum games are those in which the total benefits for all participants total zero. Baseball can be seen as a zero-sum game. If one is told that the New York Yankees and the New York Mets played an exhibition game and the Yankees won, then one also knows that the New York Mets lost. Basketball and most games in professional football are also zero-sum games because there is a winner and a loser. Poker can also be seen as a zero-sum game. If your five friends have a Friday night game of poker and one player is up $100, then you also know that the other four players have suffered a cumulative loss of $100.

Non-zero-sum games, on the other hand, are those that potentially have net results other than zero. This simply means that the loss of one player does not directly correspond to the game of another player. In a non-zero-sum game, it is possible for all the players to win or for all the players to lose. The classic illustration of a non-zero-sum game is known as the prisoner's dilemma. The prisoner's dilemma hypothesizes that two criminals (prisoner A and prisoner B) are arrested and charged with the same crime. At the police station, they are separated, and each is given the following option: if you inform on the other prisoner, you will be set free, while the other prisoner will receive a five-year sentence. Both prisoners would instinctively recognize that if they both remained silent, the police would have insufficient evidence to convict both of the crime. At worst, they would be held in the jail for several months. If, however, both prisoners informed on each other, they would probably receive a two-year sentence. Assuming that both prisoners wish to serve the minimal amount of time, their individual decisions will be dictated by what they believe will be the other prisoner's decision. There are four possible outcomes to this scenario:

1. Prisoner A informs on prisoner B while prisoner B remains silent. This is a win for prisoner A and a loss for prisoner B. This is a win-lose outcome.

2. Prisoner B informs on prisoner A while prisoner A remains silent. This is a win for prisoner B and a loss for prisoner A. This is a win-lose outcome.

3. Both prisoner A and prisoner B inform on each other. This situation essentially represents a loss for both prisoner A and prisoner B. This is a lose-lose outcome.

4. Both prisoner A and prisoner B trust each other and remain silent. This results in both prisoners doing a minimal amount of time. In effect, this is a win-win for both individuals.

The point of this brief introduction to game theory is to highlight the possibility of creating a **win-win scenario**. In the prisoner's dilemma, the key to achieving a win-win outcome is that both parties must have complete trust in each other. This concept of mutual trust plays a critical role in successful supply chain management. Far too often, both the supplier and the customer perceive the relationship as a win-lose outcome only. Customers want suppliers to provide items at the lowest possible cost, with the highest quality, delivered exactly when needed. Customers often use multiple suppliers and play them off against each other to guarantee the lowest possible price. Suppliers want to provide customers with items of the highest possible price, with acceptable quality, and delivered when it is convenient for the supplier. These attitudes produce a "dance" between the customer and the supplier, where both are trying to win even if that means that the other loses. These attitudes often stem from the fact that there is no trust between the customer and the supplier.

W. Edwards Deming, the famous management guru who was most commonly associated with the quality movement, had several interesting insights into areas that would be associated with supply chain management. As one of the few management theorists whose ideas were comprehensive enough to be synthesized into a coherent business philosophy, Deming summarized his approach to management in fourteen points. One of these points is as follows: "End the practice of awarding business on the basis of price. Instead, minimize total cost. Move toward a single supplier for any one item, with a long-term relationship of loyalty and trust."[12]

Deming argued that the move toward a single supplier for a particular part could yield significant advantages. Using a single supplier requires that a customer must sign a multiyear agreement with the supplier. This enables both the supplier and the customer to better understand each other's needs and capabilities. As this knowledge grows, the supplier can better serve the customer by improving quality, design, and service.[13] From these improvements, one can easily anticipate that there will be lower costs and higher profits. A multiyear contract with a supplier guaranteeing particular sales is invaluable to many suppliers because of the benefit of such a contract when that supplier must deal with its bank. Deming counters the argument for the need for multiple suppliers, in case a catastrophe or a disaster strikes that single supplier, by suggesting that a tight and trusting relationship will lead the supplier to develop sufficient contingency plans. Deming argues that a sense of joint responsibility comparable to a marriage comes from such trust.

Building such trust between two organizations is not easy. It will often require significant changes in one or both parties. Such change is best induced when it is clear to all participants that there is top-level management support for the new ways of doing business. Top management must articulate the shared vision between the two organizations. Top management must clearly identify the objectives and metrics to be used by both the supplier and the customer. People need to clearly understand the joint benefits from adopting the new way of business. In addition, even with electronic communication, it is highly advisable that members of both organizations meet on a regular basis and perhaps tour each other's facilities.

The new relationships that are required for the success of any supply chain management program are not easy to implement, but they are vital. Every effort must be made to adopt this win-win perspective.

win-win scenario

Outcomes where there can be multiple winners.

Video Clip 11.8

Module 6: Supply Chain Integration
How elements of a supply chain must be brought together.

View the video online at: http://www.youtube.com/v/S_yMW2b0kNk

 Video Clip 11.9

Module 7: Global Supply Chain Management
An examination of global operations.

View the video online at: http://www.youtube.com/v/ZuQ200JAViA

Video Clip 11.10

Module 8: Socially Responsible Supply Chain Management
Social responsibility and sustainability are important concepts.

View the video online at: http://www.youtube.com/v/VdbKvXh6sLU

Video Clip 11.11

Module 9: Business Processes
The moment a customer places an order through delivery.

View the video online at: http://www.youtube.com/v/JUInjQvzlkE

 Video Clip 11.12

Module 11: Quality Management
Supply chains are tasked with producing high-quality products.

View the video online at: http://www.youtube.com/v/QJNVrY_Z2NM

2.2 Managing Information in New Ways

Cost, profits, and financial ratios can provide useful insights into the overall efficiency and effectiveness of any business. However, they do not always tell the full story. A sudden spike in the price of oil, a flood that destroys a low-cost supplier, an increase in interest rates, the closing of a large plant in a small town, or a national banking crisis are all external factors that can cripple the financial viability of any business. These external factors lie beyond the control of even the best management team. Sometimes we need to be very careful about what we measure and how we should measure. Although it adds a layer of complexity to a basic accounting system, measurements that are useful for evaluating processes that serve customers can be provided.

When evaluating the supply chain of a business, there is a great need to carefully consider what metrics should be employed. Such a consideration should include at least some of the following factors:

- **Total supply chain cost.** All the operational expenditures of a cost associated with the requisite information systems.
- **Cash-to-cash cycle time.** The time between when an organization purchases raw materials and when they are paid by the customer.
- **Delivery.** The percentage of orders delivered on or before customer due dates.
- **Flexibility.** The amount of time required to handle a significant ramp up in production.[14]

supply chain operations reference (SCOR) model

A comprehensive series of metrics to evaluate the performance of a supply chain's operations.

For those who are seriously committed to maximizing the benefits from successful supply chain management, study the **supply chain operations reference (SCOR) model**. This model enables businesses to benchmark their supply chain management systems. Developed in 1996 by the Supply Chain Council in conjunction with AMR Research and Pittiglio Rabin Todd and Rath,[15] the purpose of the SCOR model is to provide methods to measure and benchmark the performance of the supply chain management system of a business. Currently, one thousand firms, universities, and government agencies participate in the continuing evolution of the SCOR model. It is predicated on three major components: process modeling, performance measurement, and the determination of best practices.

The process-modeling component begins with five essential elements that link together the supply chain: plan, source, make, deliver, and return. Plan refers to those processes associated with the design of the supply chain, planning activities associated with the other four processes, and the implementation of all these plans. These plans should enable management to identify any significant gaps and determine how these gaps will be closed. Source refers to the ordering and the acquisition of goods and services to meet anticipated demand, including purchase orders, scheduling, receipts, and storage. Make refers to those processes used to create the product or the service, including, for example, make to stock, make to order, or engineer to order. Deliver refers to those processes associated with the development and the fulfillment of customer orders, including scheduling, packaging, and shipping all orders. Lastly, return refers to those processes associated with the return of finished products by a customer. The SCOR model attempts to be as inclusive as possible with respect to these five major processes. Each process can be broken down into subcomponents. Currently, there are thirty subcomponents for the plan element, twenty-seven subcomponents for the source element, thirty-one subcomponents for the make element, sixty-one subcomponents for the deliver element, and thirty-six subcomponents for the return element. This program then goes on to identify specific metrics for nearly every subcomponent. It is the most comprehensive system of evaluation for supply chain management.

 Video Clip 11.13

Walmart Logistics
A Walmart logistics commercial.

View the video online at: http://www.youtube.com/v/mLW5MfON_64

Video Clip 11.14

Ford Manufacturing Supply Chain
A Cisco promotional video on supply chain management.

View the video online at: http://www.youtube.com/v/qyO9QSo0FjU

 Video Clip 11.15

Module 10: Measuring Performance
Supply chains are tasked with being effective, efficient, and adaptable.

View the video online at: http://www.youtube.com/v/R4HPYYR5iLw

Web Resources

Game Theory

A comprehensive set of materials from a professor's course on game theory.

www.agsm.edu.au/bobm/teaching/SGTM.html

Prisoner's Dilemma

A computer application that allows individuals to play a game based on the prisoner's dilemma.

www.gametheory.net/Mike/applets/PDilemma

SCOR Frameworks

An overview of SCOR from the Supply Chain Council.

supply-chain.org/resources/scor

The SCOR Model for Supply Chain Strategic Decisions

An article describing SCOR.

scm.ncsu.edu/scm-articles/article/the-scor-model-for-supply-chain-strategic-decisions

EXERCISES

1. Identify some examples in your life and in business of win-win scenarios.
2. How were these scenarios achieved?
3. What were the greatest threats to these scenarios?
4. Interview five small business owners and ask them if they have had any experiences with win-win scenarios and how were they achieved.
5. Ask the same five small business owners how they measure (if they do) the effectiveness of the performance of their supply chain.
6. Imagine a local bakery that produces goods for a regional supermarket chain. Examine the SCOR model and determine if it is appropriate for evaluating the bakery's supply chain.

3. THE BENEFITS AND THE RISKS OF PARTICIPATING IN A SUPPLY CHAIN

LEARNING OBJECTIVES

1. Understand the major benefits to be derived from adopting a supply chain management system.
2. Understand the challenges of creating such a system.
3. Understand the technical and managerial risks associated with supply chain management.
4. Recognize the benefits for a small business in adopting supply chain management.

3.1 The Benefits of Successful Supply Chain Management

For any small business, a commitment to developing a supply chain management system is not a small undertaking. It involves the commitment of significant financial resources for the acquisition of appropriate software. Policies and procedures must be changed in accordance with the needs of the new system. Personnel must be trained in not only using the new software but also adapting to new ways of doing business. Small businesses accept these challenges of adopting supply chain management systems because such systems are viewed as being important for long-term survival and because businesses anticipate substantial management and economic benefits.

The management benefits of supply chain management system include the following:

- **Silo busting.** By their very nature, supply chain management systems improve communication across all functions within a business. This leads to employees having a better understanding of the entire operations of a business and how their work relates to the overall benefits of the business.

- **Improve communications with suppliers and customers.** Improved communications with customers enhances the overall value provided to those customers. The improvement in customer satisfaction leads to longtime relationships, which yields significant economic benefits. Improved communications with suppliers improve the overall operational efficiency of both participants, reduce costs, and improve profits.

- **Supplier selection.** Supply chain management systems can help businesses evaluate prospective suppliers and monitor the performance of current suppliers. This capability can lead to strategic sourcing and significant cost savings plus improvement of the when- and where-needed variables.

- **Improvements in purchasing.** The automation of purchasing reduces errors and improves the economic efficiency of the purchasing function. Disciplined purchasing can allow for the full exploitation of available discounts.

- **Reduction of inventory costs.** Supply chain management systems can produce significant cost savings across all levels of inventory. Improved forecasting and scheduling will lead to increases in inventory turns and a corresponding reduction of costs.

- **Improvements in operations.** Improved quality control reduces the scrap rate, which in turn can have significant cost savings. Better production scheduling translates into producing what is needed when it is needed. The business does not have to spend additional money trying to expedite the production of particular orders to customers. The cost of goods sold is reduced in this manner. An additional benefit of supply chain management systems is that they lead to better utilization of plant and equipment. Great utilization translates into less likelihood that unneeded assets will be acquired, which has major financial benefits.

- **Error reduction.** By automating processes, billing errors and errors associated with purchasing and shipping quantities can be reduced. This not only saves money but also improves satisfaction with both suppliers and customers.

- **Improvements in transportation operations.** Accurate deliveries reduce returns and their associated costs. Sophisticated shipping models can reduce the overall cost of transportation.

- **Additional financial benefits.** Such systems can improve the collections process, which impacts customer relations, reduces bad debts, and improves cash flow.

3.2   The Risks Associated with Supply Chain Management

The major risks associated with a supply chain management system fall into two categories: technical and managerial.

Michael Porter's five forces model is a model of the major factors that contribute to an industry's overall structure. It also points to factors that might affect the overall profitability of the particular business within that industry. The greater the strength of these forces, the greater the challenge to make above average return profits for businesses in that industry. It is useful to review two of those forces—the power of suppliers and the power of buyers—and reexamine how they might influence the profitability of any business in the supply chain.

Porter identifies the following factors that might contribute to the overall strength of each force. He argued that suppliers are powerful (see Figure 11.3) when the following occurs:

- **They are concentrated.** When an industry is dominated by only a few suppliers, these suppliers generally have a greater ability to dictate terms to their customers. The mining company DeBeers, which controls more than 50 percent of the world diamond production, is able to set the selling price of diamonds for most of the world's jewelers.[16] It should be pointed out, however, that in some cases concentration, particularly a duopoly, provides an opportunity for customers to force the two competing firms to compete more readily against each other. Think of the situation of Boeing and Airbus and their relationship to their customers—various airlines. At present, there are only two major producers of commercial aircraft, and airlines sometimes obtain better deals from one manufacturer because of their desire to maintain parity in market share.

- **The size of the suppliers is large relative to the buyers.** Suppliers are powerful when they are large and sell to a set of fragmented buyers. Think of the largest oil companies that sell gasoline to independent stations. The power in this scenario lies with the large oil companies.

- **Switching costs are high.** Suppliers have power when the cost of switching to an alternative supplier is expensive. Many businesses stay with Microsoft products because to do otherwise means that they would have to repurchase new hardware and software for the entire organization.

Problems may also arise from a heavier reliance on one customer in the supply chain. Even large companies need to be aware of their relative strength in the supply chain. Rubbermaid is the most admired corporation in America, as voted by *Fortune* magazine in 1993 and 1994, yet it had significant difficulties when dealing with one of its major customers—Walmart. In the early 1990s, Rubbermaid found that the cost for a key ingredient—resin—had increased by 80 percent.[17] Walmart's almost total focus on lowering its prices led it to drop many of Rubbermaid's products. This began a downward spiral for Rubbermaid, which led to its acquisition by Newell Inc. Rubbermaid went from the status of the most admired corporation to being a basket case because it failed to recognize its excessive dependence on one customer.

Web Resources

The Benefits of Supply Chain Management

A list of benefits from SAP, a software company.

searchsap.techtarget.com/feature/Checklist-Quantifying-Supply-Chain-Management-benefits

The Risks of Supply Chain Management

A Forbes article on the risks associated with supply chain management.

www.forbes.com/2006/11/15/risks-supply-chain-strategies-biz-logistics-cx_rm_1115strategies.html

Risk and Rewards in Supply Chain Management

A Harvard working paper.

hbswk.hbs.edu/archive/4971.html

KEY TAKEAWAYS

- There are significant benefits for businesses that adopt supply chain management systems.
- The benefits stem from improved customer relations, cost cutting, and increased operational efficiencies.
- The adoption of a supply chain management perspective can pose risks.
- Businesses must consider the relative power of both their suppliers and their customers.

EXERCISES

1. Interview the owners of local businesses who say they have some form of a supply chain management system and ask them if they believe they have benefited from the system.
2. Ask them how they have benefited.
3. Ask them to identify the major problems they had with implementing and using the system.
4. Ask them if they believe they have the "power" in their supply chain or if the "power" is in the hands of their suppliers.

---

4. THE THREE THREADS

LEARNING OBJECTIVES

1. Understand how customer value is enhanced by supply chain management.
2. Understand how cash flow can be increased, in the long term, by using supply chain management.
3. Understand the various computer programs that make up a supply chain management program.
4. Recognize the risks that can stem from adopting a single supplier program.

4.1 Customer Value Implications

Throughout this text, we have emphasized the importance for small businesses to constantly focus on the notion of improving value for their customers. Successfully implementing a supply chain management system offers tremendous possibilities for not only improving value to customers but also significantly enhancing the capabilities and profitability of the small business itself. Supply chain management improves customer value in the following ways:

- **Reduced inventory.** A well-executed supply chain management system means that customers receive orders when they need them. Further, this does not necessarily imply that the supplier will be holding the inventory for the customer—although that might occur. It refers to the fact that better communication and better scheduling may enable the supplier to produce the item exactly when it is needed.

- **Improvement in the order accuracy.** Supply chain management should guarantee that when orders are shipped, the right items are shipped in the right quantity. This does not disrupt the production of the customer and eliminates product returns, which results in economic benefits for both the customer and the supplier.
- **Reduced cycle time for product development.** To ensure success, the customer and the supplier must develop new levels of trust. This trust will evolve into a long-term relationship. Both parties begin to know each other better, including each other's needs and capabilities. As this evolves, the supplier is in a better position to help the customer develop new products far more rapidly. It greatly reduces the product cycle time.
- **Financial benefits.** These value improvements all translate into significant cost savings. Cost savings experienced by the supplier can be transferred into cost savings for the customer. Relatively modest improvements in inventory reduction, reduced safety stock size, reduce stockouts, improved order fill rates, and reduced transit time can yield surprisingly large financial benefits to both parties.
- **Peace of mind.** Having a supplier that one can trust to accurately deliver items in a timely low-cost fashion, which has also developed contingency plans to cope with potential problems, is relatively unique and provides the customer with a high level of comfort. One may be unable to place an economic price on such peace of mind.

4.2 Cash-Flow Implications

It must be recognized that committing to a supply chain management system from scratch will entail a major investment. New approaches to software can reduce both the cost and the risk of such a commitment. However, businesses will want to recoup most of the investment as quickly as possible—perhaps six months or less. Given the potential for cost savings, the impact on increasing cash flow should be obvious.

What is not obvious is the potential for significant improvements in cash flow from minor improvements generated by supply chain management systems. To illustrate this, let us look at an example adapted from Coyle et al. (2009).[18] Assume that a firm is in the following situation: It ships orders to customers; if the orders are incomplete or inaccurate, the firm assumes the full cost of the return and follow-up shipping. When an incorrect shipment is made, to ameliorate their upset customers, the firm takes $100 off the bill. However, when some customers find that the order is incomplete or inaccurate, they are so upset that they cancel the order. Here are the data:

Number of orders per year	50,000
Number of items per order	25
Profit per unit ($)	30
Price reduction for incorrect order ($)	100
Back order cost per order ($)	200
Percentage of totally correct orders	90
Percentage of incorrect orders cancelled	25

It can be readily seen that the profit per order is $750 (25 × $30). We now examine the lost cash flow from the situation. The lost cash flow has several components. The first component is the back order cost, which is composed of the number of orders that will have to be back filled. The second component is associated with the losses from the incorrect orders that were canceled. The last component is the price reduction for the incorrect order.

$$\text{lost cash flow} = \text{backorder costs} + \text{cancelled sales costs} + \text{price reduction costs}$$

These can be computed as follows:

$$\text{lost cash flow} = [\text{number of orders} \times (1 - \text{percentage of totally correct orders}) \times \text{backordered cost per order}]$$

$$[\text{number of orders} \times (1 - \text{percentage of totally correct orders}) \times \text{percentage of incorrect orders cancelled} \times \text{profit per order}] + [\text{number of orders} \times (1 - \text{percentage of totally correct orders}) \times \text{price reduction for incorrect order}]$$

Now let us substitute the correct values into this equation.

$$\text{lost cash flow} = [50,000 \times (1 - .90) \times \$200] + [50,000 \times (1 - .90) \times (.25) \times \$750] + [50,000 \times (1 - .90) \times \$100]$$

$$\text{lost cash flow} = \$1,000,000 + \$937,500 + \$500,000 = \$2,437,500$$

We now assume that an "improved" supply chain management system has been installed. The percentage of correctly filled orders increases from 90 percent to 96 percent. If we substitute 96 percent into these equations, we find that the *new* lost cash flow would decrease to *$975,000*. This means that a 6 percent increase in order accuracy leads to a 60 percent decrease in the loss of cash flow.

4.3   Implications of Technology and the E-Environment

electronic data interchange

The ability to electronically transfer large "packets" of data across various locations and programs.

It should be obvious that contemporary supply chain management cannot be conducted through paper and pencil procedures. The backbone of today's supply chain management is software. Initially, it would be impossible to think of developing such systems without **electronic data interchange**. Today, the Internet serves as the basis for sharing communication between suppliers and customers. However, there is more to the technology behind supply chain management system than merely the exchange of data.

supplier relationship management

Programs that involve planning and controlling the actions with upstream suppliers, including supplier analysis, order execution, payment, and performance monitoring.

Supply chain management requires several types of software packages and the need to successfully integrate them. One can identify several major software components of a supply chain management system (see Figure 11.4). One section would be **supplier relationship management** programs. These programs involve planning and controlling the actions with upstream suppliers. Such programs would cover many aspects of procurement—supplier analysis, order execution, payment, and performance monitoring.[19] There would also be customer relationship management (CRM) software that would handle all interactions with customers. Enterprise resource planning (ERP) would handle the necessary integration of all data. ERP coordinates data flows from finance, accounting, and operations to provide management with a seamless overview of the performance of a business. It may also have a

decision support system

A program that allows for data manipulation or the use of analytical modeling tools to provide a better decision-making environment, which may involve the use of mathematical programming models to optimize decisions.

decision support system, which allows for data manipulation or the use of analytical modeling tools to provide a better decision-making environment. It may involve using mathematical programming models to optimize decisions. Another set of modules dedicated to logistics would focus on the optimal use of warehousing and shipping. These functions are sometimes handled externally by either a third- or fourth-party logistics provider.

FIGURE 11.4 Schematic for a Supply Chain Management Information System

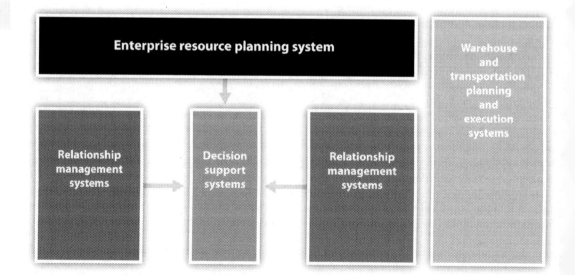

cloud-based software

Software located off-site, generally maintained by another party, and that can be accessed anywhere there is an Internet connection.

Not too long ago, the acquisition and the operation of these software packages would have been prohibitive for most small businesses from both a cost standpoint and a technical standpoint. Fortunately, software providers now recognize that small and midsize businesses represent a tremendous market for supply chain management software. It was estimated in 2008 that the demand for business enterprise software applications for small and midsized businesses would grow at a nearly 11 percent annualized growth rate until 2012.[20] Microsoft, Oracle, and SAP have developed systems that enable small to midsize companies to handle all the complexities of global supply chain management.[21] Large software vendors such as Oracle estimated that the midmarket clientele was approximately 4,500 out of their total client base of 7,000 customers. Several factors can be attributed to this rapid growth in small to midsize businesses. The first was that many software providers were willing to offer in-house installation at a predictable cost. Second and perhaps the most important factor is the increasing move to **cloud-based software**, where software resides on an external server to which the businesses are connected to via the Internet. It provides several substantial benefits to small businesses: lowers software and hardware costs, installation is significantly easier, maintenance and training costs are lower, and free upgrades may sometimes be available. The use of Internet-based systems also makes it easier to maintain lines of communications with one's suppliers and customers. Robert LaGarde, president of LaGarde E-business Solution, has stated that "using Internet technology to provide customers with online demand access to supply chain systems is critical to nurturing and growing relationships with customers."[22] What initially appeared to be a remarkably complex system of programs has now been made available to even very small businesses.

 Video Clip 11.16

Impact of RFID Technology on Supply Chain Management
The impact of RFID technology on supply chains.

View the video online at: http://www.youtube.com/v/0VbMr2gnGDE

 Video Clip 11.17

Supply Chains and Information Technology
Modern-day supply chains are tasked with responding at lightning speed.

View the video online at: http://www.youtube.com/v/SXDvHgjRNDQ

Video Clip 11.18

Future Supply Chain 2016

The main supply chain challenges for consumer products and retail for the next decade.

View the video online at: http://www.youtube.com/v/US5IO1HfmEo

Video Link 11.1

Japan: The Business Aftershocks

Japan is a small country with a supersized role in the global supply chain (a short ad precedes the video clip).

online.wsj.com/video/japan-the-business-aftershocks/
8D24FD7D-5767-4F4C-AC35-7124F8E1F571.html?mod=googlewsj

Web Resources

List of Supply Chain Management Software

A comprehensive list of SCM software with links.

www.capterra.com/supply-chain-management-software

About.com SCM Software

Supply chain management software with links to other sites.

http://logistics.about.com/gi/o.htm?zi=1/XJ/Ya&zTi=1&sdn=logistics&cdn=money&tm=75&gps=191_
1419_1259_550&f=00&tt=14&bt=1&bts=1&zu=http%3A//technology.inc.com   /managing/articles/200805/
supplychain.html

The Benefits of Supply Chain Management Software

Identifies benefits and includes option to download a report on the top fifteen ERP providers.

www.business-software.com/erp/supply-chain/benefits-of-supply-chain-erp.php

KEY TAKEAWAYS

- Supply chain management can enhance customer value in many ways.
- Cost savings brought about by supply chain management systems can produce amplified improvements in cash flow.
- Supply chain management systems can be seen as a collection of interconnected software packages.
- The advent of cloud computing can make supply chain management systems available for small businesses.

1. Interview the owners of five local businesses and ask them how supply chain management has or could enhance their customers' value.
2. For those small business owners who have a functioning supply chain management system, ask them if they have noticed improvements in cash flow attributable to the system.
3. Ask them what system(s) they use and why they went with these computer packages.
4. Ask them if they have contingency plans for the loss of key suppliers.

Disaster Watch

This chapter has emphasized that successful supply chain management requires successful integration across the supply chain. It has been argued that businesses should actively seek to have a single source supplier for particular parts and components. Having a single source supplier may result in a closer relationship that should yield significant economic benefit. Many businesses, both large and small, have moved toward, if not a single supplier, then a significantly reduced number of suppliers for particular parts. This, however, may have some serious negative consequences.

Apple introduced its new iPad 2 tablet on March 2, 2011. Little more than a week later, on March 11, Japan was struck by a major earthquake and damage from the resulting tsunami. Although the two events may seem to be unrelated, there are several connections. It was estimated that Japanese firms manufactured at least five major components in the iPad 2. Although some of these firms were not damaged by either the earthquake or the tsunami, they found that maintaining production schedules was a challenge due to curtailment and available electricity, the movement of supplies, and employees being unable to arrive at work. "These factors are having a major impact on 'delicate processes, such as semiconductor lithography,' said the report, especially as the country continues to experience aftershocks."[23] Apple was not the only firm affected by the Japanese disaster. The port of Sendai was heavily damaged, and many goods could not be shipped out. As one commentator put it, "It is a nuclear winter for the economy."[24]

Further exacerbating the situation for Apple was an explosion at Foxconn Technology Group's plant in Chengdu, China. The explosion killed three workers and injured many more. In addition, the initial estimate was that Apple might lose production of more than half a million iPad 2 units while the plant was closed for repairs.[25]

Disruptions in the supply chain need not be caused by natural disasters. They can occur because of human failings and can have significant consequences. Toys "R" Us was severely damaged in 1999 when its online customer order system proved to be inadequate for demand at Christmastime. In the same time frame, The Hershey Company, which expended approximately $100 million on developing software for its supply chain, found that attempting to develop an order system, a CRM system, and a supply chain planning system proved to be too much of a technical challenge. Because of failures in the system, Hershey missed at least $150 million in orders. Hershey was guilty of trying to implement these systems simultaneously. They had gone a "bridge too far."[26]

There is actually a field called supply chain sensitivity analysis that attempts to identify the extent of disruptions in the supply chain caused by external factors. It relies on computer simulation analysis.[27] Obviously, such an approach is beyond the capability of most small businesses.

ENDNOTES

1. John Donne, "XVII. Meditation," *The Literature Network*, accessed February 4, 2012, www.online-literature.com/donne/409.

2. John Mickletwait and Adrian Woodridge, *Witch Doctors: Making Sense of the Management Gurus* (New York: Time Books, 1996), 22.

3. Scott Webster, *Principles and Tools for Supply Chain Management* (Boston: McGraw-Hill, 2008), 62.

4. "CSCMP Supply Chain Management Definitions," *Council of Supply Chain Management Professionals*, accessed February 1, 2012, cscmp.org/aboutcscmp/definitions.asp.

5. *APICS—Operations Management Body of Knowledge Framework*, 2nd ed. (Chicago: APICS, 2009).

6. John Mentzer, William DeWitt, James Keebler, Soonhong Min, Nancy Nix, Carlo Smith, and Zach Zacharia, "Defining Supply Chain Management," *Journal of Business Logistics* 22, no. 2 (2001): 7.

7. Steve Schifferes, "Globalisation Shakes the World," *BBC News*, January 21, 2007, accessed February 1, 2012, news.bbc.co.uk/2/hi/business/6279679.stm.

8. Martin Murray, "Introduction to Supply Chain Management," *About.com*, accessed February 1, 2012, logistics.about.com/od/supplychainintroduction/a/into_scm.htm; Phillip Edwards, "Supply Chain for Small Businesses and Its Benefit," *Small and Medium Business Corner*, April 22, 2011, accessed February 1, 2012, smb-corner.com/2011/04/supply-chain-management-small-business; Joel D. Wisner, G. Keong Leong, and Keah-Choon Tan, *Principles of Supply Chain Management: A Balanced Approach* (Mason, OH: South-Western, 2004), 13.

9. Susanne Hertz and Monica Alfredsson, "Strategic Development of Third-Party Logistics Providers," *Industrial Marketing Management* 32, no. 2 (2003): 139.

10. "Fourth-Party Logistics," *Business Dictionary.com*, accessed February 27, 2012, www.businessdictionary.com/definition/fourth-party-logistics-4PL.html.

11. Cecil C. Bozarth and Robert B. Handfield, *Introduction to Operations and Supply Chain Management*, 2nd ed. (Upper Saddle River, NJ: Pearson Prentice Hall, 2007), 519.

12. Ken Boyer and Rohit Verma, *Operations and Supply Chain Management for the 21st Century* (Mason, OH: South-Western, 2009), 38.

13. W. Edwards Deming, *The New Economics for Industry, Government, Education*, 2nd ed. (Cambridge, MA: MIT Press, 2000), 232.

14. Joel D. Wisner, G. Keong Leong, and Keah-Choon Tan, *Principles of Supply Chain Management: A Balanced Approach* (Mason, OH: South-Western, 2004), 442.

15. Scott Webster, *Principles and Tools for Supply Chain Management* (Boston: McGraw-Hill, 2008), 55.

16. Mason A. Carpenter and William G. Sanders, *Strategic Management and Dynamic Perspective* (Upper Saddle River, NJ: Prentice Hall, 2008), 108.

17. Mary Ethridge, "News about the Wal-Mart Struggle," accessed February 2, 2012, www.dsausa.org/lowwage/walmart/Dec17_03.html.

18. John J. Coyle, C. John Langley, Brian Gibson, Robert A. Novak, and Edward J. Bardi, *Supply Chain Management: A Logistics Perspective*, 8th ed. (Mason, OH: South-Western, 2008), 301.

19. Joel D. Wisner, G. Keong Leong, and Keah-Choon Tan, *Principles of Supply Chain Management: A Balanced Approach* (Mason, OH: South-Western, 2004), 76.

20. "Small and Medium-Sized Business Enterprise Applications Market to Grow to $80.3 Billion by 2012," *Business Wire*, June 11, 2008, accessed February 2, 2012, www.reuters.com/article/2008/06/11/idUS117514+11-Jun-2008+BW20080611.

21. Carol Lawrence, "Enterprise Resource Planning Software Become More Accessible to Small and Midsize Companies," *McClatchy Tribune Business News*, August 8, 2010.

22. David Hayes, "When Size Doesn't Matter (in business)," *McClatchy Tribune Business News*, March 4, 2010.

23. Michelle Maisto, "Apple iPad 2 Production Hindered by Japan Earthquake: IHS iSuppli," *eWeek.com*, March 19, 2011, accessed February 2, 2012, www.eweek.com/c/a/Mobile-and-Wireless/Apple-iPad-2-Production-Hindered-by-Japan-Earthquake-IHS-iSuppli-385386.

24. Peter Müller and Alexander Neubacher, "Disaster in Japan Sends Ripples through the Global Economy," *Spiegel Online International*, March 22, 2011, accessed February 2, 2012, www.spiegel.de/international/business/0,1518,752325,00.html.

25. "Blast Could Cut iPad 2 Production by 500,000: iSuppli," *Taipei Times*, May 25, 2011, accessed February 12, 2012, www.taipeitimes.com/News/biz/archives/2011/05/25/2003504064.

26. "The 11 Greatest Supply Chain Disasters," *SupplyChainDigest*, January 2006, accessed February 2, 2012, www.scdigest.com/assets/reps/SCDigest_Top-11-SupplyChainDisasters.pdf.

27. Jack Kleijen, "Supply Chain Simulation Tools and Techniques: A Survey," *International Journal of Simulation and Process Modeling* 1, no. 1/2 (2005): 82.

CHAPTER 12
People and Organization

Flat World Knowledge

Source: Used with permission from Flat World Knowledge.

The idea for Flat World Knowledge (FWK), the publisher of this book, started on a business trip to Chicago in 2006. Co-founders Jeff Shelstad and Eric Frank, who were both working at a large educational publisher at the time, decided they wanted to move away from the limitations and the frustrations of the traditional publishing industry. Veterans of the higher education publishing industry. Their vision was to create a new publishing company that offered a lot more choices to students, professors, and authors.

"Students can't afford to pay $200 for a textbook. The old business model wasn't adapting fast enough to the Internet, where so much information was available for free or low-cost," says Jeff, referring to traditional publishers. "We knew there had to be a better way to publish high-quality material *and* eliminate price and access barriers."

Since its beginning in 2007, more than thirty employees have joined this fast-growing start-up, located just north of New York City, in Irvington, New York. The company has become a recognized pioneer in transforming higher educational publishing and textbook affordability.

FWK is upending the $8 billion college textbook industry with a new business model that focuses on affordability and personalization. Professors who assign FWK books are free to revise and edit the material to match their course and help improve student success. Students have a choice of affordable print and digital formats that they can access online or on a laptop, tablet, e-reader or smartphone for a fraction of the price that most traditional publishers charge.

Rather than hamper the company's growth, the economic downturn has actually highlighted the value of its products and the viability of its business model. Despite the bad economy, FWK has been able to raise over $30 million in venture capital. Clearly, they are doing something right.

The numbers tell the story. Since the launch of their first ten books in spring 2009 (there are more than one hundred fifteen books to date), faculty at more than two thousand institutions in forty-four countries have adopted FWK books. As a result, more than 600,000 students have benefited from affordable textbook choices that lower costs, increase access and personalize learning.

In 2010, 2011 and 2012, *EContent* magazine named FWK as one of the top one hundred companies that matter most in the digital content industry. FWK was also named 2010 Best Discount Textbook Provider by the Education Resources People's Choice Awards.

What is particularly refreshing is Jeff's philosophy about people and work. "Give talented people an opportunity to build something meaningful, the tools to do it, and the freedom to do one's best." He believes in flexibility with people and their jobs, and, to that end, employees have the option to work remotely. There is no question that FWK is an innovator in the educational publishing industry, but it also knows how to treat people well and provide a challenging environment that fosters personal growth.

Source: Interview with Jeff Shelstad, March 31, 2011; "Flatworld Knowledge Named to EContent Magazine Top 100 Digital Companies of 2010," Pressitt, December 15, 2010, accessed February 2, 2012, http://pressitt.com/smnr/ Flat-World-Knowledge-Named-to-EContent-Magazines-2010-List-of-Top-100-Digital-Companies-/2961/; Alexandra Torres, "Company Offers Alternatives to Enter the World of Knowledge," The Ticker, October 10, 2010, accessed February 2, 2012, http://www.theticker.org/mobile/ company-offers-alternatives-to-enter-the-world-of-knowledge-1.2360719; John Tozzi, "Online Startups Target College Book Costs," Bloomberg BusinessWeek, September 23, 2010, accessed February 2, 2012, www.BusinessWeek.com/smallbiz/content/sep2010/sb20100922_892919.htm.

1. PRINCIPLES OF MANAGEMENT AND ORGANIZATION

LEARNING OBJECTIVES

1. Understand the functions of management.
2. Explain the three basic leadership styles.
3. Explain the three basic levels of management.
4. Understand the management skills that are important for a successful small business.
5. Understand the steps in ethical decision making.

All small businesses need to be concerned about management principles. Management decisions will impact the success of a business, the health of its work environment, its growth if growth is an objective, and customer value and satisfaction. Seat-of-the-pants management may work temporarily, but its folly will inevitably take a toll on a business. This section discusses management principles, levels, and skills—all areas that small business owners should understand so that they can make informed and effective choices for their businesses.

1.1 What Is Management?

management

The application of planning, organizing, staffing, directing, and controlling functions in the most efficient manner possible to accomplish meaningful organizational objectives.

There is no universally accepted definition for management. The definitions run the gamut from very simple to very complex. For our purposes, we define **management** as "the application of planning, organizing, staffing, directing, and controlling functions in the most efficient manner possible to accomplish meaningful organizational objectives."[1] Put more simply, management is all about achieving organizational objectives through people and other resources.[2]

Management principles apply to all organizations—large or small, for-profit or not-for-profit. Even one-person small businesses need to be concerned about management principles because without a fundamental understanding of how businesses are managed, there can be no realistic expectation of success. Remember that the most common reason attributed to small business failure is failure on the part of management.

1.2 Management Functions

On any given day, small business owners and managers will engage in a mix of many different kinds of activities—for example, deal with crises as they arise, read, think, write, talk to people, arrange for things to be done, have meetings, send e-mails, conduct performance evaluations, and plan. Although the amount of time that is spent on each activity will vary, all the activities can be assigned to one or more of the five management functions: planning, organizing, staffing, directing, and controlling (Figure 12.1).

FIGURE 12.1 Management Functions

Planning

Planning "is the process of anticipating future events and conditions and determining courses of action for achieving organizational objectives."[3] It is the one step in running a small business that is most commonly skipped, but it is the one thing that can keep a business on track and keep it there.[4] Planning helps a business realize its vision, get things done, show when things cannot get done and why they may not have been done right, avoid costly mistakes, and determine the resources that will be needed to get things done.[5] Business planning for the small business is discussed in Chapter 5, and marketing planning is discussed in Chapter 8.

Organizing

Organizing "consists of grouping people and assigning activities so that job tasks and the mission can be properly carried out."[6] Establishing a management hierarchy is the foundation for carrying out the organizing function.

Contrary to what some people may believe, the principle of organizing is not dead. Rather, it is clearly important "to both the organization and its workers because both the effectiveness of organizations and worker satisfaction require that there be clear and decisive direction from leadership; clarity of responsibilities, authorities, and accountabilities; authority that is commensurate with responsibility and accountability; unified command (each employee has one boss); a clear approval process; and, rules governing acceptable employee behavior."[7] Except for a small business run solely by its owner, every small business needs a management hierarchy—no matter how small. Each person in the business should know who is responsible for what, have the authority to carry out his or her responsibilities, and not get conflicting instructions from different bosses. The absence of these things can have debilitating consequences for the employees in particular and the business in general.[8]

The organizational design and structure of a small business are important parts of organizing, which are discussed in Section 2.

planning

The process of anticipating future events and conditions and determining courses of action for achieving organizational objectives.

organizing

Grouping people and assigning activities so that job tasks and the mission can be properly carried out.

Video Link 12.1

Glassblowing Business Thrives

Lesson learned: Everyone should know his or her role in the business.

www.cnn.com/video/#/video/living/2010/10/15/mxp.sbs.glass.business.hln?iref=videosearch

Staffing

staffing

Selecting, placing, training, developing, compensating, and evaluating employees.

The **staffing** function involves selecting, placing, training, developing, compensating, and evaluating (the performance appraisal) employees.[9] Small businesses need to be staffed with competent people who can do the work that is necessary to make the business a success. It would also be extremely helpful if these people could be retained. Many of the issues associated with staffing in a small business are discussed in Section 4.

Directing

directing

The managerial function that initiates action.

leading

The process of influencing people to work toward a common goal.

motivating

The process of providing reasons for people to work in the best interests of an organization.

Directing is the managerial function that initiates action: issuing directives, assignments, and instructions; building an effective group of subordinates who are motivated to do what must be done; explaining procedures; issuing orders; and making sure that mistakes are corrected.[10] Directing is part of the job for every small business owner or manager. **Leading** and **motivating** work together in the directing function. Leading "is the process of influencing people to work toward a common goal [and] motivating is the process of providing reasons for people to work in the best interests of an organization."[11]

Different situations call for different leadership styles. In a very influential research study, Kurt Lewin established three major leadership styles: autocratic, democratic, and laissez-faire.[12] Although good leaders will use all three styles depending on the situation, with one style normally dominant, bad leaders tend to stick with only one style.[13]

autocratic leadership

The leader makes decisions without involving others.

Autocratic leadership occurs when a leader makes decisions without involving others; the leader tells the employees what is to be done and how it should be accomplished.[14] Lewin et al. found that this style creates the most discontent.[15] However, this style works when all the information needed for a decision is present, there is little time to make a decision, the decision would not change as a result of the participation of others, the employees are well motivated, and the motivation of the people who will carry out subsequent actions would not be affected by whether they are involved in the decision or not.[16] This leadership style should not be used very often.

democratic leadership

The leader involves other people in decision making.

Democratic leadership involves other people in the decision making—for example, subordinates, peers, superiors, and other stakeholders—but the leader makes the final decision. Rather than being a sign of weakness, this participative form of leadership is a sign of strength because it demonstrates respect for the opinions of others. The extent of participation will vary depending on the leader's strengths, preferences, beliefs, and the decision to be made, but it can be as extreme as fully delegating a decision to the team.[17] This leadership style works well when the leader has only part of the information and the employees have the other part. The participation is a win-win situation, where the benefits are mutual. Others usually appreciate this leadership style, but it can be problematic if there is a wide range of opinions and no clear path for making an equitable, final decision.[18] In experiments that Lewin et al. conducted with others, the democratic leadership style was revealed as the most effective.[19]

laissez-faire leadership (or delegative or free-reign leadership)

Leadership that minimizes the leader's involvement in decision making, but the leader is responsible for the final decision.

Laissez-faire leadership (or delegative or free-reign leadership) minimizes the leader's involvement in decision making. Employees are allowed to make decisions, but the leader still has responsibility for the decisions that are made. The leader's role is that of a contact person who provides helpful guidance to accomplish objectives.[20] This style works best when employees are self-motivated and competent in making their own decisions, and there is no need for central coordination; it presumes full trust and confidence in the people below the leader in the hierarchy.[21] However, this is not the style to use if the leader wants to blame others when things go wrong.[22] This style can be problematic because people may tend not to be coherent in their work and not inclined to put in the energy they did when having more visible and active leadership.[23]

Good leadership is necessary for all small businesses. Employees need someone to look up to, inspire and motivate them to do their best, and perhaps emulate. In the final analysis, leadership is necessary for success. Without leadership, "the ship that is your small business will aimlessly circle and eventually run out of power or run aground."[24]

Don't Be This Kind of Leader or Manager

Here are some examples of common leadership styles that should be avoided.

- **Post-hoc management.** As judge and jury, management is always right and never to blame. This approach ensures security in the leader's job. This style is very common in small companies where there are few formal systems and a general autocratic leadership style.[25]

- **Micromanagement.** Alive and well in businesses of all sizes, this style assumes that the subordinate is incapable of doing the job, so close instruction is provided, and everything is checked. Subordinates are often criticized and seldom praised; nothing is ever good enough. It is really the opposite of leadership.[26]

- **Seagull management.** This humorous term is used to describe a management style whereby a person flies in, poops on you, and then flies away.[27] When present, such people like to give criticism and direction in equal quantities—with no real understanding of what the job entails. Before anyone can object or ask what the manager really wants, he or she is off to an important meeting. Everyone is actively discouraged from saying anything, and eye contact is avoided.[28]

- **Mushroom management.** This manager plants you knee-deep (or worse) in the smelly stuff and keeps you in the dark.[29] Mushroom managers tend to be more concerned about their own careers and images. Anyone who is seen as a threat may be deliberately held back. These managers have their favorites on whom they lavish attention and give the best jobs. Everyone else is swept away and given the unpopular work. Oftentimes, mushroom managers are incompetent and do not know any better. We have all seen at least one manager of this type.

- **Kipper management.** This is the manager who is, like a fish, two-faced because employees can see only one face at a time. To senior managers, this person is typically a model employee who puts business first and himself last. To subordinates, however, the reverse is often the case. The subordinates will work hard to get things done in time, but they are blamed when things go wrong—even if it is not their fault. The kipper will be a friend when things need to get done and then stab the subordinates in the back when glory or reward is to be gained.[30] We have all seen this kind of manager, perhaps even worked for one.

Controlling

Controlling is about keeping an eye on things. It is "the process of evaluating and regulating ongoing activities to ensure that goals are achieved."[31] Controlling provides feedback for future planning activities and aims to modify behavior and performance when deviations from plans are discovered.[32] There are four commonly identified steps in the controlling process.[33] (See Figure 12.2.) **Setting performance standards** is the first step. Standards let employees know what to expect in terms of time, quality, quantity, and so forth. The second step is **measuring performance**, where the actual performance or results are determined. **Comparing performance** is step three. This is when the actual performance is compared to the standard. The fourth and last step, **taking corrective action**, involves making whatever actions are necessary to get things back on track. The controlling functions should be circular in motion, so all the steps will be repeated periodically until the goal is achieved.

controlling

The process of evaluating and regulating ongoing activities to ensure that the goals are achieved.

FIGURE 12.2 The Controlling Function

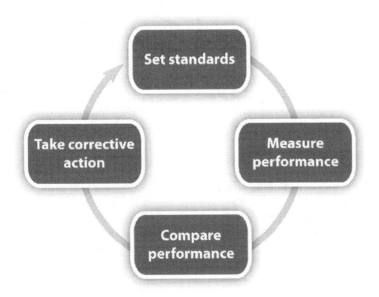

1.3 Levels of Management

As a small business grows, it should be concerned about the levels or the layers of management. Also referred to as the **management hierarchy** (Figure 12.3), there are typically three levels of management: top or executive, middle, and first-line or supervisory. To meet a company's goals, there should be coordination of all three levels.

FIGURE 12.3 The Management Hierarchy

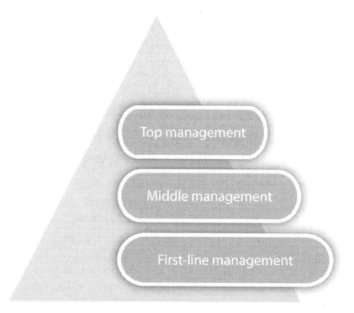

Top management, also referred to as the executive level, guides and controls the overall fortunes of a business.[34] This level includes such positions as the president or CEO, the chief financial officer, the chief marketing officer, and executive vice presidents. Top managers devote most of their time to developing the mission, long-range plans, and strategy of a business—thus setting its direction. They are often asked to represent the business in events at educational institutions, community activities, dealings with the government, and seminars and sometimes as a spokesperson for the business in advertisements. It has been estimated that top managers spend 55 percent of their time planning.[35]

Middle management is probably the largest group of managers. This level includes such positions as regional manager, plant manager, division head, branch manager, marketing manager, and project director. Middle managers, a conduit between top management and first-line management, focus on specific operations, products, or customer groups within a business. They have responsibility for developing detailed plans and procedures to implement a firm's strategic plans.[36]

First-line or supervisory management is the group that works directly with the people who produce and sell the goods and/or the services of a business; they implement the plans of middle management.[37] They coordinate and supervise the activities of operating employees, spending most of their time working with and motivating their employees, answering questions, and solving day-to-day problems.[38] Examples of first-line positions include supervisor, section chief, office manager, foreman, and team leader.[39]

In many small businesses, people often wear multiple hats. This happens with management as well. One person may wear hats at each management level, and this can be confusing for both the person wearing the different hats and other employees. It is common for the small business owner to do mostly first-level management work, with middle or top management performed only in response to a problem or a crisis, and top-level strategic work rarely performed.[40] This is not a good situation. If the small business is large enough to have three levels of management, it is important that there be clear distinctions among them—and among the people who are in those positions. The small business owner should be top management only. This will eliminate confusion about responsibilities and accountabilities.

1.4 Management Skills

Management skill "is the ability to carry out the process of reaching organizational goals by working with and through people and other organizational resources."[41] Possessing management skill is generally considered a requirement for success.[42] An effective manager is the manager who is able to master four basic types of skills: technical, conceptual, interpersonal, and decision making.

Technical skills "are the manager's ability to understand and use the techniques, knowledge, and tools and equipment of a specific discipline or department."[43] These skills are mostly related to working with processes or physical objects. Engineering, accounting, and computer programming are examples of technical skills.[44] Technical skills are particularly important for first-line managers and are much less important at the top management level. The need for technical skills by the small business owner will depend on the nature and the size of the business.

Conceptual skills "determine a manager's ability to see the organization as a unified whole and to understand how each part of the overall organization interacts with other parts."[45] These skills are of greatest importance to top management because it is this level that must develop long-range plans for the future direction of a business. Conceptual skills are not of much relevance to the first-line manager but are of great importance to the middle manager. All small business owners need such skills.

Interpersonal skills "include the ability to communicate with, motivate, and lead employees to complete assigned activities,"[46] hopefully building cooperation within the manager's team. Managers without these skills will have a tough time succeeding. Interpersonal skills are of greatest importance to middle managers and are somewhat less important for first-line managers. They are of least importance to top management, but they are still very important. They are critical for all small business owners.

The fourth basic management skill is **decision making** (Figure 12.4), the ability to identify a problem or an opportunity, creatively develop alternative solutions, select an alternative, delegate authority to implement a solution, and evaluate the solution.[47]

FIGURE 12.4 Management Decision Making

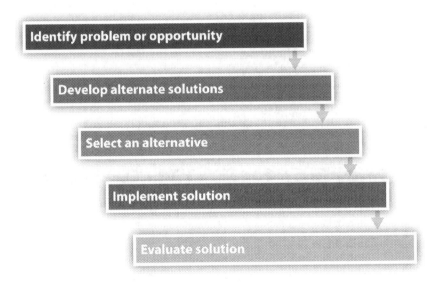

Making good decisions is never easy, but doing so is clearly related to small business success. "Decisions that are based on a foundation of knowledge and sound reasoning can lead the company into long-term prosperity; conversely, decisions that are made on the basis of flawed logic, emotionalism, or incomplete information can quickly put a small business out of commission."[48]

management skill

The ability to carry out the process of reaching organizational goals by working with and through people and other organizational resources.

technical skills

Abilities related to working with processes or physical objects.

conceptual skills

A manager's ability to see an organization as a unified whole and understand how each part of the overall organization interacts with other parts.

interpersonal skills

The ability to communicate with, motivate, and lead employees to complete assigned activities.

decision making

The ability to identify a problem or an opportunity, creatively develop alternative solutions, select an alternative, delegate authority to implement a solution, and implement and evaluate the solution.

A Framework for Ethical Decision Making

Small business decisions should be ethical decisions. Making ethical decisions requires that the decision maker(s) be sensitive to ethical issues. In addition, it is helpful to have a method for making ethical decisions that, when practiced regularly, becomes so familiar that it is automatic. The Markkula Center for Applied Ethics recommends the following framework for exploring ethical dilemmas and identifying ethical courses of action.[49] However, in many if not most instances, a small business owner or manager and an employee will usually know instinctively whether a particular decision is unethical.

Recognize an Ethical Issue

- Could this decision or situation be damaging to someone or some group? Does this decision involve a choice between a good and a bad alternative or perhaps between two "goods" or between two "bads"?
- Is this issue about more than what is legal or most efficient? If so, how?

Get the Facts

- What are the relevant facts of the case? What facts are not known? Can I learn more about the situation? Do I know enough to make a decision?
- What individuals and groups have an important stake in the outcome? Are some concerns more important? Why?
- What are the options for acting? Have all the relevant persons and groups been consulted? Have I identified creative options?

Evaluate Alternative Actions

- Which option will produce the most good and do the least harm?
- Which option best respects the rights of all who have a stake?
- Which option treats people equally or proportionately?
- Which option best serves the community as a whole, not just some members?
- Which option leads me to act as the sort of person I want to be?

Make a Decision and Test It

- Considering all these approaches, which option best addresses the situation?
- If I told someone I respect—or told a television audience—which option I have chosen, what would they say?

Act and Reflect on the Outcome

- How can my decision be implemented with the greatest care and attention to the concerns of all stakeholders?
- How did my decision turn out, and what have I learned from this specific situation?

KEY TAKEAWAYS

- Management principles are important to all small businesses.
- Management decisions will impact the success of a business, the health of its work environment, its growth if growth is an objective, and customer value and satisfaction.
- Management is about achieving organizational objectives through people.
- The most common reason attributed to small business failure is failure on the part of management.
- On any given day, a typical small business owner or manager will be engaged in some mix of planning, organizing, staffing, directing, and controlling.
- Different situations call for different leadership styles. The three major styles are autocratic, democratic, and laissez-faire. Bad leaders typically stick with one style.
- The management hierarchy is typically composed of three levels: top or executive, middle, and first-line or supervisory. If a small business is large enough to have these three levels, it is important that there be a clear distinction between them.
- Management skills are required for success. Technical, conceptual, interpersonal, and decision-making skills will be of differing importance depending on the management level.

2. ORGANIZATIONAL DESIGN

LEARNING OBJECTIVES

1. Understand why an organizational structure is necessary.
2. Understand organizational principles.
3. Explain the guidelines for organizing a small business.
4. Describe the different forms of organizational structure and how they apply to small businesses.

Organizing consists of grouping people and assigning activities so that job tasks and the mission of a business can be properly carried out. The result of the organizing process should be an overall structure that permits interactions among individuals and departments needed to achieve the goals and objectives of a business.[50] Although small business owners may believe that they do not need to adhere to the organizing principles of management, nothing could be farther from the truth.

> *Principles represent guidelines that managers can use in making decisions. They are not laws etched in stone. At times, principles can be used exactly as the way they are stated; at other times they should be modified or even completely ignored.* **Small business owners must learn through experience when and where to use [the] principles or to modify them** *[emphasis added]. Principles when used effectively and in the right context often bring organizational efficiencies and thus result in the growth of the business. Some organizing principles…would apply to small businesses as well as they would to large enterprises and would lead to similar benefits.*[51]

There is no single best way to organize. Rather, the organization decision is based on a multitude of factors, including business size, market, product mix, competition, the number of employees, history, objectives and goals, and available financial resources.[52] Each small business must decide what organizational design best fits the business.

2.1 Fundamentals of Organization

Ivancevich and Duening[53] maintain that there are several fundamental issues that managers need to consider when making any kind of organizational decision: clear objectives, coordination, formal and informal organization, the organization chart, formal authority, and centralization versus decentralization. Understanding these fundamentals can facilitate the creation of an organizational structure that is a good fit for a small business.

Clear Objectives

Objectives "give meaning to the business—and to the work done by employees—by determining what it is attempting to accomplish."[54] Objectives provide direction for organizing a firm, helping to identify the work that must be done to accomplish the objectives. This work, in turn, serves as the basis on which to make staffing decisions.

Coordination

The resources of a small business and its employees must be coordinated to minimize duplication and maximize effectiveness.[55] Coordination requires informal communication with and among employees every day. All businesses must continually coordinate the activities of others—an effort that should never be underestimated. Business leaders must make sure that employees have the answers to six fundamental questions:[56]

1. What is my job?
2. How am I doing?
3. Does anyone care?
4. How are we doing?
5. What are our vision, mission, and values?
6. How can I help?

Formal and Informal Organization

formal organization

The details of the roles and the responsibilities of all employees.

When a one-person small business adds employees, some kind of hierarchy will be needed to indicate who does what. This hierarchy often becomes the **formal organization**—that is, the details of the roles and responsibilities of all employees.[57] Formal organization tends to be static, but it does indicate who is in charge of what. This helps to prevent chaos. The formal organizational structure helps employees feel safe and secure because they know exactly what their chain of command is. The downside of a formal organizational structure is that it typically results in a slower decision-making process because of the numerous groups and people who have to be involved and consulted.[58]

informal organization

All the connections and relationships that relate to how people throughout an organization actually network to get the job done.

grapevine (or water cooler)

The informal communications network within an organization, separate from—and sometimes much faster than—formal channels of communication.

The **informal organization** is almost never explicitly stated. It consists of all the connections and relationships that relate to how people throughout the organization actually network to get a job done. The informal organization fills the gaps that are created by the formal organization.[59] Although the informal organization is not written down anywhere, it has a tremendous impact on the success of a small business because it is "composed of natural leaders who get things done primarily through the power granted to them by their peers."[60] Informal groups and the infamous grapevine are firmly embedded in the informal organization. The **grapevine (or water cooler)** "is the informal communications network within an organization,…completely separate from—and sometimes much faster than—the organization's formal channels of communication."[61] Small business owners must acknowledge the existence of the grapevine and figure out how to use it constructively.

Video Clip 12.1

Leading Outside the Lines
The formal and informal organizations need to work together to sustain peak performance over time.

View the video online at: http://www.youtube.com/v/xjSyz_GiyCg

Organization Chart

The **organization chart** is a visual representation of the formal organization of a business. The chart shows the structure of the organization and the relationships and relative ranks of its positions; it helps organize the workplace while outlining the direction of management control for subordinates.[62] Even the one-person small business can use some kind of organization chart to see what functions need to be performed; this will help ensure that everything that should be done is getting done.[63] Figure 12.5 illustrates a simple organization chart for a one-person retail business.[64]

organization chart

A visual representation of the formal organization of a business.

FIGURE 12.5 Organization Chart for a One-Person Small Business

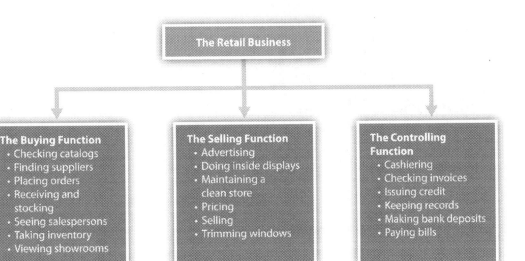

Organization charts offer the following benefits:[65]

- Effectively communicate organizational, employee, and enterprise information
- Allow managers to make decisions about resources, provide a framework for managing change, and communicate operational information across the organization
- Are transparent and predictable about what should happen in a business
- Provide a quick snapshot about the formal hierarchy in a business
- Tell everyone in the organization who is in charge of what and who reports to whom

There are, of course, several limitations to organization charts:[66]

- They are static and inflexible, often being out of date as organizations change and go through growth phases.
- They do not aid in understanding what actually happens within the informal organization. The reality is that organizations are often quite chaotic.
- They cannot cope with changing boundaries of firms due to outsourcing, information technology, strategic alliances, and the network economy.

In its early stages, a small business may choose not to create a formal organization chart. However, organization must exist even without a chart so that the business can be successful. Most small businesses find organization charts to be useful because they help the owner or the manager track growth and change in the organizational structure.[67] The real challenge is to create an organizational chart that reflects the real world. Small businesses have a definite advantage here because their size allows for more flexibility and manageability.

Video Clip 12.2

Burn Your Org Chart
Not all organizational charts reflect the real world.

View the video online at: http://www.youtube.com/v/Kx_Vfx3y7nQ

formal authority

The right to give orders and set policy.

Formal authority is "the right to give orders and set policy."[68] It is organized according to a hierarchy, typically expressed in the organization chart, where one manager may have authority over some employees while being subject to the formal authority of a superior at the same time. Formal authority also encompasses the allocation of an organization's resources to achieve its objectives.[69] The position on the organization chart will be indicative of the amount of authority and formal power held by a particular individual.

line authority

Having direct authority over lower positions in the hierarchy.

Two major types of authority that the small business owner should understand are line and staff. These authorities reflect the existing relationships between superiors and subordinates.[70] **Line authority** refers to having direct authority over lower positions in the hierarchy. "A manager with line authority is the unquestioned superior for all activities of his or her subordinates."[71] The day-to-day tasks of those with line authority involve working directly toward accomplishing an organization's mission, goals, and objectives.[72] Examples of positions with line authority are the president, the vice president of operations, and the marketing manager. In a small business, the owner or the top manager will have line authority over his or her subordinates. The extent of line authority beyond the owner or the top manager will depend on the size of the business and the organizational vision of the owner.

staff authority

Advisory only; there is no authority to take action and no responsibility for revenue generation.

Staff authority is advisory only. There is no authority to take action (except when someone is a manager of a staff function, e.g., human resources), and there is no responsibility for revenue generation. Someone with staff authority assists those with line authority as well as others who have staff authority. Examples of staff authority are human resources, legal, and accounting, each of which is relevant to a small business. Staff personnel can be extremely helpful in improving the effectiveness of line personnel. Unfortunately, staff personnel are often the first to go when cutbacks occur. As a small business grows, a decision may be made to add staff personnel because the most significant factor in determining whether or not to add personnel is the size of a business. The larger the organization, the greater the need and the ability to hire staff personnel to provide specialized expertise.[73] Small businesses, however, may prefer to hire outside service providers for staff functions such as legal and accounting services because it would be difficult to keep such people busy full time. Remember, cash flow is king.

Centralization and Decentralization

centralization

Very little authority; job activities are not delegated to subordinates.

decentralization

Authority and job activities are delegated rather than being held by a small management group.

Centralization and decentralization are about the amount of authority to delegate. **Centralization** means that little or no authority and job activities are delegated to subordinates. A relatively small number of line managers make the decisions and hold most of the authority and power. **Decentralization** is the opposite. Authority and job activities are delegated rather than being held by a small management group.[74]

Depending on various factors, organizations move back and forth on the centralization-decentralization continuum. For example, managing a crisis requires more centralized decision making because decisions need to be made quickly.[75] A noncrisis or a normal work situation would favor decentralized decision making and encourages employee empowerment and delegated authority.[76] There are no universally accepted guidelines for determining whether a centralized or a decentralized approach should be used. It has been noted, however, that "the best organizations are those that are able to shift flexibly from one level of centralization to another in response to changing external conditions."[77] Given the flexibility and the responsiveness of small businesses that originate from their size, any movement that is needed along the centralization-decentralization continuum will be much easier and quicker.

2.2 Guidelines for Organizing

Several management principles can be used as guidelines when designing an organizational structure. Although there are many principles to consider, the focus here is on unity of command, division of work, span of control, and the scalar principle. These principles are applicable to small businesses although, as has been said earlier, they should not be seen as etched in stone. They can be modified or ignored altogether depending on the business, the situation at hand, and the experience of management.[78]

Unity of Command

Unity of command means that no subordinate has more than one boss. Each person in a business should know who gives him or her the authority to make decisions and do the job. Having conflicting orders from multiple bosses will create confusion and frustration about which order to follow and result in contradictory instructions.[79] In addition, violating the unity of command will undermine authority, divide loyalty, and create a situation in which responsibilities can be evaded and work efforts will be duplicated and overlapping. Abiding by the unity of command will provide discipline, stability, and order, with a harmonious relationship—relatively speaking, of course—between superior and subordinate.[80] Unity of command makes the most sense for everyone, but it is violated on a regular basis.

unity of command

No subordinate has more than one boss.

Division of Labor

The **division of labor** is a basic principle of organizing that maintains that a job can be performed much more efficiently if the work is divided among individuals and groups so that attention and effort are focused on discrete portions of the task—that is, the jobholder is allowed to specialize.[81] The result is a more efficient use of resources and greater productivity. As mentioned earlier, small businesses are commonly staffed with people who wear multiple hats, including the owner. However, the larger the business, the more desirable it will be to have people specialize to improve efficiency and productivity. To do otherwise will be to slow down processes and use more resources than should be necessary. This will have a negative impact on the bottom line.

division of labor

A job can be performed much more efficiently if the jobholder is allowed to specialize.

Span of Control

Span of control (span of management) refers to the number of people or subordinates that a manager supervises. The span of control typically becomes smaller as a person moves up the management hierarchy. There is no magic number for every manager. Instead, the number will vary based on "the abilities of both the manager and the subordinates, the nature of the work being done, the location of the employees, and the need for planning and coordination."[82] The growing trend is to use wider spans of control. Companies are flattening their structures by reducing their layers of management, particularly middle management. This process has increased the decision-making responsibilities that are given to employees.[83] As a small business grows, there will likely be more management hierarchy unless the small business owner is committed to a flatter organization. Either approach will have implications for span of control.

span of control (span of management)

The number of people or subordinates that a manager supervises.

Scalar Principle

The **scalar principle** maintains "that authority and responsibility should flow in a clear, unbroken line from the highest to the lowest manager."[84] Abiding by this principle will result in more effective decision making and communication at various levels in the organization. Breaking the chain would result in confusion about relationships and employee frustration. Following this principle is particularly important to small businesses because the tendency may otherwise be to operate on a more informal basis because of the size of the business. This would be a mistake. Even a two-person business should pay attention to the scalar principle.

scalar principle

Authority and responsibility should flow in a clear, unbroken line from the highest manager to the lowest manager.

2.3 Types of Organization Structures

contingency approach

There is no "one best" structure appropriate for every organization. The "best" structure for an organization fits its needs for the current situation.

Knowledge about organization structures is important for a small business that is already up and running as well as a small business in its early stages. Organizations are changing every day, so small business owners should be flexible enough to change the structure over time as the situation demands, perhaps by using the **contingency approach**. "The contingency approach to the structure of current organizations suggests there is no 'one best' structure appropriate for every organization. Rather, this approach contends the 'best' structure for an organization fits its needs for the situation at the time."[85] If a small business employs fewer than fifteen people, it may not be necessary to worry too much about its organizational structure. However, if the plans for the business include hiring more than fifteen people, having an organizational structure makes good sense because it will benefit a company's owner, managers, employees, investors, and lenders.[86] There are many structure options. Functional, divisional, matrix, and network or virtual structures are discussed here.

Functional Structure

functional structure

Organized according to job or purpose in the organization.

The **functional structure** is overwhelmingly the choice of business start-ups and is probably the most common structure used today. This structure organizes a business according to job or purpose in the organization and is most easily recognized by departments that focus on a single function or goal. (See Figure 12.6 for an example of a functional structure.) A start-up business is not likely to have an organization that looks like this. There may be only one or two boxes on it, representing the founder and his or her partner (if applicable).[87] As a small business grows, the need for additional departments will grow as well.

FIGURE 12.6 An Example of a Functional Structure

Source: "Small Business Management Skills," How to Start a Business, accessed February 2, 2012, http://www.how-to-start-a-small-business.com/ small-business-management-skills.html.

The functional structure gives employees and their respective departments clear objectives and purpose for their work. People in accounting can focus on improving their knowledge and skills to perform that work. This structure has also been shown to work well for businesses that operate in a relatively stable environment.[88]

At the same time, the functional structure can create divisions between departments if conflict occurs,[89] and it can become an obstruction if the objectives and the environment of the business require coordination across departments.[90]

Divisional Structure

The **divisional structure** can be seen as a decentralized version of the functional structure. The functions still exist in the organization, but they are based on product, geographic area or territory, or customer. Each division will then have its own functional department(s).[91] (See Figure 12.7 for an example of a divisional structure.)

FIGURE 12.7 An Example of a Divisional Structure

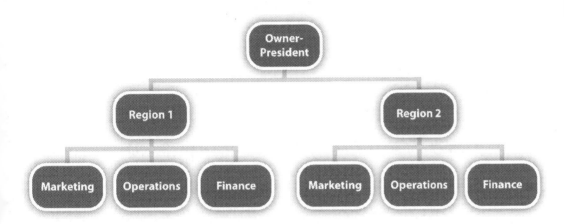

The divisional structure can work well because it focuses on individual geographic regions, customers, or products. This focus will enable greater efficiencies of operation and the building of "a common culture and esprit de corps that contributes both to higher morale and a better knowledge of the division's portfolio."[92] There are, of course, disadvantages to this structure. Competing divisions may turn to office politics, rather than strategic thinking, to guide their decision making, and divisions may become so compartmentalized as to lead to product incompatibilities.[93]

As a small business starts to grow in the diversity of its products, in the geographic reach of its markets, or in its customer bases, there is an evolution away from the functional structure to the divisional structure. However, significant growth would be needed before the divisional structure should be put into place.

Matrix Structure

The **matrix structure** combines elements of the functional and the divisional structures, bringing together specialists from different areas of a business to work on different projects on a short-term basis. Each person on the project team reports to two bosses: a line manager and a project manager. (See Figure 12.8 for an example of a matrix structure.) The matrix structure, popular in high-technology, multinational, consulting, and aerospace firms and hospitals, offers several key advantages, including the following: flexibility in assigning specialists, flexibility in adapting quickly to rapid environmental changes, the ability to focus resources on major products and problems, and creating an environment where there is a higher level of motivation and satisfaction for employees.[94] The disadvantages include the following: the violation of the "one boss" principle (unity of command) because of the dual lines of authority, responsibility, and accountability;[95] employee confusion and frustration from reporting to two bosses; power struggles between the first-line and the project managers; too much group decision making; too much time spent in meetings; personality clashes; and undefined personal roles.[96] The disadvantages notwithstanding, many companies with multiple business units, operations in multiple countries, and distribution through multiple channels have discovered that the effective use of a matrix structure is their only choice.[97]

divisional structure

A decentralized version of the functional structure in which functions still exist in an organization but are based on product, geographic area or territory, or customer.

matrix structure

Brings together specialists from different areas of a business to work on different projects on a short-term basis.

FIGURE 12.8 An Example of a Matrix Structure

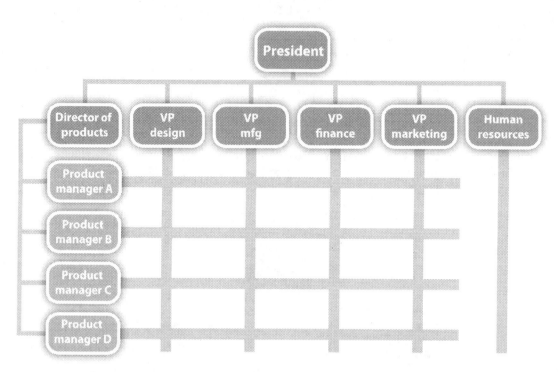

Source: "Sample Organization Charts: Matrix Organizational Structure," Vertex41.com, accessed February 2, 2012, http://www.vertex42.com/ExcelTemplates/organizational-chart.html.

The matrix structure is for project-oriented businesses, such as aerospace, construction, or small manufacturers of the job-shop variety (producers of a wide diversity of products made in small batches).

Virtual Organization

virtual organization (or network organization)

Administration is the primary function performed; other functions—such as marketing, engineering, production, and finance—are outsourced to other organizations or individuals.

The **virtual organization (or network organization)** is becoming an increasingly popular business structure as a means of addressing critical resource, personnel, and logistical issues. (See Figure 12.9 for an example of a virtual organization.) Administration is the primary function performed; other functions—such as marketing, engineering, production, and finance—are outsourced to other organizations or individuals. Individual professionals may or may not share office space, the organization is geographically distributed, the members of the organization communicate and coordinate their work through information technology, and there is a high degree of informal communication. The barriers of time and location are removed.[98]

FIGURE 12.9   An Example of a Virtual Organization

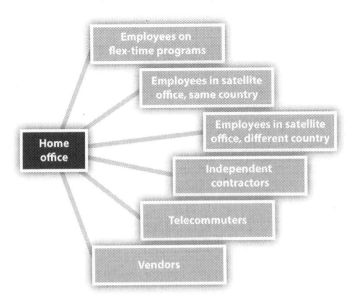

Source: "Supporting Skills," Eviton, Inc., accessed February 2, 2012, http://eviton.com/organizations.htm.

The positives associated with a virtual organization include reduced real-estate expenses, increased productivity, higher profits, improved customer service, access to global markets, environmental benefits (such as reduced gas mileage for employees, which contributes to reduced auto emissions), a wider pool of potential employees, and not needing to have all or some of the relevant employees in the same place at the same time for meetings or delivering services.[99] The negatives include setup costs; some loss of cost efficiencies; cultural issues (particularly when working in the global arena); traditional managers not feeling secure when their employees are working remotely, particularly in a crisis; feelings of isolation because of the loss of the camaraderie of the traditional office environment; and a lack of trust.[100]

The virtual organization can be quite attractive to small businesses and start-ups. By outsourcing much of the operations of a business, costs and capital requirements will be significantly reduced and flexibility enhanced. Given the lower capital requirements of a virtual business, some measures of profitability (e.g., return on investment [ROI] and return on assets [ROA]), would be significantly increased. This makes a business much more financially attractive to potential investors or banks, which might provide funding for future growth. **ROI** "is a performance measure used to evaluate the efficiency of an investment or to compare the efficiency of a number of investments."[101] **ROA** is "an indicator of how profitable a company is relative to its assets…[giving] an idea as to how efficient management is at using its assets to generate earnings."[102]

ROI

A performance measure used to evaluate the efficiency of an investment or compare the efficiency of several investments.

ROA

An indicator of how profitable a business is relative to its assets and indicates how efficient management is at using its assets to generate earnings.

Creating an Effective Business Organization Structure

Thinking and rethinking the business organization structure is important for all businesses—large or small. Conditions, products, and markets change. It is important to be flexible in creating a business structure that will best allow a business to operate effectively and efficiently. Each of the following should be considered:

- **Competitors.** Make an educated guess of the structure of competitors. Try to find out what works for them. Look at their reporting line structures and their procurement, production, marketing, and management systems. Perhaps there are some good ideas to be had.

- **Industry.** Is there a standard in an industry? Perhaps an industry lends itself to flexible organization structures, or perhaps more hierarchical structures are the norm. For example, auto manufacturers are usually set up regionally.

- **Compliance or legal requirements.** If an industry is regulated, certain elements may be required in the business structure. Even if an industry is not regulated, there may be compliance issues associated with employing a certain number of employees.

- **Investors and lending sources.** Having a business organization structure will give potential investors and funding institutions a window into how the business organizes its operations. The structure also lets investors and lenders know what kind of talent is needed, how soon they will be needed, and how the business will find and attract them.[103]

KEY TAKEAWAYS

- Organizations are changing every day, so small business owners should be flexible enough to change their structure over time as the situation demands.
- The functional structure is overwhelmingly the choice of business start-ups and is probably the most commonly used structure today.
- The functional structure organizes a business according to the job or the purpose in the organization and is most easily recognized by departments that focus on a single function or goal.
- The divisional structure is a decentralized version of the functional structure. The functions still exist, but they are based on product, geographic area or territory, or customer.
- As a small business starts to grow, there is an evolution away from the functional to the divisional structure. However, significant growth is required before the divisional structure is put into place.
- The matrix structure brings specialists from different areas of a business together to work on different projects for a short-term basis. This structure is for project-oriented businesses, such as aerospace, construction, or small manufacturers.
- In the virtual structure, administration is the primary function performed, with other functions—such as marketing, engineering, production, and finance—outsourced to other companies or individuals. This structure can be quite attractive to small businesses and start-ups.
- Creating an effective business organization structure should take the competition, the industry, compliance or legal requirements, investors, and lending sources into consideration.

EXERCISES

1. Select two small businesses that market two very different products, for example, a small manufacturer and a restaurant. Contact the manager of each business and conduct a fifteen-minute interview about the organizational structure that has been chosen. Ask each manager to describe the existing organizational structure (drawing an organization chart), explain why that structure was chosen, and reflect on the effectiveness and efficiency of the structure. Also ask each manager whether any thoughts have been given to changing the existing structure.

2. Frank Rainsford has been, in effect, the CEO of Frank's All-American BarBeQue since its inception. His major role has been that of restaurant manager, receiving support from his assistant manager Ed Tobor for the last fourteen years. Frank has two children, a son and daughter, who both worked in the restaurant as teenagers. His daughter has worked periodically at the restaurant since she graduated from high school. Frank's son, who recently lost his job, has returned to work for his father. The son produced several plans to expand the business, including the opening of a second restaurant and the extensive use of social media. After careful consideration, Frank has decided to open a second restaurant, but this has presented him with a major problem—how to assign responsibilities to personnel. His son wants to be designated the restaurant manager of the second restaurant and made the vice president of marketing. Ed Tobor also wants to be the manager of the new restaurant. His daughter has expressed an interest in being the manager of either restaurant. How should Frank resolve this problem?

3. LEGAL FORMS OF ORGANIZATION FOR THE SMALL BUSINESS

LEARNING OBJECTIVES

1. Understand the different legal forms that a small business can take.
2. Explain the factors that should be considered when choosing a legal form.
3. Understand the advantages and disadvantages of each legal form.
4. Explain why the limited liability company may be the best legal structure for many small businesses.

Every small business must select a legal form of ownership. The most common forms are sole proprietorship, partnership, and corporation. A limited liability company (LLC) is a relatively new business structure that is now allowed by all fifty states. Before a legal form is selected, however, several factors must be considered, not the least of which are legal and tax options.

3.1 Factors to Consider

The legal form of the business is one of the first decisions that a small business owner will have to make. Because this decision will have long-term implications, it is important to consult an attorney and an accountant to help make the right choice. The following are some factors the small business owner should consider before making the choice:[104]

- **The owner's vision.** Where does the owner see the business in the future (size, nature, etc.)?
- **The desired level of control.** Does the owner want to own the business personally or share ownership with others? Does the owner want to share responsibility for operating the business with others?
- **The level of structure.** What is desired—a very structured organization or something more informal?
- **The acceptable liability exposure.** Is the owner willing to risk personal assets? Is the owner willing to accept liability for the actions of others?
- **Tax implications.** Does the owner want to pay business income taxes and then pay personal income taxes on the profits earned?
- **Sharing profits.** Does the owner want to share the profits with others or personally keep them?
- **Financing needs.** Can the owner provide all the financing needs or will outside investors be needed? If outside investors are needed, how easy will it be to get them?
- **The need for cash.** Does the owner want to be able to take cash out of the business?

The final selection of a legal form will require consideration of these factors and tradeoffs between the advantages and disadvantages of each form. No choice will be perfect. Even after a business structure is determined, the favorability of that choice over another will always be subject to changes in the laws.[105]

3.2 Sole Proprietorship

A **sole proprietorship** is a business that is owned and usually operated by one person. It is the oldest, simplest, and cheapest form of business ownership because there is no legal distinction made between the owner and the business (see Table 12.1). Sole proprietorships are very popular, comprising 72 percent of all businesses and nearly $1.3 trillion in total revenue.[106] Sole proprietorships are common in a variety of industries, but the typical sole proprietorship owns a small service or retail operation, such as a dry cleaner, accounting services, insurance services, a roadside produce stand, a bakery, a repair shop, a gift shop, painters, plumbers, electricians, and landscaping services.[107] Clearly, the sole proprietorship is the choice for most small businesses.

sole proprietorship

The most basic type of business organization in which there is only one owner.

TABLE 12.1 Sole Proprietorships: A Summary of Characteristics

Liability	Taxes	Advantages	Disadvantages
Unlimited: owner is responsible for all the debts of the business.	No special taxes; owner pays taxes on profits; not subject to corporate taxes	<ul><li>Tax breaks</li><li>Owner retains all profits</li><li>Easy to start and dissolve</li><li>Flexibility of being own boss</li><li>No need to disclose business information</li><li>Pride of ownership</li></ul>	<ul><li>Owner absorbs all losses</li><li>Unlimited liability</li><li>Difficult to get financing</li><li>Management deficiencies</li><li>Lack of stability in case of injury, death, or illness</li><li>Time demands</li><li>Difficult to hire and keep highly motivated employees</li></ul>

Source: John M. Ivancevich and Thomas N. Duening, Business: Principles, Practices, and Guidelines (Mason, OH: Atomic Dog Publishing, 2007), 60; David L. Kurtz, Contemporary Business, 13th Edition Update (Hoboken, NJ: John Wiley & Sons, 2011), 163; "How to Choose the Right Business Structure for Your Small Business," National Federation of Independent Business, accessed February 3, 2012, http://bit.ly/KCvnaT; William M. Pride, Robert J. Hughes, and Jack R. Kapoor, Business (Boston: Houghton Mifflin, 2008), 150–51.

3.3 Partnership

partnership

Two or more people voluntarily operating a business as co-owners for profit.

A **partnership** is two or more people voluntarily operating a business as co-owners for profit. Partnerships make up more than 8 percent of all businesses in the United States and more than 11 percent of the total revenue.[108] Like the sole proprietorship, the partnership does not distinguish between the business and its owners (see Table 12.2). There should be a legal agreement that "sets forth how decisions will be made, profits will be shared, disputes will be resolved, how future partners will be admitted to the partnership, how partners can be bought out, and what steps will be taken to dissolve the partnership when needed."[109]

general partnership

A business composed of two or more owners who contribute the initial capital of the business and share in the profits and the losses.

There are two types of partnerships. In the **general partnership**, all the partners have unlimited liability, and each partner can enter into contracts on behalf of the other partners. A **limited partnership** has at least one general partner and one or more limited partners whose liability is limited to the cash or property invested in the partnership. Limited partnerships are usually found in professional firms, such as dentists, lawyers, and physicians, as well as in oil and gas, motion-picture, and real-estate companies. However, many medical and legal partnerships have switched to other forms to limit personal liability.[110]

limited partnership

A business format that may have several general partners and several more limited partners who do not have unlimited liability.

Before creating a partnership, the partners should get to know each other. According to Michael Lee Stallard, cofounder and president of E Pluribis Partners, a consulting firm in Greenwich, Connecticut, "The biggest mistake business partners make is jumping into business before getting to know each other...You must be able to connect to feel comfortable expressing your opinions, ideas and expectations."[111]

TABLE 12.2 Partnerships: A Summary of Characteristics

Liability	Taxes	Advantages	Disadvantages
Unlimited for general partner; limited partners risk only their original investment.	Individual taxes on business earnings; no income taxes as a business	■ Owner(s) retain all profits ■ Unlimited for general partner; limited partners risk only their original investment. Individual taxes on business earnings; no income taxes as a business ■ Easy to form and dissolve ■ Greater access to capital ■ No special taxes ■ Clear legal status ■ Combined managerial skills ■ Prospective employees may be attracted to a company if given incentive to become a partner	■ Unlimited financial liability for general partners ■ Interpersonal conflicts ■ Financing limitations ■ Management deficiencies ■ Partnership terminated if one partner dies, withdraws, or is declared legally incompetent ■ Shared decisions may lead to disagreements

Source: John M. Ivancevich and Thomas N. Duening, Business: Principles, Practices, and Guidelines (Mason, OH: Atomic Dog Publishing, 2007), 64–65; David L. Kurtz, Contemporary Business, 13th Edition Update (Hoboken, NJ: John Wiley & Sons, 2011), 163; "How to Choose the Right Business Structure for Your Small Business," National Federation of Independent Business, accessed February 3, 2012, http://bit.ly/KCvnaT; William M. Pride, Robert J. Hughes, and Jack R. Kapoor, Business (Boston: Houghton Mifflin, 2008), 154–55; "Small Business Planner—Choose a Structure," US Small Business Administration, accessed February 3, 2012, http://archive.sba.gov/smallbusinessplanner/start/chooseastructure/index.html.

3.4 Corporation

corporation

An artificial person created by law, with most of the legal rights of a real person.

A **corporation** "is an artificial person created by law, with most of the legal rights of a real person. These include the rights to start and operate a business, to buy or sell property, to borrow money, to sue or be sued, and to enter into binding contracts"[112] (see Table 12.3). Corporations make up 20 percent of all businesses in the United States, but they account for almost 90 percent of the revenue.[113] Although some small businesses are incorporated, many corporations are extremely large businesses—for example, Walmart, General Electric, Procter & Gamble, and Home Depot. Recent data show that only about one-half of the small business owners in the United States run incorporated businesses.[114]

Scott Shane, author of *The Illusions of Entrepreneurship* (Yale University Press, 2010), argues that small businesses that are incorporated have a much higher rate of success than sole proprietorships, outperforming unincorporated small businesses in terms of profitability, employment growth, sales growth, and other measures.[115] Shane maintains that being incorporated may not make sense for "tiny little businesses" because the small amount of risk may not be worth the complexity. However, Deborah Sweeney, incorporation expert for Intuit, disagrees, saying that "even the smallest eBay business has a risk of being sued" because shipping products around the country or the world can create legal problems if a shipment is lost.[116] Ultimately, it is the small business being successful that may be the biggest factor for the owner to move from a sole proprietorship to a corporation.

TABLE 12.3 Corporations: A Summary of Characteristics

Liability	Taxes	Advantages	Disadvantages
Limited;	multiple taxation	■ Limited liability ■ Skilled management team ■ Ease of raising capital ■ Easy to transfer ownership by selling stock ■ Perpetual life ■ Legal-entity status ■ Economies of large-scale operations	■ Double taxation ■ Difficult and expensive to start ■ Individual stockholder has little control over operations ■ Financial disclosure ■ Lack of personal interest unless managers are also stockholders ■ Credit limitations ■ Government regulation and increased paperwork

Source: "How—and Why—to Incorporate Your Business," Entrepreneur, accessed February 3, 2012, http://www.entrepreneur.com/article/77730; John M. Ivancevich and Thomas N. Duening, Business: Principles, Practices, and Guidelines (Mason, OH: Atomic Dog Publishing, 2007), 64–65; "How to Choose the Right Business Structure for Your Small Business," National Federation of Independent Business, accessed February 3, 2012, http://bit.ly/KCvnaT; William M. Pride, Robert J. Hughes, and Jack R. Kapoor, Business (Boston: Houghton Mifflin, 2008), 154–55.

3.5 Limited Liability Company

The **limited liability company** is a relatively new form of business ownership that is now permitted in all fifty states, although the laws of each state may differ. The LLC is a blend of a sole proprietorship and a corporation: the owners of the LLC have limited liability and are taxed only once for the business.[117] The LLC provides all the benefits of a partnership but limits the liability of each investor to the amount of his or her investment (see Table 12.4). "LLCs were created to provide business owners with the liability protection that corporations enjoy without the double taxation."[118]

According to Carter Bishop, a professor at Suffolk University Law School, who helped draft the uniform LLC laws for several states, "There's virtually no reason why a small business should file as a corporation, unless the owners plan to take the business public in the near future."[119] In the final analysis, the LLC business structure is the best choice for most small businesses. The owners will have the greatest flexibility, and there is a liability shield that protects all owners.[120]

limited liability company

An organizational form that can be limited to a single individual or several other owners or shareholders.

TABLE 12.4 Limited Liability Companies: A Summary of Characteristics

Liability	Taxes	Advantages	Disadvantages
Limited;	owners taxed at individual income tax rate	■ Limited liability ■ Taxed at individual tax rate ■ Shareholders can participate fully in managing company ■ No limit on number of shareholders ■ Easy to organize ■ LLC members can agree to share profits and losses disproportionately	■ Difficult to raise money ■ No perpetual life ■ Is dissolved at death, withdrawal, resignation, expulsion, or bankruptcy of one member unless there is a vote to continue ■ No transferability of membership without the majority consent of other members

Source: Annalyn Censky, "Business Structures 101," CNN Money, August 4, 2008, accessed February 3, 2012, http://cnnmon.ie/MDaxXN; "Limited Liability Company," Entrepreneur.com, accessed February 3, 2012, http://www.entrepreneur.com/article/24484; John M. Ivancevich and Thomas N. Duening, Business: Principles, Practices, and Guidelines (Mason, OH: Atomic Dog Publishing, 2007), 64–65; "How to Choose the Right Business Structure for Your Small Business," National Federation of Independent Business, accessed February 3, 2012, http://bit.ly/KCvnaT; William M. Pride, Robert J. Hughes, and Jack R. Kapoor, Business (Boston: Houghton Mifflin, 2008), 159.

KEY TAKEAWAYS

- Every small business must select a legal form of ownership. It is one of the first decisions that a small business owner must make.
- The most common forms of legal structure are the sole proprietorship, the partnership, and the corporation. An LLC is a relatively new business structure.
- When deciding on a legal structure, every small business owner must consider several important factors before making the choice.
- The sole proprietorship is the oldest, simplest, and cheapest form of business ownership. This business structure accounts for the largest number of businesses but the lowest amount of revenue. This is the choice for most small businesses.
- A partnership is two or more people voluntarily operating a business as co-owners for profit. There are general partnerships and limited partnerships.
- A corporation is an artificial person with most of the legal rights of a real person. Corporations make up about 20 percent of all businesses in the United States, but they account for almost 90 percent of the revenue.
- Small businesses that are incorporated outperform unincorporated small businesses in terms of profitability, employment growth, sales growth, and other measures.
- The LLC is a hybrid of a sole proprietorship and a corporation. It is the best choice for most small businesses.

EXERCISES

1. Select three small businesses of different sizes: small, medium, and large. Interview the owners, asking each about the legal structure that the owner chose and why. If any of the businesses are sole proprietorships, ask the owner if an LLC was considered. If not, try to find out why it was not considered.
2. Frank's BarBeQue is currently a sole proprietorship. Frank's son, Robert, is trying to persuade his father to either incorporate or become an LLC. Assume that you are Robert. Make a case for each legal structure and then make a recommendation to Frank. It is expected that you will go beyond the textbook in researching your response to this assignment.

4. PEOPLE

L E A R N I N G   O B J E C T I V E S

1. Understand the complexities of hiring, retaining, and terminating employees.
2. Be aware of the laws that apply to businesses of all sizes and specifically to small businesses of certain sizes.
3. Understand outsourcing: what it is; when it is a good idea; and when it is a bad idea.
4. Describe ways to improve office productivity.

The term *human resources* has been deliberately avoided in this section. This term is more appropriate for large bureaucratic organizations that tend to view their personnel as a problem to be managed. Smaller and midsize enterprise personnel, however, are not mere resources to be managed. They should not be seen as cogs in a machine that are easily replaceable. Rather, they are people to be cultivated because they are the true lifeblood of the organization.

Many small businesses operate with no employees. The sole proprietor handles the whole business individually, perhaps with help from family or friends from time to time. Deciding to hire someone will always be a big leap because there will be an immediate need to worry about payroll, benefits, unemployment, and numerous other details.[121] A small business that looks to grow will face the hiring decision again and again, and additional decisions about compensation, benefits, retention, training, and termination will become necessary. Other issues of concern to a growing small business or a small business that wants to stay pretty much where it is include things such as outsourcing, how to enhance and improve productivity, and legal matters.

4.1 Hiring New People

All businesses want to attract, develop, and retain enough qualified employees to perform the activities necessary to accomplish the organizational objectives of the business.[122] Although most small businesses will not have a department dedicated to performing these functions, these functions must be performed just the same. The hiring of the first few people may end up being pretty simple, but as the hiring continues, there should be a more formal hiring process in place.

Figure 12.10 illustrates the basics of any hiring process, whether for a sole proprietorship or a large multinational corporation.

FIGURE 12.10 Steps in the Hiring Process

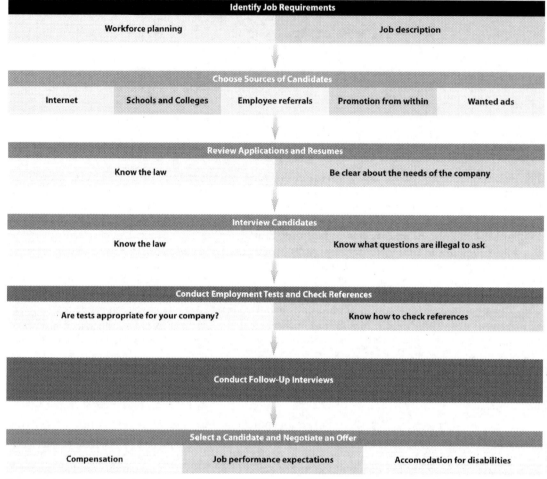

Source: Adapted from David L. Kurtz, Contemporary Business, 13th Edition Update (Hoboken, NJ: John Wiley & Sons, 2011), 289.

Identify Job Requirements

A small business owner should not proceed with hiring anyone until he or she has a clear idea of what the new hire will do and how that new hire will help attain the objectives of the business. **Workforce planning**, the "process of placing the right number of people with the right skills, experiences, and competencies in the right jobs at the right time,"[123] is a way to do that. The scope of this planning will be very limited when a business is very small, but as a business grows, it will take on much greater importance. Doing things right with the first new hire will establish a strong foundation for hiring in the future. Forecasting needs for new people, both current and future, is part of workforce planning. No forecast is perfect, but it will provide a basis on which to make hiring decisions.

As an employer, every small business should prepare a **job description** before initiating the recruitment process. A good job description describes the major areas of an employee's job or position: the duties to be performed, who the employee will report to, the working conditions, responsibilities, and the tools and equipment that must be used on the job.[124] It is important not to create an inflexible job description because it will prevent the small business owner and the employees from trying anything new and learning how to perform their jobs more productively.[125]

Choose Sources of Candidates

Because hiring a new employee is an expensive process, it is important to choose sources that have the greatest potential for reaching the people who will most likely be interested in what a small business has to offer. Unfortunately, it is not always possible to know what those sources are, so selecting a mix of sources makes good sense.

- **Internet.** The Internet offers a wealth of places to advertise a job opportunity. Monster.com, CareerBuilder.com, and LinkedIn.com are among the largest and most well-known sites, but there may be local or regional job sites that might work better, particularly if a business is very small. A business will not have the resources to bring people in from great distances. If a business has a Facebook or a Twitter presence, this is another great place to let people know about job openings. There may also be websites that specialize in particular occupations.

- **Schools and colleges.** Depending on the nature of the job, local schools and colleges are great sources for job candidates, particularly if the job is part time. Full-time opportunities may be perfect for the new high school or college graduate. It would be worth checking out college alumni offices as well because they often offer job services.

- **Employee referrals.** Referrals are always worth consideration, if only on a preliminary basis. The employee making the referral knows the business and the person being referred. Going this route can significantly shorten the search process…if there is a fit.

- **Promotion from within.** Promoting from within is a time-honored practice. The owner sends a positive signal to employees that there is room for advancement and management cares about its employees. It is significantly less costly and quicker than recruiting outside, candidates are easier to assess because more information is available, and it improves morale and organization loyalty.[126] On the downside, there may be problems between the person who is promoted and former coworkers, and the organization will not benefit from the fresh ideas of someone hired from the outside.

- **Want ads.** Want ads can be very effective for a small business, especially if a business is looking locally or regionally. The more dynamic the want ad, the more likely it will attract good candidates. Newspapers and local-reach magazines might be a business's first thoughts but also consider advertising in the newsletters of relevant professional organizations and at the career services offices of local colleges, universities, and technical colleges.

Review Applications and Résumés

When looking for the best qualified candidates, be very clear about the objectives of the business and the associated reason(s) for hiring someone new. It is also critical to know the law. Some examples are provided here. This would be a good time to consult with a lawyer to make sure that everything is done properly.

1. **Employee registration requirement.** All US employers must complete and retain Form I-9 for each individual, whether a citizen or a noncitizen, hired for employment in the United States. The employer must verify employment eligibility and identity documents presented by the employee.[127]

2. **The Civil Rights Act of 1964, the Civil Rights Act of 1991, and the Equal Employment Opportunity Act of 1972.** Attempt to provide equal opportunities for employment with regard to race, religion, age, creed, gender, national origin, or disability.[128] The closest Equal Employment Opportunity Commission (EEOC) district office should be contacted for specific information.

3. **Immigration Reform and Control Act of 1986.** This law places a major responsibility on employers for stopping illegal immigration.

Labor Laws Governing Employers

The following is a brief synopsis of some of the federal statutes governing employers that may apply to a small business. In many instances, they are related to the size of the business.[129] There are definite advantages to staying small.

The following laws apply no matter the size of the business:

- Fair Labor Standards Act
- Social Security
- Federal Insurance Contributions Act
- Medicare
- Equal Pay Act
- Immigration Reform and Control Act
- Federal Unemployment Tax Act

This additional law applies if a business has more than ten employees:

- Occupational Safety and Health Administration Act

The following additional laws apply if a business has more than fourteen employees:

- Title VII Civil Rights Act

- Americans with Disabilities Act (ADA)
- Pregnancy Discrimination Act

The following additional laws apply if a business has more than nineteen employees:

- Age Discrimination in Employment Act
- Older Worker Benefit Protection Act
- Consolidated Omnibus Budget Reconciliation Act

This additional law applies if a business has more than forty-nine employees:

- Family Medical Leave Act

The following additional laws apply if a business has more than ninety-nine employees:

- Worker Adjustment and Retraining Notification Act
- Employee Retirement Income Security Act

Interview Candidates

Just as knowing the law is important when reviewing applications and résumés, it is also important when interviewing candidates. Several interview questions are illegal to ask—for example, "Do you have dependable child care in place?" and "Do you rent or own your own home?"[130] In general, the off-limit topics in most employment interviews include religion, national origin, race, marital status, parental status, age, disability, gender, political affiliation, criminal records, and other personal information such as financial and credit history.[131] In short, keep the interview focused on the job, its requirements, and the qualifications of the candidate. Interviewing guidelines can be found at www.smallbusinessnotes.com/managing-your-business/interviewing-guidelines.html or http://www.smallbusinessnotes.com/managing-your-business/general-interview-guidelines.html.

Conduct Employment Tests and Check References

Selection tests have been used to screen applicants for more than one hundred years.[132] An effective testing program can improve accuracy in selecting employees; provide an objective means for comparing candidates; and provide information about training, development, or counseling needs. These advantages must be carefully weighed against the disadvantages: the fallibility of tests, the fact that tests can never measure everything, and many tests discriminate against minorities.[133] Each small business owner must decide whether employment tests make sense for his or her business. However, Daniel Kehrer of Work.com claims that employee testing is essential to reducing employee turnover for small businesses because preemployment screens are four times greater at predicting employee success than interviews. He notes further that high turnover rates are much more expensive for small businesses than large companies.[134] Just be sure that all employment tests can be linked to a business necessity.[135]

Checking references is a much more difficult proposition. It is a good idea to check references after the interview to objectively evaluate the candidate's qualifications, experience, and other information presented during the interview. Not checking references can result in poor hiring choices.[136]

Unfortunately, many former employers are reluctant to reveal anything other than an employee's date of hire and departure and job title,[137] but others may be willing to discuss an employee's job performance, work ethic, attendance, attitude, and other things that may be important to the prospective employer.[138]

As important as it is to check references, it is a process that is fraught with legal risk, so check with an attorney before moving forward.

Select a Candidate and Negotiate an Offer

After any desired follow-up interviews are conducted, it is time to select a candidate and negotiate an offer. There are three main issues to consider: compensation, job performance and expectations, and accommodations for disabilities.

Compensation includes wages, salaries, and benefits. Although wages and salaries are often used interchangeably, they are different. **Wages** are payments based on an hourly pay rate or the amount of output. Production employees, maintenance workers, retail salespeople (sometimes), and part-time workers are examples of employees who are paid wages.[139] **Salaries** are typically calculated weekly, biweekly, or monthly. They are usually paid to office personnel, executives, and professional employees.[140] Every small business should do its best to offer competitive wages and salaries, but a small business will generally not be able to offer wages and salaries that are comparable to those offered by large corporations and government. **Employee benefits**, such as health and disability insurance, sick leave, vacation time, child and elder care, and retirement plans, are paid entirely or in part by the company; they represent a large component of each employee's compensation.[141] Most employees have come to expect a good benefits program, even in a small business, so "the absence of a program or an inadequate program can seriously hinder a company's ability to attract and keep good personnel."[142] Not surprisingly, small businesses are also not in a position to offer the same level of benefits that can be offered by large corporations and the government. However, small businesses can still offer a good benefits program if it includes some or all the following elements: health insurance, disability insurance, life insurance, a retirement plan, flexible compensation, leave, and perks.[143] In addition, small businesses can offer benefits that only a small business can offer—for example, the flexibility to dress casually, half days on Friday, and bringing one's pet to work. Other ideas include gym memberships or lunch programs. These things have proven to increase employee loyalty, and they will fit the budget of even the smallest business.[144]

Set Performance Expectations

It is in the best interests of a business for prospective new employees to know and understand their performance expectations. This means that a business must determine what these expectations are. New employees should understand the goals of the organization and, as applicable, the department in which they will be working. It should also be made clear how the employee's work can positively impact the achievement of these goals.[145]

Make Accommodations for Disabilities

If a business is hiring someone with a disability and has fifteen or more employees, it is required by the ADA (enacted in 1990) to make reasonable workplace accommodations for employees with disabilities. Though not required, businesses with fewer than fifteen employees should consider accommodations as well.

> *Reasonable accommodations are adjustments or modifications which range from making the physical work environment accessible to restructuring a job, providing assistive equipment, providing certain types of personal assistants (e.g., a reader for a person who is blind, an interpreter for a person who is deaf), transferring an employee to a different job or location, or providing flexible scheduling.*
>
> *Reasonable accommodations are tools provided by employers to enable employees with disabilities to do their jobs. For example, employees are provided with desks, chairs, phones, and computers. An employee who is blind or who has a visual impairment might need a computer which operates by voice command or has a screen that enlarges print.[146]*

A tax credit is available to an eligible small business, and businesses may deduct the costs (up to $15,000) of removing an architectural barrier. Small businesses should check with the appropriate government agency before making accommodations to make sure that everything is done correctly.

Is a Business Hiring and Breeding Greedy and Selfish Employees?

If a business is worried about hiring a bunch of jerks, the EGOS Survey (Evaluation Gauge for Obnoxious Superstars) from *Fast Company* will help it find out. If a business owner answers truthfully, the owner can learn whether he or she is a leader of obnoxious superstars. Hiring jerks can happen in any size business.[147]

compensation

Wages, salaries, and benefits.

wages

Payments based on an hourly pay rate or the amount of output.

salary

Calculated weekly, biweekly, or monthly and usually paid to office personnel, executives, and professional employees.

employee benefits

Health and disability insurance, sick leave, vacation time, child and elder care, retirement plans and other perks paid entirely or in part by a company that represent a large component of each employee's compensation.

4.2 Retention and Termination

retention

Keeping employees.

termination

Ending the employment of
current employees against
their will.

Acquiring skilled, talented, and motivated employees will be a continuing concern for all small businesses. But the concerns do not end there. There will be issues concerning retention and termination of employment. **Retention** refers to keeping employees, and **termination** is about ending the employment of current employees against their will.

Retention

Employee retention rates play an important role in the cost of running a business. The first few years of an employee's service are the most costly because money will be spent on recruiting and training the employee. It is only after the employee has been working for some time that he or she will start making money for the business.[148]

Because of the costly and time-consuming nature of hiring new employees, many companies today increasingly emphasize retaining productive people.[149] Even the smallest of businesses should be concerned about retention because high turnover will be disruptive to the operations of the business and, as a result, may lessen the quality of the customer experience and customer satisfaction.

training

A continual process of
providing employees with
skills and knowledge they
need to perform at a high
level.

A good training and orientation program at the outset of employment can set the stage for increased retention. **Training** "is a continual process of providing employees with skills and knowledge they need to perform at a high level."[150] This continuing process is important. According to *Inc.com*, "the quality of employees and the continual improvement of their skills and productivity through training, are now widely recognized as vital factors in ensuring the long-term success and profitability of small businesses."[151] Training programs will vary greatly depending on the size and the nature of the business. However, all training programs must be based on both organizational and individual needs, spell out the problems that will be solved, and be based on sound theories of learning.[152] Many training and management development programs are not for amateurs, but the extent to which a small business can provide professionally delivered programs will be budget and needs related. In some instances, training is performed by someone who is currently doing the job—for example, using a particular machine, operating the cash register, stocking merchandise, and learning office procedures and protocols. Nothing additional is required.

Employee incentive programs are particularly important for small businesses because benefits satisfaction in small businesses typically lags behind benefits satisfaction in large corporations. A recent study[153] revealed that 81 percent of employees who are satisfied with their benefits are also satisfied with their jobs, whereas 23 percent of employees who are dissatisfied with their benefits are very satisfied with their jobs (Figure 12.11).

FIGURE 12.11 Benefits Satisfaction in Small Businesses

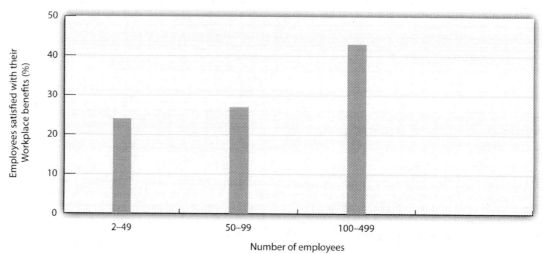

Source: "Building a Better Benefits Program without Breaking the Budget: Five Practical Steps Every Small Business Should Consider," MetLife, 2010, accessed February 3, 2012, http://www.metlife.com/assets/institutional/services/insights-and-tools/ebts/small-market-whitepaper-v2.pdf.

Given the importance of benefits to employees, small businesses need to be very creative about what kinds of incentives are offered to their employees. One of the biggest incentives may be the flexibility and camaraderie that are not available in larger businesses,[154] but to increase employee retention and attract the best and brightest, there will need to be more.[155] Creating a sense of community, offering leadership opportunities, creating a culture of recognition, and constantly offering opportunity can be powerful incentives.[156] They can be very effective at increasing employee retention, particularly when there is insufficient money to provide large raises. People want to enjoy their jobs as well as earn money, and they may care about their community and passions equally as much as their salaries. This is an opportunity for small businesses because "smaller companies may be better positioned to provide work-life balance that makes for happier, healthier employees."[157]

 Video Clip 12.3

Keeping Small Business Employees
Some ideas for keeping small business employees. They begin with a good job description.

View the video online at: http://www.youtube.com/v/O0tbAF0ZKOo

Termination

Termination or firing will always be unavoidably painful,[158] but it is a managerial duty that is sometimes necessary. In small businesses, terminations are usually carried out by the owner. They should be done promptly to preserve the health of the business.[159] Terminations can be **termination at will** or **termination for cause**.

- **Termination at will.** Employment at will means that a person does not have an employment contract. The person is employed "at the will" of the employer for as little or as long as the owner desires. It also means that a person can stop working for an employer at any time. An employer "doesn't need to give a reason for termination of an 'at will' employee, as long as the termination isn't unlawful or discriminatory…Termination can be due to a merger, workforce reduction, change in company direction and business focus, poor company performance, or any number of other legitimate reasons."[160]

- **Termination for cause.** When someone is terminated for cause, that person is being fired for a specific reason,[161] one of which may be behavior. Common causes for termination include but are not limited to stealing, lying, falsifying records, embezzlement, insubordination, deliberately violating company policies or rules, absenteeism and tardiness, unsatisfactory performance, changed job requirements, sexual harassment, and failing a drug or alcohol test.[162] Sexual harassment is a form of sex discrimination that violates Title VII of the Civil Rights Act of 1964. According to the EEOC, sexual harassment is "unwelcome sexual advances, requests for sexual favors, and other verbal or physical conduct of a sexual nature constitutes sexual harassment when submission to or rejection of this conduct explicitly or implicitly affects an individual's employment, unreasonably interferes with an individual's work performance or creates an intimidating, hostile or offensive work environment."[163]

When an employee has been terminated, the small business owner should inform the other employees. As a general rule, the less said to coworkers and other employees about an employee's termination, the better. People will be curious, but do not infringe on the terminated employee's privacy or say something that might leave a person open to legal action.[164] The best approach is to inform immediate coworkers, subordinates, and clients by simply telling them that the company no longer employs the employee. Do not mention any details but do include an explanation of how the terminated employee's duties will be carried out in the future.[165]

termination at will

The employer doesn't need to give a reason for termination as long as the termination is not unlawful or discriminatory.

termination for cause

A person is fired (terminated) for a specific reason.

4.3 Outsourcing

Outsourcing is the practice of using outside firms, some of which may be offshore, to handle work that is normally performed within a company.[166] Small business owners routinely outsource a range of services, such as landscaping; building, utility, and furniture maintenance; distribution; and cleaning.[167] Consistent with the trend set by larger corporations, small businesses are outsourcing a range of services, many of which were once considered fundamental internal functions.[168]

A major reason for outsourcing is cost reduction. Other benefits of outsourcing include increasing efficiency, enabling a company to start new projects quickly, allowing a company to focus on its core business, leveling the playing field with larger companies, and reducing risk.[169] There is no question that outsourcing can be a good idea, but outsourcing is not always a good idea.

When Is Outsourcing a Good Idea?

Outsourcing is a good idea when it allows a small business "to continue performing the functions it does best, while hiring other companies [many of which may be other small businesses] to do tasks that they can handle more competently and cost-effectively."[170] Traditionally, payroll and personnel services have been outsourced by small businesses, but small businesses now use outside providers for a much greater range of services, including the following:[171]

- **Accounting and bookkeeping.** A growth area here is outsourcing accounts receivable. This enables a small business to sell off its accounts receivable and invoices to a financing company.[172] As a small business grows, the process of collecting accounts receivable may become too cumbersome to handle without collection agencies becoming involved.[173]

- **Specialist and expert help.** Elance offers a range of services for small businesses. It has access to thousands of professionals around the world who can provide services such as graphic design, multimedia presentations, engineering, sales and marketing, writing, and translation.[174]

- **Public relations and marketing services.** These services are costly, require specialized expertise, and are not usually full-time needs.[175] Many service providers specialize in the needs of small businesses.

- **Virtual assistants.** These people are independent entrepreneurs who provide administrative, creative, or technical support. A growing phenomenon, they work on a contractual basis via online or electronic communications. Virtual Office Temps and VirtualAssistants.com are examples of companies that can connect virtual assistants with any company that is interested.[176]

- **Creating benefits package.** A tremendous amount of time and creativity would be required for a smaller company to create a benefits package that is competitive in the marketplace.[177] Given the vast complexities of health care, including health-care laws that differ by state, outsourcing this activity makes good sense.

- **Legal services.** A small business may need to consult an attorney for a variety of reasons, including the following:

    - Choosing the business structure
    - Constructing a partnership agreement
    - Obtaining a corporate charter
    - Registering a corporation's stock
    - Obtaining a trademark, a patent, or a copyright or intellectual property
    - Filing for licenses or permits at the local, state, and federal levels
    - Purchasing an existing business or real estate
    - Hiring employees, independent contractors, and other external suppliers (outsourcing)
    - Extending credit and collecting debts
    - Creating valid contracts
    - Initiating or defending against lawsuits
    - Keeping current on and compliant with business law and regulations (e.g., advertising, employment and labor, finance, intellectual property, online business law, privacy law, environmental regulations, and the Uniform Commercial Code)
    - Protecting intellectual property
    - Protecting ideas or inventions from others' infringement[178]

However, the cost of a full-time attorney would probably be prohibitive. Outsourcing these services is an appropriate choice. Some legal firms offer small businesses a flat monthly fee instead of charging them by the hour,[179] a practice that is very helpful to the small business budget.

When Is Outsourcing a Bad Idea?

Although outsourcing has benefits, there are times when it is a bad idea. For example, sales and technology development are operations that are generally best handled in-house because they are full-time needs that are at the heart of any business.[180] Outsourcing might actually end up being the more expensive alternative, leading to a financial loss instead of a gain. An example would be the cost of a highly specialized expert.[181] In addition, when outsourcing overseas, the small business owner and/or managers may not be prepared to manage projects across time differences and cultural barriers and may not have clear guidelines, expectations, and processes in place to manage product or service quality.[182]

4.4   Office Productivity

All small businesses want their employees to work better and smarter. In fact, the smaller a business is, the more efficient and effective it must be. Productivity is an issue in two places: the office and in manufacturing. Office productivity (which applies to all levels in the organization) is discussed in this section, and the role of technology is the focus. "Office" is used broadly to include, for example, physical offices, virtual offices, work situations that involve in-the-car time (e.g., realtors and salespeople), restaurant kitchens, and people who work on the sales floor in retail establishments.

Even the smallest of businesses can improve productivity by using technology, even though such use may be very limited in some instances. For example, goods and services needed to run a business can often be ordered online; e-mail can be used for customer and supplier communication; taxes can be filed online; and a simple software package like *Microsoft Communicator* allows intra- and extracompany communication via e-mail, text, and video. It will be the rare business that uses no technology.

Some have referred to technology as the road map to small business success—helping grow the business, work smarter, attract more customers, enhance customer service, and stay ahead of the competition.[183] An important component of all this is high office productivity. Efficiency and effectiveness in the office will benefit the entire business.

With the proliferation of social networks, small businesses are implementing more Facebook-like applications into their day-to-day operations.[184] Yammer, for example, "enables a company's employees to gather inside a private and secure social network that can be controlled and monitored by the employer. The goal is to increase productivity…[It] is about making people work more productively using communication that's becoming very popular in the consumer space."[185] Other similar products include Conenza and Chatter.

Some see the iPad as changing how business relationships are built—providing opportunities to connect with prospects in a more meaningful way and allowing people to collaborate with others in real time from wherever they are.[186] The iPad is also changing the way people can work. The SoundNote application allows note taking and recording a meeting simultaneously; once written, the notes can be e-mailed directly to the participants.[187] Just want to take notes? Use Evernote.[188] The iPad can be used in the kitchen of a restaurant, a café, a hotel, or a bar for finding recipes and cooking instructions, displaying recipes as PDF files, and working on budgets and cost analyses.[189] In retailing, the iPad can be used as a virtual sales assistant. In a dress department, coordinating accessories from a jewelry store or the shoe department can be accessed and recommended to the customer. Car dealers could customize a car by showing colors and finishes to the customer—all while standing in the parking lot.[190] In real estate, the iPad can be used for buyer consultations, listing presentations, tracking properties, and chatting with clients—just to name a few.[191]

Video Clip 12.4

Using the iPad for Real Estate
Some tips on how to use the iPad in real estate.

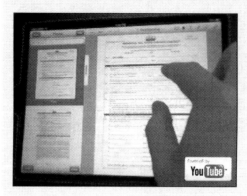

View the video online at: http://www.youtube.com/v/jlfA5lypla4

Although every small business owner may not see an immediate need for an iPad, it is a technology worth checking out. New applications for office productivity are coming out all the time.

A **smartphone** is a device that lets a person make phone calls but has other features found on a digital assistant or a computer, such as sending and receiving e-mail and editing Microsoft Office documents.[192] A popular brand is the Apple iPhone. Smartphones give a person access to company data that is normally not possible without a laptop; make it possible to accomplish more, faster; enable mobile workers to connect to company information while on the road; keep your calendar, address book, and task lists organized; and, perhaps most importantly, keep frustrations to a minimum because the technology is designed to work in tandem with a **server** and a **personal digital assistant (PDA)**.[193] A server is a computer or a series of computers that link other computers or electronic devices together.[194] A PDA is a handheld computer that acts "as an electronic organizer or day planner that is portable, easy to use and capable of sharing information with your PC."[195] Blackberry is a popular brand of the PDA. The smartphone can be used for numerous business functions, such as tracking equipment and accounts, keeping calendars and address books, connecting to the Internet, acting as a global positioning system (GPS), and running multimedia software.[196]

Like everyone else, small businesses have to do more with less. This means that effective collaboration is increasingly critical to success. Because collaboration is a daily requirement for all small businesses, the question becomes how to have productive collaboration without using up too much time and costing too much money. What is needed is a way to "spur employees to share ideas and increase productivity while protecting work-life balance."[197] A recent study reported that among companies that used collaboration tools, 72 percent reported better business performance.[198] One popular collaboration tool is web conferencing: "Web conferencing services enable users to hold collaborative meetings with interactive whiteboard tools, give sales demonstrations with real-time efficacy, stage presentations with full and select moderator control or hold enhanced, multimedia roundtable discussions…And, with recording and playback tools available in the leading Web conferencing service providers, audience members and other authorized users can access meetings, presentations and demonstrations again and again or continually reference whiteboard sessions."[199]

Although Top Ten Reviews ranked Infinite Conferencing, Netviewer Meet, and Adobe Connect Pro as the 2011 top three web conferencing services, each small business should select the product that best serves its needs and its budget.

Virtual or Telecommuting Employees

Another boon to office productivity and adding to the bottom line is the **virtual or telecommuting employee**. This is an employee that works from a location other than the traditional office. They can work from anywhere.[200] There is no agreement on the number of US workers that are already telecommuting. However, it has been estimated that 40 percent of the US workforce hold jobs that lend themselves to telecommuting.[201]

The advantages of virtual employees include the following:[202]

- Companies could save $6,500 annually per employee.

---

smartphone

A technological device that lets a person make phone calls but has other features found on a digital assistant or a computer.

server

A computer or a series of computers that link other computers or electronic devices together.

personal digital assistant (PDA)

A small mobile handheld device that provides computing and information storage and retrieval capabilities for personal and business use.

virtual or telecommuting employee

An employee who works at home, on the road, or in a satellite location for all or part of his or her regular workweek.

- Virtual employees tend to be happier, healthier, and less stressed compared to their office-bound coworkers.
- Virtual workers are significantly more productive than their office-bound colleagues. The differential is estimated at 15 percent.
- Virtual employees almost always give back more than 50 percent of the time they save by not commuting.
- Some virtual workers actually put in more time per week than those who commute.

From the perspective of the virtual employee, the advantages of telecommuting are as follows: no distractions from coworkers; no stress from office politics; spending more time with the family; saving money on transportation, parking, and clothing; and avoiding traffic or saving time by not commuting.[203]

Virtual employees offer terrific advantages to the small business owner who is always looking to cut costs and attract high-quality employees. However, it is not something that works for everyone and every kind of business. For example, a restaurant cannot have a virtual waiter...at least not yet. A small business that wants to use virtual employees must create the appropriate infrastructure—that is, technology, security, policies, behavioral protocols, performance management, and so forth—to provide the best support for telecommuting workers in how, where, and when they do their jobs.[204] For support with telecommuting challenges, small business owners can tap into The Alternative Board, an organization with three thousand small- and midsized-business owners.[205]

Video Link 12.2

Making Telecommuting Work

Looking at telecommuting from the employee and the employer perspectives.

www.cbsnews.com/video/watch/?id=10162239n?tag=bnetdomain

KEY TAKEAWAYS

- Deciding to hire someone will always be a big step because there will be an immediate need to worry about payroll, benefits, unemployment, and numerous other issues.
- The hiring process includes identifying job requirements, choosing sources of candidates, reviewing applications and résumés, interviewing candidates, conducting employment tests (if desired), checking references, conducting follow-up interviews if needed, selecting a candidate, and making an offer.
- It is very important to know employment law before proceeding with the hiring process. For example, several potential questions are illegal to ask.
- Whether it is required or not, small businesses should be willing to make accommodations for employees with disabilities.
- Retention is an important concern for all small businesses.
- When an employee is to be terminated, it is best to do it promptly.
- Outsourcing is about using outside firms, some of which may be offshore, to handle work that is normally performed within a company. Outsourcing can be either good or bad; it depends on the situation.
- Office productivity is about working smarter and better. Social networking, the iPad, smartphones, online collaboration tools, and virtual employees can all help increase productivity.

1. As the owner of a one-hundred-employee business, you just learned that some of your employees were "dumpster diving" in the trash outside a competitor's offices. In other words, they were looking for information that could provide your company with a competitive advantage. With investigation, you found out that the head of the espionage operation was a personal friend. You have decided to fire your friend immediately, along with his dumpster divers. How should you proceed with the termination of your friend and his operatives so that you will not be held liable in a lawsuit? Would you reconsider the firing of the operatives? Why or why not?[206]

2. Robert is trying to convince his father, Frank of Frank's BarBeQue, to integrate more technology into his restaurant operations because it will increase productivity. Assuming the role of Robert, select technologies that you think would be a good fit for Frank's restaurant. Prepare your recommendations for Frank.

5. THE THREE THREADS

LEARNING OBJECTIVES

1. Explain how people and organization can add to customer value.
2. Explain how decisions about people and organization can impact cash flow.
3. Explain how technology and the e-environment are impacting people and organization.

5.1 Customer Value Implications

By definition, a small business is small. The CEO and the top management team have a much greater understanding of the tasks and operations of the entire business and what their employees are doing. (Sometimes their employees wish they did not have such a good knowledge of the tasks they, the employees, are supposed to be performing.) In a small business, it is much more likely for the CEO and the top management team to have a personalized relationship with their customer base. Sometimes this functions on a one-to-one basis and is predicated on a true sense of personal friendship. This intimacy between those at the top of a small business and their customers or clientele can yield tremendous benefits for both the business and the customers. Knowing the true needs of the customer on a personalized level greatly enhances the value produced by a business.

Small business organizations are flatter and less bureaucratic. Sometimes they are less centralized. This enables frontline personnel to be closer to the customer, where they can better ascertain the needs of the customer and make decisions more quickly to satisfy those needs. This adds to the value of these businesses in the eyes of their customers because of a more positive customer experience.

In addition to being closer to the customers, the owner of a smaller business has a closer relationship with the employees. There generally is no need for a formal "human resources" department that bureaucratizes relationships. The owner knows the strengths and the weaknesses of the employees and will best use them in the business. The owner can develop personal relationships with employees that are impossible in larger organizations. This closeness can often translate into an intangible strength—loyalty. Employees who are happy with their employment will provide greater value to the customer.

5.2 Cash-Flow Implications

The simpler the organizational structure, the more positive will be the impact on cash flow. Having unnecessary positions will negatively impact small business operations in terms of not only costs but also efficiency and effectiveness.

Improper hiring and termination procedures will also adversely affect cash flow. Recruiting employees is an expensive process, so errors in the hiring process will be a drain on the cash flow of a business and, as a result, its profitability. Termination is a particularly sensitive process, so a careful and thoughtful procedure should be developed for carrying it out. Errors in either hiring or termination may open up a business to lawsuits, another major hit to cash flow and profitability.

Technology adoption for office productivity improvements (e.g., social networking, iPads, and smartphones) may adversely affect the cash flow in the short term, but (hopefully) the higher productivity should offset those losses in the longer term. As an example, recall Lloyd's Construction in

Eagan, Minnesota, from Chapter 1. The company switched to a **smartphone** system that allowed for integrated data entry and communication. The company reduced its routing and fuel costs by as much as 30 percent, and they estimated that they saved $1 million on a $50,000 investment.[207]

5.3   Implications of Technology and the E-Environment

New technology solutions are being introduced every day, many of them potentially very useful for small businesses. This chapter discussed the productivity enhancement possibilities offered by social networking, the iPad, smartphones, and collaboration tools, but the discussion was only the tip of the iceberg. Technology is so pervasive in today's workplace that ignoring it will be done at each business's peril. Mobile technology is now even pervading the hiring process; the world of recruiting via mobile technology is moving at the speed of light. The result? More and more organizations are trying to figure out how to start using mobile devices to recruit new employees.[208] The prospect of targeting all populations of people is an exciting—but certainly challenging—one.

Another interesting technology product is talent management software developed by Taleo, which is targeted to the small business to simplify recruiting, hiring, and performance management with "unmatched flexibility."[209] There are undoubtedly other similar products available. The point is that this is an example of the small business technology solutions that are available for exploration and consideration.

The e-environment is a small business facilitator extraordinaire. The web is a fabulous place, making collaboration and communication so much better and faster. It has opened the door to enhanced productivity, and a potentially important part of that is the virtual employee. Small businesses should seriously consider the advantages of virtual employees because they can help the small business expand its reach, increase employee morale, and contribute to a much better work-life balance.

KEY TAKEAWAYS

- The less bureaucratic organizational structure of small businesses tends to open the door for more personalized relationships between the CEO and other top managers and customers. This adds considerable value to the business and the customer experience.
- The simpler the organizational structure, the more positive the impact on cash flow.
- Technology investments for increased productivity will be a drain on cash flow in the short term, but productivity improvements should offset the loss in the long term.
- New technology products are being introduced every day, many of them geared to the small business. Small businesses should make it a point to learn about what's available and keep an open mind about adopting a new solution to an old problem.
- The e-environment has opened the door to multiple ways to improve office productivity, not the least of which is the virtual employee.

EXERCISE

1. Select a small business with between fifty and seventy-five employees. Set up an interview with the president or one of the other members of top management. Ask the person to describe the organizational structure of the business, and then ask him or her to discuss whether the structure helps or hinders his or her relationships with customers. Lastly, ask if there is anything about the organizational structure he or she would change—and why.

Disaster Watch

John owns a very successful electronics business. He has been in business for only three years and already has several large stores. He has seventy-five part- and full-time employees. The business thrives on a sales force that must be able to close deals, particularly on high-priced items.

Jennifer is John's administrative assistant. She has been with him from the beginning, and John considers her to be a vital element in the success of the business. He had wooed her away from another large electronics chain. On Tuesday, Jennifer requested a private meeting with him. She arrived at the meeting clearly distressed. He asked her to sit down and tell him what was troubling her. She struggled not to cry but could not hold back the tears. She recounted the following story.

Ed Smith, a salesperson, had for the last five weeks been making inappropriate and suggestive comments to her. She told John that at first she tried to dismiss and deflect Ed's comments with humor, and the humor clearly indicated that she had no interest. The result was that the comments became more frequent, more aggressive, and more vulgar. At this point (last Friday), Jennifer indicated to Ed that she found his remarks offensive and harassing. He laughed and, in the intervening days, continued the remarks, which became even more progressively lewd. It was Jennifer's opinion that Ed was incapable of understanding how inappropriate his behavior was. She believes that his presence creates a significantly hostile working environment for her and other women. She thinks it would be best for the organization if Ed were fired immediately.

John expressed his profound sympathy to Jennifer and said that he would speak to Ed right away. This clearly was not what Jennifer wanted to hear. She left John's office simply stating, "It's either him or me."

Although John was extremely sympathetic to Jennifer's position, he recognized that he had to speak to Ed to protect himself. Further, John had to consider the fact that Ed was unquestionably his best salesperson. Two hours later, John called Ed into his office and related Jennifer's story. Ed laughed it off as harmless word play, even going as far as saying, "Could you possibly see me being interested in a woman who looks like she does?" He then countered with, "Look. You know I'm your best salesman, and if I'm fired because of some slanderous comments, I'll sue." He then stormed out of John's office.

What should John do?

ENDNOTES

1. John M. Ivancevich and Thomas N. Duening, *Business: Principles, Guidelines, and Practices* (Mason, OH: Atomic Dog Publishing, 2007), 172.

2. David L. Kurtz, *Contemporary Business* (Hoboken, NJ: John Wiley & Sons, 2011), 254.

3. David L. Kurtz, *Contemporary Business* (Hoboken, NJ: John Wiley & Sons, 2011), 257.

4. "Management Principles," *Small Business Notes*, accessed February 2, 2012, www.smallbusinessnotes.com/managing-your-business/management-principles.

5. John M. Ivancevich and Thomas N. Duening, *Business: Principles, Guidelines, and Practices* (Mason, OH: Atomic Dog Publishing, 2007), 176; David L. Kurtz, *Contemporary Business* (Hoboken, NJ: John Wiley & Sons, 2011), 257.

6. John M. Ivancevich and Thomas N. Duening, *Business: Principles, Guidelines, and Practices* (Mason, OH: Atomic Dog Publishing, 2007), 176.

7. "Traditional Management Principles," *Small Business Notes*, accessed February 2, 2012, www.smallbusinessnotes.com/managing-your-business/traditional-management-principles.html.

8. "Traditional Management Principles," *Small Business Notes*, accessed February 2, 2012, www.smallbusinessnotes.com/managing-your-business/traditional-management-principles.html.

9. John M. Ivancevich and Thomas N. Duening, *Business: Principles, Guidelines, and Practices* (Mason, OH: Atomic Dog Publishing, 2007), 176.

10. John M. Ivancevich and Thomas N. Duening, *Business: Principles, Guidelines, and Practices* (Mason, OH: Atomic Dog Publishing, 2007), 177; David L. Kurtz, *Contemporary Business* (Hoboken, NJ: John Wiley & Sons, 2011), 257.

11. William M. Pride, Robert J. Hughes, and Jack R. Kapoor, *Business* (Boston: Houghton Mifflin, 2008), 224.

12. Kurt Lewin, Ronald Lippitt, and Ralph K. White, "Patterns of Aggressive Behavior in Experimentally Created 'Social Climates,'" *Journal of Social Psychology* 10, no. 2 (1939): 269–99.

13. Don Clark, "Leadership Styles," *Big Dog and Little Dog's Performance Juxtaposition*, June 13, 2010, accessed February 2, 2012, www.nwlink.com/~donclark/leader/leadstl.html.

14. Kurt Lewin, "Lewin's Leadership Styles," *Changing Minds*, accessed February 2, 2012, changingminds.org/disciplines/leadership/styles/lewin_style.htm; Don Clark, "Leadership Styles," *Big Dog and Little Dog's Performance Juxtaposition*, June 13, 2010, accessed February 2, 2012, www.nwlink.com/~donclark/leader/leadstl.html.

15. Kurt Lewin, Ronald Lippitt, and Ralph K. White, "Patterns of Aggressive Behavior in Experimentally Created 'Social Climates,'" *Journal of Social Psychology* 10, no. 2 (1939): 269–99.

16. Kurt Lewin, "Lewin's Leadership Styles," *Changing Minds*, accessed February 2, 2012, changingminds.org/disciplines/leadership/styles/lewin_style.htm; Don Clark, "Leadership Styles," *Big Dog and Little Dog's Performance Juxtaposition*, June 13, 2010, accessed February 2, 2012, www.nwlink.com/~donclark/leader/leadstl.html.

17. "Participative Leadership," *Changing Minds*, accessed February 2, 2012, changingminds.org/disciplines/leadership/styles/participative_leadership.htm.

18. Kurt Lewin, "Lewin's Leadership Styles," *Changing Minds*, accessed February 2, 2012, changingminds.org/disciplines/leadership/styles/lewin_style.htm; Don Clark, "Leadership Styles," *Big Dog and Little Dog's Performance Juxtaposition*, June 13, 2010, accessed February 2, 2012, www.nwlink.com/~donclark/leader/leadstl.html.

19. Kurt Lewin, Ronald Lippitt, and Ralph K. White, "Patterns of Aggressive Behavior in Experimentally Created 'Social Climates,'" *Journal of Social Psychology* 10, no. 2 (1939): 269–99.

20. John M. Ivancevich and Thomas N. Duening, *Business: Principles, Guidelines, and Practices* (Mason, OH: Atomic Dog Publishing, 2007), 178.

21. Kurt Lewin, "Lewin's Leadership Styles," *Changing Minds*, accessed February 2, 2012, changingminds.org/disciplines/leadership/styles/lewin_style.htm; Don Clark, "Leadership Styles," *Big Dog and Little Dog's Performance Juxtaposition*, June 13, 2010, accessed February 2, 2012, www.nwlink.com/~donclark/leader/leadstl.html.

22. Don Clark, "Leadership Styles," *Big Dog and Little Dog's Performance Juxtaposition*, June 13, 2010, accessed February 2, 2012, www.nwlink.com/~donclark/leader/leadstl.html.

23. Kurt Lewin, Ronald Lippitt, and Ralph K. White, "Patterns of Aggressive Behavior in Experimentally Created 'Social Climates,'" *Journal of Social Psychology* 10, no. 2 (1939): 269–99; Kurt Lewin, "Lewin's Leadership Styles," *Changing Minds*, accessed February 2, 2012, changingminds.org/disciplines/leadership/styles/lewin_style.htm.

24. Susan Ward, "5 Keys to Leadership for Small Business," *About.com*, accessed February 2, 2012, sbinfocanada.about.com/od/smallbusinesslearning/a/leadership1.htm.

25. "Post-hoc Management," *Changing Minds*, accessed February 2, 2012, changingminds.org/disciplines/leadership/articles/post-hoc_management.htm.

26. "Micromanagement," *Changing Minds*, accessed February 2, 2012, changingminds.org/disciplines/leadership/articles/micromanagement.htm.

27. "Leadership Styles," *Changing Minds*, accessed February 2, 2012, changingminds.org/disciplines/leadership/styles/leadership_styles.htm.

28. "Seagull Management," *Changing Minds*, accessed February 2, 2012, changingminds.org/disciplines/leadership/articles/seagull_management.htm.

29. "Leadership Styles," *Changing Minds*, accessed February 2, 2012, changingminds.org/disciplines/leadership/styles/leadership_styles.htm.

30. "Leadership Styles," *Changing Minds*, accessed February 2, 2012, changingminds.org/disciplines/leadership/styles/leadership_styles.htm.

31. William M. Pride, Robert J. Hughes, and Jack R. Kapoor, *Business* (Boston: Houghton Mifflin, 2008), 224.

32. John M. Ivancevich and Thomas N. Duening, *Business: Principles, Guidelines, and Practices* (Mason, OH: Atomic Dog Publishing, 2007), 176.

33. John M. Ivancevich and Thomas N. Duening, *Business: Principles, Guidelines, and Practices* (Mason, OH: Atomic Dog Publishing, 2007), 176; William M. Pride, Robert J. Hughes, and Jack R. Kapoor, *Business* (Boston: Houghton Mifflin, 2008), 224.

34. William M. Pride, Robert J. Hughes, and Jack R. Kapoor, *Business* (Boston: Houghton Mifflin, 2008), 226.

35. John M. Ivancevich and Thomas N. Duening, *Business: Principles, Guidelines, and Practices* (Mason, OH: Atomic Dog Publishing, 2007), 183.

36. David L. Kurtz, *Contemporary Business, 13th Edition Update* (Hoboken, NJ: John Wiley & Sons, 2011), 255.

37. David L. Kurtz, *Contemporary Business, 13th Edition Update* (Hoboken, NJ: John Wiley & Sons, 2011), 255.

38. William M. Pride, Robert J. Hughes, and Jack R. Kapoor, *Business* (Boston: Houghton Mifflin, 2008), 227.

39. David L. Kurtz, *Contemporary Business, 13th Edition Update* (Hoboken, NJ: John Wiley & Sons, 2011), 255; William M. Pride, Robert J. Hughes, and Jack R. Kapoor, *Business* (Boston: Houghton Mifflin, 2008), 227.

40. John Seiffer, "3 Levels of Management," *Better CEO*, April 14, 2006, accessed June 1, 2012, betterceo.com/2006/04/14/3-levels-of-management/.

41. Samuel C. Certo and S. Trevis Certo, *Modern Management: Concepts and Skills* (Upper Saddle River, NJ: Prentice Hall, 2012), 11.

42. Les Worral and Cary Cooper, "Management Skills Development: A Perspective on Current Issues and Setting the Future Agenda," *Leadership & Organization Development Journal* 22, no. 1 (2001): 34–39, as cited in Samuel C. Certo and S. Trevis Certo, *Modern Management: Concepts and Skills* (Upper Saddle River, NJ: Prentice Hall, 2012), 11.

43. David L. Kurtz, *Contemporary Business, 13th Edition Update* (Hoboken, NJ: John Wiley & Sons, 2011), 256.

44. Samuel C. Certo and S. Trevis Certo, *Modern Management: Concepts and Skills* (Upper Saddle River, NJ: Prentice Hall, 2012), 11.

45. David L. Kurtz, *Contemporary Business, 13th Edition Update* (Hoboken, NJ: John Wiley & Sons, 2011), 257.

46. David L. Kurtz, *Contemporary Business, 13th Edition Update* (Hoboken, NJ: John Wiley & Sons, 2011), 256.

47. John M. Ivancevich and Thomas N. Duening, *Business: Principles, Guidelines, and Practices* (Mason, OH: Atomic Dog Publishing, 2007), 188.

48. "Decision Making," *eNotes*, March 17, 2011, accessed June 1, 2012, http://www.enotes.com/decision-making-reference/decision-making-178403.

49. "A Framework for Thinking Ethically," *Santa Clara University*, accessed June 1, 2012, www.scu.edu/ethics/practicing/decision/framework.html.

50. David L. Kurtz, *Contemporary Business, 13th Edition Update* (Hoboken, NJ: John Wiley & Sons, 2011), 272.

51. Hal Babson and John Bowen, *Instructor's Manual to Accompany Business: Principles, Guidelines, and Practices* (Mason, OH: Atomic Dog Publishing, 2004), 8–9.

52. John M. Ivancevich and Thomas N. Duening, *Business: Principles, Guidelines, and Practices* (Mason, OH: Atomic Dog Publishing, 2007), 199.

53. John M. Ivancevich and Thomas N. Duening, *Business: Principles, Guidelines, and Practices* (Mason, OH: Atomic Dog Publishing, 2007), 200–204.

54. John M. Ivancevich and Thomas N. Duening, *Business: Principles, Guidelines, and Practices* (Mason, OH: Atomic Dog Publishing, 2007), 200–204.

55. William M. Pride, Robert J. Hughes, and Jack R. Kapoor, *Business* (Boston: Houghton Mifflin, 2008), 263.

56. "Reinventing the Strategic Communicator," *Strategic Communication Management*, August/September 2001, 32–35, as cited in John M. Ivancevich and Thomas N. Duening, *Business: Principles, Guidelines, and Practices* (Mason, OH: Atomic Dog Publishing, 2007), 201.

57. "Formal Organizational Structure—What Is It?," *The Business Plan*, accessed February 2, 2012, www.the-business-plan.com/formal-organizational-structure.html.

58. "Formal Organizational Structure—What Is It?," *The Business Plan*, accessed February 2, 2012, www.the-business-plan.com/formal-organizational-structure.html.

59. Marshall Goldsmith and Jon Katzenbach, "Navigating the 'Informal' Organization," *Bloomberg BusinessWeek*, February 14, 2007, accessed February 2, 2012, www.BusinessWeek.com/careers/content/feb2007/ca20070214_709560.htm.

60. Charles Hall, *Getting Results…for the Hands-On Manager* (Saranac Lake, NY: American Management Association, 1986), 40–42.

61. William M. Pride, Robert J. Hughes, and Jack R. Kapoor, *Business* (Boston: Houghton Mifflin, 2008), 264.

62. "Introduction to Organizational Charts," *OrgChart.net*, July 18, 2011, accessed February 2, 2012, www.orgchart.net/wiki/Main_Page.

63. "Organization Charts," *Small Business Notes*, accessed February 2, 2012, www.smallbusinessnotes.com/managing-your-business/organization-charts.html.

64. "Organization Charts," *Small Business Notes*, accessed February 2, 2012, www.smallbusinessnotes.com/managing-your-business/organization-charts.html.

65. "Introduction to Organizational Charts," *OrgChart.net*, March 16, 2011, accessed February 2, 2012, www.orgchart.net/wiki/Main_Page; "Organization Chart," *12 Manage—The Executive Fast Track*, accessed February 2, 2012, www.12manage.com/methods_organization_.chart.html.

66. "Organization Chart," *12Manage—The Executive Fast Track*, accessed February 2, 2012, www.12manage.com/methods_organization_.chart.html.

67. William M. Pride, Robert J. Hughes, and Jack R. Kapoor, *Business* (Boston: Houghton Mifflin, 2008), 247.

68. John M. Ivancevich and Thomas N. Duening, *Business: Principles, Guidelines, and Practices* (Mason, OH: Atomic Dog Publishing, 2007), 203.

69. Samuel C. Certo and S. Trevis Certo, *Modern Management: Concepts and Skills* (Upper Saddle River, NJ: Prentice Hall, 2012), 276; John M. Ivancevich and Thomas N. Duening, *Business: Principles, Guidelines, and Practices* (Mason, OH: Atomic Dog Publishing, 2007), 203.

70. Samuel C. Certo and S. Trevis Certo, *Modern Management: Concepts and Skills* (Upper Saddle River, NJ: Prentice Hall, 2012), 278.

71. John M. Ivancevich and Thomas N. Duening, *Business: Principles, Guidelines, and Practices* (Mason, OH: Atomic Dog Publishing, 2007), 203.

72. K. J. Henderson, "Features of the Line & Staff Organization Structure," *Chron.com*, accessed February 2, 2012, smallbusiness.chron.com/features-line-staff-organization-structure-449.html.

73. Samuel C. Certo and S. Trevis Certo, *Modern Management: Concepts and Skills* (Upper Saddle River, NJ: Prentice Hall, 2012), 278.

74. Samuel C. Certo and S. Trevis Certo, *Modern Management: Concepts and Skills* (Upper Saddle River, NJ: Prentice Hall, 2012), 283; John M. Ivancevich and Thomas N. Duening, *Business: Principles, Guidelines, and Practices* (Mason, OH: Atomic Dog Publishing, 2007), 204.

75. Zhiang Lin and Kathleen M. Carley, "Organizational Design and Adaptation in Response to Crises: Theory and Practice," *Academy of Management Proceedings*, 2001, B1–B6.

76. John M. Ivancevich and Thomas N. Duening, *Business: Principles, Guidelines, and Practices* (Mason, OH: Atomic Dog Publishing, 2007), 204.

77. Francis Fukuyama, "Why There Is No Science of Public Administration," *Journal of International Affairs*, Fall 2004, 189–201.

78. Samuel C. Certo and S. Trevis Certo, *Modern Management: Concepts and Skills* (Upper Saddle River, NJ: Prentice Hall, 2012), 33; John M. Ivancevich and Thomas N. Duening, *Business: Principles, Guidelines, and Practices* (Mason, OH: Atomic Dog Publishing, 2007), 205–206.

79. John M. Ivancevich and Thomas N. Duening, *Business: Principles, Guidelines, and Practices* (Mason, OH: Atomic Dog Publishing, 2007), 207.

80. "Principles of Management," *Management Study Guide*, accessed February 2, 2012, www.managementstudyguide.com/management_principles.htm.

81. Samuel C. Certo and S. Trevis Certo, *Modern Management: Concepts and Skills* (Upper Saddle River, NJ: Prentice Hall, 2012), 33; John M. Ivancevich and Thomas N. Duening, *Business: Principles, Guidelines, and Practices* (Mason, OH: Atomic Dog Publishing, 2007), 206.

82. Marce Kelly and Jim McGowen, *BUSN* (Mason, OH: South-Western, 2008), 206.

83. Ashim Gupta, "Organization's Size and Span of Control," *Practical Management*, January 10, 2010, accessed February 2, 2012, www.practical-management.com/Organization-Development/Organization-s-size-and-span-of-control.html; Marce Kelly and Jim McGowen, *BUSN* (Mason, OH: South-Western, 2008), 206; David L. Kurtz, *Contemporary Business, 13th Edition Update* (Hoboken, NJ: John Wiley & Sons, 2011), 275.

84. John M. Ivancevich and Thomas N. Duening, *Business: Principles, Guidelines, and Practices* (Mason, OH: Atomic Dog Publishing, 2007), 207.

85. Patricia M. Buhler, "Changing Organizational Structures and Their Impact on Managers," *Supervision*, 2011, 24–26.

86. "A Strong Business Organization Structure Is Paramount to Business Success," *The Business Plan*, accessed February 2, 2012, www.the-business-plan.com/business-organization-structure.html.

87. "Small Business Management Skills," *How to Start a Small Business*, accessed February 2, 2012, www.how-to-start-a-small-business.com/small-business-management-skills.html.

88. John M. Ivancevich and Thomas N. Duening, *Business: Principles, Guidelines, and Practices* (Mason, OH: Atomic Dog Publishing, 2007), 210; Kristie Lorette, "Organizational Structure Types in Companies," *Chron.com*, accessed February 2, 2012, smallbusiness.chron.com/organizational-structure-types-companies-2791.html.

89. Kristie Lorette, "Organizational Structure Types in Companies," *Chron.com*, accessed February 2, 2012, smallbusiness.chron.com/organizational-structure-types-companies-2791.html.

90. John M. Ivancevich and Thomas N. Duening, *Business: Principles, Guidelines, and Practices* (Mason, OH: Atomic Dog Publishing, 2007), 211.

91. Kristie Lorette, "Organizational Structure Types in Companies," *Chron.com*, accessed February 2, 2012, smallbusiness.chron.com/organizational-structure-types-companies-2791.html.

92. Jason Gillikin, "Advantages and Disadvantages of Divisional Organizational Structure," *Chron.com*, accessed February 2, 2012, smallbusiness.chron.com/advantages-disadvantages-divisional-organizational-structure-611.html.

93. Jason Gillikin, "Advantages and Disadvantages of Divisional Organizational Structure," *Chron.com*, accessed February 2, 2012, smallbusiness.chron.com/advantages-disadvantages-divisional-organizational-structure-611.html.

94. Marce Kelly and Jim McGowen, *BUSN* (Mason, OH: South-Western 2008), 208; David L. Kurtz, *Contemporary Business, 13th Edition Update* (Hoboken, NJ: John Wiley & Sons, 2011), 278; Kristie Lorette, "Organizational Structure Types in Companies," *Chron.com*, accessed February 2, 2012, smallbusiness.chron.com/organizational-structure-types-companies-2791.html.

95. Robert C. Ford and W. Alan Randolph, "Cross-Functional Structures: A Review and Integration of Matrix Organization and Project Management," *Journal of Management*, June 1992, 2.

96. John M. Ivancevich and Thomas N. Duening, *Business: Principles, Guidelines, and Practices* (Mason, OH: Atomic Dog Publishing, 2007), 214; William M. Pride, Robert J. Hughes, and Jack R. Kapoor, *Business* (Boston: Houghton Mifflin, 2008), 259.

97. Jay R. Galbraith, "Matrix Is the Ladder to Success," *Bloomberg BusinessWeek*, August 2009, accessed February 2, 2012, www.BusinessWeek.com/debateroom/archives/2009/08/matrix_is_the_l.html.

98. Manju K. Ahuja and Kathleen M. Carley, "Network Structure in Virtual Organizations," *Organization Science* 10, no. 6 (November 1999): 741–57; Les Phang, "Understanding Virtual Organizations," *ISACA Journal* 6 (2001): 42–47; William M. Pride, Robert J. Hughes, and Jack R. Kapoor, *Business* (Boston: Houghton Mifflin, 2008), 260.

99. John M. Ivancevich and Thomas N. Duening, *Business: Principles, Guidelines, and Practices* (Mason, OH: Atomic Dog Publishing, 2007), 214; Les Phang, "Understanding Virtual Organizations," *ISACA Journal* 6 (2001): 42–47.

100. John M. Ivancevich and Thomas N. Duening, *Business: Principles, Guidelines, and Practices* (Mason, OH: Atomic Dog Publishing, 2007), 214; Les Phang, "Understanding Virtual Organizations," *ISACA Journal* 6 (2001): 42–47.

101. "Return on Investment—ROI," *Investopedia*, accessed February 2, 2012, www.investopedia.com/terms/r/returnoninvestment.asp.

102. "Return on Assets—ROA," *Investopedia*, accessed February 2, 2012, www.investopedia.com/terms/r/returnonassets.asp.

103. "A Strong Business Organization Structure Is Paramount to Business Success," *The Business Plan*, accessed February 2, 2012, www.the-business-plan.com/business-organization-structure.html.

104. Karen Collins, *Exploring Business* (Irvington, NY: Flat World Knowledge, 2009), 90; "Small Business Planner: Choose a Structure," *US Small Business Association*, accessed February 3, 2012, archive.sba.gov/smallbusinessplanner/start/chooseastructure/index.html.

105. "Limited Liability Company," *Entrepreneur.com*, July 9, 2007, accessed February 3, 2012, www.entrepreneur.com/article/24484.

106. US Internal Revenue Service, "Selected Returns and Forms Filed or to Be Filed by Type During Specified Calendar Years 1980–2005," SOI Bulletin, Historical Table, Fall 2004, as cited in John M. Ivancevich and Thomas N. Duening, *Business: Principles, Guidelines, and Practices* (Mason, OH: Atomic Dog Publishing, 2007), 60.

107. John M. Ivancevich and Thomas N. Duening, *Business: Principles, Guidelines, and Practices* (Mason, OH: Atomic Dog Publishing, 2007), 60; adapted from David L. Kurtz, *Contemporary Business, 13th Edition Update* (Hoboken, NJ: John Wiley & Sons, 2011), 163.

108. William M. Pride, Robert J. Hughes, and Jack R. Kapoor, *Business* (Boston: Houghton Mifflin, 2008), 150.

109. "Small Business Planner: Choose a Structure," *US Small Business Association*, accessed February 3, 2012, archive.sba.gov/smallbusinessplanner/start/chooseastructure/index.html.

110. John M. Ivancevich and Thomas N. Duening, *Business: Principles, Guidelines, and Practices* (Mason, OH: Atomic Dog Publishing, 2007), 60; David L. Kurtz, *Contemporary Business, 13th Edition Update* (Hoboken, NJ: John Wiley & Sons, 2011), 163; William M. Pride, Robert J. Hughes, and Jack R. Kapoor, *Business* (Boston: Houghton Mifflin, 2008), 150.

111. Shelley Banjo, "Before You Tie the Knot…," *Wall Street Journal*, November 26, 2007, accessed February 3, 2012, online.wsj.com/article/SB119562612627400387.html.

112. William M. Pride, Robert J. Hughes, and Jack R. Kapoor, *Business* (Boston: Houghton Mifflin, 2008), 157.

113. Jeff Madura, *Introduction to Business* (St. Paul, MN: Paradigm Publishers International, 2010), 150.

114. Matthew Bandyk, "Turning Your Small Business into a Corporation," *US News & World Report*, March 14, 2008, accessed February 3, 2012, money.usnews.com/money/business-economy/small-business/articles/2008/03/14/turning-your-small-business-into-a-corporation.

115. Matthew Bandyk, "Turning Your Small Business into a Corporation," *US News & World Report*, March 14, 2008, accessed February 3, 2012, money.usnews.com/money/business-economy/small-business/articles/2008/03/14/turning-your-small-business-into-a-corporation.

116. Matthew Bandyk, "Turning Your Small Business into a Corporation," *US News & World Report*, March 14, 2008, accessed February 3, 2012, money.usnews.com/money/business-economy/small-business/articles/2008/03/14/turning-your-small-business-into-a-corporation.

117. "How to Choose the Right Business Structure for Your Small Business," *National Federation of Independent Business*, accessed February 3, 2012, www.nfib.com/tabid/56/?cmsid=49906.

118. "Limited Liability Company," *Entrepreneur.com*, July 9, 2007, accessed February 3, 2012, www.entrepreneur.com/article/24484.

119. Annalyn Censky, "Business Structures 101," *CNN Money*, August 4, 2008, accessed February 3, 2012, http://cnnmon.ie/MDaxXN.

120. Annalyn Censky, "Business Structures 101," *CNN Money*, August 4, 2008, accessed February 3, 2012, http://cnnmon.ie/MDaxXN.

121. "Human Resources," *Small Business Notes*, accessed June 1, 2012, www.smallbusinessnotes.com/managing-your-business/human-resources.

122. David L. Kurtz, *Contemporary Business, 13th Edition Update* (Hoboken, NJ: John Wiley & Sons, 2011), 288.

123. "Workforce Planning," accessed February 3, 2012, www.orgchart.net/wiki/Main_Page.

124. William M. Pride, Robert J. Hughes, and Jack R. Kapoor, *Business* (Boston: Houghton Mifflin, 2008), 159.

125. "Job Descriptions," *Small Business Notes*, accessed February 3, 2012, www.smallbusinessnotes.com/managing-your-business/job-descriptions.html.

126. "When Is It Better to Promote from Within Your Company?," *AllBusiness*, accessed February 3, 2012, www.allbusiness.com/human-resources/workforce-management-hiring-recruitment/1502-1.html.

127. "Hiring Issues," *Small Business Notes*, accessed February 3, 2012, www.smallbusinessnotes.com/managing-your-business/hiring-issues.html.

128. John M. Ivancevich and Thomas N. Duening, *Business: Principles, Guidelines, and Practices* (Mason, OH: Atomic Dog Publishing, 2007), 299.

129. "Labor Laws Governing Employers," *Small Business Notes*, accessed February 3, 2012, www.smallbusinessnotes.com/managing-your-business/labor-laws-governing-employers.html.

130. John M. Ivancevich and Thomas N. Duening, *Business: Principles, Guidelines, and Practices* (Mason, OH: Atomic Dog Publishing, 2007), 303.

131. "Interviewing Guidelines," *Small Business Notes*, accessed February 3, 2012, www.smallbusinessnotes.com/managing-your-business/interviewing-guidelines.html.

132. "Employment Testing and Selection," *Chron.com*, accessed February 3, 2012, smallbusiness.chron.com/employment-testing-selection-4794.html.

133. John M. Ivancevich and Thomas N. Duening, *Business: Principles, Guidelines, and Practices* (Mason, OH: Atomic Dog Publishing, 2007), 304–305.

134. "Employment Testing and Selection," *Chron.com*, accessed February 3, 2012, smallbusiness.chron.com/employment-testing-selection-4794.html.

135. "Employment Testing and Selection," *Chron.com*, accessed February 3, 2012, smallbusiness.chron.com/employment-testing-selection-4794.html.

136. "How to Request References," University of Texas at Austin Human Resource Services, accessed February 3, 2012, www.utexas.edu/hr/manager/hiring/references.html.

137. "Hiring Issues," *Small Business Notes*, accessed February 3, 2012, www.smallbusinessnotes.com/managing-your-business/hiring-issues.html.

138. Alison Doyle, "Reference Check Questions," *About.com*, accessed February 3, 2012, jobsearch.about.com/od/referencesrecommendations/a/refercheck.htm.

139. David L. Kurtz, *Contemporary Business, 13th Edition Update* (Hoboken, NJ: John Wiley & Sons, 2011), 294–95.

140. David L. Kurtz, *Contemporary Business, 13th Edition Update* (Hoboken, NJ: John Wiley & Sons, 2011), 295.

141. David L. Kurtz, *Contemporary Business, 13th Edition Update* (Hoboken, NJ: John Wiley & Sons, 2011), 296.

142. "Employee Benefits," *Small Business Notes*, accessed February 3, 2012, www.smallbusinessnotes.com/managing-your-business/employee-benefits.html.

143. "Employee Benefits," *Small Business Notes*, accessed February 3, 2012, www.smallbusinessnotes.com/managing-your-business/employee-benefits.html.

144. "Improve Your Employee Retention Rate," *Small Business Notes*, accessed February 3, 2012, www.smallbusinessnotes.com/managing-your-business/improve-your-employee-retention-rate.html.

145. "Setting Clearer Performance Expectations," *SmallBusinessLand.com*, accessed February 3, 2012, www.smallbusinessland.com/article/setting-clearer-performance-expectations.html.

146. "What Is Reasonable Accommodation?," *Marines*, accessed February 27, 2012, www.marines.mil/unit/hqmc/hr/Pages/EEO_Reasonable_Accommodation.aspx.

147. Robert I. Sutton, "Quiz: Are You Hiring and Breeding Greedy and Selfish Employees?," *Fast Company*, September 2, 2010, accessed February 3, 2012, www.fastcompany.com/article/quiz-are-you-hiring-and-breeding-greedy-and-selfish-employees.

148. "Improve Your Employee Retention Rate," *Small Business Notes*, accessed February 3, 2012, www.smallbusinessnotes.com/managing-your-business/improve-your-employee-retention-rate.html.

149. John M. Ivancevich and Thomas N. Duening, *Business: Principles, Guidelines, and Practices* (Mason, OH: Atomic Dog Publishing, 2007), 295.

150. John M. Ivancevich and Thomas N. Duening, *Business: Principles, Guidelines, and Practices* (Mason, OH: Atomic Dog Publishing, 2007), 309.

151. "Training and Development," *Inc.com*, accessed February 3, 2012, www.inc.com/encyclopedia/training-and-development.html.

152. John M. Ivancevich and Thomas N. Duening, *Business: Principles, Guidelines, and Practices* (Mason, OH: Atomic Dog Publishing, 2007), 309.

153. "Building a Better Benefits Program without Breaking the Budget: Five Practical Steps Every Small Business Should Consider," *MetLife*, 2010, accessed February 3, 2012, www.metlife.com/assets/institutional/services/insights-and-tools/ebts/small-market-whitepaper-v2.pdf.

154. "Employee Incentives for Small Business," *Yahoo! Voices*, May 24, 2007, accessed February 3, 2012, voices.yahoo.com/employee-incentives-small-business-359161.html.

155. Sharon McLoone, "How Do I…Offer Employee Incentives," *Washington Post*, December 4, 2008, voices.washingtonpost.com/small-business/2008/12/how_do_i_offer_employee_incenti.html.

156. "Employee Incentive Programs on a Small Business Budget," *Small Business Notes*, accessed February 3, 2012, www.smallbusinessnotes.com/managing-your-business/employee-incentive-programs-on-a-small-business-budget.html.

157. "Report: Cost-Effective Benefits Strategies for Small Businesses," *ESBJournal.com*, October 19, 2010, accessed February 3, 2012, esbjournal.com/2010/10/report-cost-effective-benefits-strategies-for-small-businesses.

158. "Employee Termination," *Inc.com*, accessed February 3, 2012, www.inc.com/encyclopedia/employee-termination.html.

159. "Employee Termination," *Inc.com*, accessed February 3, 2012, www.inc.com/encyclopedia/employee-termination.html.

160. "Employees: Job Termination Rights FAQs," *Lawyers.com*, accessed February 3, 2012, labor-employment-law.lawyers.com/wrongful-termination/Employees-Job-Termination-Rights-FAQ.html#10.

161. Alison Doyle, "Terminated for Cause," *About.com*, accessed February 3, 2012, jobsearch.about.com/od/jobloss/g/terminatedforcause.htm.

162. Alison Doyle, "Terminated for Cause," *About.com*, accessed February 3, 2012, jobsearch.about.com/od/jobloss/g/terminatedforcause.htm; "Employee Termination," *Inc.com*, accessed February 3, 2012, www.inc.com/encyclopedia/employee-termination.html.

163. "Facts about Sexual Harassment," *US Equal Employment Opportunity Commission*, June 27, 2002, accessed February 3, 2012, www.eeoc.gov/facts/fs-sex.html.

164. "Employee Termination: Informing Other Employees," *Small Business Notes*, accessed February 3, 2012, www.smallbusinessnotes.com/managing-your-business/employee-termination-informing-other-employees.html.

165. "Employee Termination: Informing Other Employees," *Small Business Notes*, accessed February 3, 2012, www.smallbusinessnotes.com/managing-your-business/employee-termination-informing-other-employees.html.

166. "The Benefits of Outsourcing for Small Businesses," *New York Times*, January 1, 2008, accessed February 3, 2012, www.nytimes.com/allbusiness/AB5221523_primary.html.

167. Joanna L. Krotz, "Tips for Outsourcing Your Small-Business Needs," *Microsoft*, accessed February 3, 2012, www.microsoft.com/business/en-us/resources/management/recruiting-staffing/tips-for-outsourcing-your-small-business-needs.aspx?fbid=WTbndqFrlli#T; David L. Kurtz, *Contemporary Business, 13th Edition Update* (Hoboken, NJ: John Wiley & Sons, 2011), 303.

168. David L. Kurtz, *Contemporary Business, 13th Edition Update* (Hoboken, NJ: John Wiley & Sons, 2011), 303.

169. "The Benefits of Outsourcing for Small Businesses," *New York Times*, January 1, 2008, accessed February 3, 2012, www.nytimes.com/allbusiness/AB5221523_primary.html.

170. David L. Kurtz, *Contemporary Business, 13th Edition Update* (Hoboken, NJ: John Wiley & Sons, 2011), 303.

171. Joanna L. Krotz, "Tips for Outsourcing Your Small-Business Needs," *Microsoft*, accessed February 3, 2012, www.microsoft.com/business/en-us/resources/management/recruiting-staffing/tips-for-outsourcing-your-small-business-needs.aspx?fbid=WTbndqFrlli#T.

172. Peter Emerson, "Accounts Receivable Outsourcing," *Streetdirectory.com*, accessed February 3, 2012, www.streetdirectory.com/travel_guide/162839/banking/accounts_receivable_outsourcing.html.

173. "When Does Outsourcing Accounts Receivables Make Sense," *Streetdirectory.com*, accessed February 3, 2012, www.streetdirectory.com/travel_guide/16826/outsourcing/when_does_outsourcing_accounts_receivables_make_sense.html.

174. Joanna L. Krotz, "Tips for Outsourcing Your Small-Business Needs," *Microsoft*, accessed February 3, 2012, www.microsoft.com/business/en-us/resources/management/recruiting-staffing/tips-for-outsourcing-your-small-business-needs.aspx?fbid=ZR0tpRAO-q#T.

175. "When Does Outsourcing Accounts Receivables Make Sense," *Streetdirectory.com*, accessed February 3, 2012, www.streetdirectory.com/travel_guide/16826/outsourcing/when_does_outsourcing_accounts_receivables_make_sense.html.

176. Adapted from Joanna L. Krotz, "Tips for Outsourcing Your Small-Business Needs," *Microsoft*, accessed February 3, 2012, www.microsoft.com/business/en-us/resources/management/recruiting-staffing/tips-for-outsourcing-your-small-business-needs.aspx?fbid=ZR0tpRAO-q#T.

177. "Benefits Packages for Emerging Businesses: Creating Long-Term Value for Your Employees," *Monster Hiring Center*, accessed February 3, 2012, grahambippart.files.wordpress.com/2010/03/benefitsfinal_6_12_07.pdf.

178. "Business Law and Regulations," *US Small Business Association*, accessed February 3, 2012, www.sba.gov/category/navigation-structure/starting-managing-business/starting-business/business-law-regulations; "Small Business Planner: Protect Your Ideas," *US Small Business Administration*, accessed February 3, 2012, www.sba.gov/smallbusinessplanner/start/protectyourideas/index.html; adapted from William M. Pride, Robert J. Hughes, and Jack R. Kapoor, *Business* (Boston: Houghton Mifflin, 2008), 159.

179. Rob Johnson, "Legal Advice…on a Budget," *Wall Street Journal*, November 15, 2010, accessed February 3, 2012, online.wsj.com/article/SB10001424052748703615104575329193640764492.html?mod=wsj_SmallBusiness_MIDDLETopStories.

180. "When Does Outsourcing Accounts Receivables Make Sense," *Streetdirectory.com*, accessed February 3, 2012, www.streetdirectory.com/travel_guide/16826/outsourcing/when_does_outsourcing_accounts_receivables_make_sense.html.

181. "When Outsourcing Is Not a Good Idea," *Streetdirectory.com*, accessed February 3, 2012, www.streetdirectory.com/travel_guide/16669/outsourcing/when_outsourcing_is_not_a_good_idea.html.

182. "The Benefits of Outsourcing for Small Businesses," *New York Times*, January 1, 2008, accessed February 3, 2012, www.nytimes.com/allbusiness/AB5221523_primary.html.

183. "Technology: Your Roadmap to Small-Business Success," *Intel*, accessed February 3, 2012, www.intel.com/content/www/us/en/world-ahead/world-ahead-small-business-success-article.html.

184. Donna Fuscaldo, "Using Social Networking to Boost Office Productivity," *Fox Business*, November 12, 2010, accessed February 3, 2012, smallbusiness.foxbusiness.com/entrepreneurs/2010/11/12/using-social-networking-boost-office-productivity.

185. Donna Fuscaldo, "Using Social Networking to Boost Office Productivity," *Fox Business*, November 12, 2010, accessed February 3, 2012, smallbusiness.foxbusiness.com/entrepreneurs/2010/11/12/using-social-networking-boost-office-productivity.

186. Brent Leary, "The iPad: Changing How We Build Business Relationships," *Inc.com*, May 2010, accessed February 3, 2012, www.inc.com/hardware/articles/201005/leary.html.

187. Ken Burgin, "20 Ways an iPad can Improve Your Restaurant, Café, Hotel or Bar," *ProfitableHospitality.com*, March 14, 2011, accessed February 3, 2012, profitablehospitality.com/news/index.php/kitchen-management/20-ways-an-ipad-can-improve-your-restaurant-cafe-hotel-or-bar.

188. Michael Hyatt, "How to Use Evernote with an iPad to Take Meeting Notes," accessed February 3, 2012, michaelhyatt.com/how-to-use-evernote-with-an-ipad-to-take-meeting-notes.html.

189. Ken Burgin, "20 Ways an iPad can Improve Your Restaurant, Café, Hotel or Bar," *ProfitableHospitality.com*, March 14, 2011, accessed February 3, 2012, profitablehospitality.com/news/index.php/kitchen-management/20-ways-an-ipad-can-improve-your-restaurant-cafe-hotel-or-bar.

190. Natalie Zmuda, "iPad Poised to Revolutionize Retail Industry," *Business Insider*, April 24, 2010, accessed February 3, 2012, www.businessinsider.com/ipad-poised-to-revolutionize-retail-industry-2010-4.

191. Patrick Woods, "Tips for Using the iPad for Real Estate," *PatrickWoods.com*, July 5, 2010, www.patrickwwoods.com/tips-for-using-the-ipad-for-real-estate.

192. Liane Cassavoy, "What Is a Smartphone?," *About.com*, accessed February 3, 2012, cellphones.about.com/od/glossary/g/smart_defined.htm.

193. Christopher Elliott, "5 Ways Smartphones & Servers Boost Productivity," *Microsoft*, accessed February 3, 2012, www.microsoft.com/business/en-us/resources/technology/communications/smartphones-and-business-productivity.aspx?fbid=WTbndqFrlI.

194. "Server (Computing)," *Wikipedia*, February 2010, accessed February 3, 2012, en.wikipedia.org/wiki/Server_(computing).

195. Craig Freudenrich and Carmen Carmack, "How PDAs Work," accessed February 2, 2012, electronics.howstuffworks.com/gadgets/travel/pda.htm.

196. Craig Freudenrich and Carmen Carmack, "How PDAs Work," accessed February 2, 2012, electronics.howstuffworks.com/gadgets/travel/pda.htm.

197. "Evaluating Shift to Online Communication Tools," *Pgi.com*, accessed February 3, 2012, www.pgi.com/us/en/content/download/7845/130408/file/PGi_WhitePaper_Return%28on%2BCollaboration_v05.pdf.

198. "Evaluating Shift to Online Communication Tools," *Pgi.com*, accessed February 3, 2012, www.pgi.com/us/en/content/download/7845/130408/file/PGi_WhitePaper_Return%28on%2BCollaboration_v05.pdf.

199. "Web Conferencing Review," *Top Ten Reviews*, accessed February 3, 2012, web-conferencing-services.toptenreviews.com.

200. Ruth Mayhew, "What Are the Advantages & Disadvantages of Virtual Offices and Telecommuting?" *Chron.com*, accessed May 30, 2012, http://smallbusiness.chron.com/advantages-disadvantages-virtual-offices-telecommuting-1167.html.

201. "Analysis Shows Telecommuting Can Cut Persian Gulf Oil Use by Almost Half," *Telecommute Connecticut*, accessed May 30, 2012, http://www.telecommutect.com/employers/telecommuting_saves_gas.php; Peter Suciu, "Telecommuting Can Save Employers Money, Too," *AllBusiness.com*, March 9, 2011, accessed February 3, 2012, www.allbusiness.com/labor-employment/working-hours-patterns-telecommuting/15480193-1.html.

202. "Flexible Telecommuting Has Many Benefits for Your Small Business," *AllBusiness.com*, March 9, 2011, accessed February 3, 2012, www.allbusiness.com/labor-employment/working-hours-patterns-telecommuting/11493643-1.html; Peter Suciu, "Telecommuting Can Save Employers Money, Too," *AllBusiness.com*, March 9, 2011, accessed February 3, 2012, www.allbusiness.com/labor-employment/working-hours-patterns-telecommuting/15480193-1.html; James Ware and Charles Grantham, "Flexible Work: Rhetoric and Reality," *Tech Republic*, accessed February 3, 2012, www.techrepublic.com/whitepapers/flexible-work-rhetoric-and-reality/384538.

203. Arnold Anderson, "Advantages of Telecommuting Jobs," *Chron.com*, accessed May 30, 2012, http://smallbusiness.chron.com/advantages-telecommuting-jobs-765.html.

204. Stegmeier Consulting Group, "The Business Case for Web Commuting: How to Reduce Workplace Costs and Increase Workforce Performance," *Computer World*, accessed February 3, 2012, www.computerworld.com/pdfs/Citrix_Business_Case_Web_Commuting.pdf.

205. "Flexible Telecommuting Has Many Benefits for Your Small Business," *AllBusiness.com*, March 9, 2011, accessed February 3, 2012, www.allbusiness.com/labor-employment/working-hours-patterns-telecommuting/11493643-1.html.

206. Adapted from Karen Collins, *Exploring Business* (Irvington, NY: Flat World Knowledge, 2009), 42.

207. Jonathan Blum, "Running an Entire Business from Smartphones," *CNN Money*, March 12, 2008, accessed February 3, 2012, money.cnn.com/2008/03/11/smbusiness/mobile_phone_software.fsb/index.htm.

208. Julie Bos, "Top Trends in Staffing: Is Your Organization Prepared for What Lies Ahead?," *Workforce Management* 90, no. 2 (2011): 33–38.

209. "Taleo Business Edition," *Taleo.com*, accessed February 3, 2012, www.taleo.com/solutions/taleo-business-edition.

CHAPTER 13
The Search for Efficiency and Effectiveness

Carrot Creative

Source: Used with permission from Carrot Creative.

The *small* in small business refers only to the number of employees or the volume of sales. It seldom refers to the level of enthusiasm, the amount of creativity, or the ability to innovate. A great example of this is Carrot Creative, a new social media agency headquartered in the Dumbo section of Brooklyn, New York. Mike Germano and Robert Gaafar started their first company while Mike was a college student and serving as a city councilman in Hamden, Connecticut. They developed sites that enabled students to sell used textbooks and rate their professors. In 2005, they opened Carrot Creative. When it was in its infancy, Carrot Creative was not a traditional marketing agency, and social media barely existed. The social media industry, as a whole, is one of the most innovative and fast-paced industries in the world, forcing companies such as Carrot Creative to stay ahead of the curve and adapt quickly.

From the very beginning, Carrot Creative has been innovative and progressive—not only because of its founders and team members but also out of necessity. It started with no available business model to copy, no rules to follow, and no resources on which to rely. They had one rule: do not accept the status quo. Carrot Creative was designed to become what its founders envisioned and what the market needed. They view themselves as a business that is always open to a challenge. They dare anyone to present them with a problem that they cannot solve. Germano, in a recent interview, put it this way, "We help brands build on social networks, teach them and help them in great ways for them to have conversations with their customers and really turn brands into people."[1]

Some of the brands that they have signed include Crayola, the National Football League, Major League Baseball, AOL, Disney, PepsiCo, Budweiser, the Islands of the Bahamas, and Ford Motor Company. Creative Carrot was the driving force behind Ford's social media campaign for its new Fiesta vehicle. This *small* business has partnerships with some of the world's largest advertising agencies and public relations (PR) firms. They also have the honor to be on the forefront of designing the very tools that define social media. They view their title as an official "Facebook Preferred Developer" as just icing on the cake.

Today, Carrot Creative remains on top of the creative game by giving all its employees the freedom to create in their own way. It keeps creativity flowing by cultivating an environment and culture that removes the idea of micromanaging and gives each Carrot Creative employee the freedom, trust, and responsibility for their own work and actions. One never knows when creativity will strike, but it certainly will not be inside a cubicle or under someone's thumb. Creativity flows through individual expression and personal work style. The Carrot Creative office is designed for just those things. There is space to work on couches, in a room of Astroturf, and private offices with maple desks, and, most importantly, the ability to be freely collaborative. As Germano said, "We appreciate the individual nature of small companies."[2]

1. PERSONAL EFFICIENCY AND EFFECTIVENESS

LEARNING OBJECTIVES

1. Recognize the difference between effectiveness and efficiency.
2. Understand the differences among first-, second-, third-, and fourth-generation time-management systems.
3. Learn how using an activity log to see how time is spent.
4. Learn the dos and don'ts of time management.

effective

Achieving the outcomes that someone wishes to produce.

efficient

Producing the desired results with the minimum expenditure of energy, time, money, personnel, or material.

Open any basic management textbook, and there will always be a discussion of the importance for an organization to be both **effective** and **efficient**. These are fundamental concepts. An organization demonstrates effectiveness when it achieves the outcomes that it wishes to produce.[3] Efficiency is "the capacity of an organization, institution or business to produce the desired results with the minimum expenditure of energy, time, money, personnel, material, etc."[4] In discussing the distinction between the two concepts, Peter Drucker once said, "Efficiency is doing things right; effectiveness is doing the right things."[5] Regardless of the exact definition of these concepts, it should be clear that any business should strive to be both effective and efficient.

It is important to recognize that for any given endeavor, one can be effective and but not efficient and vice versa. This can be illustrated with the following example. Two students are working in their college mail room. Each is given a stack of five hundred individual class schedules that are to be sorted and placed in the mailboxes of the undergraduate students. They are told that when they are done, they will be given another job. The first student is meticulous and carefully checks that each class schedule goes to the right recipient. She completes the job in 4.5 hours. The second student is less careful about accuracy and makes several errors by putting the wrong schedule in the wrong box. However, he completes his work in 3 hours. The first student was effective because the task was to get the right schedule to the right student. The second student was more efficient, if efficiency is measured in the number of schedules dispensed per hour.

In the late 1950s and early 1960s, two important works on the nature of a firm introduced an expanded concept known as "organizational slack."[6] Slack was seen as the excess capacity maintained by an organization. By definition, slack implies that an organization is not perfectly efficient. Some argue that slack provides resources for innovation and change. Others see it as a buffer for a firm.[7] Although these debates might make for interesting academic discussions, it must be recognized that most small businesses do not have the luxury of maintaining any appreciable slack. Their survival hinges on being *both* highly effective and highly efficient. Therefore, any technique, program, or methodology that improves those ends is vital to the well-being of a small business.

1.1 Time Management

Strategy is the art of making use of time and space. I am less concerned about the latter than the former. Space we can recover, lost time never.[8]

- *Napoleon*

Throughout this chapter, the focus will be on the simple fact that one of the great enemies in life—particularly a businessperson's life—is the existence and acceptance of waste. One of the resources that we can least afford to waste is time. In many ways, time is the most precious of all resources. Other resources can often be purchased or acquired, but time cannot be purchased. Once lost, time can never be recaptured. Time, as a resource, should be of particular importance for the small business owner.

If one is serious about maximizing the use of time, then one should consider two venues: use a time-management system and avoid what are referred to as "time wasters." The term *time-management system* is a broad concept and covers many different approaches. Regardless of the approach used, its adoption provides multiple benefits. As one author puts it—"'**Time management**' involves working on the right things [effectiveness] and doing them the best way [efficiency]."[9] Steven Covey, author of *First Things First*,[10] a "bible" for time management, identifies four generations of time-management systems. He defines a **first-generation time-management system** as being composed of essentially a list of tasks that must be done. A **second-generation time-management system** ties deadlines to those tasks. A **third-generation time-management system** incorporates task prioritization. Many businesspeople are familiar with paper-and-pencil or computerized systems for listing tasks, noting their due dates, and prioritizing them in terms of relative importance. Covey argues for a **fourth-generation time-management system**. This system is designed to bring balance into the personal and the professional lives of individuals. It is best illustrated by Covey's 2 × 2 matrix, where one axis is composed of tasks that can be categorized as *urgent* or *not urgent*. The other axis is composed of tasks that can be characterized as either *important* or *not important* (see Figure 13.1). He emphasizes that those tasks that might be found in the *important/not urgent* quadrant (quadrant 2) might be critical to an individual's well-being. Unfortunately, because they are listed as *not urgent*, they might fall by the wayside. His goal is to produce a "balanced manager." This balance refers to what he argues are the four fundamental human needs: physical needs, social needs, mental needs, and spiritual needs. His approach to time management is based on valuing relationships and recognizing that the proper management of relationships will reduce the amount of time wasted in activities.

time management

Working on the right things (effectiveness) and doing them the best way (efficiency).

first-generation time-management system

A system composed of essentially a list of tasks that must be done.

second-generation time-management system

A system that ties deadlines to those tasks that must be done.

third-generation time-management system

A system that incorporates a system of prioritization to tasks that must be done.

fourth-generation time-management system

A system designed to bring balance into the personal and professional life of an individual.

FIGURE 13.1 Time-Management Matrix

	Urgent	**Not Urgent**
Important	**Quadrant 1** **Manage** Quadrant of Necessity • Crises • Pressing problems • Deadline driven projects, meetings, preparations	**Quadrant 2** **Focus** Quadrant of Quality • Preparation • Prevention • Values clarification • Relationship building through re-creation • Empowerment
Not Important	**Quadrant 3** **Avoid** Quadrant of Deception • Interruptions, some phone calls • Some mail, some reports • Some meetings • Many proximate, pressing matters • Many popular activities	**Quadrant 4** **Avoid** Quadrant of Waste • Trivia, busy work • Junk mail • Some phone calls • Time wasters • "Escape" activities

Source: Steven Covey, A. Roger Merrill, and Rebecca R. Merrill, First Things First (New York: Simon and Shuster, 1994), 37; James Cooper, "3 Vital Time Management Principles for Small Business Owners & Entrepreneurs," mimosaPLANET, December 2, 2010, accessed February 4, 2012, http://mimosaplanet.com/Small-Business-Blog/bid/55824/3-Vital-Time-Management-Principles-for-Small-Business-Owners-Entrepreneurs.html.

Covey advocates that an individual should have a deep understanding of what is important in one's life and recognize that, on any day, one will assume different roles. Both elements need to be incorporated into the time-management system. For Covey, we all have to assume different roles in our personal and professional lives. The objective is to identify what these roles require time-wise and how they can be successfully integrated. To achieve integration, we need to better understand ourselves. Covey suggests that developing a personal mission statement is vital to achieving balance. Some characteristics of such a statement might include the following:

- What represents the deepest and best within a person?
- What is an expression of a person's unique capacity to contribute to one's family, the organization, and the world at large?
- What represents pursuits that are higher than self-interest?
- What integrates all four fundamental human needs?
- What principles produce quality-of-life results?
- What inspires a person?

The following is an example of a personal mission statement that uses the Covey approach:

I am at my best when I am challenged by a task that has some significance.

I will try to prevent times when I have to work with individuals who think only of their own advancement.

I will enjoy my work when my company provides customers with value and earns a profit.

I will find enjoyment in my personal life when I feel that I have done something that benefits all members of my immediate family.

I will find opportunities that will allow my firm to double its sales every three years.

I can do anything I set my mind to; I will grow my business to the point where I can retire when I am 55.

My life's journey is building my business and providing a comfortable life for my family.

I will be a person who has created a business that provides value to its customers, and I will be an individual who made his family understand how much he loved them.

My most important future contribution to others will be that I expanded my business's operations so that I might provide opportunities and gainful employment for additional workers.

I will stop procrastinating and start working on the following:

- *Broadening the products offered by my business*
- *Being more tolerant of others who hold conflicting opinions*
- *Developing plans for my retirement*

I will strive to incorporate the following attributes into my life:

- *The ability to make all individuals who work for my business feel as though their views are valued and counted.*
- *Illustrate to others that one does not have to limit oneself to a narrow domain of interests.*
- *Never give up regardless of the difficulty of a situation.*

I will constantly renew myself by focusing on the four dimensions of my life:

- *Exercise*
- *Greater tolerance for others*
- *Find more time for reading*
- *Control my temper*

Covey's complete system of time management is comprehensive and is supported by both paper-and-pencil and software support materials.

If Covey's comprehensive approach appears to be initially overwhelming, where else might a person begin to improve their time-management skills? An excellent—in fact a critical—takeoff point would be to ask the following question: "Where has the time gone?" How often have we asked ourselves or heard others pose this question, and how often are we unable to answer it? Until one has a solid idea of how time is spent, it is impossible to manage time effectively. It is comparable to beginning a journey to a location without knowing the exact starting point. An excellent way of knowing how time is spent is to use an activity log.

An **activity log** involves writing down every task and activity a person is involved with during a day. It also requires noting when these activities occurred during the day and how long they lasted. It would be very useful to also comment on one's emotional state and energy level while performing these tasks and activities. The log should be maintained for a period of time—generally one or two weeks. At the end of this period, analyze how time was spent. This analysis should look for some common threads:

- How much time per day or week is spent on particular activities?
- When during the day did you feel the most productive?
- When during the day did you feel the least productive or have the most disruptions to workflow?
- What activities were individuals who created these disruptions to workflow?
- What activities seem to provide little or no value?

activity log

A technique that involves writing down every task and activity that one is involved with during a day.

The goal of this analysis is to identify what task or activity should be eliminated and when, if there is a pattern to productivity, a high-value challenging task should be scheduled. The activity log should provide useful insights into how a person should structure time flow.[11] As one author put it, "Find your rhythm and schedule around."[12]

After identifying workflow patterns, then seriously begin planning for time management. The first stage of this process involves identifying the required tasks to be performed across various time horizons, such as the upcoming year, month, week, or day. Draw on Covey and others to include a broad spectrum of life activities, not just work-oriented activities.[13]

In addition to identifying these tasks, it is vital that a person prioritize these tasks. Some tasks are clearly more important than others. As an example, securing a major sale would have a much higher priority than selecting the appropriate stationery for a business. The next step is determining—or more likely estimating—how much time and what resources will be required to complete the tasks. Use these estimates of time to generate a to-do list specifying the completion date for the tasks and the activities. Plan on working within realistic blocks of time.[14] When dealing with a large complex project, learn to break it down into manageable segments and components.

It is one thing to create a prioritized time schedule; it is something entirely different to successfully follow such a schedule. Time management involves learning how to consistently carry out these tasks while avoiding the many time-robbing traps that exist in all our lives.[15]

The following are some dos and don'ts of time management:

- **Learn to "chunk."** Chunking is a process by which similar activities are grouped into common blocks of time. As an example, one might schedule several activities associated with the financial operations of the business—such as paying bills, tallying receipts, and so forth—together during a specific time period.[16]

- **Learn to delegate.** A common complaint leveled at entrepreneurs and small business owners is their propensity to be involved in every aspect of the business. The effective use of one's time will involve recognizing that one person cannot do everything. It is important to learn how to delegate a particular task to subordinates. The challenge is to properly supervise the subordinates so that the task is carried out as desired.[17]

- **Learn to say "no."** It is often said that the most important word for a manager to learn is the word *no*. Time management involves discipline. It means that at times we must stop activities that would become time robbers.[18] What about the colleague who drifts into your work space and asks, "Do you have a few minutes?" When we know that this colleague will be talking more about his or her own personal life rather than work-related activities, then we must have the courage to say, "Sorry, but I do not have the time." In periods of time pressure, we must even find strength to forgo some activities, such as going out to lunch.[19]

- **Learn to not procrastinate.** For many of us, this is the great challenge. It is best dealt with by maintaining a clear focus on the required tasks. This is why a to-do list of tasks tied with prioritization is so important. One way to deal with procrastination is to concentrate on one task and staying with the task until it is complete.[20] Another form of procrastination is the willing acceptance of wasting time. Waiting is a form of wasting time if one is not engaged in some useful activity while waiting for some other outcome—such as working while on hold during a phone call.[21]

- **Learn to manage e-mail.** One of the greatest sources of time wasting is the improper management of e-mail. The ping announcing a new e-mail message often lures one away from productive work to read the message. One should plan set blocks of time during the day to handle e-mail. Outside these blocks, one should not open any e-mail. E-mail should be approached so that each item can be dealt with once and then eliminated.[22] One should also be prepared to "on deadline days…put up the equivalent of a 'do not disturb sign.'"[23]

- **Learn to find private time.** It is vital that an individual find time where to be alone with one's own thoughts and work in isolation without interruptions. Time to think allows the small business owner to think about the "big picture."[24] This type of break can actually improve one's efficiency and effectiveness.[25] As with e-mail, one must be prepared to demand no interruptions.

In addition to these suggestions, one should learn to use some form of time-management system: a paper-and-pencil system, such as a day planner; a computer-based system; or a system that works on one's smartphone or an iPad. Select one system and stay with it.[26]

Do not become addicted to the rush of constantly being *busy*. For some individuals, there is confusion between being "on the go" and actually accomplishing what one needs to accomplish. Many of these people view themselves as successful multitaskers. This ability to **multitask** is often referred to as a modern-day requisite skill. However, the reality is that multitasking appears to reduce one's productivity. Some studies indicate that multitasking prolongs the accomplishment of a list of tasks by as

multitask

The ability to handle several tasks simultaneously.

much as 20 percent to 40 percent.[27] A better use of one's time is to focus on one task at a time.[28] In conclusion, it is important to recognize that one should not expect to achieve a perfect allocation of one's time, especially as unexpected events arise. The best that can be hoped for is that "we can actually manage ourselves."[29]

 ### Video Clip 13.1

Time-Management Tips Are Really Self-Management Tips!
Harvard Business Publishing covers time management.

View the video online at: http://www.youtube.com/v/bf2HBoYDKRk

 ### Video Clip 13.2

Secrets of Effective Time Management
Several time-management techniques are discussed.

View the video online at: http://www.youtube.com/v/wy7Hxqgr-54

Web Resources

Eleven Time-Management Tips, Part 1: Coming to Grips with the Time Management Myth

This site provides useful tips on successful time management.

sbinfocanada.about.com/cs/timemanagement/a/timemgttips.htm

Three Vital Time-Management Principles for Small Business Owners and Entrepreneurs

What principles are key for small business owners and entrepreneurs?

mimosaplanet.com/Small-Business-Blog/bid/55824/
3-Vital-Time-Management-Principles-for-Small-Business-Owners-Entrepreneurs.html

Time Management

Learn how to schedule and manage time wisely and effectively, avoid procrastination, and improve productivity.

www.powerhomebiz.com/leadership/time.htm

Time-Management Tips for Small Business Owners

Tips that focus on small businesses.

ezinearticles.com/?Time-Management-Tips-For-Small-Business-Owners&id=4849540

Time Management

A sampling of links on time management.

www.businesstown.com/time/time.asp

KEY TAKEAWAYS

- An effective organization achieves the outcomes it wishes to produce.
- Efficiency is the ability of any organization to produce the desired results with the minimum expenditure of resources.[30]
- Time-management systems have evolved through four generations of models.
- Using an activity log can assist anyone in learning how to better manage time.
- Learning the dos and don'ts of time management can significantly improve one's efficiency.

EXERCISES

1. Create a time log for a five-day period. Analyze this log and see how you spend time.
2. Identify what you believe to be your own biggest time wasters and how you intend to deal with them.
3. If you do not currently use a formal time-management system, look at several paper-and-pencil or digital versions, evaluate them, and describe which you would select and why.

2. CREATIVITY

LEARNING OBJECTIVES

1. Understand the three fundamental innovation strategies.
2. Understand what supports creativity in individuals and businesses.
3. Learn what may repress creativity in individuals.
4. Learn about some tools that may help individuals and organizations become more creative.

Money never starts an idea; it is the idea that starts the money.[31]
- Owen Laughlin

Thomas Friedman—the author of *That Used to Be Us*,[32] *Hot, Flat, and Crowded*[33] and *The World Is Flat*[34] —and other pundits consistently argue that the future belongs to those societies and businesses that can best capitalize on creativity and innovation. It is a great tragedy that we often think of creativity and innovation in terms of new technologies only. We fail to realize that creativity and innovation can occur anywhere within a business. There is a story—perhaps it is an urban legend—about a member of the cleaning staff for a company that manufactures shampoo. This employee brought a suggestion to the attention of an executive on the marketing team. The employee pointed out that the instructions on the back of the bottle of shampoo said—"Lather and rinse" and suggested that it should read "Lather, rinse, and repeat." It may be apocryphal and somewhat unethical, but, if true, it would have led to a significant increase in sales. We recount this legend not to advocate any form of chicanery but to point out that creative insights may come from anyone and anywhere. Creativity is not limited to scientists, engineers, designers, or top executives. It is a property that all human beings possess. Likewise, creativity need not be singularly channeled into new high-tech products or advanced designs. Innovation may pursue different strategies. There are three fundamental innovation strategies for firms: **need seeker**, **market reader**, and **technology driver**.[35] Need seeker firms actively interact with their present and future customers and carefully listen to them so that they can develop new products and services. These firms tend to be the first in the market. A market reader firm maintains a close relationship with its customers and provides them value through small innovative changes. A technology-driven firm is a business that puts money into research and development to produce revolutionary breakthroughs and/or incremental changes. Such a firm spends more time and effort in anticipating future customer needs and carefully listening to what customers believe they want at this point in time. None of these three innovation strategies is clearly superior to the other. It is interesting to know, however, that none of these strategies precludes or minimizes the potential contribution that could come from a small business. If one examines the three innovation strategies, it could be clearly argued that small businesses have an advantage over their larger rivals for the first two strategies. Both rely on a business having a deep and intimate understanding of the needs and desires of its customers. Small businesses also are better positioned to actively listen to their customers and, because of their size, respond more rapidly. Even the third innovation strategy often is the domain of the smaller business. Think of the number of technological breakthroughs that were initiated by smaller firms (at least, smaller at that time) than the large behemoths.

At one level, creativity should be thought of as a rare flower that should be nurtured at both the individual level and the organizational level. Many businesses create an environment that not only does not foster creativity among its personnel but also actively crushes it. Such firms punish any failure, which increases fear in the personnel to try something new. These firms fail to reward innovative successes. They foster groupthink, often responding with the following reply: "We have always done it this way." The leadership team believes that leaders are the only ones responsible for creative actions. This type of organization is toxic to creativity.

Before examining the tools and techniques that might enhance creativity, it is important to understand what personal and organizational factors might inhibit creativity.

- **Accepting the belief that one may not be creative.** At a recent sports event, the coach of the team wore a t-shirt that had the following saying: "If you believe you can do something or if you believe you can't do something, you are right." Individuals who tell themselves that they are not creative are producing a self-fulfilling prophecy. They will not even attempt to break through barriers that might preclude them from having brilliant, creative, and innovative ideas. It is absolutely vital for the small business owner to be open to the possibility of his or her own tremendous creativity.

- **Acceptance of the current situation.** Sometimes we assume that the current situation is not only fully acceptable but also the only way that it can be. With that type of mental framework, we never will be in a position even to ask, "How could the situation be made better?" This corresponds with the old idiom, "If it ain't broke, don't fix it." A creative mind is always operating under the assumption that things can be different and can be made better.

- **Self-censorship.** This is a situation when an idea occurs to us, but we initially consider it too outlandish or too impractical to successfully implement. We dismiss the idea without any further consideration. One does not even take the opportunity to record the idea. We engage in self-sabotage of our own creativity by dismissing our own ideas out of hand.

- **Allowing ideas to die.** It is not enough to have a creative idea. One must have the courage to defend the idea and the fortitude to see it through to fruition. Unfortunately, individuals adopt the philosophy of W. C. Fields: "If at first you don't succeed, try, try again. Then quit. No use being a damn fool about it."[36] A good counterexample of this failure to pursue ideas is the genesis of FedEx. Fred Smith, FedEx's CEO and founder, was an economics major at Yale University. While there in 1965, Smith wrote a term paper outlining the concept behind FedEx. Legend has it that this paper received a grade of C. Most students would feel that this grade was a

need seeker

A firm that actively interacts with its present and future customers and carefully listens to them so that it can develop new products and services.

market reader

A firm that maintains a close relationship with its customers and provides them value through small innovative changes.

technology driver

A business that puts money into research and development to produce revolutionary breakthroughs and/or incremental changes.

clear indication that the concept was infeasible, but Fred Smith was not persuaded, and nine years later he began FedEx. It is not enough to be creative; one also must be courageous.

- ✴ **Not maintaining a record of ideas.** What is called inspiration may be rather fickle. Ideas may come to us in the most unlikely of places and at unexpected times. Individuals should be prepared to make note of these ideas as they come. It might simply require having a notepad available at all times or a digital recorder to take down ideas. Sometimes it is useful to write out the ideas, place them where they are visually accessible, and return to them at some point in the future.

brainstorming

A group process by which individuals produce solutions to problems without any restriction placed on their possible options.

Perhaps one of the most commonly used creativity tools is **brainstorming**, an approach that emphasizes collaboration within a group. Brainstorming begins by specifying a problem or issue—for example, "How can we boost sales at the restaurant?"; "What can be done to reduce customer complaints?"; or "Why do these particular types of defects keep occurring?" Then one brings together personnel who are directly familiar with the problem or the issue. Sometimes it might be advisable to bring in people not directly familiar with the problem or the issue because they may bring a totally different perspective that might enhance the overall creativity of the problem-solving exercise. The room where the brainstorming exercise is held should be equipped with a whiteboard, or a computer with a projector, or a simple flip chart. The moderator or the facilitator of the brainstorming session should restate the problem. Individuals should be able to shout out possible solutions. The facilitator writes them down or types them into the computer, which is then projected so that all people can see the proposals. The most critical point of the brainstorming session is the openness with which the group accepts any and all ideas. No matter how bizarre or off-the-wall a suggestion might appear to be, no one is allowed to criticize it. Even if an idea is simply crazy, participants do not have the latitude to make any negative remarks. After all the ideas have been presented and written down, the group begins a process of winnowing down the number of suggestions to a smaller number, perhaps five.[37] In the real world, most decisions cannot be done with respect to a simple, single criterion. As an example, one might evaluate the five possible solutions with respect to cost. In the freewheeling environment of brainstorming, one possible solution might yield the lowest cost but might be illegal. Before evaluating the reduced set of solutions, the group must identify all the criteria that would be useful in determining the solutions. Examples of such criteria might be cost, viability, the probability of implementing the solution within a given timeline, or customer acceptance. Once these criteria have been identified, the group can then scale (numerically evaluate) each solution with respect to the criteria. Such an approach should help the group identify the overall best solution. This is the most basic and most common format for brainstorming. Other variations exist that are designed to deal with some possible deficiencies of classical brainstorming, such as naturally reticent members.[38]

mind mapping

A diagram that specifies all the types of relationships among key elements of a problem or an issue.

Another useful approach to stimulate creative thinking about a problem or an issue is **mind mapping**. This technique is used widely in a variety of contexts, including creative writing courses. It is a visual model that uses words, phrases, tasks, or concepts centered on an idea or a problem. A node or a figure representing the core notion is drawn at the center. Ideas that are related to this central notion are drawn off, as branches, to the sides. These secondary ideas, in turn, may generate other offshoots. This continues until all interrelationships are mapped on the diagram. Figure 13.2 is a mind map that might have been drawn for Frank's All-American BarBeQue, when it was considering an expansion.

FIGURE 13.2 Mind Map for Expanding Frank's All-American BarBeQue

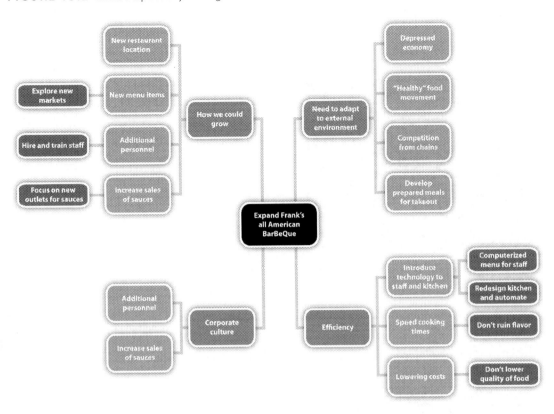

The Financial Monitor from Simione Consultants

William Simione Jr., the founding member of Simione Consultants (see the opening vignette of Chapter 9), has always believed that there has been a need for the home health and hospice industries to have timely financial benchmarks. Recognizing that this need was not being met, Simione started Financial Monitor LLC in 2009. This company launched a product known as the *Financial Monitor*. This is an excellent example of a business using its creativity to develop a new business. Using the company's expertise in the home health and hospice industries, Simione designed a program that would benchmark clients' quarterly financial reports against industry standards. Two principals, William Simione III and David Berman, have managed the development of the *Financial Monitor*. In 2009, Rob Simione was added to the *Financial Monitor* team as the senior manager.

The long-term goal of the *Financial Monitor* is to become the industry's major database for financial information. Currently, Simione has a database of 160 providers. With this information, Simione not only provides clients with meaningful financial information but also provides the home health and hospice industry with data that can be used in advocacy efforts on both national and state levels. Simione has begun to work with both the National Association for Home Care and Hospice and several state associations to have the *Financial Monitor* help them in their advocacy efforts. The short-term goal is to have five hundred home health and hospice agencies on the *Financial Monitor* by end of 2011, and the long-range goal is to have in excess of five thousand on it by the end of 2014.

Video Clip 13.3

TED Fullerton—Matthew Jenusaitis—Importance of Creativity in Business
A discussion of the importance of creativity in business. It is seventeen minutes—but very good.

View the video online at: http://www.youtube.com/v/eLNL3znhG6Y

 Video Clip 13.4

TEDxPugetSound—Edgar Papke—Creativity and the Human Art of Business
Discusses how to match creativity and motivation. Another long video, but it has excellent ideas.

View the video online at: http://www.youtube.com/v/STWvCCbGUzk

Web Resources

Let Creativity & Imagination Grow Your Business

Discusses the importance of creativity for business development.

www.theopensite.com/marketing-business-promotion/small-business-imagination-creativity

Passion & Creativity Go a Long Way for Small Business Owners

Reviews the critical role of passion for start-ups.

www.catalystmarketers.com/passion-creativity-small-business-owners

Creativity: Breaking the Mental Blocks

How to overcome barriers to creativity.

www.smallbusinessadvocate.com/small-business-articles/creativity-breaking-the-mental-blocks-694

KEY TAKEAWAYS

- All members of an organization can be creative.
- Organizations need to develop environments that support and nurture creativity.
- Mental blocks can stifle an individual's creative capability.
- Tools such as brainstorming and mind mapping can enhance the creativity of groups.

EXERCISES

1. What do you believe are your own personal blocks to being more creative?
2. Brainstorm with several colleagues and come up with five innovative concepts for a local restaurant.
3. Draw a mind map for how you might become better in managing time.

3.   ORGANIZATIONAL EFFICIENCY

LEARNING OBJECTIVES

1. Understand the eight dimensions of product quality.
2. Understand the five dimensions of service quality.
3. Learn about the Deming philosophy of quality management.
4. Learn about the fundamentals of Six Sigma quality management.

When considering effectiveness or efficiency improvements on an organizational level, one generally thinks in terms of programs: projects with some battery of tools and techniques. Quite often, the businessperson is confronted with choosing from a cornucopia of the most recent business fads. The fad de jour is tried and often found wanting. Eventually, businesspeople become inured to the latest hot trend, continue with their standard operations, and become less willing to try something new. This is extremely unfortunate because some of these programs offer the opportunity for significant improvements. Two such programs are quality management and lean thinking. Both approaches grew out of manufacturing environments. Most of the articles and books about them tend to emphasize manufacturing-based examples. However, this does not mean that they are limited to that domain. More and more service industries are recognizing that the adoption of quality management and/or lean thinking offers tremendous benefits in effectiveness and efficiency. The same can also be said about the acceptance of these business models by smaller firms. Although some quality and lean programs are presented as complete and complex systems requiring extensive training routines, many small businesses have adopted the underlying concepts without resorting to significant expenditures. They recognized that the promulgation of the underlying principles of quality and lean management can yield significant returns without significant expenditures.

3.1   Quality Management

Quality is never an accident; it is always the result of high intention sincere effort intelligent direction and skillful execution; it represents the wise choice of many alternatives the cumulative experience of many masters of craftsmanship. Quality also marks the search for an ideal after necessity has been satisfied and mere usefulness achieved.[39]

- William A. Foster

Throughout this text, the concept of customer value has been emphasized. Intimately linked to customer value is the notion of quality. Therefore, it is extremely unfortunate that for most people, businesspeople included, the term *quality* is either totally misunderstood or viewed from a rather narrow perspective. This stems from two reasons. The first is based on a correct assumption that quality is defined by the user (customer); however, many then go on to believe that because quality is subjective, it then becomes impossible to define. The second problem centers on the tendency to view quality, particularly in products, as singularly the result of the use of costly raw materials, components, careful craftsmanship, and detailed processes. It is assumed that together these expensive elements must necessarily produce a quality but costly outcome. In this belief system, if one wants to identify the quality of the product, one has to look only at the price tag. Quality is synonymous with cost. This is a huge error because, as will be shown, a true commitment to quality can reduce costs and expenses—and do so quite significantly.

Quality in Small Business

To see the practical benefits of using the principles of quality management for small businesses, one can simply review the winners of the Malcolm Baldrige Award. This award, started in 1987, seeks to acknowledge businesses that have a solid commitment to quality. Awards were initially given in the categories of manufacturing, service, and small businesses; subsequently, three more categories were added: education, nonprofits, and health care. A sampling of two recent winners in the small business category clearly shows that the smaller enterprise can produce spectacular results by adopting quality management.

K&N Management, a 2010 winner, operates two fast-casual restaurants in Austin, Texas. With a strong commitment to quality, such as using iPads to gather quick survey data from customers, K&N saw its sales increase from $3 million in 2000 to over $7.5 million in 2010. Its gross profit was consistently related to quality. In 2010, K&N was named the "best place to work in Austin."[40]

The 2009 winner in the small business category was MidwayUSA, an online retailer for gun owners and hunters. Again, MidwayUSA's commitment to quality has produced some impressive results. The firm has a customer retention rate of 98 percent. It had a growth rate of 25 percent for 2008, compared to a 10 percent rate for its nearest competitor. From 2003 to 2008, MidwayUSA saw its net profits increase from 2.5 percent to 10 percent.[41]

These Baldrige award winners are only a few of the indicators that a focus on quality translates into improved customer satisfaction, improved employee satisfaction, and significant improvements to a firm's financials.

Without a fundamental understanding of what quality really means, it is impossible to achieve it—consistently. So how should one approach a useful definition of the term *quality*? Many authors suggest that when discussing quality, it is useful to distinguish between product quality and service quality. Today, there may be no clear-cut distinction between exclusively product-based businesses or exclusively service-based businesses. Few products can be viewed in isolation from supporting services. As an example, an automobile manufacturer clearly produces a product; however, few manufacturers would survive long if they totally excluded the area of follow-up services, such as vehicle maintenance across a car's lifetime. Likewise, many service businesses rely on ancillary products. An investment company provides a service; however, it may also provide its clients with investment perspective reports. Many view McDonald's as essentially a service company—the service being the delivery of fast food; obviously, the ancillary product is the food.

The literature indicates that rather than having a unitary definition of quality, it is important to identify the dimensions of quality. In a seminal 1984 article, David Garvin identified eight dimensions of product quality: **performance**, **features**, **reliability**, **conformance**, **durability**, **serviceability**, **aesthetics**, and **perceived quality**.[42] Table 13.1 describes what these dimensions mean and gives examples. Garvin recognized that no consumer will find all eight dimensions equally important. However, to ensure success, a business must identify which of the eight dimensions are important to its customers. As an example, if we are dealing with a product such as a heart pacemaker, customers would be most interested in the reliability and durability dimensions of that product. If a customer is buying a car for street drag racing only, then that person's focus would be on the performance dimensions of the vehicle.

TABLE 13.1   The Eight Dimensions of Product Quality

Dimension	Characteristics	Examples
Performance	The primary measurable operating characteristics of a product.	The following outcomes for each category are of greatest importance to consumers: ■ **Car.** Miles per gallon or acceleration time to go from 0 to 60 miles per hour ■ **Light bulb.** Wattage ■ **Laptop computer.** Amount of memory or speed of processor ■ **Copier.** Pages per minute or cost per page
Features	The secondary operating characteristics of a product.	The following outcomes for each category may not be initially seen as critical but often influence the purchasing decision of a consumer: ■ **Car.** Comfort of ride or the number of cupholders ■ **Light bulb.** The shade of light given off ■ **Laptop computer.** Size or brightness of the screen ■ **Copier.** Ease of use
Reliability	The probability that a product will function for a given period of time or how often it breaks down. This is most often measured by the mean time between failures (MTBF). This is the expectation of how long a product is expected to last.	■ **Light bulb.** Expected lifetime ■ **Electric watch.** Time between replacing batteries ■ **Copier.** Time between replacing toner cartridge or printer drum
Conformance	The extent to which a product matches established standards. This is viewed by many as the critical component of quality and is the basis of statistical process control.	■ **Car.** How well replacement parts match original equipment manufacturer components ■ **Laptop computer.** Voltage measurements

performance

The primary measurable operating characteristics of a product.

features

The secondary operating characteristics of a product.

reliability (product)

The probability that a product will function for a given period of time or how often it breaks down.

conformance

The extent to which a product matches established standards.

durability

The expectation of how long a product will last and how it will function under various working conditions.

serviceability

The speed, competence, and courtesy of repairs or maintenance of a product.

aesthetics

How a product looks, feels, sounds, tastes, or smells.

perceived quality

The concept of quality most influenced by brand names, advertising, and commonly held perceptions concerning a product.

Dimension	Characteristics	Examples
Durability	The expectation of how long a product will last and how it will function under various working conditions. This dimension refers to how well a product lasts over time and under different environments.	■ **Car.** Expected lifetime of engine or tires; how a car functions under temperature extremes ■ **Laptop computer.** Functionality after being dropped
Serviceability	The speed, competence, and courtesy of repairs or maintenance of a product. This dimension corresponds to the ancillary service component of products.	■ **Car.** The conduct of scheduled maintenance or repairs ■ **Laptop computer.** Speed of return to computer after repairs; intact files after repair
Aesthetics	This is how a product looks, feels, sounds, tastes, or smells. This is the most subjective of the eight dimensions. This dimension means that it is extremely important to consider design issues with respect to any product.	■ **Car.** The attractiveness of the exterior style of the vehicle; the luxuriousness of the dashboard ■ **Laptop computer.** Stylish exterior; unique colors; uniqueness of its operations, such as a new type of input device
Perceived quality	Consumers often do not have direct evidence of objective measures of a product's quality—both tangible and intangible measures. This concept of quality is most influenced by brand names, advertising, and commonly held perceptions concerning a product. Powerful brands often provide the perception that a product is of higher quality.	■ **Car.** Rolls-Royce: finest quality car produced and commands a premium price ■ **Aspirin.** Compare prices for same number of tablets: generic bottle versus brand name version—price difference due to perceived quality.

SERVQUAL

A market research instrument that plays a prominent role in improving quality in service environments.

Another approach to examining quality, this time in the service context, is to explicitly consider quality as a comparison between a customer's expectations and a customer's perception of performance. Parasuraman, Zeithaml, and Berry argued in their 1985 seminal article that there were ten determinants (dimensions) of service quality: reliability, responsiveness, competence, access, courtesy, communication, credibility, security, knowing the customer, and tangibles.[43] After some major research, they reduced this set to five dimensions: **tangibles, reliability, responsiveness, assurance,** and **empathy**.[44] Again, it is critical to note that customers will not view all five dimensions as equally important. In fact, the relative rank of these dimensions may differ significantly across industries. The approach of Zeithaml et al. has become well known as the **SERVQUAL** instrument, and it plays a prominent role in improving quality in service environments. The five service quality dimensions are given in Table 13.2. This SERVQUAL system explains the notion that quality is associated with a gap between expectations and perceptions. It identifies the following five types of gaps that a service organization should examine and attempt to minimize:

1. The gap between what customers expect and what a business believes are its customers' expectations

2. The gap between a business's evaluation of its own performance and how its customers evaluate its performance

3. The gap between a customer's experience and a business's specified level of performance

4. The gap between the communicated level of service by a business and what a customer actually experiences

5. The gap between a customer's expectation and actual experience.

From looking at these five gaps, it should be obvious that a full utilization of the SERVQUAL instrument is quite a challenge and might be beyond the capacity of most small businesses. That does not mean, however, that a business interested in providing its customers with quality service cannot apply some of the elements of the SERVQUAL instrument or use it as a conceptual template.

TABLE 13.2 The Dimensions of Service Quality

Dimension	Characteristics	Examples
Tangibles	The physical appearance of the facility, personnel, and communications media.	The first thing customers notice is appearances. This may involve the cleanliness of a facility, how brightly lit it is, the width of the aisles, or how personnel are dressed. A cheaply designed website may convey a totally inappropriate message about a business. It should be remembered that a business has only one chance to make a first impression. At its start, McDonald's emphasized not speed of service but the cleanliness of its facilities.
Reliability	The ability to perform the service correctly and consistently.	Reliability means performing the service correctly each and every time. One failure with a customer may destroy his or her faith in the capability of a business. FedEx emphasizes its guarantee to get a package there overnight—*each and every time*. An accounting firm must make sure that its clients' tax returns are done properly and submitted on time.
Responsiveness	The speed and courtesy to customer inquiries.	A customer who is put on "hold" for any length of time is on the path to becoming an ex-customer. This dimension requires all personnel to be well mannered and focus on the needs of the customer. Disney trains its park staff to recognize that they are not responding for the sixtieth time to the same inquiry; they are responding for the first time to the sixtieth individual who is asking that question.
Assurance	The extent to which the customer trusts and has confidence in the service provider.	A medical facility's survival depends on its customers' belief that they are receiving excellent medical care. The same is true for any professional service. Trust is built over time and is a fragile commodity.
Empathy	The extent and quality of individualized attention given to a customer.	Empathy should be thought of in terms of a doctor's "bedside manner." Customers want to be thought of as individuals, not as numbers. Businesses should avoid using preprinted labels on envelopes because this clearly conveys the image of a mass mailing.

tangibles

The physical appearance of a facility, the personnel, and communications media.

reliability (service)

The ability to perform the service correctly and consistently.

responsiveness

The speed and courtesy to customer inquiries.

assurance

The extent to which a customer trusts and has confidence in the service provider.

empathy

The extent of the quality of individualized attention given to a customer.

When using the term *quality management*, we should recognize that there is no universally consistent notion of how one can produce quality products and services. In fact, the quality management movement has been evolving for nearly a century. Perhaps the best way of tracing this evolution is to examine the contributions of some of the key proponents of quality. One of the first bodies of work that should be reviewed is that of Walter A. Shewhart (1891–1967). Similar to two other "quality gurus"—W. Edwards Deming and Joseph Juran (the authors are hesitant to use the term *guru* because this might question the true value of the work of these individuals)—Shewhart worked for Western Electric Company, a division of AT&T.[45] There he developed what is now known as **statistical process control (SPC)**, a mathematical approach that measures how well products conform to previously determined standards. The goal here is to develop a control chart that would enable an operator to distinguish between the random change associated with any manufacturing process and specifically assignable causes of such change. As an example, a machine produces 0.25-inch diameter bolts. Not all the manufactured bolts will be exactly 0.25 inches in diameter. There will be some natural variation around this value. Rather than test the diameter of every bolt, in SPC, a sample of bolts is tested on a regular basis. Based on statistical analysis, one can determine if this sample is within acceptable limits around the 0.25-inch value. If a sample is not within these acceptable limits, then the machine is shut down, and every effort is made to determine the assignable cause—faulty materials, machine error, or operator error. The benefit of this approach is that one can determine, with a high degree of accuracy, the operational characteristics of the system without the expense of testing every item produced. A full discussion of all aspects of SPC is beyond the focus of this text.

statistical process control (SPC)

A mathematical approach that measures how well products conform to previously determined standards.

PDCA cycle

A series of steps to ensure continuous improvement.

Shewhart's two books, *Economic Control of Quality of Manufactured Product*[46] and *Statistical Method from the Viewpoint of Quality Control*,[47] are still available in print and are viewed as the foundation works in the field.

Shewhart also made major contributions in the way we think about implementing a quality program in any organization. He advocated a systematic approach structured in four cyclical phases. This approach is sometimes referred to as the **PDCA cycle** (see Figure 13.3) or the Deming cycle. (Yet the Deming cycle is an improper name for the PDCA cycle.) The PDCA cycle calls for a cycle of continuous improvement. The first step is to *plan* for a change that would lead to improvement. The planning process requires data collection to make a decision. Regardless of the approach to quality management, all decision making must be data driven. The second step in the cycle is the *do* phase. This entails implementing the change. It also implies that a business will implement that change on an experimental basis, meaning that the organization would run a pilot program rather than implementing it throughout the entire organization. The third phase of the cycle is *check*. This means that after a sufficient period of time following the initial implementation phase, the results are evaluated to ascertain if the change produced the desired effect. If that answer is positive, then the organization moves onto the fourth stage of the cycle (*act*), where the changes are implemented throughout the entire organization. At the end of the *act* phase, the process is repeated with respect to some new problem area.

FIGURE 13.3 The PDCA Cycle

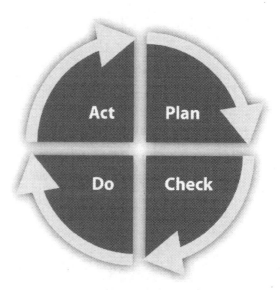

The two other quality gurus who worked with Shewhart at Western Electric Company, as previously mentioned, were Joseph Juran and W. Edwards Deming. Juran's numerous contributions to the field include the first standard reference work in the field of quality management: *The Quality Control Handbook*.[48] He also developed the Juran Trilogy, an approach to quality management that involves three phases: quality control, quality improvement, and quality planning.

Deming was born in 1900 and received an engineering degree from the University of Wyoming and a doctorate from Yale University. During his career, he worked for Western Electric Company, Bell Labs, and the US Department of Agriculture. During the Second World War, he taught SPC methods to thousands of engineers and plant personnel. After the war, Deming worked in Japan with Douglas McArthur's Office of Supreme Command of Allied Powers. Several years later, he returned to Japan and worked with Japanese scientists and engineers and taught them about SPC. Deming's work with the Japanese improved his understanding of what must transpire in a business organization to ensure quality products and services.[49] The Japanese recognized his accomplishments by creating the Deming Prize, which is awarded to organizations that exemplify a commitment to quality.

Many consider Deming as the world's preeminent proponent of quality. In fact, many see him as one of the most important business thinkers of the twentieth century. In a November 1999 issue, *Fortune* identified Deming, along with Peter Drucker and Frederick Taylor, as three individuals who had more impact on the operations of businesses than any CEO. In its April 22, 1991, edition, *US News & World Report* covered nine important turning points in human history. The final point was Deming's impact on the Japanese quality movement.[50]

What distinguishes Deming from all other quality theorists is his comprehensiveness known as **the Deming method**. It has been stated that Deming proposed an alternative philosophy of doing business. He argued that one should believe that the purpose of a business is to delight a customer. If customers are delighted, then profits will follow. The Deming philosophy was summarized in his fourteen points, which are given in Table 13.3.

the Deming method

The philosophy and the techniques to ensure quality that were enunciated by W. Edwards Deming.

TABLE 13.3 Deming's Fourteen Points

#	Point	Explanation
1	Create constancy of purpose toward improvement of product and service, with the aim to become competitive and to stay in business, and to provide jobs.	Deming believed that a firm must have a strong future focus. It should be willing to innovate all areas of operations, services, and products with the purpose of improvement and corresponding cost reduction. It must be willing on all levels to invest in these activities.
2	Adopt the new philosophy. We are in a new economic age. Western management must awaken to the challenge, must learn their responsibilities, and take on leadership for change.	Businesses can no longer accept given levels of errors, defects, and mistakes. This means that a small business must challenge its own beliefs about acceptable levels of failure.
3	Cease dependence on inspection to achieve quality. Eliminate the need for inspection on a mass basis by building quality into the product in the first place.	Inspecting 100 percent of the finished goods produced by a business is wasteful, costly, and without purpose. A business should focus on evaluating every process that is used to produce the product or the service. Using SPC and sampling will achieve better results than 100 percent inspection at a far lower cost. See Section 4.
4	End the practice of awarding business on the basis of price tag. Instead, minimize total cost. Move toward a single supplier for any one item, on the long-term relationship of loyalty and trust.	Low price has no meaning if a customer is buying poor quality. It is better to find a business that can ensure the quality of the goods (or services) rather than attempting to play off several suppliers to achieve a lower price. In Chapter 11, this is a central tenet.
5	Improve constantly and forever the system of production and service, to improve quality and productivity, and thus constantly decrease cost.	The focus of a quality management program should be on processes rather than merely looking at outcomes. The goal is to consistently improve these processes. This will result in lower cost and better utilization of labor.
6	Institute training on the job.	A training program should recognize that people learn in different ways. The training program should be tailored to the learning style of the employees. The central focus of any training program throughout an organization should be to make employees aware of the problems associated with variation.
7	Institute leadership. The aim of supervision should be to help people and machines and gadgets to do a better job. Supervision of management is in need of an overhaul, as well as supervision of production workers.	Businesses have little trouble finding managers and supervisors; the problem is finding leaders. Leadership involves a deep and thorough understanding of the work that is to be done. Leaders provide the vision to employees that enable them to carry out their work with pride.
8	Drive out fear, so that everyone may work effectively for the company.	Fear is often systemic in organizations. It could be the fear of losing one's job. It can be the fear of making a mistake. It could be the fear of displeasing a supervisor. In all cases, this fear prevents employees from taking an initiative and being innovative. In the long run, this can be fatal for any organization.
9	Break down barriers between departments. People in research, design, sales, and production must work as a team, to foresee problems of production and in use that may be encountered with the product or service.	If people in different functional areas of a business do not know what the others are doing, they cannot adopt the perspective that focuses on what is good for the business at large. They focus on only what is good for their silo. A failure to understand the duties and responsibilities of people in other segments of the business means that people engage in finger-pointing rather than aggressively attempting to solve problems on a system-wide basis.
10	Eliminate slogans, exhortations, and targets for the workforce asking for zero defects and new levels of productivity. Such exhortations only create adversarial relationships, as the bulk of the causes of low quality and low productivity belong to the system and thus lie beyond the power of the work force.	Exhorting people to work harder is pointless if there are fundamental flaws or problems with the system they are working in. People recognize this and resent it. It makes them doubt the sincerity and intelligence of management.

#	Point	Explanation
11	a. Eliminate work standards (quotas) on the factory floor. Substitute leadership. b. Eliminate management by objective. Eliminate management by numbers, numerical goals. Substitute leadership.	Work standards that do not include a quality component may be detrimental to the operation of a business. Refer to the example at the beginning of this chapter. The second student was superior on the measure of the number of schedules sorted per hour; however, the students who received the wrong schedule would take a dim view of the capability of the college. Deming feels that this holds true for not only production workers but also management. Using the wrong set of numbers that drive the business may drive the business into insolvency.
12	a. Remove barriers that rob the hourly paid worker of his right to pride in workmanship. The responsibility of supervisors must be changed from sheer numbers to quality. b. Remove barriers that rob people in management and engineering of their right to pride in workmanship. This means, inter alia, abolishment of the annual or merit rating and management by objective.	Employees who do not have a chance for some dignity associated with their work are unlikely to take pride in their work. Pride forces individuals to perform tasks correctly and spot errors. Pride should foster individual initiative to improve processes and quality.
13	Institute a vigorous program of education and self-improvement.	Training programs should be available for all levels of employees. Training should not be limited to short-term outcomes; it should focus on providing a deep understanding of the key processes of a business.
14	Put everybody in the company to work to accomplish the transformation. The transformation is everybody's job.	Quality should never be seen as the responsibility of management or a specialized group, such as quality assurance. It is everyone's job.

Source: W. Edwards Deming, Out of Crisis (Cambridge, MA: MIT Press, 1982), 23–24.

The last quality theorist who should be discussed is Philip Crosby. Crosby was an executive at ITT and the Martin Company. His approach to quality reflected a practicing manager's perspective. Although he is often associated (correctly) with the zero-defect program, his great contribution can be found in his first book *Quality Is Free*.[51] In this text, Crosby argued that the definition of quality should be based on conformance to quality, and nonconformance is highly expensive. He estimates that the cost of nonconformance can run as high as 30 percent of revenue.[52] This figure includes costs associated with rework, scrap, warranties, lost goodwill, reputation, and customers. He further argues that expenditures on quality to guarantee conformance to requirements will always be less than the cost of nonconformance; therefore, quality should be seen as being free. Crosby was embraced by many American executives because of his emphasis on the practical and his formal acknowledgment of the importance of the bottom line. His approach is often referred to as **Total Quality Management**.

Implementing quality management concepts in American business has had a long and somewhat checkered history. In the last four decades, total quality and continuous quality movements have blossomed in popularity and then quickly died. Two decades ago, Walter Lareau argued that many American businesses, particularly large businesses, have an almost pathological antipathy toward quality management because some of its (quality) fundamental principles run totally counter to corporate belief systems, namely, customers are a pain and employees are an even bigger pain.[53] In the intervening time, however, it appears that one approach to quality has captured the imagination of many businesses—both large and small. This quality program is known as **Six Sigma**.

Although Six Sigma is often associated, at least in the public's mind, with General Electric, it began at Motorola in the 1980s and was spearheaded by William Smith.[54] The term *sigma* (σ) comes from SPC and represents the concept of the **standard deviation**. Six standard deviations away from specifications signify that the process produces only 3.4 defects per million opportunities. This is a remarkable accomplishment. Imagine a restaurant that is open 12 hours a day, 365 days per year. On average, the restaurant serves 1 meal every 55 seconds or about 800 meals per day. It would take them approximately 3.4 years to serve one million meals. So if this restaurant was operating at a Six Sigma level, it would make a mistake in taking an order *only once a year*. Six Sigma draws on a battery of tools and techniques derived from SPC and earlier quality management programs. Six Sigma's mantra for

total quality management

A catchall term that covers a variety of methods and approaches to improve organizational quality.

Six Sigma

A quality management program created by the Motorola Corporation that seeks to reduce defects to the Six Sigma level, which translates as no more than 3.4 defects per million parts.

standard deviation

A statistical measure of dispersal about the mean. It is used in SPC models.

continuous improvement involves what is referred to as the *DMAIC* cycle (see Figure 13.4), where D stands for design, M stands for measurement, A stands for analyze, I stands for improve, and C stands for control. Clearly, this concept is derived from the Shewhart cycle.

FIGURE 13.4 The DMAIC Cycle

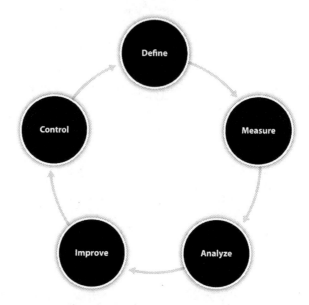

What was different about the Six Sigma program was that all these tools and techniques were packaged in a coherent program. There was a heavy emphasis on quick results and the ability to demonstrate to management tangible cost savings. Six Sigma involves committed training programs that promote statistical tools and management techniques. Graduates of the most basic certification training program are referred to as "green belts," a term derived from the martial arts. Those who receive more advanced training are known as "black belts."[55] Given that Six Sigma is closely associated with large corporate entities and complex training programs, one might think that it would be irrelevant for smaller enterprises. Nothing could be further from the truth. Six Sigma offers a systematic and pragmatic approach for quality improvement in the smaller firm.[56]

 Video Clip 13.5

Six Sigma—The Essence Of
An overview of Six Sigma and a discussion of how organizations use it.

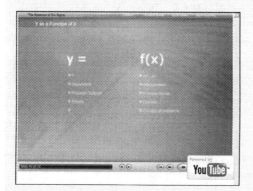

View the video online at: http://www.youtube.com/v/Z6stEYP25Fg

Video Clip 13.6

Pizza Anyone? Six Sigma DMAIC Strategy Introduction
Explains Six Sigma's DMAIC strategy in simple, nontechnical terms using the familiar setting of a pizza restaurant business.

View the video online at: http://www.youtube.com/v/PesZs-DwgXE

 Video Clip 13.7

Six Sigma Interview with Jack Welch
Jack Welch, former CEO of General Electric, talks about implementing Six Sigma at General Electric.

View the video online at: http://www.youtube.com/v/aNMULFcLuIM

Web Resources

PDCA Cycle

A description of the Shewhart cycle.

asq.org/learn-about-quality/project-planning-tools/overview/pdca-cycle.html

Deming's Fourteen Points

Discusses Deming's fourteen points and includes links to allied topics.

leanandkanban.wordpress.com/2011/07/15/demings-14-points

Seven Basic Quality Tools

These seven tools get to the heart of implementing quality principles.

asq.org/learn-about-quality/seven-basic-quality-tools/overview/overview.html

Seven New Management and Planning Tools

Ways to promote innovation, communicate information, and successfully plan major projects.

asq.org/learn-about-quality/quality-tools.html

KEY TAKEAWAYS

- Quality for manufactured goods may be defined by using the eight dimensions of product quality.
- Quality in services may be defined by using the five dimensions of service quality.
- Quality should be seen as a continuing cycle (PDCA) of improvement.
- Quality guru W. Edwards Deming offers a complete philosophy of quality management in the workplace.
- The costs of quality improvements are always less than the costs of poor quality; hence quality is free.
- Six Sigma is a modern and highly practical approach to quality improvements.

EXERCISES

1. Take the eight dimensions of product quality and rank them in terms of relative importance for the following products: a heart pacemaker, a minivan, a laptop computer for high school students, an army assault rifle, an office copy machine, a light bulb, a jet engine, and a pocket lighter.
2. Take the five dimensions of service quality and rank them in terms of relative importance for the following services: a bank, a college classroom, a walk-in clinic, a divorce lawyer's office, a cell phone service, a credit card company, a financial advisor, and a computer repair company.
3. Assume that your college or university suddenly decided to fully accept the Deming philosophy. How would it have to change? What do you think would be the first change that a student would notice? How would a particular course change if an instructor adopted the Deming philosophy?

4. GOING LEAN

LEARNING OBJECTIVES

1. Understand the basic logic of lean thinking.
2. Understand the sources of waste for a manufactured product.
3. Understand the sources of waste for a service.
4. Learn about the five Ss of lean.

Waste is worse than loss. The time is coming when every person who lays claim to ability will keep the question of waste before him constantly. The scope of thrift is limitless. [57]
- *Thomas A. Edison*

The most dangerous kind of waste is the waste we do not recognize. [58]
- *Shigeo Shingo*

lean thinking

A management approach that seeks to eliminate all forms of waste from operations.

Another organization-wide movement that has become popular at a global level during the last two decades is the concept of **lean thinking**. This concept was first introduced to American businesspeople in the book *The Machine That Changed the World: The Story of Lean Production—Toyota's Secret Weapon in the Global Car Wars That Is Now Revolutionizing World Industry.* [59] This book focused on the global automobile industry. It highlighted the significant differences in productivity between Japanese firms, Toyota in particular, and their American and European rivals. At the time the book was written, Toyota was half the size of General Motors; today, on a global basis, Toyota is larger than General Motors. The book highlighted the approach adopted by Toyota, which is, as articulated by Taiichi Ohno, its developer, centered on "the absolute elimination of waste."

Although lean is most closely associated with Toyota, its central principles are applicable for any small and midsize enterprise. Audubon Media Corporation is a publisher of cookbooks. It adopted a program that included a variety of lean techniques. In a two-year period, it increased sales by 25 percent without increasing staffing, reduced lead time by at least 50 percent, and increased available floor space by 20 percent through inventory reduction and more efficient redesign. Corporate Image, a manufacturer of packaging, adopted lean methods and reduced lead times by over 35 percent and reduced costs by nearly $180,000 in one year. [60]

Lean thinking is predicated on five major principles. [61] The first principle can be summarized as follows: *know who your customers are and know how they define value.* This principle coincides nicely with the underlying philosophy of the quality movement, namely, placing the customer first. Without understanding what the customer wants and what the customer values, an organization runs the risk of producing a wasteful quantity of goods and services that the customer does not want or need.

The second principle of lean thinking centers on *determining and visualizing the value stream*. The **value stream** is the entire set of activities associated with the production of goods and services. The goal of such mapping is to identify any and all activities that provide no value to the customer. Once those nonvalue activities have been identified, they are to be eliminated. Students are required, every semester, to go to their advisor and begin the process to register for the next semester or prepare for graduation. Imagine mapping out every step in that process. Having done that, colleges and universities could probably find some steps or activities that do not add value. In a lean operation, those steps would be eliminated. One could also think in terms of the process that most patients face when going to some type of medical facility. They are often required to fill out multiple forms that require the same information. In Figure 13.5, we provide an example of a value stream map for the process of supplying hospitals with blood.

value stream

The entire set of activities associated with the production of goods and services.

FIGURE 13.5 Value Stream Map for Supplying Hospitals with Blood

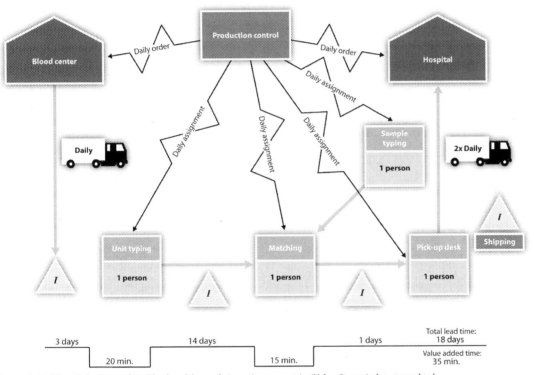

Source: Derived from Value Stream, http://facultyweb.berry.edu/jgrout/processmapping/Value_Stream/value_stream.html

The third principle of lean thinking argues that every effort should be made to *make the remaining steps flow*. The term *flow* here refers to the notion that from design to delivery to the customer, all steps and activities should be structured in such a way that there will be minimal or nonexistent downtime, waste, or waiting within or between the steps.[62] This is perhaps the most challenging of all the five principles of lean thinking. To make operations flow in a seamless manner often requires substantive changes in production and service processes. In fact, it may require substantive changes to the structure of a business.

The fourth principle involves a **pull system** *triggered by customer needs*. The term *pull* means that the production of goods and services is triggered by customer demand. This aspect of lean is what is commonly referred to as just-in-time inventory. The central idea is that the entire value stream is fired up only by customer demand. Thus inventory throughout the system is minimized.

pull system

The production of the goods and services are triggered by customer demand.

The fifth and last principle is *pursuing perfection*. This clearly shows that lean thinking is not totally separate and divorced from the concepts of total quality management or Six Sigma. This last principle advocates that removing the impediments to quality will mean a significant reduction in waste. Like Crosby's work, lean advocates often talk of striving for zero defects.

One of the first steps in any lean program is identifying where waste exists within the system. Taiichi Ohno and Shigeo Shingo, the two cofounders of the Toyota Production System, identified seven possible sources of waste: **transportation, inventory, motion, waiting, overprocessing, overproduction,** and **defects.** (A nice mnemonic to remember these seven sources is TIM WOOD.) Table 13.4 identifies and gives examples of the original seven sources of waste used throughout Toyota.

transportation waste

The movement of components and parts that is not associated with their transformation.

inventory waste

Materials not being actively used to meet customer demand represent a waste of capital.

motion waste

Unnecessary motion by employees and equipment.

waiting waste

Components or products not being processed.

overprocessing waste

A component or a product that requires more time to process than the standard estimate.

overproduction waste

Producing more than a customer wants at a particular point in time.

defects waste

The waste and expense of producing defects.

TABLE 13.4 Seven Sources of Manufacturing Wastes

Type of Waste	Description	Examples
Transportation	The movement of components and parts not associated with their transformation. Unnecessary movement (that which is not required by the customer) runs the risk of damage.	When looking for suppliers, Toyota takes into consideration their proximity to its production plants. Toyota plants are designed so that suppliers can bring their items directly to where they will be used on the factory floor.
Inventory	The three types of inventory—raw materials, work in process, and finished goods—are all forms of investment. When these inventories are not being actively used to meet customer demand, they represent a waste of capital.	Just-in-time inventory strives to produce inventory according to the demand of the customer. Every effort is made to smooth production processes so that there is no need to produce any component in bulk quantities. Many restaurants cook meals only when ordered by the customer. This minimizes leftovers.
Motion	This term refers to employees and equipment, not components or products. Unnecessary motion is a waste of time and money. Like transportation, it runs the risk of damage to the final product or the employees.	Excess movement by workers or machinery is to be avoided. Workers and equipment are positioned so that they are in close proximity and movements are minimized. Machines are sometimes grouped in a U-shape so that one worker can operate them with minimal movement.
Waiting	If components or products are not being processed, then there is waiting. This represents a waste of investment.	Eliminating this form of waste is the reason for the concept of "flow." Production processes need to be redesigned to minimize the time spent waiting. Special paints are used that dry quickly so that vehicles can move on to the next processing step without having to wait.
Overprocessing	A component or a product that requires more time to process than the standard estimate represents a waste. This concept also involves the notion that using inappropriate or excessively complex manufacturing processes or tools also represent a form of waste.	The essence here can be summarized by KISS—keep it simple, stupid. This is a well-known engineering principle whereby "less is more." The process can be accomplished with a simple machine preferable to a complex machine. Simplicity accomplishes the task, minimizes the chance for failure, and reduces waste. A classic example of this would be the engineers who were asked to determine the volume of a complex part. Some began by taking accurate measurements to compute the volume of some segments of the part. Another engineer simply tossed the part into a bucket of water and measured the volume of water displaced.
Overproduction	Producing more than the customer wants at a particular point in time is a source of waste. Some businesses have set up operations where they believe that production in large batches is the most economically efficient method. This generally means large inventory levels. Overproduction is seen by some as the driving force behind the other six sources of waste. Lean thinking tasks them to reexamine these basic assumptions.	A manufacturer has a good idea of the annual demand of a particular part. Setting up the machine that is used to produce this part is an expense proposition. Financial analysis indicates that the company should produce one batch of the part every quarter (three months' worth of supply). A three-month supply of the part means that a considerable portion sits in inventory for a long period of time. This quantity of inventory may also mask any defects in manufacturing. It would take quite a while to go through this batch before one would realize that the batch might have had problems in production. A company that focused on reducing the setup cost of the machine could then produce smaller batches, which, in turn, would produce lower inventory levels and therefore catch quality problems earlier.
Defects	Defects in products produce expensive waste—rework costs, scrapping costs, or excess warranty costs.	Here is where lean thinking and quality management merge. Poor quality of product and service represents a dramatic waste.

The continued references to the Toyota Production System might lead the reader to believe that lean thinking is appropriate only for the manufacturing environment. That would be profoundly misleading because lean has tremendous applicability to service, particularly in the areas of health care, banking, and retail. Some authors believe that these seven sources of waste are absolutely applicable to service environments.[63] Others have suggested that the original seven sources of manufacturing waste be modified to cover the service environment, as follows: delay, duplication, unnecessary motion, unclear communication, incorrect inventory, errors, and opportunity lost.[64] These seven sources and corresponding examples are described in Table 13.5.

TABLE 13.5 Seven Sources of Service Waste

Type of Waste	Description	Examples
Delay	Any instance in which a customer must wait for any aspect of the service.	One walks into a fast-food restaurant and finds a long queue (line). Any service time spent in that queue is a delay. Another example of the delay would be waiting on the phone to speak to a sales representative.
Duplication	When a customer has to repeat any activity unnecessarily.	Patients in a medical facility who have to repeatedly fill out forms would be an example of duplication. A website requires customer input of information, but then the website crashes, causing the customer to reinput the information is another example. Such instances are extremely annoying to most consumers.
Unnecessary motion	A customer who is shuttled between a variety of operations and where each move does not substantially add to value.	A customer wishes to lodge a complaint. The customer calls the complaint department and then is moved from one sales representative to another. This type of frustration may cause customers to drop the service.
Unclear communication	The failure to provide clear instructions for any stage of the service environment.	Unclear communication, particularly with respect to instructions to customers, is contained in the entire service experience. Examples would include instructions that are filled with jargon or that easily confuse customers.
Incorrect inventory	Services often have ancillary products. If a product is not available, the customer has to wait for it.	A customer places an online order for multiple items. At the time of the order, the customer is told that all the items are available and will be shipped at once. When the customer receives the order, not all the items are in the shipment, and some items are on backorder. "Murphy's Law" would dictate that the items on backorder are the ones the customer most wanted.
Errors	Any errors or mistakes associated with either the ancillary goods or the service itself.	Telling a customer that the repair service will arrive between 10 a.m. and 1 p.m. and then showing up at 4 p.m. is the type of error that few customers are willing to forgive or forget.
Opportunity lost	Every engagement with the customer in a service environment is an opportunity to succeed or fail. Failure can be associated with a bad behavioral interaction with the customer, ignorance about the service, or providing incorrect information to the customer.	Services differ from products in many ways. One of the most important is that quality services tend to be in real time. In manufacturing, one can test the product before it is shipped. This does not always occur in services. A few words from a rude clerk can describe the customer's vision of the company. Subsequent apologies may do nothing to erase this negative image. Providing customers with the wrong information, even about minor details, can also destroy their perception of a company.

Lean thinking uses several techniques to achieve its ends. We have mentioned **value stream** mapping. Other techniques include just-in-time inventory control, **quick changeover** (a program to reduce setup times to make it more attractive to produce in smaller batches), **Kaisen** (a Japanese term that refers to any program that seeks small improvements on a regular basis rather than a huge quality initiative), and **visual management** (a program of visually presenting key metrics to all personnel so that they can be aware of any and all progress). One technique that has broad application in both manufacturing and service environments is known as the 5 Ss. The five Ss refer to Japanese terms for, in effect, housekeeping.[65] The five Ss, which together strive for simplicity and neatness to improve efficiency and effectiveness, are as follows:

- **Seiei or organization.** Only those tools and equipment that are absolutely needed are available at any one time. All other equipment is stored away until needed.

- **Seiton or orderliness.** Every part is in its correct place. The Japanese use pegboards to store tools. They sometime draw an outline of the tool on the board so that it is returned to its correct place.

- **Seiso or cleanliness.** Work environments are kept immaculate. This is done to reinforce the notion of perfect. Some factory floors are painted white so that anything dropped or any litter becomes immediately apparent.

---

delay

In services, this corresponds to the waiting waste concept.

duplication

Anytime a customer must repeat any activity unnecessarily.

unnecessary motion

A customer is shuttled between a variety of operations and where each move does not substantially add to value.

unclear communication

The failure to provide clear instructions for any stage of a service.

incorrect inventory

A product is not available to the customer, causing the customer to wait for it.

errors

In services, this corresponds to defects.

opportunity lost

An engagement with the customer to a service environment that is a failure.

quick changeover

A program to reduce setup times to make it more attractive to produce in smaller batches.

Kaisen

A Japanese term that refers to any program that seeks small improvements on a regular basis rather than a huge quality initiative.

visual management

A program where key metrics are presented visually to all personnel so they can be aware of any and all progress.

- **Seitetsu or standardized cleanup.** This is a reinforcement of the prior three points. Starting in Japanese kindergartens, children are required to clean their classroom—together—before they are released to go home.
- **Shitsuke or discipline.** A program to adhere to set procedures because of pride in one's own work.

More and more businesses are realizing that lean thinking and quality are not two distinct management approaches but two extremely complementary models. One finds more and more references to a concept known as Lean Six Sigma, which is a program that combines aspects of both lean thinking and quality management. It recognizes that lean by itself cannot bring processes under control, and Six Sigma significantly reduces process time or capital investment.[66] Both approaches offer benefits to small businesses that cannot be ignored if these businesses want to remain viable in an increasingly competitive world.

 Video Clip 13.8

Lean Process Improvement—Funny
A silent comedy to illustrate lean principles.

View the video online at: http://www.youtube.com/v/CJSZj9bShAI

 Video Clip 13.9

Building a Lean Culture
Lean requires change throughout an organization.

View the video online at: http://www.youtube.com/v/AlETNIjBzmU

Video Clip 13.10

Lean Office: Applying Lean to Business Processes
Lean is not limited to manufacturing but can be applied to office management.

View the video online at: http://www.youtube.com/v/cLys-mCSHFQ

Web Resources

Introduction to Lean

A great introduction to lean concepts by a consulting firm.

www.leanthinking.info/aboutlean.html

Glossary of Lean Tools

Definitions of key terms.

www.shopwerkssoftware.com/lean_glossary.aspx

Bringing "Lean" Principles to Service Industries

The application of lean concepts to the service environment.

hbswk.hbs.edu/item/5741.html

Achieving a "Lean Service" Breakthrough

An example of lean concepts applied to the service environment.

www.stratform.com/lean_services.htm

KEY TAKEAWAYS

- Lean thinking represents a program to eliminate all forms of waste in an organization.
- For any production or service process, one could map out all the currently existing steps and then remove those that do not add value to the customer.
- There are seven sources of waste in manufacturing processes.
- There are seven sources of waste in service processes.

EXERCISES

1. Interview several local small business owners about how they try to minimize waste.
2. Pick a particular college course you are currently taking and identify sources of waste in that class. How could you redesign that college class to minimize those wastes?
3. Discuss how the 5 Ss approach could be used in your personal life to improve efficiency and effectiveness.

5. PERSONNEL EFFICIENCY

LEARNING OBJECTIVES

1. Understand the importance of meetings.
2. Understand why meetings fail.
3. Understand the importance of an agenda.
4. Learn about behavioral issues in meetings.

If you had to identify, in one word, the reason why the human race has not achieved, and never will achieve, its full potential, that word would be "meetings."[67]
  - *Dave Barry*

Meetings are indispensable when you don't want to do anything.[68]
  - *John Kenneth Galbraith*

5.1 Managing Meetings

As a business grows, it will—in all probability—increase the number of its employees. As the employee base grows, there is increased demand to coordinate activities, exchange information, and engage in decision-making activities. These usually occur at meetings, and one would think that these would be straightforward events. Yet the reality is that many managers and employees come to dread participation at meetings. Data indicate that many, if not most, meetings fail to produce the desired outcome. A study conducted in 1993 found that executives were seen as a spending seventeen hours per week in meetings, and one-third felt that time was wasted.[69] Another survey of thirty-eight thousand managers found that 66 percent felt that the meetings they attend were a waste of time.[70] Still another study found that managers spend as much as 40 percent of their work time in meetings, but only 64 percent of those meetings were seen as achieving their intended outcome;[71] another study found that executives were spending as much as 70 percent of their time at meetings, but only 40 percent of those meetings had clear objectives, and only 28 percent of those meetings with objectives actually met them.[72] Yet 80 percent of the participants viewed running a successful meeting as a crucial test of manager's abilities.[73] These figures are particularly tragic because so many meetings occur in the business world. One estimate puts the number of meetings, on a daily basis, globally, at 73 million.[74] These are rather depressing figures, but the clear lesson for small business owners is that they cannot afford the luxury of not running their meetings effectively.

The good news is that the successful management of a meeting is a learnable skill.[75] Conducting an effective meeting requires that a manager focus on both procedural and behavioral issues. We will first look at procedural issues associated with running a meeting. Before considering holding a meeting, ask the following question: "Is this meeting really necessary?" Frequent meetings are sometimes held merely out of habit.[76] Can the goals of a meeting be achieved by other mechanisms?[77] These might include using the Internet; e-mail; teleconferencing; or technologies, such as MS Communicator, which allows for bulletin board interaction, voice communication, and videoconferencing. Interestingly, for all the complaints about meetings, a recent study indicated that face-to-face meetings were seen by 95 percent of those surveyed as being positive, especially in the interest of developing long-term relationships.[78]

After deciding that a meeting is necessary, it is important to determine the nature of that meeting. Meetings may have many different types of goals. They can be directed to problem solving, decision making, conflict resolution, providing information, or generating new ideas.[79] This is necessary because the nature of the meeting will drive its structure and internal dynamics. As an example, if a meeting is directed to a decision-making task, it should probably proceed in two parts. The first portion should be directed toward identifying solutions, while the second portion should focus on what might be the best solution.[80] The next decision would be to determine who will participate in the meeting. Ideally, this list would be limited to those who would be directly affected by the outcome of the meeting; however, in the case of informational meetings, the list may be expanded to those who will be directly or indirectly affected. The next decision is associated with determining who will be assigned particular roles in the meeting. The chair is the individual who calls the meeting, provides the initial agenda, and specifies the purpose of the meeting. It may be useful to assign the role of facilitator to an individual. This neutral person can push the meeting along, particularly when conflict arises. It is desirable to have people trained as facilitators and rotate this position among facilitators.[81] Another important role is the individual who is officially assigned to take notes. The notes of the meeting should be written up and sent to all participants in the meeting within two business days. This position should also be rotated among the participants of the meeting. It also might be advisable to assign the role of timekeeper to an individual. The timekeeper has the task of limiting the amount of time spent on any-one agenda item to the previously agreed-on time frame.[82]

Perhaps the most important activity prior to the actual meeting is the proper structuring of an **agenda**. In another study, 75 percent of those surveyed said that a good agenda is critical for a success-ful meeting.[83] The agenda is the formal strategic plan for a meeting. It is the mechanism for ensuring that a meeting is focused on relevant topics. A failure to have a clear focus will guarantee that the parti-cipants will have a sense that nothing had been accomplished.[84] Focus stems from having everyone understand a meeting's purpose and what one intends to achieve.[85] Items on the agenda should be prioritized in terms of their importance, which is often done by allocating a specific amount of time to each agenda item.[86] Any and all resources that will be required for the meeting should be identified along with the individuals who are responsible for securing the resources. The roles of chair, timekeep-er, note taker, and facilitator (where possible) should be assigned in advance. The agenda should be sent out at least five business days before the meeting so that participants can gather the required in-formation. This timeline also allows for people to make suggestions for changing the agenda. It is also highly advisable to make it a policy that all participants arrive on time at the beginning of the meet-ing.[87]

Allowing individuals to contribute to the agenda will provide them with a sense that they are con-tributing.[88] In setting the timeline for the different items on the agenda, it is advisable that one allow for a few extra minutes at the end of the meeting to discuss how well the meeting went and how it could be improved.[89] These few moments should be expanded into a formal system. Assessing meet-ing effectiveness can be done through an external observer conducting an evaluation, focus groups, or surveys.[90] Figure 13.6 provides a format for a part of the overall agenda that addresses some of the previous suggestions. It is available as an agenda format wizard in Microsoft Word 2007.

agenda

A document the outlines the purpose, membership, and required resources for an upcoming meeting.

FIGURE 13.6 Agenda Format

Expansion Plans

6/26/2012
10:00 AM to 11:00 AM
Main Meeting Room

Meeting called by: Frank Rainsford	Type of meeting: Information and Decision Making
Facilitator: Frank Rainsford Timekeeper: Alice Jacobs	Note taker: Bill Rogers

Attendees:
F. Rainsford, R. Rainsford, J. Enders, A.Jacobs, L.Rogers, W. Rogers

Please read:
1. Real Estate Report for Darien Commercial Properties
2. Contractors Responses to Our RFP
3. Budget Estimate for Remodeling Properties
4. Gantt Chart for Remodeling Project

Please bring:
1. Personal Analysis of Real Estate Properties
2. Critiques of Contractors' Proposals
3. Critique of Budget for Remodeling

Agenda Topics		
Review of Available Properties	Jack Enders	15
Evaluation of Possible Contractors	Bill Rogers	15
Funding Requirements	Alice Jacobs	15
Develop Time Line for Next Stage	Lucy Rogers	15
Review	Frank Rainsford	5

Agenda Topics

Review of Available Properties	Jack Enders	15 minutes

Discussion: Review and critique possible commercial properties in Darien

Conclusions:

Action Items:	Person Responsible:	Deadline:
Final selection of property	Frank Rainsford 9/26/1012	

Evaluation of Possible Contractors	Bill Rogers	15

Discussion: Evaluate proposals to remodel commercial properties from the three contractors that provided responses to our RFP

Conclusions: Evaluate economic viability of all three proposals

Action Items:	Person Responsible:	Deadline:
Enter into negotiations with winning contractor	Frank and Robert Rainsford	10/15/2011

Funding Requirements	Alice Jacobs	15

Discussion: Review Budget estimates for Remodeling and purchase of new equipment

Conclusions: Evaluate accuracy of budget estimates

Action Items:	Person Responsible:	Deadline:
Review comments and revise budget estimates	Alice Jacobs	9/31/2012

Develop Time Line for Next Stage	Lucy Rogers	10

Discussion: Review Gantt Timeline for New Restaurant Project

Conclusions:

Action Items:	Person Responsible:	Deadline:

Develop Time Line for Next Stage	Lucy Rogers	10

Discussion: Review Gantt Chart time line for new restaurant project

Conclusions: Revise and resubmit

Action Items:	Person Responsible:	Deadline:
Generate revised Gantt Chart	Lucy Rogers	7/11/2011

Video Clip 13.11

Business Management and Leadership Skills: How to Conduct an Effective Meeting
The basics of meeting management.

View the video online at: http://www.youtube.com/v/FjCuLhgJBUE

 Video Clip 13.12

Conducting Effective Small Scale Meetings
How to conduct a meeting, even in one's home.

View the video online at: http://www.youtube.com/v/bFVcQU7rq7A

 Video Clip 13.13

How to Avoid Meetings That Suck
How to escape the traps behind bad meetings.

View the video online at: http://www.youtube.com/v/BVHIMxW6D8w

Web Resources

Managing Business Meetings

An excellent list of suggestions on business meetings.

www.cbsnews.com/8301-505125_162-51057051/managing-business-meetings/?tag=bnetdomain

Managing Your Meeting Monsters

Identifying the types of personalities at meetings.

www.impactfactory.com/p/business_meeting_skills_training_development/friends_111-1107-40530.html

KEY TAKEAWAYS

- Poorly run meetings are common and costly.
- Successful meetings require structure and an agenda.
- The agenda should identify the purpose of the meeting, the participants and their roles, the requisite resources, and agenda topics with timelines.
- Behavioral issues must always be considered when managing a meeting.

EXERCISES

1. Interview the owners of five businesses and determine what percentage of meetings they attend they find to be "effective."
2. Ask them what constitutes a *bad* meeting.
3. Ask them what constitutes a *good* meeting.
4. Create an agenda for a meeting with a fellow student who came up with an idea for a new business.

6. THE THREE THREADS

LEARNING OBJECTIVES

1. Understand that in addition to quality management and lean thinking, creativity, time management, and well-executed meetings can improve value to customers.
2. Understand that quality management and lean programs can produce significant increases in operational efficiency that increases positive cash flow.
3. Learn about computer tools that can improve time management, creativity, quality management, and lean operations.

When all think alike, then no one is thinking.[91]
   - *Walter Lippman*

6.1 Customer Value Implications

It should be clear that quality management and lean thinking have the notion of customer value at their cores. Both approaches actively incorporate needs and wants into the design of products and services and, even more importantly, into the design of the processes used to create these products and services. Regardless of what quality program one adopts for an organization, the issue of customer value is the single most important question. Lean thinking also recognizes the vital importance of first identifying the customer's notion of value so that any activity that does not add value is ruthlessly eliminated. As one article put it, "Lean enterprise never misses an opportunity to capture information about customers."[92]

The linkages between quality management, lean thinking, and customer value, therefore, should be obvious. What is less obvious is the connection between customer value and topics such as creativity, time management, and running meetings effectively. Nonetheless, indirect connections do exist. Without creativity, there will not be any new product development, and there will be no innovations in design, packaging, promotion, or distribution that can be so vital to the enhancement of value.

Owners, managers, supervisors, and employees who cannot manage their time effectively or efficiently will be unable to provide appropriate attention to improving customer value. Poorly run meetings are inefficient and degrade morale; neither is a recipe for enhancing customer value.

6.2   Cash-Flow Implications

The old saying "time is money" may be shopworn, but it is an absolute truism. Wasting time inexorably turns into a waste of money. Poor time management means that time is wasted, which costs the individual and the organization.

In a depressed economy, both large and small firms attempt to preserve cash flow by adopting a program of cost cutting. This often begins with laying off employees. However, this presents a rather significant problem. As Nancy Koehn, a business historian at Harvard business School, points out, "If demand picks up, you can't exploit it because you don't have the resources."[93] Lean thinking offers an alternative to cost cutting by reducing staff. Lean thinking, a focus on more intelligent cost-cutting, and the efficient use of all business resources have produced significant results, such as an 80 percent to a 90 percent reduction in inventory investment, an 80 percent to a 90 percent reduction in manufacturing lead times, a 50 percent reduction in space requirements, and a 50 percent reduction in material handling equipment. Such results translate into tremendous cost savings.[94]

Firms that have used the principles of the Toyota Production System have also found that they can achieve a 50 percent reduction in human effort and a 200 percent to a 500 percent improvement in quality. One small manufacturer, Gelman Sciences, adopted a lean approach to operations, and during a nine-month period, one section of the company saw inventory turns go from twenty to fifty-seven, inventory value dropped from $86,000 to $33,000, and lead time dropped from three to four weeks to one to three days.[95] Estee Bedding Company applied lean concepts to its operations and reduced its labor cost as a percentage of sales by one-half; Ameripay, a payroll service firm, saw sales increase from $1.8 million to $6 million in three years.[96] Some small businesses that are part of a larger supply change may find their movement toward lean thinking supported by firms that are further up the supply chain. In the 1990s, Pratt & Whitney initiated a program to assist smaller firms in its supply chain by requiring them to move to more of a lean focus.[97] Even small foreign firms are beginning to recognize the economic benefits from adopting lean methodologies. A polyvinyl chloride manufacturer in Thailand adopted a lean management program and saw its average production time per unit decline from forty-four minutes to twenty-three minutes while decreasing the number of operators from fifty to forty-one.[98] The concepts behind lean thinking, with its focus on efficiencies, should dictate that a small business should automate as many processes—such as bookkeeping—as possible and rely on outsourcing when feasible.[99]

One does not have to commit to major organizational programs, such as a quality management system or lean thinking, to find ways to save on cash flow. Earlier in this chapter we cited two studies. One said that better than one-third of executives believed that all meetings were a waste, while the second study said that two-thirds of all meetings were a waste. We split the difference between these two studies and arrive at a figure that one-half of all meetings are perceived as useless. This can have significant cash-flow implications, even for small firms.

Let us illustrate this through a simple example. The owner of a small hardware store believes it is important to have weekly meetings with the store's supervisor and five employees. Let us assume that the owner values his or her time at $70 per hour. The supervisor's value is given at $35 an hour, while each employee's time is valued at $10 per hour. Employees are expected to produce 2.5 times their pay. This means that a 1-hour meeting should be valued at $282.50 [$70/hour + 2.5 × (5 employees × $10/hour) + 2.5 × (1 supervisor × $35/hour)]. Assuming 52 meetings per year, the total opportunity cost for these meetings is $14,690. If one-half of those meetings are a waste, then the business is losing nearly $7,350 a year. There are many areas throughout a firm's operations that can be evaluated to reduce wasteful activities and improve its cash-flow position.

6.3   Implications of Technology and the E-Environment

Time-management systems are available in a variety of paper-and-pencil and software formats. They generally allow for listing to-do tasks, setting due dates, identifying required resources, and prioritizing their importance. Some allow for a project format, where one can break down the project into smaller interrelated tasks. Many of them provide the capability to synchronize this information across several computers and smartphones. This would allow a person to have the time-management system available on an office computer, a home computer, and in the pocket (smartphone). One system is based on Covey's fourth-generation approach to time management.

Multiple software packages are geared to assist individuals and groups who wish to improve their creativity. There are packages to help with brainstorming in its various forms. Numerous companies provide mind-mapping software in a variety of formats: computers, iPads, and even smartphones.

Quality management encompasses many tools and techniques, far more than could ever be covered in this chapter. There are packages geared just for statistical process control (SPC) models. Some can receive data from a process and then automatically inform the operator of a "drift" from conformance to standards. In addition to SPC models, other packages include tools that are used to improve quality. These packages range from less than $100 to many thousands of dollars.

Web Resources

Achieve

A time-management system.

www.effexis.com/achieve/planner.htm

My Life Organized

A time-management system.

www.mylifeorganized.net

PlanPlus for Outlook v7

A time-management system (based on Covey's fourth-generation time-management system).

franklincoveysoftware.com/individual/individual-products/planplus-for-outlook-v7

SciPlore

Mind-mapping software.

en.wikipedia.org/wiki/SciPlore_MindMapping

MindManager

Mind-mapping software.

en.wikipedia.org/wiki/MindManager

MindMaple

Mind-mapping software.

en.wikipedia.org/wiki/MindMaple

MindMapper

Mind-mapping software.

en.wikipedia.org/wiki/MindMapper

Creative Whack Pack

Brainstorming software app for the iPad.

itunes.apple.com/us/app/creative-whack-pack/id307306326?mt=8

Mind View 4

Brainstorming software.

www.matchware.com/mv3be_landing.php?gclid=CKyWyorEiasCFWUZQgodAQjG1Q

Sigma Magic

Quality management software plus lean components.

www.sigmamagic.com

Sigma XL

Quality management software

www.sigmaxl.com

SPC XL

Quality management software add-in for Excel.

www.sigmazone.com/spcxl.htm

Lean Tuppas Software

Quality management software.

www.tuppas.com/lean-manufacturing-software/lean-manufacturing-software.htm

KEY TAKEAWAYS

- Customer value can be enhanced not only through organizational programs such as quality management and lean thinking but also by increasing creativity, time-management skills, and meeting effectiveness.
- Quality management and lean programs can generate efficiencies that produce significant cost savings.
- Software exists that can assist with improving one's own time management.
- Similar programs are available to improve the creativity of teams and support both quality and lean improvement programs.

EXERCISES

1. Evaluate several computerized time-management systems and write a report covering your selection process.
2. Evaluate several creativity packages and select one that you might buy. Write a one-page paper that talks about why you selected this package.
3. Assume you are a small manufacturer of hypodermic needles. You have sixty employees, and sales are $23 million. You are nervous about overseas competitors, whose products are getting better. You want to further improve your quality and may be interested in applying lean thinking to your operations. Evaluate several software packages and write a report specifying why you support the acquisition of this package.

Disaster Watch

Successful small business owner often rapidly acquire a sixth sense—one that warns them of impending dangers. They begin to sense when there are changes in consumer preferences, when there is a need for an infusion of additional financial resources, or when closer attention needs to be paid to cash flow. These are fundamental issues, and the failure to recognize them will lead to disaster. Subtler issues associated with operations are sometimes missed, and just because they are less obvious does not mean that they cannot be as dangerous. Small businesses can die when they fail to focus on the necessity of being efficient. As said by one commentator, "As the economy grows leaner, this focus on efficiency is paramount to SMEs [small and mid-sized enterprises], and may indicate chances of business sustainability."[100]

In Section 1, time was identified as perhaps the most vital resource, since once lost it can never be recovered. This perspective may be particularly true for small businesses. Most small businesses are under tremendous financial pressures. They normally don't have the luxury of having large staffs, and this means that much of the work falls on the shoulders of the owner. Those owners who cannot effectively manage their time are asking for problems in their business and personal lives.[101] Their businesses can suffer because the owners don't have sufficient time to generate new business.[102] Family life suffers because the owner's inability to successfully manager his or her time translates into time inefficiently spent at work.

Small business is often touted, correctly, as the driving mechanism for innovation in this country. The implication is that innovation and creativity in small business is limited to the development of new products and services. This belief can be disastrous for any small business because it may preclude creative innovations in other areas, such as operations and marketing. Recognizing this as a possibility, IBM has begun to operate "boot camps" to instruct smaller business how to fully exploit social media to drive sales.[103]

A failure to maintain a clear focus on quality can have disastrous consequences. While quality in and of itself may not guarantee success, its absence, in the long run, will guarantee failure. Given the complexity of many quality programs and tools, small businesses should overcome a reticence to bring outside quality experts in-house.[104]

Lastly, businesses—large and small—can be slowly poisoned by an unending stream of poorly managed meetings. Those types of meetings waste managers' and employees' precious time and can wreck morale.

ENDNOTES

1. Julie Kanfer, "Brooklyn Tech: Carrot Creative's Mike Germano," *Brooklyn Heights Blog*, May 14, 2010, accessed February 4, 2012, brooklynheightsblog.com/archives/18448.

2. Julie Kanfer, "Brooklyn Tech: Carrot Creative's Mike Germano," *Brooklyn Heights Blog*, May 14, 2010, accessed February 4, 2012, brooklynheightsblog.com/archives/18448.

3. Amitai Etzioni, *Modern Organizations* (Englewood Cliffs, NJ: Prentice Hall, 1964), 17.

4. "Efficiency, Organizational," *Mondofacto*, December 12, 1998, accessed February 4, 2012, www.mondofacto.com/facts/dictionary?efficiency%2C+organizational.

5. "Peter Drucker Quotes," *Brainy Quote*, accessed February 4, 2012, www.brainyquote.com/quotes/authors/p/peter_drucker.html.

6. James G. March and Herbert A. Simon, *Organizations* (New York: John Wiley & Sons, 1958), 46; Richard M. Cyert and James G. March, *A Behavioral Theory of the Firm* (Oxford, UK: Blackwell, 1963), 121.

7. Joseph L. C. Cheng and Idalene F. Kesner, "Organizational Slack and Response to Environmental Shifts: The Impact of Resource Allocation Patterns," *Journal of Management* 23, no. 1 (1997): 1–18.

8. "Napoleon Speaks on Increasing Market Share," *Stealing Share, Inc.*, accessed June 1, 2012, http://www.stealingshare.com/pages/Napoleon%20Strategy%20works.htm.

9. Peggy Duncan, *The Time Management Memory Jogger* (Salem, NH: Goal/QPC Publishers, 2008), xi.

10. Steven Covey, A. Roger Merrill, and Rebecca R. Merrill, *First Things First* (New York: Simon and Shuster, 1994), 35.

11. "Activity Logs: Finding Out How You Really Spend Your Time," *Mind Tools*, accessed February 4, 2012, www.mindtools.com/pages/article/newHTE_03.htm.

12. "5 Time-Management Tricks," *Shifting Careers*, December 12, 2007, accessed February 4, 2012, shiftingcareers.blogs.nytimes.com/2007/12/12/5-time-management-tricks.

13. Rachna D. Jain, "10 Ways for Entrepreneurs to Find More Time," *PowerHomeBiz.com*, September 9, 2003, accessed February 4, 2012, www.powerhomebiz.com/vol124/findtime.htm.

14. Susan Giurleo, "11 Time Management Tips for Small Business Success," *DrSusanGiurleo.com*, April 11, 2011, accessed February 4, 2012, drsusangiurleo.com/11-time-management-tips-for-small-business-success.

15. Donald Wetmore, "Some Time Savers," *PowerHomeBiz.com*, accessed February 4, 2012, www.powerhomebiz.com/vol70/timesavers.htm.

16. Rachna D. Jain, "10 Ways for Entrepreneurs to Find More Time," *PowerHomeBiz.com*, September 9, 2003, accessed February 4, 2012, www.powerhomebiz.com/vol124/findtime.htm.

17. Susan Giurleo, "11 Time Management Tips for Small Business Success," *DrSusanGiurleo.com*, April 11, 2011, accessed February 4, 2012, drsusangiurleo.com/11-time-management-tips-for-small-business-success.

18. Carol Halsey, "The Greatest Technique of Time Management," *PowerHomeBiz.com*, accessed February 4, 2012, www.powerhomebiz.com/vol94/time.htm.

19. "5 Time-Management Tricks," *Shifting Careers*, December 12, 2007, accessed February 4, 2012, shiftingcareers.blogs.nytimes.com/2007/12/12/5-time-management-tricks.

20. "5 Time-Management Tricks," *Shifting Careers*, December 12, 2007, accessed February 4, 2012, shiftingcareers.blogs.nytimes.com/2007/12/12/5-time-management-tricks.

21. Susan Giurleo, "11 Time Management Tips for Small Business Success," *DrSusanGiurleo.com*, April 11, 2011, accessed February 4, 2012, drsusangiurleo.com/11-time-management-tips-for-small-business-success.

22. "5 Time-Management Tricks," *Shifting Careers*, December 12, 2007, accessed February 4, 2012, shiftingcareers.blogs.nytimes.com/2007/12/12/5-time-management-tricks.

23. "5 Time-Management Tricks," *Shifting Careers*, December 12, 2007, accessed February 4, 2012, shiftingcareers.blogs.nytimes.com/2007/12/12/5-time-management-tricks.

24. Rachna D. Jain, "10 Ways for Entrepreneurs to Find More Time," *PowerHomeBiz.com*, September 9, 2003, accessed February 4, 2012, www.powerhomebiz.com/vol124/findtime.htm.

25. "10 Time Management Mistakes: Avoiding Common Pitfalls," *Mind Tools*, accessed February 4, 2012, www.mindtools.com/pages/article/time-management-mistakes.htm.

26. Donald Wetmore, "Some Time Savers," *PowerHomeBiz.com*, accessed February 4, 2012, www.powerhomebiz.com/vol70/timesavers.htm.

27. "10 Time Management Mistakes: Avoiding Common Pitfalls," *Mind Tools*, accessed February 4, 2012, www.mindtools.com/pages/article/time-management-mistakes.htm.

28. "20 Quick Tips for Better Time Management," *Stepcase Lifehack*, accessed March 12, 2012, www.lifehack.org/articles/lifehack/20-quick-tips-for-better-time-management.html#.

29. Susan Ward, "11 Time Management Tips: Part 1: Coming to Grips with the Time Management Myth," *About.com*, accessed February 4, 2012, sbinfocanada.about.com/cs/timemanagement/a/timemgttips.htm.

30. "Efficiency, Organizational," *Mondofacto*, December 12, 1998, accessed February 4, 2012, www.mondofacto.com/facts/dictionary?efficiency%2C+organizational.

31. "Owen Laughlin Quotes," *Searchquotes*, accessed February 4, 2012, www.searchquotes.com/quotation/Money_never_starts_an_idea._It_is_always_the_idea_that_starts_the_money/17400.

32. Thomas Friedman and Michael Mandelbaum, *That Used to Be Us: How America Fell Behind the World It Invented and How We Can Come Back* (New York: Farrar, Straus and Giroux, 2011).

33. Thomas Friedman, *Hot, Flat, and Crowded: Why We Need a Green Revolution—and How It Can Renew America* (New York: Farrar, Straus and Giroux, 2008).

34. Thomas Friedman, *The World Is Flat: A Brief History of the Twenty-First Century* (New York: Farrar, Straus and Giroux, 2005).

35. Barry Jaruzelski and Kevin Dehoff, "The Global Innovation 1000: How the Top Innovators Keep Winning," *Strategy+Business (Booz & Company)*, November 3, 2010, accessed February 4, 2012, www.strategy-business.com/article/10408?gko=08375.

36. "W. C. Fields Quotes," *Goodreads*, accessed February 4, 2012, www.goodreads.com/author/quotes/82951.W_C_Fields.

37. Jeffrey P. Baumgartner, "The Step by-Step Guide to Brainstorming," *The Wonderful World of Jeffery Paul Baumgartner*, accessed February 4, 2012, jpb.com/creative/brainstorming.php.

38. "Brainstorming: Generating Many Radical, Creative Ideas," *Mind Tools*, accessed February 4, 2012, www.mindtools.com/brainstm.html.

39. "William A. Foster—'Quality Is Never an Accident…,'" *Quotegasm*, accessed February 4, 2012, www.quotegasm.com/william-a-foster/william-a-foster-quality-is-never-an-accident.

40. "2010 Award Recipient: K&N Management," *Malcolm Baldrige*, accessed February 4, 2012, www.baldrige.nist.gov/PDF_files/2010_K&N_Management_Profile.pdf.

41. "2009 Award Recipient: MidwayUSA," *Malcolm Baldrige*, accessed February 4, 2012, www.baldrige.nist.gov/PDF_files/MidwayUSA_Profile.pdf.

42. David Garvin, "What Does 'Product Quality' Really Mean?," *Sloan Management Review* 26, no. 1 (1984): 25–43.

43. A. Parasuraman, Valerie A. Zeithaml, and Leonard L. Berry, "A Conceptual Model of Service Quality and Its Implications for Future Research," *Journal of Marketing* 49 (1985): 41.

44. Valerie A. Zeithaml, A. Parasuraman, and Leonard L. Berry, *Delivering Quality Service: Balancing Customer Perceptions and Expectations* (New York: Free Press, 1990), 38.

45. "Walter A. Shewhart," *ASQ*, accessed February 4, 2012, asq.org/about-asq/who-we-are/bio_shewhart.html.

46. Walter A. Shewhart, *Economic Control of Quality of Manufactured Product* (New York: D. Van Nostrand Company, 1931).

47. Walter A. Shewhart, *Statistical Method from the Viewpoint of Quality Control* (Long Island, NY: Dover Publications, 1980).

48. "Joseph M. Juran," *Juran Institute Inc.*, accessed February 4, 2012, www.juran.com/about_juran_institute_our_founder.html.

49. Robert B. Austenfeld Jr., "W. Edwards Deming: The Story of a Truly Remarkable Person," *International Quality Federation*, May 10, 2011, accessed February 4, 2012, www.iqfnet.org/Ff4203.pdf.

50. "History's Hidden Turning Points," *Leadership Alliance*, accessed March 2, 2012, www.leadershipalliance.com/demingnews.htm.

51. Philip Crosby, *Quality Is Free* (New York: McGraw-Hill, 1979).

52. Philip B. Crosby, "Quality Is Free—If You Understand It," *Philip Crosby Associates II Inc.*, accessed February 4, 2012, www.wppi.org/wphistory/philipcrosby/QualityIsFreeIfYouUnderstandit.pdf.

53. Walter Lareau, *American Samurai: Why Every American Executive Must Fight for Quality* (New York: Warner Books, 1991), 47.

54. Wolf Akpose, "A History of Six Sigma," December 2010, accessed February 4, 2012, www.todaysengineer.org/2010/Dec/six-sigma.asp.

55. "Six Sigma Training, History, Definitions: Six Sigma and Quality Management Glossary," *BusinessBalls.com*, accessed February 4, 2012, www.businessballs.com/sixsigma.htm.

56. Greg Brue, "Six Sigma for Small Business," *Entrepreneur Press*, 2006, accessed February 4, 2012, www.entrepreneur.com/downloads/assist/six_sigma_for_smallbusiness.pdf.

57. Thomas Edison, "Thomas A Edison Quotes," *Brainy Quote*, accessed February 5, 2012, www.brainyquote.com/quotes/quotes/t/thomasaed149058.html.

58. Shigeo Shingo, "Lean Quote: A Simple Quote…An Important Idea…," *Matt Hrivnak.com*, accessed February 5, 2012, matthrivnak.com/2008/03/19/a-simple-quotean-important-idea.

59. James P. Womack, Daniel T. Jones, and Daniel Roos, *The Machine That Changed the World: The Story of Lean Production—Toyota's Secret Weapon in the Global Car Wars That Is Now Revolutionizing World Industry* (New York, Harper Perennial, 1990).

60. Jim Black, "Kaizen (Continuous Improvement) for Small- and Medium-Sized Companies," *CIRAS News* 33, no. 2 (1999), accessed February 4, 2012, www.ciras.iastate.edu/publications/management/Kaizen.asp.

61. "The Five Principles of Lean Thinking," *Cardiff University*, accessed February 4, 2012, www.cardiff.ac.uk/lean/principles/index.html.

62. "The Principles of Lean Thinking: Tools and Techniques for Advanced Manufacturing," *Industial Technology Centre*, accessed February 4, 2012, www.itc.mb.ca/downloads/resources_by_topic/princ_lean%20thinking/PrinciplesofLeanThinkingRevD2004.pdf.

63. Michael George, *Lean Six Sigma for Service: How to Use Lean Speed and Six Sigma Quality to Improve Services and Transactions* (New York: McGraw-Hill, 2003), 76.

64. "Seven Wastes of Service | Customer Perception," *Lean Manufacturing Tools*, accessed February 5, 2012, leanmanufacturingtools.org/81/seven-wastes-of-service-customer-perceptio.

65. "5S Check List," *Systems2win*, accessed March 9, 2012, www.systems2win.com/solutions/5S.htm.

66. Michael George, *Lean Six Sigma for Service: How to Use Lean Speed and Six Sigma Quality to Improve Services and Transactions* (New York: McGraw-Hill, 2003), 6.

67. "Wanderings: Dave Barry Learned All This in 50 Years," *Brent Zupp*, accessed February 6, 2012, www.wanderings.net/notebook/Main/ThingsLearn50YearsDaveBarry.

68. Nancy Roman, "Meetings: How to Waste Time at Work," *Cornelius & Associates*, accessed June 1, 2012, www.corneliusassoc.com/articles/Meetings%20waste%20time.pdf.

69. Roy Woodard, "Meetings, Bloody Meetings," *Credit Control* 15, no. 5 (1993): 1.

70. Robert F. Moran Jr., "Meetings: The Bane of the Workplace, It Doesn't Have to Be," *Library Administration & Management* 20, no. 3 (2006): 135–39, accessed February 6, 2012, journals.tdl.org/llm/article/view/1637/917.

71. Judith Lindenberger, "Make the Most of Your Meetings," *Office Solutions* 24, no. 3 (2007): 40.

72. Stuart Levine, "Make Meetings Less Ready," *HR Magazine* 52, no. 1 (2007): 107.

73. Stuart Levine, "Make Meetings Less Ready," *HR Magazine* 52, no. 1 (2007): 107.

74. Charlie Hawkins, "'F' Words for Effective Meetings," *Journal for Quality and Participation* 22, no. 5 (1999): 56.

75. Roy Woodard, "Meetings, Bloody Meetings," *Credit Control* 14, no. 5 (1993): 1.

76. Kelley Robertson, "How to Run an Effective Sales Meeting," *Changing Minds*, June 7, 2009, accessed February 4, 2012, changingminds.org/articles/articles09/effective_sales_metting.htm.

77. Stuart Levine, "Make Meetings Less Ready," *HR Magazine* 52, no. 1 (2007): 107.

78. Jay Boehmer, "Harvard Study Shows Face-to-Face Meeting Value, Rising Virtual Interest," *Successful Meetings*, accessed February 6, 2012, www.successfulmeetings.com/Event-Planning/Technology-Solutions/Articles/Harvard-Study-Shows-Face-To-Face-Meeting-Value,-Rising-Virtual-Interest.

79. T. L. Stanley, "Make Your Meetings Effective," *SuperVision* 67, no. 4 (2005): 6; Curt Smith, "Effective Meetings—Not an Oxymoron!" *Manage* 51, no. 1 (1999): 10.

80. Robert F. Moran Jr., "Meetings: The Bane of the Workplace, It Doesn't Have to Be," *Library Administration & Management* 20, no. 3 (2006): 135–39, accessed February 6, 2012, journals.tdl.org/llm/article/view/1637/917.

81. Charlie Hawkins, "'F' Words for Effective Meetings," *Journal for Quality and Participation* 22, no. 5 (1999): 56.

82. Wayne Chaneski, "Productive Meetings—Back to Basics," *Modern Machine Shop* 79, no. 11 (2007): 52, accessed February 6, 2012, www.mmsonline.com/columns/productive-meetingsback-to-basics.

83. Judith Lindenberger, "Make the Most of Your Meetings," *Office Solutions* 24, no. 3 (2006): 40.

84. Jim Sullivan, "Focused Agenda Can Energize Manager Meetings," *Nations Restaurant News* 37, no. 5 (2003), accessed February 6, 2012, findarticles.com/p/articles/mi_m3190/is_5_37/ai_97392571.

85. Anonymous, "Running Meetings Effectively," *The British Journal for Administration Management*, October/November 2005, 25.

86. Charlie Hawkins, "'F' Words for Effective Meetings," *Journal for Quality and Participation* 22, no. 5 (1999): 56.

87. Max Messner, "Conducting Effective Meetings," *Strategic Finance* 82, no. 12 (2001): 8, accessed February 6, 2012, findarticles.com/p/articles/mi_hb6421/is_12_82/ai_n28842307.

88. Kelley Robertson, "How to Run an Effective Sales Meeting," *Changing Minds*, June 7, 2009, accessed February 4, 2012, changingminds.org/articles/articles09/effective_sales_metting.htm.

89. Charlie Hawkins, "'F' Words for Effective Meetings," *Journal for Quality and Participation* 22, no. 5 (1999): 56.

90. Joseph Allen, Steven Regelberg, and John Scott, "Mind Your Meetings," *Quality Progress*, April 2008, 42, 4, 51.

91. Walter Lippman, "When All Think Alike, Then No One Is Thinking," *Uneven Chopsticks*, accessed February 6, 2012, unevenchopsticks.com/when-all-think-alike-then-no-one-is-thinking.

92. Christer Karlsson and Pär Ahlstrom, "A Lean and Smaller Global Firm?," *International Journal of Operations and Production Management* 17, no. 10 (1997): 940.

93. Sarah E. Needleman, "Three Best Ways to Get Lean," *Wall Street Journal*, March 25, 2000, accessed February 6, 2012, online.wsj.com/article/SB10001424052748704094104575143680597058528.html.

94. Lawrence P. Etkin, Farhard M. E. Raiszadeh, and Harold R. Hunt Jr., "Just-in-Time: A Timely Opportunity for Small Manufacturers," *Industrial Management* 32, no. 1 (1990): 16.

95. Matthew Zayko, Douglas Broughman, and Walter Hancock, "Lean Manufacturing Yields World-Class Improvements for Small Manufacturing," *IIE Solutions* 29, no. 4 (1997): 36.

96. John T. Slania, "Lean Firms Look to Ride Recovery," *Crain's Chicago Business* 27, no. 2 (2004): SB6.

97. Mario Emiliani, "Supporting Small Businesses in Their Transition to Lean Production," *Supply Chain Management* 5, no. 2 (2000): 66–71.

98. Nanchanok Wongsamuth, "Nawaplastic Pushes Lean Management," *McClatchy Tribune Business News*, July 31, 2010.

99. Matt Dotson and Brandon Kennington, "Eliminating Waste Using Lean Concepts for Small Business," *Automate My Small Business*, November 9, 2009, accessed February 4, 2012, automatemysmallbusiness.com/eliminating-waste-using-lean-concepts-for-small-business.

100. Renee O'Farrell, "Problems of Small Scale Industries," *eHow*, accessed March 7, 2012, www.ehow.com/about_5368391_problems-small-scale-industries.html.

101. Richard Sandusky, "The Problems That Small Business Owners Face," *eHow*, accessed March 7, 2012, www.ehow.com/list_6521178_problems-small-business-owners-face.html.

102. Rod Kurtz, "Solving Time Management Problems," *BusinessWeek.com*, accessed March 7, 2012, www.BusinessWeek.com/smallbiz/tips/archives/2007/01/solving_time_management_problems.html.

103. Market Watch: Wall Street Journal, "IBM Launches Global Boot Camps to Help Small and Midsize Businesses Build Social Media Skills," *Wall Street Journal*, accessed March 7, 2012.

104. Diane Kulisek, "Top Three Small Business Quality Problems," *CAPAtrak* (blog), accessed March 7, 2012, capatrak.wordpress.com/2009/12/21/top-three-small-business-quality-problems.

CHAPTER 14

Icebergs and Escapes

SoBe

Source: Used with permission from John Bello.

John Bello and Tom Schwalm founded SoBe Beverages in Norwalk, Connecticut, in 1996. The name is an abbreviation of South Beach, the well-known upscale area in Miami, Florida. John describes SoBe as playfully irreverent, having brand equity with meaning, a cult brand that resonates in the marketplace. He attributes the company's success to some luck, missteps by the competition, being aggressive, and tapping into a cultural shift.

SoBe tapped into a cultural shift toward healthier living and wellness and the rise of companies like General Nutrition that focused on wellness products: vitamins, supplements, minerals, and herbs. Their first product, Black Tea 3G, contained ginseng, guarana, and ginkgo. Orange Carrot, another of SoBe's first successful products, is a blend of orange and carrot juices enhanced with calcium, chromium picolinate, and carnitine. An extensive line of other flavors was added. All ingredients were linked to specific health benefits.

The first two years of operation saw SoBe losing money, but by the end of 1997, the company was on fire. In five years, the company went from $0 to $300 million in sales, and it became a national brand. SoBe was competing effectively at a premium price. Coca-Cola, Pepsi, Arizona, and other brands took notice. Within three years, Coca-Cola was talking to SoBe about a possible strategic partnership. There were fifteen meetings, only two of which were with marketing. The rest were with corporate lawyers (John calls them "sales preventers") and regulators. At the end of 1999, Minute Maid presented the proposal to the Coca-Cola board. Surprisingly, it was rejected. Coca-Cola saw no reason to go beyond carbonated soft drinks, and there were also some leadership issues. Back to square one.

John and Tom started looking at liquidation because of pressure from investors who wanted their money. But there were other reasons they thought about selling. They were not interested in managing a disparate group of investors—bankers, investors, and private equity companies. With 250 employees, the company was growing into something they did not want it to be—and they were not having as much fun. In 2000, the market was flattening, so with a big brand image, it was a good time to get out. They also wanted to get into larger markets, such as schools and golf clubs, but only big companies could get them into a broader marketplace. They hired an investment bank and again went into negotiations with Coca-Cola as a strategic partner. The situation became very complicated and frustrating. Ultimately, a deal with Coca-Cola was again a no-go.

All was not lost. Pepsi (and others) had expressed an interest. John made a presentation to forty people at Pepsi—rather than the multiple presentations he had to make to Coca-Cola—and within two weeks, they had a deal. SoBe was sold in 2000 to Pepsi for an impressive $370 million…a very nice return on an investment of $7 million in cash and $1 million in trade-out services. Part of the deal was that John would stay on at Pepsi for two years to manage the brand, but after one day, it was clear to him that he was not going to be managing anything. Things were moved into committee, and the corporate bureaucracy took over. John likened the experience to "Making Ho Chi Minh a general in the US Army," that is, he had a very different way of doing things. He is independent, is unconventional, speaks his mind, and would rather do things and make them work—an approach that tends to be at odds with the culture in large corporations.

SoBe inspired a whole line of functional beverages that people like to buy to make them feel smarter, healthier, and sexier. The company helped to build careers that have lasted. John is very happy with his legacy…and with his piece of the $370 million sale price.

Source: Interview with John Bello, cofounder of SoBe, August 23, 2011.

Most textbooks on small business and entrepreneurship emphasize, quite correctly, the benefits and joys of owning and operating one's own business. However, they often neglect to cover many of the challenges of continuing to operate a business successfully—the icebergs that can sink a business. The first half of this chapter covers one of the biggest icebergs: a natural or a man-made disaster and the disaster planning that should precede it. Being able to anticipate a disaster will contribute significantly to its effective handling so that a business can survive.

Even if a small business survives a disaster or another kind of iceberg, the owner may still wish to walk away. If a business does not survive, the owner will have no choice but to walk away. There may be other reasons forcing the owner to walk away, or escape, as well. The second half of this chapter discusses the forced escape and the other end of the spectrum—when things go so well that the business owner is ready to move on to another phase of his or her life. In both cases, an exit strategy will be required.

1. ICEBERGS

LEARNING OBJECTIVES

1. Understand the kinds of disasters that can face a small business.
2. Understand why disaster planning is important to a small business.
3. Describe the process of disaster planning.
4. Describe the sources of disaster assistance for small businesses.

A natural or a man-made disaster is but the tip of the iceberg. Planning for the complexity of what lies below the tip is important for every small business. Small- to medium-sized businesses are the most vulnerable in the event of a disaster.[1] It has been estimated by the US Department of Labor that 40 percent of businesses never reopen following a disaster. At least 25 percent of the remaining companies will close within two years. The Association of Records Managers and Administrators estimated that over 60 percent of small businesses that experience a major disaster close by the end of two years.[2]

Given these odds, planning for disaster recovery makes great sense—even if, in the end, walking away makes the most sense. If a small business owner decides to rebuild, the process can begin after human health and safety are restored, the electricity is back on, and transportation is up and running. Everyone will want life to return to normal following the destruction, but that may not be possible for every small business. The market may change. Conditions may change, and a business must change to succeed in disaster recovery.[3]

1.1 Disaster Planning

In the film *Apollo 13*, astronauts and engineers went through seemingly endless simulations of what might go wrong on a flight to the moon. The astronauts complained that some of the scenarios were unrealistic and almost impossible to occur. But when a near disaster occurred on Apollo 13, the engineers and astronauts were confronted with a problem that had never been considered; however, because of their prior experience with disaster training, they were able to develop a solution.

Rather than being negative, anticipating what can go wrong can be profoundly positive through either prevention or quickly responding to a crisis. The wise small business owner should appreciate Murphy's Law ("Anything that can go wrong will go wrong") and Murphy's first corollary ("And it will go wrong at the worst possible moment"). The most pragmatic small business owner will also realize that Murphy was an optimist.

The Federal Emergency Management Agency declared 741 natural disasters in the United States for the period 2000 to 2011. Of that number, 66 percent were declared across the following six states: Texas (#1), California, Oklahoma, New York, Florida, and Louisiana (#6). However, every state and territory was represented.[4] Planning for the aftermath of severe storms, flooding (e.g., perhaps snow melts too fast), fire, a hurricane or a tornado, a terrorist attack, or—in some areas—an earthquake is the key to getting back to business with a minimum of disruption. Not all businesses will face the same likelihood of these disasters occurring, but everyone faces the possibility of fire, severe storms, and flooding. Every situation will be unique, with the complexity of issues depending on the particular industry, size, location, and scope of a business.[5] The widespread nature of a the typical disaster means that public services, such as police, fire fighters, and medical assistance, will be unable to reach everyone right away. A business might be going it alone for a while.[6]

According to a recent poll conducted by the National Federation of Independent Business, man-made disasters affect 10 percent of small businesses, and natural disasters have impacted more than 30 percent of all small businesses in the United States.[7] **Man-made disasters** are disastrous events caused directly and principally by one or more identifiable deliberate or negligent human actions.[8] They include such things as arson, radiation contamination, terrorism, structural collapse due to engineering failures, civil disorder, and industrial hazards.[9] The better prepared a business is, the faster it will be able to recover and resume operations…if that is the decision. Having a disaster plan can mean the difference between being shut down for a few days and going out of business entirely.[10]

man-made disaster

A disastrous event caused directly and principally by one or more identifiable deliberate or negligent human actions.

A Disaster Planning Success Story

Joe Bogner of Dodge City, Kansas, learned the importance of disaster planning firsthand. He owns Western Beverage, Inc., a beverage distribution company serving twenty-nine counties in western Kansas. In 2002, Western Beverage sustained millions of dollars in fire damage. Yet the company resumed deliveries after just three days. Bogner was named the Kansas City Small Businessperson of the Year for 2006, partially because of his company's ability to respond to adversity. As his nomination package stated, "Setting up plans of action and following through are Joe's way of life. He has proven and is continuing to prove that dreams can come true."[11]

Four key facts about disaster planning must be kept in mind: (1) disasters will occur, (2) an owner must have a plan *before* the disaster occurs, (3) react with urgency but do not panic, and (4) ride it out.[12] If an owner is committed to having a disaster plan for a business, the plan and process can be structured in a variety of ways. For this section, however, the recommendations on Ready.gov serve as the structure for our discussion. These recommendations reflect the Emergency Preparedness Business Continuity Standard (NFPA 1600) developed by the National Fire Protection Association and endorsed by the American National Standards Institute and the Department of Homeland Security.[13] The recommendations are divided into three areas: plan to stay in business, talk to the people, and protect the investment. The topics discussed here are presented in Figure 14.1. They have the greatest immediacy for a small business.

FIGURE 14.1 Disaster Planning

Plan to stay in business	Talk to your people	Protect your investment
• Be informed • Continuity planning	• Involve co-workers • Crisis communication • Employee health	• Insurance coverage • Facilities, buildings, and plants • Cybersecurity

Source: http://www.ready.gov/business.

1.2 Plan to Stay in Business

A business owner has invested a tremendous amount of time, money, resources, and emotions into building a business, so he or she will want to be able to survive a natural or man-made disaster. This requires taking a proactive approach so that the chances of the business surviving are increased. Unfortunately, nothing can be done to guarantee the survival of a business because there is no way to know what kind of disaster may occur—or when. There is also no way to know what kind of business environment the owner will face after the disaster. There are, however, several things can be done to increase those chances of survival. Resist the temptation to put emergency planning on the back burner.

Be Informed

It is important to look realistically at the types of disasters that might affect a business internally and externally and prepare a risk assessment. Consider the natural disasters that are most common in the areas where the business operates and think about the business's vulnerability to man-made disasters. Fires are the most common disasters in the United States, and they are extremely destructive to businesses,[14] but an owner may not be aware that a community is very vulnerable to flooding from snow melt or that the proximity to a chemical plant makes a business vulnerable to the results of explosions. This is why it is important to prepare a risk assessment so that the business can plan accordingly.

Make a Continuity Plan

It is said that a business continuity plan is the least expensive insurance any business can have—especially a small business—because it costs virtually nothing to produce.[15] The better the continuity planning is before a disaster, the greater the chances that a business will survive and recover. There are many things that can be done.[16] The following is not an exhaustive list:

1. Carefully assess how the business functions. Document internal key personnel and backups (i.e., the personnel without whom a business absolutely cannot function). The list should be as large as necessary but as small as possible.

2. Identify suppliers, shippers, resources, and other businesses that are interacted with on a daily basis. Document these and other external contacts, such as bankers, attorneys, information technology (IT) consultants, utilities, and municipal and community offices (police, fire, etc.) that may be needed for assistance.

3. Identify people who can telecommute. Take steps to ensure that critical staff can telecommute if necessary.

4. Plan for payroll continuity.

5. Document critical equipment. Personal computers, fax machines, special printers and scanners, and software are critical to most businesses. An accurate inventory will help a business restore critical equipment.

6. Make sure that all data and critical documents are protected. Critical documents include articles of incorporation and other legal papers, utility bills, banking information, and human resources documents; all these will be required to start over again. The Small Business Administration (SBA) recommends that vital business records—information stored on paper and computer—should be copied and saved at an offsite location at least fifty miles away from the main business site.[17] Companies such as Carbonite can store records "on the cloud."

7. Identify a contingency location where business can be conducted while the primary office is unavailable. Many hotels have well-equipped business facilities that can be used, but remember that other businesses may need to do the same thing. It is good to have a contingency plan for a contingency location.

8. Put all the information together. The continuity plan is an important document, a copy of which should be given to all key personnel. Do not distribute the plan to people who do not need to have it. The plan will contain sensitive and secure information that could be used by a disgruntled employee for inappropriate purposes.

9. Plan to change the plan. There will always be events that could not have been factored into the plan. For example, the contingency site is damaged beyond use or the business's bank is in an area that will be without power for days. Situations such as these will require immediate changes to the plan.

10. Review and revise the plan.

1.3 Talk to People

Without good communication, the internal and external structure of a business—and its daily operations—will face challenges that may ultimately lead to its downfall.[18] Strong communication skills are, therefore, a vital part of business success. When first starting out, the owner will need good communication skills to attract and keep new customers. As the business grows and new employees are required, these skills will be needed to hire, motivate, and retain good staff.[19] It is for this reason that the employees of a business should play a central role in creating a disaster plan.

Involve Coworkers

Providing for the well-being of all employees is one of the best ways to ensure that a business will recover from a disaster. A business must be able to communicate with them before, during, and after a disaster. There are several recommendations for doing this, including the following:[20]

- Employees from all levels in the organization should be involved.
- Internal communications tools, such as newsletters and intranets, should be used to communicate emergency plans and procedures.
- Set up procedures to warn people, being sure to plan how to warn employees who are hearing impaired, are otherwise disabled, or do not speak English.
- Encourage employees to find an alternate way of getting to and from work in case their usual way of transportation is interrupted.
- Keep a record of employee emergency contact information with other important documents.

Write a Crisis Communication Plan

The owner must decide how the business will contact suppliers, creditors, other employees, local authorities, customers, media, and utility companies during and after the disaster. One easy way to do this is to assign key employees to make designated contacts. Provide a list of these key employees and contacts to each affected employee and keep a copy with other protected contacts. Each key employee should also keep a copy of the list at home. In addition,[21] do the following:

- Make sure that top executives have all the relevant information needed to protect employees, customers, vendors, and nearby facilities.
- Update customers on whether and when products will be received and services rendered.
- Let public officials know what the business is prepared to do to help in the recovery effort.
- Let public officials know whether the business will need emergency assistance to conduct essential business activity.

Support Employee Health—and the Owner's Health

Disasters often result in business disorientation and environmental detachment, with the psychological trauma of key decision makers leading to company inflexibility (perhaps inability) to deal with the change required to move forward.[22] If the owner or other key personnel experience posttraumatic stress disorder, it can cripple a business's decision-making ability.

No matter the disaster, there will be psychological effects (e.g., fear, stress, depression, anxiety, and difficulty in making decisions) as well as—depending on the nature of the disaster—physical effects such as injuries, burns, exposure to toxins, and prolonged pain.[23] As a result, the owner and the employees may have special recovery needs. To support those needs, do the following:[24]

- Provide for time at home to care for family needs, if necessary.
- Have an open-door policy that facilitates seeking care when needed.
- Reestablish routines as best as possible.
- Offer special counselors to help people address their fears and anxieties.
- Take care of yourself. Leaders tend to experience increased stress after a disaster. The leader's own health and recovery are also important to both family and the business as a whole.

1.4   Protect the Investment

Last but certainly not least, take steps to protect the business and secure its physical assets. Among the things that can be done, having appropriate insurance coverage; securing facilities, buildings, and plants; and improving cybersecurity are at the top of the list.

Insurance Coverage

Having inadequate insurance coverage can leave a business vulnerable to a major financial loss if it is damaged, destroyed, or simply interrupted for a period of time. Because insurance policies vary, meet with an insurance agent who understands the needs of a particular business.[25]

business interruption insurance

Protects a business in the event of a natural disaster, a fire, or other extenuating circumstances that affects the ability of a company to conduct business.

- Review coverage for things such as physical losses, flood coverage, and business interruption. Normal hazard insurance does not cover floods, so make sure the business has the right insurance.[26] **Business interruption insurance** protects a business in the event of a natural disaster, a fire, or other extenuating circumstances that affect the ability of a company to conduct business.[27] Small business owners should seriously consider this type of insurance because it can provide enough money to meet overhead and other expenses while out of commission. The premiums for these policies are based on a company's income.[28]
- Understand what the insurance policy covers and what it does not cover.
- Add coverage as necessary.
- Understand the deductible and make adjustments as appropriate.
- Think about how creditors and employees will be paid.
- Plan how to pay yourself if the business is interrupted.
- Find out what records the insurance provider will require after an emergency and store them in a safe place. It would be a good idea to take pictures of your physical facilities, equipment, buildings, and plant so that insurance claims can be processed quickly. These pictures will also provide a good basis for putting the operation back into working order.

Secure Facilities, Buildings, and Plants

One cannot predict what will happen in the case of a disaster, but there are steps that can be taken in advance to help protect a business's physical assets, including the following:[29]

- Fire extinguishers and smoke detectors should be installed in appropriate places.
- Building and site maps with critical utility and emergency routes clearly marked should be available in multiple locations—and they should be protected with other important documents.
- Think about whether automatic fire sprinklers, alarm systems, closed circuit television, access control, security guards, or other security measures would make sense.
- Secure the entrance and the exit for people, products, supplies, and anything else that comes into and leaves the business.
- Teach employees to quickly identify suspect packages and letters, for example, packages and letters with misspelled words, no return address, the excessive use of tape, and strange coloration or odor. Have a plan for how such packages and letters are to be handled.

Improve Cybersecurity

Many, perhaps most, small businesses will have data and IT systems that may require specialized expertise. They need to be protected. The industry, size, and scope of a business will determine the complexity of cybersecurity, but even the smallest business can be better prepared.[30] Small businesses are the most vulnerable to cybersecurity breaches because they have the weakest security systems, thereby making them easier online targets.[31]

Video Clip 14.1

Cybersecurity
An overview of cybersecurity.

View the video online at: http://www.youtube.com/v/le0bRyXNrTs

Video Link 14.1

Chubb Group of Insurance Companies

The Chubb Group of Insurance Companies provides a very good video discussion of cybersecurity.

www.chubb.com/businesses/csi/chubb822.html

Every computer can be vulnerable to attack. The consequences can range from simple inconvenience to financial catastrophe.[32] There are several things that can be done to protect a business, its customers, and its vendors, including the following:[33]

- **Explore cybersecurity liability insurance.** This coverage is available at reasonable rates to protect against credit card identity theft, with limits up to $5 million. This insurance will cover the loss of digital assets plus expenses for public relations, damages, and service interruption. It will also protect customers. The notification of customers whose credit was compromised is included plus any legal costs and a year of credit monitoring for each individual affected. Although other cybersecurity insurance policies can cover data loss, applicants must break down loss estimates on an hourly basis because most breaches are resolved in hours, not days. This is not an easy thing to do.

- **Use antivirus software and keep it up to date.** If an owner is not already doing this, he or she should probably have a mental examination.

- **Do not open e-mail from unknown sources.** Always be suspicious of unexpected e-mails that include attachments, whether or not they are from a known source. When in doubt, delete the file and the attachment—and then empty the computer's deleted items file. This should be a procedure that all employees know about and follow. The owner must do it as well.

- **Use hard-to-guess passwords.** An application for cyberinsurance requires, among other things, answering the following question: "Are passwords required to be at least seven characters in length, alphanumeric, and free of consecutive characters?" (Check yes or no.) Whether or not a business plans to apply for cyberinsurance, instituting this kind of password policy is well worth consideration.

KEY TAKEAWAYS

- Small- to medium-sized businesses are the most vulnerable in the event of a disaster.
- Some estimates claim that over 60 percent of small businesses that experience a major disaster close by the end of the second year.
- Planning for disaster recovery makes great sense for protecting a business.
- Every state and territory has experienced disasters. Planning for the aftermath is the key to getting back to business with a minimum of disruption. However, every situation will be unique.
- Man-made disasters affect 10 percent of small businesses, while natural disasters have impacted more than 30 percent of all small businesses in the United States.
- A man-made disaster is a disastrous event caused directly and principally by one or more identifiable deliberate or negligent human actions—for example, arson, terrorism, and structural collapse.
- The better prepared a business is, the faster it will recover from a disaster and resume operations. Having a disaster plan can mean the difference between being shut down for a few days and going out of business entirely.
- Even the smallest business should have a disaster plan.
- The three main areas that an owner should focus on in a disaster plan are the plan to stay in business, talk to people, and protect the investment.

EXERCISE

Frank's BarBeQue just missed being impacted by a tornado that ripped through southwestern Connecticut. Many small businesses were lost, never to reopen, while others sustained major physical and economic damage. Frank's son, Robert, asked his father about whether he was prepared for something like that. Frank's response was troubling. Although he kept some important documents in a safety deposit box at the bank, there was little planning or protection. Robert explained the importance of disaster planning, but Frank was overwhelmed by the prospect of the process.

Robert contacted a local university and arranged with its school of business for a team of five students to prepare a disaster plan for Frank's BarBeQue. He presented the project idea to his father and was relieved that his dad was willing to participate. It was clearly understood that no proprietary or confidential information would be shared with the students.

1. Assume that you are the leader of the team. Describe the approach you will take and the recommendations that you will make. It is expected that you will go beyond the information provided in the text. Creativity is strongly encouraged.

2. DISASTER ASSISTANCE

LEARNING OBJECTIVE

1. Learn about the sources of disaster assistance for the physical and/or economic losses of small business.

Do not assume that all small businesses will qualify for disaster loan assistance or that insurance will cover the costs of all losses. A small business owner may have to depend on other forms of financial assistance—for example, savings, friends, and family.[34] However, if a small business has sustained economic injury after a disaster, it may be eligible for financial assistance from the Small Business Administration (SBA). If a business is located in a declared disaster area, the owner may apply for a long-term, low-interest loan to repair or replace damaged property.[35]

FIGURE 14.2 Disaster Damage

© *Thinkstock*

2.1 Physical and Economic Injury Disaster Loans

In the case of a physical disaster, a small business owner may apply for a low-interest SBA loan of up to $2 million to repair or replace damaged real estate, equipment, inventory, and fixtures: "The loan may be increased by as much as 20 percent of the total amount of disaster damage to real estate and/or leasehold improvements, as verified by SBA, to protect property against future disasters of the same type. These loans will cover uninsured and or under-insured losses."[36] It is also possible that small business disaster relief loans may be available at the local, county, regional, or state level.[37]

The SBA can also help small businesses that were not damaged physically but have suffered economically.[38] An Economic Injury Disaster Loan of up to $2 million can be granted to meet necessary financial obligations—expenses the business would have paid if the disaster had not occurred.

The interest rate on both Physical and Economic Injury Disaster Loans will not exceed 4 percent if you do not have credit available elsewhere. Repayment can be up to 30 years, but this will depend on the business's ability to repay the loan. For businesses that may have credit available elsewhere, the interest rate will not exceed 8 percent. SBA determines whether the applicant has credit available elsewhere.[39]

2.2 Disaster Assistance from the Internal Revenue Service

The Internal Revenue Service (IRS) provides some disaster assistance and emergency relief for businesses through special tax law provisions, especially when the federal government declares their location to be a major disaster area. The IRS may grant additional time to file returns and pay taxes. While doing disaster planning, check the latest special tax law provisions that may help a business recover financially from the impact of a major disaster.[40] It would also be a good idea to check out what kind of record keeping the IRS requires so that a business will be fully prepared should it be necessary to take advantage of what the IRS offers.

2.3 SCORE Business Advice

Disaster recovery will push the limits of a small business…and then some. Locate the closest offices of **SCORE (Service Corps of Retired Executives)**—a nonprofit association dedicated to educating entrepreneurs and helping small businesses start, grow, and succeed nationwide—and enlist their support. SCORE provides confidential business counseling services at no charge.[41]

2.4 Online Disaster Assistance

DisasterAssistance.gov is a one-stop web portal, self-described as access to disaster help and resources, that details over sixty different forms of assistance from seventeen US government agencies where a business owner can apply for SBA loans through online applications, receive referral information on forms of assistance that do not have online applications, or check the progress and status of online applications.[42]

Benefits.gov wants to let survivors and disaster relief workers know about the many disaster relief programs that are available. There are questions for a small business owner who has suffered damage because of a natural disaster to answer to find out which government benefits the business may be eligible to receive. The site also provides a link to DisasterAssistance.gov.[43]

KEY TAKEAWAYS

- Do not assume that a small business will qualify for disaster loan assistance or that insurance will cover the costs of all losses. A small business owner may have to depend on others for financial assistance—for example, friends, family, and savings.
- A small business owner may apply for a low-interest SBA loan of up to $2 million to repair or replace damaged real estate. The interest rate on this loan will not exceed 4 percent if credit is not available elsewhere.
- The SBA also provides financial assistance to small businesses that were not damaged physically but suffered economic losses. The interest rate on this loan will also not exceed 4 percent if the business does not have credit available elsewhere.
- The IRS provides disaster assistance and emergency relief through special tax provisions.
- It would be worthwhile checking out SCORE for assistance.
- Online disaster assistance is available through two website portals: DisasterAssistance.gov and Benefits.gov.

EXERCISE

1. As part of the disaster management plan, Robert has asked the student team to prepare a specific plan for obtaining disaster assistance under the assumption that both physical and economic damages will occur. Review the various options and the material from the previous section in this chapter and then make specific recommendations. It is expected that you will go beyond the information presented in the text.

---

3. ESCAPES: GETTING OUT OF THE BUSINESS

LEARNING OBJECTIVES

1. Identify the situations in which an owner may choose to get out of business.
2. Identify and understand the situations that may lead to being forced out of business.
3. Understand the resources that can help an owner make a decision.

There are many reasons why an owner might want to walk away from a business; the choice is oftentimes the owner's. Perhaps the owner wants to sell the business before retirement. Perhaps someone has approached the owner with a terrific offer. Perhaps investors are pressuring the owner for their money. Perhaps no one in the owner's family wants to take over the business. Perhaps it is no longer fun; the entrepreneurial spirit is gone, and the owner's passion has changed. It could be that either the owner or the team is not committed to making things work.[44] Perhaps the owner would like to cash out the equity built in the business.[45] There are many other reasons as well:

- The owner is spending more time fixing nominal problems, it feels as if he or she is working backward, and no end seems in sight.

- Instead of being the most optimistic person on the team, the owner starts taking a negative view on most of the decisions the team is making about future prospects for growth.

- Continuing with the business may have serious, lasting personal repercussions, such as threatening one's marriage, familial relationships, or health. The potential risk is no longer worth the reward.

- The owner sees the writing on the wall: no repeat or referral customers, no positive feedback from any source, or no demand for the business's product or service. Positive feedback can take many forms: word of mouth, referrals, favorable press, favorable posts and reviews on Facebook and Twitter, and plenty of inquiries. If a business owner is not satisfying customers and attracting new ones, why be in business at all?

3.1   When Walking Away Is Not the Owner's Choice

There will also be those times when walking away from a business may not be the owner's choice.

- **The owner wants no one else to run the business and is unwilling to give up equity.** Every small business founder faces the **founder's dilemma**—that is, the dilemma between making money and controlling the business.[46] It is tough to do both because they tend to be incompatible goals. Founders often make decisions that conflict with maximizing wealth.[47] If an owner wants to make a lot of money from a business, the owner will need to give up more **equity** (the money put into the business) to attract investors, which requires relinquishing control as equity is given away; investors may alter the board membership of a business.[48] To retain control of a business, the owner will have to keep more equity, relying on his or her own capital instead of taking money from investors. The result will be less capital to increase a company's value, but he or she will be able to run the company.[49]

  In a recent study of 212 new ventures, it was found that in three years, 50 percent of the founders were no longer the CEO, only 20 percent were still "in the corner office," and fewer than 25 percent led their company's initial public offering (IPO). Four out of five found themselves being forced to step down at some point.[50] Although specific to new ventures, this information has a clear message for all small business founders/owners: wanting to make a lot of money while still controlling and running the business are not compatible goals. One must decide which goal is most important, understanding that the choice of letting someone else run the business will likely result in being forced to step down…and perhaps out of the business altogether.

- **The owner is facing bankruptcy.** One study[51] found that firms with less sophisticated owners or managers with respect to experience and training increases the likelihood of bankruptcy as do a deteriorating market and having less access to capital. There can be other reasons as well—for example, employee theft, fraud, or a consumer liability lawsuit that drains a company's assets.

- **The owner may be the cause.** The owner could be killing the company or, at the very least, shooting himself or herself in the foot. There are several ways in which this could happen:[52] (1) micromanaging, which may lead to, for example, employees presenting problems or issues but no solutions, unusually high turnover, and never receiving a project that the owner does not change; (2) spending money in the wrong places—for example, spending money on items not needed, such as a fancier location, hiring more staff than needed, and attending costly trade shows with limited or no return on investment; (3) chasing after every customer instead of focusing on the ideal and regular customers that should be reached; (4) the owner is not on top of the numbers, perhaps because he or she is not financially minded and has not taken the time to become financially minded or hire someone as the finance person; and (5) the owner is not a people person, perhaps being a "my way or the highway" kind of person who invests no emotion or warmth when dealing with employees and colleagues, or is an egomaniac.

- **The owner is seriously ill.** Being ill will raise doubts about a company's future, and new businesses are the most vulnerable.[53] If there is no one in the owner's family who is interested in or willing to take over the business, this can add additional stress to the situation.

- **The industry dies or implodes.** Sometimes the demand for a service or a product just dies—for example, web-consulting companies during the dot-com bust in 2000 and 2001.[54] Henrybuilt Corporation, a Seattle firm that specialized in designing kitchens from $30,000 to $100,000, saw

founder's dilemma

The choice between making money or controlling and running a business.

equity

The amount of money invested in a firm.

its sales come to a standstill in 2008. Everyone was cancelling projects. The company modified its product and was able to survive.[55]

3.2 Resources to Help Make a Decision

The decision to walk away from a business—whether that decision is voluntary or forced—is not an easy one to make. Consult with an appropriate mix of individuals; a partner or partners if applicable, your spouse, your family, an attorney, an accountant, and perhaps someone from SCORE. Each individual can offer a different perspective and different counsel. Ultimately, however, the decision is the owner's.

One thing is for certain. Whether the escape is voluntary or forced, there should be an exit strategy.

KEY TAKEAWAYS

- Escaping from a business is the owner's choice when, for example, he or she wants to sell the business before retirement, someone has approached the owner with a terrific offer, investors are pressuring the owner for their money, no family member wants to take over the business, or it is not fun anymore.
- An escape may be forced when, for example, an owner wants no one else to run the business and is unwilling to give up equity or is facing bankruptcy or is seriously ill.
- The owner should consult with a mix of resources before making a decision.

EXERCISE

1. You are the twenty-eight-year-old founder of a very successful, five-year-old software company. For the last three years, sales have doubled in each year. Last year's sales were $75 million. A major high-tech firm wants to buy your company. They will offer cash and will sweeten the offer by allowing you the option of being CEO for at least two years. How much would the firm have to offer you to take this deal? How would you know if it was a fair offer? Would you exercise the option to act as CEO for the two years? If you took the offer, what would be your life plans?

4. EXIT STRATEGIES

LEARNING OBJECTIVES

1. Understand the importance of an exit strategy.
2. Explain the exit strategies that a small business can consider.

The most emotional topic a small business owner will face while building a business—and the hardest decision to make—is when and how to exit the business. This very personal decision should be considered while building the business because this decision will impact many other decisions made along the way.[56] Ultimately, however, an exit strategy must be developed whether or not it is considered along the way. The strategy should be developed early in the business, and it should be reviewed and changed periodically because conditions change. Unfortunately, many small business owners have no exit strategy. This will make an already very emotional decision and process even more difficult.

There are many exit strategies that a small business owner can consider. Liquidation or walk away, family succession, selling the business, bankruptcy, and taking the company public are discussed here. Selecting an exit strategy is important because the way in which an owner exits can affect the following:[57]

- The value that the owner and/or shareholders (if any) can realize from a business
- Whether a cash deal, deferred payments, or staged payments are received
- The future success of the business and its products or services (unless one is closing the business)
- Whether the owner wants to retain any involvement in or control of the business
- Tax liabilities

FIGURE 14.3 Leaving a Business

© *Thinkstock*

FIGURE 14.4 Possible Exit Strategies

The best exit strategy (see Figure 14.4) is the one that is the best match to a small business and the owner's personal and professional goals. The owner must first decide what he or she wants to walk away with—for example, money, management control, or intellectual property. If interested only in money, selling the business on the open market or to another business may be the best choice. If, on the other hand, one's legacy and seeing the small business continue are important, family succession or selling the business to the employees might be a better solution.[58]

4.1   Liquidation or Walkaway

liquidation

The sale of a business's assets.

walkaway

A small business that is closed with all debts paid.

goodwill

An intangible asset that reflects the value of intangible assets, such as a strong brand name, good customer relations, good employee relations, patents, intellectual property, the size and the quality of the customer list, and market penetration.

badwill

The negative effect felt by a company when it is found out that a company has done something not in accord with good business practices.

There are times when a small business owner may decide that enough is enough, so he or she simply calls it quits, closes the business doors, and calls it a day.[59] This happens all the time, to hundreds of businesses every day—for example, a small shop, a restaurant, a small construction company, a shoe store, a gift shop, a consignment shop, a nail salon, a bakery, or a video store.[60] This closing of the business involves **liquidation**, the selling of all assets. If all debts are paid, it can also be referred to as a **walkaway**.

To make any money with the liquidation exit strategy, a business must have valuable assets to sell—for example, land or expensive equipment. The name of the business may have some value, so it could be purchased by someone for pennies on the dollar and restarted with different owners. There is also a possibility that there may be a substantial amount of goodwill or even badwill if a business has been around for a long time. **Goodwill** is an intangible asset that reflects the value of intangible assets, such as a strong brand name, good customer relationships, good employee relationships, patents, intellectual property, size and quality of the customer list, and market penetration.[61] However, if a business is simply closed, the value of the goodwill will drop, and the selling price will be lower than it would have been prior to the business being closed.[62]

Badwill is the negative effect felt by a company when it is found out that a company has done something not in accord with good business practices. Although badwill is typically not expressed in a dollar amount, it can result in such things as decreased revenue; the loss of clients, customers, and suppliers; the loss of market share; the loss of credit; federal or state indictments for crimes committed; and censure by the community.[63] For the small business owner who wants to close under these circumstances, there will be nothing much to sell but tangible assets because the business will have very little, if any, market value.

In all instances of liquidation, the proceeds from the sale of assets must first be used to repay creditors. The remaining money is divided among the shareholders (if any), the partners (if any), and the owner.[64] In an ideal walkaway situation, the following occurs:[65]

- All bills are paid off (or scheduled).
- All taxes are paid, and the various levels of government are informed of the closure.
- Contracts, leases, and the like are fulfilled or formally terminated.
- Employees are let go to find other jobs.
- Assets or inventory is depleted.
- No lawsuits are consuming money and time.
- Customers are placed so that they get needed goods or services.
- If needed, insurance is continued to cover unexpected claims after the firm closes.

The walkaway is the cleanest and best way to exit, but it is not always possible for all businesses that decide to close their doors. There will, of course, always be those instances in which the owner closes the business and takes off, leaving a mess behind.

Any small business owner thinking about liquidation should consider the pros and cons, which are as follows:[66]

- **Pros**
  - It is easy and natural. Everything comes to an end.
  - No negotiations are involved.
  - There are no worries about the transfer of control.

- **Cons**
  - Get real! It is a waste. At most, the owner will get the market value of the company's assets.
  - Things such as client lists, the owner's reputation, and business relationships may be very valuable. Liquidation destroys them without an opportunity to recover their value.
  - Other shareholders, if any, may be less than thrilled about how much is left on the table.
  - If a company's brand has any value, there is a loyal or sizeable customer base, or there is a stable core of employees, an owner would be significantly better off selling the company.

4.2 Family Succession

Many small business owners dream of passing the business to a family member. Keeping the business in the family allows the owner's legacy to live on, which is clearly an attractive option. Family succession as an exit strategy also allows the owner an opportunity to groom the successor; the owner might even retain some influence and involvement in the business if desired.[67] However, given that very few family firms survive beyond the first generation and even fewer survive into the third generation,[68] **succession** is the most critical issue facing family firms.[69] Succession is the transference of leadership from one generation to the next to ensure continuity of family ownership of the business.[70]

A sudden decision to hand over the business to a family member is unwise. The owner will be burdened with problems that will likely lead to business failure. Succession in family firms is a multistage, complex process that should begin even before the heirs enter the business, and effects extend beyond the point in time when they are named as successors. Many factors are involved, and the succession should evolve over a long period of time.[71] Further, because succession is usually followed by changes in the organization, particularly the change in the top position, it is thought to be an indicator of the future of the business. The better prepared and committed the successor is, the greater the likelihood of a successful succession process and business.[72] The quality of interpersonal relationships, successors' expectations, and the role of the predecessor are also relevant to success.[73]

The ideal is for the family business to have engaged in formal **succession planning**: planning for the family business to be transferred to a family member or members. The failure to plan for succession is seen as a fundamental human resource problem as well as the primary cause for the poor survival rate of family businesses.[74] Unfortunately, a very small percentage of family businesses plan appropriately for succession, and those that do frequently have mental, not written, plans.[75] A discussion of succession planning is in Chapter 3.

succession

Passing the business to the next generation.

succession planning

Planning for the family business to be transferred to a family member or members.

Video Clip 14.2

How to Pass On a Family Business

The owner of the Casanova Restaurant in Carmel, California, talks about his business and his hopes of passing it on to his children.

View the video online at: http://www.youtube.com/v/Il16MJeZOOQ

4.3 Bankruptcy

Feeling the need to file for bankruptcy is a tough pill for any small business owner to swallow. **Bankruptcy** is an extreme form of business termination that uses a legal method for closing a business and paying off creditors when the business is failing and the debts are substantially greater than the assets.[76] Because bankruptcy is a complicated legal process, it is important to get an attorney involved as soon as possible. There may be options other than bankruptcy, and consulting with an attorney will help. The owner must understand how bankruptcy works and the options that are available. It is also good to know that not all bankruptcies are voluntary; creditors can petition the court for a business to declare bankruptcy.[77]

Chapter 7 small business bankruptcy, more commonly referred to as liquidation, is appropriate when a business is failing, has no future, and has no substantial assets. This form of bankruptcy makes sense only if the owner wants to walk away. It is particularly suited to sole proprietorships and other small businesses in which the business is essentially an extension of its owner's skills.[78] Under Chapter

bankruptcy

An extreme form of business termination that uses a legal method for closing a business and paying off creditors when a business is failing and the debts are substantially greater than the assets.

7 bankruptcy law, a trustee will take a business apart, selling assets to satisfy outstanding debts and discharging debts that cannot be satisfied with the assets that are available.[79]

Chapter 11 small business bankruptcy allows an owner to run a business with court oversight. The owner loses control of the firm, but it continues to operate. The owner is protected from creditors in the short term because the court orders an automatic stay that prevents the creditors from seizing your assets. Unfortunately, the outcome is not pleasant. The owner is out as manager, and the creditors end up owning the business. If the owner cannot pay the $75,000+ in legal fees, the judge will probably order liquidation, so the result is the same as a Chapter 7.[80] This form of bankruptcy applies to sole proprietorships, corporations, and partnerships.[81]

The amount that creditors can collect will depend on how a business is structured. If a business is a sole proprietorship, the owner's personal assets may be used to pay off business debts, depending on the chosen bankruptcy option. If a business is a corporation, a limited liability company, or some form of a partnership, the owner's personal assets are protected and cannot be used to pay off business debts.[82]

4.4 Alternatives to Bankruptcy

Instead of going the bankruptcy route, a small business owner could do the following things:[83]

- **Negotiate debt.** This involves trying to reorganize a business's finances outside a legal proceeding. The owner can work with the creditors to renegotiate the terms of payment and the amount owed to each creditor. If a business is basically profitable but the debt situation is due to an unusual circumstance, such as a lawsuit or a temporary industry slowdown, this could be a successful solution.

- **Improve operations.** If the owner is in a position to fix the cash problem by fixing the underlying problems in the business, it may not be necessary to declare bankruptcy. An owner should look at cash-flow controls; eliminate unprofitable products, services, and divisions; and restructure into a leaner and meaner organization.

- **Turn around and restructure the business.** This alternative combines debt negotiation and operational improvement—perhaps the best choice. By doing both things at the same time, an owner will be in an even stronger position to improve the balance sheet, cash flow, and profitability—and avoid insolvency.

4.5 Taking a Company Public

initial public offering (IPO)

A stock offering in which the owner or owners of equity in the formerly private company have their private holdings transferred into issues tradable on public markets.

An **initial public offering (IPO)** is a stock offering in which the owner or owners of equity in a formerly private company have their private holdings transferred into issues tradable in public markets, such as the New York Stock Exchange (NYSE).[84] From the initial owners' perspective, an IPO is often seen as liquidation, but it is also a money event for a company. For this reason, an IPO makes sense only if a small business can benefit from a substantial infusion of cash.[85]

IPOs receive lots of press, even though they are really very rare. In a typical year, there may be 200 IPOs, perhaps even less. Consider the following data:[86]

- 2008: 32 IPOs
- 2009: 63 IPOs
- 2010: 157 IPOs
- 2011: 159 IPOs[87]

Why are the numbers so small?[88] The IPO process is costly, labor intensive, and usually requires an up-front investment of more than $100,000. Detailed reports are required on a business's financials, staffing, marketing, operations, management, and so forth. Preparing these reports typically costs hundreds of thousands of dollars, sometimes millions, every year. The Sarbanes-Oxley Act alone, a product of the Enron scandal, costs even the smallest companies several hundred thousand dollars in consulting fees. Lastly, many companies are not valued very highly on the stock market.

When thinking about an IPO, consider the following pros and cons:[89]

- **Pros**
  - The owner will be on the cover of *Newsweek*.
  - The stock will be worth in the tens—or even hundreds—of millions of dollars.
  - Venture capitalists will finally stop bugging the owner as they frantically try to ensure their shares will retain value.

- **Cons**
  - Only a very few number of small businesses actually have this option available to them because there are so few IPOs in the United States each year.
  - A business needs financial and accounting rigor from day one that is way beyond what many small business owners put in place.
  - The owner will spend most of his or her time selling the company, not running it.
  - Investment bankers take 6 percent off the top, and the transaction costs of an IPO can run into the millions.

Stever Robbins of *Entrepreneur* paints an amusing but very dismal picture of what is actually involved in an IPO.[90]

> You start by spending millions just preparing for the road show, where you grovel to convince investors your stock should be worth as much as possible…Unlike an acquisition, where you craft a good fit with a single suitor, here you are romancing hundreds of Wall Street analysts. If the romance fails, you've blown millions. And if you succeed, you end up married to the analysts. You call that a life?
>
> Once public, you bow and scrape to the analysts. These earnest 28-year-olds—who haven't produced anything of value since winning their fifth grade limerick contest—will study your every move, soberly declaring your utter incompetence at running the business you've built over decades. It's one thing to receive this treatment from your loving spouse. It's quite another to receive it from Smith Barney.
>
> We won't even talk about the need to conform to Sarbanes-Oxley, or the 6 percent underwriting fees you'll pay to investment bankers, or lockout periods, or how markets can tank your wealth despite having a healthy business, or how IPO-raised funds distort your income statement, or…
>
> In short, IPOs are not only rare, they're a pain in the backside. They make the headlines in the very, very rare cases that they produce 20-year-old billionaires. But when you're founding [and running] your company, consider them just one of many exit strategies. Realize that there are a lot of ways to skin a cat, and just as many ways to get value out of your company. Think ahead, surely, but do it with sanity and gravitas. And if you find yourself tempted to start looking for more office space in preparation for your IPO in 18 months, call me first. I'll talk you down until the paramedic arrives.

For some small businesses, although not many, an IPO might make sense—and may even be necessary. For most, however, an IPO is clearly not a viable exit strategy.

4.6 Selling the Business

Another possible exit strategy is selling the business. Although the sale of a business is sometimes described as the end of entrepreneurship or as failure or defeat,[91] selling the business can also be a relief and the beginning of the next phase of the owner's personal and professional life. As in the case of SoBe (highlighted at the beginning of this chapter), the owners sold the business because, among other things, it was becoming something they did not want it to be—and it was no longer fun. Whatever the reason, an owner can sell a business only once, so be sure that it is the right exit strategy. The owner should address the following questions:[92]

1. **Can the business be sold?** There are many things that make a business attractive to buyers: a solid history of profitability, a large and loyal base of customers, a good reputation, a competitive

advantage (e.g., intellectual property rights, patents, long-term contracts with clients, and exclusive distributorships), opportunities for growth, a desirable location, a skilled workforce, and a loyal workforce. If a business does not have at least some of these things or others of equal value, it will not likely generate much interest in the market.

2. **Is the owner ready to sell or does the owner need to sell?** Selling a business, when it is a choice, requires emotional and financial readiness. The owner must think about what life will be like after the business is sold. What will be a source of income? How will time be spent? Has the owner "sold out" or could more have been done with the business? Does the owner love what he or she is doing? Many small business owners suffer real remorse after handing their businesses over to a new owner. Selling the business because the owner is forced to will engender very different emotional and financial challenges.

3. **What is the business worth?** The owner may have no idea. For example, the owner of a small professional services firm felt the firm was worth more than $1 million. After a lengthy search, however, the owner received less than one-half that amount from the buyer. On the other side of the coin, the owner of an information technology (IT) company planned to sell the company to an employee for $200,000. However, after advertising the business for sale nationwide, the owner sold it for one dollar shy of $1 million.

It is recommended that an owner start planning for a sale at least three to four years in advance. Sometimes, even five years is not long enough. It is very easy to become overly attached to a business, so it will be difficult to see how the business really looks to an outsider.[93] Selling a business is an art and a science. If the asking price is too high, this may signal to potential buyers that the owner is not really interested in selling. Because there are several methods used to value a business, it is a good idea to hire a professional.[94]

There are different ways to sell a business (see Figure 14.5). Acquisition, friendly buyout, selling to the employees, and selling on the open market are discussed here. Be aware, however, that if a business is floundering and it is well known that the business is having major problems paying bills, **vulture capitalists** might start circling. A vulture capitalist is a **venture capitalist** who invests in floundering firms in the hope that they will turn around.[95] A venture capitalist is an investor who either provides capital to start-up ventures or supports small companies to expand but does not have access to public funding. Venture capitalists typically expect higher returns because they are taking additional risks.[96]

vulture capitalists

A venture capitalist who invests in floundering firms in the hope that they will turn around.

venture capitalist

Individuals who provide money for start-up businesses or additional capital for a business to grow. They invest to make not only a profit but also returns that are substantially greater than those found in the market.

FIGURE 14.5 Four Ways to Sell a Small Business

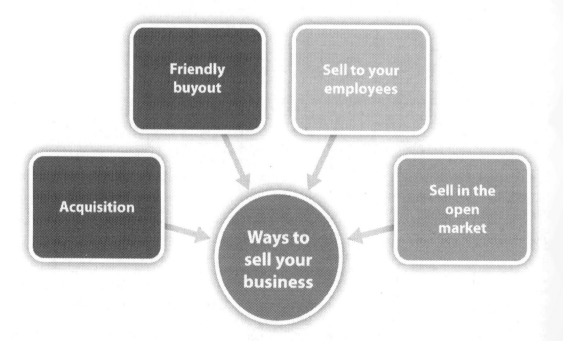

Acquisition

When one business buys another business, as in the case of Pepsi buying SoBe, it is called an **acquisition**. Businesses buy other businesses for all kinds of reasons—for example, as a quick path to expansion or diversification or to get rid of the competition. When Pepsi was considering acquiring SoBe, their first thought was to kill the brand. But the bottlers convinced them otherwise, saying that it was a very strong brand.[97]

Acquisition is one of the most common exit strategies for a small business. One key to success is to target the potential acquirer(s) in advance, position the business accordingly, and convince the acquirer that the small business is worth the asking price.[98] Another way to become the target of an acquisition is to be successful in the marketplace. This happened with SoBe. Coca-Cola, Pepsi, Arizona, and Campbell's all expressed an interest after SoBe became a national brand. Pepsi ended up being the acquirer in the end.[99]

In an acquisition, the owner negotiates the price—a good thing because public markets value a business relative to its industry, which limits the value of a business. In an acquisition, however, there is no limit on the perceived value of a company. Why? The person making the acquisition decision is rarely the owner of the acquiring company, so there is no problem with the checkbook. It is someone else's money.

When thinking about an acquisition, consider the following pros and cons:

- Pros[100]

    - If a business has strategic value to an acquirer, it may pay far more than the business is worth to anyone else.
    - If multiple acquirers are in a bidding war, the owner can raise the price "to the stratosphere."

- Cons[101]

    - If the owner organizes the business around a specific acquirer, the business may be unattractive to other buyers.
    - Acquisitions are messy and often difficult when cultures and systems clash in the merged company. Although not a small business example, the Warner-AOL combination was a failure largely due to a major culture clash.
    - Acquisitions are frequently accompanied by noncompete agreements and other strings that, while making the owner rich, can make life unpleasant for a while. Noncompete agreements are enforceable, but their enforcement depends on the applicable facts and circumstances—including which state's law governs.[102]

Friendly Buyout

A **friendly buyout** occurs when ownership is transferred to family members, customers, employees, current managers, children, or friends. It is still considered selling the business, but the terms and nature of the transaction are usually very different. No matter who the "friendly" buyer may be, figure on starting to plan early—and engage a professional before, during, and after the sale.[103]

When thinking about friendly buyout, consider the following pros and cons:

- Pros[104]

    - The owner knows much more about the buyer, and the buyer knows the owner. There is less due diligence required.
    - The buyer will most likely preserve what is important about the business.
    - If management buys the business, it has a commitment to make it work.

- Cons[105]

    - The owner will be less objective about the buyer and more likely to let his or her guard down in negotiations and planning. The owner leaves too much money on the table.
    - If the owner sells to a friend, the friend will be less than thrilled when discovering, for example, decades' worth of unpaid taxes.
    - Selling to family can tear a company apart with jealousies and promotions that put emotion ahead of business needs.

acquisition

When another business buys a business.

friendly buyout

The transfer of ownership to family members, customers, employees, children, or friends.

Selling to Employees

Selling the business to employees and/or managers is another option to consider. "Arranging an employee buyout can be a win-win situation as they get an established business they know a great deal about already and you get enthusiastic buyers that want to see your business continue to thrive."[106] The owner can accomplish this process by setting up an employee stock option plan (ESOP), a stock equity plan that lets employees buy ownership in the business. However, because the owner is giving control of the business to the employees, a transition plan is critical to make sure that they are ready to carry on the business after the owner leaves. It is a good idea to hire an ESOP specialist. Keep in mind, though, that only corporations are eligible to form an ESOP. An ESOP is expensive to set up and maintain, so this might not be the best choice.[107]

If an ESOP is not appealing or the business is not eligible to have an ESOP, selling the business could be as simple as having a current employee take it over. The owner could also consider a **worker-owned cooperative**, in which interested employees become members of a cooperative that buys the business.[108] In the case of Select Machine of Brimfield, Ohio, "[the owners] sold 30 percent of their stock to the co-op in the first of several installments. The co-op took out loans in the amount of $324,000, which were personally guaranteed by the sellers. The loans were paid off out of company profits over three years; subsequent installments have been owner-financed. Today the co-op owns 59 percent of the company's stock, and sale of an additional 10 percent is now on the table."[109]

For a worker-owned cooperative to work, the business owner(s) must be totally committed to the sale of the business to the employees. It is a good option if the business is small (fewer than twenty-five employees), profitable, relatively debt free, already has a culture of participatory management, and the owners are willing to stay on throughout the transition.[110]

Selling on the Open Market

Selling a business on the open market is the most popular exit strategy for small businesses.[111] Unfortunately, it has been estimated that 75 percent of US businesses do not sell,[112] so if this is how the owner wants to sell the business, it must be marketed in a way that maximizes its value in the eyes of a potential buyer.

An owner also needs to spread the word. Most savvy business buyers use the Internet to research available businesses for sale, so post the sale notice on the two largest websites:[113] BizBuySell.com, self-described as the "Internet's Largest Business for Sale Marketplace," and BizQuest.com, self-described as the "Original Business for Sale Website."

---

worker-owned cooperative

Interested employees who become members of a cooperative that buys a business.

KEY TAKEAWAYS

- The most emotional topic an owner will face when building a business—and the hardest decision he or she will probably have to make—is when and how to exit.
- An exit strategy should be planned while running the business. Unfortunately, many small businesses do not have an exit plan.
- There are many exit strategies that a small business owner can consider, including liquidation or walkaway, family succession, selling the business, bankruptcy, and taking a company public.
- The best exit strategy is the one that best matches the small business and the owner's personal and professional goals.
- Liquidation is the selling of all assets. If all debts are paid, it can also be referred to as a walkaway. Walking away is the cleanest and best way to exit a business.
- Family succession is the transference of leadership from one generation to the next to ensure continuity of family ownership in the business. It is a critical issue in family businesses because few family firms survive beyond the first generation and even fewer survive into the third generation.
- The failure to plan for succession is seen as a basic human resource problem as well as the primary cause for the poor survival rate of family businesses.
- Bankruptcy is an extreme exit strategy that uses a legal method for closing a business and paying off creditors when a business is failing and the debts are substantially greater than the assets.
- Debt negotiations, operational improvements, or business turnaround and restructuring are alternatives to bankruptcy.
- An IPO is a stock offering in which the owner or owners of equity in a business have their private holdings transferred into issues tradable in public markets, such as the NYSE.
- There are several options for selling a business: acquisition, friendly buyout, selling to the employees, and selling in the open market.
- An acquisition is when another business buys a business. In an acquisition, there is no limit on the perceived value of the business.
- A friendly buyout is the transfer of ownership to family members, customers, employees, current managers, children, or friends—but it is still a sale.
- Selling to the employees can be a win-win situation because they get an established business that they know a great deal about already, and the owner gets enthusiastic buyers who want to see a business continue to thrive.
- Selling in the open market is the most popular exit strategy for small businesses.
- It has been estimated that 75 percent of small businesses do not sell, so a business must market in a way that maximizes its value in the eyes of the potential buyer.

EXERCISE

1. Two executives of a regional food company are regular customers and big fans of Frank's All-American BarBeQue. They recently learned that Frank has been selling his sauces in local grocery stores and have been a big hit. The executives bought jars of each flavor, took them back to their company, and talked to the people who would decide about adding products to their line. Everyone loved the sauces, and there was definite interest in acquiring the sauce-making side of Frank's business. It would fill a hole in their product line that they had been looking to fill.

   The company contacted Frank about its interest, and Frank—with some urging from his son, Robert—is thinking about it. It would provide Frank with a nice retirement (when he decides to do that), money for his son and daughter, and a legacy. How should Frank proceed?

ENDNOTES

1. "Planning Can Cut Disaster Recovery Time, Expense," *US Small Business Administration*, accessed February 6, 2012, archive.sba.gov/idc/groups/public/documents/sba_homepage/serv_da_dprep_howtoprep.pdf.

2. Darrell Zahorsky, "Disaster Recovery Decision Making for Small Business," *About.com*, accessed February 6, 2012, sbinformation.about.com/od/disastermanagement/a/disasterrecover.htm.

3. Darrell Zahorsky, "Disaster Recovery Decision Making for Small Business," *About.com*, accessed February 6, 2012, sbinformation.about.com/od/disastermanagement/a/disasterrecover.htm.

4. "Declared Disasters by Year and State," *Federal Emergency Management Agency*, accessed February 6, 2012, www.fema.gov/news/disaster_totals_annual.fema.

5. "Planning Can Cut Disaster Recovery Time, Expense," *US Small Business Administration*, accessed February 6, 2012, archive.sba.gov/idc/groups/public/documents/sba_homepage/serv_da_dprep_howtoprep.pdf.

6. F. John Reh, "Survive the Unthinkable through Crisis Planning," *About.com*, accessed February 6, 2012, management.about.com/cs/communication/a/PlaceBlame1000.htm.

7. Darrell Zahorsky, "Disaster Recovery Decision Making for Small Business," *About.com*, accessed February 6, 2012, sbinformation.about.com/od/disastermanagement/a/disasterrecover.htm.

8. "Man-Made Disaster," *BusinessDictionary.com*, accessed February 6, 2012, www.businessdictionary.com/definition/man-made-disaster.html.

9. "Anthropogenic Hazard," *Wikipedia*, accessed February 6, 2012, en.wikipedia.org/wiki/List_of_man-made_disasters.

10. "Disaster Preparedness: FAQs," *US Small Business Administration*, accessed February 6, 2012, sbaonline.sba.gov/services/disasterassistance/disasterpreparedness/serv_da_dprep_howcaniprep.html.

11. "Planning Can Cut Disaster Recovery Time, Expense," *US Small Business Administration*, accessed February 6, 2012, archive.sba.gov/idc/groups/public/documents/sba_homepage/serv_da_dprep_howtoprep.pdf.

12. F. John Reh, "Survive the Unthinkable through Crisis Planning," *About.com*, accessed February 6, 2012, management.about.com/cs/communication/a/PlaceBlame1000.htm.

13. "Plan For and Protect Your Business," *Ready.gov*, accessed February 29, 2012, www.ready.gov/business.

14. "Fires," *American Red Cross*, accessed February 6, 2012, www.sdarc.org/HowWeHelp/DisasterPreparedness/Fire/tabid/31/Default.aspx.

15. "How to Create a Business Continuity Plan," *wikiHow*, accessed February 6, 2012, www.wikihow.com/Create-a-Business-Continuity-Plan.

16. "Plan For and Protect Your Business," *Ready.gov*, accessed February 29, 2012, www.ready.gov/business; "How to Create a Business Continuity Plan," *wikiHow*, accessed February 6, 2012, www.wikihow.com/Create-a-Business-Continuity-Plan.

17. "Disaster Preparedness: FAQs," *US Small Business Administration*, accessed June 1, 2012, http://archive.sba.gov/services/disasterassistance/disasterpreparedness/serv_da_dprep_howcaniprep.html.

18. Kristie Lorette, "Importance of Good Communication in Business," *Chron.com*, accessed February 6, 2012, smallbusiness.chron.com/importance-good-communication-business-1403.html.

19. Leslie Schwab, "Small Business: The Importance of Strong Communication Skills," *Helium*, June 20, 2009, accessed February 6, 2012, www.helium.com/items/1486526-strong-communication-skills-are-required-for-success-in-small-business.

20. "Plan For and Protect Your Business," *Ready.gov*, accessed February 29, 2012, www.ready.gov/business.

21. "Plan For and Protect Your Business," *Ready.gov*, accessed February 29, 2012, www.ready.gov/business.

22. Darrell Zahorsky, "Disaster Recovery Decision Making for Small Business," *About.com*, accessed February 6, 2012, sbinformation.about.com/od/disastermanagement/a/disasterrecover.htm.

23. John H. Ehrenreich, "Coping with Disasters: A Guidebook to Psychosocial Intervention," *Toolkit Sport for Development*, October 2001, accessed February 6, 2012, www.toolkitsportdevelopment.org/html/resources/7B/7B83B250-3EB8-44C6-AA8E-CC6592C53550/CopingWithDisaster.pdf.

24. "Plan For and Protect Your Business," *Ready.gov*, accessed February 29, 2012, www.ready.gov/business.

25. "Insurance Coverage Review Worksheet," *Ready.gov*, accessed February 6, 2012, www.ready.gov/sites/default/files/documents/files/InsuranceReview_Worksheet.pdf.

26. "Disaster Preparedness: FAQs," *US Small Business Administration*, accessed June 1, 2012, http://archive.sba.gov/services/disasterassistance/disasterpreparedness/serv_da_dprep_howcaniprep.html.

27. "Business Interruption Insurance," *Entrepreneur*, accessed February 6, 2012, www.entrepreneur.com/encyclopedia/term/82292.html.

28. "Business Interruption Insurance," *Entrepreneur*, accessed February 6, 2012, www.entrepreneur.com/encyclopedia/term/82282.html.

29. "Plan For and Protect Your Business," *Ready.gov*, accessed February 29, 2012, www.ready.gov/business.

30. "Plan For and Protect Your Business," *Ready.gov*, accessed February 29, 2012, www.ready.gov/business.

31. "CyberSecurity by Chubb," *Chubb Group of Insurance Companies*, accessed February 6, 2012, www.chubb.com/businesses/csi/chubb822.html.

32. "Plan For and Protect Your Business," *Ready.gov*, accessed February 29, 2012, www.ready.gov/business.

33. "Plan For and Protect Your Business," *Ready.gov*, accessed February 29, 2012, www.ready.gov/business; "Cyber Security Liability Insurance," *Wall Street Journal*, March 18, 2010, as cited in Robert Hess and Company Insurance Brokers, May 6, 2010, accessed February 6, 2012, robhessco.com/183/cyber-security-liability-insurance/; Eric Schwartzel, "Cybersecurity Insurance: Many Companies Continue to Ignore the Issue," *Pittsburg Post-Gazette*, June 22, 2010, accessed February 6, 2012, www.post-gazette.com/pg/10173/1067262-96.stm.

34. Darrell Zahorsky, "Disaster Recovery Decision Making for Small Business," *About.com*, accessed February 6, 2012, sbinformation.about.com/od/disastermanagement/a/disasterrecover.htm.

35. "Disaster Assistance For Businesses of All Sizes," *US Small Business Administration*, accessed February 28, 2012, archive.sba.gov/idc/groups/public/documents/sba_homepage/serv_da_dprep_factsheethome.pdf.

36. "Disaster Assistance For Businesses of All Sizes," *US Small Business Administration*, accessed February 28, 2012, archive.sba.gov/idc/groups/public/documents/sba_homepage/serv_da_dprep_factsheethome.pdf.

37. See, for example, the small business loans that are available through the Union County Economic Development Corporation (Union, New Jersey) for disaster assistance: scotchplains.patch.com/articles/union-county-makes-small-business-loans-available.

38. "Demand Grows for Disaster Loans," *Wall Street Journal*, September 7, 2011, accessed February 6, 2012, blogs.wsj.com/in-charge/2011/09/07/demand-grows-for-disaster-loans/?mod=google_news_blog.

39. "Disaster Assistance For Businesses of All Sizes," *US Small Business Administration*, accessed February 28, 2012, archive.sba.gov/idc/groups/public/documents/sba_homepage/serv_da_dprep_factsheethome.pdf.

40. "Disaster Assistance and Emergency Relief for Individuals and Businesses," *Internal Revenue Service*, accessed February 6, 2012, www.irs.gov/businesses/small/article/0,id=156138,00.html.

41. "About SCORE," *SCORE*, accessed February 6, 2012, www.score.org/about-score.

42. "Disaster Assistance and Emergency Relief for Individuals and Businesses," *Internal Revenue Service*, accessed February 6, 2012, www.irs.gov/businesses/small/article/0,id=156138,00.html; "What Is DisasterAssistance.gov," *DisasterAssistance.gov*, accessed February 6, 2012, www.disasterassistance.gov.

43. "Disaster Assistance and Emergency Relief for Individuals and Businesses," *Internal Revenue Service*, accessed February 6, 2012, www.irs.gov/businesses/small/article/0,id=156138,00.html; "Looking for Benefits?," accessed February 6, 2012, www.benefits.gov.

44. "Knowing When to Throw in the Towel," *Fox Business*, May 2, 2011, accessed February 6, 2012, smallbusiness.foxbusiness.com/entrepreneurs/2011/05/02/knowing-throw-towel.

45. Timothy Faley, "Making Your Exit," *Inc.*, March 1, 2006, accessed February 6, 2012, www.inc.com/resources/startup/articles/20060301/tfaley.html; "Knowing When to Throw in the Towel," *Fox Business*, May 2, 2011, accessed February 6, 2012, smallbusiness.foxbusiness.com/entrepreneurs/2011/05/02/knowing-throw-towel.

46. Dan Bigman, "On the Hunt," *Forbes* 185, no. 2 (2009): 56–59.

47. Noam Wasserman, "The Founder's Dilemma," *Harvard Business Review*, February 2008, 1–8.

48. Noam Wasserman, "The Founder's Dilemma," *Harvard Business Review*, February 2008, 1–8.

49. Noam Wasserman, "The Founder's Dilemma," *Harvard Business Review*, February 2008, 1–8.

50. Dan Bigman, "On the Hunt," *Forbes* 185, no. 2 (2009): 56–59; Noam Wasserman, "The Founder's Dilemma," *Harvard Business Review*, February 2008, 1–8.

51. Richard Carter and Howard Van Auken, "Small Firm Bankruptcy," *Journal of Small Business Management* 44, no. 4 (2006): 493–512.

52. Geoff Williams, "Dead Zone," *Entrepreneur*, March 2007, accessed February 6, 2012, www.entrepreneur.com/magazine/entrepreneur/2007/march/174716.html.

53. Leigh Buchanan, "A Fight for Survival: When the Boss Gets Cancer," *Inc.*, July/August 2009, 106, 108.

54. Joel Spolsky, "The Day My Industry Died," *Inc.*, July/August 2009, 37–38.

55. Sarah E. Needleman, Vanessa O'Connell, Emily Maltby, and Angus Loten, "And the Most Innovative Entrepreneur Is...," *Wall Street Journal*, November 14, 2011, accessed February 6, 2012, online.wsj.com/article/SB10001424052970203716204577013501641346794.html.

56. Timothy Faley, "Making Your Exit," *Inc.*, March 1, 2006, accessed February 6, 2012, www.inc.com/resources/startup/articles/20060301/tfaley.html.

57. "Consider Your Exit Strategy When Starting Up: Why You Need an Exit Strategy," *Business Link*, accessed February 6, 2012, www.businesslink.gov.uk/bdotg/action/detail?itemid=1073792644&type=RESOURCES.

58. Susan Ward, "Exit Strategies for Your Small Business," *About.com*, accessed June 1, 2012, sbinfocanada.about.com/od/businessplanning/a/exitstrategies.htm.

59. Steven Robbins, "Exit Strategies for Your Business," *Entrepreneur*, June 27, 2005, accessed February 6, 2012, www.entrepreneur.com/article/78512.

60. Andrew Clarke, "Exit Strategies for Small Business Owners," *Experts.com*, 2006, accessed February 6, 2012, www.experts.com/Articles/Exit-Strategies-for-Small-Business-Owners-By-Andrew-Clarke.

61. "Goodwill," *Investopedia*, accessed February 6, 2012, www.investopedia.com/terms/g/goodwill.asp.

62. Andrew Clarke, "Exit Strategies for Small Business Owners," *Experts.com*, 2006, accessed February 6, 2012, www.experts.com/Articles/Exit-Strategies-for-Small-Business-Owners-By-Andrew-Clarke.

63. "Badwill," *Investopedia*, accessed February 6, 2012, www.investopedia.com/terms/b/badwill.asp.

64. Stever Robbins, "Exit Strategies for Your Business," *Entrepreneur*, June 27, 2005, accessed February 6, 2012, www.entrepreneur.com/article/78512.

65. Jerome A. Katz and Richard P. Green, *Entrepreneurial Small Business* (New York: McGraw-Hill Irwin, 2009), 663.

66. Andrew Clarke, "Exit Strategies for Small Business Owners," *Experts.com*, 2006, accessed February 6, 2012, www.experts.com/Articles/Exit-Strategies-for-Small-Business-Owners-By-Andrew-Clarke; Stever Robbins, "Exit Strategies for Your Business," *Entrepreneur*, June 27, 2005, accessed February 6, 2012, www.entrepreneur.com/article/78512.

67. Susan Ward, "Exit Strategies for Your Small Business," *About.com*, accessed February 6, 2012, sbinfocanada.about.com/od/businessplanning/a/exitstrategies.htm.

68. Sue Birley, "Succession in the Family Firm: The Inheritor's View," *Journal of Small Business Management* 24, no. 3 (1986): 36–43; Manfred F. R. Kets de Vries, "The Dynamics of Family Controlled Firms: The Good News and the Bad News," *Organizational Dynamics* 21, no. 3 (1993), 59–68; Michael H. Morris, Roy O. Williams, Jeffrey A. Allen, and Ramon A. Avila, "Correlates of Success in Family Business Transitions," *Journal of Business Venturing* 12 (1997): 385–401.

69. Wendy C. Handler, "Succession in Family Business: A Review of the Literature," *Family Business Review* 7, no. 2 (1994): 133–57.

70. Stanley M. Davis, "Entrepreneurial Succession," *Administrative Science Quarterly* 13 (1968): 402–16, as cited in A. Bakr Ibrahim, Khaled Soufani, Panikkos Poutziouris, and Jose Lam, "Qualities of an Effective Successor: The Role of Education and Training," *Education and Training* 46, no. 8/9 (2004): 474–80.

71. A. Bakr Ibrahim, Khaled Soufani, Panikkos Poutziouris, and Jose Lam, "Qualities of an Effective Successor: The Role of Education and Training," *Education and Training* 46, no. 8/9 (2004): 474–80; Katiuska Cabrera-Suarez, "Leadership Transfer and the Successor's Development in the Family Firm," *The Leadership Quarterly* 16 (2005): 71–96.

72. Katiuska Cabrera-Suarez, "Leadership Transfer and the Successor's Development in the Family Firm," *The Leadership Quarterly* 16 (2005): 71–96.

73. Katiuska Cabrera-Suarez, "Leadership Transfer and the Successor's Development in the Family Firm," *The Leadership Quarterly* 16 (2005): 71–96.

74. A. Bakr Ibrahim, Khaled Soufani, Panikkos Poutziouris, and Jose Lam, "Qualities of an Effective Successor: The Role of Education and Training," *Education and Training* 46, no. 8/9 (2004): 474–80.

75. Stephan van der Merwe, Elmarie Venter, and Suria M. Ellis, "An Exploratory Study of Some of the Determinants of Management Succession Planning in Family Businesses," *Management Dynamics* 18, no. 4 (2009): 2–17.

76. Jerome A. Katz and Richard P. Green, *Entrepreneurial Small Business* (New York: McGraw-Hill Irwin, 2009), 663.

77. "Bankruptcy," *US Small Business Administration*, accessed February 6, 2012, www.sba.gov/content/bankruptcy.

78. Caron Beesley, "Bankruptcy Options for the Small Business Owner," *AllBusiness.com*, February 5, 2009, accessed February 6, 2012, www.allbusiness.com/company-activities-management/company-structures-ownership/11772426-1.html; "Small Business Bankruptcy…You Have Choices," *Daniel B. James Group*, accessed February 6, 2012, www.small-business-bankruptcy.com.

79. Caron Beesley, "Bankruptcy Options for the Small Business Owner," *AllBusiness.com*, February 5, 2009, accessed February 6, 2012, www.allbusiness.com/company-activities-management/company-structures-ownership/11772426-1.html; "Small Business Bankruptcy…You Have Choices," *Daniel B. James Group*, accessed February 6, 2012, www.small-business-bankruptcy.com.

80. "Small Business Bankruptcy…You Have Choices," *Daniel B. James Group*, accessed February 6, 2012, www.small-business-bankruptcy.com.

81. Caron Beesley, "Bankruptcy Options for the Small Business Owner," *AllBusiness.com*, February 5, 2009, www.allbusiness.com/company-activities-management/company-structures-ownership/11772426-1.html.

82. "Bankruptcy," *US Small Business Administration*, accessed February 6, 2012, www.sba.gov/content/bankruptcy.

83. "Small Business Bankruptcy…You Have Choices," *Daniel B. James Group*, accessed February 6, 2012, www.small-business-bankruptcy.com.

84. Timothy Faley, "Making Your Exit," *Inc.*, March 1, 2006, accessed February 6, 2012, www.inc.com/resources/startup/articles/20060301/tfaley.html.

85. Timothy Faley, "Making Your Exit," *Inc.*, March 1, 2006, accessed February 6, 2012, www.inc.com/resources/startup/articles/20060301/tfaley.html.

86. "IPOs in 2011," *Upcoming-IPOs.com*, August 23, 2011, accessed February 6, 2012, upcoming-ipos.com/ipos-in-2011; Trent Tillman, "2010 Year-End U.S. IPO Review and 2011 Outlook," *Syndicate Trader*, March 4, 2011, accessed February 6, 2012, syndicatetrader.wordpress.com/2011/03/04/2010-year-end-u-s-ipo-review-and-2011-outlook.

87. Douglas W. Campbell, "2011 IPO Review & 2012 Outlook," *Triad Securities*, January 6, 2012, accessed February 28, 2012, www.triadsecurities.com/ipo_review/20120106.

88. Andrew Clarke, "Exit Strategies for Small Business Owners," *Experts.com*, 2006, accessed February 6, 2012, www.experts.com/Articles/Exit-Strategies-for-Small-Business-Owners-By-Andrew-Clarke.

89. Stever Robbins, "Exit Strategies for Your Business," *Entrepreneur*, June 27, 2005, accessed February 6, 2012, www.entrepreneur.com/article/78512.

90. Stever Robbins, "Exit Strategies for Your Business," *Entrepreneur*, June 27, 2005, accessed February 6, 2012, www.entrepreneur.com/article/78512.

91. J. G. Pellegrin, "Toward a Model of Making and Executing the Decision to Sell: An Exploratory Study of the Sale of Family Owned Companies" (PhD diss.), Lausanne Business School, Switzerland, 1999, as cited in Christian Niedermeyer, Peter Jaskiewicz, and Sabine B. Klein, "'Can't Get to Satisfaction?' Evaluating the Sale of the Family Business from the Family's Perspective and Driving Implications for New Venture Activities," *Entrepreneurship & Regional Development* 22, no. 3–4 (2010): 293–320.

92. Barbara Taylor, "How to Sell Your Business," *New York Times*, January 7, 2010, accessed February 6, 2012, www.nytimes.com/2010/01/07/business/smallbusiness/07guide.html; Anthony Tjan, "The Founder's Dilemma: To Sell or Not to Sell?," *Harvard Business Review*, February 18, 2011, accessed February 6, 2012, blogs.hbr.org/tjan/2011/02/the-founders-dilemma-to-sell-o.html.

93. Andrew Clarke, "Exit Strategies for Small Business Owners," *Experts.com*, 2006, accessed February 6, 2012, www.experts.com/Articles/Exit-Strategies-for-Small-Business-Owners-By-Andrew-Clarke.

94. Barbara Taylor, "How to Sell Your Business," *New York Times*, January 7, 2010, accessed February 6, 2012, www.nytimes.com/2010/01/07/business/smallbusiness/07guide.html.

95. "Vulture Capitalist," *Investopedia*, accessed February 6, 2012, www.investopedia.com/terms/v/vulturecapitalist.asp; "Vulture Capitalist," *Urban Dictionary*, November 12, 2009, accessed February 6, 2012, www.urbandictionary.com/define.php?term=Vulture%20Capitalist.

96. "Venture Capitalist," *Investopedia*, accessed February 6, 2012, www.investopedia.com/terms/v/venturecapitalist.asp.

97. Interview with John Bello, cofounder of SoBe, August 23, 2011.

98. Susan Ward, "Exit Strategies for Your Small Business," *About.com*, accessed February 6, 2012, sbinfocanada.about.com/od/businessplanning/a/exitstrategies.htm.

99. Interview with John Bello, cofounder of SoBe, August 23, 2011.

100. Stever Robbins, "Exit Strategies for Your Business," *Entrepreneur*, June 27, 2005, accessed February 6, 2012, www.entrepreneur.com/article/78512.

101. Stever Robbins, "Exit Strategies for Your Business," *Entrepreneur*, June 27, 2005, accessed February 6, 2012, www.entrepreneur.com/article/78512.

102. George W. Keeley, "Non-Compete Agreements: Are They Enforceable?," *KK&R*, accessed February 29, 2012, www.kkrlaw.com/articles/noncomp.htm.

103. Andrew Clarke, "Exit Strategies for Small Business Owners," *Experts.com*, 2006, accessed February 6, 2012, www.experts.com/Articles/Exit-Strategies-for-Small-Business-Owners-By-Andrew-Clarke; Stever Robbins, "Exit Strategies for Your Business," *Entrepreneur*, June 27, 2005, accessed February 6, 2012, www.entrepreneur.com/article/78512.

104. Andrew Clarke, "Exit Strategies for Small Business Owners," *Experts.com*, 2006, accessed February 6, 2012, www.experts.com/Articles/Exit-Strategies-for-Small-Business-Owners-By-Andrew-Clarke; Stever Robbins, "Exit Strategies for Your Business," *Entrepreneur*, June 27, 2005, accessed February 6, 2012, www.entrepreneur.com/article/78512.

105. Andrew Clarke, "Exit Strategies for Small Business Owners," *Experts.com*, 2006, accessed February 6, 2012, www.experts.com/Articles/Exit-Strategies-for-Small-Business-Owners-By-Andrew-Clarke; Stever Robbins, "Exit Strategies for Your Business," *Entrepreneur*, June 27, 2005, accessed February 6, 2012, www.entrepreneur.com/article/78512.

106. Susan Ward, "Exit Strategies for Your Small Business," *About.com*, accessed February 6, 2012, sbinfocanada.about.com/od/businessplanning/a/exitstrategies.htm.

107. Monica Mehta, "Alternative Exits for Business Owners," *Bloomberg BusinessWeek*, July 27, 2010, accessed February 6, 2012, www.BusinessWeek.com/smallbiz/content/jul2010/sb20100727_564778.htm.

108. Barbara Taylor, "A Creative Way to Sell Your Business," *New York Times*, October 29, 2010, accessed February 6, 2012, boss.blogs.nytimes.com/2010/10/29/a-creative-way-to-sell-your-business.

109. Barbara Taylor, "A Creative Way to Sell Your Business," *New York Times*, October 29, 2010, accessed February 6, 2012, boss.blogs.nytimes.com/2010/10/29/a-creative-way-to-sell-your-business.

110. Barbara Taylor, "A Creative Way to Sell Your Business," *New York Times*, October 29, 2010, accessed February 6, 2012, boss.blogs.nytimes.com/2010/10/29/a-creative-way-to-sell-your-business.

111. Susan Ward, "Exit Strategies for Your Small Business," *About.com*, accessed February 6, 2012, sbinfocanada.about.com/od/businessplanning/a/exitstrategies.htm.

112. Harvey Zemmel, "Top 7 Ways to Maximize Your Exit Strategy for Maximum Profit," *About.com*, accessed February 6, 2012, sbinfocanada.about.com/od/sellingabusiness/a/exitstrategyhz.htm.

113. Barbara Taylor, "A Creative Way to Sell Your Business," *New York Times*, October 29, 2010, accessed February 6, 2012, boss.blogs.nytimes.com/2010/10/29/a-creative-way-to-sell-your-business.

CHAPTER 15
Going Global: Yes or No?

Center Rock Inc.

Source: Reprinted with permission from Center Rock, Inc.

Brandon Fisher, the founder of Center Rock Inc., is shown on the left side in the picture. The man to his right is Richard Soppe, the senior drilling application engineer. The number 33 is the number of Chilean miners who were rescued in 2010. Brandon and his company, now at seventy-five employees, are true American heroes.

Center Rock manufactures and distributes a complete line of air drilling tools and products. At its state-of-the-art manufacturing facility in Pennsylvania, they build stock and made-to-order products that are used by leading drilling, oil and gas, foundation, construction, roadway, and mining contractors across North America, Europe, Asia, Russia, and Australia. Fisher entered the global market four years ago as a way to expand the business. He was able to finance the expansion internally, so financing was not an issue.

Center Rock Inc., founded in 1998 by then twenty-six-year-old Brandon Fisher, began as a drilling company. He designed and built his own horizontal drilling rig and, shortly thereafter, began focusing on making Center Rock an air and rock drilling supplier and manufacturer. He recognized the need for a manufacturing company that was reactive to customer needs, with innovative products and 24/7 customer service and support. Working with his high-tech engineering and design team, Fisher created a company different from its competitors with its unique products and service capabilities.

"I love what I do," says Fisher. "There is always a challenge in this industry to find new ways to drill into the earth, and the challenge feeds the excitement."[1]

1.   US SMALL BUSINESS IN THE GLOBAL ENVIRONMENT

LEARNING OBJECTIVES

1. Understand and appreciate the role of small businesses in the global environment.
2. Learn about the global growth opportunities for small businesses.
3. Understand the advantages and the disadvantages of a small business going global.

Although small businesses make up a disproportionately large share of the number of companies that export and import, this represents only about 1 percent of the total number of small businesses. Thus many small businesses have yet to compete globally. The opportunities are there. "So much of what America makes is in great demand," said US Commerce Secretary Gary Locke in an interview, adding further that the growth potential for small companies is outside the United States. Dale Hayes, vice president of US marketing for UPS concurs, observing that the demand for high-quality American products is huge.[2] It may be that a small business is already competing globally because foreign-owned companies are competing in our own backyards.[3]

Yet the global marketplace is not relevant to most small businesses. Given that 99 percent of the small businesses in the United States are not operating globally—preferring to grow (if they want to) locally, regionally, and perhaps nationally—it is reasonable to conclude that going global will interest only a few. Those few, however, must undertake careful analyses before jumping into the global arena.

1.1   The Small Business Global Presence

It may seem to many that the global market is the domain of the large corporations, but the statistics tell a very different story. Small businesses actually account for close to 97.6 percent of US exporters and 32.8 percent of the value of US exports as well as 97.1 percent of all identified importers and 31.9 percent of the known import value.[4] Consider the following additional facts:[5]

- Small businesses account for 96.4 percent of all manufacturing exporters, which is 17.2 percent of the sector's $562 billion in exports.
- Nearly 100 percent (99.2 percent) of exporting wholesalers were small businesses, which is 61.1 percent of the sector's $218 billion in exports.
- Of other companies with exports, 96.9 percent were small businesses. These companies include manufacturing companies of prepackaged software and books, freight forwarders and other transportation service firms, business services, engineering and management services, gas and oil extraction companies, coal mining companies, and communication services, to name a few.
- Small businesses account for 93.6 percent of all manufacturing importers, which is 12.9 percent of the sector's $602 billion in imports.
- Nearly 100 percent (99.2 percent) of wholesaler importers were small businesses, contributing 56.8 percent of the sector's $451 billion in imports.
- Small businesses accounted for 94.3 percent of the companies that both exported and imported, accounting for 29 percent of the export value and 27 percent of the import value.

This tells us that small businesses are very active in the global marketplace, and small business success in international markets is extremely important to the welfare of the United States.[6] Although it is true that small businesses are major users of imported goods, the focus of this chapter is on small business exporting because exporting can be an effective way to diversify the customer base, manage market fluctuations, grow, and become more competitive.[7]

Small businesses are limited in the products and the services that they export. Small business exports are concentrated in four main product categories: computers and electronic products, chemicals, machinery, and transportation equipment. However, the leading product categories in terms of market share were wood products, apparel and accessories, tobacco products, beverages, and leather products.[8]

foreign affiliate

A branch or a subsidiary of the parent company established outside the national boundaries of the parent company's home market.

Although the United States is one of the world's largest participants in global services trade, very little information exists with respect to services exports by small businesses. What is known is that it is increasingly common for most US services firms to establish a **foreign affiliate**—a branch or a subsidiary of the parent company established outside the national boundaries of the parent company's home market—because most services are better supplied in close proximity to the principal or final customers.[9] Additionally, in some business sectors, foreign regulations may restrict the delivery of some services to affiliates only. For example, to comply with domestic solvency requirements, some countries require that personal lines of insurance be carried out only by affiliates. Another example is the protection of intellectual property rights. This is often accomplished through the services of affiliates, thus intellectual property is kept in-house.[10]

What is particularly interesting is that most of the service exporting occurs in businesses with 0–19 employees, with the least service exporting done by small businesses with 300–499 employees. This may be the exact opposite of what you would expect.

1.2   The Advantages of Going Global

The flexibility of a smaller company may make it possible to meet the demands of global markets and redefine a company's programs more quickly than might occur in the larger **multinational corporation**.[11] A multinational corporation is a company that operates on a worldwide scale without ties to any specific nation or region; it is organized under the laws of its own country.[12] This flexibility of the smaller company is particularly true of the **micromultinationals**, a relatively new category of tiny companies that operate globally, having a presence and people in multiple countries.[13]

These micromultinationals outsource virtually everything to specialists all over the world and sell to people all over the world through the Internet.[14] The Internet is inexpensive technology, and the services designed to help small businesses make it possible for the small company to operate across borders with the same effectiveness and efficiencies as large businesses.[15]

> **multinational corporation**
>
> A company that operates on a worldwide scale without ties to any specific nation or region and organized under the laws of its own country.
>
> **micromultinationals**
>
> Tiny companies that operate globally, having a presence and people in multiple countries.

Micromultinationals

Generation Alliance is a branding and design firm that provides services to clients all over the world. They have core employees in Australia and specialist contractors in New Zealand, the United Kingdom, Germany, Switzerland, Jamaica, Dubai, and Singapore. One of their more interesting projects was to rebrand the country of Botswana for the global market.[16]

Jadience sells a line of health and skincare products that has its roots in traditional oriental medicine. Their physical products are sent to customers, mostly spas, in the United States, Canada, and Mexico.[17]

Worketc operates in the large and competitive business software market. Their focus is small businesses, selling web-based customer relationship management (CRM), project management, billing, shared calendars, help desk, and document management software. The company is headquartered in Sydney, Australia, and it claims happy customers in sixteen countries. The United States accounts for 86 percent of its customers.[18]

There are many reasons why small businesses should consider going global:[19]

- A small business that thinks and sells only domestically may be reaching only a small share of its potential customers because 95 percent of the world's consumers live outside the United States.
- Exporting enables companies to diversify their portfolios and weather changes in the domestic economy. This stabilizes seasonal and cyclical market fluctuations.
- Exporting helps small businesses grow and become more competitive in all their markets, which reduces the dependence on existing markets.
- Exporting increases sales and profits, also extending the sales potential of existing products. Research has shown that exporting can expand total sales 0.6 percent to 1.3 percent faster than would otherwise be the case.
- Exporting companies are able to sell excess production capacity.
- Exporting companies are nearly 8.5 percent less likely to go out of business.
- There are higher worker earnings as well, which contributes to the betterment of the community.

According to the US Small Business Administration (SBA),[20] US exporting businesses experience faster annual employment growth by 2 to 4 percentage points over their nonexporting counterparts. Workers employed in exporting companies have better paying jobs and better opportunities for advancement. Research has estimated that blue-collar worker earnings in firms that export are 13 percent higher than those in nonexporting plants, 23 percent higher when comparing large plants, and 9 percent higher when comparing small plants. White-collar employees also benefit from higher salaries, 18 percent more than their nonexporting counterparts. Less skilled workers also earn more at companies that export. Lastly, the benefits that all workers receive at exporting plants are 37 percent higher and include improved medical insurance and paid leave.

Video Link 15.1

Why Export?

Why small businesses should consider entering the global marketplace.

www.inc.com/exporting/whyexport.htm

1.3 The Disadvantages of Going Global

There is no question that the benefits of going global are considerable. However, disadvantages or barriers must also be considered. For example, a small business will incur additional costs, such as modifying its product or its packaging (perhaps even changing the name of its product so that it does not convey negative meanings outside the United States), developing new promotional materials, administrative costs (such as hiring staff to launch the export expansion and dedicating personnel for traveling), traveling to foreign locations (very important), and shipping.[21] It may also be necessary for the owner to subordinate short-term profits to long-term gains, wait longer for payments, apply for additional financing, and obtain special export licenses.[22] There will be differences in consumer needs, wants, and usage patterns for products; differences in consumer response to the elements of the marketing mix and differences in the legal environment may conflict with those of the United States.[23] Then, of course, there are cultural and language issues along with the all-too-familiar fear of the unknown.[24] A recent survey of exporting and nonexporting members of the National Small Business Association (NSBA) and the Small Business Exporters Association (SBEA) reported the following main barriers to small businesses selling their goods and/or services to foreign customers:[25]

- I do not have goods and/or services that are exportable: 49 percent.
- I do not know much about it and am not sure where to start: 38 percent.
- I would worry too much about getting paid: 29 percent.
- It is too costly: 27 percent.
- It would take too much time away from my regular, domestic sales: 17 percent.
- I cannot obtain financing to offer products or services to foreign customers: 7 percent.

Three things were identified as the single largest challenge: worrying about getting paid (26 percent), feeling that exporting is confusing and difficult to do (24 percent), and having limited goods and/or services that are exportable (18 percent).

Richard Ginsburg in the SBA's Office of International Trade has commented that most US small businesses simply do not understand the value of taking their business global, further noting that "the number-one barrier to trade is the psychological acceptance that global business is necessary."[26]

Small businesses also face some resource constraints that reduce their ability to export. For example, small businesses are more likely than larger firms to face scarcities of financial and human resources that limit their ability to take advantage of global opportunities. Limited personnel, the inability to meet quality standards, the lack of financial backing, and insufficient knowledge of foreign markets are important constraints affecting the ability of small businesses to export.[27] Fortunately, being proactive, innovative, and willing to take risks have helped small businesses overcome export impediments and improve export performance.[28]

The disadvantages of going global may warrant a go-slow approach, but they should not be viewed as knockout factors. If a business's financial situation is weak, the timing may not be right for becoming an exporter…but perhaps exporting makes sense in the future. In any case, very careful thinking should precede the decision to export.

2010 Winner of the Growth through Global Trade Award

Source: SteelMaster Buildings. Reprinted with permission.

The UPS Growth through Global Trade Award recognizes businesses with fewer than five hundred employees that are excelling in international trade. The inaugural winner was SteelMaster Buildings LLC, in Virginia Beach, Virginia, a manufacturer, designer, and supplier. The UPS award was followed up by two other national awards and four regional awards related to SteelMaster's increases in global trade plus a mention in a September 2010 speech by the former US Secretary of Commerce, Gary Locke, at a trade conference. The company earned first place in the 2011 Export Video Contest cosponsored by the SBA and VISA.

Building Beyond Our Borders
Video contest winning entry.

View the video online at: http://www.youtube.com/v/sLbFRRHnUzg

SBA Exporting Video Contest
Video contest finalist entries.

View the video online at: http://www.youtube.com/v/jyqVdV_6Hyg

SteelMaster employs fifty people, excluding distributors. It exports to more than forty countries and has distributorship relationships in more than fifty international markets (e.g., South Korea, Romania, Mexico, Angola, Chile, Peru, Slovakia, South Sudan, and Australia). This distributor network has provided an important source of market differentiation. Since the company began exporting in 2006, in response to the very competitive and saturated US market, the company's revenue has quadrupled, and exporting now represents over 20 percent of its total revenue. In addition,

- The SteelMaster website is user-friendly and offers a bilingual choice for Spanish-speaking viewers. Live chat is also available. In addition, various parts of the website have been translated to other languages (i.e., Korean, French, Romanian, Portuguese, and Arabic) to serve the company's international customers in their own languages.

- SteelMaster buildings are environmentally friendly and can be recycled. Green buildings are offered that protect against nonuniform weathering and reduce energy loads on buildings due to a long-term, bright service that helps heat reflectivity.

- SteelMaster's Galvalume Plus coated steel has been approved by the ENERGY STAR program for both low-slope and high-slope applications.

- The SteelMaster product can be easily used in the wake of natural disasters, such as earthquakes, flooding, or hurricanes. The company has participated in humanitarian relief efforts, specifically in Haiti.[29] The company stands ready to provide safe and reliable construction solutions to people in need around the world.

KEY TAKEAWAYS

- Small businesses make up a disproportionately large share of the number of companies that export and import. However, this is only about 1 percent of the total number of small businesses.
- The growth potential for small companies outside the United States is huge because of the demand for high-quality American products.
- Small businesses account for close to 98 percent of US exporters and 33 percent of the value of US exports.
- Small business success in international trade is extremely important to the welfare of the United States.
- There are many advantages and disadvantages of a small business going global. These must be analyzed very carefully before deciding to enter the global marketplace.
- A recent survey of small business owners revealed that the number one barrier to exporting was the feeling that their businesses did not have exportable goods and/or services. The number one challenge was worrying about getting paid.

EXERCISE

1. Go to www.trade.gov/mas/ian/statereports. Select your state and prepare a profile of small business exporting. Review additional sites as well, for example, websites sponsored by your state's commerce and/ or economic development departments. When looking at government sites, you may see the term *small- and medium-sized businesses* or something similar. They are simply referring to businesses with fewer than five hundred employees. This is the small business group for your purposes.

2. WHAT YOU SHOULD KNOW BEFORE GOING GLOBAL

LEARNING OBJECTIVES

1. Learn about the different ways that a business can export.
2. Understand the importance of an industry analysis.
3. Understand that it is important to carefully assess a business.
4. Learn about the marketing decisions that must be made.
5. Learn about the kinds of legal and political issues that will affect the exporting activities of a business.
6. Understand why the currency exchange rate is important to determining price.
7. Learn about the different sources of financing.

Although expanding into global markets offers many important benefits, not the least of which is increased profits, it will also introduce new complexities into the operations of a small business. There are several key decisions (see Figure 15.1) that will need to be made, including the following:[30]

- Determine which foreign market(s) to enter.
- Analyze the expenditures required to enter a new market and determine the source(s) of financing.
- Determine the best way to organize the overseas operation in concert with the US organization.
- Determine the extent to which, if any, the marketing mix will need to be adapted to the needs of the foreign market(s).
- Figure out the best way for the business to get paid.

These decisions, and others, will be based on an assessment of the ways to export, an analysis of the industry and the business, marketing and cultural factors, legal and political conditions, currency exchange issues, and sources of financing.

Video Link 15.2

A Family Business Goes Global

A small business specializing in leather-care products gets a lesson in expanding beyond its old fashioned clientele.

money.cnn.com/video/fsb/2008/09/10/fsb.pecard.makeover.fsb

FIGURE 15.1 Factors Affecting the Decision to Go Global

2.1   Ways to Export

Small businesses can choose from two basic ways to export: directly or indirectly.[31] There are advantages and disadvantages of each that should be understood before making a choice.

Direct Exporting

In **direct exporting**, a small business exports directly to a customer who is interested in buying a particular product. The small business owner makes all the arrangements for shipping and distributing the product overseas, is responsible for the marketing research, and collects payment. This approach gives the owner greater control over the entire transaction and entitles him or her to higher profits—although these higher profits are accompanied by the need to invest significantly more resources and efforts (see Table 15.1). It also requires a significantly changed internal organizational structure, which entails more risk.[32]

direct exporting

Exporting directly to a customer who is interested in buying a product.

TABLE 15.1 Advantages and Disadvantages of Direct Exporting

Advantages	Disadvantages
Potential profits are greater because intermediaries are eliminated.	It takes more time, energy, and money than an owner may be able to afford.
The owner has a greater degree of control over all aspects of the transaction.	It requires more "people power" to cultivate a customer base.
The owner knows customers, and the customers know the owner. Customers feel more secure in doing business directly with the owner.	Servicing the business will demand more responsibility from every level in the organization. The owner is held accountable for whatever happens. There is no buffer zone.
Business trips are much more efficient and effective because an owner can meet directly with the customer responsible for selling the product.	The owner may not be able to respond to customer communications as quickly as a local agent can.
The owner knows whom to contact if something is not working. The owner gets slightly better protection for trademarks, patents, and copyrights.	The owner must handle all the logistics of the transaction. If it is a technological product, the owner must be prepared to respond to technical questions and provide on-site start-up training and ongoing support services.
The owner is presented as fully committed and engaged in the export process and develops a better understanding of the marketplace. As a business develops in the foreign market, the owner has greater flexibility to improve or redirect marketing efforts.	

Source: Laurel Delaney, "Direct Exporting: Advantages and Disadvantages to Direct Exporting," About.com, accessed February 7, 2012,

http://importexport.about.com/od/DevelopingSalesAndDistribution/a/Direct-Exporting-Advantages-And-Disadvantages-To-Direct-Exporting.htm.

Indirect Exporting

indirect exporting

Entering into an agreement with an agent, a distributor, or a traditional exporting house for the purpose of selling (or marketing and selling) the products in the target market.

Indirect exporting involves entering "into an agreement with an agent, distributor, or a traditional exporting house for the purpose of selling (or marketing and selling) the products in the target market."[33] Many small businesses choose this option, at least at the outset. It is the simplest approach, particularly when a business does not have the necessary human and financial resources to promote products in foreign markets in any other way (see Table 15.2).[34] The easiest way to export indirectly is to sell to an intermediary in the United States because the business will normally not be responsible for collecting payment from the overseas customer or coordinating the shipping logistics.[35]

TABLE 15.2 Advantages and Disadvantages of Indirect Exporting

Advantages	Disadvantages
Does not require a lot of organizational effort or staff workers.	Not all types of goods lend themselves to indirect exporting (e.g., technically complex goods and services).
The producer of the goods is subject to only small dangers and risk (e.g., a short-term drop in the exchange rate).	The profits of a business will be lower, and control over foreign sales is lost.
It is an almost risk-free way to begin. It demands minimal involvement in the export process. It allows the owner to continue to concentrate on its domestic business.	A business very rarely knows who its customers are, thus losing the opportunity to tailor its offerings to their evolving needs.
The business has limited liability for product marketing problems. There is always someone else at which to point the finger.	When an owner visits, he or she is a step removed from the actual transaction and feels out of the loop.
The owner learns on the fly about international marketing. Depending on the type of intermediary with which the owner is dealing, the owner does not have to be concerned with shipment and other logistics.	The intermediary might be offering products similar to a particular business's products, including directly competitive products, to the same customers instead of providing exclusive representation.
A business can field-test its products for export potential. In some instances, the local agent can field technical questions and provide necessary product support.	The long-term outlook and goals for an export program can change rapidly, and if a business has put its product in someone else's hands, it is hard to redirect efforts accordingly.

Source: CBS Investment, "Advantages and Disadvantages of Direct and Indirect Exports," CBS Investment, accessed February 7, 2012,

http://www.cbsinvestment.com/advantages-and-disadvantages-of-direct-and-indirect-exports/; Laurel Delaney, Start and Run a Profitable Exporting

Business (Vancouver, BC: Self-Counsel Press, 1998), chapter 8.

2.2   Industry Analysis

Before jumping into the global pond, it is a good idea to identify where an industry currently is and then look at the trends and directions that are predicted over the next three years. This will be true whether a business is only on the ground, only online, or both brick and click.

A business should try to determine how competitive an industry is in the global market.[36] Try to get as good a picture of the market as possible because the better informed a business is, the better its chances of a successful global entry. Learn a product's potential in a given market, where the best prospects for success seem to be, and common business practices.[37]

A small business owner may be reticent about conducting market research before going global, particularly if domestic research efforts have been limited or nonexistent. However, the global market is a very different animal compared to the domestic market. It is even more important to conduct thorough market research to help identify possible risks in advance so that the appropriate steps can be taken to avoid mistakes. This ultimately portrays the business as forward-thinking, trustworthy, and credible.[38]

- Several resources should be consulted. However, the best guide to exporting for the small business comes from the US government.[39]
- The SBA is a great place to start to find information to help a business break into the global game. The information on exporting and importing is comprehensive and easily understood.
- The US government portal Export.gov provides online trade resources and one-on-one assistance for global businesses. Export.gov provides particularly helpful information on regulations, licenses, and trade data and analysis. Trade data can help a business identify the best countries to target for exports. A business can gauge the size of the market for a product or a service and develop a pricing strategy to become competitive.[40]
- The US International Trade Commission offers market information, trade leads, and overseas business contacts. Trade professionals are available to help a business every step of the way with information counseling that can reduce costs, risks, and the mystery of exporting.[41]
- The US Department of Commerce provides trade opportunities for US business, export-related assistance, and market information.[42]
- Information about protecting intellectual property abroad can be found at http://www.stopfakes.gov. This is important because counterfeiting and piracy cost the world economy approximately $650 billion per year.[43]

Other sources to be consulted include people in the same business or industry, industry-specific magazines, trade fairs, seminars,[44] and export training and technical assistance that is available to small businesses through the states and the federal government. The Federation of International Trade Associations is a global trade portal that provides trade leads, market research, links to eight thousand import/export websites, and even travel services. WorldBid.com describes itself as the largest network of international trade marketplaces in the world, providing trade leads and new business contacts.[45]

The Internet makes it possible to gather and view tremendous amounts of information. If a business is thinking seriously about going global, there is no better time to take advantage of this quick-and-easy access than now.

Video Link 15.3

Knowing the Export Environment

Government experts identify challenges and debunk some myths.

www.inc.com/exporting/exportsuccess.htm

2.3   Business Assessment: Are You Ready?

It is important to honestly self-evaluate a business to determine whether it is really ready to go global or not…or at least not yet.[46] If a business is thinking about expanding globally, it is probably already doing something right to have reached this point. However, that does not preclude the importance of assessing its strengths and its weaknesses to determine the approach that should be taken in the global market.[47] This will be true no matter what role e-commerce plays in a business. Even a micromultinational business should assess its strengths and its weaknesses, although its instantaneous presence as a global business means that the assessment must be done at start-up and then must continue as products and services move from country to country.

There are several issues that should be addressed. The following are some of the questions that should be asked:[48]

- Why is a business successful in the domestic market? What is its growth rate? What are its strengths?

- What products have export potential? Do the products fill a niche that is exclusive to the US market? Are they packaged in a way that can be understood by non-English-speaking consumers? Do they violate any cultural taboos or contain ingredients that will prohibit their sale in a foreign market? Identify the key selling features of the products, identify the needs that they satisfy, and identify any selling constraints.

- What are the competitive advantages of a particular business's products over other domestic and international businesses?

- What competitive products are sold abroad and by whom?

- Does the product require complementary goods and technologies? If so, who will provide them?

- How will the business provide customer service?

- Can production handle a wider demographic? Can the business increase output without sacrificing quality?

- Does the business have the money to market globally?

- Is the entire business (including all staff) committed to a global effort?

If a product is an industrial good, a business will want to know things such as what firms will likely use it, whether its use or life might be affected by climate, and whether geography will present transportation problems that will affect purchase. In the case of a consumer good, a business will want to know who will consume it; how frequently it will be purchased; whether it will be restricted abroad; whether climate or geography will negatively impact accessibility for purchase; and—perhaps most importantly—whether it conflicts with traditions, taboos, habits, or the beliefs of customers abroad.[49]

A helpful tool to assess readiness is the export questionnaire available at www.export.gov/begin/assessment.asp. This questionnaire highlights characteristics common to successful exporters and identifies areas that need to be strengthened to improve export activities.

Video Link 15.4

Where Will Your Next Customer Come From?

Small businesses looking to grow should look beyond US borders to find new customers.

www.sba.gov/content/where-will-your-next-customer-come

2.4 Marketing

value proposition

The set of benefits offered to customers to satisfy their needs and wants consisting of some combination of products, services, information, and experiences.

Just as it is necessary to offer a different marketing mix (see Figure 15.2) for different target markets, it will generally be necessary to adapt the marketing mix to the global market in general and different countries in particular. A business's unique **value proposition** (the set of benefits offered to customers to satisfy their needs and wants consisting of some combination of products, services, information, and experiences)[50] is what will differentiate one marketplace offering from the competition. Given the more diversified competition in the global marketplace, identifying the value proposition is even more critical—and most likely more difficult—than in the domestic market.[51]

FIGURE 15.2 The Marketing Mix

Product

The ideal situation is when a product developed for the US market can be sold in a foreign country without any changes. Although some kinds of products can be introduced with no changes (e.g., cameras, consumer electronics, and many machine tools),[52] most products usually have to be altered in some way to meet conditions in a foreign market.[53] From a small business perspective, the owner will want to market products that do not require drastic changes to be accepted. Relatively minor packaging changes, such as size or the language on the package, can be made inexpensively, but more drastic changes should be avoided. If a product must be changed drastically to market it globally, conduct an in-depth cost analysis to determine whether the additional costs will outweigh the anticipated benefits.[54] If a product is a food or a beverage, for example, is the business prepared to make the changes necessary to appeal to widely varying tastes?[55]

Products need to be adapted for many reasons, including the following:[56]

- Different physical or mandated requirements must be met (e.g., electrical goods will need to be rewired for different voltage systems).
- The legal, economic, political, technological, and climatic requirements of the local marketplace vary (e.g., varying laws will set specific packaging sizes and safety and quality standards).
- The product or the company name must translate flawlessly to the new target market so that it does not convey an unintended, perhaps very negative, meaning. One of the most well-known examples of a translation blunder is the Chevy Nova. In Spanish, "nova" means "no go."
- The package label may need to be changed. Imagine the horror of a well-known baby food producer that introduced small jars of baby food in Africa when it found out that the consumers inferred from the baby picture on the jars that the jars contained ground-up babies. This shows us that even big companies can make big mistakes.
- A change in flavor or fragrance may be necessary to bring a product in line with what is expected in a culture. The pine and hints of ammonia or chlorine scents that are popular in the United States were flops in Japan because many Japanese sleep on the floor on futons. With their heads so close to the floor, a citrus scent is more pleasing.

The less economically developed a market happens to be, the greater may be the need for product adaptation. Research has found that only one in ten products can be marketed in developing countries without some kind of product adaptation.[57]

Cultural Differences

It is important to know that cultural and social differences are intertwined with the perceived value and importance that a market places on a product.[58] "A product is more than a physical item: It is a bundle of satisfactions (or *utilities*) that the buyer receives. These include its form, taste, color, odor, and texture; how it functions in use; the package; the label; the warranty; the manufacturer's and retailer's servicing; the confidence or prestige enjoyed by the brand; the manufacturer's reputation; the country of origin; and any other symbolic utility received from the possession or use of the goods. In short, the market relates to more than a product's physical form and primary function."[59]

The values, customs, rituals, language, and taboos within a culture will determine the acceptability of a product or a service. Cultural sensitivity is particularly important in cyberspace. Website visitors may come from anywhere in the world. Icons and gestures that seem friendly to US visitors may shock people from other cultures. For example, a high-five hand gesture would be insulting to a visitor from Greece.[60] Knives and scissors should not be given as gifts in South America because they symbolize the severing of a friendship.[61]

The **psychological attributes** of a product (features that have little to do with the primary function of the product but add value to customer satisfaction, e.g., color, size, design, brand name, and price)[62] can also vary across cultures, and the meaning and the value assigned to those attributes can be positive or negative. It may be necessary to adapt the nonphysical features of the product to maximize the positive meanings and eliminate the negative ones.[63] When Coca-Cola, the number one global brand, introduced Diet Coke to Japan, it found that Japanese women do not like to admit to dieting. Further, the idea of diet was associated with medicine and sickness. Coca-Cola ended up changing the name to Coke Light.[64] This happened in Europe as well, so if a product is associated with weight loss, a business must be very careful with its marketing.

The Package

The package for a product includes its design, colors, labeling, trademarks, brand name, size, product information, and the actual packaging materials. There are many reasons why a package may have to be adapted for a particular country. There may be laws that stipulate a specific type of bottle or can, package sizes, measurement units, extraheavy packaging, and the use of particular words on the label.[65] In some cases, the expense of package adaptation may be cost prohibitive for entering a market. Consider the following examples:[66]

- In Japan, a poorly packaged product is seen as an indicator of product quality.
- Prices are required to be printed on the labels in Venezuela, but putting prices on labels or in any way suggesting the retail price in Chile is illegal.
- A soft-drink company from the United States incorporated six-point stars as decoration on its package labels. But it had inadvertently offended some of its Arab customers who interpreted the stars as symbolizing pro-Israeli sentiment.
- Soft drinks are sold in smaller sizes in Japan to accommodate the smaller Japanese hand.
- Descriptive words such as giant or jumbo on a package or a label may be illegal in some countries.

The message here is clear. Before going global with a product, examine the packaging so that each element is in compliance with appropriate laws and regulations so that nothing will offend prospective customers.

Global Packaging

Canada's oldest candymaker, Ganong Brothers, is located about one mile from Maine. The company chairman, David Ganong, can see the US border from his office window. You would think it would be easy for Ganong Brothers to sell to the US market. Not so. In Canada, nutritional labels read *5 mg*, with a space between the number and the unit of measurement. Ganong's jellybeans cannot get into America unless the label reads *5mg*, without the space. This difference, as well as differences in Canada's nutritional guidelines, means that Ganong must produce and package its US products separately, which reduces its efficiency. Small differences can and do have a significant effect on cross-border trade. This may be the reason why there is not as much trade between the United States and Canada as you would think.[67] This notwithstanding, however, Canada remains the number one exporting destination for US small businesses.[68]

The Business Website

As part of product preparations, a business will need to make its website ready for international business. Remember that the website is a very cost-effective way to sell a product or a service across borders. Here are four ways to ready the website:[69]

1. **Internationalize website content.** A business must account for language differences, and cultural differences may require different graphics and different colors. One way to deal with the additional costs is to translate text or provide country-specific sites only for the country or countries where the most products are sold. One organization that provides resources to help

businesses localize their products and resources is the Globalization and Localization Association.

2. **Calculate the buyer's costs and estimate shipping.** Shipping internationally will take longer, is more complicated, and will be more expensive than shipping domestically. Fortunately, there are shipping management software packages available that will automatically figure the costs and delivery times for overseas orders, giving a close estimate. Large shipping carriers, such as UPS and FedEx, offer such software; other companies include E4X Inc., eCustoms, and Kewill Systems Plc.[70]

3. **Optimize site and search marketing for international web visitors.** With the increase in cross-border selling, websites can be optimized for visitors from specific countries, and techniques can be used to attract international visitors through search engines and search ads. This is a growing specialty among search marketers. A business should definitely check out the cost of hiring such a marketer as a consultant. It would be well worth the investment.

4. **Comply with government export regulations.** A business does not need government approval to sell most goods and services across international borders. There are, of course, notable exceptions. For example, the US government restricts defense or military goods, and agricultural, plant, and food items may have restrictions or special labeling requirements. Such restrictions should be addressed on the website. It may be necessary to restrict the sale of certain products to certain countries only.

Video Link 15.5

Finding Your First Customer

To find the first customer, visit the selected country.

www.inc.com/exporting/findingfirst.htm

Translation Blunders in Global Marketing

We often hear it said that something was lost in the translation. Here are some global marketing examples of translation blunders. Something important to note is that most of these blunders were committed by the "big guys," companies that are extremely marketing-savvy—proof positive that no one is immune from this kind of error.

- When Coca-Cola was first translated phonetically into Chinese, the result was a phrase that meant "bite the wax tadpole." When Coca-Cola discovered the error, the company was able to find a close phonetic equivalent that could be loosely translated as "happiness in the mouth."[71]

- When Pope John Paul II visited Miami in 1987, an ambitious entrepreneur wanted to sell t-shirts with the logo, "I saw the Pope" in Spanish. The entrepreneur forgot that the definite article in Spanish has two genders. Instead of printing "El Papa" ("the Pope"), he printed "La Papa" ("the potato"). Needless to say, there was no market for t-shirts that read "I saw the potato."[72]

- Sunbeam got into trouble when it did not change the name of its Mist-Stick curling iron when marketing it in Germany. As it turned out, "mist" is German slang for manure. Not surprisingly, German women did not want to use a manure stick in their hair.[73]

- A proposed new soap called "Dainty" in English came out as "aloof" in Flemish (Belgium), "dimwitted" in Farsi (Iran), and "crazy person" in Korean. The product was dropped.[74] The company either did not have the resources to research a new name or did not want to take the time and incur the costs to do so.

- Kellogg's Bran Buds sounded like "burned farmer" in Swedish.[75]

Given that misunderstanding foreign languages can destroy a brand, it is worth the investment to hire someone who is proficient in the native language in the intended market—including the use of slang. This will help a small business avoid a fatal mistake because it does not have the resources of the big companies to fix the mistakes.[76] This concern must be extended to the web presence as well because the website is an integral part of the product.

Price

Pricing for the global market is not an easy thing to do. Many factors must be taken into account, the first of which are traditional price considerations: fixed and variable costs, competition, company objectives, proposed positioning strategies, the target group, and willingness to pay.[77] Add to these factors things such as the additional costs that are incurred due to taxes, tariffs, transportation, retailer margin, and currency fluctuation risks;[78] the nature of the product or industry, the location of production facility, and the distribution system;[79] the psychological effects of price; the rest of the marketing mix; and the price transparency created by the Internet[80] and a business can begin to appreciate the challenges of global price setting. About the only thing that can be seen as a certainty is that a small business should expect the price of its product or service to be different, usually higher, in a foreign market.[81] The specifics of that difference need to be worked out carefully, with thorough analysis.

Setting the right price for a product or a service is critical to success. It will be a challenge to navigate the pricing waters of each different country—to learn why, for example, a product sells for $16 in the United States but $23 in Britain.

Place

distribution process

The physical handling and distribution of goods, the passage of ownership or title, and the buying and selling negotiations between producers and middlemen and middlemen and customers.

As challenging as distribution may be for a small business in the domestic market, it is even more so for the global market. No matter the product, it has to go through a **distribution process**—the physical handling and distribution of goods, the passage of ownership or title, and the buying and selling negotiations between producers and middlemen and middlemen and customers.[82] It would make sense to be able to take advantage of existing transportation systems, retailers, and suppliers to sell goods and provide services. Unfortunately, adequate distribution systems do not exist in all countries, so a business will need to develop ways to get products to customers in as cost-effective a manner as possible.[83]

Video Link 15.6

Getting Your Product from Here to There

Small businesses rely on freight forwarding and shipping experts to move products around the world.

www.inc.com/exporting/heretothere.htm

Before deciding on a channel or channels of distribution, a business needs information. The following are some basic questions as a starting point:

- Is the selected market dominated by major retailers or is the retail sector made up of small independent retailers?[84]
- How many intermediaries will be involved? In Japan, for example, a product must go through approximately five different types of wholesalers before it reaches the final consumer.[85]
- Can we use the manufacturer, wholesaler, retailer, or consumer channel or can we export directly to a retailer?
- Should we work with a foreign partner? Unless a business plans to establish a retail operation on foreign soil, it will need to establish business-to-business (B2B) sales relationships. Then products can be sold directly to foreign retailers or foreign distributors who will sell to those retailers. A foreign partner can provide valuable insights about local import regulations, product marketability, and local customs. The US Department of Commerce website contains directories of foreign buyers.[86] Small businesses excel at forming strategic partnerships.[87]
- Where can we attend a trade show or a trade mission? Going to these events can help a business find distribution channels.
- Is the Internet commonly used to distribute my product?

Video Link 15.7

Understanding Partnerships and Distributors

Partnerships help many thriving US businesses overseas.

www.inc.com/exporting/partnerships.htm

Video Link 15.8

Identifying Marketing Channels/Activities

How research and planning inform business growth.

www.inc.com/exporting/marketingchannels.htm

In the final analysis, the behavior of distribution channel members will be the result of the interaction between cultural, economic, political, legal, and marketing environments. A small business that is looking to go global—or is already there—will encounter channel structures that range from a minimally developed marketing infrastructure, such as in emerging markets, to highly complex, multilayered systems, such as in Japan.[88]

When deciding to enter the global marketplace, a determination must be made as to whether the current channel structure in the selected country (or countries) will meet the business's needs or whether some additional arrangements will be needed. The means of distribution will necessarily be a country-by-country decision. No matter the arrangement, however, figure on the costs being greater than in the United States.

Promotion

It is understandable that a small business owner may want to use the same integrated marketing communications (IMC) programs used in the home market to inform customers in foreign markets and persuade them to buy. This "one voice" approach offers the advantage of enabling a business or a product to gain broader recognition in the global marketplace; it also helps reduce costs, minimize redundancies in personnel, and maximize the speed of implementation.[89] However, things are not that easy. Cultural, social, language, and legal differences from country to country will usually make it necessary to modify IMC messages to not offend current or prospective customers. Modification is more of a challenge for the small business because the resources needed to make the changes are more limited.

A business communicates with its customers through some combination of its website, advertising, publicity, public relations, sales promotion, sales personnel, e-mail, and social media. The actual mix will be a function of the selected country or countries. For example, in some less-developed countries, the major portion of the promotional effort in rural and less-accessible parts of the market is sales promotion; in other markets, product sampling works especially well when the product concept is new or has a very small market share.[90] In Saudi Arabia, there is an appreciation for fancy packaging, and point-of-sale advertising elicits the best reaction.[91] However, the appropriateness of IMC activities for a small business will depend on the product being marketed, the industry in which it is competing, and the country in which it hopes to sell the product.

Of all the four Ps, decisions involving advertising are thought to be those most often affected by cultural differences in foreign markets. Consumers respond in terms of their culture, style, feelings, value systems, attitudes, beliefs, and perceptions. Because advertising's function is to interpret or translate the qualities of products and services in terms of consumer needs, wants, desires, and aspirations, emotional appeals, symbols, persuasive approaches, and other characteristics in an advertisement must coincide with cultural norms if the ad is to be effective.[92]

Examples abound of international advertising mistakes that have offended different cultures. Three are presented here. Although they are linked to large corporations, there are lessons to be learned by small businesses. No business is immune from making mistakes from time to time.

- Burger King ran in-store ads for three restaurants in Spain that depicted the Hindu goddess Lakshami on top of a ham sandwich. The caption read, "a snack that is sacred." Many Hindus are vegetarian and were offended by the ad. Burger King pulled it.[93]

- Burger King ran a campaign in Europe for the Texican Whopper that featured a lanky American cowboy; a short, round Mexican draped in a cape resembling Mexico's flag; and the caption, "the taste of Texas with a little spicy Mexican." There was an immediate uproar, with the Mexican ambassador to Spain objecting publicly.[94]

- During a time when Fiat was trying to take advantage of auto sales growth in China, it released an ad in Italy in which actor Richard Gere drove a Lancia Delta from Hollywood to Tibet. The ad did not air in China, but it caused an online uproar nonetheless. Richard Gere is hated in China because he is an outspoken supporter of the Dalai Lama. His selection as the Fiat spokesperson was a major faux pas by Fiat.[95]

The reality of international advertising is that its cost and the effort required to prepare and place the ads correctly may be prohibitive for most small businesses, therefore pushing the emphasis on other elements of the IMC mix. However, a business will not know that for sure until it does the proper research before making a decision. Consider the characteristics of the target market, how the market uses media in that country, and which media are actually available. Some countries do not have commercial television, and some do not have advertising in newspapers. There will be newspaper and magazine circulation differences from country to country; in countries with a low literacy rate, radio and television advertising (if available) will be more effective than print media.[96]

Fortunately, small businesses that want to go global can look to social media for assistance. The social web is a low-cost way to catapult a small business brand into the global arena.[97] Facebook, the most popular social networking site in the world, has developed a self-serve advertising tool that has created the greatest interest among small businesses that might not have had the means to launch a global advertising campaign before. This would be a good place to start—along with a map of the world's most popular media applications country by country and culture by culture, which is available at www.appappeal.com/the-most-popular-app-per-country/social-networking.

No matter the mix of the IMC program, and no matter whether a business is business-to-consumer (B2C) or B2B, the way a business communicates internationally will be a major determinant of success. Each IMC component is a communication channel in its own right. A business must consider the appropriateness of each message in each channel. For example, is the message adequate? Does it contain correct cultural interpretations? Are the colors and graphics right? In the case of advertising, have the media been chosen that match the behavior of the intended audience? Have you correctly assessed the needs and wants or the thinking processes of the target market?[98]

Careful consideration of these and other communication issues will not guarantee success, but it should help reduce the chances of making a major marketing blunder.

2.5 Legal and Political Issues

It is impossible for any small business to know all the laws that pertain to exporting from the United States. Thus it is important to consult an attorney who is knowledgeable about the legal implications of globalization: international trade laws, tax laws, local regulations,[99] international border restrictions, customs rules, and duties and taxes.[100]

To varying degrees, each small business must be concerned with the following. However, this list is not exhaustive; it is a sampling only.

- The Foreign Corrupt Practices Act makes it illegal for companies to pay bribes to foreign officials, candidates, or political parties. The challenge for all US businesses is that bribery is a common business practice in many countries, even though it is illegal.[101] Interestingly, private business bribes are tax deductible in Germany as long as the German businessperson discloses both his or her identity and the recipient of the bribe(s). Although it is supposedly rarely used, it is available.[102]

- Specific licenses and permits are required or additional paperwork must be completed if the following specific products are exported or imported: agricultural products, automobiles (not a likely product for a small business), chemicals, defense products, food and beverage products, industrial goods, and pharmaceutical and biotechnology products.[103]

- There is heightened sensitivity since September 11, 2011, about exporting products that could even remotely be used in a military or a terrorist capacity.[104]

- Brand names, trademarks, products, processes, designs, and formulas are among the more valuable assets a small business can possess. These need to be protected—domestically and internationally. US officials estimate that $300 billion of intellectual property assets are ripped off every year.[105]

- There are commercial laws within countries related to marketing, environmental issues, and antitrust.

Video Link 15.9

Understanding Legal Considerations

Important legal considerations for small businesses that want to go global.

www.inc.com/exporting/legal.htm

In addition to legal considerations, no small business can conduct global business without understanding the influence of the political environments in which it will be operating.[106] Every nation has the sovereign right to grant or withhold permission to do business within its political boundaries and control where its citizens do business, so the political environment of countries is necessarily a critical concern to any small business.[107] Political issues include the stability of government policies (a stable and friendly government being the ideal), the forms of government (with some being more open to foreign commerce than others), political parties and their influence on economic policy, the degree of nationalism (the greater the nationalism, the greater the bias against foreign business and investments may be), fear and/or animosity that is targeted toward a specific country, and trade disputes.[108] One or all these things create political risk that must be assessed. The most severe political risk is confiscation, the seizing of a company's assets without payment.[109]

2.6 Currency Exchange Issues

The **exchange rate** is the rate at which one country's currency can be exchanged for the currency of another country.[110] For example, assume that on a particular day, $1 exchanged for 0.75643 euros and 49.795 Indian rupees.[111] These exchange rates then changed the next day, when $1 exchanged for 0.6891 euros and 49.845 Indian rupees, meaning that the value of the US dollar *increased* in value with respect to the euro and *decreased* in value against the Indian rupee. Currency exchange rates change daily, and they are important because currency fluctuations can present additional problems for the small business looking to go global. The appreciation and depreciation of a currency will have an effect on the prices of goods and services. For example, as the dollar declines in value against the euro, the price of goods and services from the European Union for US customers will increase, likely reducing their purchases.[112] The following are other implications of exchange rate fluctuations:[113]

- Inattention to exchange rates in long-term contracts could result in large unintended discounts.
- Rapid and unexpected currency fluctuations can make pricing in local currencies very difficult.
- Shifts in exchange rates can influence the attractiveness of various business decisions, not the least of which is whether doing business in a particular country is worthwhile.

Different strategies may be needed when the dollar is weak versus when it is strong. For example, when the US dollar is weak, a business should stress price benefits. When the dollar is strong, a business can engage in nonprice competition by improving quality, delivery, and after-sale services.[114] To navigate these challenging currency exchange waters, it will be necessary to tap into accounting and finance expertise.

> **exchange rate**
>
> The rate at which one country's currency can be exchanged for the currency of another country.

2.7 Sources of Financing

How a business finances an export project is often a critical factor in its success. Financing decisions extend to working capital and export transactions. Working capital is needed to finance operations before and after a sale, and money is needed to sustain a business until it is paid for the goods and services that have been provided (export transactions). The International Trade Association in the US Department of Commerce identifies the following factors as important to consider when making financing decisions.[115]

- **The need for financing to make the sale.** Offering favorable payment terms can make a product more competitive.
- **The length of time the product is being financed.** The term of the loan required determines how long a business will have to wait before the buyer pays for the product, which will influence the choice of how to finance the transaction.
- **The cost of different methods of financing.** Interest rates and fees will vary, and a business should probably expect to assume some of the financing costs. Before providing an invoice to the buyer, a business must understand how these costs will affect price and profit.
- **The risks associated with financing the transaction.** The riskier the transaction, the more difficult and costly it will be for a business to finance it because there will likely be a higher chance for default. The level of risk will be influenced by several things, not the least of which is the political and economic stability of the buyer's country. In risky situations, the financing provider may require the most secure method of payment—a letter of credit or export credit insurance.
- **The need for preshipment financing and postshipment working capital.** Working capital could experience unexpected and severe strains with the production of an unusually large order or a surge of orders. Inadequate working capital can limit exporting growth—even during normal periods.

Where to Go

Small businesses have reported that problems with access to financing for their exporting operations are a major barrier to exporting. The difficulties they experience in obtaining both trade finance and working capital often prevent small businesses from financing purchases by foreign buyers. This encourages foreign buyers to choose suppliers that are able to extend credit. Small businesses must also face the perception of lending institutions that they are a higher risk than larger companies coupled with a lack of familiarity with exporting by community banks.[116]

Despite any anticipated difficulties, small businesses need to find export financing. They can look for financing in several places. The first place to look is internally. Does it already have the funds to finance global efforts? If the answer is yes, then all is well. This was the case for Center Rock, the small business featured at the beginning of this chapter. If the answer is no, which will most likely be the case, it will be necessary to look for external financing. A range of options is available for small businesses to consider (see Table 15.3). As you will see, most financing sources are available from the government. A small business must become familiar with the financing, insurance, and grant programs that are available to help it finance transactions and carry out export operations.[117]

TABLE 15.3 Sources of Export Financing for the Small Business

Source	Information
Extending credit to foreign buyers working with commercial banks	Liberal financing can enhance export competitiveness, but extending credit must be weighed carefully. Some commercial bank services used to finance domestic business, including revolving lines of credit for working capital, are often needed to finance export sales until payment is received. However, commercial banks prefer to establish an ongoing business relationship instead of financing solely on the basis of an individual order. Most US banks do not lend against export orders, export receivables, or letters of credit.
Export Express 7(a) Loan Programs	Offered by the SBA, this streamlined program helps small businesses develop or expand their export markets. A business may be able to obtain SBA-backed financing for loans and lines of credit up to $500,000.
Export Working Capital Program (EWCP) 7(a) Loan Programs	This SBA loan program targets small businesses that are able to generate export sales but need additional working capital to support these sales. The SBA provides lenders guarantees of up to 90 percent on export loans to ensure that qualified exporters do not lose viable export sales due to a lack of working capital.
International Trade Loan Program 7(a) Loan Programs	Loans are available for businesses that plan to start or continue exporting or have been adversely affected by competition from imports. The loan proceeds must enable the borrower to be in a better position to compete. The program offers borrowers a maximum SBA-guaranteed portion of $1.75 million.
Export-Import Bank	An independent federal agency that provides working capital loan guarantees, export-credit insurance, and other forms of financing for US exporters of all sizes. The funds are aimed at offsetting the added risks of doing business abroad, from complex trade rules to unpaid bills.
Using export intermediaries	Many export intermediaries, for example, trading companies and export management companies, can help finance export sales. The intermediaries may provide short-term financing or may purchase the goods to be exported directly from the manufacturer, thus eliminating any risks to the manufacturer that are associated with the export transaction as well as the need for financing.

Source: "Export Financing," US Small Business Administration, accessed February 7, 2012, http://www.sba.gov/content/export-financing-0; US Department of Commerce, A Basic Guide to Exporting, 10th ed. (Washington, DC: International Trade Association, 2008), 194, 197; "More Small Businesses Seek Export Financing," Wall Street Journal, May 20, 2011, accessed February 7, 2012, http://blogs.wsj.com/in-charge/2011/05/20/more-small-businesses-seek-export-financing.

Video Link 15.10

Financing

Some of the ways small businesses can finance their exporting projects.

www.inc.com/exporting/financing.htm

KEY TAKEAWAYS

- Expanding into global markets introduces new complexities into small business operations.
- The decision to go global should be based on an assessment of the ways to export, an analysis of the industry and a particular company, marketing and cultural factors, legal and political conditions, currency exchange rates, and sources of financing.
- There are two basic ways to export: direct or indirect. In direct exporting, a small business exports directly to a customer who is interested in buying the product. Indirect exporting involves using a middleman for marketing and selling the product in the target market.
- Industry analysis involves looking at where an industry currently is and the trends and directions predicted over the next three years so that a business can try to determine how competitive an industry is in the global market.
- It is important to honestly self-evaluate a business to determine whether it is ready to go global or not.
- It will generally be necessary to adapt the marketing mix to the global market in general and different countries in particular.
- Legal issues include international trade laws, tax laws, and local regulations.
- No small business can conduct global business without understanding the influence of the political environments in which it will be operating.
- Currency exchange rates are important because currency fluctuations can present additional problems for a small business that is looking to go global. In particular, the appreciation and depreciation of a currency will have an effect on the prices of goods and services.
- How a business finances an export project is often a critical factor in its success.
- Working capital is needed before and after the sale, and money is needed until the goods and services that have been provided have been paid for.
- Many—perhaps most—of the sources for small business exporting activity are governmental.

EXERCISES

1. Comment on the following: a small business owner firmly believes that because a product is successful in Chicago, Illinois, it will be successful in Tokyo or Berlin.[118] Be as specific as you can in your comments.
2. There has been tremendous growth in online business, which has introduced new elements to the legal climate of global business. Patents, brand names, copyrights, and trademarks are difficult to monitor because there are no boundaries with the Internet. What steps could a small business take to protect its trademarks and brands in this environment? Prepare at least five suggestions.[119]
3. Find a local small business that exports its products. Talk to the owner about his or her experiences. Ask questions such as the following: What convinced you to export? How did you decide on the product(s) to export? Did you have to adapt your product(s) in any way? What were the greatest barriers you had to face?

3. KEY MANAGEMENT DECISIONS AND CONSIDERATIONS

LEARNING OBJECTIVES

1. Understand the organizational support that will be needed for exporting activities.
2. Understand the need to select the best market to entry.
3. Identify and describe each possible market entry strategy.
4. Learn about the different approaches to getting paid.
5. Appreciate the importance of business etiquette when traveling to visit customers.
6. Understand the importance of an export plan.

After a business decides to jump into the global pond, several key management decisions must be made (Figure 15.3). Among them are organization for the global project, selecting the best market to enter, the level of involvement desired, and how to get paid. There should also be consideration of global etiquette and travel.

FIGURE 15.3 Management Decisions

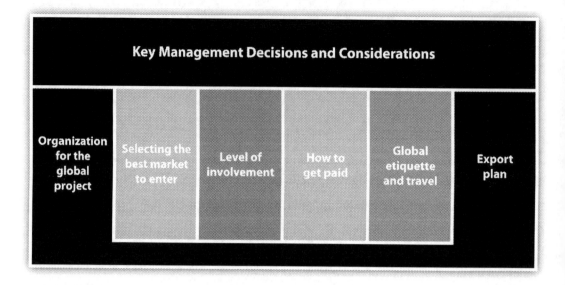

Several important questions about the global venture should be answered before making any management decisions or considerations.[120] Less than satisfactory answers to these questions may put the global venture in jeopardy.

1. Do the company's reasons for pursuing export markets include solid objectives, such as increasing sales volume or developing a broader, more stable customer base, or are the reasons frivolous, such as the owner wants an excuse to travel?

2. How committed is top management to the export effort? Is it viewed as a quick fix for a slump in domestic sales? Will the company neglect its export customers if domestic sales pick up?

3. What are management's expectations for the export effort? Will they expect export operations to become self-sustaining quickly? If so, how quickly?

4. What level of return on investment is expected from the export project?

3.1 Organization for the Global Project

It will be important to have some kind of structure or team within the business to handle the global side of the business. It does not have to be large, but it should be dedicated to ensuring that export sales are adequately serviced, and there should be a clear indication of who will be responsible for the organization and staffing.[121] Having the right resources for the global effort is critical, so a business should make the most of skills already held by staff members, for example, languages or familiarity with a range of foreign currencies. If these and other needed skills are not already available on staff, a small business should seek assistance from external experts.[122]

Other organizational issues that small businesses must address before going abroad include the following:[123]

- **Getting internal buy-in.** Because going overseas to do business is a larger undertaking than many businesses realize, make sure that senior management and the people who are responsible for implementing and supporting the overseas effort know what the goals are and what is expected of them with respect to oversight and management. Knowing how much senior management time should be and could be allocated is an important part of getting internal buy-in. Look for support from people in all functions of the business.

- **Making sure that the full costs of overseas hiring are understood.** If people from overseas will be hired, employment regulations and practices are very different. For example, outside the United States, employment benefits often represent a larger percentage of an employee's salary than in the United States; in the European Union, for example, a full-blown employment contract is needed, not just an offer letter. This tilts the balance of power to the employee at the expense of the company, making termination very difficult. Understanding the full ramifications of hiring people outside the United States has significant implications for a company's financial success.

- **Thinking about how the business will manage overseas employees' expectations.** Different time zones and countries wreak havoc with keeping employees on the same page. Employees hired locally may have very different ideas about what is considered acceptable than a US employee does. Unless expectations and responsibilities are clearly conveyed at the beginning, problems will undoubtedly arise. They may anyway, but perhaps they will not be as serious.

3.2   Market Selection

A business must select the best market(s) to enter. The three largest markets for US products are Canada, Japan, and Mexico, but these countries may not be the largest or best markets for a particular product.[124] If a business is not sure where the best place for doing global business is, one good approach is to find out where domestic competitors have been expanding internationally. Although moving into the same market(s) may make good sense, a good strategy might also be to go somewhere else. Three key US government databases that can identify the countries that represent significant export potential for a product are as follows:[125]

1. The SBA's Automated Trade Locator Assistance System
2. Foreign Trade Report FT925
3. The US Department of Commerce's National Trade Data Bank

After identifying the country or countries that may offer the best market potential for a product, serious market research should be conducted. A business should look at all the following factors: demographic, geographic, political, economic, social, cultural, market access, distribution, production, and the existence or absence of **tariffs** and nontariff trade barriers. Tariffs are taxes imposed on imported goods so that the price of imported goods increases to the level of domestic goods. Tariffs can be particularly critical in selecting a particular country because the tariff may make it impossible for a US small business to profitably sell its products in a particular country.

Nontariff trade barriers are laws or regulations enacted by a country to protect its domestic industries against foreign competition.[126] These barriers include such things as import licensing requirements; fees; government procurement policies; border taxes; and packaging, labeling, and marking standards.[127]

tariffs

Taxes imposed on imported goods so that the price of imported goods increases to the level of domestic goods.

nontariff trade barriers

Laws or regulations enacted by a country to protect its domestic industries against foreign competition.

3.3   Market Entry Strategies

A small business must decide how it wants to enter the selected foreign market(s). Several choices might look attractive for a business (see Figure 15.4). Direct and indirect exporting, strategic alliances, joint ventures, and direct foreign investment are discussed in this section. The benefits and risks associated with each strategy depend on many factors. Among them are the type of product or service being produced; the need for product or service support; and the foreign economic, political, business, and cultural environment to be penetrated. A firm's level of resources and commitment and the degree of risk it is willing to incur will help determine the strategy that the business thinks will work best.[128]

FIGURE 15.4 Examples of Export Market Entry Strategies

Direct exporting and indirect exporting are discussed in Section 2.

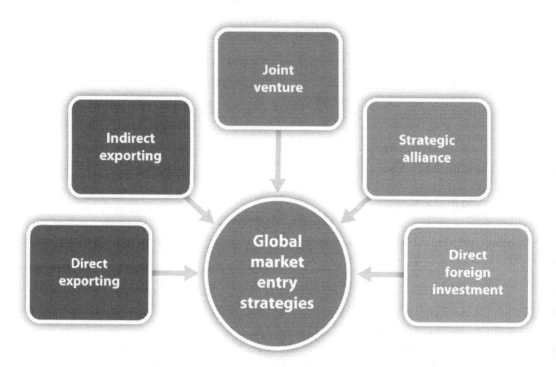

- A **joint venture (JV)** is a partnership with a foreign firm formed to achieve a specific goal or operate for a specific period of time. A legal entity is created, with the partners agreeing to share in the management of the JV, and each partner holds an equity position. Each company retains its separate identity. Among the benefits are immediate market knowledge and access, reduced risk, and control over product attributes. On the negative side, JV agreements across national borders can be extremely complex, which requires a very high level of commitment by all parties.[129] Because some countries have restrictions on the foreign ownership of corporations, a JV may be the only way a small business can purchase facilities in another country.[130]

- A **strategic alliance** is very similar to a JV in that it is a partnership formed to create competitive advantage on a worldwide basis.[131] An agreement is signed between two corporations, but a separate business entity is not created.[132] The business relationship is based on cooperation out of mutual need, and there is shared risk in achieving a common objective. Growing at a rate of about 20 percent per year, strategic alliances are created for many reasons (e.g., opportunities for rapid expansion into new markets, reduced marketing costs, and strategic competitive moves).[133] "Small businesses excel at forming strategic partnerships and alliances which make them look bigger than they are and offer their customers a global reach."[134]

- **Direct foreign investment** is exactly what it sounds like: investment in a foreign country. If a business is interested in manufacturing locally to take advantage of low-cost labor, gain access to raw materials, reduce the high costs of transportation to market, or gain market entry, direct foreign investment is something to be considered. However, the complicated mix of considerations and risks—for example, the growing complexity and contingencies of contracts and degree of product differentiation—makes decisions about foreign investments increasingly difficult.[135]

3.4 Getting Paid

Being paid in full and on time is of obvious importance to a business, so the level of risk that it is willing to assume in extending credit to customers is a major consideration.[136] The credit of a buyer will always be a concern, but potentially more worrisome is the lessened recourse a business will have when it comes to collecting unpaid international debts. Extra caution must be exercised. Both the business owner and the buyer must agree on the terms of the sale in advance.[137]

The primary methods of payment for international transactions are payment in advance (the most secure), letters of credit, documentary collection (drafts), consignment, and open account (the least secure), which are described as follows:[138]

- **Cash in advance.** This is the ideal method of payment because a company is relieved of collection problems and has immediate use of the money. Unfortunately, it tends to be an option only when the manufacturing process is specialized, lengthy, or capital intensive and requires partial or progress payments. Wire transfers are commonly used, and many exporters accept credit cards.

- **Documentary letter of credit.** This is an internationally recognized instrument issued by a bank on behalf of its client, the purchaser. A letter of credit represents the bank's guarantee to pay the seller, provided that the conditions specified in the letter are fulfilled.

- **Documentary collection or draft.** This involves the use of a draft, drawn by the seller on the buyer. It requires the buyer to pay the face amount either on sight (sight draft) or on a specified date in the future (time draft). The draft is an unconditional order to make payment in accordance with its terms, which specify the documents needed before title to the goods will be passed. All terms of payment should be clearly specified so that confusion and delay are avoided.

- **Open account.** With an open account, the exporter bills the customer, who is then expected to pay under agreed-on terms at a future date after the goods are manufactured and delivered (usually with fifteen, thirty, or sixty days). This payment method works well if the buyer is well established, has a long and favorable payment record, or has been thoroughly checked for being creditworthy. This approach is considered risky in international business because a business has limited recourse if debts are unpaid. Small businesses considering this option must examine the political, economic, and commercial risks very thoroughly.

- **Consignment sales.** Goods are shipped to a foreign distributor, which sells them on behalf of the exporter. Title to the goods remains with the exporter until they are sold, at which point payment is sent to the exporter. The exporter has the greatest risk and least control over the goods with this method, and payment may take a while. Risk insurance should be seriously considered with consignment sales.

When buyers default on their payments, it can be time-consuming, difficult, and expensive to obtain payments. A business should contact the buyer and try to negotiate payment. If negotiation fails and the amount of the debt is large enough to make a difference in that business, obtain the assistance and advice of the business's bank, legal counsel, and the US Commercial Service, an organization that can resolve payment problems informally. If arbitration becomes necessary, the International Chamber of Commerce is the place to go. It handles most international arbitrations and is usually acceptable to foreign companies because it is not affiliated with any single country.[139]

3.5 Business Etiquette and Travel

Having a successful global business requires getting to know the history, the culture, and the customs of the country or countries in which a business hopes to expand. Each country is different from another and the United States in some ways. Some of these differences have been discussed earlier in this chapter. Among the cultural differences to be faced are business styles, attitudes toward business relationships and punctuality, negotiating styles, gift-giving customers, greetings, the significance of gestures, the meanings of colors and numbers, and customs regarding titles. For example, engaging in small talk before conducting business is standard practice in Saudi Arabia, and gift giving is an important part of doing business in Japan.[140]

Before traveling to the chosen country or countries, knowing any and all cultural differences is critical. It is also important to educate stateside employees who will be working with international customers.

Being successful in global operations will depend on the relationships that are built. The best way to build them is by traveling to the selected country. Travel there…but do so with the cultural knowledge and understanding that will allow the conduct of business without inadvertently offending a potential customer.

Video Link 15.11

Meet Your Customers: Traveling There

Building relationships for success in exporting businesses.

www.inc.com/exporting/travelingthere.htm

3.6   The Export Plan

After deciding to sell products or services abroad, a carefully researched export plan is a source of direction. An export plan helps a business act on—rather than react to—the challenges and risks encountered in global business. The plan will also help a business obtain financial assistance and find investors, strategic partners, and JV partners that may be needed for success.[141]

There are many elements of an export plan, including a description of the company; its market and industry; its objectives; information on its products or services; an analysis of the target market and industry, including trends and forecasts; an examination of competitors and their strengths and weaknesses; international marketing strategies, including customer profiling and the development of sales and distribution channels; employment and training issues; after-sales and customer service, and financial requirements and forecasts.[142] "Many companies launch their export activities haphazardly and are unsuccessful in their early efforts because of poor or no planning, which often leads them to abandon exporting altogether."[143]

Video Link 15.12

Providing Good Customer Service

Small business owners talk about what they have learned by serving international customers.

www.inc.com/exporting/customerservice.htm

A business's first export plan should be simple, only a few pages because important market data and planning elements may not be easily available or completely unavailable. The plan should be written and seen as a flexible management document, not a static document that sits on a shelf somewhere gathering dust. Objectives need to be compared against actual results, just as a business would do with its marketing plan and its overall business plan. A business should be open to revising the plan as necessary as new information becomes available and experience is gained.[144]

Video Link 15.13

Creating an Export Business Plan

Small business owners agree that developing a strategic plan is the first step toward exporting success.

www.inc.com/exporting/businessplan.htm

KEY TAKEAWAYS

- Before taking a business global, desire to pursue export markets for good rather than frivolous reasons.
- Management commitment must be present for successful global operations.
- A business must decide on some kind of structure to handle its global side. It should be dedicated to ensuring that export sales are adequately serviced.
- Getting internal buy-in is critical.
- A business will need to select the best market(s) to enter. Although Canada, Japan, and Mexico are the largest markets for US products, these countries may not be the best markets for specific products or services.
- Tariffs and nontariff trade barriers can pose serious constraints.
- A business must decide how to enter a foreign market. For example, it can choose direct and indirect exporting, strategic alliances, JVs, and direct foreign investment.
- Being paid in full and on time is of obvious importance, especially considering the difficulties a business will encounter in collecting an unpaid international debt. The most secure method of payment is cash in advance. The least secure is an open account.
- Learning and understanding the business etiquette of the country or countries to which a business is exporting is a very important part of building business relationships.
- A carefully researched export plan is a source of direction, and it will help a business act on—rather than react to—the challenges and risks it will encounter in global business.

1. Go to the Coca-Cola website (www.coca-cola.com/en/index.html) and select one website from each of the following geographic areas: Latin America, Europe, Eurasia, Africa, and Asia Pacific. Compare the home pages of these sites to the US home page—even though you will not understand the language (unless you are bilingual). Look at the graphics, layout, and uses of color. What are the similarities? What are the differences? To what would you attribute the differences? How would these similarities and differences inform the design of a small business website for conducting global business?

4. THE THREE THREADS

LEARNING OBJECTIVES

1. Understand how to contribute to customer value in exporting activities.
2. Explain how exporting can impact cash flow.
3. Explain how technology and the e-environment impact exporting.

4.1 Customer Value Implications

Always remember that customers make the decision about whether the appropriate value is present, and that value will always be as they perceive it. Carefully adapting a product to the targeted country for an exporting venture is an important first step in providing customer value. This means knowing about the sources of value in a product or a service and then acting on them. It can mean a minor product adaptation—for example, serving beer in McDonald's in Germany or wine in McDonald's in France and Italy—or a new twist on distribution—for example, Procter & Gamble selling shampoo in single-use tubes in newsstands in India. Although these are large-company examples, the experiences can be easily translated into small business exporting practice.

Another important source of customer value is the company website. Whether the website is the only selling platform of a business or is part of a brick-and-click exporting business, foreign buyers are much more likely to buy if a business's website is in their language. Although translation and country-specific sites can be a costly proposition, the text, graphics, and colors of the website can either enhance or detract from an exporting business. A small business owner should find out what organizational services and website designers can provide assistance. It may be possible to link the website to the Google translation tool to get a rough translation in seconds.[145]

Once a sale is made, do not make the mistake of thinking that it is the end of the relationship between the business and an overseas customer. Providing after-sale service must be an integral part of a company's export strategy from the very beginning.[146] This service should include regular thank-yous for their business; a plan for regular communication; and offering customers 24/7 availability via some combination of fax, Twitter, e-mail alerts, a wiki, a Skype account, and telephone voicemail services where messages can be retrieved around the clock. This level of access will be of great value to foreign customers because it lets them know that you are reliable, dependable, ready to serve, and willing to minimize risk. It is this proper care and feeding of customers that will keep them coming back because the business provides value that makes it worth their while.[147]

There is something else to consider as well. Research has shown that global online shoppers demand live customer service, with this service being more important than price.[148] This has implications not only for how customer service is designed for the targeted country for exports but for buyers from other countries as well.

4.2 Cash-Flow Implications

A small business exporter will face the same cash-flow challenges that affect any small business, but being an exporter presents additional cash-flow challenges that are unique to selling products overseas. One of these challenges comes from the value-added tax (VAT) in Europe. Having the proper VAT registration can be key because all non–European Union businesses must collect and remit the VAT on applicable transactions. A business is required to charge the VAT, and compliance requires periodic VAT filings, which means keeping VAT records on file and available for inspection by local tax authorities and anyone else who has reason and authority to inspect them. A failure to comply can result in significant penalties and cash-flow problems.[149]

Shipping costs pose another threat to cash flow. Shipping products overseas is very expensive, with the fees sometimes being as high as the cost of shipping the merchandise itself. Add to that the differences in currencies and taxes, and a business is faced with the possibility of having to pay all or most of the shipping costs up front. While waiting for customers to pay, paying these costs will have a negative impact on cash flow.[150] Fortunately, there are cost-cutting approaches available. For example, Michael Katz, a small business owner who ships portfolio and art cases overseas, was able to reduce the extra expenses by negotiating a discount with UPS, cutting his shipping costs to 50 percent of the list rate.[151]

4.3 Implications of Technology and the E-Environment

Inexpensive technology and the Internet have made it possible for small businesses to operate internationally with some of the same efficiencies as larger companies.[152] The global reach of the Internet makes it cost-effective for small businesses to sell products and services overseas. Small businesses can broaden their presence internationally by adopting e-commerce and e-business practices that are user-friendly for non-English-speaking countries.[153]

The small business owner can also look to several other sources of assistance for global endeavors. Consider the following three examples:

1. The self-service advertising product developed by Facebook gives small businesses an opportunity to reach a global audience.[154]

2. Shipping management software packages will automatically figure the costs and the delivery times for overseas orders, giving a close estimate. They also convert the currency for the buyer. Integrating this software into the website of a small business will provide a seamless experience for the customer, making an important contribution to customer value.[155]

3. The Internet and mobile devices lower information and communication costs, providing new channels of distribution and permitting 24/7 global reach through Twitter, wikis, e-mail alerts, and Skype.

KEY TAKEAWAYS

- A small business can offer customer value in its global activities by carefully adapting its products to the targeted country, having a website that caters to the language and culture of the buyers, and providing excellent after-sale service.
- The small business faces potential cash-flow problems from the VAT and shipping costs.
- Inexpensive technology and the Internet have made it possible for small businesses to operate internationally with some of the same efficiencies as larger companies.

EXERCISES

1. How can mobile devices be used to help the exporting operations of a small business?
2. How does the advertising product developed by Facebook work? How can it help increase the global reach of a small business? What are the costs for a small business?

Disaster Watch

Michael has been very successful with his exporting business. Instead of choosing Canada, Japan, or Mexico, the top three countries for small business exporting, he decided on Babalacala, a small country in the Middle East that has a history of political stability even though it has been ruled by one man for more than thirty-five years. The risk has been worth it so far. Michael identified the demand for his product, and he was right on target with his marketing research.

Michael has a small manufacturing plant that employs 150 locals and 5 people from the United States. He has successfully adapted his product to the local cultural, legal, and economic environments. His prices and promotion strategy are good fits, and his distribution structure—with some minor tweaking—is proving to be very efficient and effective. Needless to say, Michael and his investors are very happy campers.

But not for much longer.

Michael awakened one morning to a large-scale revolt against the current governor of Babalacala. The streets of the capital city were filled with protestors. Things were peaceful at first, but violence erupted in the afternoon. Many of Michael's local workers left the factory to protest or because they were afraid. Telecommunications were out, transportation was spotty, and there was only intermittent power. Most of the local stores closed. The word on the street was that the protestors were in for the long haul. They planned to keep protesting until the current governor resigned or left the country.

What should Michael do? He has a lot of money, time, and passion invested in his exporting business, and there are investors to think about. He does not want to leave Babalacala, but this is a serious situation.

ENDNOTES

1. "About Us," *Center Rock Inc.*, accessed February 7, 2012, www.centerrock.com/content/about-us; e-mail correspondence with Brandon Fisher, July 28, 2011.

2. Paul Davidson, "Small Businesses Look Across Borders to Add Markets," *USA Today*, April 12, 2011, accessed February 7, 2012, www.usatoday.com/money/economy/2011-04-06-small-businesses-go-international.htm; Rieva Lesonsky, "Increased Opportunities for Small-Business Exports," *Small Business Trends*, June 27, 2010, accessed February 7, 2012, smallbiztrends.com/2010/06/opportunities-small-business-exports.html.

3. "Breaking into the Trade Game: A Small Business Guide to Exporting," *US Small Business Administration*, 2005, accessed February 7, 2012, archive.sba.gov/idc/groups/public/documents/sba_homepage/serv_entire.pdf.

4. "Profile of U.S. Importing and Exporting Companies, 2008–2009 Highlights," *US Census Bureau*, April 12, 2011, accessed February 7, 2012, www.census.gov/foreign-trade/Press-Release/edb/2009/2009Highlights.pdf.

5. "Profile of U.S. Importing and Exporting Companies, 2008–2009 Highlights," *US Census Bureau*, April 12, 2011, accessed February 7, 2012, www.census.gov/foreign-trade/Press-Release/edb/2009/2009Highlights.pdf.

6. "Breaking into the Trade Game: A Small Business Guide to Exporting," *US Small Business Administration*, 2005, accessed February 7, 2012, archive.sba.gov/idc/groups/public/documents/sba_homepage/serv_entire.pdf.

7. US Department of Commerce, *A Basic Guide to Exporting*, 10th ed. (Washington, DC: International Trade Association, 2008), i.

8. "Small and Medium-Sized Enterprises: Overview of Participation in U.S. Exports," *US International Trade Commission*, January 2010, accessed February 7, 2012, www.usitc.gov/publications/332/pub4125.pdf.

9. "Small and Medium-Sized Enterprises: Overview of Participation in U.S. Exports," *US International Trade Commission*, January 2010, accessed February 7, 2012, www.usitc.gov/publications/332/pub4125.pdf.

10. "Small and Medium-Sized Enterprises: Overview of Participation in U.S. Exports," *US International Trade Commission*, January 2010, accessed February 7, 2012, www.usitc.gov/publications/332/pub4125.pdf.

11. Philip R. Cateora and John L. Graham, *International Marketing* (New York: McGraw-Hill Irwin, 2007), 312.

12. William M. Pride, Robert J. Hughes, and Jack R. Kapoor, *Business* (Boston: Houghton Mifflin, 2007), 94.

13. Anita Campbell, "The Trend of the Micro-Multinationals," *Small Business Trends*, February 20, 2007, accessed February 7, 2012, smallbiztrends.com/2007/02/the-trend-of-the-micro-multinationals.html; Bernard Lunn, "Introducing the Tales of Micro-Nationals," *Small Business Trends*, July 7, 2010, accessed February 7, 2012, smallbiztrends.com/2010/07/introducing-the-tales-of-micro-multinationals.html.

14. Bernard Lunn, "Introducing the Tales of Micro-Nationals," *Small Business Trends*, July 7, 2010, accessed February 7, 2012, smallbiztrends.com/2010/07/introducing-the-tales-of-micro-multinationals.html.

15. Anita Campbell, "Preparing Your Business to Go Global," *Small Business Trends*, November 19, 2010, accessed February 7, 2012, smallbiztrends.com/2010/11/preparing-your-business-to-go-global.html.

16. Bernard Lunn, "Tales of Micro-Multinationals: Generation Alliance," *Small Business Trends*, July 7, 2010, accessed February 7, 2012, smallbiztrends.com/2010/07/tales-of-micro-multinationals-generation-alliance.html.

17. Bernard Lunn, "Tales of Micro-Multinationals: Jadience," *Small Business Trends*, July 15, 2010, accessed February 7, 2012, smallbiztrends.com/2010/07/tales-of-micro-multinationals-jadience.html.

18. Bernard Lunn, "Tales of Micro-Multinationals: Worketc," *Small Business Trends*, July 21, 2010, accessed February 7, 2012, smallbiztrends.com/2010/07/micro-multinationals-worketc.html; "The Why of What We're About," *Worketc*, accessed February 7, 2012, www.worketc.com/about_us.

19. "Benefits of Exporting," *Export.gov*, March 31, 2011, accessed February 7, 2012, export.gov/about/eg_main_016807.asp; Laurel Delaney, "A How-To on Expanding Your Business Globally," *The Global Small Business Blog*, January 11, 2011, accessed February 7, 2012, borderbuster.blogspot.com/2011/01/how-to-on-expanding-your-business.html; Steve Strauss, "Globalization Is Good for (Small) Business," *USA Today*, May 17, 2004, accessed February 7, 2012, www.usatoday.com/money/smallbusiness/columnist/strauss/2004-05-17-globalization_x.htm; "Breaking into the Trade Game: A Small Business Guide to Exporting," *US Small Business Administration*, 2005, accessed February 7, 2012, archive.sba.gov/idc/groups/public/documents/sba_homepage/serv_entire.pdf.

20. "Breaking into the Trade Game: A Small Business Guide to Exporting," *US Small Business Administration*, 2005, accessed February 7, 2012, archive.sba.gov/idc/groups/public/documents/sba_homepage/serv_entire.pdf.

21. Laurel Delaney, "A How-To on Expanding Your Business Globally," *The Global Small Business Blog*, January 11, 2011, accessed February 7, 2012, borderbuster.blogspot.com/2011/01/how-to-on-expanding-your-business.html; Strategic Name Development, Inc., "Global Linguistic Analysis" (2011), accessed February 7, 2012, www.namedevelopment.com/global-linguistic-analysis.html.

22. "Breaking into the Trade Game: A Small Business Guide to Exporting," *US Small Business Administration*, 2005, accessed February 7, 2012, archive.sba.gov/idc/groups/public/documents/sba_homepage/serv_entire.pdf.

23. "Global Marketing," *SmallBusiness.com*, accessed February 7, 2012, smallbusiness.com/wiki/Global_marketing.

24. Rieva Lesonsky, "Increased Opportunities for Small-Business Exports," *Small Business Trends*, June 27, 2010, accessed February 7, 2012, smallbiztrends.com/2010/06/opportunities-small-business-exports.html.

25. "2010 Small Business Exporting Survey," *NSBA and SBEA*, March 11, 2010, accessed February 7, 2012, www.nsba.biz/docs/2010_small_business_exporting_survey_001.pdf.

26. Kevin Morris, "Small Business Owner Takes His Green Energy Business Global," *AllBusiness.com*, April 22, 2011, accessed February 7, 2012, www.allbusiness.com/small-green-energy-business/15572754-1.html.

27. "Breaking into the Trade Game: A Small Business Guide to Exporting," *US Small Business Administration*, 2005, accessed February 7, 2012, archive.sba.gov/idc/groups/public/documents/sba_homepage/serv_entire.pdf.

28. "Breaking into the Trade Game: A Small Business Guide to Exporting," *US Small Business Administration*, 2005, accessed February 7, 2012, archive.sba.gov/idc/groups/public/documents/sba_homepage/serv_entire.pdf.

29. Shannon Coursey, "Has Your Small Business Taken Big Steps to Grow Globally?," *UPS Upside*, January 10, 2011, accessed February 7, 2012, blog.ups.com/2011/01/10/has-your-small-business-taken-big-steps-to-grow-globally/; Laurel Delaney, "And the Winner for the Growth through Global Trade Award Goes To...," *The Global Small Business Blog*, January 24, 2011, accessed February 7, 2012, borderbuster.blogspot.com/2011/01/and-winner-for-growth-through-global.html; interview with Michelle Wickum, director of marketing, SteelMaster Buildings, January 5, 2012; SteelMaster company materials provided by Michelle Wickum, Director of Marketing, January 5, 2012.

30. Adapted from David L. Kurtz, *Contemporary Business* (Hoboken, NJ: John Wiley & Sons, 2011), 121.

31. Laurel Delaney, "A How-To on Expanding Your Business Globally," *The Global Small Business Blog*, January 11, 2011, accessed February 7, 2012, borderbuster.blogspot.com/2011/01/how-to-on-expanding-your-business.html.

32. Laurel Delaney, "A How-To on Expanding Your Business Globally," *The Global Small Business Blog*, January 11, 2011, accessed February 7, 2012, borderbuster.blogspot.com/2011/01/how-to-on-expanding-your-business.html; Laurel Delaney, "Direct Exporting: Advantages and Disadvantages to Direct Exporting," *About.com*, accessed February 7, 2012, importexport.about.com/od/DevelopingSalesAndDistribution/a/Direct-Exporting-Advantages-And-Disadvantages-To-Direct-Exporting.htm; "The Advantages of Direct Exporting," *vcShipping.com*, accessed February 7, 2012, www.vcshipping.com/export/the-advantages-of-direct-exporting.html.

33. Team Canada Inc., "10 Steps to Successful Exporting," *About.com*, accessed February 7, 2012, sbinfocanada.about.com/od/canadaexport/a/10exportsteps.htm.

34. CBS Investment, "Advantages and Disadvantages of Direct and Indirect Exports," *CBS Investment*, accessed February 7, 2012, www.cbsinvestment.com/advantages-and-disadvantages-of-direct-and-indirect-exports/; Laurel Delaney, "A How-To on Expanding Your Business Globally," *The Global Small Business Blog*, January 11, 2011, accessed February 7, 2012, borderbuster.blogspot.com/2011/01/how-to-on-expanding-your-business.html.

35. Laurel Delaney, *Start and Run a Profitable Exporting Business* (Vancouver, BC: Self-Counsel Press, 1998): chapter 8.

36. Laurel Delaney, "A How-To on Expanding Your Business Globally," *The Global Small Business Blog*, January 11, 2011, accessed February 7, 2012, borderbuster.blogspot.com/2011/01/how-to-on-expanding-your-business.html.

37. "6 Steps to Begin Exporting," *US Small Business Administration*, accessed February 7, 2012, www.sba.gov/content/6-steps-begin-exporting.

38. Tricia Phillips, "Biz Bureau Gives Top Tips on Going Global with Your Business," *Mirror*, January 26, 2011, accessed February 7, 2012, www.mirror.co.uk/advice/money/2011/01/26/biz-bureau-gives-top-tips-on-going-global-with-your-business-115875-22875517.

39. "A Small Business Guide to Exporting: Part 1—Getting Started," *AllBusiness.com*, accessed February 7, 2012, www.allbusiness.com/economy-economic-indicators/money-currencies/11790828-1.html.

40. "Trade Data and Analysis," *Export.gov*, March 3, 2011, accessed February 7, 2012, export.gov/tradedata/index.asp.

41. "Session 11: Global Expansion," *My Own Business*, accessed February 7, 2012, www.myownbusiness.org/global_expansion/index.html.

42. "Session 11: Global Expansion," *My Own Business*, accessed February 7, 2012, www.myownbusiness.org/global_expansion/index.html.

43. "Session 11: Global Expansion," *My Own Business*, accessed February 7, 2012, www.myownbusiness.org/global_expansion/index.html.

44. Laurel Delaney, "A How-To on Expanding Your Business Globally," *The Global Small Business Blog*, January 11, 2011, accessed February 7, 2012, borderbuster.blogspot.com/2011/01/how-to-on-expanding-your-business.html.

45. "Session 11: Global Expansion," *My Own Business*, accessed February 7, 2012, www.myownbusiness.org/global_expansion/index.html.

46. "Is Your Small Business Ready to Go Global?," *Small Business CEO*, February 7, 2011, accessed February 7, 2012, www.smbceo.com/2011/02/07/global-business-2.

47. Laurel Delaney, "A How-To on Expanding Your Business Globally," *The Global Small Business Blog*, January 11, 2011, accessed February 7, 2012, borderbuster.blogspot.com/2011/01/how-to-on-expanding-your-business.html.

48. Laurel Delaney, "A How-To on Expanding Your Business Globally," *The Global Small Business Blog*, January 11, 2011, accessed February 7, 201; borderbuster.blogspot.com/2011/01/how-to-on-expanding-your-business.html; "Starting an Export Business," *Gaebler.com*, May 19, 2011, accessed February 7, 201, www.gaebler.com/Starting-an-Export-Business.htm; William M. Pride, Robert Hughes, and Jack R. Kapoor, *Business* (Boston: Houghton Mifflin, 2008), 96; "Is Your

Small Business Ready to Go Global?," *Small Business CEO*, February 7, 2011, accessed February 7, 2012, www.smbceo.com/2011/02/07/global-business-2.

49. Laurel Delaney, "A How-To on Expanding Your Business Globally," *The Global Small Business Blog*, January 11, 2011, accessed February 7, 2012, borderbuster.blogspot.com/2011/01/how-to-on-expanding-your-business.html.

50. Philip Kotler and Kevin Lane Keller, *Marketing Management* (Upper Saddle River, NJ: Pearson Prentice Hall, 2009), 13.

51. Jennifer LeClaire, "How to Take Your Small Business Global," *E-Commerce Times*, June 20, 2006, accessed February 7, 2012, www.ecommercetimes.com/story/50910.html%20?wlc=1305842348.

52. Philip Kotler and Kevin Lane Keller, *Marketing Management* (Upper Saddle River, NJ: Pearson Prentice Hall, 2009), 611.

53. John M. Ivancevich and Thomas N. Duening, *Business: Principles, Guidelines, and Practices* (Mason, OH: Atomic Dog Publishing, 2007), 49.

54. "All About Global Marketing," *BusinessKnowledgeSource.com*, accessed February 7, 2012, www.businessknowledgesource.com/marketing/all_about_global_marketing_032164.html.

55. Arundhati Parmar, "Dependent Variables: Sound Global Strategies Rely on Certain Factors," *Marketing News*, September 2002, 2.

56. Philip R. Cateora and John L. Graham, *International Marketing* (New York: McGraw-Hill Irwin, 2007), 341, 351, 353; "Global Linguistic Analysis," *Strategic Name Development*, accessed February 7, 2012, www.namedevelopment.com/global-linguistic-analysis.html.

57. Philip R. Cateora and John L. Graham, *International Marketing* (New York: McGraw-Hill Irwin, 2007), 341.

58. Philip R. Cateora and John L. Graham, *International Marketing* (New York: McGraw-Hill Irwin, 2007), 343.

59. C. K. Prahalad, *The Fortune at the Bottom of the Pyramid* (Philadelphia: Wharton School Publishing, 2005), as cited in Philip R. Cateora and John L. Graham, *International Marketing* (New York: McGraw-Hill Irwin, 2007), 343.

60. David L. Kurtz, *Contemporary Business* (Hoboken, NJ: John Wiley & Sons, 2011), 109.

61. David L. Kurtz, *Contemporary Business* (Hoboken, NJ: John Wiley & Sons, 2011), 109.

62. Philip R. Cateora and John L. Graham, *International Marketing* (New York: McGraw-Hill Irwin, 2007), 343.

63. Philip R. Cateora and John L. Graham, *International Marketing* (New York: McGraw-Hill Irwin, 2007), 343.

64. Philip R. Cateora and John L. Graham, *International Marketing* (New York: McGraw-Hill Irwin, 2007), 343.

65. Philip R. Cateora and John L. Graham, *International Marketing* (New York: McGraw-Hill Irwin, 2007), 352.

66. Philip R. Cateora and John L. Graham, *International Marketing* (New York: McGraw-Hill Irwin, 2007), 352–53.

67. Ryan Underwood, "Creating a Smart Export Strategy," *Inc.*, May 3, 2011, accessed February 7, 2012, www.inc.com/magazine/20110501/author-pankaj-ghemawat-on-global-expansion-for-small-exporters.html.

68. "Small and Medium-Sized Enterprises: Overview of Participation in U.S. Exports," *US International Trade Commission*, January 2010, accessed February 7, 2012, www.usitc.gov/publications/332/pub4125.pdf.

69. Anita Campbell, "How to Make Your Website Ready for International Business," *Small Business Trends*, October 29, 2010, accessed February 7, 2012, smallbiztrends.com/2010/10/website-ready-international-business.html.

70. Paul Demery, "Anchors Aweigh," *Internet Retailer*, January 31, 2008, accessed February 7, 2012, www.internetretailer.com/2008/01/31/anchors-aweigh.

71. "Translation Problems in Global Marketing," *My Opera*, November 14, 2006, accessed February 7, 2012, my.opera.com/kitkreuger/blog/2006/11/14/translation-problems-in-global-marketing.

72. "Translation Problems in Global Marketing," *My Opera*, November 14, 2006, accessed February 7, 2012, my.opera.com/kitkreuger/blog/2006/11/14/translation-problems-in-global-marketing.

73. Philip Kotler and Kevin Lane Keller, *Marketing Management* (Upper Saddle River, NJ: Pearson Prentice Hall, 2009), 613.

74. Karen Collins, *Exploring Business* (Irvington, NY: Flat World Knowledge, 2009), 72.

75. John Freivalds, "What's in a Name?," *Business Library*, April 1996, accessed February 7, 2012, findarticles.com/p/articles/mi_m4422/is_n4_v13/ai_18512264.

76. Jeffrey Gangemi, "Avoiding Faux Pas When Exporting," *Bloomberg BusinessWeek*, June 27, 2007, accessed February 7, 2012, www.businessweek.com/smallbiz/content/jun2007/sb20070627_897013.htm?campaign_id=rss_smlbz.

77. "The International Marketing Mix," *Learn Marketing*, accessed February 7, 2012, www.learnmarketing.net/internationalmarketingmix.htm.

78. John M. Ivancevich and Thomas N. Duening, *Business: Principles, Guidelines, and Practices* (Mason, OH: Atomic Dog Publishing, 2007), 40; Philip Kotler and Kevin Lane Keller, *Marketing Management* (Upper Saddle River, NJ: Pearson Prentice Hall, 2009), 616.

79. Eric Mitchell, "The Pricing Advisor," *The Pricing Advisor Newsletter*, accessed February 7, 2012, members.pricingsociety.com/articles/Pricing-for-Global-Markets.pdf.

80. "The International Marketing Mix," *Learn Marketing*, accessed February 7, 2012, www.learnmarketing.net/internationalmarketingmix.htm.

81. John M. Ivancevich and Thomas N. Duening, *Business: Principles, Guidelines, and Practices* (Mason, OH: Atomic Dog Publishing, 2007), 50.

82. Philip R. Cateora and John L. Graham, *International Marketing* (New York: McGraw-Hill Irwin, 2007), 396.

83. John M. Ivancevich and Thomas N. Duening, *Business: Principles, Guidelines, and Practices* (Mason, OH: Atomic Dog Publishing, 2007), 50.

84. "The International Marketing Mix," *Learn Marketing*, accessed February 7, 2012, www.learnmarketing.net/internationalmarketingmix.htm.

85. "The International Marketing Mix," *Learn Marketing*, accessed February 7, 2012, www.learnmarketing.net/internationalmarketingmix.htm.

86. Ryan Underwood, "Creating a Smart Export Strategy," *Inc.*, May 3, 2011, accessed February 7, 2012, www.inc.com/magazine/20110501/author-pankaj-ghemawat-on-global-expansion-for-small-exporters.html.

87. Laurel Delaney, "Global Guru: Shaking Things Up. Making Things Happen," *Change This*, October 2004, accessed February 7, 2012, changethis.com/manifesto/6.03.GlobalGuru/pdf/6.03.GlobalGuru.pdf.

88. Philip R. Cateora and John L. Graham, *International Marketing* (New York: McGraw-Hill Irwin, 2007), 396.

89. John M. Ivancevich and Thomas N. Duening, *Business: Principles, Guidelines, and Practices* (Mason, OH: Atomic Dog Publishing, 2007), 50; "Global Marketing," *SmallBusiness.com*, accessed February 7, 2012, smallbusiness.com/wiki/Global_marketing.

90. Philip R. Cateora and John L. Graham, *International Marketing* (New York: McGraw-Hill Irwin, 2007), 468.

91. Marian Katz, "No Women, No Alcohol; Learn Saudi Taboos before Placing Ads," *Abstracts, Business International*, 1986, accessed June 1, 2012, www.faqs.org/abstracts/Business-international/No-women-no-alcohol-learn-Saudi-taboos-before-placing-ads.html.

92. Philip R. Cateora and John L. Graham, *International Marketing* (New York: McGraw-Hill Irwin, 2007), 473.

93. Emily Bryson York, "Burger King's MO: Offend, Earn Media, Apologize, Repeat," *Ad Age Global*, July 8, 2009, accessed February 7, 2012, adage.com/article/global-news/advertising-burger-king-draws-ire-hindus-ad/137801.

94. Shaun Rein, "Learn from Burger King's Advertising Fiasco," *Forbes*, April 20, 2009, accessed February 7, 2012, www.forbes.com/2009/04/20/advertising-global-mistakes-leadership-managing-marketing.html.

95. Shaun Rein, "Learn from Burger King's Advertising Fiasco," *Forbes*, April 20, 2009, accessed February 7, 2012, www.forbes.com/2009/04/20/advertising-global-mistakes-leadership-managing-marketing.html.

96. John M. Ivancevich and Thomas N. Duening, *Business: Principles, Guidelines, and Practices* (Mason, OH: Atomic Dog Publishing, 2007), 50.

97. Susan Gunelius, "Building Your Brand with Social Media," *Reuters*, January 4, 2011, accessed February 7, 2012, www.reuters.com/article/2011/01/05/idUS162459562201 10105.

98. Adapted from Philip R. Cateora and John L. Graham, *International Marketing* (New York: McGraw-Hill Irwin, 2007), 479.

99. "Small Business Globalization: Should You Pursue Global Markets?," *more-for-small business.com*, accessed February 7, 2012, www.more-for-small-business.com/small-business-globalization-should-you-pursue-global-markets.html.

100. Paul Demery, "Anchors Aweigh," *Internet Retailer*, January 31, 2008, accessed February 7, 2012, www.internetretailer.com/2008/01/31/anchors-aweigh.

101. Philip R. Cateora and John L. Graham, *International Marketing* (New York: McGraw-Hill Irwin, 2007), 203.

102. Joshua Ritchie, "The 5 Most Bizarre Tax Deductions around the World," *Mint Software Inc.*, December 15, 2009, accessed June 1, 2012, http://www.mint.com/blog/trends/the-5-most-bizarre-tax-deductions-around-the-world/.

103. "Exporting/Importing Specific Products," *US Small Business Administration*, accessed February 7, 2012, www.sba.gov/content/exportingimporting-specific-products.

104. "For Entrepreneurs: Starting an Export Business," *Gaebler.com*, May 19, 2011, accessed February 7, 2012, www.gaebler.com/Starting-an-Export-Business.htm.

105. Philip R. Cateora and John L. Graham, *International Marketing* (New York: McGraw-Hill Irwin, 2007), 193.

106. Philip R. Cateora and John L. Graham, *International Marketing* (New York: McGraw-Hill Irwin, 2007), 158.

107. Philip R. Cateora and John L. Graham, *International Marketing* (New York: McGraw-Hill Irwin, 2007), 158.

108. Philip R. Cateora and John L. Graham, *International Marketing* (New York: McGraw-Hill Irwin, 2007), 159-165.

109. Philip R. Cateora and John L. Graham, *International Marketing* (New York: McGraw-Hill Irwin, 2007), 166.

110. John M. Ivancevich and Thomas N. Duening, *Business: Principles, Guidelines, and Practices* (Mason, OH: Atomic Dog Publishing, 2007), 39.

111. "Euro," *X-rates.com*, accessed March 5, 2012, www.x-rates.com/d/EUR/table.html%20X-rates.com; "Indian Rupee," *X-Rates*, accessed March 5, 2012, www.x-rates.com/d/INR/table.html.

112. John M. Ivancevich and Thomas N. Duening, *Business: Principles, Guidelines, and Practices* (Mason, OH: Atomic Dog Publishing, 2007), 39.

113. Philip R. Cateora and John L. Graham, *International Marketing* (New York: McGraw-Hill Irwin, 2007), 537; David L. Kurtz, *Contemporary Business* (Hoboken, NJ: John Wiley & Sons, 2011), 113.

114. Philip R. Cateora and John L. Graham, *International Marketing* (New York: McGraw-Hill Irwin, 2007), 538.

115. US Department of Commerce, *A Basic Guide to Exporting*, 10th ed. (Washington, DC: International Trade Association, 2008), 193–94.

116. "Small and Medium-Sized Enterprises: Overview of Participation in U.S. Exports," *US International Trade Commission*, January 2010, accessed February 7, 2012, www.usitc.gov/publications/332/pub4125.pdf.

117. "6 Steps to Begin Exporting," *US Small Business Administration*, accessed February 7, 2012, www.sba.gov/content/6-steps-begin-exporting.

118. Adapted from Philip R. Cateora and John L. Graham, *International Marketing* (New York: McGraw-Hill Irwin, 2007), 367.

119. David L. Kurtz, *Contemporary Business* (Hoboken, NJ: John Wiley & Sons, 2011), 133.

120. "Management Issues Involved in the Export Decision," *Export.gov*, March 31, 2011, accessed February 7, 2012, export.gov/exportbasics/eg_main_017455.asp.

121. "Management Issues Involved in the Export Decision," *Export.gov*, March 31, 2011, accessed February 7, 2012, export.gov/exportbasics/eg_main_017455.asp.

122. Tricia Phillips, "Biz Bureau Gives Top Tips on Going Global with Your Business," *Mirror*, January 26, 2011, accessed February 7, 2012, www.mirror.co.uk/advice/money/2011/01/26/biz-bureau-gives-top-tips-on-going-global-with-your-business-115875-22875517.

123. Denise O'Berry, "Is Now the Time to Expand to Global Markets?," *AllBusiness.com*, April 14, 2008, accessed February 7, 2012, www.allbusiness.com/company-activities-management/company-strategy/8518731-1.html; Anita Campbell, "Smaller and Younger Companies Get Overseas Presence," *Small Business Trends*, December 7, 2007, accessed February 7, 2012, smallbiztrends.com/2007/12/smaller-and-younger-companies-get-overseas-presence.html; "Management Issues Involved in the Export Decision," *Export.gov*, March 31, 2011, accessed February 7, 2012, export.gov/exportbasics/eg_main_017455.asp.

124. Laurel Delaney, "A How-To on Expanding Your Business Globally," *The Global Small Business Blog*, January 11, 2011, accessed February 7, 2012, borderbuster.blogspot.com/2011/01/how-to-on-expanding-your-business.html.

125. Laurel Delaney, "A How-To on Expanding Your Business Globally," *The Global Small Business Blog*, January 11, 2011, accessed February 7, 2012, borderbuster.blogspot.com/2011/01/how-to-on-expanding-your-business.html.

126. Laurel Delaney, "A How-To on Expanding Your Business Globally," *The Global Small Business Blog*, January 11, 2011, accessed February 7, 2012, borderbuster.blogspot.com/2011/01/how-to-on-expanding-your-business.html.

127. Philip R. Cateora and John L. Graham, *International Marketing* (New York: McGraw-Hill Irwin, 2007), 40.

128. "Exporting Basics," *SmallBusiness.com*, February 6, 2010, accessed February 7, 2012, smallbusiness.com/wiki/Exporting_basics.

129. Philip R. Cateora and John L. Graham, *International Marketing* (New York: McGraw-Hill Irwin, 2007), 329; William M. Pride, Robert J. Hughes, and Jack R. Kapoor, *Business* (Boston: Houghton Mifflin, 2008), 93; "Joint Ventures and Strategic Alliances," *Fukuda Law Firm*, accessed February 7, 2012.

130. John M. Ivancevich and Thomas N. Duening, *Business: Principles, Guidelines, and Practices* (Mason, OH: Atomic Dog Publishing, 2007), 47.

131. William M. Pride, Robert J. Hughes, and Jack R. Kapoor, *Business* (Boston: Houghton Mifflin, 2008), 93).

132. "Joint Ventures and Strategic Alliances," *Fukuda Law Firm*, accessed February 7, 2012.

133. Philip R. Cateora and John L. Graham, *International Marketing* (New York: McGraw-Hill Irwin, 2007), 327.

134. Laurel Delaney, "Global Guru: Shaking Things Up. Making Things Happen," *Change This*, October 19, 2004, accessed February 7, 2012, changethis.com/manifesto/6.03.GlobalGuru/pdf/6.03.GlobalGuru.pdf.

135. Philip R. Cateora and John L. Graham, *International Marketing* (New York: McGraw-Hill Irwin, 2007), 332.

136. US Department of Commerce, *A Basic Guide to Exporting*, 10th ed. (Washington, DC: International Trade Association, 2008), 177.

137. Laurel Delaney, "A How-To on Expanding Your Business Globally," *The Global Small Business Blog*, January 11, 2011, accessed February 7, 2012, borderbuster.blogspot.com/2011/01/how-to-on-expanding-your-business.html.

138. Laurel Delaney, "A How-To on Expanding Your Business Globally," *The Global Small Business Blog*, January 11, 2011, accessed February 7, 2012, borderbuster.blogspot.com/2011/01/how-to-on-expanding-your-business.html; US Department of Commerce, *A Basic Guide to Exporting*, 10th ed. (Washington, DC: International Trade Association, 2008), 178–80, 182–83.

139. US Department of Commerce, *A Basic Guide to Exporting*, 10th ed. (Washington, DC: International Trade Association, 2008), 184.

140. US Department of Commerce, *A Basic Guide to Exporting*, 10th ed. (Washington, DC: International Trade Association, 2008), 211.

141. "10 Steps to Successful Exporting," *About.com*, accessed February 7, 2012, sbinfocanada.about.com/od/canadaexport/a/10exportsteps.htm.

142. "10 Steps to Successful Exporting," *About.com*, accessed February 7, 2012, sbinfocanada.about.com/od/canadaexport/a/10exportsteps.htm.

143. US Department of Commerce, *A Basic Guide to Exporting*, 10th ed. (Washington, DC: International Trade Association, 2008), 18.

144. US Department of Commerce, *A Basic Guide to Exporting*, 10th ed. (Washington, DC: International Trade Association, 2008), 18.

145. Anita Campbell, "How to Make Your Website Ready for International Business," *Small Business Trends*, October 29, 2010, accessed February 7, 2012, smallbiztrends.com/2010/10/website-ready-international-business.html.

146. US Department of Commerce, *A Basic Guide to Exporting*, 10th ed. (Washington, DC: International Trade Association, 2008), 219.

147. Laurel Delaney, "Building Global Bonds One Customer at a Time," *Small Business Trends*, June 27, 2008, accessed February 7, 2012, smallbiztrends.com/2008/06/global-customer-bonds.html.

148. "Webinar: Online Retail and the ROI of Live Help—Why Global Online Shoppers Demand Live Customer Service," accessed February 7, 2012, www.retailcustomerexperience.com/whitepapers/2508/Webinar-Online-Retail-and-the-ROI-of-Live-Help-Why-Global-Online-Shoppers-Demand-Live-Customer-Service.

149. Denise O'Berry, "Is Now the Time to Expand to Global Markets?," *AllBusiness.com*, April 14, 2008, accessed February 7, 2012, www.allbusiness.com/company-activities-managements/company-strategy/8518731-1.html.

150. Anita Campbell, "How to Make Your Website Ready for International Business," *Small Business Trends*, October 29, 2010, accessed February 7, 2012, smallbiztrends.com/2010/10/website-ready-international-business.html.

151. Elise Craig, "How to Get Your Small Business into the Export Game," *CBS Money Watch*, March 3, 2011, accessed February 7, 2012, www.cbsnews.com/8301-505143_162-46540438/how-to-get-your-small-business-into-the-export-game.

152. Anita Campbell, "Preparing Your Business to Go Global," *Small Business Trends*, November 19, 2010, accessed February 7, 2012, smallbiztrends.com/2010/11/preparing-your-business-to-go-global.html.

153. US Department of Commerce, *A Basic Guide to Exporting*, 10th ed. (Washington, DC: International Trade Association, 2008), 219.

154. "Small Business News: The Global View," *Small Business Trends*, January 18, 2011, accessed February 7, 2012, smallbiztrends.com/2011/01/small-business-news-the-global-view.html.

155. Anita Campbell, "How to Make Your Website Ready for International Business," *Small Business Trends*, October 29, 2010, accessed February 7, 2012, smallbiztrends.com/2010/10/website-ready-international-business.html.

Appendix: A Sample Business Plan

The following business plan for Frank's All-American BarBeQue was built using Business Plan Pro software. It is for the purpose of illustration and does not represent the full capabilities of the software.

1. EXECUTIVE SUMMARY

Frank's All-American BarBeQue has operated for decades in the southern Connecticut shore region. With a tradition of superlative food at fair prices served in a family-friendly atmosphere, the owners now believe it is time to open a second restaurant and expand the production and the distribution of Frank's signature barbecue sauces. This second restaurant will be in Darien, Connecticut, and will be nearly twice as large, in terms of seating capacity, as the current Fairfield restaurant. The company also plans to ramp up production of its sauces and increase their sales fourfold in the next three years.

1.1 Objectives

The owners of Frank's All-American BarBeQue and other investors plan to put $160,000 of their own money into the second restaurant and expand the production of the signature sauces. They seek to raise an addition $175,000 from a bank loan that will be repaid in two years.

1.2 Mission

Vision Statement

To produce the best barbecue food in New England.

Mission Statement

The mission of Frank's All-American BarBeQue is to provide the southern Connecticut shore region with the finest barbecue food in four major regional styles at affordable prices in a family-friendly setting. As we grow, we will never forget and remain faithful to those factors that have made us a success.

1.3 Keys to Success

Frank's All-American BarBeQue has been in business for nearly forty years. It has weathered good times and bad times through all types of economic conditions. We have survived because Frank's has remained committed to several principles.

- The only objective of a restaurant is to serve the finest food it can prepare. Good food—not more gimmicks or advertising—brings in customers and, more importantly, *keeps* customers.
- Preparing the finest foods means a commitment to excellence, which means obtaining the best ingredients and a dedication to cooking barbecue properly, which means cooking carefully and *slowly*.
- In addition to providing the finest food, we remain committed to providing excellent service. To us, this means friendly and knowledgeable staff members who make the customers feel like they are dining with family.
- We provide the right atmosphere. Our goal is to have a setting that says "barbecue." We do not provide a fancy setting; our basic setting complements the food we serve.

1.4 Company Summary

Frank's All-American BarBeQue has been a highly successful restaurant in Fairfield, Connecticut, for nearly forty years. It was started and is still managed by Frank Rainsford. Its food and sauces have won awards at both regional and national barbecue cook-offs. In addition, Frank's has been voted the best barbecue establishment in Connecticut numerous times by many local newspapers and magazines.

The management team of Frank's All-American BarBeQue has decided that *now* is the time to expand to an additional location. After careful analysis, a second Frank's All-American BarBeQue can and should be opened in Darien, Connecticut. This restaurant will be larger and geared to better tap into the growing premade, take-home dinner market.

In the last few years, Frank's has been selling its four signature barbecue sauces—Texan, Memphis, Kansas City, and Carolina—in local supermarkets. Although this represents a small portion of overall revenues, sales have been growing at a remarkable pace. This market must be exploited. Preliminary market research indicates that this segment of the business will grow at 20 percent per year for the next five years.

1.5 Company Ownership

Presently, Frank's All-American BarBeQue is a limited liability partnership with Frank Rainsford and his wife Betty as owners. Each has a 50 percent share in the business.

The plans for expansion will bring in capital from three other investors: Robert Rainsford, Susan Rainsford Rogers, and Alice Jacobs. Robert Rainsford and Susan Rainsford Rogers are the son and daughter of Frank and Betty. Both have extensive work experience at Frank's. Alice Jacobs has been the restaurant's accountant for over twenty years.

To assist the financing of the expansion, Robert Rainsford and Susan Rainsford Rogers will each invest $50,000, while Alice Jacobs will invest $60,000.

The new limited liability partnership will result in the investors holding the following equity percentages:

Frank Rainsford	40.00%
Betty Rainsford	40.00%
Robert Rainsford	6.25%
Susan Rainsford Rogers	6.25%
Alice Jacobs	7.50%

1.6 Company History

Frank's All-American BarBeQue was founded in 1972 by Frank Rainsford. Although a native New Englander, Frank learned about cooking barbecue while serving in the US Air Force. During his twelve years of service, he traveled across the country and learned about the four major styles of American barbecue—Texas, Memphis, Kansas City, and Carolina. His plan was to introduce people in southern Connecticut to *real* barbecue that entailed high-quality meats properly cooked and smoked over an appropriate length of time.

In the beginning, Frank's All-American BarBeQue was a small facility; it could seat about thirty people. It was located near the Fairfield railroad station and was the first full-service barbecue restaurant in Fairfield. Frank's placed an emphasis on featuring the food; it had a highly simplified decor where the tables were covered with butcher paper, not linen tablecloths. The restaurant was an immediate hit, received considerable local press, and won several food awards. This success enabled Frank's to move to a larger facility in Fairfield on the town's main thoroughfare—Boston Post Road. The new location was a midsize restaurant of about eighty seats. Frank has built this location into a relatively successful and locally well-known enterprise. It has been at the present location since the early 1980s. It shares a parking lot with several other stores in the small mall in which it is located.

Frank's has won many awards at regional and national barbecue cook-offs (for both the food and the sauces), which is unusual for a barbecue business in New England. The restaurant has been written up, repeatedly, in the local and New York papers for the quality of its food and its four signature barbecue sauces. In the last few years, Frank's has sold small lots of these sauces in local supermarkets. They have been distributed because of Frank's personal connections with the store managers. Frank Rainsford has been approached by a major regional supermarket to sell his sauces. The supermarket is willing to find a facility that could produce Frank's sauces in significantly larger volumes, which would represent a substantial increase in the sales of sauces. Table 16.1 provides a summary of key financial figures for the last three years—2008 to 2010. Figure 16.1 illustrates these key numbers for that period of time.

TABLE 16.1 Past Performance of Frank's All-American BarBeQue

Past Performance	2008	2009	2010
Sales	$1,637,610	$1,696,564	$1,793,268
Gross margin	$851,557	$909,358	$943,259
Gross margin %	52.00%	53.60%	52.60%
Operating expenses	$542,080	$577,315	$600,408
Inventory turnover	13.20	12.10	12.90
Balance Sheet	**2008**	**2009**	**2010**
Current Assets			
Cash	$102,665	$125,172	$102,665
Inventory	$391,238	$331,045	$345,678
Other current assets	$278,372	$230,074	$278,372
Total current assets	$772,275	$686,291	$726,715
Long-Term Assets			
Long-term assets	$504,580	$388,820	$423,675
Accumulated depreciation	$180,856	$135,739	$145,765
Total long-term assets	$323,724	$253,081	$277,910
Total assets	$1,095,999	$939,372	$1,004,625
Current Liabilities			
Accounts payable	$155,534	$132,206	$145,321
Current borrowing	$170,000	$150,000	$135,000
Other current liabilities (interest free)	$81,888	$63,972	$74,329
Total current liabilities	$407,422	$346,178	$354,650
Long-term liabilities	$220,000	$190,000	$175,000
Total liabilities	$627,422	$536,178	$529,650
Paid-in capital	$75,000	$75,000	$75,000
Retained earnings	$281,838	$234,377	$287,114
Earnings	$111,739	$93,817	$112,861
Total capital	$468,577	$403,194	$474,975
Total capital and liabilities	$1,095,999	$939,372	$1,004,625
Other Inputs			
Payment Days	30	30	30

FIGURE 16.1 Past Performance Chart

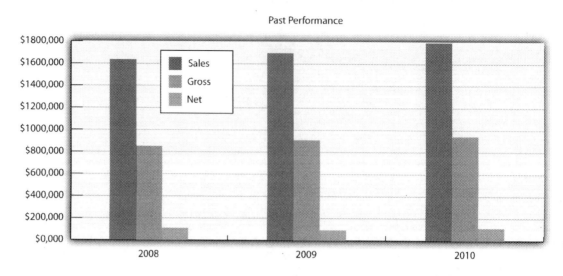

1.7   Company Locations and Facilities

Frank's All-American BarBeQue has been in Fairfield, Connecticut, for decades. It has a reputation throughout the southern Connecticut shore region for excellent food and has received numerous awards. The management team determined that a second location could tap into this local name recognition. Several towns in the region were evaluated for total population, population density, family income, and home value. These factors were considered because of their impact on generating traffic and consumers being able to pay for meals that are priced slightly higher than typical fast-food outlets. In addition, the average family size and the percentage of family households were considered because Frank's is a family restaurant. Lastly, data were gathered on the average travel time to and from work for residents and the real estate tax rate. Because the new location of Frank's will emphasize prepared meals, we felt that individuals with longer commutes would be more likely to order meals and pick them up at Frank's. A summary of these data is provided in Table 16.2 and Table 16.3.

After thorough analysis, it was concluded that Darien, Connecticut, would be the best location for the new branch of Frank's All-American BarBeQue. It has a high-income population and a high population density, and a large percentage of its inhabitants are members of family households. They have longer commuting times, which increase the potential need for prepared meals.

TABLE 16.2 Demographic Data for Selected Connecticut Towns—Part 1

Item	Fairfield	Westport	Easton	Darien	Norwalk
Population	57,578	25.884	7,383	19,375	83,802
Population density	1,917	1,293	269	1,508	3,675
Income	$108,209	$155,322	$162,688	$180,474	$79,693
House value	$589,179	$1,169,081	$868,622	$1,430,589	$504,100
Percentage of family households	72.6%	74.6%	84.3%	81.7%	64.1%
Travel time (minutes)	31.3	39.4	34.8	36.4	25.4
Real estate tax rate	1.3%	0.9%	1.3%	0.8%	1.1%
Family size	3.07	2.70	3.0	3.0	2.50

TABLE 16.3 Demographic Data for Selected Connecticut Towns—Part 2

Item	Stamford	Weston	Wilton	Trumbull	State of Connecticut
Population	121,026	10,199	17,771	34,422	3,574,097
Population density	3,206	515	659	478	739/sq. mile
Income	$81,206	$190,080	$183,252	$103,019	$68,595
House value	$612,900	$1,198,615	$1,044,316	$492,623	$306,000
Percentage of family households	63.8%	84.9%	82.3%	81.5%	67.7%
Travel time (minutes)	24.0	41.6	39.2	27.1	
Real estate tax rate	0.7%	1.1%	1.2%	1.5%	1.8%
Family size	2.50	3.0	3.25	2.80	

A specific location has been identified in Darien for the second Frank's All-American BarBeQue. It is in a small mall and is large enough to have a seating capacity of 150–160 plus takeout facilities. The mall has more than adequate parking for future customers. The mall is located three blocks from the Metro-North Darien railroad station and is four blocks from the I-95 exit. It is therefore well positioned to attract traffic from both car and rail commuters. The lease fee for a three-year contract is very reasonable for a property of this size.

1.8 Products and Services

Frank's All-American BarBeQue specializes in the finest barbecue served in a family-friendly format. It uses the finest cuts of meats that are free of any growth hormones. It is known for a variety of slow-smoked and slow-cooked meats, such as ribs, beef, pulled pork, and chicken. These are served with Frank's famous and award-winning sauce varieties, which represent the four major styles of barbecue cooking. Frank's is also noted for its side dishes and desserts.

Our goal is to expand operations to a second location in Darien, Connecticut. This outlet will be significantly larger and will have a section devoted to takeout meals.

1.9 Competitive Comparison

There are approximately forty specialty barbecue restaurants in Connecticut. They are spread throughout the state, but only four (including Frank's All-American BarBeQue) are in the southern shore region. The three competitors are smaller operations. None of the barbecue restaurants in Connecticut have the history, reputation, acclaim, or awards that match Frank's All-American BarBeQue. It is not an exaggeration to say that Frank's is the preeminent barbecue restaurant in Connecticut. It has a loyal following that reaches as far as New York City.

Frank's is the only barbecue restaurant in Connecticut where supermarkets are vying for the right to market Frank's signature barbecue sauces. This sideline business promises to be extremely profitable and support the overall marketing efforts for both locations of Frank's All-American BarBeQue.

1.10 Fulfillment

Frank's All-American BarBeQue has always been committed to providing the absolute best in barbecue food. This has meant assuring the highest quality ingredients in food preparation. Frank has established a decades-long relationship with suppliers in the New York and Connecticut areas. He selects nothing but the choicest selections of beef, pork, and chicken. He has always made sure that his meats come from suppliers who are committed to quality ingredients and who never use growth hormones. This long-term relationship with a variety of key suppliers enables Frank to secure the best cuts at reasonable prices. Frank is equally careful in using the finest spices for his barbecue sauces. The same is true for all the side dishes that Frank's All-American BarBeQue offers its customers.

This commitment to quality is not limited to the selection of meats and ingredients. Frank and his staff recognize that top-quality barbecue food requires a knowledgeable and deep commitment to cooking the food properly. All meats must be cooked and smoked slowly. This requires time, effort, expense, and commitment, but the results are spectacular. Some cuts of meat at Frank's may require as many as eleven hours of preparation and cooking. Excellence is not achieved without a commitment to effort. This effort has been recognized with numerous awards at national barbecue cook-offs. Frank has clearly recognized that the meal is clearly a function of the quality of the meat, quality ingredients, and careful preparation.

1.11 Future Products and Services

Frank's All-American BarBeQue is ready to accept new challenges. Opening a second restaurant will significantly increase sales, but the second location is only the beginning of new directions for Frank's. Although Frank has been selling his regional barbecue sauces in local outlets for years, he is now ready to sign a contract with a major regional supermarket chain to market and sell these sauces throughout New England. Preliminary studies indicate that Frank can anticipate a 20 percent annual growth rate in the sales of sauces for the next five years.

With the growth of two-income families, less and less time is available to prepare meals at home. Recognizing this simple fact, Frank's All-American BarBeQue plans to offer a variety of prepackaged barbecue meals that can be picked up at the restaurant and reheated at home. As part of its new commitment to a web-based presence, customers will be able to order these meals by regular phone, with smartphones, or through the Internet. Customers will be able to select from a list of prepackaged dinner meals or any combination of items. Customers can designate the time to pick up the meals, and the meals will be ready for them. This service promises significant revenue growth.

1.12 Market Analysis Summary

Since the 1930s, the American public has spent at least 5 percent of its disposable income on eating out. Even with annual fluctuations, this is a strong indicator of the viability of this industry. This can be best illustrated by reviewing industry results for the last few years.

Both 2009 and 2010 were difficult years for the restaurant industry. In 2008, sales increased by 3.8 percent. However, sales fell by nearly 0.75 percent in 2009. *This was the first year in the history of the industry that sales actually declined.* The restaurant industry's sales in 2009 were $566 billion, down from over $570 billion. Prices rose by 2.2 percent in 2009. The increase in sales for 2010 was 0.5 percent, and price increases stabilized at 0.75 percent.

It is anticipated that there will be significant price competition in every segment of the restaurant industry. Some analysts argued that the poor performances for the restaurant industry in both 2009 and 2010 could be attributed to declines in both business and personal travel. Hotel occupancy rates in 2009 were down by nearly 10 percent. A study conducted by the National Restaurant Association argued that 20 percent of the sales in casual dining restaurants might be due to travelers and visitors. Frank's All-American BarBeQue relies to a far lesser extent on travelers as customers. A rough estimate based on credit card receipts, for the period 2006–2010, indicated that travelers represented less than 2 percent of Frank's sales. The pressure on the restaurant industry has been felt by many chain restaurants, which significantly curtailed their expansion plans.

Even though the recession was in full bloom in 2009, many food prices rose and rose significantly. Beef prices rose between 4 percent and 12 percent, while pork prices rose between 5 percent and 13 percent. Numerous studies have indicated that the increase in commodity prices will not be a transitory phenomenon.

With 925,000 food service locations in operation in the United States, this translates into 1 restaurant for every 330 Americans.

The health-care reform bill passed in 2010 should, in the near future, provide some relief for restaurants by creating a system that will assume greater responsibility by individuals to pay for their own health-care coverage.

Restaurants must also be much more cautious in the future about the possibility of hiring illegal aliens. As a whole, the National Restaurant Association supports immigration reform. However, it is concerned that any legislation should not limit a restaurant's ability to hire workers. It is also concerned about the cost to assure worker eligibility.

The Mintel Group, a market research firm, found that consumers who are interested in quality opt for independent restaurants over chain outlets. An increasing consumer focus on health translates into an emphasis on natural ingredients. In the barbecue industry, this translates into naturally raised meats (i.e., the avoidance of artificial growth hormones in cattle), which are a hallmark of Frank's All-American BarBeQue.

The National Restaurant Association estimated that sales in full-service restaurants in 2010 would exceed $184 billion—an increase of 1.2 percent from 2009 sales.

Several macroeconomic factors make opening a restaurant in Darien attractive, including the following:

- **Increases in the growth domestic product (GDP).** The GDP is estimated to grow 1.7 percent in 2011 and 1.5 percent in 2012. The estimates for Fairfield County are significantly higher.

- **Disposable personal income.** The national level of personal income should rise nearly 4 percent in 2011, and there is an expectation of 3 percent growth in 2012. These numbers appear to be much stronger in the Fairfield County area.

Although 2010 was not a banner year for the restaurant industry—it was one where more restaurants closed than opened each month—there was one bright spot: Chain barbecue restaurants grew between 2 percent and 3 percent—an auspicious sign even for independent operators.

The home meal replacement market and the existing investment in restaurant equipment provide a nice growth opportunity for restaurants. It is been estimated that takeout sales in limited service chain restaurants might be as large as 60 percent of total sales. The same study found that takeout food has been growing twice as fast as the overall restaurant industry. Natural competitors in this market are supermarkets that offer prepackaged meals. However, we feel that few—if any—supermarkets provide the quality barbecue food that can be found at Frank's.

1.13   Market Segmentation

Frank's All-American BarBeQue views its major market segment as suburbanites in the south shore region of Connecticut. One way of further segmenting the market is by the type of meal being provided. Table 16.4 provides estimated growth rates for each type of meal (plus sauce sales) and projected number of meals (and jars of sauce) for the period 2011 to 2015. Figure 16.2 illustrates the relative contributions.

TABLE 16.4 Market Analysis

Potential Customers	Growth	2011	2012	2013	2014	2015
Lunch	8%	17,000	18,275	19,646	21,119	22,703
Dinner	5%	40,000	42,000	44,100	46,305	48,620
Takeout	20%	10,000	12,000	14,400	17,280	20,736
Sauces	15%	12,000	13,800	15,870	18,251	20,989
Total	9.37%	79,000	86,075	94,016	102,955	113,048

FIGURE 16.2 Market Analysis

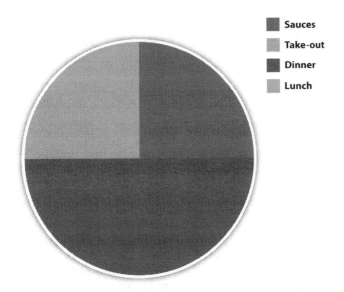

Sauces
Take-out
Dinner
Lunch

Market Needs

We believe that the market centers on excellent barbecue food served at reasonable prices and served in a family-friendly manner. We further believe that a growing segment of the market will want prepared meals that can be conveniently picked up and served at home. Table 16.4 provides a projected breakdown of the potential customers for the next five years. This breakdown is predicated on the type of meals served and includes the sale of sauces. We provide estimated growth rates and forecasted sale of meals (and bottles of sauces) for the period 2011 to 2015. Figure 16.2 shows the breakdown of the number of meals by type in 2015.

1.14   Web Plan Summary

Presently, Frank's All-American BarBeQue has a very simple website. The website provides minimal information—listing some of the menu items and the restaurant's telephone number. It was created eight years ago by a college student who was working at Frank's.

Robert Rainsford's professional expertise is in the area of website development. After graduating from college, Robert was hired by a firm that specialized in developing web and social media presences for other companies. He worked for that firm in New York City for seven years. Robert rose rapidly through the company's ranks, eventually becoming one of its vice presidents. His expertise in this area will enable Frank's All-American BarBeQue to significantly enhance its web presence. Rather than just having a website that identifies the restaurant's location and telephone number, along with a brief summary of its menu, the new website will be far richer in content and capability. It will provide a complete menu listing, identifying all items with corresponding images. The new website will enable customers to place orders through the Internet for lunch, dinner, or takeout items. The section devoted to takeout items will enable a customer to purchase prepared meals or choose from all items on the menu to develop a prepackaged meal. Customers will be able to identify the time that they will arrive for the pickup.

The website will have links to the Facebook and Twitter accounts of Frank's All-American BarBeQue. These connections will enhance its social media presence. Customers will be asked to post comments about their dining experience and suggestions on how Frank's can improve its operations and service. It will enable Frank's to expand operations and still maintain the same close customer relationship that currently exists at the Fairfield restaurant.

1.15   Website Marketing Strategy

The new web presence for Frank's All-American BarBeQue will be geared to developing a new level of customer relationships. Customers at both restaurants will be asked to fill out forms where they will supply an e-mail address and a birthdate. (This information can also be supplied through Frank's new website.) This information will enable Frank's to keep customers informed of specials and offer coupons and the new rewards card program for special occasions, such as holidays or birthdays.

We view the website of Frank's All-American BarBeQue as a major component of enhancing our relationship with our customers. It should provide convenience to customers through their ability to see what is on the menu, identify new specials, and order meals and pick them up at their convenience. The use of social media will expand awareness of Frank's and enable it to develop closer relationships with present and future customers.

1.16   Development Requirements

Robert Rainsford tapped into his expertise in social media and has already developed a far more sophisticated website for Frank's All-American BarBeQue. He has secured the necessary server capacity to handle additional traffic on the website. In addition, he has set up several social media accounts for Frank's All-American BarBeQue, including Facebook and Twitter. Robert also created a program linked to a database that will monitor customer purchases through the rewards card program. This program will send out birthday notices and discounts to customers and will inform them of their current status in the rewards card program.

Robert contacted several former colleagues at his former place of employment and has identified several candidates for the role of website manager. This individual will be responsible for updating the website and the social media sites on a daily basis. He or she will also be responsible for analyzing the flow of information that comes through these sites and preparing management reports.

1.17   Strategy and Implementation Summary

The core strategy of Frank's All-American BarBeQue is to continue what has made it a success at a new location. Simply put, our strategy is to provide our customers with the finest barbecue food in Connecticut, at reasonable prices, in a family-friendly environment. In addition, we hope to improve our ability to meet customer needs by making life more convenient for our customers. We believe that these fundamentals are universally applicable.

1.18 SWOT Analysis

A strengths, weaknesses, opportunities, and threats (SWOT) analysis was undertaken for Frank's All-American BarBeQue.

Strengths

The key strength of Frank's All-American BarBeQue is the quality of its food and service. It has been the recipient of numerous local and national awards for its foods and sauces. Other strengths include a highly knowledgeable management team with expertise in operating a barbecue restaurant, a close working relationship with suppliers of premier cuts of meats, and a loyal clientele in the south shore region.

Weaknesses

The weaknesses associated with this business plan center on operating an additional restaurant with a much larger capacity than the Fairfield, Connecticut, restaurant. The second location will require an experienced restaurant manager. This plan calls for a significant increase in prepared (takeout) meals. Orders will be placed either by phone or through the website. Current personnel have little experience in ratcheting up the takeout portion of the business.

Opportunities

This business plan offers significant opportunities for Frank's All-American BarBeQue. A second, larger location will translate into a significant increase in sales. Finalizing a business relationship with the regional supermarket chain will enable Frank's to significantly increase the production and the sales of its signature sauces. The sales of sauces are expected to increase by 20 percent per year for the next five years.

Threats

Any expansion with the opening of a new location always entails some risk. The principals of Frank's All-American BarBeQue will be investing a significant amount of capital and will be borrowing money from a bank to open a second location. It is strongly believed that the second location will capitalize on the success of the Fairfield restaurant and will become a success.

1.19 Competitive Edge

The competitive edge of Frank's All-American BarBeQue resides mainly in the quality of its food and its commitment to serve the food in a family-friendly environment. The quality of its food is unmatched in the entire state. No other barbecue restaurant has received the awards and the accolades that Frank's All-American BarBeQue has received for the past forty years. Its reputation for quality gives it an edge that no other barbecue restaurant or chain can match.

1.20 Marketing Strategy

The target market for Frank's All-American BarBeQue is essentially suburban families in the south shore region of Connecticut. These people appreciate the finest barbecue food at reasonable prices. It is expected that an important group within this target market will be families with two incomes whose busy schedules would make prepared meals a very attractive option. We further assume that this market is technically sophisticated and will appreciate the convenience of ordering these meals via the Internet.

A key component of the marketing strategy of Frank's All-American BarBeQue is to use the Internet and technology to enhance the relationship with its customer base. Frank's will use the website, Facebook, Twitter, and e-mails to inform customers of special food items or discounts based on holidays and customers' birthdays. We intend to use the website as a mechanism to gain an improved insight into customer needs and wants.

Frank's All-American BarBeQue will also initiate a rewards card program. Customers will sign up for the rewards card program either at the two locations or online. They can use this program every time they make a purchase either at the restaurants or online. After a set number of visits (seven), customers will be entitled to either discounts or free items. The rewards card program will enable Frank's All-American BarBeQue to track customers' buying patterns and anticipate the ways in which they can better serve their customers.

1.21 Sales Forecasts

We provide a five-year forecast of the dollar value of sales broken down by the two restaurants and the sauces in Table 16.5. Figure 16.3 illustrates a forecast for the breakdown of sales on monthly basis in 2011, and Figure 16.4 illustrates the breakdown of sales for the next five years.

TABLE 16.5 Sales Forecast

Sales	2011	2012	2013	2014	2015
Frank's (Fairfield)	$1,907,183	$1,954,863	$2,003,734	$2,053,827	$2,105,173
Frank's (Darien)	$2,222,000	$2,555,300	$2,810,830	$3,091,913	$3,401,104
Sauces	$62,500	$75,000	$90,000	$108,000	$130,000
Total sales	$4,191,683	$4,585,163	$4,904,564	$5,253,740	$5,636,277
Direct Cost of Sales	**2011**	**2012**	**2013**	**2014**	**2015**
Frank's (Fairfield)	$953,594	$977,430	$1,001,867	$1,026,914	$1,052,587
Frank's (Darien)	$1,111,000	$1,277,650	$1,405,415	$1,545,957	$1,700,552
Sauces	$31,250	$37,500	$45,000	$54,000	$64,800
Subtotal direct cost of sales	$2,095,844	$2,292,580	$2,452,282	$2,626,871	$2,817,939

FIGURE 16.3 Monthly Sales for Two Restaurants and Sauces

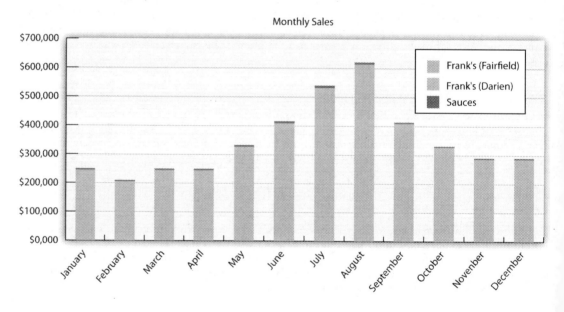

FIGURE 16.4   Five-Year Forecast of Sales for Two Restaurants and Sauces

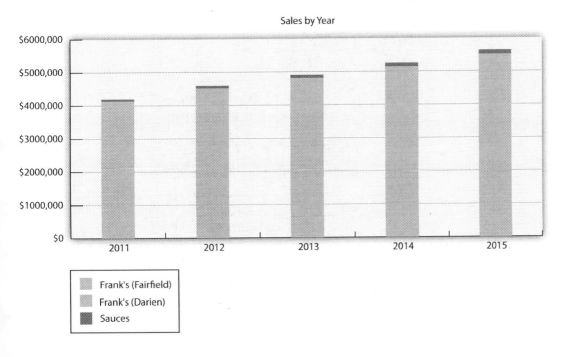

1.22   Management Summary

Currently, Frank Rainsford is the CEO and chief operating officer of Frank's All-American BarBeQue. He is also the restaurant manager at the Fairfield restaurant. During the week, his daughter (Susan Rainsford Rogers) often replaces Frank as the restaurant manager. The Fairfield restaurant has a full-time cook who operates under Frank's supervision, and two other full-time employees function as waiters and waitresses. These full-time employees are supplemented by six part-time employees.

Under the new management structure, Frank Rainsford will hold the position of CEO. His wife, Betty Rainsford, will be designated the president and chief operating officer. Their daughter, Susan Rainsford Rogers, will be given the title vice president for operations. She will be responsible for the day-to-day operations of the Darien, Connecticut, restaurant. Robert Rainsford will have the title of vice president of marketing. He will be responsible for all marketing activities and the operation of the website. Alice Jacobs will be the vice president of finance and the comptroller of Frank's All-American BarBeQue.

1.23   Organizational Structure

The new management structure of Frank's All-American BarBeQue is a basic functional layout appropriate for this type of business and is shown in Figure 16.5.

FIGURE 16.5 Organizational Chart

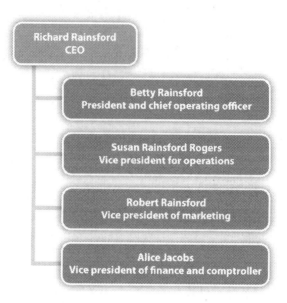

1.24   Personnel Plan

Table 16.6 is a five-year breakdown of the types and costs of personnel.

TABLE 16.6 Forecasts of Personnel

Personnel Plan	2011	2012	2013	2014	2015
Cooks Personnel					
Cook (Fairfield)	$54,000	$54,600	$55,000	$55,500	$56,000
Cook (Darien)	$66,000	$66,000	$66,500	$67,000	$67,500
Subtotal	$120,000	$120,600	$121,500	$122,500	$123,500
Servers Personnel					
Full-time servers (Fairfield)	$28,800	$28,800	$16,000	$17,500	$18,000
Full-time servers (Darien)	$57,600	$57,600	$24,500	$25,000	$2,600
Part-time servers both locations	$192,000	$192,000	$192,000	$192,000	$192,000
Subtotal	$278,400	$278,400	$232,500	$234,500	$212,600
General and Administrative Personnel					
Restaurant manager (Fairfield)	$42,000	$42,000	$43,000	$43,500	$44,000
Restaurant manager (Darien)	$54,000	$54,600	$56,000	$56,500	$57,000
Subtotal	$96,000	$96,600	$99,000	$100,000	$101,000
Total people	39	39	39	39	39
Total payroll	$494,400	$495,600	$453,000	$457,000	$437,100

1.25   Financial Plan

Frank's All-American BarBeQue will be financing the creation of a second restaurant through a combination of private investment and a bank loan. The private investment will raise $160,000, and Frank's will seek another $175,000 as a two-year loan. These funds will be used to pay for equipment and leasing expenses associated with opening a second restaurant.

1.26   Important Assumptions

The assumptions associated with the grow rates of sales each year for the next five years are the keys to the financial planning process. We began with very modest assumptions of 8 percent growth in lunch sales and 5 percent growth in dinner sales. We anticipate fairly vigorous growth in takeout meals (20 percent) and sauces (15 percent). Although these are large growth rates, we do not feel that they are unrealistic.

1.27   Key Financial Indicators

Figure 16.6 provides historical (2008–2010) and forecasted (2011–2015) values for the key financial indicators.

FIGURE 16.6   Key Financial Indicators

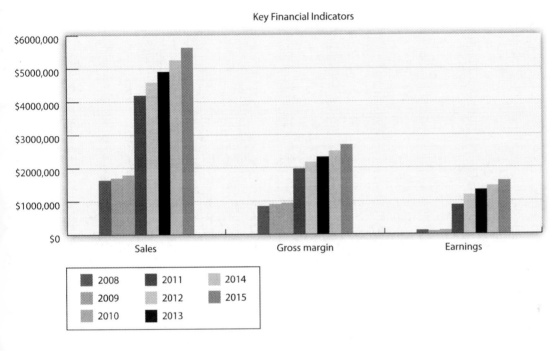

1.28   Breakeven Analysis

In Table 16.7 and Figure 16.7, we show the results of our breakeven analysis for Frank's All-American BarBeQue. The results indicate that with sales of approximately $110,000 each month, Frank's All-American BarBeQue will break even.

TABLE 16.7   Breakeven Analysis

Monthly revenue	$112,627
Assumptions	
Average variable cost	50%
Estimated monthly fixed cost	$56,313

FIGURE 16.7 Breakeven Analysis

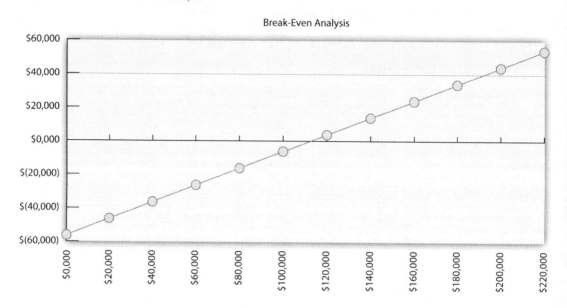

Break-Even Analysis

1.29 Projected Profit and Loss

Our analysis anticipates significant growth in profits in the next five years with the opening of a second Frank's All-American BarBeQue in Darien. The profit margins should increase from in excess of $850,000 in 2011 to nearly $1,600,000 by 2015 and should be in excess of 20 percent for all five years. A complete analysis of the profit and loss statements is in Table 16.8. The annual profits are illustrated in Figure 16.8.

TABLE 16.8 Profit and Loss

Pro Forma Profit and Loss	2011	2012	2013	2014	2015
Sales	$4,191,683	$4,585,163	$4,904,564	$5,253,740	$5,636,277
Direct cost of sales	$2,095,844	$2,292,580	$2,452,282	$2,626,871	$2,817,939
Cooks payroll	$120,000	$120,600	$121,500	$122,500	$123,500
Other costs of sales	$0	$0	$0	$0	$0
Total cost of sales	$2,215,844	$2,413,180	$2,573,782	$2,749,371	$2,941,439
Gross margin	$1,975,839	$2,171,983	$2,330,782	$2,504,369	$2,694,838
Gross margin %	47.14%	47.37%	47.52%	47.67%	47.81%
Operating Expenses					
Servers payroll	$278,400	$278,400	$232,500	$234,500	$212,600
Advertising/promotion	$0	$0	$0	$0	$0
Other servers expenses	$0	$0	$0	$0	$0
Total servers expenses	$278,400	$278,400	$232,500	$234,500	$212,600
Servers %	6.64%	6.07%	4.74%	4.46%	3.77%
General and Administrative Expenses					
General and administrative payroll	$96,000	$96,600	$99,000	$100,000	$101,000
Marketing/promotion	$12,000	$0	$0	$0	$0
Depreciation	$0	$0	$0	$0	$0
Rent	$180,000	$0	$0	$0	$0
Utilities	$13,200	$0	$0	$0	$0
Insurance	$22,000	$0	$0	$0	$0
Payroll taxes	$74,160	$74,340	$67,950	$68,550	$65,565
Other general and administrative expenses	$0	$0	$0	$0	$0
Total general and administrative expenses	$397,360	$170,940	$166,950	$168,550	$166,565
General and administrative %	9.48%	3.73%	3.40%	3.21%	2.96%
Other Expenses					
Other payroll	$0	$0	$0	$0	$0
Consultants	$0	$0	$0	$0	$0
Other expenses	$0	$0	$0	$0	$0
Total other expenses	$0	$0	$0	$0	$0
Other %	0.00%	0.00%	0.00%	0.00%	0.00%
Total operating expenses	$675,760	$449,340	$399,450	$403,050	$379,165
Profit before interest and taxes	$1,300,079	$1,722,643	$1,931,332	$2,101,319	$2,315,673
EBITDA (Earnings Before Interest, Taxes, Depreciation, and Amortization)	$1,300,079	$1,722,643	$1,931,332	$2,101,319	$2,315,673
Interest expense	$43,755	$34,995	$30,980	$30,980	$30,980
Taxes incurred	$376,897	$506,294	$570,106	$621,102	$685,408
Net profit	$879,427	$1,181,354	$1,330,246	$1,449,237	$1,599,285
Net profit/sales	20.98%	25.76%	27.12%	27.58%	28.37%

FIGURE 16.8 Yearly Profits

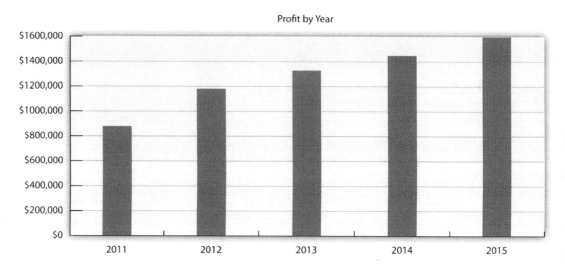

1.30　Projected Cash Flow

Table 16.9 is a five-year forecast of cash flows for Frank's All-American BarBeQue. The forecast shows extremely strong and positive cash flows for each year.

TABLE 16.9 Cash Flow Forecast

Pro Forma Cash Flow					
Cash Received	**2011**	**2012**	**2013**	**2014**	**2015**
Cash from Operations					
Cash sales	$4,191,683	$4,585,163	$4,904,564	$5,253,740	$5,636,277
Subtotal cash from operations	$4,191,683	$4,585,163	$4,904,564	$5,253,740	$5,636,277
Subtotal cash received	$4,366,683	$4,585,163	$4,904,564	$5,253,740	$5,636,277
Expenditures	**2011**	**2012**	**2013**	**2014**	**2015**
Expenditures from Operations					
Cash spending	$494,400	$495,600	$453,000	$457,000	$437,100
Bill payments	$2,500,504	$2,911,392	$3,085,406	$3,338,682	$3,587,794
Subtotal spent on operations	$2,994,904	$3,406,992	$3,538,406	$3,795,682	$4,024,894
Other liabilities principal repayment	$54,000	$54,000	$54,000	$0	$0
Long-term liabilities principal repayment	$87,600	$87,600	$0	$0	$0
Subtotal cash spent	$3,296,504	$3,548,592	$3,592,406	$3,795,682	$4,024,894
Net cash flow	$1,070,179	$1,036,571	$1,312,158	$1,458,058	$1,611,383
Cash balance	$1,172,844	$2,209,415	$3,521,573	$4,979,631	$6,591,014

1.31　Projected Balance Sheet

Table 16.10 is a balance sheet forecast for Frank's All-American BarBeQue.

TABLE 16.10 Balance Sheet Forecast

Pro Forma Cash Flow					
Assets	**2011**	**2012**	**2013**	**2014**	**2015**
Current Assets					
Cash	$1,172,844	$2,209,415	$3,521,573	$4,979,631	$6,591,014
Inventory	$72,421	$79,197	$109,296	$117,245	$125,954
Other current assets	$278,372	$278,372	$278,372	$278,372	$278,372
Total current assets	$1,523,636	$2,566,983	$3,909,241	$5,375,249	$6,995,341
Long-Term Assets					
Long-term assets	$583,675	$583,675	$583,675	$583,675	$583,675
Accumulated depreciation	$145,765	$145,765	$145,765	$145,765	$145,765
Total long-term assets	$437,910	$437,910	$437,910	$437,910	$437,910
Total assets	$1,961,546	$3,004,893	$4,347,151	$5,813,159	$7,433,251
Liabilities and Capital	**2011**	**2012**	**2013**	**2014**	**2015**
Current Liabilities					
Accounts payable	$189,416	$193,009	$259,021	$275,791	$296,597
Current borrowing	$135,000	$135,000	$135,000	$135,000	$135,000
Other current liabilities	$20,329	($33,671)	($87,671)	($87,671)	($87,671)
Subtotal current liabilities	$344,745	$294,338	$306,350	$323,120	$343,926
Long-term liabilities	$262,400	$174,800	$174,800	$174,800	$174,800
Total liabilities	$607,145	$469,138	$481,150	$497,920	$518,726
Paid-in capital	$75,000	$75,000	$75,000	$75,000	$75,000
Retained earnings	$399,975	$1,279,402	$2,460,755	$3,791,002	$5,240,239
Earnings	$879,427	$1,181,354	$1,330,246	$1,449,237	$1,599,285
Total capital	$1,354,402	$2,535,755	$3,866,002	$5,315,239	$6,914,524
Total liabilities and capital	$1,961,546	$3,004,893	$4,347,151	$5,813,159	$7,433,251
Net worth	$1,354,402	$2,535,755	$3,866,002	$5,315,239	$6,914,524

These figures clearly demonstrate that the proposed opening of a second restaurant is more than economically viable; it is an extremely lucrative project that promises to increase the net worth of the firm by 500 percent in five years.

Index

ABC classification system
26

accessibility
29, 96, 188, 216, 244, 466

accounting
11-14, 25-31, 75, 91-93, 109, 144, 148, 201-202, 223, 267-303, 316, 322-326, 336, 341, 348, 359, 364-367, 371, 382, 409, 449, 458, 473

accounts payable
145, 275-277, 305, 489, 503

accounts receivables
267, 274, 293, 391-392

accrual accounting
25, 30, 270-274, 300

acquisition
15, 41, 123, 223, 297, 302-304, 310-312, 316, 342-348, 430, 449-453

actionability
188

activity log
394-400

activity-based costing system
322

advertising
47, 62-63, 91, 116, 121-124, 139, 143, 154, 159-160, 166, 172, 186, 196, 210, 219-222, 226, 232, 249, 253, 258-260, 265-266, 279, 286-287, 377, 382, 393, 407-408, 450, 471-472, 482-487, 501

advertising media
219

aesthetics
38-41, 204, 407-408

affiliate marketing
220

agenda
389, 422-427, 432

all-in-one e-commerce platform solution
109

analytics
61, 109, 116, 205, 259-265

angel investors
131-132, 269, 305, 310

asset management or efficiency ratios
291-295

assets
17, 21, 26, 88-89, 144-145, 268, 273-282, 291-293, 302-305, 317-319, 325, 335, 345, 352, 369-371, 380, 390-391, 438-439, 443-448, 453, 472-473, 489, 503

assurance
41, 333, 408-409, 413

augmented layer
195

autocratic leadership
356

badwill
446, 455

balance sheet
131, 144-148, 268, 273-279, 283, 288-291, 317-319, 448, 489, 502-503

bankruptcy
12, 21, 31, 147, 305, 310, 374, 443-448, 453-455

banner ads
220, 249-253, 257-260

benchmarking
328

birth
10, 17-19, 49, 129, 143

blog
31, 53, 60-61, 66, 111, 115-117, 124, 152, 181, 220-223, 230-233, 263-265, 300, 396-399, 431-432, 484-486

blog advertising
220

brainstorming
153, 402-405, 429-431

brand
20, 24, 60, 64-69, 90-91, 97, 101-104, 125-127, 159-162, 169-172, 176-179, 184-201, 206-210, 217-225, 231, 239-240, 244-252, 260, 264-265, 384, 407-408, 433-434, 446, 451, 467-475, 485

brand equity
198, 218, 247, 264, 433

breakeven analysis
254-255, 261, 265, 313-316, 321, 326, 333-334, 499-500

brick-and-click business
94-99, 219, 226, 481

brokerage model
97

browser safe colors
204

business ethics
19-23, 32, 115-116

business intelligence
92-93, 112-115

business interruption insurance
438, 454

business process reengineering
328

business-to-business (B2B)
95, 113, 136, 164, 190, 211, 470

business-to-consumer (B2C)
95, 175, 190, 195, 211, 223

business-to-government (B2G)

buying center
1

C-corporation
303-3

CAMPARI
311-3

cash
4-6, 13-18, 24-26, 30-32, 48, 61-63, 70, 85-86, 112-1
131, 144-151, 172, 178-180, 201, 227-229, 233, 262-3
312, 317-318, 322-326, 341, 345-351, 364, 371-372, 3
386-387, 427-430, 434, 443-448, 479-482, 489, 502-

cash flow
4-6, 13-17, 24-26, 30-32, 61-63, 85-86, 112-113, 1
149-151, 172, 178-180, 201, 227, 233, 262-263, 267-3
318, 323-326, 345-351, 364, 386-387, 427-430, 4
481-482, 502-

cash-based accounting
25, 30,

cash-flow management
13-14, 25-26, 150,

cash-flow projections statement

cash-flow statement
131, 144-148, 273, 281

centralization
18, 361

channel pricing

cloud computing
63, 298, 323-324

cloud-based software
296, 34

compensation
72-78, 82-90, 225, 299, 37

competitive advantage
4, 28, 32, 43, 54, 66-70, 86, 97, 106, 120-123, 14
193-194, 208, 244-246, 333, 38

conceptual skills

conditional value
38-3

conformance
196, 271, 406-4

consumer
32, 37-40, 50, 54-55, 60-62, 66, 91, 95, 101, 108, 1
136, 146, 156-175, 186-199, 210-214, 220-2
247-252, 303, 331, 338, 350, 383, 406-407, 430, 4
466-4

consumer behavior
32, 163-1

consumer-to-business (C2B)

onsumer-to-consumer (C2C)
95

ontent
4, 8-11, 15, 22-24, 32, 41, 56, 61, 76, 88-90, 95, 106-115, 141, 180-185, 202-207, 223-233, 265, 326, 353, 389-392, 455, 466-468, 474, 484-486, 494

ntingency approach
366

ntingency planning
81, 260-261, 265

ntrolling
348, 354-361, 443

re layer
195

rporation
7, 24, 66, 84, 167, 271, 301-306, 326, 345, 370-375, 382, 390, 413-416, 443, 448, 454, 459

st focus
124-128

st leadership
124-129

t of capital
316-317, 326

t of goods sold (COGS)
278

t-based pricing
209-210, 232

wdfunding
228, 233

ural competence
75

ent assets
145, 274-277, 291, 489, 503

ent liabilities
145, 275-277, 291, 489, 503

omer
3-57, 61-66, 74, 81, 85-86, 91-102, 106-113, 117-121, 125-127, 138, 142-165, 169-186, 190-199, 206-233, -254, 260-263, 270, 281, 295-301, 322-323, 327-354, 3-360, 367-370, 380-387, 401-412, 416-421, 427-432, 443-446, 457-459, 463-469, 475-482, 486, 494-495

omer experience
163, 169-173, 179-182, 186, 190, 198-199, 221-227, 247, 380, 386-387

mer lifetime value
47-48, 54, 66

mer loyalty
9, 48, 62-63, 96-99, 163, 171-174, 179-181, 199, 246, 252

mer outsourcing
113

mer relationship management
63-66, 81, 92-93, 109, 150, 331, 335, 348, 459

customer relationship management (CRM)
63, 81, 92-93, 331, 335, 348, 459

customer segment pricing
159

customer value
4-6, 24-25, 30-49, 54-56, 61-66, 85-86, 92, 112-113, 120-121, 125-126, 142-143, 149-150, 154-156, 163, 178-182, 186, 209, 216, 227-229, 233, 240, 262-263, 295, 300, 322, 327, 335, 346, 350, 354, 360, 386, 405, 427-430, 481-482

customer value proposition
262-263

cybercrime
103-108, 116

decentralization
364-365

decision making
4-6, 22-26, 30, 49, 61, 69-70, 74, 82-84, 93, 141, 152, 296, 302, 313, 325, 354-360, 364-367, 389, 410, 422, 454

decision support system
348

decline
13, 17-19, 145, 201, 209, 274, 292, 316-319, 428

defects waste
402, 412-413, 417-419

delay
106, 207, 335, 418-419, 479

democratic leadership
356

depreciation
145, 273-280, 313, 473-475, 489, 501-503

differential response
188

differentiation
19, 124-128, 154, 162, 171, 184-194, 198-201, 207-208, 230, 461, 478

differentiation focus
124-128

digital technology
4-5, 24-30, 61-63, 86, 99, 108, 112-113, 178-179, 227-228, 262-263, 296, 323

direct channel
212-213, 217

direct competition
210, 245

direct exporting
463-464, 475-478, 484

direct foreign investment
477-480

direct marketing
54, 91, 143, 219-226, 233, 258-259

directing
354-356, 360

discount pricing
209-210, 232

distribution
7, 29, 41, 111, 116, 121, 126-130, 143, 158-161, 174, 178, 190, 210-217, 227-228, 246-248, 252-253, 304, 329-338, 367, 382, 428, 435, 470-471, 477-482, 487

distribution process
470

division of labor
18, 365

divisional structure
367-370

domain name registration
100

domain name selection
100

duplication
362, 418-419

durability
190, 196, 406-408

dynamic pricing
208

e-business
1-4, 24-33, 86, 91-117, 149-150, 297, 349, 482

e-commerce
5-6, 24-33, 86, 91-117, 149-150, 176, 297, 465, 482-485

e-commerce business model
96-99

e-commerce platform
108-109

e-environment
26, 61-63, 85-86, 113, 178-179, 227-228, 262-263, 296, 323, 348, 386-387, 428, 481-482

e-mail advertising
219-220

e-marketing
99, 186-187, 196, 202, 230-232

e-procurement
323-326

earnings before taxes (EBT)
279, 318

effective
5-6, 14, 23-26, 99-102, 124-127, 158, 175, 184-189, 193, 203-205, 210, 215, 220-221, 225-231, 235-236, 252, 257-258, 262-264, 292, 322-324, 328, 334, 343, 354-359, 365-370, 377-384, 391-394, 398-400, 422, 426-427, 432-434, 455-458, 464, 468-472, 482

efficient
28, 64, 79, 93, 215, 227, 237-238, 262, 267-269, 293, 302, 314-315, 322-323, 334, 343, 354, 360, 365, 369, 383, 394, 416-418, 428-430, 464, 482

electronic data interchange
348

electronic transactions
92-93, 101

emotional value
38, 156

empathy
408-409

employee benefits
333, 379, 391

enterprise resource planning (ERP)
92-93, 328, 336, 348

epistemic value
38-39, 156

equity
26, 71, 84, 132, 145, 193, 198, 218, 240, 247, 264, 273-277, 282, 287, 291-292, 300-304, 309-311, 316-321, 326, 433, 443-444, 448, 452-453, 478, 488

equity loans
26

errors
101, 106, 172, 195, 205, 268, 345, 386, 394, 412-413, 419

ethics
19-24, 32, 73, 103, 108, 115-116, 161, 360, 389

ethics policy (code of conduct or code of ethics)
22

even-odd pricing
209-210

exchange rate
462, 473

executive summary
141, 149, 239, 261-264, 487

existence
13-19, 43, 47, 55, 60-61, 130, 136-138, 143, 176, 242, 362, 394, 477

expense control
25-26

expense forecast
254-256

external factors
13-15, 341, 351

external marketing environment
161

extranet
29, 94, 115

family business
45, 68-90, 119, 447, 455, 463

features
18, 38, 112, 116, 125, 147, 153, 192-195, 206-207, 218, 222-225, 231, 245, 384, 390, 406-407, 466-468

finance
7, 11-17, 66, 75, 93, 141, 225, 231, 252, 268, 300-311, 316, 324-326, 330, 348, 368-370, 382, 432, 443, 457, 473-474, 497

financial accounting
269, 273, 290, 300

financial inadequacy
13-15

financial leverage
291-295, 309, 313-316, 321

financial leverage ratios
291-295

first-generation time-management system
395

first-line or supervisory management
358

fixed assets
145, 274-275, 281, 293

fixed costs
172, 201, 247, 254, 313-315, 322, 333-334

focus group
64, 175, 254, 423

foreign affiliate
458

formal authority
361-364

formal competence
75

formal organization
362-363

founder's dilemma
443, 454-455

fourth-generation time-management system
395, 429

friendly buyout
450-453

full-service web developer
100

functional structure
366-370

functional value
38, 156

game theory
338-339, 343-344

general partnership
303-304, 372

geographic pricing
209-210

goodwill
21, 145, 275, 413, 446, 455

grapevine (or water cooler)
362

graphics
202-207, 231, 237, 468, 472, 481

green business practice
1

gross profit
144-145, 278-279, 292-293, 317-320, 4

growth
7, 11, 15-19, 29-33, 71, 77, 82, 86, 91-95, 108-1 115-116, 129-131, 138, 143-146, 150-152, 161, 1 201-204, 223, 227-230, 237-249, 281-284, 292, 305, 3 323-326, 330-331, 348-349, 353-354, 360-363, 367-3 382, 406, 443, 450, 457-462, 466, 470-475, 484, 491-4 498-5

historic cash-flow statement

holistic marketing concept
154-

hosting
100, 109, 115, 150,

incentive marketing model

income statement
131, 144, 148, 273-274, 278-281, 288-291, 317-320,

incorrect inventory

indirect channel
213

indirect competition

indirect exporting
464, 475

individual consumers or end users (busine to-consumer [B2C])

industry life cycle
16-

informal organization
36

initial public offering (IPO)
44

innovation
6-10, 17-19, 29-31, 38-41, 46, 53-61, 66, 115, 12 153-154, 169-172, 181, 197, 201, 394, 400-40 4

inseparability

intangibility

intangible assets
145, 2

integrated marketing communications (
218, 2

integration
28-33, 86, 116, 150, 179, 186, 218, 324, 331-340, 3

intellectual property
96, 101-104, 108, 115-116, 246, 261, 382, 445-446, 450, 458, 465, 472

interactive marketing
219, 223-226, 233

intermediaries
160, 212-217, 329, 464, 470, 474

internal marketing environment
160, 247, 382

interpersonal skills
359

interrole conflict
83

intranet
93-94, 115

introduction
19, 32, 52, 64-66, 131-133, 141, 192, 201, 232, 247-249, 277-280, 336-339, 352, 389-390, 415, 421

inventory
25-29, 35, 39, 94, 114, 125, 145, 149, 160, 183, 196, 209-211, 215-217, 232, 262, 268-274, 289-293, 305-306, 327-335, 345-347, 416-419, 428, 436, 441, 446, 489, 503

inventory control
25-28, 125, 215-217, 269, 334-335, 419

inventory waste
25-29, 35, 39, 94, 114, 125, 145, 149, 160, 183, 196, 209-211, 215-217, 232, 262, 268-274, 289-293, 305-306, 327-335, 345-347, 416-419, 428, 436, 441, 446, 489, 503

job description
376, 381

joint venture (JV)
478

jurisdiction
101-102, 116

just-in-time
335, 417-419, 432

kaizen
419

key to success
142, 241, 248, 261, 487

laissez-faire leadership (or delegative or free-rein leadership)
356

layout
39, 106, 169, 203, 207, 231, 481, 497

leading
5, 83, 186, 239, 267, 356, 362, 383-384, 437, 457-458

lean inventory management
26

lean methodologies
328, 335, 428

lean thinking
405, 416-421, 427-431

learning organization
328

liabilities
145, 261, 268, 273-277, 291, 303, 445, 489, 502-503

life-cycle stage
165-166

limited liability company
304, 370-374, 390, 448

limited partnership
303, 372

line authority
364

liquidation
216, 433, 446-448, 453

liquidity
25, 274, 291-295

liquidity ratios
291-295

loading speed
207

logistics
211, 215-218, 232, 329-337, 342, 346-352, 464

long-term assets
145, 274-275, 489, 503

loss leader
209

man-made disaster
434-436, 440, 454

management
1-502

management by objectives
328

management hierarchy
355-360, 365

management skill
359

managerial accounting
269, 290

managerial inadequacy
11-15

market reader
401

market segmentation
43-48, 66, 154-158, 163, 181, 187-189, 493

market summary
241-242, 261

market value ratios
291, 295

marketable securities
145, 274-277

marketing
1-6, 13-19, 24, 29-32, 37, 41, 45-55, 61-66, 75, 91-93, 97-99, 105, 109, 114-117, 121, 127-130, 138, 143, 148-149, 153-267, 324, 352-358, 364, 368-370, 382, 393, 401-404, 430-433, 448, 457-486, 491-497, 501

marketing communications
218-220, 224-229

marketing communications mix
218-220, 224-226

marketing concept
154-155, 163

marketing environment
66, 154, 160-163, 174, 255

marketing management
32, 66, 154-157, 162-166, 181-182, 219, 230-233, 264-265, 352, 485

marketing mix
154, 158-166, 173, 178, 184-189, 193-194, 207-211, 218, 227, 231, 243-253, 261, 460-462, 466-467, 475, 485

marketing objectives
162, 184-187, 194, 230, 237, 247-252, 261

marketing plan
129, 143, 149, 162, 185, 194, 230, 235-265, 480

marketing research
49, 158, 173-177, 182, 187-188, 235, 254, 463, 482

marketing strategy
37, 91, 154, 162-163, 174, 182-233, 239-254, 261, 265, 494-495

marketing strategy pyramid
251-252, 265

materials requirement planning
335

matrix structure
367-370

maturity
16-19, 201

measurability
38, 188

micromultinationals
459

middle management
358, 365

midlife
17-19

mind mapping
402-405

mission statement
142, 149-152, 186, 240, 261-264, 396, 487

mobile commerce (m-commerce)
95

mobile shopping solution
179

monetary component of cost
39

motion waste
219, 357, 372, 417-419, 482

motivating
356-358

multichannel distribution system (or hybrid channel)
215

multinational corporation
375, 459

multitask
398

need seeker
401

negative or destructive conflict
82

net present value
48, 54, 318

net present value (NPV)
318

net profit
145, 279, 292-293, 317-320, 501

news site advertising
220

niche market
158, 163, 189, 230, 242, 267, 289

non-zero-sum game
338

nontariff trade barriers
477-480

notes payable
145, 275

notes receivable
145, 274

online market maker
95

operating expenses
144-145, 279, 292, 489, 501

operating profit
279-280, 292-293

operations
1, 7-8, 12-14, 26-29, 40-41, 45, 67-68, 81, 86, 92-99, 103,
112-113, 120, 127-128, 132, 136, 142-158, 188, 211, 256,
267-268, 273, 279-281, 286-289, 293-305, 310-311, 316,
322-325, 329-348, 352, 358, 364-369, 373, 380-386,
397-398, 405-412, 416-419, 427-435, 440, 448, 462,
473-482, 491-497, 502

opportunity lost
419

order fulfillment
99, 106, 112

organization chart
361-364, 370, 390

organizational life cycle (OLC)
17

organizing
120, 303, 354-355, 360-361, 365

ossification
17-19

other revenues and expenses
279

outsourcing
108, 113, 127, 331-334, 363, 369, 375, 382-385, 391-392

overprocessing waste
417-418

overproduction waste
418

owner's equity
145, 273-277, 291-292

packaging
55-56, 61, 104, 159, 194-198, 216, 231, 342, 416, 428, 460,
467-471, 477

partnership
303-304, 317, 370-374, 382, 433, 448, 478, 488

PDCA cycle
410, 415

peer-to-peer (P2P)
95

penetration pricing
209

perceived quality
209, 406-408

perception
24, 30-32, 46, 85-86, 165-166, 176, 191, 195, 408, 419, 432,
474

performance
16-22, 28-31, 38-41, 56, 77-78, 83-84, 90, 155-158, 192,
196, 200-202, 207-208, 257, 265, 290-291, 295, 321, 326,
330, 336-338, 342-344, 348, 354-357, 361-362, 369,
378-392, 406-409, 460, 489-490

perishability
197

personal digital assistant (PDA)
384

personal factors
165-166

personal selling
219, 224-228, 233

physical distribution (logistics)
215

place
2, 11, 17-18, 23, 35-37, 45, 49, 73, 85-86, 94, 98-105, 12
129-130, 143, 158-166, 172, 176-178, 185-186, 193-19
203-207, 211, 216-217, 224-227, 240-242, 247-25
260-265, 286-290, 301, 347, 367-370, 375-378, 383, 38
402, 406, 412, 419, 438, 449, 461, 465, 470-479, 4

planning
1, 5, 14-19, 25-31, 54, 79-96, 115, 119-123, 129-1
143-152, 171, 176, 181, 187, 202, 211, 220, 230-2
235-237, 252, 260-261, 265, 283, 297, 301-302, 309, 3
328-329, 335-336, 342, 348-360, 365, 376, 391, 398, 4
415, 432-436, 440-441, 447-455, 470, 480, 4

positioning
154, 162, 184-195, 202-203, 208-209, 230, 250-251,

positive or constructive conflict

prepaid expenses
145,

prestige pricing (or premium pricing)

price
21-26, 36-41, 45, 100, 120, 125, 136-139, 143-
154-163, 175-180, 190-194, 201, 206-220, 226-227,
245-246, 252-254, 262, 274, 286, 296-297, 305-
312-317, 322-324, 333, 339-341, 345-347, 353, 406-
412, 433-434, 446, 450-451, 462, 468-473, 477, 481

price skimming

price transparency
208

price-quality signaling

pricing objectives
20

primary marketing research

privacy
96-99, 103-108, 112, 217, 38

procurement
28-29, 95, 323-329, 333-334, 338, 348, 36

product decline stage

product design
66, 194-197, 207-2

product development (incubation) stage

product growth stage

product introduction stage

product life cycle (PLC)

product maturity stage

roduct reliability
106

rofessional manager
75

rofitability ratios
291-295

romotion
, 74, 121, 143, 158-163, 178, 194-195, 207, 214, 218-222, 26, 232, 252-253, 259-263, 279, 330, 377, 404, 428, 471, 501

oprietary research report
175

ychic component
40

ychological attributes
468

ychological or individual factors
165-166

blic relations (PR)
219-221, 247, 393

blicity
159, 219-222, 226, 471

system
417

e-play business
94-99, 219, 226

litative forecasting methods
137

lity
22-24, 38-41, 45, 50-52, 66-70, 82-85, 91, 99, 106-109, 116, 125-127, 131, 142, 155-162, 166, 170, 190-197, 3-210, 218, 227, 231, 240-246, 250, 262-263, 300-302, 314, 328-334, 339-341, 345, 353, 357, 380, 385, 396, 405-420, 427-432, 446-447, 457-462, 466-468, 473, 488-495

ity function deployment (QFD)
50

atitative forecasting methods
137

changeover
419

-response (QR) code
227-228

-frequency identity device (RFID)
27

nd
199, 459

ables management
25-26

nce group
165-166

ility (product)
38-41, 64, 106-107, 190, 195-196, 406-409

reliability (service)
38-41, 64, 106-107, 190, 195-196, 406-409

reputation management
222-223

resource maturity
16-19

responsiveness
365, 408-409

retained earnings
145, 275-280, 300, 306, 489, 503

retention
21, 47, 54, 109, 172, 248, 375, 380-381, 385, 391, 406

ROA
313, 317-322, 369, 390

ROI
36-37, 237, 258-260, 265, 369, 390, 486

S-corporation
303-304

salary
25, 69, 73, 77-78, 82, 87, 113, 144, 279, 290, 304, 313, 379-381, 459, 476

sales conversion rate
107

sales forecast
139-141, 254-256, 261, 496

sales promotion
159, 219-220, 226, 232, 259, 471

scalar principle
365

scenario planning
133, 146-147

SCORE (Service Corps of Retired Executives)
442

search engine optimization
100, 229

search engine placement
100

second-generation time-management system
395

secondary marketing research
175

Secure Sockets Layer (SSL)
106

self-concept
165-166

server
95, 229, 349, 384, 392, 494

serviceability
406-408

SERVQUAL
408-409

shopping cart abandonment
217

shopping environment
39, 165-166, 172

site interactivity
205

site navigation
205

situation analysis
241-243, 255-261

situational factors
157, 165-166

Six Sigma
405, 413-420, 431-432

small business
1-502

Small Business Administration
6-8, 31, 89, 131, 135, 237, 305, 326, 372, 391, 436, 454-455, 459, 474, 484-486

small business failure
11-15, 25, 31, 354, 360

small business growth stages
16

small business success
11-15, 32, 152, 173, 359, 383, 431, 458, 462

smartphone
27, 110, 117, 227-228, 353, 384-387, 392, 398, 429

social factors
161, 165-166

social media
52, 63-66, 107-109, 117, 143, 150, 159, 166-169, 180-182, 206, 220-226, 233, 244, 249, 253, 257-260, 265, 324, 370, 393, 430-432, 471-472, 485, 494

social media advertising
220

social value
38, 156

societal marketing concept
154-155

sole proprietorship
303, 371-375, 448

span of control (span of management)
365

stability
70, 74-75, 188, 365, 371, 472-473, 482

staff authority
364

staffing
15, 354-356, 360-361, 391-392, 416, 448, 476

standard deviation
413

statistical process control (SPC)
429

strategic alliance
478

strategy
1, 15-18, 33, 37, 66, 75, 81-83, 91-97, 108-110, 115-116, 120-132, 143, 148-154, 159-163, 174, 180-233, 239-254, 261-265, 312, 338, 358, 394, 401, 415, 431-434, 444-455, 465, 475-477, 481-486, 494-495

substantiality
188

success
6, 11-25, 31-36, 40, 44-45, 49, 56-59, 70, 74, 78-82, 90, 99, 106-109, 115, 119, 124-133, 138, 142-152, 158, 173, 177, 186, 190, 194-197, 201-208, 218-223, 237, 241, 248, 261, 265, 276-279, 298, 304, 311-314, 327, 339, 344-347, 353-362, 373, 378-392, 406, 423, 430-437, 445-447, 451-458, 462-465, 470-480, 487-488, 494-495

success-disengagement substage
17

success-growth substage
17

succession
70-73, 79-84, 89, 119, 445-447, 453-455

succession planning
79-84, 89, 119, 447, 455

supplier relationship management
348

supply chain management
92-93, 112-115, 216, 323, 327-352, 432

supply chain operations reference (SCOR) model
342

survival
14-19, 24, 30-31, 61, 112, 120, 124, 129, 145-150, 205, 264, 298-301, 324, 344, 394, 409, 436, 447, 453-454

SWOT analysis
241, 246-248, 261-264, 495

symbolic layer
195

take-off
16-19

tangibles
408-409

target market
49, 100, 154, 158, 162-164, 170, 174, 185-192, 196-202, 208-220, 230, 237-241, 247-252, 256, 261-262, 464-467, 471-475, 480, 495

tariffs
330, 469, 477-480

technical skills
13, 78, 359

technology driver
401

termination
375, 380-381, 386, 391, 447, 476

termination at will
381

termination for cause
381

the Deming method
328, 411

third-generation time-management system
395

time component
40

time management
394-400, 427-432

times interest earned ratio
292

top management
339, 358-359, 386-387, 476

Total customer benefit
25

Total customer cost
25

total quality management
328, 413, 417

touch points
169-173

training
8, 23, 32, 71, 75, 81, 87, 115, 144-146, 225-228, 245, 250, 267-269, 297-298, 312, 349, 356, 375-380, 391, 405, 412-414, 431, 435, 443, 455, 464-465, 480

transportation waste
8-12, 31, 80, 160, 195, 215-218, 232, 333-337, 345, 385, 417-418, 434-437, 458, 469-470, 478, 483

typeface
204

typography
106, 202-207, 231

unclear communication
419

unity of command
365-367

unnecessary motion
418-419

usability
196, 202-207, 231

user interface
205, 231

value proposition
39-47, 54, 97, 171, 262-263, 466

value stream
417-4

values
7, 12, 20-23, 31-32, 36-37, 43, 50, 54, 66-70, 74-80, 8
138, 142, 147, 157, 161, 199, 208, 240, 278, 291-295, 3(
313, 317, 348, 362, 417, 428, 468, 4

variability

variable costs
201, 209, 254, 313-314, 334, 4

venture capitalist
26, 49, 132, 144, 305, 310, 450,

venture capitalists
124, 129-132, 144, 269, 305, 449-

virtual merchant model

virtual or telecommuting employee

virtual organization (or network organization)

vision statement
142, 185-186, 240, 261

visual management

voice of the customer (VOC)

vulture capitalists

wages
70, 78, 136, 145, 275, 286-287, 304, 33.

waiting waste
229, 296, 323, 398, 417-41

walkaway
44

Web 1.0

Web 2.0
67, 99, 108-1

webinars or webcasts

website objectives
202-2

website security
1

wholesalers
160, 164, 212-215, 4

wiki
94, 111, 115, 181-182, 264, 300, 389-392, 4

win-win scenario

word-of-mouth communication

159, 219, 226

worker-owned cooperative

452

workforce planning

376, 391

youth

17-19

zero-sum game

338